14. vi. 58

THE COLLECTED WORKS

OF

C. G. JUNG

VOLUME 11

EDITORS

SIR HERBERT READ

MICHAEL FORDHAM, M.D., M.R.C.P.

GERHARD ADLER, PH.D.

Jean Fouquet: *The Trinity with the Virgin Mary*

From the Book of Hours of Etienne Chevalier (Chantilly)

The mandala encloses the three identical male figures composing the Trinity and a fourth, female figure, together with the four symbols of the Evangelists, three in the form of animals and one (Matthew) in the form of an angel. Mary is Queen of the Angels. (Cf. pp. 64ff. and 107ff.)

PSYCHOLOGY AND RELIGION: WEST AND EAST

C. G. JUNG

TRANSLATED BY R. F. C. HULL

ROUTLEDGE & KEGAN PAUL

LONDON

BROADWAY HOUSE, 68–74 CARTER LANE
LONDON E.C.4

THIS EDITION IS BEING PUBLISHED BY ROUTLEDGE & KEGAN PAUL LTD., IN ENGLAND AND FOR THE BOLLINGEN FOUNDATION BY PANTHEON BOOKS INC., IN THE UNITED STATES OF AMERICA. THE PRESENT VOLUME IS NUMBER 11 OF THE COLLECTED WORKS, AND IS THE SEVENTH TO APPEAR.

PRINTED IN THE U. S. A.

EDITORIAL NOTE

The title *Psychology and Religion: West and East* calls for comment, since no single volume can cover Jung's publications on a subject that takes so prominent a place in all his later works. To a full understanding of Jung's thesis on religion a thorough grasp of his theory of the archetypes is essential, as well as a knowledge of several other of the volumes of the Collected Works, of which *Aion* and *Psychology and Alchemy* may be singled out.

It could, therefore, be said that the Editors would have been better advised to group all these works under the general title *Psychology and Religion,* rather than confine this title to a single volume. It will not be out of place to remember that Jung's definition of religion is a wide one. Religion, he says, is "a careful and scrupulous observation of what Rudolf Otto aptly termed the *numinosum.*" From this standpoint, Jung was struck by the contrasting methods of observation employed by religious men of the East and by those of the predominantly Christian West.

The main part of the title is that of the Terry Lectures for 1937, its general applicability being evident; but the volume has a particular aim, which the subtitle *West and East* clarifies. Thus the division into two parts, "Western Religion" and "Eastern Religion," reflecting Jung's idea that the two are radically different.

In the original "Psychology and Religion," which introduces Part One, Jung expounds the relation between Christianity and alchemy. This connection he has worked out in greater detail in *Psychology and Alchemy,* where he says that "alchemy seems like a continuation of Christian mysticism carried on in the subterranean darkness of the unconscious." There follow in this volume "A Psychological Approach to the Dogma of the Trinity," translated for the first time into English, and "Transformation Symbolism in the Mass," which presents alchemical and Aztec parallels to the Christian ritual. Part One ends with the provocative essay "Answer to Job." These three works, all original researches of distinctive importance, are especially significant because they penetrate to the heart of Christian symbolism and shed new light on its psychological meaning. Part One also contains two forewords, of particular interest because the books they introduce both illustrate the relevance of Jung's work for religious thinking; a short essay on the Swiss saint, Brother Klaus; and two essays on the relation between psychotherapy and religious healing.

It is worthy of note that most of the works on Eastern religion in Part Two are commentaries or forewords, in contrast with the authoritative tone of Jung's writings on Christianity and alchemy. This fact confirms what should be clear from all his work: that his main interest has been in the psychology of Western man and so in his religious life and development.

It may be a matter for surprise that the foreword to the *I Ching,* which closes the volume, is included here; it is a document that would scarcely be termed religious, in the common usage of that word. If, however, Jung's definition cited above be kept in mind, and if it be remembered that the earlier interpretations of what is now known as synchronicity were essentially religious in Jung's sense and that the *I Ching* was studied by the most illustrious of the Eastern sages, the intention of the Editors will be apparent. Jung's commentary on *The Secret of the Golden Flower* might equally well have come into the second part of this volume, but because of the many analogies between this Taoist text and alchemy, the Editors have placed it in Volume 13, *Alchemical Studies.*

*

Grateful acknowledgment is made to the School of American Research, Santa Fe, New Mexico, for a quotation from the Anderson and Dibble translation of Sahagùn; to the Clarendon Press, Oxford, for passages from M. R. James, *The Apocryphal New Testament;* the Oxford University Press, for Professor Jung's commentary on *The Tibetan Book of the Great Libera-*

tion; and the Harvill Press and the Henry Regnery Company for Professor Jung's foreword to *God and the Unconscious.*

The frontispiece is from a photograph by Giraudon, Paris, of an illustration in the Book of Hours of Etienne Chevalier, Condé Museum, Chantilly.

TRANSLATOR'S NOTE

I wish to make grateful acknowledgment to the following persons, whose various translations have been consulted to a greater or less degree during the preparation of this volume; Miss Monica Curtis, for help derived from her perceptive translation of extensive portions of "Transformation Symbolism in the Mass," published as Guild Lecture No. 69 by the Guild of Pastoral Psychology, London, and of which certain passages are incorporated here almost verbatim; Father Victor White, O.P., for the use of his translation of the foreword to his book *God and the Unconscious;* Dr. Horace Gray, for reference to his translation of "Brother Klaus" in the *Journal of Nervous and Mental Diseases;* Mr. W. S. Dell and Mrs. Cary F. Baynes, for reference to their translation of "Psychotherapists or the Clergy" in *Modern Man in Search of a Soul;* Dr. James Kirsch, for making available to me his private translation of "Answer to Job," prepared for members of a seminar he conducted at Los Angeles, 1952–53, and also for his helpful criticism during personal discussions; Mrs. Cary F. Baynes, for reference to her translation of "Yoga and the West" in *Prabuddha Bharata* and for the use with only minor alterations of her translation of the foreword to the *I Ching;* Miss Constance Rolfe, for reference to her translation of the foreword to Suzuki's *Introduction to Zen Buddhism;* and Mrs. Carol Baumann, for reference to her translation of "The Psychology of Eastern Meditation" in *Art and Thought.* Acknowledgment is also made to Mr. A. S. B. Glover for his translations of many Latin passages throughout as well as for the index.

TABLE OF CONTENTS

III

Translated from "Das Wandlungssymbol in der Messe," *Von den Wurzeln des Bewusstseins* (Zurich: Rascher, 1954).

IV

V

VI

PART TWO: EASTERN RELIGION

VII

VIII

PART ONE

WESTERN RELIGION

I

PSYCHOLOGY AND RELIGION

[Originally written in English and delivered in 1937, at Yale University, New Haven, Connecticut, as the fifteenth series of "Lectures on Religion in the Light of Science and Philosophy" under the auspices of the Dwight Harrington Terry Foundation. The lectures were published for the Terry Foundation by the Yale University Press (and by Oxford University Press, London) in 1938. They were then translated into German by Felicia Froboese, and the translation, revised by Toni Wolff and augmented by Professor Jung, was published at Zurich, 1940, as *Psychologie und Religion*. The present version is based on both the original English and the German versions and contains the revisions and additions of the latter.—EDITORS.]

1. THE AUTONOMY OF THE UNCONSCIOUS

1 As it seems to be the intention of the founder of the Terry Lectures to enable representatives of science, as well as of philosophy and other spheres of human knowledge, to contribute to the discussion of the eternal problem of religion, and since Yale University has bestowed upon me the great honour of delivering the Terry Lectures for 1937, I assume that it will be my task to show what psychology, or rather that special branch of medical psychology which I represent, has to do with or to say about religion. Since religion is incontestably one of the earliest and most universal expressions of the human mind, it is obvious that any psychology which touches upon the psychological structure of human personality cannot avoid taking note of the fact that religion is not only a sociological and historical phenomenon, but also something of considerable personal concern to a great number of individuals.

2 Although I have often been called a philosopher, I am an empiricist and adhere as such to the phenomenological standpoint. I trust that it does not conflict with the principles of scientific empiricism if one occasionally makes certain reflections which go beyond a mere accumulation and classification of experience. As a matter of fact I believe that experience is not even possible without reflection, because "experience" is a process of assimilation without which there could be no under-

standing. As this statement indicates, I approach psychological matters from a scientific and not from a philosophical standpoint. Inasmuch as religion has a very important psychological aspect, I deal with it from a purely empirical point of view, that is, I restrict myself to the observation of phenomena and I eschew any metaphysical or philosophical considerations. I do not deny the validity of these other considerations, but I cannot claim to be competent to apply them correctly.

3 I am aware that most people believe they know all there is to be known about psychology, because they think that psychology is nothing but what they know of themselves. But I am afraid psychology is a good deal more than that. While having little to do with philosophy, it has much to do with empirical facts, many of which are not easily accessible to the experience of the average man. It is my intention to give you a few glimpses of the way in which practical psychology comes up against the problem of religion. It is self-evident that the vastness of the problem requires far more than three lectures, as the necessary elaboration of concrete detail takes a great deal of time and explanation. My first lecture will be a sort of introduction to the problem of practical psychology and religion. The second is concerned with facts which demonstrate the existence of an authentic religious function in the unconscious. The third deals with the religious symbolism of unconscious processes.

4 Since I am going to present a rather unusual argument, I cannot assume that my audience will be fully acquainted with the methodological standpoint of the branch of psychology I represent. This standpoint is exclusively phenomenological, that is, it is concerned with occurrences, events, experiences—in a word, with facts. Its truth is a fact and not a judgment. When psychology speaks, for instance, of the motif of the virgin birth, it is only concerned with the fact that there is such an idea, but it is not concerned with the question whether such an idea is true or false in any other sense. The idea is psychologically true inasmuch as it exists. Psychological existence is subjective in so far as an idea occurs in only one individual. But it is objective in so far as that idea is shared by a society—by a *consensus gentium*.

5 This point of view is the same as that of natural science. Psychology deals with ideas and other mental contents as zool-

ogy, for instance, deals with the different species of animals. An elephant is "true" because it exists. The elephant is neither an inference nor a statement nor the subjective judgment of a creator. It is a phenomenon. But we are so used to the idea that psychic events are wilful and arbitrary products, or even the inventions of a human creator, that we can hardly rid ourselves of the prejudiced view that the psyche and its contents are nothing but our own arbitrary invention or the more or less illusory product of supposition and judgment. The fact is that certain ideas exist almost everywhere and at all times and can even spontaneously create themselves quite independently of migration and tradition. They are not made by the individual, they just happen to him—they even force themselves on his consciousness. This is not Platonic philosophy but empirical psychology.

6 In speaking of religion I must make clear from the start what I mean by that term. Religion, as the Latin word denotes, is a careful and scrupulous observation of what Rudolf Otto [1] aptly termed the *numinosum,* that is, a dynamic agency or effect not caused by an arbitrary act of will. On the contrary, it seizes and controls the human subject, who is always rather its victim than its creator. The *numinosum*—whatever its cause may be—is an experience of the subject independent of his will. At all events, religious teaching as well as the *consensus gentium* always and everywhere explain this experience as being due to a cause external to the individual. The *numinosum* is either a quality belonging to a visible object or the influence of an invisible presence that causes a peculiar alteration of consciousness. This is, at any rate, the general rule.

7 There are, however, certain exceptions when it comes to the question of religious practice or ritual. A great many ritualistic performances are carried out for the sole purpose of producing at will the effect of the *numinosum* by means of certain devices of a magical nature, such as invocation, incantation, sacrifice, meditation and other yoga practices, self-inflicted tortures of various descriptions, and so forth. But a religious belief in an external and objective divine cause is always prior to any such performance. The Catholic Church, for instance, administers the sacraments for the purpose of bestowing their spiritual blessings upon the believer; but since this act would amount to

1 *The Idea of the Holy.*

enforcing the presence of divine grace by an indubitably magical procedure, it is logically argued that nobody can compel divine grace to be present in the sacramental act, but that it is nevertheless inevitably present since the sacrament is a divine institution which God would not have caused to be if he had not intended to lend it his support.[2]

8 Religion appears to me to be a peculiar attitude of mind which could be formulated in accordance with the original use of the word *religio,* which means a careful consideration and observation of certain dynamic factors that are conceived as "powers": spirits, daemons, gods, laws, ideas, ideals, or whatever name man has given to such factors in his world as he has found powerful, dangerous, or helpful enough to be taken into careful consideration, or grand, beautiful, and meaningful enough to be devoutly worshipped and loved. In colloquial speech one often says of somebody who is enthusiastically interested in a certain pursuit that he is almost "religiously devoted" to his cause; William James, for instance, remarks that a scientist often has no creed, but his "temper is devout." [3]

9 I want to make clear that by the term "religion" [4] I do not mean a creed. It is, however, true that every creed is originally based on the one hand upon the experience of the *numinosum* and on the other hand upon *πίστις,* that is to say, trust or loyalty, faith and confidence in a certain experience of a numinous nature and in the change of consciousness that ensues. The conversion of Paul is a striking example of this. We might say, then, that the term "religion" designates the attitude peculiar to a consciousness which has been changed by experience of the *numinosum.*

2 *Gratia adiuvans* and *gratia sanctificans* are the effects of the *sacramentum ex opere operato.* The sacrament owes its undoubted efficacy to the fact that it is directly instituted by Christ himself. The Church is powerless to connect the rite with grace in such a way that the sacramental act would produce the presence and effect of grace. Consequently the rite performed by the priest is not a *causa instrumentalis,* but merely a *causa ministerialis.*

3 "But our esteem for facts has not neutralized in us all religiousness. It is itself almost religious. Our scientific temper is devout." *Pragmatism,* p. 14.

4 "Religion is that which gives reverence and worship to some higher nature [which is called divine]." Cicero, *De inventione rhetorica,* II, 53, 161. For "testimony given under the sanction of religion on the faith of an oath" cf. Cicero, *Pro Coelio,* 55.

10 Creeds are codified and dogmatized forms of original religious experience.[5] The contents of the experience have become sanctified and are usually congealed in a rigid, often elaborate, structure of ideas. The practice and repetition of the original experience have become a ritual and an unchangeable institution. This does not necessarily mean lifeless petrifaction. On the contrary, it may prove to be a valid form of religious experience for millions of people for thousands of years, without there arising any vital necessity to alter it. Although the Catholic Church has often been accused of particular rigidity, she nevertheless admits that dogma is a living thing and that its formulation is therefore capable of change and development. Even the number of dogmas is not limited and can be multiplied in the course of time. The same holds true of the ritual. Yet all changes and developments are determined within the framework of the facts as originally experienced, and this sets up a special kind of dogmatic content and emotional value. Even Protestantism, which has abandoned itself apparently to an almost unlimited emancipation from dogmatic tradition and codified ritual and has thus split into more than four hundred denominations—even Protestantism is bound at least to be Christian and to express itself within the framework of the belief that God revealed himself in Christ, who suffered for mankind. This is a definite framework with definite contents which cannot be combined with or supplemented by Buddhist or Islamic ideas and feelings. Yet it is unquestionably true that not only Buddha and Mohammed, Confucius and Zarathustra, represent religious phenomena, but also Mithras, Attis, Cybele, Mani, Hermes, and the deities of many other exotic cults. The psychologist, if he takes up a scientific attitude, has to disregard the claim of every creed to be the unique and eternal truth. He must keep his eye on the human side of the religious problem, since he is concerned with the original religious experience quite apart from what the creeds have made of it.

11 As I am a doctor and a specialist in nervous and mental diseases, my point of departure is not a creed but the psychology of the *homo religiosus,* the man who takes into account and carefully observes certain factors which influence him and, through

[5] Heinrich Scholz (*Die Religionsphilosophie des Als-Ob*) insists on a similar standpoint. Cf. also Pearcy, *A Vindication of Paul.*

him, his general condition. It is easy to denominate and define these factors in accordance with historical tradition or ethnological knowledge, but to do the same thing from the standpoint of psychology is an uncommonly difficult task. What I can contribute to the question of religion is derived entirely from my practical experience, both with my patients and with so-called normal persons. As our experience with people depends to a large extent upon what we do with them, I can see no other way of proceeding than to give you at least a general idea of the line I take in my professional work.

12 Since every neurosis is connected with man's most intimate life, there will always be some hesitation when a patient has to give a complete account of all the circumstances and complications which originally led him into a morbid condition. But why shouldn't he be able to talk freely? Why should he be afraid or shy or prudish? The reason is that he is "carefully observing" certain external factors which together constitute what one calls public opinion or respectability or reputation. And even if he trusts his doctor and is no longer shy of him, he will be reluctant or even afraid to admit certain things to *himself,* as if it were dangerous to become conscious of himself. One is usually afraid of things that seem to be overpowering. But is there anything in man that is stronger than himself? We should not forget that every neurosis entails a corresponding amount of demoralization. If a man is neurotic, he has lost confidence in himself. A neurosis is a humiliating defeat and is felt as such by people who are not entirely unconscious of their own psychology. And one is defeated by something "unreal." Doctors may have assured the patient, long ago, that there is nothing the matter with him, that he does not suffer from a real heart-disease or from a real cancer. His symptoms are quite imaginary. The more he believes that he is a *malade imaginaire,* the more a feeling of inferiority permeates his whole personality. "If my symptoms are imaginary," he will say, "where have I picked up this confounded imagination and why should I put up with such a perfect nuisance?" It is indeed pathetic to have an intelligent man almost imploringly assure you that he is suffering from an intestinal cancer and declare at the same time in a despondent voice that of course he knows his cancer is a purely imaginary affair.

13 Our usual materialistic conception of the psyche is, I am

afraid, not particularly helpful in cases of neurosis. If only the soul were endowed with a subtle body, then one could at least say that this breath- or vapour-body was suffering from a real though somewhat ethereal cancer, in the same way as the gross material body can succumb to a cancerous disease. That, at least, would be something real. Medicine therefore feels a strong aversion for anything of a psychic nature—either the body is ill or there is nothing the matter. And if you cannot prove that the body is really ill, that is only because our present techniques do not enable the doctor to discover the true nature of the undoubtedly organic trouble.

14 But what, actually, is the psyche? Materialistic prejudice explains it as a mere epiphenomenal by-product of organic processes in the brain. Any psychic disturbance must therefore be an organic or physical disorder which is undiscoverable only because of the inadequacy of our present methods of diagnosis. The undeniable connection between psyche and brain gives this point of view a certain weight, but not enough to make it an unshakable truth. We do not know whether there is a real disturbance of the organic processes in the brain in a case of neurosis, and if there are disorders of an endocrine nature it is impossible to say whether they might not be effects rather than causes.

15 On the other hand, it cannot be doubted that the real causes of neurosis are psychological. Not so long ago it was very difficult to imagine how an organic or physical disorder could be relieved by quite simple psychological means, yet in recent years medical science has recognized a whole class of diseases, the psychosomatic disorders, in which the patient's psychology plays the essential part. Since my readers may not be familiar with these medical facts I may instance a case of hysterical fever, with a temperature of 102°, which was cured in a few minutes through confession of the psychological cause. A patient with psoriasis extending over practically the whole body was told that I did not feel competent to treat his skin trouble, but that I should concentrate on his psychological conflicts, which were numerous. After six weeks of intense analysis and discussion of his purely psychological difficulties, there came about as an unexpected by-product the almost complete disappearance of the skin disease. In another case, the patient had recently undergone an

operation for distention of the colon. Forty centimetres of it had been removed, but this was followed by another extraordinary distention. The patient was desperate and refused to permit a second operation, though the surgeon thought it vital. As soon as certain intimate psychological facts were discovered, the colon began to function normally again.

16 Such experiences make it exceedingly difficult to believe that the psyche is nothing, or that an imaginary fact is unreal. Only, it is not there where a near-sighted mind seeks it. It exists, but not in physical form. It is an almost absurd prejudice to suppose that existence can only be physical. As a matter of fact, the only form of existence of which we have immediate knowledge is psychic. We might well say, on the contrary, that physical existence is a mere inference, since we know of matter only in so far as we perceive psychic images mediated by the senses.

17 We are surely making a great mistake when we forget this simple yet fundamental truth. Even if a neurosis had no cause at all other than imagination, it would, none the less, be a very real thing. If a man imagined that I was his arch-enemy and killed me, I should be dead on account of mere imagination. Imaginary conditions do exist and they may be just as real and just as harmful or dangerous as physical conditions. I even believe that psychic disturbances are far more dangerous than epidemics or earthquakes. Not even the medieval epidemics of bubonic plague or smallpox killed as many people as certain differences of opinion in 1914 or certain political "ideals" in Russia.

18 Although the mind cannot apprehend its own form of existence, owing to the lack of an Archimedean point outside, it nevertheless exists. Not only does the psyche exist, it is existence itself.

19 What, then, shall we say to our patient with the imaginary cancer? I would tell him: "Yes, my friend, you are really suffering from a cancer-like thing, you really do harbour in yourself a deadly evil. However, it will not kill your body, because it is imaginary. But it will eventually kill your soul. It has already spoilt and even poisoned your human relations and your personal happiness and it will go on growing until it has swallowed your whole psychic existence. So that in the end you will not be a human being any more, but an evil destructive tumour."

20 It is obvious to our patient that he is not the author of his morbid imagination, although his theoretical turn of mind will certainly suggest that he is the owner and maker of his own imaginings. If a man is suffering from a real cancer, he never believes himself to be responsible for such an evil, despite the fact that the cancer is in his own body. But when it comes to the psyche we instantly feel a kind of responsibility, as if we were the makers of our psychic conditions. This prejudice is of relatively recent date. Not so very long ago even highly civilized people believed that psychic agencies could influence our minds and feelings. There were ghosts, wizards, and witches, daemons and angels, and even gods, who could produce certain psychological changes in human beings. In former times the man with the idea that he had cancer might have felt quite differently about his idea. He would probably have assumed that somebody had worked witchcraft against him or that he was possessed. He never would have thought of himself as the originator of such a fantasy.

21 As a matter of fact, I take his cancer to be a spontaneous growth, which originated in the part of the psyche that is not identical with consciousness. It appears as an autonomous formation intruding upon consciousness. Of consciousness one might say that it is our own psychic existence, but the cancer has *its* own psychic existence, independent of ourselves. This statement seems to formulate the observable facts completely. If we submit such a case to an association experiment,[6] we soon discover that man is not master in his own house. His reactions will be delayed, altered, suppressed, or replaced by autonomous intruders. There will be a number of stimulus-words which cannot be answered by his conscious intention. They will be answered by certain autonomous contents, which are very often unconscious even to himself. In our case we shall certainly discover answers that come from the psychic complex at the root of the cancer idea. Whenever a stimulus-word touches something connected with the hidden complex, the reaction of the conscious ego will be disturbed, or even replaced, by an answer coming from the complex. It is just as if the complex were an autonomous being capable of interfering with the intentions of

[6] Cf. my "Studies in Word Association."

the ego. Complexes do indeed behave like secondary or partial personalities possessing a mental life of their own.

22 Many complexes are split off from consciousness because the latter preferred to get rid of them by repression. But there are others that have never been in consciousness before and therefore could never have been arbitrarily repressed. They grow out of the unconscious and invade the conscious mind with their weird and unassailable convictions and impulses. Our patient belonged to the latter category. Despite his culture and intelligence, he was a helpless victim of something that obsessed and possessed him. He was unable to help himself in any way against the demonic power of his morbid idea. It proliferated in him like a carcinoma. One day the idea appeared and from then on it remained unshakable; there were only short intervals when he was free from it.

23 The existence of such cases does something to explain why people are afraid of becoming conscious of themselves. There might really be something behind the screen—one never knows—and so people prefer "to consider and observe carefully" the factors external to their consciousness. In most people there is a sort of primitive δεισιδαιμονία with regard to the possible contents of the unconscious. Beneath all natural shyness, shame, and tact, there is a secret fear of the unknown "perils of the soul." Of course one is reluctant to admit such a ridiculous fear. But one should realize that this fear is by no means unjustified; on the contrary, it is only too well founded. We can never be sure that a new idea will not seize either upon ourselves or upon our neighbours. We know from modern as well as from ancient history that such ideas are often so strange, indeed so bizarre, that they fly in the face of reason. The fascination which is almost invariably connected with ideas of this sort produces a fanatical obsession, with the result that all dissenters, no matter how well meaning or reasonable they are, get burnt alive or have their heads cut off or are disposed of in masses by the more modern machine-gun. We cannot even console ourselves with the thought that such things belong to the remote past. Unfortunately they seem to belong not only to the present, but, quite particularly, to the future. "Homo homini lupus" is a sad yet eternal truism. There is indeed reason enough for man to be afraid of the impersonal forces lurking in his unconscious. We

are blissfully unconscious of these forces because they never, or almost never, appear in our personal relations or under ordinary circumstances. But if people crowd together and form a mob, then the dynamisms of the collective man are let loose—beasts or demons that lie dormant in every person until he is part of a mob. Man in the mass sinks unconsciously to an inferior moral and intellectual level, to that level which is always there, below the threshold of consciousness, ready to break forth as soon as it is activated by the formation of a mass.

24 It is, to my mind, a fatal mistake to regard the human psyche as a purely personal affair and to explain it exclusively from a personal point of view. Such a mode of explanation is only applicable to the individual in his ordinary everyday occupations and relationships. If, however, some slight trouble occurs, perhaps in the form of an unforeseen and somewhat unusual event, instantly instinctual forces are called up, forces which appear to be wholly unexpected, new, and strange. They can no longer be explained in terms of personal motives, being comparable rather to certain primitive occurrences like panics at solar eclipses and the like. To explain the murderous outbreak of Bolshevism, for instance, as a personal father-complex appears to me singularly inadequate.

25 The change of character brought about by the uprush of collective forces is amazing. A gentle and reasonable being can be transformed into a maniac or a savage beast. One is always inclined to lay the blame on external circumstances, but nothing could explode in us if it had not been there. As a matter of fact, we are constantly living on the edge of a volcano, and there is, so far as we know, no way of protecting ourselves from a possible outburst that will destroy everybody within reach. It is certainly a good thing to preach reason and common sense, but what if you have a lunatic asylum for an audience or a crowd in a collective frenzy? There is not much difference between them because the madman and the mob are both moved by impersonal, overwhelming forces.

26 As a matter of fact, it only needs a neurosis to conjure up a force that cannot be dealt with by rational means. Our cancer case shows clearly how impotent man's reason and intellect are against the most palpable nonsense. I always advise my patients to take such obvious but invincible nonsense as the manifesta-

tion of a power and a meaning they have not yet understood. Experience has taught me that it is much more effective to take these things seriously and then look for a suitable explanation. But an explanation is suitable only when it produces a hypothesis equal to the morbid effect. Our patient is confronted with a power of will and suggestion more than equal to anything his consciousness can put against it. In this precarious situation it would be bad strategy to convince him that in some incomprehensible way he is at the back of his own symptom, secretly inventing and supporting it. Such a suggestion would instantly paralyse his fighting spirit, and he would get demoralized. It is far better for him to understand that his complex is an autonomous power directed against his conscious personality. Moreover, such an explanation fits the actual facts much better than a reduction to personal motives. An apparently personal motivation does exist, but it is not made by his will, it just happens to him.

27 When in the Babylonian epic Gilgamesh's arrogance and hybris defy the gods, they create a man equal in strength to Gilgamesh in order to check the hero's unlawful ambition. The very same thing has happened to our patient: he is a thinker who has settled, or is always going to settle, the world by the power of his intellect and reason. His ambition has at least succeeded in forging his own personal fate. He has forced everything under the inexorable law of his reason, but somewhere nature escaped and came back with a vengeance in the form of an unassailable bit of nonsense, the cancer idea. This was the clever device of the unconscious to keep him on a merciless and cruel leash. It was the worst blow that could be dealt to all his rational ideals and especially to his belief in the all-powerful human will. Such an obsession can only occur in a person who makes habitual misuse of reason and intellect for egotistical power purposes.

28 Gilgamesh, however, escaped the vengeance of the gods. He had warning dreams to which he paid attention. They showed him how he could overcome his enemy. Our patient, living in an age when the gods have become extinct and have fallen into bad repute, also had such dreams, but he did not listen to them. How could an intelligent man be so superstitious as to take dreams seriously! The very common prejudice against dreams is

but one symptom of a far more serious undervaluation of the human psyche in general. The marvellous development of science and technics is counterbalanced by an appalling lack of wisdom and introspection. It is true that our religion speaks of an immortal soul; but it has very few kind words to say for the human psyche as such, which would go straight to eternal damnation were it not for a special act of Divine Grace. These two important factors are largely responsible for the general undervaluation of the psyche, but not entirely so. Older by far than these relatively recent developments are the primitive fear of and aversion to everything that borders on the unconscious.

29 Consciousness must have been a very precarious thing in its beginnings. In relatively primitive societies we can still observe how easily consciousness gets lost. One of the "perils of the soul," [7] for instance, is the loss of a soul. This is what happens when part of the psyche becomes unconscious again. Another example is "running amok," [8] the equivalent of "going berserk" in Germanic saga.[9] This is a more or less complete trance-state, often accompanied by devastating social effects. Even a quite ordinary emotion can cause considerable loss of consciousness. Primitives therefore cultivate elaborate forms of politeness, speaking in a hushed voice, laying down their weapons, crawling on all fours, bowing the head, showing the palms. Even our own forms of politeness still exhibit a "religious" consideration of possible psychic dangers. We propitiate fate by magically wishing one another a good day. It is not good form to keep the left hand in your pocket or behind your back when shaking hands. If you want to be particularly ingratiating you use both hands. Before people of great authority we bow with uncovered head, i.e., we offer our head unprotected in order to propitiate the powerful one, who might quite easily fall sudden prey to a fit of uncontrollable violence. In war-dances primitives can become so excited that they may even shed blood.

30 The life of the primitive is filled with constant regard for the ever-lurking possibility of psychic danger, and the procedures employed to diminish the risks are very numerous. The setting up of tabooed areas is an outward expression of this fact. The

[7] Frazer, *Taboo and the Perils of the Soul,* pp. 30ff.; Crawley, *The Idea of the Soul,* pp. 82ff.; Lévy-Bruhl, *Primitive Mentality.*

[8] Fenn, *Running Amok.*

[9] Ninck, *Wodan und germanischer Schicksalsglaube.*

innumerable taboos are delimited psychic areas which are meticulously and fearfully observed. I once made a terrific mistake when I was with a tribe on the southern slopes of Mount Elgon, in East Africa. I wanted to inquire about the ghost-houses I frequently found in the woods, and during a palaver I mentioned the word *selelteni,* meaning 'ghost.' Instantly everybody was silent and painfully embarrassed. They all looked away from me because I had spoken aloud a carefully hushed-up word, and had thus invited most dangerous consequences. I had to change the subject in order to be able to continue the meeting. The same men assured me that they never had dreams; they were the prerogative of the chief and of the medicine man. The medicine man then confessed to me that he no longer had any dreams either, they had the District Commissioner instead. "Since the English are in the country we have no dreams any more," he said. "The District Commissioner knows everything about war and diseases, and about where we have got to live." This strange statement is based on the fact that dreams were formerly the supreme political guide, the voice of *Mungu,* 'God.' Therefore it would have been unwise for an ordinary man to suggest that he had dreams.

31 Dreams are the voice of the Unknown, ever threatening new schemes, new dangers, sacrifices, warfare, and other troublesome things. An African Negro once dreamt that his enemies had taken him prisoner and burnt him alive. The next day he called his relatives together and implored them to burn him. They consented so far as to bind his feet together and put them in the fire. He was of course badly crippled but had escaped his foes.[10]

32 There are any amount of magical rites that exist for the sole purpose of erecting a defence against the unexpected, dangerous tendencies of the unconscious. The peculiar fact that the dream is a divine voice and messenger and yet an unending source of trouble does not disturb the primitive mind in the least. We find obvious remnants of this primitive thinking in the psychology of the Hebrew prophets.[11] Often enough they hesitate to listen to the voice. And it was, we must admit, rather hard on a pious man like Hosea to marry a harlot in order to obey the

10 Lévy-Bruhl, *How Natives Think,* and *Primitive Mentality,* ch. 3, "Dreams," pp. 97ff.

11 Haeussermann, *Wortempfang und Symbol in der alttestamentlichen Prophetie.*

Lord's command. Since the dawn of humanity there has been a marked tendency to limit this unruly and arbitrary "supernatural" influence by means of definite forms and laws. And this process has continued throughout history in the form of a multiplication of rites, institutions, and beliefs. During the last two thousand years we find the institution of the Christian Church taking over a mediating and protective function between these influences and man. It is not denied in medieval ecclesiastical writings that a divine influx may occur in dreams, but this view is not exactly encouraged, and the Church reserves the right to decide whether a revelation is to be considered authentic or not.[12] In spite of the Church's recognition that

12 In his excellent treatise on dreams and their functions, Benedictus Pererius, S.J. (*De Magia; De Observatione Somniorum et de Divinatione Astrologica libri tres,* 1598) says: "For God is not constrained by such laws of time, nor does he await opportune moments for his operation; for he inspires dreams where he will, when he will, and in whomsoever he will" (p. 147). The following passage throws an interesting light on the relation of the Church to the problem of dreams: "For we read in Cassian's 22nd Collation, that the old governors and directors of the monks were well versed in seeking out and testing the causes of certain dreams" (p. 142). Pererius classifies dreams as follows: "Many [dreams] are natural, some are of human origin, and some are even divine" (p. 145). There are four causes of dreams: (1) An affection of the body. (2) An affect or vehement commotion of the mind caused by love, hope, fear, or hatred (pp. 126ff.). (3) The power and cunning of the demon, i.e. of a heathen god or the Christian devil. ("For the devil is able to know natural effects which will needs come about at some future time from fixed causes; he can know those things which he himself is going to bring about at a later time; he can know things, both present and past, which are hidden from men, and make them known to men in dreams" [p. 129]. Concerning the diagnosis of demonic dreams, the author says: "It can be surmised that dreams are sent by the devil, firstly if dreams often occur which signify future or hidden events, knowledge whereof is advantageous not to any useful end whether for oneself or for others, but only for the vain display of curious information, or even for the doing of some evil act . . ." [p. 130].) (4) Dreams sent by God. Concerning the signs indicating the divine nature of a dream, the author says: ". . . from the importance of the matters made known by the dream, especially if, in the dream, those things are made known to a man of which certain knowledge can come to him only by God's leave and bounty. Of such sort are those things which in the schools of the theologians are called contingent future events; further, the secrets of the heart which are wholly hidden from all men's understanding; and lastly, those highest mysteries of our faith which are known to no man unless he be taught them by God [!] . . . That this [is divine] is especially declared by a certain enlightenment and moving of the spirits, whereby God so illumines the mind, so acts upon the will, and so assures the dreamer of the

certain dreams are sent by God, she is disinclined, and even averse, to any serious concern with dreams, while admitting that some might conceivably contain an immediate revelation. Thus the change of mental attitude that has taken place in recent centuries is, from this point of view at least, not wholly unwelcome to the Church, because it effectively discouraged the earlier introspective attitude which favoured a serious consideration of dreams and inner experiences.

credibility and authority of his dream that he so clearly recognizes and so certainly judges God to be its author that he not only desires to believe it, but must believe it without any doubt whatsoever" (pp. 131ff.). Since the demon, as stated above, is also capable of producing dreams accurately predicting future events, the author adds a quotation from Gregory the Great (*Dialogorum Libri IV*, cap. 48, in Migne, *P.L.*, vol. 77, col. 412): "Holy men discern between illusions and revelations, the very words and images of visions, by a certain inward sensibility, so that they know what they receive from the good spirit and what they endure from the deceiver. For if a man's mind were not careful in this regard, it would plunge itself into many vanities through the deceiving spirit, who is sometimes wont to foretell many true things, in order that he may entirely prevail to ensnare the soul by some one single falsity" (p. 132). It seemed to be a welcome safeguard against this uncertainty if dreams were concerned with the "highest mysteries of our faith." Athanasius, in his biography of St. Anthony, gives us some idea of how clever the devils are in foretelling future events. (Cf. Budge, *The Book of Paradise*, I, pp. 37ff.) The same author says they sometimes appear even in the shape of monks, singing psalms, reading the Bible aloud, and making disturbing remarks about the moral conduct of the brethren (pp. 33ff. and 47). Pererius, however, seems to trust his own criterion, for he continues: "As therefore the natural light of our minds enables us clearly to discern the truth of first principles, so that they are embraced by our assent immediately and without any argument; so in dreams sent by God the divine light shining upon our minds brings it about that we understand and believe with certainty that those dreams are true and of God." He does not touch on the delicate question of whether *every* unshakable conviction derived from a dream necessarily proves the divine origin of the dream. He merely takes it for granted that a dream of this sort would naturally exhibit a character consistent with the "highest mysteries of our faith," and not perchance with those of another one. The humanist Kaspar Peucer (in his *Commentarius de praecipuis generibus divinationum*, 1560) is far more definite and restrictive in this respect. He says (p. 270): "Those dreams are of God which the sacred scriptures affirm to be sent from on high, not to every one promiscuously, nor to those who strive after and expect revelations of their own opinion, but to the Holy Patriarchs and Prophets by the will and judgment of God. [Such dreams are concerned] not with light matters, or with trifles and ephemeral things, but with Christ, the governance of the Church, with empires and their well ordering, and other remarkable events; and to these God always adds sure testimonies, such as the gift of interpretation and other things, by

33 Protestantism, having pulled down so many walls carefully erected by the Church, immediately began to experience the disintegrating and schismatic effect of individual revelation. As soon as the dogmatic fence was broken down and the ritual lost its authority, man had to face his inner experience without the protection and guidance of dogma and ritual, which are the very quintessence of Christian as well as of pagan religious experience. Protestantism has, in the main, lost all the finer shades of traditional Christianity: the mass, confession, the greater part of the liturgy, and the vicarious function of priesthood.

34 I must emphasize that this statement is not a value-judgment and is not intended to be one. I merely state the facts. Protestantism has, however, intensified the authority of the Bible as a substitute for the lost authority of the Church. But as history has shown, one can interpret certain biblical texts in many ways. Nor has scientific criticism of the New Testament been very helpful in enhancing belief in the divine character of the holy scriptures. It is also a fact that under the influence of a so-called

---

which it is clear that they are not rashly to be objected to, nor are they of natural origin, but are divinely inspired." His crypto-Calvinism is palpably manifest in his words, particularly when one compares them with the natural theology of his Catholic contemporaries. It is probable that Peucer's hint about "revelations" refers to certain heretical innovations. At any rate, in the next paragraph, where he deals with dreams of diabolical origin, he says these are the dreams "which the devil shows nowadays to Anabaptists, and at all times to Enthusiasts and suchlike fanatics." Pererius with more perspicacity and human understanding devotes one chapter to the question "Whether it be lawful for a Christian man to observe dreams?" (pp. 142ff.) and another to the question "To what kind of man does it belong to interpret dreams aright?" (pp. 245ff.). In the first he reaches the conclusion that important dreams should be considered. I quote his words: "Finally, to consider whether the dreams which ofttimes disturb us and move us to evil courses are put before us by the devil, as likewise on the other hand to ponder whether those by which we are aroused and incited to good, as for example to celibacy, almsgiving, and entering the religious life, are sent us by God, is the part not of a superstitious mind, but of one that is religious, prudent, and careful and solicitous for its salvation." Only stupid people would observe all the other futile dreams. In the second chapter, he answers that nobody should or could interpret dreams "unless he be divinely inspired and instructed." "Even so," he adds, "the things of God knoweth no man, but the Spirit of God" (I Cor. 2:11). This statement, eminently true in itself, reserves the art of interpretation to such persons as are endowed by their office with the gift of the Holy Spirit. It is obvious, however, that a Jesuit author could not envisage a descent of the Holy Spirit outside the Church.

scientific enlightenment great masses of educated people have either left the Church or become profoundly indifferent to it. If they were all dull rationalists or neurotic intellectuals the loss would not be regrettable. But many of them are religious people, only incapable of agreeing with the existing forms of belief. Otherwise, one could hardly explain the remarkable effect of the Buchman movement on the more-or-less educated Protestant classes. The Catholic who has turned his back on the Church usually develops a secret or manifest leaning towards atheism, whereas the Protestant follows, if possible, a sectarian movement. The absolutism of the Catholic Church seems to demand an equally absolute negation, whereas Protestant relativism permits of variations.

35 It may perhaps be thought that I have gone a bit too far into the history of Christianity, and for no other purpose than to explain the prejudice against dreams and inner experiences. But what I have just said might have been part of my conversation with our cancer patient. I told him that it would be better to take his obsession seriously instead of reviling it as pathological nonsense. But to take it seriously would mean acknowledging it as a sort of diagnostic statement of the fact that, in a psyche which really existed, trouble had arisen in the form of a cancer-like growth. "But," he will certainly ask, "what could that growth be?" And I shall answer: "I do not know," as indeed I do not. Although, as I mentioned before, it is surely a compensatory or complementary unconscious formation, nothing is yet known about its specific nature or about its content. It is a spontaneous manifestation of the unconscious, based on contents which are not to be found in consciousness.

36 My patient is now very curious how I shall set about getting at the contents that form the root of the obsession. I then inform him, at the risk of shocking him severely, that his dreams will provide us with all the necessary information. We will take them as if they issued from an intelligent, purposive, and, as it were, personal source. This is of course a bold hypothesis and at the same time an adventure, because we are going to give extraordinary credit to a discredited entity—the psyche—whose very existence is still denied by not a few contemporary psychologists as well as by philosophers. A famous anthropologist, when I showed him my way of proceeding, made the typical remark:

"That's all very interesting indeed, but dangerous." Yes, I admit it is dangerous, just as dangerous as a neurosis. If you want to cure a neurosis you have to risk something. To do something without taking a risk is merely ineffectual, as we know only too well. A surgical operation for cancer is a risk too, and yet it has to be done. For the sake of better understanding I have often felt tempted to advise my patients to think of the psyche as a subtle body in which subtle tumours can grow. The prejudiced belief that the psyche is unimaginable and consequently less than air, or that it is a more or less intellectual system of logical concepts, is so great that when people are not conscious of certain contents they assume these do not exist. They have no confidence and no belief in a reliable psychic functioning outside consciousness, and dreams are thought to be only ridiculous. Under such conditions my proposal arouses the worst suspicions. And indeed I have heard every argument under the sun used against the vague spectres of dreams.

37 Yet in dreams we find, without any profound analysis, the same conflicts and complexes whose existence can also be demonstrated by the association test. Moreover, these complexes form an integral part of the existing neurosis. We have, therefore, reason to believe that dreams can give us at least as much information as the association test can about the content of a neurosis. As a matter of fact, they give very much more. The symptom is like the shoot above ground, yet the main plant is an extended rhizome underground. The rhizome represents the content of a neurosis; it is the matrix of complexes, of symptoms, and of dreams. We have every reason to believe that dreams mirror exactly the underground processes of the psyche. And if we get there, we literally get at the "roots" of the disease.

38 As it is not my intention to go any further into the psychopathology of neuroses, I propose to choose another case as an example of how dreams reveal the unknown inner facts of the psyche and of what these facts consist. The dreamer was another intellectual, of remarkable intelligence and learning. He was neurotic and was seeking my help because he felt that his neurosis had become overpowering and was slowly but surely undermining his morale. Fortunately his intellectual integrity had not yet suffered and he had the free use of his fine intelligence. For this reason I set him the task of observing and recording his

dreams himself. The dreams were not analysed or explained to him and it was only very much later that we began their analysis. Thus the dreams I am going to relate have not been tampered with at all. They represent an entirely uninfluenced natural sequence of events. The patient had never read any psychology, much less any analytical psychology.

39 Since the series consists of over four hundred dreams, I could not possibly convey an impression of the whole material; but I have published elsewhere a selection of seventy-four dreams containing motifs of special religious interest.[13] The dreamer, it should be said, was a Catholic by education, but no longer a practising one, nor was he interested in religious problems. He was one of those scientifically minded intellectuals who would be simply amazed if anybody should saddle them with religious views of any kind. If one holds that the unconscious has a psychic existence independent of consciousness, a case such as that of our dreamer might be of particular interest, provided we are not mistaken in our conception of the religious character of certain dreams. And if one lays stress on the conscious mind alone and does not credit the unconscious with an independent existence, it will be interesting to find out whether or not the dreams really derive their material from conscious contents. Should the facts favour the hypothesis of the unconscious, one could then use dreams as possible sources of information about the religious tendencies of the unconscious.

40 One cannot expect dreams to speak of religion as we know it. There are, however, two dreams among the four hundred that obviously deal with religion. I will now give the text which the dreamer himself had taken down:

All the houses have something theatrical about them, with stage scenery and decorations. The name of Bernard Shaw is mentioned. The play is supposed to take place in the distant future. There is a notice in English and German on one of the sets:

13 "Dream Symbols of the Individuation Process." [Orig. in *Eranos-Jahrbuch 1935.* A revised and expanded version of this appears in *Psychology and Alchemy,* as Part II.—EDITORS.] Although the dreams cited here are mentioned in the above publication, they are examined there from a different standpoint. Since dreams have many aspects they can be studied from various angles.

This is the universal Catholic Church.
It is the Church of the Lord.
All those who feel that they are the instruments of the Lord may enter.

Under this is printed in smaller letters: "The Church was founded by Jesus and Paul"—like a firm advertising its long standing.

I say to my friend, "Come on, let's have a look at this." He replies, "I do not see why a lot of people have to get together when they're feeling religious." I answer, "As a Protestant you will never understand." A woman nods emphatic approval. Then I see a sort of proclamation on the wall of the church. It runs:

Soldiers!

When you feel you are under the power of the Lord, do not address him directly. The Lord cannot be reached by words. We also strongly advise you not to indulge in any discussions among yourselves concerning the attributes of the Lord. It is futile, for everything valuable and important is ineffable.

(Signed) *Pope* . . . (Name illegible)

Now we go in. The interior resembles a mosque, more particularly the Hagia Sophia: no seats—wonderful effect of space; no images, only framed texts decorating the walls (like the Koran texts in the Hagia Sophia). One of the texts reads "Do not flatter your benefactor." The woman who had nodded approval bursts into tears and cries, "Then there's nothing left!" I reply, "I find it quite right!" but she vanishes. At first I stand with a pillar in front of me and can see nothing. Then I change my position and see a crowd of people. I do not belong to them and stand alone. But they are quite clear, so that I can see their faces. They all say in unison, "We confess that we are under the power of the Lord. The Kingdom of Heaven is within us." They repeat this three times with great solemnity. Then the organ starts to play and they sing a Bach fugue with chorale. But the original text is omitted; sometimes there is only a sort of coloratura singing, then the words are repeated: "Everything else is paper" (meaning that it does not make a living impression on me). When the chorale has faded away the gemütlich *part of the ceremony begins; it is almost like a students' party. The people are all cheerful and equable. We move about, converse, and greet one another, and wine (from an episcopal seminary) is served with other refreshments. The health of the Church is drunk and, as if to express everybody's pleasure at the increase in membership, a loudspeaker blares a ragtime melody with the refrain, "Charles is also with us now." A priest explains to me: "These somewhat trivial amusements are officially approved and permitted. We must adapt a little to American methods. With a large crowd such as we have here this is inevitable. But we differ in principle from the American churches by our decidedly anti-ascetic tendency." Thereupon I awake with a feeling of great relief.*

41 There are, as you know, numerous works on the phenomenology of dreams, but very few that deal with their psychology. This for the obvious reason that a psychological interpretation of dreams is an exceedingly ticklish and risky business. Freud has made a courageous attempt to elucidate the intricacies of dream psychology with the help of views which he gathered in the field of psychopathology.[14] Much as I admire the boldness of his attempt, I cannot agree either with his method or with its results. He explains the dream as a mere façade behind which something has been carefully hidden. There is no doubt that neurotics hide disagreeable things, probably just as much as normal people do. But it is a serious question whether this category can be applied to such a normal and world-wide phenomenon as the dream. I doubt whether we can assume that a dream is something other than it appears to be. I am rather inclined to quote another Jewish authority, the Talmud, which says: "The dream is its own interpretation." In other words *I take the dream for what it is.* The dream is such a difficult and complicated thing that I do not dare to make any assump-

14 Freud, *The Interpretation of Dreams.* Silberer (*Der Traum,* 1919) presents a more cautious and more balanced point of view. As to the difference between Freud's and my own views, I would refer the reader to my little essay on this subject, "Freud and Jung: Contrasts." Further material in *Two Essays on Analytical Psychology,* pp. 18ff.; Kranefeldt, *Secret Ways of the Mind;* Gerhard Adler, *Entdeckung der Seele;* and Toni Wolff, "Einführung in die Grundlagen der komplexen Psychologie," in *Die kulturelle Bedeutung der komplexen Psychologie.*

tions about its possible cunning or its tendency to deceive. The dream is a natural occurrence, and there is no earthly reason why we should assume that it is a crafty device to lead us astray. It occurs when consciousness and will are to a large extent extinguished. It seems to be a natural product which is also found in people who are not neurotic. Moreover, we know so little about the psychology of the dream process that we must be more than careful when we introduce into its explanation elements that are foreign to the dream itself.

42 For all these reasons I hold that our dream really is speaking of religion and that it intends to do so. Since the dream has a coherent and well-designed structure, it suggests a certain logic and a certain intention, that is, it has a meaningful motivation which finds direct expression in the dream-content.

43 The first part of the dream is a serious statement in favour of the Catholic Church. A certain Protestant point of view—that religion is just an individual experience—is discouraged by the dreamer. The second, more grotesque part is the Church's adaptation to a decidedly worldly standpoint, and the end is a statement in favour of an anti-ascetic tendency which would not and could not be backed up by the real Church. Nevertheless the dreamer's anti-ascetic priest makes it a matter of principle. Spiritualization and sublimation are essentially Christian principles, and any insistence upon the contrary would amount to blasphemous paganism. Christianity has never been worldly nor has it ever looked with favour on good food and wine, and it is more than doubtful whether the introduction of jazz into the cult would be a particular asset. The "cheerful and equable" people who peripatetically converse with each other in more or less Epicurean style remind one much more of an ancient philosophical ideal which is rather distasteful to the contemporary Christian. In the first and second part the importance of masses or crowds of people is emphasized.

44 Thus the Catholic Church, though highly recommended, appears coupled with a strange pagan point of view which is irreconcilable with a fundamentally Christian attitude. The actual irreconcilability does not appear in the dream. It is hushed up as it were by a cosy ("gemütlich") atmosphere in which dangerous contrasts are blurred and blended. The Protestant conception of an individual relationship to God is swamped by mass organiza-

tion and a correspondingly collective religious feeling. The insistence on crowds and the insinuation of a pagan ideal are remarkable parallels to things that are actually happening in Europe today. Everybody was astonished at the pagan tendencies of modern Germany because nobody knew how to interpret Nietzsche's Dionysian experience. Nietzsche was but one of the thousands and millions of Germans yet unborn in whose unconscious the Teutonic cousin of Dionysus—Wotan—came to birth during the Great War.[15] In the dreams of the Germans whom I treated then I could clearly see the Wotanistic revolution coming on, and in 1918 I published an article in which I pointed out the peculiar kind of new development to be expected in Germany.[16] Those Germans were by no means people who had studied *Thus Spake Zarathustra,* and certainly the young people who resurrected the pagan sacrifices of sheep knew nothing of Nietzsche's experience.[17] That is why they called their god Wotan and not Dionysus. In Nietzsche's biography you will find irrefutable proof that the god he originally meant was really Wotan, but, being a philologist and living in the seventies and eighties of the nineteenth century, he called him Dionysus. Looked at from a comparative point of view, the two gods have much in common.

45 There is apparently no opposition to collective feeling, mass religion, and paganism anywhere in the dream of my patient, except for the Protestant friend who is soon reduced to silence. One curious incident merits our attention, and that is the unknown woman who at first backs up the eulogy of Catholicism and then suddenly bursts into tears, saying: "Then there's nothing left," and vanishes without returning.

15 Cf. the relation of Odin as the god of poets, seers, and raving enthusiasts, and of Mimir, the Wise One, to Dionysus and Silenus. The word Odin has a root-connection with Gall. οὐᾶτεις, Ir. *fāith,* L. *vates,* similar to μάντις and μαίνομαι. Ninck, *Wodan und germanischer Schicksalsglaube,* pp. 30ff.

16 "The Role of the Unconscious."

17 Cf. my "Wotan" (*Neue Schweizer Rundschau,* 1936; an abbreviated version in the *Saturday Review of Literature,* Oct. 16, 1937; subsequently published in *Essays on Contemporary Events,* 1947). The Wotan parallels in Nietzsche's work are to be found in the poem "To the Unknown God" (*Werke,* ed. Baeumler, V, p. 457); *Thus Spake Zarathustra,* trans. by Thomas Common, pp. 293ff., 150, and 185f.; and the Wotan dream of 1859 in Elisabeth Foerster-Nietzsche, *Der werdende Nietzsche,* pp. 84ff.

46 Who is this woman? To the dreamer she is a vague and unknown person, but when he had that dream he was already well acquainted with her as the "unknown woman" who had frequently appeared in previous dreams.

47 As this figure plays a great role in men's dreams, it bears the technical name of the "anima," [18] with reference to the fact that, from time immemorial, man in his myths has expressed the idea of a male and female coexisting in the same body. Such psychological intuitions were usually projected in the form of the divine syzygy, the divine pair, or in the idea of the hermaphroditic nature of the creator.[19] Edward Maitland, the biographer of Anna Kingsford, relates in our own day an inner experience of the bisexual nature of the Deity.[20] Then there is Hermetic philosophy with its hermaphrodite and its androgynous inner man,[21] the *homo Adamicus,* who, "although he appears in

18 Cf. My *Two Essays,* Part II, ch. 2; *Psychological Types,* Defs. 48, 49; "Archetypes of the Collective Unconscious"; and "Concerning the Archetypes."

19 Cf. my "Concerning the Archetypes."

20 Maitland, *Anna Kingsford,* I, pp. 129ff.

21 The statement about the hermaphroditic nature of the Deity in *Corpus Hermeticum,* Lib. I (ed. Scott, *Hermetica,* I, p. 118): "For the first Mind was bisexual," is probably taken from Plato, *Symposium,* XIV. It is questionable whether the later medieval representations of the hermaphrodite stem from "Poimandres" (*Hermetica,* I), since the hermaphrodite figure was practically unknown in the West before the *Poimander* was printed by Marsilio Ficino in 1471. It is possible, however, that one of the few scholars of those days who understood Greek got the idea from one of the Greek codices then extant, as for instance the Codex Laurentianus 71, 33, the Codex Parisinus Graecus 1220, or the Codices Vaticanus Graecus 237 and 951, all from the 14th century. There are no older codices. The first Latin translation by Marsilio Ficino had a sensational effect. But before that date we have the hermaphroditic symbols from the Codex Germanicus Monacensis 598, dated 1417. It seems to me more probable that the hermaphrodite symbol derives from Arabic or Syriac MSS. translated in the 11th or 12th century. In the old Latin "Tractatulus Avicennae," which is strongly influenced by Arabic tradition, we find: "[The elixir] is a voluptuous serpent impregnating itself" (*Artis auriferae,* I, 1593, p. 406). Although the author was a Pseudo-Avicenna and not the authentic Ibn Sina (970–1037), he is one of the Arabic-Latin sources for medieval Hermetic literature. We find the same passage in "Rosinus ad Sarratantam" (*Artis aurif.,* I, p. 309). "Rosinus" is an Arabic-Latin corruption of "Zosimos," a Greek neo-Platonic philosopher of the 3rd century. His treatise "Ad Sarratantam" belongs to the same class of literature, and since the history of these texts is still shrouded in darkness, nobody can say who copied from whom. The *Turba philosophorum,* Sermo LXV, a Latin text of Arabic

masculine form, always carries about with him Eve, or his wife, hidden in his body," as a medieval commentator on the *Hermetis Tractatus aureus* says.[22]

48 The anima is presumably a psychic representation of the minority of female genes in a man's body. This is all the more probable since the same figure is not to be found in the imagery of a woman's unconscious. There is a corresponding figure, however, that plays an equivalent role, yet it is not a woman's image but a man's. This masculine figure in a woman's psychology has been termed the "animus." [23] One of the most typical manifestations of both figures is what has long been called "animosity." The anima causes illogical moods, and the animus produces irritating platitudes and unreasonable opinions. Both are frequent dream-figures. As a rule they personify the unconscious and give it its peculiarly disagreeable or irritating character. The unconscious in itself has no such negative qualities. They appear only when it is personified by these figures and when they begin to influence consciousness. Being only partial personalities, they have the character either of an inferior woman or of an inferior man—hence their irritating effect. A man experiencing this influence will be subject to unaccountable

origin, makes the same allusion: "The composite brings itself forth." (Ruska, *Turba philosophorum,* 1931, p. 165.) So far as I can judge, the first text that definitely mentions the hermaphrodite is the "Liber de arte chymica" of the 16th century (*Artis aurif.,* I, pp. 575ff.). On p. 610 it says: "For that Mercurius is all metals, male and female, and an hermaphroditic monster even in the marriage of soul and body." Of the later literature I mention only Hieronymus Reusner, *Pandora* (1588); "Splendor Solis" (*Aureum vellus,* 1598); Michael Maier, *Symbola aureae mensae* (1617) and *Atalanta fugiens* (1618); J. D. Mylius, *Philosophia reformata* (1622).

22 The "Tractatus aureus Hermetis" is of Arabic origin and does not belong to the *Corpus Hermeticum.* Its history is unknown (first printed in *Ars chemica,* 1566). Dominicus Gnosius wrote a commentary on the text in his *Hermetis Trismegisti Tractatus vere Aureus de Lapide philosophici secreto* (1610). On p. 101 he says: "As a shadow continually follows the body of one who walks in the sun . . . so our Adamic hermaphrodite, though he appears in masculine form, nevertheless always carries about with him Eve, or his feminine part, hidden in his body." This commentary, together with the text, is reproduced in Manget, *Bibliotheca chemica curiosa,* I (1702), pp. 401ff.

23 There is a description of both these figures in *Two Essays,* Part II, pp. 186ff. See also *Psychological Types,* Def. 48, and Emma Jung, "Ein Beitrag zum Problem des Animus."

moods, and a woman will be argumentative and produce opinions that are beside the mark.[24]

49 The negative reaction of the anima to the church dream indicates that the dreamer's feminine side, his unconscious, disagrees with his conscious attitude. The disagreement started with the text on the wall: "Do not flatter your benefactor," which the dreamer agreed with. The meaning of the text seems sound enough, so that one does not understand why the woman should feel so desperate about it. Without delving further into this mystery, we must content ourselves for the time being with the statement that there is a contradiction in the dream and that a very important minority has left the stage under vivid protest and pays no more attention to the proceedings.

50 We gather, then, from the dream that the unconscious functioning of the dreamer's mind has produced a pretty flat compromise between Catholicism and pagan *joie de vivre*. The product of the unconscious is manifestly not expressing a fixed point of view or a definite opinion, rather it is a dramatic exposition of an act of reflection. It could be formulated perhaps as follows: "Now what about this religious business? You are a Catholic, are you not? Is that not good enough? But asceticism—well, well, even the church has to adapt a little—movies, radio, spiritual five o'clock tea and all that—why not some ecclesiastical wine and gay acquaintances?" But for some secret reason this awkward mystery woman, well known from many former dreams, seems to be deeply disappointed and quits.

51 I must confess that I find myself in sympathy with the anima. Obviously the compromise is too cheap and too superficial, but it is characteristic of the dreamer as well as of many other people to whom religion does not matter very much. Religion was of no concern to my patient and he certainly never expected that it would concern him in any way. But he had come to me because of a very alarming experience. Being highly rationalistic and intellectual he had found that his attitude of mind and his philosophy forsook him completely in the face of his neurosis and its demoralizing forces. He found nothing in his whole

24 Anima and animus do not only occur in negative form. They may sometimes appear as a source of enlightenment, as messengers (ἄγγελοι), and as mystagogues. [Cf. Jung, *Aion*, par. 33 (Swiss edn., p. 34); "Psychology of the Transference," p. 293.—EDITORS.]

Weltanschauung that would help him to gain sufficient control of himself. He was therefore very much in the situation of a man deserted by his hitherto cherished convictions and ideals. It is by no means extraordinary that under such conditions a man should return to the religion of his childhood in the hope of finding something helpful there. It was, however, not a conscious attempt or decision to revivify his earlier religious beliefs. He merely dreamed it; that is, his unconscious produced a peculiar statement about his religion. It is just as if the spirit and the flesh, the eternal enemies in a Christian consciousness, had made peace with each other in the form of a curious mitigation of their contradictory nature. Spirituality and worldliness come together in unexpected amity. The effect is slightly grotesque and comical. The inexorable severity of the spirit seems to be undermined by an almost antique gaiety perfumed with wine and roses. At all events the dream describes a spiritual and worldly atmosphere that dulls the sharpness of a moral conflict and swallows up in oblivion all mental pain and distress.

52 If this was a wish-fulfilment it was surely a conscious one, for it was precisely what the patient had already done to excess. And he was not unconscious of this either, since wine was one of his most dangerous enemies. The dream, on the other hand, is an impartial statement of the patient's spiritual condition. It gives a picture of a degenerate religion corrupted by worldliness and mob instincts. There is religious sentimentality instead of the *numinosum* of divine experience. This is the well-known characteristic of a religion that has lost its living mystery. It is readily understandable that such a religion is incapable of giving help or of having any other moral effect.

53 The over-all aspect of the dream is definitely unfavourable, although certain other aspects of a more positive nature are dimly visible. It rarely happens that dreams are either exclusively positive or exclusively negative. As a rule one finds both aspects, but usually one is stronger than the other. It is obvious that such a dream provides the psychologist with enough material to raise the problem of a religious attitude. If our dream were the only one we possess we could hardly hope to unlock its innermost meaning, but we have quite a number of dreams in our series which point to a remarkable religious problem. I never, if I can help it, interpret one dream by itself. As a rule a

dream belongs in a series. Since there is a continuity of consciousness despite the fact that it is regularly interrupted by sleep, there is probably also a continuity of unconscious processes—perhaps even more than with the events of consciousness. In any case my experience is in favour of the probability that dreams are the visible links in a chain of unconscious events. If we want to shed any light on the deeper reasons for the dream, we must go back to the series and find out where it is located in the long chain of four hundred dreams.

54 We find our dream wedged in between two important dreams of an uncanny quality. The dream before reports that there is a gathering of many people and that a peculiar ceremony is taking place, apparently of magical character, for the purpose of "reconstructing the gibbon." The dream after is concerned with a similar theme—the magical transformation of animals into human beings.[25]

55 Both dreams are intensely disagreeable and very alarming to the patient. Whereas the church dream manifestly moves on the surface and expresses opinions which in other circumstances could just as well have been thought consciously, these two dreams are strange and remote in character and their emotional effect is such that the dreamer would avoid them if possible. As a matter of fact, the text of the second dream says: "If one runs away, all is lost." Curiously enough, this remark coincides with that of the unknown woman: "Then there's nothing left." The inference to be drawn from these remarks is that the church dream was an attempt to escape from other dream ideas of a much deeper significance. These ideas appear in the dreams occurring immediately before and after it.

[25] [Cf. *Psychology and Alchemy*, pars. 164ff., 183ff.—EDITORS.]

2. DOGMA AND NATURAL SYMBOLS

56 The first of these dreams—the one preceding the church dream—speaks of a ceremony whereby an ape is to be reconstructed. To explain this point sufficiently would require too many details. I must, therefore, restrict myself to the mere statement that the "ape" refers to the dreamer's instinctual personality,[1] which he had completely neglected in favour of an exclusively intellectual attitude. The result had been that his instincts got the better of him and attacked him at times in the form of uncontrollable outbursts. The "reconstruction" of the ape means the rebuilding of the instinctual personality within the framework of the hierarchy of consciousness. Such a reconstruction is only possible if accompanied by important changes in the conscious attitude. The patient was naturally afraid of the tendencies of the unconscious, because hitherto they had revealed themselves to him in their most unfavourable form. The church dream that followed represents an attempt to seek refuge from this fear in the shelter of a church religion. The third dream, in speaking of the "transformation of animals into human beings," obviously continues the theme of the first one; that is, the ape is reconstructed solely for the purpose of being transformed later into a human being. In other words, the pa-

1 [Cf. *Psychology and Alchemy*, par. 175.—EDITORS.]

tient has to undergo an important change through the reintegration of his hitherto split-off instinctuality, and is thus to be made over into a new man. The modern mind has forgotten those old truths that speak of the death of the old man and the making of a new one, of spiritual rebirth and such-like old-fashioned "mystical absurdities." My patient, being a scientist of today, was more than once seized by panic when he realized how much he was gripped by such thoughts. He was afraid he was going mad, whereas the man of two thousand years ago would have welcomed such dreams and rejoiced in the hope of a magical rebirth and renewal of life. But our modern attitude looks back arrogantly upon the mists of superstition and of medieval or primitive credulity, entirely forgetting that we carry the whole living past in the lower storeys of the skyscraper of rational consciousness. Without the lower storeys our mind is suspended in mid air. No wonder it gets nervous. The true history of the mind is not preserved in learned volumes but in the living psychic organism of every individual.

57 I must admit, however, that the idea of renewal took on shapes that could easily shock a modern mind. It is indeed difficult, if not impossible, to connect "rebirth," as we understand it, with the way it is depicted in the dreams. But before we discuss the strange and unexpected transformation there hinted at, we should turn our attention to the other manifestly religious dream to which I alluded before.

58 While the church dream comes relatively early in the long series, the following dream belongs to the later stages of the process.[2] This is the literal text:

I come to a strange, solemn house—the "House of the Gathering." Many candles are burning in the background, arranged in a peculiar pattern with four points running upward. Outside, at the door of the house, an old man is posted. People are going in. They say nothing and stand motionless in order to collect themselves inwardly. The man at the door says of the visitors to the house, "When they come out again they are cleansed." I go into the house myself and find I can concentrate perfectly. Then a voice says: "What you are doing is dangerous. Religion is not a tax to be paid so that you can rid yourself of the woman's

2 [Cf. ibid., par. 293.—EDITORS.]

image, for this image cannot be got rid of. Woe unto them who use religion as a substitute for the other side of the soul's life; they are in error and will be accursed. Religion is no substitute; it is to be added to the other activities of the soul as the ultimate completion. Out of the fulness of life shall you bring forth your religion; only then shall you be blessed!" While the last sentence is being spoken in ringing tones I hear distant music, simple chords on an organ. Something about it reminds me of Wagner's Fire Music. As I leave the house I see a burning mountain and I feel: "The fire that is not put out is a holy fire" (*Shaw,* Saint Joan).

59 The patient was deeply impressed by this dream. It was a solemn and powerful experience for him, one of several which produced a far-reaching change in his attitude to life and humanity.

60 It is not difficult to see that this dream forms a parallel to the church dream. Only this time the church has become a house of solemnity and self-collection. There are no indications of ceremonies or of any other known attributes of the Catholic Church, with the sole exception of the burning candles, which are arranged in a symbolic form probably derived from the Catholic cult.[3] They form four pyramids or points, which perhaps anticipate the final vision of the flaming mountain. The appearance of the number four is, however, a regular feature in the patient's dreams and plays a very important role. The holy fire refers to Bernard Shaw's *Saint Joan,* as the dreamer himself observes. The unquenchable fire, on the other hand, is a well-known attribute of the Deity, not only in the Old Testament, but also as an *allegoria Christi* in an uncanonical logion cited in Origen's *Homilies:*[4] "Ait ipse salvator: qui iuxta me est, iuxta ignem est, qui longe est a me, longe est a regno" (the Saviour himself says: Whoever is near to me is near to the fire; whoever is far from me is far from the kingdom). Since the time of Heraclitus life has been conceived as a *πῦρ ἀεὶ ζῶν,* an ever-

3 A bishop is allowed four candles for a private mass. Some of the more solemn forms of the Mass, such as the *Missa cantata,* also have four. Still higher forms have six or seven.

4 Origen, *In Jeremiam homiliae,* XX, 3, in Migne, *P.G.,* vol. 13, col. 532. Also in James, *The Apocryphal New Testament,* p. 35.

living fire; and as Christ calls himself "The Life," the uncanonical saying is quite understandable. The fire signifying "life" fits into the frame of the dream, for it emphasizes that "fulness of life" is the only legitimate source of religion. Thus the four fiery points function almost as an icon denoting the presence of the Deity or an equivalent being. In the system of Barbelo-Gnosis, four lights surround the Autogenes (the Self-Born, or Uncreated).[5] This strange figure may correspond to the Monogenes of Coptic Gnosis, mentioned in the Codex Brucianus. There too the Monogenes is characterized as a quaternity symbol.

61 As I said before, the number four plays an important role in these dreams, always alluding to an idea akin to the Pythagorean tetraktys.[6]

62 The *quaternarium* or quaternity has a long history. It appears not only in Christian iconology and mystical speculation[7] but plays perhaps a still greater role in Gnostic philosophy[8]

[5] Irenaeus, *Against Heresies,* trans. by Keble, p. 81.

[6] Cf. Zeller, *Die Philosophie der Griechen,* where all the sources are collected. "Four is the origin and root of eternal nature" (I, p. 291). Plato derives the human body from the four. According to the Neoplatonists, Pythagoras himself called the soul a square (Zeller, III, II, p. 120).

[7] The "four" in Christian iconography appears chiefly in the form of the four evangelists and their symbols, arranged in a rose, circle, or melothesia, or as a tetramorph, as for instance in the *Hortus deliciarum* of Herrad of Landsberg and in works of mystical speculation. Of these I mention only: (1) Jakob Böhme, *XL Questions concerning the Soule* (1647). (2) Hildegard of Bingen, Codex Luccensis, fol. 372, and Codex Heidelbergensis, "Scivias," representations of the mystic universe; cf. Singer, *Studies in the History and Method of Science.* (3) The remarkable drawings of Opicinus de Canistris in the Codex Palatinus Latinus 1993, Vatican; cf. Salomon, *Weltbild und Bekenntnisse eines avignonesischen Klerikers des 14. Jahrhunderts.* (4) Heinrich Khunrath, *Vom hylealischen, das ist, pri-materialischen catholischen, oder algemeinen natürlichen Chaos* (1597), pp. 204 and 281, where he says the "Monas catholica" arises from the rotation of the "Quaternarium" and interprets it as an image and allegory of Christ (further material in Khunrath, *Amphitheatrum sapientiae aeternae,* 1604). (5) The speculations about the cross: "It is said . . . that the cross was made of four kinds of wood," St. Bernard, *Vitis mystica,* cap. XLVI, in Migne, *P.L.,* vol. 184, col. 752; cf. W. Meyer, *Die Geschichte des Kreuzholzes vor Christus,* p. 7. For the quaternity see also Dunbar, *Symbolism in Mediaeval Thought and Its Consummation in the Divine Comedy.*

[8] Cf. the systems of Isidorus, Valentinus, Marcus, and Secundus. A most instructive example is the symbolism of the Monogenes in the Codex Brucianus (Bodleian Library, Oxford, MS. Bruce 96), trans. by C. A. Baynes, *A Coptic Gnostic Treatise,* pp. 59ff., 70ff.

and from then on down through the Middle Ages until well into the eighteenth century.[9]

63 In the dream under discussion, the quaternity appears as the most significant exponent of the religious cult created by the unconscious.[10] The dreamer enters the "House of the Gathering" alone, instead of with a friend as in the church dream. Here he meets an old man, who had already appeared in an earlier dream as the sage who had pointed to a particular spot on the earth where the dreamer belonged. The old man explains the character of the cult as a purification ritual. It is not clear from the dream-text what kind of purification is meant, or from what it should purify. The only ritual that actually takes place seems to be a concentration or meditation, leading up to the ecstatic phenomenon of the voice. The voice is a frequent occurrence in this dream-series. It always utters an authoritative declaration or command, either of astonishing common sense or of profound philosophic import. It is nearly always a final statement, usually coming toward the end of a dream, and it is, as a rule, so clear and convincing that the dreamer finds no argument against it. It has, indeed, so much the character of indisputable truth that it can hardly be understood as anything except a final and trenchant summing up of a long process of unconscious deliberation and weighing of arguments. Fre-

9 I am thinking of the mystical speculations about the four "roots" (the rhizomata of Empedocles), i.e., the four elements or four qualities (wet, dry, warm, cold), peculiar to Hermetic or alchemical philosophy. Descriptions in Petrus Bonus, *Pretiosa margarita novella* (1546); Joannes Pantheus, *Ars transmutationis metallicae* (1519), p. 5, based on a *quaternatio;* Raymund Lull, "Theorica et practica" (*Theatrum chemicum,* IV, 1613, p. 174), a *quaternatio elementorum* and of chemical processes; Michael Maier, *Scrutinium chymicum* (1687), symbols of the four elements. The last-named author wrote an interesting treatise called *De circulo physico quadrato* (1616). There is much the same symbolism in Mylius, *Philosophia reformata* (1622). Pictures of the Hermetic redemption in the form of a tetrad with symbols of the four evangelists (from Reusner's *Pandora* and the Codex Germanicus Monacensis 598) are reproduced in *Psychology and Alchemy,* figs. 231 and 232; quaternity symbolism, ibid., pp. 208ff. Further material in Kuekelhaus, *Urzahl und Gebärde.* Eastern parallels in Zimmer, *Kunstform und Yoga im indischen Kultbild;* Wilhelm and Jung, *The Secret of the Golden Flower.* The literature on the symbolism of the cross is also relevant here.

10 This sentence may sound presumptuous, for I seem to be forgetting that we are concerned here with a single and unique dream from which no far-reaching conclusions can be drawn. My conclusions, however, are based not on this dream alone but on many similar experiences to which I have alluded elsewhere.

quently the voice issues from an authoritative figure, such as a military commander, or the captain of a ship, or an old physician. Sometimes, as in this case, there is simply a voice coming apparently from nowhere. It was interesting to see how this very intellectual and sceptical man accepted the voice; often it did not suit him at all, yet he accepted it unquestioningly, even humbly. Thus the voice revealed itself, in the course of several hundred carefully recorded dreams, as an important and even decisive spokesman of the unconscious. Since this patient is by no means the only one I have observed who exhibited the phenomenon of the voice in dreams and in other peculiar states of consciousness, I am forced to admit that the unconscious is capable at times of manifesting an intelligence and purposiveness superior to the actual conscious insight. There can be no doubt that this is a basic religious phenomenon, observed here in a person whose conscious mental attitude certainly seemed most unlikely to produce religious phenomena. I have not infrequently made similar observations in other cases and I must confess that I am unable to formulate the facts in any other way. I have often met with the objection that the thoughts which the voice represents are no more than the thoughts of the individual himself. That may be; but I would call a thought my own only when *I* have thought it, just as I would call money my own only when I have earned or acquired it in a conscious and legitimate manner. If somebody gives me the money as a present, then I shall certainly not say to my benefactor, "Thank you for my money," although to a third person I might say afterwards: "This is my own money." With the voice I am in a similar situation. The voice gives me certain contents, exactly as if a friend were informing me of his ideas. It would be neither decent nor truthful to suggest that what he says are my own ideas.

64 This is the reason why I differentiate between what I have produced or acquired by my own conscious effort and what is clearly and unmistakably a product of the unconscious. Someone may object that the so-called unconscious mind is merely my own mind and that, therefore, such a differentiation is superfluous. But I am not at all convinced that the unconscious mind is merely *my* mind, because the term "unconscious" means that I am not even conscious of it. As a matter of fact, the concept of the unconscious is an assumption for the sake of convenience.

In reality I am totally unconscious of—or, in other words, I do not know at all—where the voice comes from. Not only am I incapable of producing the phenomenon at will, I am unable to anticipate what the voice will say. Under such conditions it would be presumptuous to refer to the factor that produces the voice as *my* unconscious or *my* mind. This would not be accurate, to say the least. The fact that you perceive the voice in your dream proves nothing at all, for you can also hear the noises in the street, which you would never think of calling your own.

65 There is only one condition under which you might legitimately call the voice your own, and that is when you assume your conscious personality to be a part of a whole or to be a smaller circle contained in a bigger one. A little bank-clerk, showing a friend around town, who points to the bank building with the words, "And this is *my* bank," is making use of the same privilege.

66 We may suppose that human personality consists of two things: first, consciousness and whatever this covers, and second, an indefinitely large hinterland of unconscious psyche. So far as the former is concerned, it can be more or less clearly defined and delimited; but as for the sum total of human personality, one has to admit the impossibility of a complete description or definition. In other words, there is bound to be an illimitable and indefinable addition to every personality, because the latter consists of a conscious and observable part which does not contain certain factors whose existence, however, we are forced to assume in order to explain certain observable facts. The unknown factors form what we call the unconscious part of the personality.

67 Of what those factors consist we have no idea, since we can observe only their effects. We may assume that they are of a psychic nature comparable to that of conscious contents, yet there is no certainty about this. But if we suppose such a likeness we can hardly refrain from going further. Since psychic contents are conscious and perceivable only when they are associated with an ego, the phenomenon of the voice, having a strongly personal character, may also issue from a centre—but a centre which is not identical with the conscious ego. Such reasoning is permissible if we conceive of the ego as being subordi-

nated to, or contained in, a supraordinate self as centre of the total, illimitable, and indefinable psychic personality.

68 I do not enjoy philosophical arguments that amuse by their own complications. Although my argument may seem abstruse, it is at least an honest attempt to formulate the observed facts. To put it simply one could say: Since we do not know everything, practically every experience, fact, or object contains something unknown. Hence, if we speak of the totality of an experience, the word "totality" can refer only to the conscious part of it. As we cannot assume that our experience covers the totality of the object, it is clear that its absolute totality must necessarily contain the part that has not been experienced. The same holds true, as I have mentioned, of every experience and also of the psyche, whose absolute totality covers a greater area than consciousness. In other words, the psyche is no exception to the general rule that the universe can be established only so far as our psychic organism permits.

69 My psychological experience has shown time and again that certain contents issue from a psyche that is more complete than consciousness. They often contain a superior analysis or insight or knowledge which consciousness has not been able to produce. We have a suitable word for such occurrences—intuition. In uttering this word most people have an agreeable feeling, as if something had been settled. But they never consider that you do not *make* an intuition. On the contrary, it always comes to you; you *have* a hunch, it has come of itself, and you only catch it if you are clever or quick enough.

70 Consequently, I explain the voice, in the dream of the sacred house, as a product of the more complete personality of which the dreamer's conscious self is a part, and I hold that this is the reason why the voice shows an intelligence and a clarity superior to the dreamer's actual consciousness. This superiority is the reason for the absolute authority of the voice.

71 The message of the voice contains a strange criticism of the dreamer's attitude. In the church dream, he made an attempt to reconcile the two sides of life by a kind of cheap compromise. As we know, the unknown woman, the anima, disagreed and left the scene. In the present dream the voice seems to have taken the place of the anima, making not a merely emotional protest but a masterful statement on two kinds of religion. According

to this statement, the dreamer is inclined to use religion as a substitute for the "woman's image," as the text says. The "woman" refers to the anima. This is borne out by the next sentence, which speaks of religion being used as a substitute for "the other side of the soul's life." The anima is the "other side," as I explained before. She is the representative of the female minority hidden below the threshold of consciousness, that is to say, in the unconscious. The criticism, therefore, would read as follows: "You try religion in order to escape from your unconscious. You use it as a substitute for a part of your soul's life. But religion is the fruit and culmination of the completeness of life, that is, of a life which contains both sides."

72 Careful comparison with other dreams of the same series shows unmistakably what the "other side" is. The patient always tried to evade his emotional needs. As a matter of fact he was afraid they might get him into trouble, for instance into marriage, and into other responsibilities such as love, devotion, loyalty, trust, emotional dependence, and general submission to the soul's needs. All this had nothing to do with science or an academic career; moreover, the word "soul" was nothing but an intellectual obscenity, not fit to be touched with a barge pole.

73 The "mystery" of the anima is the mysterious allusion to religion. This was a great puzzle to my patient, who naturally enough knew nothing of religion except as a creed. He also knew that religion can be a substitute for certain awkward emotional demands which one might circumvent by going to church. The prejudices of our age are visibly reflected in the dreamer's apprehensions. The voice, on the other hand, is unorthodox, indeed shockingly unconventional: it takes religion seriously, puts it on the very apex of life, a life containing "both sides," and thus upsets his most cherished intellectual and rationalistic prejudices. This was such a revolution that my patient was often afraid he would go crazy. Well, I should say that we—knowing the average intellectual of today and yesterday—can easily sympathize with his predicament. To take the "woman's image"—in other words, the unconscious—seriously into account, what a blow to enlightened common sense! [11]

[11] Cf. the *Hypnerotomachia Poliphili* (1499). This book is supposed to have been written by a monk of the 15th century. It is an excellent example of an anima-romance. [Fierz-David's study *The Dream of Poliphilo* treats it as such.—EDITORS.]

74 I began his personal treatment only after he had observed the first series of about three hundred and fifty dreams. Then I got the whole backwash of his upsetting experiences. No wonder he wanted to run away from his adventure! But, fortunately, the man had *religio,* that is, he "carefully took account of" his experience and he had enough *πίστις*, or loyalty to his experience, to enable him to hang on to it and continue it. He had the *great advantage of being neurotic* and so, whenever he tried to be disloyal to his experience or to deny the voice, the neurotic condition instantly came back. He simply could not "quench the fire" and finally he had to admit the incomprehensibly numinous character of his experience. He had to confess that the unquenchable fire was "holy." This was the *sine qua non* of his cure.

75 One might, perhaps, consider this case an exception inasmuch as fairly complete human beings are exceptions. It is true that an overwhelming majority of educated people are fragmentary personalities and have a lot of substitutes instead of the genuine goods. But being like that meant a neurosis for this man, and it means the same for a great many other people too. What is ordinarily called "religion" is a substitute to such an amazing degree that I ask myself seriously whether this kind of "religion," which I prefer to call a creed, may not after all have an important function in human society. The substitute has the obvious purpose of replacing *immediate experience* by a choice of suitable symbols tricked out with an organized dogma and ritual. The Catholic Church maintains them by her indisputable authority, the Protestant "church" (if this term is still applicable) by insistence on belief in the evangelical message. So long as these two principles work, people are effectively protected against immediate religious experience.[12] Even if something of the sort should happen to them, they can refer to the Church, for she would know whether the experience came from God or from the devil, and whether it is to be accepted or rejected.

76 In my profession I have encountered many people who have had immediate experience and who would not and could not submit to the authority of ecclesiastical decision. I had to go

[12] Ecclesiastical vestments are not for adornment only, they also serve to protect the officiating priest. "Fear of God" is no groundless metaphor, for at the back of it there is a very real phenomenology. Cf. Exodus 20:18f.

with them through the crises of passionate conflicts, through the panics of madness, through desperate confusions and depressions which were grotesque and terrible at the same time, so that I am fully aware of the extraordinary importance of dogma and ritual, at least as methods of mental hygiene. If the patient is a practising Catholic, I invariably advise him to confess and to receive communion in order to protect himself from immediate experience, which might easily prove too much for him. With Protestants it is usually not so easy, because dogma and ritual have become so pale and faint that they have lost their efficacy to a very great extent. There is also, as a rule, no confession, and the clergy share the common dislike of psychological problems and also, unfortunately, the common ignorance of psychology. The Catholic "director of conscience" often has infinitely more psychological skill and insight. Protestant parsons, moreover, have gone through a scientific training at a theological faculty which, with its critical spirit, undermines naïveté of faith, whereas the powerful historical tradition in a Catholic priest's training is apt to strengthen the authority of the institution.

77 As a doctor I might, of course, espouse a so-called "scientific" creed, holding that the contents of a neurosis are nothing but repressed infantile sexuality or will to power. By thus depreciating these contents, it would be possible, up to a point, to shield a number of patients from the risk of immediate experience. But I know that this theory is only partially true, which means that it formulates only certain aspects of the neurotic psyche. And I cannot tell my patients what I myself do not fully believe.

78 Now people may ask me: "But if you tell your practising Catholic to go to the priest and confess, you are telling him something you do not believe"—that is, assuming that I am a Protestant.

79 In order to answer this critical question I must first of all explain that, if I can help it, I never preach my belief. If asked I shall certainly stand by my convictions, but these do not go beyond what I consider to be my actual knowledge. I believe only what I *know*. Everything else is hypothesis and beyond that I can leave a lot of things to the Unknown. They do not bother me. But they would begin to bother me, I am sure, if I felt that I *ought* to know about them. If, therefore, a patient is convinced

of the exclusively sexual origin of his neurosis, I would not disturb him in his opinion because I know that such a conviction, particularly if it is deeply rooted, is an excellent defence against an onslaught of immediate experience with its terrible ambiguity. So long as such a defence works I shall not break it down, since I know that there must be cogent reasons why the patient has to think in such a narrow circle. But if his dreams should begin to destroy the protective theory, I have to support the wider personality, as I have done in the case of the dream described. In the same way and for the same reason I support the hypothesis of the practising Catholic while it works for him. In either case, I reinforce a means of defence against a grave risk, without asking the academic question whether the defence is an ultimate truth. I am glad when it works and so long as it works.

80 With our patient, the Catholic defence had broken down long before I ever touched the case. He would have laughed at me if I had advised him to confess or anything of that sort, just as he laughed at the sexual theory, which he had no use for either. But I always let him see that I was entirely on the side of the voice, which I recognized as part of his future greater personality, destined to relieve him of his one-sidedness.

81 For a certain type of intellectual mediocrity characterized by enlightened rationalism, a scientific theory that simplifies matters is a very good means of defence because of the tremendous faith modern man has in anything which bears the label "scientific." Such a label sets your mind at rest immediately, almost as well as *Roma locuta causa finita:* "Rome has spoken, the matter is settled." In itself any scientific theory, no matter how subtle, has, I think, less value from the standpoint of psychological truth than religious dogma, for the simple reason that a theory is necessarily highly abstract and exclusively rational, whereas dogma expresses an irrational whole by means of imagery. This guarantees a far better rendering of an irrational fact like the psyche. Moreover, dogma owes its continued existence and its form on the one hand to so-called "revealed" or immediate experiences of the "Gnosis" [13]—for instance, the God-man, the Cross, the Virgin Birth, the Immaculate Conception,

13 Gnosis, as a special kind of knowledge, should not be confused with "Gnosticism."

the Trinity, and so on, and on the other hand to the ceaseless collaboration of many minds over many centuries. It may not be quite clear why I call certain dogmas "immediate experiences," since in itself a dogma is the very thing that precludes immediate experience. Yet the Christian images I have mentioned are not peculiar to Christianity alone (although in Christianity they have undergone a development and intensification of meaning not to be found in any other religion). They occur just as often in pagan religions, and besides that they can reappear spontaneously in all sorts of variations as psychic phenomena, just as in the remote past they originated in visions, dreams, or trances. Ideas like these are never invented. They came into being before man had learned to use his mind purposively. Before man learned to produce thoughts, thoughts came to him. *He did not think—he perceived his mind functioning.* Dogma is like a dream, reflecting the spontaneous and autonomous activity of the objective psyche, the unconscious. Such an expression of the unconscious is a much more efficient means of defence against further immediate experiences than any scientific theory. The theory has to disregard the emotional values of the experience. The dogma, on the other hand, is extremely eloquent in just this respect. One scientific theory is soon superseded by another. Dogma lasts for untold centuries. The suffering God-Man may be at least five thousand years old and the Trinity is probably even older.

82 Dogma expresses the soul more completely than a scientific theory, for the latter gives expression to and formulates the conscious mind alone. Furthermore, a theory can do nothing except formulate a living thing in abstract terms. Dogma, on the contrary, aptly expresses the living process of the unconscious in the form of the drama of repentance, sacrifice, and redemption. It is rather astonishing, from this point of view, that the Protestant schism could not have been avoided. But since Protestantism became the creed of the adventurous Germanic tribes with their characteristic curiosity, acquisitiveness, and recklessness, it seems possible that their peculiar nature was unable to endure the peace of the Church, at least not for any length of time. It looks as if they were not yet advanced enough to suffer a process of salvation and to submit to a deity who was made visible in the magnificent structure of the Church.

There was, perhaps, too much of the Imperium Romanum or of the Pax Romana in the Church—too much, at least, for their energies, which were and still are insufficiently domesticated. It is quite likely that they needed an unmitigated and less controlled experience of God, as often happens to adventurous and restless people who are too youthful for any form of conservatism or domestication. They therefore did away with the intercession of the Church between God and man, some more and some less. With the demolition of protective walls, the Protestant lost the sacred images that expressed important unconscious factors, together with the ritual which, from time immemorial, has been a safe way of dealing with the unpredictable forces of the unconscious. A vast amount of energy was thus liberated and instantly went into the old channels of curiosity and acquisitiveness. In this way Europe became the mother of dragons that devoured the greater part of the earth.

83 Since those days Protestantism has become a hotbed of schisms and, at the same time, of rapid advances in science and technics which cast such a spell over man's conscious mind that it forgot the unpredictable forces of the unconscious. The catastrophe of the first World War and the extraordinary manifestations of profound spiritual malaise that came afterwards were needed to arouse a doubt as to whether all was well with the white man's mind. Before the war broke out in 1914 we were all quite certain that the world could be righted by rational means. Now we behold the amazing spectacle of states taking over the age-old totalitarian claims of theocracy, which are inevitably accompanied by suppression of free opinion. Once more we see people cutting each other's throats in support of childish theories of how to create paradise on earth. It is not very difficult to see that the powers of the underworld—not to say of hell—which in former times were more or less successfully chained up in a gigantic spiritual edifice where they could be of some use, are now creating, or trying to create, a State slavery and a State prison devoid of any mental or spiritual charm. There are not a few people nowadays who are convinced that mere human reason is not entirely up to the enormous task of putting a lid on the volcano.

84 This whole development is fate. I would not lay the blame either on Protestantism or on the Renaissance. But one thing is

certain—that modern man, Protestant or otherwise, has lost the protection of the ecclesiastical walls erected and reinforced so carefully since Roman days, and because of this loss has approached the zone of world-destroying and world-creating fire. Life has become quickened and intensified. Our world is shot through with waves of uneasiness and fear.

85 Protestantism was, and still is, a great risk and at the same time a great opportunity. If it goes on disintegrating as a church, it must have the effect of stripping man of all his spiritual safeguards and means of defence against immediate experience of the forces waiting for liberation in the unconscious. Look at all the incredible savagery going on in our so-called civilized world: it all comes from human beings and the spiritual condition they are in! Look at the devilish engines of destruction! They are invented by completely innocuous gentlemen, reasonable, respectable citizens who are everything we could wish. And when the whole thing blows up and an indescribable hell of destruction is let loose, nobody seems to be responsible. It simply happens, and yet it is all man-made. But since everybody is blindly convinced that he is nothing more than his own extremely unassuming and insignificant conscious self, which performs its duties decently and earns a moderate living, nobody is aware that this whole rationalistically organized conglomeration we call a state or a nation is driven on by a seemingly impersonal, invisible but terrifying power which nobody and nothing can check. This ghastly power is mostly explained as fear of the neighbouring nation, which is supposed to be possessed by a malevolent fiend. Since nobody is capable of recognizing just where and how much he himself is possessed and unconscious, he simply projects his own condition upon his neighbour, and thus it becomes a sacred duty to have the biggest guns and the most poisonous gas. The worst of it is that he is quite right. All one's neighbours are in the grip of some uncontrolled and uncontrollable fear, just like oneself. In lunatic asylums it is a well-known fact that patients are far more dangerous when suffering from fear than when moved by rage or hatred.

86 The Protestant is left to God alone. For him there is no confession, no absolution, no possibility of an expiatory *opus divinum* of any kind. He has to digest his sins by himself; and, because the absence of a suitable ritual has put it beyond his

reach, he is none too sure of divine grace. Hence the present alertness of the Protestant conscience—and this bad conscience has all the disagreeable characteristics of a lingering illness which makes people chronically uncomfortable. But, for this very reason, the Protestant has a unique chance to make himself conscious of sin to a degree that is hardly possible for a Catholic mentality, as confession and absolution are always at hand to ease excess of tension. The Protestant, however, is left to his tensions, which can go on sharpening his conscience. Conscience, and particularly a bad conscience, can be a gift from heaven, a veritable grace if used in the interests of the higher self-criticism. And self-criticism, in the sense of an introspective, discriminating activity, is indispensable in any attempt to understand your own psychology. If you have done something that puzzles you and you ask yourself what could have prompted you to such an action, you need the sting of a bad conscience and its discriminating faculty in order to discover the real motive of your behaviour. It is only then that you can see what motives are governing your actions. The sting of a bad conscience even spurs you on to discover things that were unconscious before, and in this way you may be able to cross the threshold of the unconscious and take cognizance of those impersonal forces which make you an unconscious instrument of the wholesale murderer in man. If a Protestant survives the complete loss of his church and still remains a Protestant, that is to say a man who is defenceless against God and no longer shielded by walls or communities, he has a unique spiritual opportunity for immediate religious experience.

87 I do not know whether I have succeeded in conveying what the experience of the unconscious meant to my patient. There is, however, no objective criterion by which such an experience can be valued. We have to take it for what it is worth to the person who has the experience. Thus you may be impressed by the fact that the apparent futility of certain dreams should mean something to an intelligent person. But if you cannot accept what he says, or if you cannot put yourself in his place, you should not judge his case. The *genius religiosus* is a wind that bloweth where it listeth. There is no Archimedean point from which to judge, since the psyche is indistinguishable from its manifestations. The psyche is the object of psychology, and—

fatally enough—also its subject. There is no getting away from this fact.

88 The few dreams I have chosen as examples of what I call "immediate experience" certainly look very insignificant to the unpractised eye. They are not spectacular, and are only modest witnesses to an individual experience. They would cut a better figure if I could present them in their sequence, together with the wealth of symbolic material that was brought up in the course of the entire process. But even the sum total of the dreams in the series could not compare in beauty and expressiveness with any part of a traditional religion. A dogma is always the result and fruit of many minds and many centuries, purified of all the oddities, shortcomings, and flaws of individual experience. But for all that, the individual experience, by its very poverty, is immediate life, the warm red blood pulsating today. It is more convincing to a seeker after truth than the best tradition. Immediate life is always individual since the carrier of life is the individual, and whatever emanates from the individual is in a way unique, and hence transitory and imperfect, particularly when it comes to spontaneous psychic products such as dreams and the like. No one else will have the same dreams, although many have the same problem. But just as no individual is differentiated to the point of absolute uniqueness, so there are no individual products of absolutely unique quality. Even dreams are made of collective material to a very high degree, just as, in the mythology and folklore of different peoples, certain motifs repeat themselves in almost identical form. I have called these motifs "archetypes," [14] and by this I mean forms or images of a collective nature which occur practically all over the earth as constituents of myths and at the same time as autochthonous, individual products of unconscious origin. The archetypal motifs presumably derive from patterns of the human mind that are transmitted not only by tradition and migration but also by heredity. The latter hypothesis is indispensable, since even complicated archetypal images can be reproduced spontaneously without there being any possibility of direct tradition.

89 The theory of preconscious primordial ideas is by no means my own invention, as the term "archetype," which stems from

[14] Cf. *Psychological Types,* Def. 26. [Also "On the Nature of the Psyche" (1954/55 edn., pp. 423ff.).—EDITORS.]

the first centuries of our era, proves.[15] With special reference to psychology we find this theory in the works of Adolf Bastian [16] and then again in Nietzsche.[17] In French literature Hubert and Mauss,[18] and also Lévy-Bruhl,[19] mention similar ideas. I only gave an empirical foundation to the theory of what were formerly called primordial or elementary ideas, "catégories" or "habitudes directrices de la conscience," "représentations collectives," etc., by setting out to investigate certain details.

90 In the second of the dreams discussed above, we met with an archetype which I have not yet considered. This is the peculiar arrangement of the burning candles in four pyramid-like points. The arrangement emphasizes the symbolic importance of the number four by putting it in place of the altar or iconostasis where one would expect to find the sacred images. Since the temple is called the "House of the Gathering," we may assume that this character is expressed if the image or symbol appears

15 The term "archetypus" is used by Cicero, Pliny, and others. It appears in the *Corpus Hermeticum,* Lib. I (Scott, *Hermetica,* I, p. 116, 8a) as a definitely philosophical concept: "Thou knowest in thy mind the *archetypal form* [τὸ ἀρχέτυπον εἶδος], the beginning before the beginning, the unbounded."

16 *Das Beständige in den Menschenrassen,* p. 75; *Die Vorstellungen von der Seele,* p. 306; *Der Völkergedanke im Aufbau einer Wissenschaft vom Menschen; Ethnische Elementargedanken in der Lehre vom Menschen.*

17 "In sleep and in dreams we pass through the whole thought of earlier humanity. . . . I mean, as a man now reasons in dreams, so humanity also reasoned for many thousands of years when awake: the first cause which occurred to the mind as an explanation of anything that required explanation was sufficient and passed for truth. . . . This atavistic element in man's nature continues to manifest itself in our dreams, for it is the foundation upon which the higher reason has developed and still develops in every individual. Dreams carry us back to remote conditions of human culture and afford us a ready means of understanding it better." Nietzsche, *Human All-Too-Human,* I, pp. 24–25, trans. by Zimmern and Cohn, modified.

18 Hubert and Mauss, *Mélanges d'Histoire des Religions,* p. xxix: "Constantly set before us in language, though not necessarily explicit in it, . . . the categories . . . generally exist rather under the form of habits that guide consciousness, themselves remaining unconscious. The notion of *mana* is one of these principles; it is a datum of language; it is implied in a whole series of judgments and reasonings concerned with attributes that are those of mana. We have described mana as a category, but it is a category not confined to primitive thought; and today, in a weakened degree, it is still the primal form that certain other categories which always function in our minds have covered over: those of substance, cause . . ." etc.

19 Lévy-Bruhl, *How Natives Think.*

in the place of worship. The tetraktys—to use the Pythagorean term—does indeed refer to an "inner gathering," as our patient's dream clearly demonstrates. The symbol appears in other dreams, usually in the form of a circle divided into four or containing four main parts. In other dreams of the same series it takes the form of an undivided circle, a flower, a square place or room, a quadrangle, a globe, a clock, a symmetrical garden with a fountain in the centre, four people in a boat, in an aeroplane, or at a table, four chairs round a table, four colours, a wheel with eight spokes, an eight-rayed star or sun, a round hat divided into eight parts, a bear with four eyes, a square prison cell, the four seasons, a bowl containing four nuts, the world clock with a disc divided into $4 \times 8 = 32$ partitions, and so on.[20]

91 These quaternity symbols occur no less than seventy-one times in a series of four hundred dreams.[21] My case is no exception in this respect. I have observed many cases where the number four occurred and it always had an unconscious origin, that is, the dreamer got it first from a dream and had no idea of its meaning, nor had he ever heard of the symbolic importance of the number four. It would of course be a different thing with the number three, since the Trinity represents a symbolic number known to everybody. But for us, and particularly for a modern scientist, four conveys no more than any other number. Number symbolism and its venerable history is a field of knowledge completely outside our dreamer's intellectual interests. If under such conditions dreams insist upon the importance of four, we have every right to call its origin an unconscious one. The numinous character of the quaternity is obvious in the second dream. From this we must conclude that it points to a meaning which we have to call "sacred." Since the dreamer was unable to trace this peculiar character to any conscious source, I apply a comparative method in order to elucidate the meaning of the symbolism. It is of course impossible to give a complete account of this procedure here, so I must restrict myself to the barest hints.

20 For the psychology of the tetraktys, see *The Secret of the Golden Flower,* pp. 96–105; *Two Essays,* Part II, pp. 225ff.; and Hauer, "Symbole und Erfahrung des Selbstes in der Indo-Arischen Mystik."

21 [A selection of these dreams is to be found in *Psychology and Alchemy,* pp. 47ff.—EDITORS.]

92 Since many unconscious contents seem to be remnants of historical states of mind, we need only go back a few hundred years in order to reach the conscious level that forms the parallel to our dreams. In our case we step back not quite three hundred years and find ourselves among scientists and natural philosophers who were seriously discussing the enigma of squaring the circle.[22] This abstruse problem was itself a psychological projection of something much older and completely unconscious. But they knew in those days that the circle signified the Deity: "God is an intellectual figure whose centre is everywhere and the circumference nowhere,"[23] as one of these philosophers said, repeating St. Augustine. A man as introverted and introspective as Emerson[24] could hardly fail to touch on the same idea and likewise quote St. Augustine. The image of the circle—regarded as the most perfect form since Plato's *Timaeus,* the prime authority for Hermetic philosophy—was assigned to the most perfect substance, to the gold, also to the *anima mundi* or *anima media natura,* and to the first created light. And because the macrocosm, the Great World, was made by the creator "in a form round and globose,"[25] the smallest part of the whole, the point, also possesses this perfect nature. As the philosopher says: "Of all shapes the simplest and most perfect is the sphere, which rests in a point."[26] This image of the Deity dormant and

22 There is an excellent presentation of the problem in Maier, *De circulo* (1616).

23 [On the source of this saying, see par. 229, n. 6, below.—EDITORS.]

24 Cf. his essay "Circles" (*Essays,* Everyman edn., p. 167).

25 Plato, *Timaeus,* 7; Steeb, *Coelum Sephiroticum Hebraeorum* (1679), p. 15.

26 Steeb, p. 19. Maier (*De circulo,* p. 27) says: "The circle is a symbol of eternity or an indivisible point." Concerning the "round element," see *Turba philosophorum,* Sermo XLI (ed. Ruska, p. 148), where the "rotundum which turns copper into four" is mentioned. Ruska says there is no similar symbol in the Greek sources. This is not quite correct, since we find a στοιχεῖον στρογγύλον (round element) in the περὶ ὀργάνων of Zosimos (Berthelot, *Alch. grecs,* III, xlix, 1). The same symbolism may also occur in his ποίημα (Berthelot, III, v bis), in the form of the περιηκονισμένον, which Berthelot translates as "objet circulaire." (The correctness of this translation, however, is doubtful.) A better parallel might be Zosimos' "omega element." He himself describes it as "round" (Berthelot, III, xlix, 1).

The idea of the creative point in matter is mentioned in Sendivogius, "Novum lumen" (*Musaeum hermeticum,* 1678, p. 559; cf. *The Hermetic Museum Restored and Enlarged,* trans. by A. E. Waite, II, p. 89: "For there is in every body a centre, the seeding-place or spermatic point." This point is a "point born of God" (p. 59). Here we encounter the doctrine of the "panspermia" (all-embracing

concealed in matter was what the alchemists called the original chaos, or the earth of paradise, or the round fish in the sea,[27] or the egg, or simply the *rotundum*. That round thing was in possession of the magical key which unlocked the closed doors of matter. As is said in the *Timaeus,* only the demiurge, the perfect being, is capable of dissolving the tetraktys, the embrace of the four elements.[28] One of the great authorities since the thirteenth century, the *Turba philosophorum,* says that the *rotundum* can dissolve copper into four.[29] Thus the much-sought-for *aurum philosophicum* was round.[30] Opinions were divided as to the procedure for procuring the dormant demiurge. Some hoped to lay hold of him in the form of a *prima materia* containing a particular concentration or a particularly suitable variety of this substance. Others endeavoured to produce the round substance by a sort of synthesis, called the *coniunctio;* the anonymous author of the *Rosarium philosophorum* says: "Make a round circle of man and woman, extract therefrom a quadrangle and from it a triangle. Make the circle round, and you will have the Philosophers' Stone." [31]

seed-bed), about which Athanasius Kircher, S.J. (*Mundus subterraneus,* 1678, II, p. 347) says: "Thus from the holy words of Moses . . . it appears that God, the creator of all things, in the beginning created from nothing a certain Matter, which we not unfittingly call Chaotic . . . within which something . . . confused lay hidden as if in a kind of panspermia . . . as though he brought forth afterward from the underlying material all things which had already been fecundated and incubated by the divine Spirit. . . . But he did not forthwith destroy the Chaotic Matter, but willed it to endure until the consummation of the world, as at the first beginning of things so to this very day, a panspermia replete with all things. . . ." These ideas lead us back to the "descent" or "fall of the deity" in the Gnostic systems. Cf. Bussell, *Religious Thought and Heresy in the Middle Ages,* pp. 559ff.; Reitzenstein, *Poimandres,* p. 50; Mead, *Pistis Sophia,* pp. 36ff., and *Fragments of a Faith Forgotten,* p. 470.

27 "There is in the sea a round fish, lacking bones and sinews, and it hath in itself a fatness" (the *humidum radicale*—the *anima mundi* imprisoned in matter). From "Allegoriae super Turbam," *Art. aurif.,* I (1593), p. 141.

28 *Timaeus* 7.

29 See above, n. 22.

30 "For as the heaven which is visible is round in form and motion . . . so is the Gold" (Maier, *De circulo,* p. 39).

31 *Rosarium philosophorum* (*Art. aurif.,* II, p. 261). This treatise is ascribed to Petrus Toletanus, who lived in Toledo about the middle of the 13th century. He is said to have been either an older contemporary or a brother of Arnold of Villanova, the famous physician and philosopher. The present form of the *Rosarium,* based on the first printing of 1550, is a compilation and probably does not date

93 This marvellous stone was symbolized as a perfect living being of hermaphroditic nature corresponding to the Empedoclean σφαῖρος, the εὐδαιμονέστατος θεός and all-round bisexual being in Plato.[32] As early as the beginning of the fourteenth century, the *lapis* was compared by Petrus Bonus to Christ, as an *allegoria Christi.*[33] In the *Aurea hora,* a Pseudo-Thomist tract from the thirteenth century, the mystery of the stone is rated even higher than the mysteries of the Christian religion.[34] I mention these facts merely to show that the circle or globe containing the four was an allegory of the Deity for not a few of our learned forefathers.

94 From the Latin treatises it is also evident that the latent demiurge, dormant and concealed in matter, is identical with the so-called *homo philosophicus,* the second Adam.[35] He is the spiritual man, Adam Kadmon, often identified with Christ. Whereas the original Adam was mortal, because he was made of the corruptible four elements, the second Adam is immortal, because he consists of one pure and incorruptible essence. Thus Pseudo-Thomas says: "The Second Adam passed from the pure elements into eternity. Therefore, since he consists of a simple and pure essence, he endures forever."[36] The same treatise quotes a Latinized Arabic author called Senior, a famous authority

back further than the 15th century, though certain parts may have originated early in the 13th century.

32 *Symposium* XIV.

33 Petrus Bonus in Janus Lacinius, *Pretiosa margarita novella* (1546). For the *allegoria Christi,* see *Psychology and Alchemy,* "The Lapis-Christus Parallel."

34 *Beati Thomae de Aquino Aurora sive Aurea hora.* Complete text in the rare printing of 1625: *Harmoniae Inperscrutabilis Chymico-philosophicae sive Philosophorum Antiquorum Consentientium Decas I* (Francofurti apud Conrad Eifridum. Anno MDCXXV). (British Museum 1033 d.11.) The interesting part of this treatise is the first part, "Tractatus parabolarum," which was omitted on account of its "blasphemous" character from the printings of *Artis auriferae* in 1572 and 1593. In the so-called Codex Rhenovacensis (Zurich Central Library), about four chapters of the "Parabolarum" are missing. The Codex Parisinus Fond. Lat. 14006 (Bibliothèque nationale) contains a complete text.

35 A good example is the commentary of Gnosius on the "Tractatus aureus Hermetis," reproduced in *Theatr. chem.,* IV, pp. 672ff., and in Manget, *Bibl. chem.,* I, pp. 400ff.

36 In *Aurea hora* (see n. 34). Zosimos (Berthelot, *Alch. grecs,* III, xlix, 4–5), quoting from a Hermetic writing, says that ὁ θεοῦ υἱὸς πανταγενόμενος was Adam or Thoth, who was made of the four elements and the four cardinal points. Cf. *Psychology and Alchemy,* pp. 348ff.

throughout the Middle Ages, as saying: "There is one substance which never dies, because it abides in continued increase," and interprets this substance as the second Adam.[37]

95 It is clear from these quotations that the round substance searched for by the philosophers was a projection very similar to our own dream symbolism. We have historical documents which prove that dreams, visions, and even hallucinations were often mixed up with the great philosophic opus.[38] Our forefathers, being even more naïvely constituted than ourselves, projected their unconscious contents directly into matter. Matter, however, could easily take up such projections, because at that time it was a practically unknown and incomprehensible entity. And whenever man encounters something mysterious he projects his own assumptions into it without the slightest self-criticism. But since chemical matter nowadays is something we know fairly well, we can no longer project as freely as our ancestors. We have, at last, to admit that the tetraktys is something psychic; and we do not yet know whether, in a more or less distant future, this too may not prove to be a projection. For the time being we must be satisfied with the fact that an idea of God which is entirely absent from the conscious mind of modern man returns in a form known consciously three hundred or four hundred years ago.

96 I do not need to emphasize that this piece of history was completely unknown to my dreamer. One could say with the classical poet: "Naturam expelles furca tamen usque recurret" (Drive out nature with a pitchfork and she always turns up again).[39]

97 The idea of those old philosophers was that God manifested himself first in the creation of the four elements. They were symbolized by the four partitions of the circle. Thus we read in a Coptic treatise of the Codex Brucianus [40] concerning the Only-Begotten (Monogenes or Anthropos):

> This same is he who dwelleth in the Monad, which is in the Setheus [creator], and which came from the place of which none can say where it is. . . . From Him it is the Monad came, in the manner of a ship, laden with all good things, and in the manner of a field, filled or planted with every kind of tree, and in the manner of a city,

37 In *Aurea hora*. For the full Latin title, see n. 34 above.

38 Cf. *Psychology and Alchemy*, pp. 235ff.

39 Horace, *Epistles*, I, x, 24.

40 Baynes, ed., *A Coptic Gnostic Treatise*, pp. 22, 89, 94.

filled with all races of mankind . . . And to its veil which surroundeth it in the manner of a defence there are twelve Gates . . . This same is the Mother-City (μητρόπολις) of the Only-Begotten.

In another place the Anthropos himself is the city and his members are the four gates. The Monad is a spark of light (σπινθήρ), an atom of the Deity. The Monogenes is thought of as standing upon a τετράπεζα, a platform supported by four pillars, corresponding to the Christian quaternarium of the Evangelists, or to the Tetramorph, the symbolic steed of the Church, composed of the symbols of the four evangelists: the angel, eagle, ox or calf, and lion. The analogy with the New Jerusalem of the Apocalypse is obvious.

98 The division into four, the synthesis of the four, the miraculous appearance of the four colours, and the four stages of the work—*nigredo, dealbatio, rubefactio,* and *citrinitas*—are constant preoccupations of the old philosophers.[41] Four symbolizes the parts, qualities, and aspects of the One. But why should my patient recapitulate these old speculations?

99 I do not know why he should. I only know that this is not an isolated case; many others under my observation or under that of my colleagues have spontaneously produced the same symbolism. I naturally do not think that it originated three or four hundred years ago. That was simply another epoch when this same archetypal idea was very much in the foreground. As a matter of fact, it is much older than the Middle Ages, as the *Timaeus* proves. Nor is it a classical or an Egyptian heritage, since it is to be found practically everywhere and in all ages. One has only to remember, for instance, how great an importance was attributed to the quaternity by the American Indians.[42]

100 Although the quaternity is an age-old and presumably prehistoric symbol,[43] always associated with the idea of a world-creating deity, it is—curiously enough—rarely understood as such by those moderns in whom it occurs. I have always been particularly interested to see how people, if left to their

41 The *Rosarium philosophorum* is one of the first attempts at a synopsis and gives a fairly comprehensive account of the medieval quaternity.

42 Cf., for instance, the 5th and 8th Annual Reports of the Smithsonian Institution, Bureau of Ethnology, Washington (1887 and 1892).

43 Cf. the paleolithic (?) "sun wheels" of Rhodesia.

own devices and not informed about the history of the symbol, would interpret it to themselves. I was careful, therefore, not to disturb them with my own opinions, and as a rule I discovered that they took it to symbolize *themselves* or rather *something in themselves.* They felt it belonged intimately to themselves as a sort of creative background, a life-producing sun in the depths of the unconscious. Though it was easy to see that certain mandala-drawings were almost an exact replica of Ezekiel's vision, it very seldom happened that people recognized the analogy even when they knew the vision—which knowledge, by the way, is pretty rare nowadays. What one could almost call a systematic blindness is simply the effect of the prejudice that God is *outside* man. Although this prejudice is not exclusively Christian, there are certain religions which do not share it at all. On the contrary they insist, as do certain Christian mystics, on the essential identity of God and man, either in the form of an *a priori* identity or of a goal to be attained by certain practices or initiations, as known to us, for instance, from the metamorphoses of Apuleius, not to speak of certain yoga methods.

101 The use of the comparative method shows without a doubt that the quaternity is a more or less direct representation of the God who is manifest in his creation. We might, therefore, conclude that the symbol spontaneously produced in the dreams of modern people means something similar—*the God within.* Although the majority of the persons concerned do not recognize this analogy, the interpretation might nevertheless be correct. If we consider the fact that the idea of God is an "unscientific" hypothesis, we can easily explain why people have forgotten to think along such lines. And even if they do cherish a certain belief in God they would be deterred from the idea of a God within by their religious education, which has always depreciated this idea as "mystical." Yet it is precisely this "mystical" idea which is forced upon the conscious mind by dreams and visions. I myself, as well as my colleagues, have seen so many cases developing the same kind of symbolism that we cannot doubt its existence any longer. My observations, moreover, date back to 1914, and I waited fourteen years before alluding to them publicly.[44]

102 It would be a regrettable mistake if anybody should take my

44 [In his commentary to *The Secret of the Golden Flower,* first pub. (in German) in 1929.—EDITORS.]

observations as a kind of proof of the existence of God. They prove only the existence of an archetypal God-image, which to my mind is the most we can assert about God psychologically. But as it is a very important and influential archetype, its relatively frequent occurrence seems to be a noteworthy fact for any *theologia naturalis.* And since experience of this archetype has the quality of numinosity, often in very high degree, it comes into the category of religious experiences.

103 I cannot refrain from calling attention to the interesting fact that whereas the central Christian symbolism is a Trinity, the formula presented by the unconscious is a quaternity. In reality the orthodox Christian formula is not quite complete, because the dogmatic aspect of the evil principle is absent from the Trinity and leads a more or less awkward existence on its own as the devil. Nevertheless it seems that the Church does not exclude an inner relationship between the devil and the Trinity. A Catholic authority expresses himself on this question as follows: "The existence of Satan, however, can only be understood in relation to the Trinity." "Any theological treatment of the devil that is not related to God's trinitarian consciousness is a falsification of the actual position." [45] According to this view, the devil possesses personality and absolute freedom. That is why he can be the true, personal "counterpart of Christ." "Herein is revealed a new freedom in God's being: he freely allows the devil to subsist beside him and permits his kingdom to endure for ever." "The idea of a mighty devil is incompatible with the conception of Yahweh, but not with the conception of the Trinity. The mystery of one God in Three Persons opens out a new freedom in the depths of God's being, and this even makes possible the thought of a personal devil existing alongside God and in opposition to him." [46] The devil, accordingly, possesses an autonomous personality, freedom, and eternality, and he has these metaphysical qualities so much in common with God that he can actually subsist in opposition to him. Hence the relationship or even the (negative) affinity of the devil with the Trinity can no longer be denied as a Catholic idea.

104 The inclusion of the devil in the quaternity is by no means a modern speculation or a monstrous fabrication of the unconscious. We find in the writings of the sixteenth-century natural

[45] Koepgen, *Die Gnosis des Christentums,* pp. 189, 190.

[46] Ibid., pp. 185ff.

philosopher and physician, Gerard Dorn, a detailed discussion of the symbols of the Trinity and the quaternity, the latter being attributed to the devil. Dorn breaks with the whole alchemical tradition inasmuch as he adopts the rigidly Christian standpoint that Three is One but Four is not, because Four attains to unity in the *quinta essentia.* According to this author the quaternity is in truth a "diabolical fraud" or "deception of the devil," and he holds that at the fall of the angels the devil "fell into the realm of quaternity and the elements" (*in quaternariam et elementariam regionem decidit*). He also gives an elaborate description of the symbolic operation whereby the devil produced the "double serpent" (the number 2) "with the four horns" (the number 4). Indeed, the number 2 is the devil himself, the *quadricornutus binarius.*[47]

105 Since a God identical with the individual man is an exceedingly complex assumption bordering on heresy,[48] the "God

[47] Dorn thinks that God created the *binarius* on the second day of Creation, when he separated the upper waters from the lower, and that this was the reason why he omitted to say on the evening of the second day what he said on all the others, namely that "it was good." The emancipation of the *binarius,* Dorn holds, was the cause of "confusion, division, and strife." From the *binarius* issued "its quaternary offspring (*sua proles quaternaria*). Since the number 2 is feminine, it also signified Eve, whereas the number 3 was equated with Adam. Therefore the devil tempted Eve first: "For [the devil] knew, being full of all guile, that Adam was marked with the *unarius,* and for this cause he did not at first attack him, for he greatly doubted whether he could do anything against him. Moreover, he was not ignorant that Eve was divided from her husband as a natural binary from the unity of its ternary [*tanquam naturalem binarium ab unario sui ternarii*]. Accordingly, armed with a certain likeness of binary to binary, he made his attack on the woman. For all even numbers are feminine, of which two, Eve's proper and original number, is the first." (Dorn, "De tenebris contra naturam et vita brevi," *Theatr. chem.,* 1602, I, p. 527. In this treatise and the one that follows it, "De Duello Animi cum Corpore," pp. 535ff., the reader will find everything I have mentioned here.) The reader will have noticed how Dorn, with great cunning, discovers in the *binarius* a secret affinity between the devil and woman. He was the first to point out the discord between threeness and fourness, between God as Spirit and Empedoclean nature, thus—albeit unconsciously—cutting the thread of alchemical projection. Accordingly, he speaks of the *quaternarius* as "fundamental to the medicine of the infidels." We must leave it an open question whether by "infidels" he meant the Arabs or the pagans of antiquity. At any rate Dorn suspected that there was something ungodly in the quaternity, which was intimately associated with the nature of woman. Cf. my remarks concerning the "virgo terrae" in the next section.

[48] I am not referring here to the dogma of the human nature of Christ.

within" also presents a dogmatic difficulty. But the quaternity as produced by the modern psyche points directly not only to the God within, but to the identity of God and man. Contrary to the dogma, there are not three, but four aspects. It could easily be inferred that the fourth represents the devil. Though we have the logion "I and the Father are one: who seeth me seeth the Father," it would be considered blasphemy or madness to stress Christ's dogmatic humanity to such a degree that man could identify himself with Christ and his homoousia.[49] But this is precisely what seems to be meant by the natural symbol. From an orthodox standpoint, therefore, the natural quaternity could be declared a *diabolica fraus,* and the chief proof of this would be its assimilation of the fourth aspect which represents the reprehensible part of the Christian cosmos. The Church, it seems to me, probably has to repudiate any attempt to take such conclusions seriously. She may even have to condemn any approach to these experiences, since she cannot admit that Nature unites what she herself has divided. The voice of Nature is clearly audible in all experiences of the quaternity, and this arouses all the old mistrust of anything even remotely connected with the unconscious. Scientific investigation of dreams is simply the old oneiromancy in new guise and therefore just as objectionable as any other of the "occult" arts. Close parallels to the symbolism of dreams can be found in the old alchemical treatises, and these are quite as heretical as dreams.[50] Here, it would seem, was reason enough for secrecy and protective metaphors.[51] The symbolic statements of the old alchemists issue from the same unconscious as modern dreams and are just as much the voice of nature.

106 If we were still living in a medieval setting where there was not much doubt about the ultimate things and where every history of the world began with Genesis, we could easily brush

49 This identification has nothing to do with the Catholic conception of the assimilation of the individual's life to the life of Christ and his absorption into the *corpus mysticum* of the Church. It is rather the opposite of this view.

50 I am thinking chiefly of works that contain alchemical legends and didactic tales. A good example would be Maier's *Symbola aureae mensae* (1617), with its symbolic *peregrinatio* (pp. 569ff.).

51 So far as I know, there are no complaints in alchemical literature of persecution by the Church. The authors allude usually to the tremendous secret of the magistery as a reason for secrecy.

aside dreams and the like. Unfortunately we live in a modern setting where all the ultimate things are doubtful, where there is a prehistory of enormous extension, and where people are fully aware that if there is any numinous experience at all, it is the experience of the psyche. We can no longer imagine an empyrean world revolving round the throne of God, and we would not dream of seeking for him somewhere behind the galactic systems. Yet the human soul seems to harbour mysteries, since to an empiricist all religious experience boils down to a peculiar psychic condition. If we want to know anything of what religious experience means to those who have it, we have every chance nowadays of studying it in every imaginable form. And if it means anything, it means everything to those who have it. This is at any rate the inevitable conclusion one reaches by a careful study of the evidence. One could even define religious experience as that kind of experience which is accorded the highest value, no matter what its contents may be. The modern mind, so far as it stands under the verdict "extra ecclesiam nulla salus," will turn to the psyche as the last hope. Where else could one obtain experience? And the answer will be more or less of the kind which I have described. The voice of nature will answer and all those concerned with the spiritual problem of man will be confronted with new and baffling problems. Because of the spiritual need of my patients I have been forced to make a serious attempt to understand some of the symbols produced by the unconscious. As it would lead much too far to embark on a discussion of the intellectual and ethical consequences, I shall have to content myself with a mere sketch.

107 The main symbolic figures of a religion are always expressive of the particular moral and mental attitude involved. I would mention, for instance, the cross and its various religious meanings. Another main symbol is the Trinity. It is of exclusively masculine character. The unconscious, however, transforms it into a quaternity, which is at the same time a unity, just as the three persons of the Trinity are one and the same God. The natural philosophers of antiquity represented the Trinity, so far as it was *imaginata in natura,* as the three ἀσώματα or "spirits," also called "volatilia," namely water, air, and fire. The fourth constituent, on the other hand, was τὸ σώματον, the earth or the body.

They symbolized the latter by the Virgin.[52] In this way they added the feminine element to their physical Trinity, thereby producing the quaternity or *circulus quadratus,* whose symbol was the hermaphroditic *rebis,*[53] the *filius sapientiae.* The natural philosophers of the Middle Ages undoubtedly meant earth and woman by the fourth element. The principle of evil was not openly mentioned, but it appears in the poisonous quality of the *prima materia* and in other allusions. The quaternity in modern dreams is a creation of the unconscious. As I explained in the first chapter, the unconscious is often personified by the anima, a feminine figure. Apparently the symbol of the quaternity issues from her. She would be the matrix of the quaternity, a θεοτόκος or Mater Dei, just as the earth was understood to be the Mother of God. But since woman, as well as evil, is excluded from the Deity in the dogma of the Trinity, the element of evil would form part of the religious symbol if the latter should be a quaternity. It needs no particular effort of imagination to guess the far-reaching spiritual consequences of such a development.

52 Cf. *Psychology and Alchemy,* fig. 232, showing the glorification of the body in the form of the Assumption of the Virgin (from Reusner, *Pandora,* 1588). St. Augustine used the earth to symbolize the Virgin: "Truth is arisen from the earth, for Christ is born of a virgin" (*Sermones,* 189, II, in Migne, *P.L.,* vol. 38, col. 1006). Likewise Tertullian: "That virgin earth, not yet watered by the rains nor fertilized by the showers" (*Adversus Judaeos,* 13, in Migne, *P.L.,* vol. 2, col. 655).

53 The *rebis* ('made of two') is the philosophers' stone, for in it the masculine and the feminine nature are united. [Cf. *Psychology and Alchemy,* p. 232 and fig. 125.—EDITORS.]

3. THE HISTORY AND PSYCHOLOGY OF A NATURAL SYMBOL

108 Although I have no wish to discourage philosophical curiosity, I would rather not lose myself in a discussion of the ethical and intellectual aspects of the problem raised by the quaternity symbol. Its psychological importance is far-reaching and plays a considerable role in practical treatment. While we are not concerned here with psychotherapy, but with the religious aspect of certain psychic phenomena, I have been forced through my studies in psychopathology to dig out these historical symbols and figures from the dust of their graves.[1] When I was a young alienist I should never have suspected myself of doing such a thing. I shall not mind, therefore, if this long discussion of the quaternity symbol, the *circulus quadratus,* and the heretical attempts to improve on the dogma of the Trinity seem to be somewhat far-fetched and exaggerated. But, in point of fact, my whole discourse on the quaternity is no more than a regrettably short and inadequate introduction to the final and crowning example which illustrates my case.

109 Already at the very beginning of our dream-series the circle appears. It takes the form, for instance, of a serpent, which describes a circle [2] round the dreamer. It appears in later dreams

1 Cf. *Symbols of Transformation.*

2 A recurrence of the ancient symbol of the uroboros, 'tail-eater.'

as a clock, a circle with a central point, a round target for shooting practice, a clock that is a *perpetuum mobile,* a ball, a globe, a round table, a basin, and so on. The square appears also, about the same time, in the form of a city square or a garden with a fountain in the centre. Somewhat later it appears in connection with a circular movement: [3] people walking round in a square; a magic ceremony (the transformation of animals into human beings) that takes place in a square room, in the corners of which are four snakes, with people again circulating round the four corners; the dreamer driving round a square in a taxi; a square prison cell; an empty square which is itself rotating; and so on. In other dreams the circle is represented by rotation—for instance, four children carry a "dark ring" and walk in a circle. Again, the circle appears combined with the quaternity, as a silver bowl with four nuts at the four cardinal points, or as a table with four chairs. The centre seems to be particularly emphasized. It is symbolized by an egg in the middle of a ring; by a star consisting of a body of soldiers; by a star rotating in a circle, the cardinal points of which represent the four seasons; by the pole; by a precious stone, and so on.

110 All these dreams lead up to one image which came to the patient in the form of a sudden visual impression. He had had such glimpses or visualizations on several occasions before, but this time it was a most impressive experience. As he himself says: "It was an impression of the most sublime harmony." In such a case it does not matter at all what *our* impression is or what *we* think about it. It only matters how the patient feels about it. It is *his* experience, and if it has a deeply transforming influence upon his condition there is no point in arguing against it. The psychologist can only take note of the fact and, if he feels equal to the task, he might also make an attempt to understand why such a vision had such an effect upon such a person. The vision was a turning point in the patient's psychological development. It was what one would call—in the language of religion—a conversion.

111 This is the literal text of the vision:

[3] An Eastern parallel is the "circulation of the light" mentioned in the Chinese alchemical treatise, *The Secret of the Golden Flower,* edited by R. Wilhelm and myself.

There is a vertical and a horizontal circle, having a common centre. This is the world clock. It is supported by the black bird.[4]

The vertical circle is a blue disc with a white border divided into 4 × 8 = 32 partitions. A pointer rotates upon it.

The horizontal circle consists of four colours. On it stand four little men with pendulums, and round about it is laid the ring that was once dark and is now golden (formerly carried by four children).

The world clock has three rhythms or pulses:

1.	*The small pulse:*	*the pointer on the blue vertical disc advances by 1/32.*
2.	*The middle pulse:*	*one complete rotation of the pointer. At the same time the horizontal circle advances by 1/32.*
3.	*The great pulse:*	*32 middle pulses are equal to one complete rotation of the golden ring.*

112 The vision sums up all the allusions in the previous dreams. It seems to be an attempt to make a meaningful whole of the formerly fragmentary symbols, then characterized as circle, globe, square, rotation, clock, star, cross, quaternity, time, and so on.

113 It is of course difficult to understand why a feeling of "most sublime harmony" should be produced by this abstract structure. But if we think of the two circles in Plato's *Timaeus,* and of the harmonious all-roundness of his *anima mundi,* we might find an avenue to understanding. Again, the term "world clock" suggests the antique conception of the musical harmony of the spheres. It would thus be a sort of cosmological system. If it were a vision of the firmament and its silent rotation, or of the steady movement of the solar system, we could readily understand and appreciate the perfect harmony of the picture. We might also assume that the platonic vision of the cosmos was faintly glimmering through the mist of a dreamlike consciousness. But there is something in the vision that does not quite accord with the harmonious perfection of the platonic picture. The two circles are each of a different nature. Not only is their

[4] This refers to a previous vision, where a black eagle carried away a golden ring. [For this entire clock vision, cf. *Psychology and Alchemy,* pars. 307ff.—EDITORS.]

movement different, but their colour too. The vertical circle is blue and the horizontal one containing four colours is golden. The blue circle might easily symbolize the blue hemisphere of the sky, while the horizontal circle would represent the horizon with its four cardinal points, personified by the four little men and characterized by the four colours. (In a former dream, the four points were represented once by four children and another time by the four seasons.) This picture immediately calls to mind the medieval representations of the world in the form of a circle or in the shape of the *rex gloriae* with the four evangelists, or the *melothesia*,[5] where the horizon is formed by the zodiac. The representation of the triumphant Christ seems to be derived from similar pictures of Horus and his four sons.[6] There are also Eastern analogies: the Buddhist mandalas or circles, usually of Tibetan origin. These consist as a rule of a circular padma or lotus which contains a square sacred building with four gates, indicating the four cardinal points and the seasons. The centre contains a Buddha, or more often the conjunction of Shiva and his Shakti, or an equivalent *dorje* (thunderbolt) symbol.[7] They are yantras or ritualistic instruments for the purpose of contemplation, concentration, and the final transformation of the yogi's consciousness into the divine all-consciousness.[8]

114 However striking these analogies may be, they are not entirely satisfactory, because they all emphasize the centre to such an extent that they seem to have been made in order to express the importance of the central figure. In our case, however, the centre is empty. It consists only of a mathematical point. The parallels I have mentioned depict the world-creating or world-ruling deity, or else man in his dependence upon the celestial constellations. Our symbol is a clock, symbolizing time. The

5 The "blood-letting manikins" are *melothesiae*. [These are the little figures which medieval physicians used to draw inside a circle or mandala on the part of the body affected, when bleeding or "cupping" a patient. *Melothesia* is the "assignment of parts of the body to the tutelage of signs or planets" (Liddell and Scott, *Greek-English Lexicon*, p. 1099). Woodcuts of *melothesiae* are reproduced in Jacobi, ed., *Paracelsus: Selected Writings*, figs. 36 and 45.—EDITORS.]

6 Budge, *Osiris and the Egyptian Resurrection*, I, 3; *The Egyptian Book of the Dead* (facsimile), pl. 5. In a manuscript from the 7th century (Gellone), the evangelists are represented with the heads of their symbolic animals instead of human heads.

7 There is an example in *The Secret of the Golden Flower*.

8 *Shrīchakrasambhāra Tantra*, ed. by Avalon.

only analogy I can think of to such a symbol is the design of the horoscope. It too has four cardinal points and an empty centre. And there is another remarkable correspondence: rotation is often mentioned in the previous dreams, and this is usually reported as moving to the left. The horoscope has twelve houses that progress numerically to the left, that is, counter-clockwise.

115 But the horoscope consists of one circle only and moreover contains no contrast between two obviously different systems. So the horoscope too is an unsatisfactory analogy, though it sheds some light on the time aspect of our symbol. We would be forced to give up our attempt to find psychological parallels were it not for the treasure-house of medieval symbolism. By a lucky chance I came across a little-known medieval author of the early fourteenth century, Guillaume de Digulleville, prior of a monastery at Châlis, a Norman poet who wrote three "Pélerinages" between 1330 and 1355.[9] They are called *Les Pélerinages de la vie humaine, de l'âme,* and *de Jésus Christ.* In the last canto of the *Pélerinage de l'âme* we find a vision of paradise.

116 Paradise consists of forty-nine rotating spheres. They are called "siècles," centuries, being the prototypes or archetypes of the earthly centuries. But, as the angel who serves as a guide to Guillaume explains, the ecclesiastical expression "in saecula saeculorum" means eternity and not ordinary time. A golden heaven surrounds all the spheres. When Guillaume looked up to the golden heaven he suddenly became aware of a small circle, only three feet wide and of the colour of sapphire. He says of this circle: "It came out of the golden heaven at one point and reentered it at another, and it made the whole tour of the golden heaven." Evidently the blue circle was rolling like a disc upon a great circle which intersected the golden sphere of heaven.

117 Here, then, we have two different systems, the one golden, the other blue, and the one cutting through the other. What is the blue circle? The angel again explains to the wondering Guillaume:

[9] Abbé Joseph Delacotte, *Guillaume de Digulleville, Trois romans-poèmes du XIVe siècle.* [A 15th-cent. verse translation of the "Pilgrimage" by John Lydgate was published by the Early English Text Society (1899–1904). For other early English translations, published in recent times, see the *Oxford History of English Literature,* II, part i, p. 308.—EDITORS.]

Ce cercle que tu vois est le calendrier,
Qui en faisant son tour entier,
Montre des Saints les journées
Quand elles doivent être fetées.
Chacun en fait le cercle un tour,
Chacune étoile y est pour jour,
Chacun soleil pour l'espace
De jours trente ou zodiaque.

(This circle is the calendar
Which spinning round the course entire
Shows the feast day of each saint
And when it should be celebrate.
Each saint goes once round all the way,
Each star you see stands for a day,
And every sun denotes a spell
Of thirty days zodiacal.)

118 The blue circle is the ecclesiastical calendar. So here we have another parallel—the element of time. It will be remembered that time, in our vision, is characterized or measured by three pulses. Guillaume's calendar circle is three feet in diameter. Moreover, while Guillaume is gazing at the blue circle, three spirits clad in purple suddenly appear. The angel explains that this is the feast-day of the three saints, and he goes on to discourse about the whole zodiac. When he comes to the sign of the Fishes he mentions the feast of the twelve fishermen which precedes that of the Holy Trinity. Whereupon Guillaume tells the angel that he has never quite understood the symbol of the Trinity. He asks him to be good enough to explain this mystery. Whereupon the angel answers: "Well, there are three principal colours: green, red, and golden." One can see them united in the peacock's tail. And he goes on: "The almighty King who puts three colours in one, cannot he also make one substance to be three?" The golden colour, he says, belongs to the Father, the red to the Son, and the green to the Holy Ghost.[10] Then the angel warns the poet not to ask any more questions and disappears.

119 We know, happily enough, from the angel's teaching, that three has to do with the Trinity. So we also know that our

10 The Holy Ghost is the cause of the *viriditas* (greenness). Cf. below, pp. 91–92.

former digression into the field of mystical speculation on the Trinity was not far off the mark. At the same time we meet with the motif of the colours, but unfortunately our patient has four, whereas Guillaume, or rather the angel, speaks only of three—gold, red, and green. Here we might quote the opening words of the *Timaeus:* "Three there are, but where is the fourth?" Or we could quote the very same words from Goethe's *Faust,* from the famous Cabiri scene in Part II, where the Cabiri bring the vision of that mysterious "streng Gebilde," the "severe image," from the sea.

120 The four little men of our vision are dwarfs or Cabiri. They represent the four cardinal points and the four seasons, as well as the four colours and the four elements. In the *Timaeus,* as also in *Faust* and the *Pélerinage,* something seems to be wrong with the number four. The missing fourth colour is obviously blue. It is the one that belongs to the series yellow, red, and green. Why is blue missing? What is wrong with the calendar? or with time? or with the colour blue? [11]

121 Poor old Guillaume has evidently been stumped by the same problem. Three there are, but where is the fourth? He was eager to learn something about the Trinity—which, as he says, he had never quite understood. And it is slightly suspicious that the angel is in such a hurry to get away before Guillaume can ask any more awkward questions.

122 Well, I suppose Guillaume was unconscious when he went to heaven, otherwise he surely would have drawn certain conclusions from what he saw. Now what did he actually see? First he saw the spheres or "siècles" inhabited by those who had at-

[11] Gerhard Dorn had a similar conception of circular figures intersecting and disturbing one another: on the one hand the circular system of the Trinity and on the other the devil's attempt to construct a system of his own. He says: "It is to be noted, moreover, that the centre is unary, and its circle is ternary, but whatever is inserted between the centre [and the circumference], and enters the enclosed realm, is to be taken as binary, be it another circle . . . or any other figure whatever." So the devil fabricated a circle of sorts for himself and tried to devise a circular system with it, but for various reasons the attempt failed. In the end all he produced was the "figure of a twofold serpent lifting up four horns, and therefore is the kingdom of the monomachy [*monomachiae regnum*] divided against itself." Being the *binarius* in person, the devil could hardly have produced anything else. ("De Duello," *Theatrum chemicum,* 1602, I, p. 547.) Already in the alchemy of Zosimos the devil appears as ἀντίμιμος, the imitator, ape of God. (Berthelot, *Alch. grecs,* III, xlix, 9. Cf. also Mead, *Pistis Sophia, passim.*)

tained eternal bliss. Then he beheld the heaven of gold, the "ciel d'or," and there was the King of Heaven sitting upon a golden throne and, beside him, the Queen of Heaven sitting upon a round throne of *brown crystal.* This latter detail refers to the fact that Mary is supposed to have been taken up to heaven with her body, as the only mortal being permitted to unite with the body before the resurrection of the dead. The king is usually represented as the triumphant Christ in conjunction with his bride, the Church. But the all-important point is that the king, being Christ, is at the same time the Trinity, and that the introduction of a fourth person, the Queen, makes it a quaternity. The royal pair represents in ideal form the unity of the Two under the rule of the One—"binarius sub monarchia unarii," as Dorn would say. Moreover, in the brown crystal, the "realm of quaternity and the elements" into which the "four-horned binarius" was cast has been exalted to the throne of the supreme intercessor, Mary. Consequently the quaternity of the natural elements appears not only in close conjunction with the *corpus mysticum* of the bridal Church or Queen of Heaven —often it is difficult to distinguish between the two—but in immediate relationship to the Trinity.[12]

123 Blue is the colour of Mary's celestial cloak; she is the earth covered by the blue tent of the sky.[13] But why should the Mother of God not be mentioned? According to the dogma she is only *beata,* not divine. Moreover, she represents the earth, which is also the body and its darkness. That is the reason why she, the all-merciful, has the power of attorney to plead for all sinners, but also why, despite her privileged position (it is not possible for the angels to sin), she has a relationship with the Trinity which is rationally not comprehensible, since it is so close and yet so distant. As the matrix, the vessel, the earth, she can be interpreted allegorically as the *rotundum,* which is characterized by the four cardinal points, and hence as the globe with the four quarters, God's footstool, or as the "four-square" Heavenly City, or the "flower of the sea, in which Christ lies

12 A peculiar coincidence of three and four is to be found in Wernher vom Niederrhein's allegory of Mary, where, besides the three men in the burning fiery furnace, a fourth appears who is interpreted as Christ. Cf. Salzer, *Die Sinnbilder und Beiworte Mariens,* p. 21.

13 Eisler, *Weltenmantel und Himmelszelt,* I, pp. 85ff.

hidden" [14]—in a word, as a mandala. This, according to the Tantric idea of the lotus, is feminine, and for readily understandable reasons. The lotus is the eternal birthplace of the gods. It corresponds to the Western rose in which the King of Glory sits, often supported by the four evangelists, who correspond to the four quarters.

124 From this precious piece of medieval psychology we gain some insight into the meaning of our patient's mandala. It unites the four and they function together harmoniously. My patient had been brought up a Catholic and thus, unwittingly, he was confronted with the same problem which caused not a little worry to old Guillaume. It was, indeed, a great problem to the Middle Ages, this problem of the Trinity and the exclusion, or the very qualified recognition, of the feminine element, of the earth, the body, and matter in general, which were yet, in the form of Mary's womb, the sacred abode of the Deity and the indispensable instrument for the divine work of redemption. My patient's vision is a symbolic answer to this age-old question. That is probably the deeper reason why the image of the world clock produced the impression of "most sublime harmony." It was the first intimation of a possible solution of the devastating conflict between matter and spirit, between the desires of the flesh and the love of God. The miserable and ineffectual compromise of the church dream is completely overcome in this mandala vision, where all opposites are reconciled. If we hark back to the old Pythagorean idea that the soul is a square,[15] then the mandala would express the Deity through its threefold rhythm and the soul through its static quaternity, the circle divided into four colours. And thus its innermost meaning would simply be the *union of the soul with God.*

125 As the world clock also represents the *quadratura circuli* and the *perpetuum mobile,* both these preoccupations of the medieval mind find adequate expression in our mandala. The golden circle and its contents represent the quaternity in the form of the four Cabiri and the four colours, and the blue circle represents the Trinity and the movement of time, according to Guillaume. In our case, the hand of the blue circle has the

14 Salzer, p. 66.

15 Zeller, *Die Philosophie der Griechen,* III, ii, p. 120. According to Archytas, the soul is a circle or sphere.

fastest movement, while the golden circle moves slowly. Whereas the blue circle seems to be somewhat incongruous in Guillaume's golden heaven, the circles in our case are harmoniously combined. The Trinity is now the life, the "pulse" of the whole system, with a threefold rhythm based, however, on thirty-two, a multiple of four. This agrees with the view I expressed before, that the quaternity is the *sine qua non* of divine birth and, consequently, of the inner life of the Trinity. Thus circle and quaternity on one side and the threefold rhythm on the other interpenetrate so that each is contained in the other. In Guillaume's version the Trinity is obvious enough, but the quaternity is concealed in the duality of the King and Queen of Heaven. What is more, the blue colour does not belong to the queen but to the calendar, which represents time and is characterized by trinitarian attributes. There seems to be a mutual interpenetration of symbols, just as in our case.

126 Interpenetrations of qualities and contents are typical not only of symbols in general, but also of the *essential similarity* of the contents symbolized. Without this similarity no interpenetration would be possible at all. We therefore find interpenetration also in the Christian conception of the Trinity, where the Father appears in the Son, the Son in the Father, the Holy Ghost in Father and Son, or both these in the Holy Ghost as the Paraclete. The progression from Father to Son and the Son's appearance on earth at a particular moment would represent the time element, while the spatial element would be personified by the Mater Dei. (The mother quality was originally an attribute of the Holy Ghost, and the latter was known as Sophia-Sapientia by certain early Christians.[16] This feminine quality could not be completely eradicated; it still adheres to the symbol of the Holy Ghost, the *columba spiritus sancti*). But the quaternity is entirely absent from the dogma, though it appears in early ecclesiastical symbolism. I refer to the cross with equal arms enclosed in the circle, the triumphant Christ with the four evangelists, the tetramorph, and so on. In later ecclesiastical symbolism the *rosa mystica,* the *vas devotionis,* the *fons*

16 Cf. the invocation in the Acts of Thomas (Mead, *Fragments of a Faith Forgotten,* pp. 422ff.). Also the "seat of wisdom" in the Litany of Loreto, and the readings from Proverbs on Mary's feast-days, e.g., the Immaculate Conception (Prov. 8:22–35).

signatus, and the *hortus conclusus* appear as attributes of the Mater Dei and of the spiritualized earth.[17]

127 It would hardly be worth while to look at all these relationships in a psychological light if the conceptions of the Trinity were nothing more than the ingenuities of human reason. I have always taken the view that they belong to the type of revelation to which Koepgen has recently given the name of "Gnosis" (not to be confused with Gnosticism). Revelation is an "unveiling" of the depths of the human soul first and foremost, a "laying bare"; hence it is an essentially psychological event, though this does not, of course, tell us what *else* it might be. That lies outside the province of science. My view comes very close to Koepgen's lapidary formula, which moreover bears the ecclesiastical imprimatur: "The Trinity is a revelation not only of God but at the same time of man." [18]

128 Our mandala is an abstract, almost mathematical representation of some of the main problems discussed in medieval Christian philosophy. The abstraction goes so far, indeed, that if it had not been for the help of Guillaume's vision we might have overlooked its widespread system of roots in human history. The patient did not possess any real knowledge of the historical material. He knew only what anybody who had received a smattering of religious instruction in early childhood would know. He himself saw no connection between his world clock and any religious symbolism. One can readily understand this, since the vision contains nothing at first sight that would remind anyone of religion. Yet the vision itself came shortly after the dream of the "House of the Gathering." And that dream was the answer to the problem of three and four represented in a still earlier dream. There it was a matter of a rectangular space, on the four sides of which were four goblets filled with coloured water. One was yellow, another red, the third green, and the fourth colourless. Obviously blue was missing, yet it had been connected with the three other colours in a previous vision, where a bear appeared in the depths of a cavern. The bear had four eyes emitting red, yellow, green, and

[17] For the Gnostics the quaternity was decidedly feminine. Cf. Irenaeus, *Against Heresies,* I, ch. xi (Keble trans., p. 36).

[18] *Die Gnosis des Christentums,* p. 194.

blue light. Astonishingly enough, in the later dream the blue colour had disappeared. At the same time the customary square was transformed into an oblong, which had never appeared before. The cause of this manifest disturbance was the dreamer's resistance to the feminine element represented by the anima. In the dream of the "House of the Gathering" the voice confirms this fact. It says: "What you are doing is dangerous. Religion is not the tax you pay in order to get rid of the woman's image, for this image cannot be got rid of." The "woman's image" is exactly what we would call the "anima." [19]

129 It is normal for a man to resist his anima, because she represents, as I said before, the unconscious and all those tendencies and contents hitherto excluded from conscious life. They were excluded for a number of reasons, both real and apparent. Some are suppressed and some are repressed. As a rule those tendencies that represent the antisocial elements in man's psychic structure—what I call the "statistical criminal" in everybody—are suppressed, that is, they are consciously and deliberately disposed of. But tendencies that are merely repressed are usually of a somewhat doubtful character. They are not so much antisocial as unconventional and socially awkward. The reason why we repress them is equally doubtful. Some people repress them from sheer cowardice, others from conventional morality, and others again for reasons of respectability. Repression is a sort of half-conscious and half-hearted letting go of things, a dropping of hot cakes or a reviling of grapes which hang too high, or a looking the other way in order not to become conscious of one's desires. Freud discovered that repression is one of the main mechanisms in the making of a neurosis. Suppression amounts to a conscious moral choice, but repression is a rather immoral "penchant" for getting rid of disagreeable decisions. Suppression may cause worry, conflict and suffering, but it never causes a neurosis. Neurosis is always a substitute for legitimate suffering.

130 If one discounts the "statistical criminal," there still remains the vast domain of inferior qualities and primitive tendencies which belong to the psychic structure of the man who is less

[19] See *Psychological Types*, Defs. 48 and 49. [Also *Aion*, par. 19 (Swiss edn., pp. 25f.)—EDITORS.]

ideal and more primitive than we should like to be.[20] We have certain ideas as to how a civilized or educated or moral being should live, and we occasionally do our best to fulfil these ambitious expectations. But since nature has not bestowed the same blessings upon each of her children, some are more and others less gifted. Thus there are people who can just afford to live properly and respectably; that is to say, no manifest flaw is discoverable. They either commit minor sins, if they sin at all, or their sins are concealed from them by a thick layer of unconsciousness. One is rather inclined to be lenient with sinners who are unconscious of their sins. But nature is not at all lenient with unconscious sinners. She punishes them just as severely as if they had committed a conscious offence. Thus we find, as the pious Henry Drummond[21] once observed, that it is highly moral people, unaware of their other side, who develop particularly hellish moods which make them insupportable to their relatives. The odour of sanctity may be far reaching, but to live with a saint might well cause an inferiority complex or even a wild outburst of immorality in individuals less morally gifted. Morality seems to be a gift like intelligence. You cannot pump it into a system to which it is not indigenous.

131 Unfortunately there can be no doubt that man is, on the whole, less good than he imagines himself or wants to be. Everyone carries a shadow, and the less it is embodied in the individual's conscious life, the blacker and denser it is. If an inferiority is conscious, one always has a chance to correct it. Furthermore, it is constantly in contact with other interests, so that it is continually subjected to modifications. But if it is repressed and isolated from consciousness, it never gets corrected, and is liable to burst forth suddenly in a moment of unawareness. At all events, it forms an unconscious snag, blocking the most well-meant attempts.

132 We carry our past with us, to wit, the primitive and inferior man with his desires and emotions, and it is only with an enormous effort that we can detach ourselves from this burden. If it comes to a neurosis, we invariably have to deal with a consid-

[20] A special instance is the "inferior function." See *Psychological Types,* Def. 40. [And *Aion,* pars. 13ff. (Swiss edn., pp. 22ff.).—EDITORS.]

[21] Widely known because of his book *Natural Law in the Spiritual World.* The quotation comes from *The Greatest Thing in the World.*

erably intensified shadow. And if such a person wants to be cured it is necessary to find a way in which his conscious personality and his shadow can live together.

133 This is a very serious problem for all those who are themselves in such a predicament or have to help sick people back to normal life. Mere suppression of the shadow is as little of a remedy as beheading would be for headache. To destroy a man's morality does not help either, because it would kill his better self, without which even the shadow makes no sense. The reconciliation of these opposites is a major problem, and even in antiquity it bothered certain minds. Thus we know of an otherwise legendary personality of the second century, Carpocrates,[22] a Neoplatonist philosopher whose school, according to Irenaeus, taught that good and evil are merely human opinions and that the soul, before its departure from the body, must pass through the whole gamut of human experience to the very end if it is not to fall back into the prison of the body. It is as if the soul could only ransom itself from imprisonment in the somatic world of the demiurge by complete fulfilment of all life's demands. The bodily existence in which we find ourselves is a kind of hostile brother whose conditions must first be known. It was in this sense that the Carpocratians interpreted Matthew 5:25f. (also Luke 12:58f.): "Agree with thine adversary quickly, whiles thou art in the way with him; lest at any time the adversary deliver thee to the judge, and the judge deliver thee to the officer, and thou be cast into prison. Verily I say unto thee, Thou shalt by no means come out thence, till thou hast paid the uttermost farthing." Remembering the other Gnostic doctrine that no man can be redeemed from a sin he has not committed, we are here confronted with a problem of the very greatest importance, obscured though it is by the Christian abhorrence of anything Gnostic. Inasmuch as the somatic man, the "adversary," is none other than "the other in me," it is plain that the Carpocratian mode of thought would lead to the following interpretation of Matthew 5:22f.: "But I say unto you, That whosoever is angry with *himself* without a cause shall be in danger of the judgment: and whosoever shall say to *himself*, Raca, shall be in danger of the council: but whosoever shall say, Thou fool, shall be in danger of hell fire. Therefore if thou bring thy gift to the altar,

22 Irenaeus, *Against Heresies*, XXV (Keble trans., p. 75).

and there rememberest that *thou hast aught against thyself,* leave there thy gift before the altar, and go thy way; first be reconciled to *thyself,* and then come and offer thy gift. Agree with *thyself* quickly, whiles thou art in the way with *thyself;* lest at any time *thou deliverest thyself* to the judge." From here it is but a step to the uncanonical saying: "Man, if indeed thou knowest what thou doest, thou art blessed; but if thou knowest not, thou art cursed, and a transgressor of the law." [23] But the problem comes very close indeed in the parable of the unjust steward, which is a stumbling-block in more senses than one. "And the lord commended the unjust steward, because he had done wisely" (Luke 16:8). In the Vulgate the word for 'wisely' is *prudenter,* and in the Greek text it is φρονίμως (prudently, sensibly, intelligently). There's no denying that practical intelligence functions here as a court of ethical decision. Perhaps, despite Irenaeus, we may credit the Carpocratians with this much insight, and allow that they too, like the unjust steward, were commendably aware of how to save face. It is natural that the more robust mentality of the Church Fathers could not appreciate the delicacy and the merit of this subtle and, from a modern point of view, immensely practical argument. It was also dangerous, and it is still the most vital and yet the most ticklish ethical problem of a civilization that has forgotten why man's life should be sacrificial, that is, offered up to an idea greater than himself. Man can live the most amazing things if they make sense to him. But the difficulty is to create that sense. It must be a conviction, naturally; but you find that the most convincing things man can invent are cheap and ready-made, and are never able to convince him against his personal desires and fears.

134 If the repressed tendencies, the shadow as I call them, were obviously evil, there would be no problem whatever. But the shadow is merely somewhat inferior, primitive, unadapted, and awkward; not wholly bad. It even contains childish or primitive qualities which would in a way vitalize and embellish human existence, but it is "not done." The educated public, the flower of our present civilization, has detached itself from its roots, and is about to lose its connection with the earth as well. There

[23] James, trans., *The Apocryphal New Testament,* p. 33.

is no civilized country nowadays where the lowest strata of the population are not in a state of unrest and dissent. In a number of European nations such a condition is overtaking the upper strata too. This state of affairs demonstrates our psychological problem on a gigantic scale. Inasmuch as collectivities are mere accumulations of individuals, their problems are accumulations of individual problems. One set of people identifies itself with the superior man and cannot descend, and the other set identifies itself with the inferior man and wants to get to the top.

135 Such problems are never solved by legislation or by tricks. They are solved only by a general change of attitude. And the change does not begin with propaganda and mass meetings, or with violence. It begins with a change in individuals. It will continue as a transformation of their personal likes and dislikes, of their outlook on life and of their values, and only the accumulation of these individual changes will produce a collective solution.

136 The educated man tries to repress the inferior man in himself, not realizing that by so doing he forces the latter into revolt. It is characteristic of my patient that he once dreamt of a military party that wanted "to strangle the left completely." Somebody remarks that the left is weak enough anyway, but the military party answers that this is just why it ought to be strangled completely. The dream shows how my patient dealt with his own inferior man. This is clearly not the right method. The dream of the "House of the Gathering," on the contrary, shows a religious attitude as the correct answer to his question. The mandala seems to be an amplification of this particular point. Historically, as we have seen, the mandala served as a symbol to clarify the nature of the deity philosophically, or to represent the same thing in a visible form for the purpose of adoration, or, as in the East, as a yantra for yoga practices. The wholeness ("perfection") of the celestial circle and the squareness of the earth, combining the four principles or elements or psychic qualities,[24] express completeness and union. Thus the mandala has the status of a "uniting symbol." [25] As the union of

24 In Tibetan Buddhism the four colours are associated with psychic qualities (the four forms of wisdom). Cf. my psychological commentary to the *Tibetan Book of the Dead,* below, p. 522.

25 See *Psychological Types,* Def. 51.

God and man is expressed in the symbol of Christ or the cross,[26] we would expect the patient's world clock to have a similar reconciling significance. Prejudiced by historical analogies, we would expect a deity to occupy the centre of the mandala. The centre is, however, empty. The seat of the deity is unoccupied, in spite of the fact that, when we analyse the mandala in terms of its historical models, we arrive at the god symbolized by the circle and the goddess symbolized by the square. Instead of "goddess" we could also say "earth" or "soul." Despite the historical prejudice, however, the fact must be insisted upon that (as in the "House of the Gathering," where the place of the sacred image was occupied by the quaternity) we find no trace of a deity in the mandala, but, on the contrary, a mechanism. I do not believe that we have any right to disregard such an important fact in favour of a preconceived idea. A dream or a vision is just what it seems to be. It is not a disguise for something else. It is a natural product, which is precisely a thing without ulterior motive. I have seen many hundreds of mandalas, done by patients who were quite uninfluenced, and I have found the same fact in an overwhelming majority of cases: there was never a deity occupying the centre. The centre, as a rule, is emphasized. But what we find there is a symbol with a very different meaning. It is a star, a sun, a flower, a cross with equal arms, a precious stone, a bowl filled with water or wine, a serpent coiled up, or a human being, but never a god.[27]

137 When we find a triumphant Christ in the rose window of a medieval church, we rightly assume that this must be a central symbol of the Christian cult. At the same time we also assume that any religion which is rooted in the history of a people is as much an expression of their psychology as the form of political government, for instance, that the people have developed.

26 The cross has also the meaning of a boundary-stone between heaven and hell, since it is set up in the centre of the cosmos and extends to all sides. (Cf. Kroll, *Gott und Hölle,* p. 18, n. 3.) The Tibetan mandala occupies a similar central position, its upper half rising up to heaven out of the earth (like the hemispherical stupas at Sanchi, India), with hell lying below. I have often found the same construction in individual mandalas: the light world on top, the dark below, as if they were projecting into these worlds. There is a similar design in Jakob Böhme's "reversed eye" or "philosophical mirror" (*XL Questions concerning the Soule,* 1647).

27 [Cf. the illustrations in Jung, "On Mandala Symbolism."—EDITORS.]

If we apply the same method to the modern mandalas that people have seen in dreams or visions, or have developed through "active imagination," [28] we reach the conclusion that mandalas are expressions of a certain attitude which we cannot help calling "religious." Religion is a relationship to the highest or most powerful value, be it positive or negative. The relationship is voluntary as well as involuntary, that is to say you can accept, consciously, the value by which you are possessed unconsciously. That psychological fact which wields the greatest power in your system functions as a god, since it is always the overwhelming psychic factor that is called "God." As soon as a god ceases to be an overwhelming factor he dwindles to a mere name. His essence is dead and his power is gone. Why did the gods of antiquity lose their prestige and their effect on the human soul? Because the Olympians had served their time and a new mystery began: God became man.

138 If we allow ourselves to draw conclusions from modern mandalas we should ask people, first, whether they worship stars, suns, flowers, and snakes. They will deny this, and at the same time they will assert that the globes, stars, crosses, and the like are symbols for a *centre in themselves*. And if asked what they mean by this centre, they will begin to stammer and to refer to this or that experience which may turn out to be something very similar to the confession of my patient, who found that the vision of his world clock had left him with a wonderful feeling of perfect harmony. Others will confess that a similar vision came to them in a moment of extreme pain or profound despair. To others again it is the memory of a sublime dream or of a moment when long and fruitless struggles came to an end and a reign of peace began. If you sum up what people tell you about their experiences, you can formulate it this way: They came to themselves, they could accept themselves, they were able to become reconciled to themselves, and thus were reconciled to adverse circumstances and events. This is almost like what used to be expressed by saying: He has made his peace with God,

28 This is a technical term referring to a method I have proposed for raising unconscious contents to consciousness. [Cf. "The Relations between the Ego and the Unconscious," pp. 220ff.; "The Psychological Aspects of the Kore" (1950/51 edn., pp. 228ff.), and *Mysterium Coniunctionis* (Swiss edn., II, pp. 307ff.).—EDITORS.]

he has sacrificed his own will, he has submitted himself to the will of God.

139 A modern mandala is an involuntary confession of a peculiar mental condition. There is no deity in the mandala, nor is there any submission or reconciliation to a deity. The place of the deity seems to be taken by the wholeness of man.[29]

140 When one speaks of man, everybody means his own ego-personality—that is, his personality so far as he is conscious of it—and when one speaks of others one assumes that they have a very similar personality. But since modern research has acquainted us with the fact that individual consciousness is based on and surrounded by an indefinitely extended unconscious psyche, we must needs revise our somewhat old-fashioned prejudice that man is nothing but his consciousness. This naïve assumption must be confronted at once with the critical question: *Whose* consciousness? The fact is, it would be a difficult task to reconcile the picture I have of myself with the one which other people have of me. Who is right? And who is the real individual? If we go further and consider the fact that man is also what neither he himself nor other people know of him—an unknown something which can yet be proved to exist—the problem of identity becomes more difficult still. Indeed, it is quite impossible to define the extent and the ultimate character of psychic existence. When we now speak of man we mean the indefinable whole of him, an ineffable totality, which can only be formulated symbolically. I have chosen the term "self" to designate the totality of man, the sum total of his conscious and unconscious contents.[30] I have chosen this term in accordance with Eastern philosophy,[31] which for centuries has occupied itself with the problems that arise when even the gods cease to incarnate. The philosophy of the Upanishads corresponds to a psychology that long ago recognized the relativity of the gods.[32] This is not to be confused with a stupid error like atheism. The

29 For the psychology of the mandala, see my commentary on *The Secret of the Golden Flower* (1931 edn., pp. 96ff.) [Also "On Mandala Symbolism" (Swiss edn., pp. 187ff.).—EDITORS.]

30 See *Psychological Types,* Def. 51. [Also "The Relations between the Ego and the Unconscious," par. 274; *Aion,* pars. 43ff. (Swiss edn., pp. 44ff.)—EDITORS.]

31 Cf. Hauer, "Symbole und Erfahrung des Selbstes," p. 33.

32 Concerning the concept of the "relativity of God," see *Psychological Types* (1923 edn., pp. 297ff.).

world is as it ever has been, but our consciousness undergoes peculiar changes. First, in remote times (which can still be observed among primitives living today), the main body of psychic life was apparently in human and in nonhuman objects: it was projected, as we should say now.[33] Consciousness can hardly exist in a state of complete projection. At most it would be a heap of emotions. Through the withdrawal of projections, conscious knowledge slowly developed. Science, curiously enough, began with the discovery of astronomical laws, and hence with the withdrawal, so to speak, of the most distant projections. This was the first stage in the despiritualization of the world. One step followed another: already in antiquity the gods were withdrawn from mountains and rivers, from trees and animals. Modern science has subtilized its projections to an almost unrecognizable degree, but our ordinary life still swarms with them. You can find them spread out in the newspapers, in books, rumours, and ordinary social gossip. All gaps in our actual knowledge are still filled out with projections. We are still so sure we know what other people think or what their true character is. We are convinced that certain people have all the bad qualities we do not know in ourselves or that they practise all those vices which could, of course, never be our own. We must still be exceedingly careful not to project our own shadows too shamelessly; we are still swamped with projected illusions. If you imagine someone who is brave enough to withdraw all these projections, then you get an individual who is conscious of a considerable shadow. Such a man has saddled himself with new problems and conflicts. He has become a serious problem to himself, as he is now unable to say that *they* do this or that, *they* are wrong, and *they* must be fought against. He lives in the "House of the Gathering." Such a man knows that whatever is wrong in the world is in himself, and if he only learns to deal with his own shadow he has done something real for the world. He has succeeded in shouldering at least an infinitesimal part of the gigantic, unsolved social problems of our day. These problems are mostly so difficult because they are poisoned by mutual projections. How can anyone see straight when he does not even see himself and the darkness he unconsciously carries with him into all his dealings?

33 This fact accounts for the theory of animism.

141 Modern psychological development leads to a much better understanding as to what man really consists of. The gods at first lived in superhuman power and beauty on the top of snow-clad mountains or in the darkness of caves, woods, and seas. Later on they drew together into one god, and then that god became man. But in our day even the God-man seems to have descended from his throne and to be dissolving himself in the common man. That is probably why his seat is empty. Instead, the common man suffers from a hybris of consciousness that borders on the pathological. This psychic condition in the individual corresponds by and large to the hypertrophy and totalitarian pretensions of the idealized State. In the same way that the State has caught the individual, the individual imagines that he has caught the psyche and holds her in the hollow of his hand. He is even making a science of her in the absurd supposition that the intellect, which is but a part and a function of the psyche, is sufficient to comprehend the much greater whole. In reality the psyche is the mother and the maker, the subject and even the possibility of consciousness itself. It reaches so far beyond the boundaries of consciousness that the latter could easily be compared to an island in the ocean. Whereas the island is small and narrow, the ocean is immensely wide and deep and contains a life infinitely surpassing, in kind and degree, anything known on the island—so that if it is a question of space, it does not matter whether the gods are "inside" or "outside." It might be objected that there is no proof that consciousness is nothing more than an island in the ocean. Certainly it is impossible to prove this, since the known range of consciousness is confronted with the unknown extension of the unconscious, of which we only know that it exists and by the very fact of its existence exerts a limiting influence on consciousness and its freedom. Wherever unconsciousness reigns, there is bondage and possession. The immensity of the ocean is simply a comparison; it expresses in allegorical form the capacity of the unconscious to limit and threaten consciousness. Empirical psychology loved, until recently, to explain the "unconscious" as mere absence of consciousness—the term itself indicates as much—just as shadow is an absence of light. Today accurate observation of unconscious processes has recognized, with all other ages before us, that the unconscious possesses a creative autonomy such as a

mere shadow could never be endowed with. When Carus, von Hartmann and, in a sense, Schopenhauer equated the unconscious with the world-creating principle, they were only summing up all those teachings of the past which, grounded in inner experience, saw the mysterious agent personified as the gods. It suits our hypertrophied and hybristic modern consciousness not to be mindful of the dangerous autonomy of the unconscious and to treat it negatively as an absence of consciousness. The hypothesis of invisible gods or daemons would be, psychologically, a far more appropriate formulation, even though it would be an anthropomorphic projection. But since the development of consciousness requires the withdrawal of all the projections we can lay our hands on, it is not possible to maintain any non-psychological doctrine about the gods. If the historical process of world despiritualization continues as hitherto, then everything of a divine or daemonic character outside us must return to the psyche, to the inside of the unknown man, whence it apparently originated.

142 The materialistic error was probably unavoidable at first. Since the throne of God could not be discovered among the galactic systems, the inference was that God had never existed. The second unavoidable error is psychologism: if God is anything, he must be an illusion derived from certain motives—from will to power, for instance, or from repressed sexuality. These arguments are not new. Much the same thing was said by the Christian missionaries who overthrew the idols of heathen gods. But whereas the early missionaries were conscious of serving a new God by combatting the old ones, modern iconoclasts are unconscious of the one in whose name they are destroying old values. Nietzsche thought himself quite conscious and responsible when he smashed the old tablets, yet he felt a peculiar need to back himself up with a revivified Zarathustra, a sort of alter ego, with whom he often identifies himself in his great tragedy *Thus Spake Zarathustra*. Nietzsche was no atheist, but his God was dead. The result of this demise was a split in himself, and he felt compelled to call the other self "Zarathustra" or, at times, "Dionysus." In his fatal illness he signed his letters "Zagreus," the dismembered god of the Thracians. The tragedy of *Zarathustra* is that, because his God died, Nietzsche himself became a god; and this happened because he was no atheist. He

was of too positive a nature to tolerate the urban neurosis of atheism. It seems dangerous for such a man to assert that "God is dead": he instantly becomes the victim of inflation.[34] Far from being a negation, God is actually the strongest and most effective "position" the psyche can reach, in exactly the same sense in which Paul speaks of people "whose God is their belly" (Phil. 3:19). The strongest and therefore the decisive factor in any individual psyche compels the same belief or fear, submission or devotion which a God would demand from man. Anything despotic and inescapable is in this sense "God," and it becomes absolute unless, by an ethical decision freely chosen, one succeeds in building up against this natural phenomenon a position that is equally strong and invincible. If this psychic position proves to be absolutely effective, it surely deserves to be named a "God," and what is more, a spiritual God, since it sprang from the freedom of ethical decision and therefore from the mind. Man is free to decide whether "God" shall be a "spirit" or a natural phenomenon like the craving of a morphine addict, and hence whether "God" shall act as a beneficent or a destructive force.

143 However indubitable and clearly understandable these psychic events or decisions may be, they are very apt to lead people to the false, unpsychological conclusion that it rests with them to decide whether they will *create* a "God" for themselves or not. There is no question of that, since each of us is equipped with a psychic disposition that limits our freedom in high degree and makes it practically illusory. Not only is "freedom of the will" an incalculable problem philosophically, it is also a misnomer in the practical sense, for we seldom find anybody who is not influenced and indeed dominated by desires, habits, impulses, prejudices, resentments, and by every conceivable kind of complex. All these natural facts function exactly like an Olympus full of deities who want to be propitiated, served, feared and worshipped, not only by the individual owner of this assorted pantheon, but by everybody in his vicinity. Bondage and possession are synonymous. Always, therefore, there is something in the psyche that takes possession and limits or suppresses our moral freedom. In order to hide this undeniable

34 Concerning the concept "inflation," see "The Relations between the Ego and the Unconscious," pp. 140ff.

but exceedingly unpleasant fact from ourselves and at the same time pay lip-service to freedom, we have got accustomed to saying apotropaically, "*I have* such and such a desire or habit or feeling of resentment," instead of the more veracious "Such and such a desire or habit or feeling of resentment *has me.*" The latter formulation would certainly rob us even of the illusion of freedom. But I ask myself whether this would not be better in the end than fuddling ourselves with words. The truth is that we do not enjoy masterless freedom; we are continually threatened by psychic factors which, in the guise of "natural phenomena," may take possession of us at any moment. The withdrawal of metaphysical projections leaves us almost defenceless in the face of this happening, for we immediately identify with every impulse instead of giving it the name of the "other," which would at least hold it at arm's length and prevent it from storming the citadel of the ego. "Principalities and powers" are always with us; we have no need to create them even if we could. It is merely incumbent on us to *choose* the master we wish to serve, so that his service shall be our safeguard against being mastered by the "other" whom we have not chosen. We do not *create* "God," we *choose* him.

144 Though our choice characterizes and defines "God," it is always man-made, and the definition it gives is therefore finite and imperfect. (Even the idea of perfection does not posit perfection.) The definition is an image, but this image does not raise the unknown fact it designates into the realm of intelligibility, otherwise we would be entitled to say that we had created a God. The "master" we choose is not identical with the image we project of him in time and space. He goes on working as before, like an unknown quantity in the depths of the psyche. We do not even know the nature of the simplest thought, let alone the ultimate principles of the psyche. Also, we have no control over its inner life. But because this inner life is intrinsically free and not subject to our will and intentions, it may easily happen that the living thing chosen and defined by us will drop out of its setting, the man-made image, even against our will. Then, perhaps, we could say with Nietzsche, "God is dead." Yet it would be truer to say, "He has put off our image, and where shall we find him again?" The interregnum is full of danger, for the natural facts will raise their claim in the form

of various -isms, which are productive of nothing but anarchy and destruction because inflation and man's hybris between them have elected to make the ego, in all its ridiculous paltriness, lord of the universe. That was the case with Nietzsche, the uncomprehended portent of a whole epoch.

145 The individual ego is much too small, its brain is much too feeble, to incorporate all the projections withdrawn from the world. Ego and brain burst asunder in the effort; the psychiatrist calls it schizophrenia. When Nietzsche said "God is dead," he uttered a truth which is valid for the greater part of Europe. People were influenced by it not because he said so, but because it stated a widespread psychological fact. The consequences were not long delayed: after the fog of -isms, the catastrophe. Nobody thought of drawing the slightest conclusions from Nietzsche's pronouncement. Yet it has, for some ears, the same eerie sound as that ancient cry which came echoing over the sea to mark the end of the nature gods: "Great Pan is dead." [35]

146 The life of Christ is understood by the Church on the one hand as an historical, and on the other hand as an eternally existing, mystery. This is especially evident in the sacrifice of the Mass. From a psychological standpoint this view can be translated as follows: Christ lived a concrete, personal, and unique life which, in all essential features, had at the same time an archetypal character. This character can be recognized from the numerous connections of the biographical details with worldwide myth-motifs. These undeniable connections are the main reason why it is so difficult for researchers into the life of Jesus to construct from the gospel reports an individual life divested of myth. In the gospels themselves factual reports, legends, and myths are woven into a whole. This is precisely what constitutes the meaning of the gospels, and they would immediately lose their character of wholeness if one tried to separate the individual from the archetypal with a critical scalpel. The life of Christ is no exception in that not a few of the great figures of history have realized, more or less clearly, the archetype of the hero's life with its characteristic changes of fortune. But the ordinary man, too, unconsciously lives archetypal forms, and if these are no longer valued it is only because of the prevailing psychological ignorance. Indeed, even the fleeting phenomena

[35] Plutarch, *De defectu oraculorum*, 17.

of dreams often reveal distinctly archetypal patterns. At bottom, all psychic events are so deeply grounded in the archetype and are so much interwoven with it that in every case considerable critical effort is needed to separate the unique from the typical with any certainty. Ultimately, every individual life is at the same time the eternal life of the species. The individual is continuously "historical" because strictly time-bound; the relation of the type to time, on the other hand, is irrelevant. Since the life of Christ is archetypal to a high degree, it represents to just that degree the life of the archetype. But since the archetype is the unconscious precondition of every human life, its life, when revealed, also reveals the hidden, unconscious ground-life of every individual. That is to say, what happens in the life of Christ happens always and everywhere. In the Christian archetype all lives of this kind are prefigured and are expressed over and over again or once and for all. And in it, too, the question that concerns us here of God's death is anticipated in perfect form. Christ himself is the typical dying and self-transforming God.

147 The psychological situation from which we started is tantamount to "Why seek ye the living among the dead? He is not here" (Luke 24:5f.). But where shall we find the risen Christ?

148 I do not expect any believing Christian to pursue these thoughts of mine any further, for they will probably seem to him absurd. I am not, however, addressing myself to the happy possessors of faith, but to those many people for whom the light has gone out, the mystery has faded, and God is dead. For most of them there is no going back, and one does not know either whether going back is always the better way. To gain an understanding of religious matters, probably all that is left us today is the psychological approach. That is why I take these thought-forms that have become historically fixed, try to melt them down again and pour them into moulds of immediate experience. It is certainly a difficult undertaking to discover connecting links between dogma and immediate experience of psychological archetypes, but a study of the natural symbols of the unconscious gives us the necessary raw material.

149 God's death, or his disappearance, is by no means only a Christian symbol. The search which follows the death is still repeated today after the death of a Dalai Lama, and in antiquity

it was celebrated in the annual search for the Kore. Such a wide distribution argues in favour of the universal occurrence of this typical psychic process: the highest value, which gives life and meaning, has got lost. This is a typical experience that has been repeated many times, and its expression therefore occupies a central place in the Christian mystery. The death or loss must always repeat itself: Christ always dies, and always he is born; for the psychic life of the archetype is timeless in comparison with our individual time-boundness. According to what laws now one and now another aspect of the archetype enters into active manifestation, I do not know. I only know—and here I am expressing what countless other people know—that the present is a time of God's death and disappearance. The myth says he was not to be found where his body was laid. "Body" means the outward, visible form, the erstwhile but ephemeral setting for the highest value. The myth further says that the value rose again in a miraculous manner, transformed. It appears as a miracle, for, when a value disappears, it always seems to be lost irretrievably. So it is quite unexpected that it should come back. The three days' descent into hell during death describes the sinking of the vanished value into the unconscious, where, by conquering the power of darkness, it establishes a new order, and then rises up to heaven again, that is, attains supreme clarity of consciousness. The fact that only a few people see the Risen One means that no small difficulties stand in the way of finding and recognizing the transformed value.

150 I showed earlier, with the help of dreams, how the unconscious produces a natural symbol, technically termed a mandala, which has the functional significance of a union of opposites, or of mediation. These speculative ideas, symptomatic of an activated archetype, can be traced back to about the time of the Reformation, which we find them formulated in the alchemical treatises as symbolic geometrical figures which sought to express the nature of the *Deus terrenus,* the philosophers' stone. For instance, we read in the commentary to the *Tractatus aureus:*

> This one thing to which the elements must be reduced is that little circle holding the place of the centre in this squared figure. It is a mediator making peace between enemies or the elements, that they may love one another in a meet embrace. He alone brings about the

squaring of the circle, which many hitherto have sought, but few have found.[36]

Of this "mediator," the wonderful stone, Orthelius says:

For as . . . the supernatural and eternal good, Christ Jesus our Mediator and Saviour, who delivers us from eternal death, from the devil, and from all evil, partakes of two natures, the divine and the human, so likewise is that earthly saviour composed of two parts, the heavenly and the earthly. With these he has restored us to health, and delivers us from diseases heavenly and earthly, spiritual and corporeal, visible and invisible.[37]

Here the "saviour" does not come down from heaven but out of the depths of the earth, i.e., from that which lies below consciousness. These philosophers suspected that a "spirit" was imprisoned there, in the vessel of matter; a "white dove" comparable to the Nous in the krater of Hermes, of which it is said: "Plunge into this krater, if thou canst, by recognizing to what end thou wast created,[38] and by believing that thou wilt rise up to Him, who hath sent the krater down to earth." [39]

151 This Nous or spirit was known as "Mercurius," [40] and it is to this arcanum that the alchemical saying refers: "Whatever the wise seek is in mercury." A very ancient formula, attributed by Zosimos to the legendary Ostanes, runs: "Go to the waters of the Nile, and there thou wilt find a stone that hath a spirit [pneuma]." A commentator explains that this refers to quicksilver (*hydrargyron,* mercury).[41] This spirit, coming from God, is also the cause of the "greenness," the *benedicta viriditas,* much praised by the alchemists. Mylius says of it: "God has breathed into created things . . . a kind of germination, which is the viridescence." In Hildegard of Bingen's Hymn to the Holy Ghost, which begins "O ignis Spiritus paraclite," we read: "From you the clouds rain down, the heavens move, the stones have their moisture, the waters give forth streams, and the earth

36 Manget, *Bibliotheca chemica curiosa,* I (1702), p. 408.

37 *Theatrum chemicum,* VI (1661), p. 431.

38 Cf. the very similar formula in the "Fundamentum" of St. Ignatius Loyola's *Spiritual Exercises.*

39 *Corpus Hermeticum,* IV, 4.

40 Mercury is "wholly aerial and spiritual." Theobald de Hoghelande, "De alchemiae difficultatibus," *Theatr. chem.,* I (1602), p. 183.

41 Berthelot, *Alch. grecs,* III, vi, 5.

sweats out greenness." This water of the Holy Ghost played an important role in alchemy since the remotest times, as the ὕδωρ θεῖον or *aqua permanens,* a symbol of the spirit assimilated to matter, which according to Heraclitus turned to water. The Christian parallel was naturally Christ's blood, for which reason the water of the philosophers was named "spiritualis sanguis." [42]

152 The arcane substance was also known simply as the *rotundum,* by which was understood the *anima media natura,* identical with the *anima mundi.* The latter is a *virtus Dei,* an organ or a sphere that surrounds God. Of this Mylius says: "[God has] love all round him. Others have declared him to be an intellectual and fiery spirit,[43] having no form, but transforming himself into whatsoever he wills and making himself equal to all things; who by a manifold relation is in a certain measure bound up with his creatures." [44] This image of God enveloped by the anima is the same as Gregory the Great's allegory of Christ and the Church: "A woman shall compass a man" (Jeremiah 31:22).[45] This is an exact parallel to the Tantric conception of Shiva in the embrace of his Shakti.[46] From this fundamental image of the male-female opposites united in the centre is derived another designation of the lapis as the "hermaphrodite"; it is also the basis for the mandala motif. The extension of God as the *anima media natura* into every individual creature means that there is a divine spark, the scintilla,[47] indwelling even in

42 Mylius, *Philosophia reformata,* p. 42; Hildegard's hymn in Daniel, *Thesaurus,* V, pp. 201–2; Dorn, "Congeries," *Theatr. chem.,* I, p. 584; "Turba philosophorum," *Artis auriferae,* I (1593), p. 89.

43 Originally a Platonic idea.

44 Mylius, p. 8.

45 St. Gregory, *Expositiones in librum I Regum,* I, i, 1; Migne, *P.L.,* vol. 79, col. 23.

46 Barbelo or Ennoia plays the role of the anima in Barbelo-Gnosis. Bousset thinks the name "Barbelo" is a corruption of *parthenos,* 'virgin.' It is also translated as 'God is in the Four.'

47 This idea was formulated in the conception of the "anima in compedibus," the fettered or imprisoned soul. (Cf. Dorn, "Speculativa philosophia," *Theatr. chem.,* I, pp. 272, 298; "De spagirico artificio," etc., ibid., I, pp. 457, 497.) So far, I have found no evidence that the medieval natural philosophers based themselves consciously on any heretical traditions. But the parallels are astonishing. Those "enchained in Hades" are mentioned very early on, in the Comarius text dating from the 1st century (Berthelot, *Alch. grecs,* IV, xx, 8.) For the spark in the darkness and the spirit imprisoned in matter, see Leisegang, *Die Gnosis,* pp. 154f. and 233. A similar motif is the conception of the "natura abscondita," which is dis-

dead matter, in utter darkness. The medieval natural philosophers endeavoured to make this spark rise up again as a divine image from the "round vessel." Such ideas can only be based on the existence of unconscious psychic processes, for otherwise we simply could not understand how the same ideas crop up everywhere. Our dream-example shows that such images are not inventions of the intellect; rather, they are natural revelations. And they will probably be found again and again in exactly the same way. The alchemists themselves say that the *arcanum* is sometimes revealed in a dream.[48]

153 The old natural philosophers not only felt pretty clearly, but actually said, that the miraculous substance whose essential nature they symbolized by a circle divided into four parts, was man himself. The "Aenigmata philosophorum"[49] speaks of the *homo albus* who is formed in the hermetic vessel. This "white man" is the equivalent of the priest figure in the visions of Zosimos. In the Arabic-transmitted "Book of Krates"[50] we find an equally significant allusion in the dialogue between the spiritual and the worldly man (corresponding to the *pneumatikos* and *sarkikos* of the Gnostics). The spiritual man says to the worldly man: "Are you capable of knowing your soul in a complete manner? If you knew it as is fitting, and if you knew what makes it better, you would be able to recognize that the names which the philosophers formerly gave it are not its true names. . . . O dubious names which resemble the true names, what errors and agonies you have provoked among men!" The names refer in turn to the philosophers' stone. A treatise ascribed to Zosimos, though it more likely derives from the

coverable in man and in all things, and is of the same nature as the anima. Thus Dorn ("De spagirico artificio," p. 457) says: "In the body of man there is hidden a certain substance of heavenly nature known to very few." In his "Philosophia speculativa" (p. 298) the same author says: "There is in natural things a certain truth not seen by the outward eye but perceived by the mind alone. Of this the philosophers had experience, and found its virtue to be such that it worked miracles." The idea of the "hidden nature" occurs already in Pseudo-Democritus. (Berthelot, II, iii, 6.)

48 A classical example is the "Visio Arislei" (*Art. aurif.*, I, pp. 146ff.). Also the visions of Zosimos (Berthelot, III, i–vi; and my "Some Observations on the Visions of Zosimos." Revelation of the magistery in a dream in Sendivogius, "Parabola" (*Bibliotheca chemica curiosa*, II, 1702, p. 475).

49 *Art. aurif.*, I, p. 151.

50 Berthelot, *La Chimie au moyen âge*, III, p. 50.

Arabic-Latinist school of literature, says unmistakably of the stone: "Thus it comes from man, and you are its mineral (raw material); in you it is found, and from you it is extracted . . . and it remains inseparably in you." [51] Solomon Trismosin expresses it most clearly of all:

> Study what thou art,
> Whereof thou art a part,
> What thou knowest of this art,
> This is really what thou art.
> All that is without thee
> Also is within.
> Thus wrote Trismosin.[52]

154 And Gerhard Dorn cries out: "Transform yourselves into living philosophical stones!" [53] There can hardly be any doubt that not a few of those seekers had the dawning knowledge that the secret nature of the stone was man's own self. This "self" was evidently never thought of as an entity identical with the ego, and for this reason it was described as a "hidden nature" dwelling in inanimate matter, as a spirit, daemon,[54] or fiery spark. By means of the philosophical *opus,* which was mostly thought of as a mental one,[55] this entity was freed from darkness and imprisonment, and finally it enjoyed a resurrection, often represented in the form of an apotheosis and equated with the resurrection of Christ.[56] It is clear that these ideas can have

51 "Rosinus ad Sarratantam," *Art. aurif.,* I, p. 311.

52 *Aureum vellus* (1598), p. 5. Trans. by J. K. in *Splendor solis* (1920).

53 "Speculativa philosophia," *Theatr. chem.,* I, p. 267.

54 Olympiodorus (Berthelot, *Alch. grecs,* II, iv, 43).

55 *Cf. Psychology and Alchemy,* pp. 243ff.

56 Mylius (*Phil. ref.,* p. 106) says that the masculine and feminine components of the stone must first be killed "that they may be brought to life again in a new and incorruptible resurrection, so that thereafter they may be immortal." The stone is also compared to the future resurrected body as a "corpus glorificatum." The "Aurea hora," or "Aurora consurgens" (*Art. aurif.,* I, p. 200) says it is "like to a body which is glorified in the day of judgment." Cf. de Hoghelande, *Theatr. chem.,* I, p. 189; "Consilium coniugii," *Ars chemica* (1566), p. 128; "Aurea hora," *Art. aurif.,* I, p. 195; Djabir, "Le Livre de la miséricorde," in Berthelot, *La Chimie au moyen âge,* III, p. 188; "Le Livre d'Ostanès," in ibid., p. 117; Comarius, in Berthelot, *Alch. grecs,* IV, xx, 15; Zosimos, in ibid., III, viii, 2, and III, i, 2; *Turba phil.,* ed. Ruska, p. 139; Michael Maier, *Symbola aureae mensae* (1617), p. 599; *Rosarium philosophorum* (1550), fol. 2a, IV, illustration.

nothing to do with the empirical ego, but are concerned with a "divine nature" quite distinct from it, and hence, psychologically speaking, with a consciousness-transcending content issuing from the realm of the unconscious.

155 With this we come back to our modern experiences. They are obviously similar in nature to the basic medieval and classical ideas, and can therefore be expressed by the same, or at any rate similar, symbols. The medieval representations of the circle are based on the idea of the microcosm, a concept that was also applied to the stone.[57] The stone was a "little world" like man himself, a sort of inner image of the cosmos, reaching not into immeasurable distances but into an equally immeasurable depth-dimension, i.e., from the small to the unimaginably smallest. Mylius therefore calls this centre the "punctum cordis." [58]

156 The experience formulated by the modern mandala is typical of people who cannot project the divine image any longer. Owing to the withdrawal and introjection of the image they are in danger of inflation and dissociation of the personality. The round or square enclosures built round the centre therefore have the purpose of protective walls or of a *vas hermeticum,* to prevent an outburst or a disintegration. Thus the mandala denotes and assists exclusive concentration on the centre, the self. This is anything but egocentricity. On the contrary, it is a much needed self-control for the purpose of avoiding inflation and dissociation.

157 The enclosure, as we have seen, has also the meaning of what is called in Greek a *temenos,* the precincts of a temple or any isolated sacred place. The circle in this case protects or isolates an inner content or process that should not get mixed up with things outside. Thus the mandala repeats in symbolic form archaic ways and means which were once concrete realities. As I have already mentioned, the inhabitant of the *temenos* was a god. But the prisoner, or the well-protected dweller in the mandala, does not seem to be a god, since the symbols used—stars, crosses, globes, etc.—do not signify a god but an obviously important part of the human personality. One might almost say that man himself, or his innermost soul, is the prisoner or the

57 "Aphorismi Basiliani," *Theatr. chem.,* IV (1613), p. 368; de Hoghelande, ibid., I (1602), p. 178; Dorn, "Congeries," ibid., I, p. 585; and many other places.
58 *Philosophia reformata* (1622), p. 21.

protected inhabitant of the mandala. Since modern mandalas are amazingly close parallels to the ancient magical circles, which usually have a deity in the centre, it is clear that in the modern mandala man—the deep ground, as it were, of the self—is not a substitute but a symbol for the deity.

158 It is a remarkable fact that this symbol is a natural and spontaneous occurrence and that it is always an essentially unconscious product, as our dream shows. If we want to know what happens when the idea of God is no longer projected as an autonomous entity, this is the answer of the unconscious psyche. The unconscious produces the idea of a deified or divine man who is imprisoned, concealed, protected, usually depersonalized, and represented by an abstract symbol. The symbols often contain allusions to the medieval conception of the microcosm, as was the case with my patient's world clock, for instance. Many of the processes that lead to the mandala, and the mandala itself, seem to be direct confirmations of medieval speculation. It looks as if the patients had read those old treatises on the philosophers' stone, the divine water, the *rotundum,* the squaring of the circle, the four colours, etc. And yet they have never been anywhere near alchemical philosophy and its abstruse symbolism.

159 It is difficult to evaluate such facts properly. They could be explained as a sort of regression to archaic ways of thinking, if one's chief consideration was their obvious and impressive parallelism with medieval symbolism. But whenever such regressions occur, the result is always inferior adaptation and a corresponding lack of efficiency. This is by no means typical of the psychological development depicted here. On the contrary, neurotic and dissociated conditions improve considerably and the whole personality undergoes a change for the better. For this reason I do not think the process in question should be explained as regression, which would amount to saying that it was a morbid condition. I am rather inclined to understand the apparently retrograde connections of mandala psychology [59] as the continuation of a process of spiritual development which began in the early Middle Ages, and perhaps even further back,

59 Koepgen (see above, p. 59n.), rightly speaks of the "circular thinking" of the Gnostics. This is only another term for totality or "all-round" thinking, since, symbolically, roundness is the same as wholeness.

in early Christian times. There is documentary evidence that the essential symbols of Christianity were already in existence in the first century. I am thinking of the Greek treatise entitled: "Comarius, the Archpriest, teaches Cleopatra the Divine Art." [60] The text is of Egyptian origin and bears no trace of Christian influence. There are also the mystical texts of Pseudo-Democritus and Zosimos.[61] Jewish and Christian influences are noticeable in the last-named author, though the main symbolism is Neoplatonist and is closely connected with the philosophy of the *Corpus Hermeticum*.[62]

160 The fact that the symbolism connected with the mandala traces its near relatives back to pagan sources casts a peculiar light upon these apparently modern psychological occurrences. They seem to continue a Gnostic trend of thought without being supported by direct tradition. If I am right in supposing that every religion is a spontaneous expression of a certain predominant psychological condition, then Christianity was the formulation of a condition that predominated at the beginning of our era and lasted for several centuries. But a particular psychological condition which predominates for a certain length of time does not exclude the existence of other psychological conditions at other times, and these are equally capable of religious expression. Christianity had at one time to fight for its life against Gnosticism, which corresponded to another psychological condition. Gnosticism was stamped out completely and its remnants are so badly mangled that special study is needed to get any insight at all into its inner meaning. But if the historical roots of our symbols extend beyond the Middle Ages they are certainly to be found in Gnosticism. It would not seem to me illogical if a psychological condition, previously suppressed, should reassert itself when the main ideas of the suppressive condition begin to lose their influence. In spite of the suppression of the Gnostic heresy, it continued to flourish throughout the Middle Ages under the disguise of alchemy. It is a well-known fact that alchemy consisted of two parts which complement one another—on the one hand chemical research proper and on the other the

60 Berthelot, *Alch. grecs,* IV, xx. According to F. Sherwood Taylor, in "A Survey of Greek Alchemy," pp. 109ff., this is probably the oldest Greek text of the 1st century. Cf. also Jensen, *Die älteste Alchemie.*

61 Berthelot, III, i.

62 Scott, *Hermetica.*

"theoria" or "philosophia."[63] As is clear from the writings of Pseudo-Democritus in the first century, entitled *τὰ φυσικὰ καὶ τὰ μυστικά*,[64] the two aspects already belonged together at the beginning of our era. The same holds true of the Leiden papyri and the writings of Zosimos in the third century. The religious or philosophical views of ancient alchemy were clearly Gnostic. The later views seem to cluster round the following central idea: The *anima mundi,* the demiurge or divine spirit that incubated the chaotic waters of the beginning, remained in matter in a potential state, and the initial chaotic condition persisted with it.[65] Thus the philosophers, or the "sons of wisdom" as they

[63] *Psychology and Alchemy,* pp. 276ff.

[64] Berthelot, *Alch. grecs,* II, i f.

[65] Very early among the Greek alchemists we encounter the idea of the "stone that has a spirit" (Berthelot, *Alch. grecs,* III, vi). The "stone" is the *prima materia,* called *hyle* or chaos or *massa confusa.* This alchemical terminology was based on Plato's *Timaeus.* Joannes C. Steeb (*Coelum sephiroticum Hebraeorum,* 1679) says: "Neither earth, nor air, nor fire, nor water, nor those things which are made of these things nor those things of which these are made, should be called the *prima materia,* which must be the receptacle and the mother of that which is made and that which can be beheld, but a certain species which cannot be beheld and is formless and sustains all things" (p. 26). The same author calls the *prima materia* "the primeval chaotic earth, Hyle, Chaos, the abyss, the mother of things. . . . That first chaotic matter . . . was watered by the streams of heaven, and adorned by God with numberless Ideas of the species." He explains how the spirit of God descended into matter and what became of him there (p. 33): "The spirit of God fertilized the upper waters with a peculiar fostering warmth and made them as it were milky. . . . The fostering warmth of the Holy Spirit brought about, therefore, in the waters that are above the heavens [*aquis supracoelestibus;* cf. Genesis 1:7], a virtue subtly penetrating and nourishing all things, which, combining with light, generated in the mineral kingdom of the lower regions the mercurial serpent [this could refer just as well to the caduceus of Aesculapius, since the serpent is also the origin of the *medicina catholica,* the panacea], in the vegetable kingdom the blessed greenness [chlorophyll], in the animal kingdom a formative virtue, so that the supracelestial spirit of the waters united in marriage with light may justly be called the soul of the world." "The lower waters are darksome, and absorb the outflowings of light in their capacious depths" (p. 38). This doctrine is based on nothing less than the Gnostic legend of the Nous descending from the higher spheres and being caught in the embrace of Physis. The Mercurius of the alchemists is winged ("volatile"). Abu'l-Qāsim Muhammad (*Kitāb al'ilm al muktasab,* etc., ed. Holmyard), speaks of "Hermes, the volatile" (p. 37), and in many other places he is called a "spiritus." Moreover, he was understood to be a Hermes *psychopompos,* showing the way to Paradise (Michael Maier, *Symbola,* p. 592). This is very much the

called themselves, took their *prima materia* to be a part of the original chaos pregnant with spirit. By "spirit" they understood a semimaterial pneuma, a sort of "subtle body," which they also called "volatile" and identified chemically with oxides and other dissoluble compounds. They called this spirit Mercurius, which was chemically quicksilver—though "Mercurius noster" was no ordinary Hg!—and philosophically Hermes, the god of revelation, who, as Hermes Trismegistus, was the arch-authority on

---

role of a redeemer, which was attributed to the Nous in "Ερμοῦ πρὸς Τάτ." (Scott, *Hermetica,* I, pp. 149ff.). For the Pythagoreans the soul was entirely devoured by matter, except for its reasoning part. (Zeller, *Die Philosophie der Griechen,* III, II, p. 138.)

In the old "Commentariolum in Tabulam smaragdinam" (*Ars chemica*), Hortulanus speaks of the "massa confusa" or the "chaos confusum" from which the world was created and from which also the mysterious *lapis* is generated. The *lapis* was identified with Christ from the beginning of the 14th century (Petrus Bonus, *Pretiosa margarita,* 1546). Orthelius (*Theatr. chem.,* VI, p. 431) says: "Our Saviour Jesus Christ . . . partakes of two natures. . . . So likewise is that earthly saviour made up of two parts, the heavenly and the earthly." In the same way the Mercurius imprisoned in matter was identified with the Holy Ghost. Johannes Grasseus ("Arca arcani," *Theatr. chem.,* VI, p. 314) quotes: "The gift of the Holy Spirit, that is the lead of the philosophers which they call the lead of the air, wherein is a resplendent white dove which is called the salt of the metals, in which consists the magistery of the work."

Concerning the extraction and transformation of the Chaos, Christopher of Paris ("Elucidarius artis transmutatoriae," *Theatr. chem.,* VI, p. 228) writes: "In this Chaos the said precious substance and nature truly exists potentially, in a single confused mass of the elements. Human reason ought therefore to apply itself to bringing our heaven into actuality." "Our heaven" refers to the microcosm and is also called the "quintessence." It is "incorruptible" and "immaculate." Johannes de Rupescissa (*La Vertu et la Propriété de la Quinte Essence,* 1581) calls it "le ciel humain." It is clear that the philosophers projected the vision of the golden and blue circle onto their *aurum philosophicum* (which was named the "rotundum"; see Maier, *De circulo,* 1616, p. 15) and onto the blue quintessence. The terms chaos and *massa confusa* were in general use, according to the testimony of Bernardus Sylvestris, a contemporary of William of Champeaux (1070–1121). His work, *De mundi universitate libri duo,* had a widespread influence. He speaks of the "confusion of the primary matter, that is, Hyle" (p. 5, li. 18), the "congealed mass, formless chaos, refractory matter, the face of being, a discolored mass discordant with itself" (p. 7, li. 18–19), "a mass of confusion" (p. 56, XI, li. 10). Bernardus also mentions the *descensus spiritus* as follows: "When Jove comes down into the lap of his bride, all the world is moved and would urge the soil to bring forth" (p. 51, li. 21–22). Another variant is the idea of the King submerged or concealed in the sea (Maier, *Symbola,* p. 380; "Visio Arislei," *Art. aurif.,* I, pp. 146ff.).

alchemy.[66] Their aim was to extract the original divine spirit out of the chaos, and this extract was called the *quinta essentia, aqua permanens,* *ὕδωρ θεῖον, βαφή* or *tinctura.* A famous alchemist, Johannes de Rupescissa (d. 1375),[67] calls the quintessence "le ciel humain," the human sky or heaven. For him it was a blue liquid and incorruptible like the sky. He says that the quintessence is of the colour of the sky "and our sun has adorned it, as the sun adorns the sky." The sun is an allegory of gold. He says: "This sun is true gold." He continues: "These two things joined together influence in us . . . the condition of the Heaven of heavens, and of the heavenly Sun." His idea is, obviously, that the quintessence, the blue sky with the golden sun in it, evokes corresponding images of the heaven and the heavenly sun in ourselves. It is a picture of a blue and golden microcosm,[68] and I take it to be a direct parallel to Guillaume's celestial vision. The colours are, however, reversed; with Rupescissa the disc is golden and the sky blue. My patient, therefore, having a similar arrangement, seems to lean more towards the alchemical side.

161 The miraculous liquid, the divine water, called sky or heaven, probably refers to the supra-celestial waters of Genesis 1:7. In its functional aspect it was thought to be a sort of baptismal water which, like the holy water of the Church, possesses a creative and transformative quality.[69] The Catholic Church

66 For instance, the genius of the planet Mercury reveals the mysteries to Pseudo-Democritus. (Berthelot, *Alch. grecs,* I, Introduction, p. 236.)

67 J. de Rupescissa, *La Vertu,* p. 19.

68 Djabir, in *La Livre de la Miséricorde,* says that the philosophers' stone is equal to a microcosm. (Berthelot, *La Chimie au moyen âge,* III, p. 179.)

69 It is difficult not to assume that the alchemists were influenced by the allegorical style of patristic literature. They even claimed some of the Fathers as representatives of the Royal Art, for instance Albertus Magnus, Thomas Aquinas, Alanus de Insulis. A text like the "Aurora consurgens" is full of allegorical interpretations of the scriptures. It has even been ascribed to Thomas Aquinas. Nevertheless, water was in fact used as an allegory of the Holy Spirit: "Water is the living grace of the Holy Spirit" (Rupert, Abbot of Deutz, in Migne, *P.L.,* vol. 169, col. 353). "Flowing water is the Holy Spirit" (Bruno, Bishop of Würzburg, in Migne, *P.L.,* vol. 142, col. 293). "Water is the infusion of the Holy Spirit" (Garnerius of St. Victor, in Migne, *P.L.,* vol. 193, col. 279). Water is also an allegory of Christ's humanity (Gaudentius, in Migne, *P.L.,* vol. 20, col. 983). Very often water appears as dew (*ros Gedeonis*), and dew, likewise, is an allegory of Christ:

still performs the rite of the *benedictio fontis* on Holy Saturday before Easter.[70] The rite consists in a repetition of the *descensus spiritus sancti in aquam.* The ordinary water thereby acquires the divine quality of transforming and giving spiritual rebirth to man. This is exactly the alchemical idea of the divine water, and there would be no difficulty whatever in deriving the *aqua permanens* of alchemy from the rite of the *benedictio fontis* were it not that the former is of pagan origin and certainly the older of the two. We find the miraculous water mentioned in the first treatises of Greek alchemy, which belong to the first century.[71] Moreover the descent of the spirit into Physis is a Gnostic legend that greatly influenced Mani. And it was possibly through Manichean influences that it became one of the main ideas of Latin alchemy. The aim of the philosophers was to transform imperfect matter chemically into gold, the panacea, or the *elixir vitae,* but philosophically or mystically into the

---

"Dew is seen in the fire" (Romanus, *De theophania,* in Pitra, *Analecta sacra,* I, p. 21). "Now has Gideon's dew flowed on earth" (Romanus, *De nativitate,* ibid., p. 237). The alchemists thought that their *aqua permanens* was endued with a virtue which they called "flos" (flower). It had the power of changing body into spirit and giving it an incorruptible quality (*Turba phil.,* ed. Ruska, p. 197). The water was also called "acetum" (acid), "whereby God finished his work, whereby also bodies take on spirit and are made spiritual" (*Turba,* p. 126). Another name for it is "spiritus sanguis" (blood spirit, *Turba,* p. 129). The *Turba* is an early Latin treatise of the 12th century, translated from an originally Arabic compilation dating back to the 9th and 10th centuries. Its contents, however, stem from Hellenistic sources. The Christian allusion in "spiritualis sanguis" might be due to Byzantine influence. *Aqua permanens* is quicksilver, *argentum vivum* (Hg). "Our living silver is our clearest water" (*Rosarium phil.,* in *Art. aurif.,* II, p. 213). The *aqua* is also called fire (ibid., p. 218). The body, or substance, is transformed by water and fire, a complete parallel to the Christian idea of baptism and spiritual transformation.

70 Missale Romanum. The rite is old and was known as the "lesser (or greater) blessing of salt and water" from about the 8th century.

71 In "Isis the Prophetess to her Son Horus" (Berthelot, *Alch. grecs,* I, xiii), an angel brings Isis a small vessel filled with transparent water, the arcanum. This is an obvious parallel to the krater of Hermes (*Corpus Hermeticum,* I) and of Zosimos (Berthelot, III, li, 8), which was filled with *nous.* In the *φυσικὰ καὶ μυστικά* of Pseudo-Democritus (Berthelot, II, i, 63), the divine water is said to effect a transformation by bringing the "hidden nature" to the surface. And in the treatise of Comarius we find the miraculous waters that produce a new springtime (Berthelot, Traductions, p. 281).

divine hermaphrodite, the second Adam,[72] the glorified, incorruptible body of resurrection,[73] or the *lumen luminum*,[74] the illumination of the human mind, or *sapientia*. As I have shown, together with Richard Wilhelm, Chinese alchemy produced the same idea, that the goal of the *opus magnum* is the creation of the "diamond body." [75]

162 All these parallels are an attempt to put my psychological observations into their historical setting. Without the historical connection they would remain suspended in mid air, a mere curiosity, although one could find numerous other modern parallels to the dreams described here. For instance, there is the following dream of a young woman. The initial dream was mainly concerned with the memory of an actual experience, a baptizing ceremony in a Protestant sect that took place under particularly grotesque and even repulsive conditions. The associations were a precipitate of all the dreamer's disappointments with religion. But the dream that came immediately after showed her a picture which she did not understand and could not relate to the previous dream. One could have aided her understanding by the simple device of prefacing her second dream with the words "on the contrary." This was the dream: *She was in a planetarium, a very impressive place overhung by the vault of the sky. In the sky two stars were shining; a white one, which was Mercury, but the other star emitted warm red*

72 Gnosius (in *Hermetis Trismegisti Tractatus vere Aureus, cum Scholiis Dominici Gnosii*, 1610, pp. 44 and 101) speaks of "Hermaphroditus noster Adamicus" when treating of the quaternity in the circle. The centre is the "mediator making peace between enemies," obviously a uniting symbol (cf. *Psychological Types*, 1923 edn., pp. 234ff. and Def. 51). [Also *Aion*, par. 304 (Swiss edn., pp. 282ff.—EDITORS.] The hermaphrodite is born of the "self-impregnating dragon" (*Art. aurif.*, I, p. 303), who is none other than Mercurius, the *anima mundi*. (Maier, *Symbola*, p. 43; Berthelot, I, 87.) The uroboros is an hermaphroditic symbol. The hermaphrodite is also called the Rebis ("made of two"), frequently depicted in the form of an apotheosis (for instance in the *Rosarium*, in *Art. aurif.*, II, pp. 291 and 359; Reusner, *Pandora*, 1588, p. 253).

73 The "Aurora consurgens" (Part I) says, quoting Senior: "There is one thing which never dies, for it lives by continual increase, when the body shall be glorified in the final resurrection of the dead. . . . Then shall the second Adam say to the first and to his children: Come ye blessed of my Father," etc.

74 Alphidius (12th cent.?): "Of them is born the modern light (*lux moderna*), to which no light is like in all the world." (*Rosarium*, in *Art. aurif.*, II, p. 248; "Tractatus aureus," *Ars chem.*)

75 Jung and Wilhelm, *The Secret of the Golden Flower.*

waves of light and was unknown to her. She now saw that the walls underneath the vault were covered with frescoes. But she could recognize only one of them: it was an antique picture of the tree-birth of Adonis.

163 The "red waves of light" she took to be "warm feelings," i.e., love, and she now thought the star must have been Venus. She had once seen a picture of the tree-birth in a museum and had fancied that Adonis, as the dying and resurgent god, must also be a god of rebirth.

164 In the first dream, then, there was violent criticism of Church religion, followed in the second dream by the mandala vision of a world clock—which is what a planetarium is in the fullest sense. In the sky the divine pair stands united, he white, she red, thus reversing the famous alchemical pair, where he is red and she is white, whence she was called Beya (Arabic *al baida,* 'the White One'), and he was called "servus rubeus," the 'red slave,' although, as Gabricius (Arabic *kibrit,* 'sulphur'), he is her royal brother. The divine pair makes one think of Guillaume de Digulleville's Christian allegory. The allusion to the tree-birth of Adonis corresponds to those dreams of my patient which had to do with mysterious rites of creation and renewal.[76]

165 So in principle these two dreams largely repeat the thought-processes of my patient, although having nothing in common with the latter except the spiritual malaise of our time. As I have already pointed out, the connection of spontaneous modern symbolism with ancient theories and beliefs is not established by direct or indirect tradition, nor even by a secret tradition as has sometimes been surmised, though there are no tenable proofs of this.[77] The most careful inquiry has never revealed any possibility of my patients' being acquainted with the relevant literature or having any other information about such ideas. It seems that their unconscious worked along the same line of thought which has manifested itself time and again in the last two thousand years. Such a continuity can only exist if we assume a certain unconscious condition as an inherited *a priori* factor. By this I naturally do not mean the inheritance of ideas, which would be difficult if not impossible to prove. I

[76] Cf. *Psychology and Alchemy,* Part II.

[77] Waite, *The Secret Tradition in Alchemy.*

suppose, rather, the inherited quality to be something like the formal possibility of producing the same or similar ideas over and over again. I have called this possibility the "archetype." Accordingly, the archetype would be a structural quality or condition peculiar to a psyche that is somehow connected with the brain.[78]

166 In the light of these historical parallels the mandala symbolizes either the divine being hitherto hidden and dormant in the body and now extracted and revivified, or else the vessel or the room in which the transformation of man into a divine being takes place. I know such formulations are fatally reminiscent of the wildest metaphysical speculations. I am sorry if it sounds crazy, but this is exactly what the human psyche produces and always has produced. Any psychology which assumes it can do without these facts must exclude them artificially. I would call this a philosophical prejudice, inadmissible from the empirical point of view. I should perhaps emphasize that we do not establish any metaphysical truth with these formulations. It is merely a statement that the psyche functions in such a way. And it is a fact that my patient felt a great deal better after the vision of the mandala. If you understand the problem it solved for him, you can also understand why he had such a feeling of "sublime harmony."

167 I would not hesitate for a moment to suppress all speculations about the possible consequences of an experience as abstruse and remote as the mandala, if this were feasible. But for me, unfortunately, this type of experience is neither abstruse nor remote. On the contrary, it is an almost daily occurrence in my profession. I know a fair number of people who have to take their experience seriously if they want to live at all. They can only choose between the devil and the deep blue sea. The devil is the mandala or something equivalent to it and the deep blue sea is their neurosis. The well-meaning rationalist will point out that I am casting out the devil with Beelzebub and replacing an honest neurosis by the swindle of a religious belief. As to the former charge, I have nothing to say in reply, being no metaphysical expert. But as to the latter one, I beg leave to point out that it is not a question of belief but of experience. Religious experience is absolute; it cannot be disputed. You can only say that

78 Cf. my "Psychological Factors Determining Human Behaviour."

you have never had such an experience, whereupon your opponent will reply: "Sorry, I have." And there your discussion will come to an end. No matter what the world thinks about religious experience, the one who has it possesses a great treasure, a thing that has become for him a source of life, meaning, and beauty, and that has given a new splendour to the world and to mankind. He has *pistis* and peace. Where is the criterion by which you could say that such a life is not legitimate, that such an experience is not valid, and that such *pistis* is mere illusion? Is there, as a matter of fact, any better truth about the ultimate things than the one that helps you to live? That is the reason why I take careful account—*religio!*—of the symbols produced by the unconscious. They are the one thing that is capable of convincing the critical mind of modern man. And they are convincing for a very old-fashioned reason: They are *overwhelming,* which is precisely what the Latin word *convincere* means. The thing that cures a neurosis must be as convincing as the neurosis, and since the latter is only too real, the helpful experience must be equally real. It must be a very real illusion, if you want to put it pessimistically. But what is the difference between a real illusion and a healing religious experience? It is merely a difference of words. You can say, for instance, that life is a disease with a very bad prognosis: it lingers on for years, only to end with death; or that normality is a general constitutional defect; or that man is an animal with a fatally overgrown brain. This kind of thinking is the prerogative of habitual grumblers with bad digestions. No one can know what the ultimate things are. We must therefore take them as we experience them. And if such experience helps to make life healthier, more beautiful, more complete and more satisfactory to yourself and to those you love, you may safely say: "This was the grace of God."

68 No transcendental truth is thereby demonstrated, and we must confess in all humility that religious experience is *extra ecclesiam,* subjective, and liable to boundless error. Yet, if the spiritual adventure of our time is the exposure of human consciousness to the undefined and indefinable, there would seem to be good reasons for thinking that even the Boundless is pervaded by psychic laws, which no man invented, but of which he has "gnosis" in the symbolism of Christian dogma. Only heedless fools will wish to destroy this; the lover of the soul, never.

II

A PSYCHOLOGICAL APPROACH TO THE DOGMA OF THE TRINITY

Noli foras ire, in teipsum redi;
in interiore homine habitat veritas.

(Go not outside, return into thyself:
Truth dwells in the inward man.)

—St. Augustine,
Liber de vera religione, xxix (72)

INTRODUCTION

169 The present study grew up out of a lecture I gave at the Eranos meeting in 1940, under the title "On the Psychology of the Idea of the Trinity." The lecture, though subsequently published,[1] was no more than a sketch, and it was clear to me from the beginning that it needed improving. Hence I felt under a kind of moral obligation to return to this theme in order to treat it in a manner befitting its dignity and importance.

170 From the reactions the lecture provoked, it was plain that some of my readers found a psychological discussion of Christian symbols objectionable even when it carefully avoided any infringement of their religious value. Presumably my critics would have found less to object to had the same psychological treatment been accorded to Buddhist symbols, whose sacredness is just as indubitable. Yet, what is sauce for the goose is sauce for the gander. I have to ask myself also, in all seriousness, whether it might not be far more dangerous if Christian symbols were made inaccessible to thoughtful understanding by being banished to a sphere of sacrosanct unintelligibility. They can easily become so remote from us that their irrationality turns

[1] "Zur Psychologie der Trinitätsidee," *Eranos-Jahrbuch 1940–41* (Zurich, 1942). [Later revised and expanded as "Versuch zu einer psychologischen Deutung des Trinitätsdogmas," *Symbolik des Geistes* (Zurich, 1948), pp. 321–446, from which version the present translation is made.—EDITORS.]

into preposterous nonsense. Faith is a charisma not granted to all; instead, man has the gift of thought, which can strive after the highest things. The timid defensiveness certain moderns display when it comes to thinking about symbols was certainly not shared by St. Paul or by many of the venerable Church Fathers.[2] This timidity and anxiety about Christian symbols is not a good sign. If these symbols stand for a higher truth—which, presumably, my critics do not doubt—then science can only make a fool of itself if it proceeds incautiously in its efforts to understand them. Besides, it has never been my intention to invalidate the meaning of symbols; I concern myself with them precisely because I am convinced of their psychological validity. People who merely believe and don't think always forget that they continually expose themselves to their own worst enemy: doubt. Wherever belief reigns, doubt lurks in the background. But thinking people welcome doubt: it serves them as a valuable stepping-stone to better knowledge. People who can believe should be a little more tolerant with those of their fellows who are only capable of thinking. Belief has already conquered the summit which thinking tries to win by toilsome climbing. The believer ought not to project his habitual enemy, doubt, upon the thinker, thereby suspecting him of destructive designs. If the ancients had not done a bit of thinking we would not possess any dogma about the Trinity at all. The fact that a dogma is on the one hand believed and on the other hand is an object of thought is proof of its vitality. Therefore let the believer rejoice that others, too, seek to climb the mountain on whose peak he sits.

171 My attempt to make the most sacred of all dogmatic symbols, the Trinity, an object of psychological study is an undertaking of whose audacity I am very well aware. Not having any theological knowledge worth mentioning, I must rely in this respect on the texts available to every layman. But since I have no intention of involving myself in the metaphysics of the Trinity, I am free to accept the Church's own formulation of the dogma, without having to enter into all the complicated metaphysical speculations that have gathered round it in the course of history. For the purposes of psychological discussion the elaborate ver-

2 Of the older ones I refer chiefly to Clement of Alexandria (d. *c.* 216), Origen (d. 253), and Pseudo-Dionysus the Areopagite (d. end of 5th cent.).

sion contained in the Athanasian Creed would be sufficient, as this shows very clearly what Church doctrine understands by the Trinity. Nevertheless, a certain amount of historical explanation has proved unavoidable for the sake of psychological understanding. My chief object, however, is to give a detailed exposition of those psychological views which seem to me necessary if we are to understand the dogma as a symbol in the psychological sense. Yet my purpose would be radically misunderstood if it were conceived as an attempt to "psychologize" the dogma. Symbols that have an archetypal foundation can never be reduced to anything else, as must be obvious to anybody who possesses the slightest knowledge of my writings. To many people it may seem strange that a doctor with a scientific training should interest himself in the Trinity at all. But anyone who has experienced how closely and meaningfully these *représentations collectives* are bound up with the weal and woe of the human soul will readily understand that the central symbol of Christianity must have, above all else, a psychological meaning, for without this it could never have acquired any universal meaning whatever, but would have been relegated long ago to the dusty cabinet of spiritual monstrosities and shared the fate of the many-armed and many-headed gods of India and Greece. But since the dogma stands in a relationship of living reciprocity to the psyche, whence it originated in the first place, it expresses many of the things I am endeavouring to say over again, even though with the uncomfortable feeling that there is much in my exposition that still needs improvement.

1. PRE-CHRISTIAN PARALLELS

I. BABYLONIA

172 In proposing to approach this central symbol of Christianity, the Trinity, from the psychological point of view, I realize that I am trespassing on territory that must seem very far removed from psychology. But everything to do with religion, everything it says, impinges so closely on the human soul that psychology cannot, in my opinion, afford to overlook it. A conception like the Trinity pertains so much to the realm of theology that the only one of the profane sciences to pay any attention to it nowadays is history. Indeed, most people have ceased even to think about dogma, especially about a concept as hard to visualize as the Trinity. Even among professing Christians there are very few who think seriously about the Trinity as a matter of dogma and would consider it a possible subject for reflection—not to mention the educated public. A recent exception is Georg Koepgen's very important book, *Die Gnosis des Christentums,*[1] which, unfortunately, soon found its way onto the Index despite the episcopal "Placet." For all those who are seriously concerned to understand dogmatic ideas, this book of Koepgen's is a perfect example of thinking which has fallen under the spell of trinitarian symbolism.

[1] Salzburg, 1939.

173 Triads of gods appear very early, at a primitive level. The archaic triads in the religions of antiquity and of the East are too numerous to be mentioned here. Arrangement in triads is an archetype in the history of religion, which in all probability formed the basis of the Christian Trinity. Often these triads do not consist of three different deities independent of one another; instead, there is a distinct tendency for certain family relationships to arise within the triads. I would mention as an example the Babylonian triads, of which the most important is Anu, Bel, and Ea. Ea, personifying knowledge, is the father of Bel ("Lord"), who personifies practical activity.[2] A secondary, rather later triad is the one made up of Sin (moon), Shamash (sun), and Adad (storm). Here Adad is the son of the supreme god, Anu.[3] Under Nebuchadnezzar, Adad was the "Lord of heaven and earth." This suggestion of a father-son relationship comes out more clearly at the time of Hammurabi: Marduk, the son of Ea, was entrusted with Bel's power and thrust him into the background.[4] Ea was a "loving, proud father, who willingly transferred his power and rights to his son." [5] Marduk was originally a sun-god, with the cognomen "Lord" (Bel); [6] he was the mediator between his father Ea and mankind. Ea declared that he knew nothing that his son did not know.[7] Marduk, as his fight with Tiamat shows, is a redeemer. He is "the compassionate one, who loves to awaken the dead"; the "Great-eared," who hears the pleadings of men. He is a helper and healer, a true saviour. This teaching about a redeemer flourished on Babylonian soil all through the Christian era and goes on living today in the religion of the Mandaeans (who still exist in Mesopotamia), especially in their redeemer figure Manda d' Hayya or Hibil Ziwa.[8] Among the Mandaeans he appears also as a light-bringer and at the same time as a world-creator.[9] Just as, in the Babylonian epic, Marduk fashions the universe out of Tiamat, so Mani, the Original Man, makes heaven and earth from the skin, bones, and excrement of the children of darkness.[10] "The all-round influence which the myth of Marduk

2 Jastrow, *Die Religion Babyloniens und Assyriens,* I, p. 61.

3 Ibid., pp. 102, 143f. 4 P. 112. 5 P. 130. 6 P. 112.

7 P. 130. Cf. John 16:15.

8 Jeremias, *The Old Testament in the Light of the Ancient East,* I, p. 137.

9 Cf. John 1:3. 10 Kessler, *Mani,* pp. 267ff.

had on the religious ideas of the Israelites is surprising." [11]

174 It appears that Hammurabi worshipped only a dyad, Anu and Bel; but, as a divine ruler himself, he associated himself with them as the "proclaimer of Anu and Bel," [12] and this at a time when the worship of Marduk was nearing its height. Hammurabi felt himself the god of a new aeon [13]—the aeon of Aries, which was then beginning—and the suspicion is probably justified that tacit recognition was given to the triad Anu-Bel-Hammurabi.[14]

175 The fact that there is a secondary triad, Sin-Shamash-Ishtar, is indicative of another intra-triadic relationship. Ishtar [15] appears here in the place of Adad, the storm god. She is the mother of the gods, and at the same time the daughter [16] of Anu as well as of Sin.

176 Invocation of the ancient triads soon takes on a purely formal character. The triads prove to be "more a theological tenet than a living force." [17] They represent, in fact, the earliest beginnings of theology. Anu is the Lord of heaven, Bel is the Lord of the lower realm, earth, and Ea too is the god of an "underworld," but in his case it is the watery deep.[18] The knowledge that Ea personifies comes from the "depths of the waters." According to one Babylonian legend, Ea created Uddushunamir, a creature of light, who was the messenger of the gods on Ishtar's journey to hell. The name means: "His light (or rising) shines." [19] Jeremias connects him with Gilgamesh, the hero who was more than half a god.[20] The messenger of the gods was usually called Girru (Sumerian "Gibil"), the god of fire. As such he has an ethical aspect, for with his purifying fire he destroys evil. He too is a son of Ea, but on the other hand he is also described as a son of Anu. In this connection it is worth mentioning that Marduk as well has a dual nature, since in one

11 Roscher, *Lexikon,* II, 2, cols. 2371f., s.v. "Marduk."

12 Jastrow, p 139. Cf. John 1 : 18.

13 Cf. the Christian fish-symbol.

14 "Anu and Bel called me, Hammurabi, the exalted prince, the worshipper of the Gods, to go forth like the sun . . . to enlighten the land." Harper, *The Code of Hammurabi,* p. 3.

15 Cf. the invocation of the Holy Ghost as "Mother" in the Acts of Thomas (James, *The Apocryphal New Testament,* p. 376). Also the feminine nature of Sophia, who frequently represents the Holy Ghost.

16 Cf. Mary as creature and as Θεοτόκος.

17 Jastrow, p. 141.

18 P. 61.

19 P. 133.

20 Jeremias, I, pp. 247ff.

hymn he is called Mar Mummi, 'son of chaos.' In the same hymn his consort Sarpanitu is invoked along with Ea's wife, the mother of Marduk, as the "Silver-shining One." This is probably a reference to Venus, the *femina alba*. In alchemy the *albedo* changes into the moon, which, in Babylonia, was still masculine.[21] Marduk's companions were four dogs.[22] Here the number four may signify totality, just as it does in the case of the four sons of Horus, the four seraphim in the vision of Ezekiel, and the four symbols of the evangelists, consisting of three animals and one angel.

II. EGYPT

177 The ideas which are present only as intimations in Babylonian tradition are developed to full clarity in Egypt. I shall pass lightly over this subject here, as I have dealt with the Egyptian prefigurations of the Trinity at greater length elsewhere, in an as yet unfinished study of the symbolical bases of alchemy.[1] I shall only emphasize that Egyptian theology asserts, first and foremost, the essential unity (homoousia) of God as father and son, both represented by the king.[2] The third person appears in the form of Ka-mutef ("the bull of his mother"), who is none other than the *ka*, the procreative power of the deity. In it and through it father and son are combined not in a triad but in a triunity. To the extent that Ka-mutef is a special manifestation of the divine *ka*, we can "actually speak of a triunity of God, king, and *ka*, in the sense that God is the father, the king is the son, and *ka* the connecting-link between them." [3] In his concluding chapter Jacobsohn draws a parallel between this Egyptian idea and the Christian credo. Apropos the passage "qui conceptus est de Spiritu Sancto, natus ex Maria virgine," he

21 Cf. Mary's connections with the moon in Rahner, *Griechische Mythen in christlicher Deutung*, pp. 200ff., and "Mysterium Lunae," p. 80.

22 A possible reference to the realm of the dead on the one hand and to Nimrod the mighty hunter on the other. See Roscher, *Lexikon*, II, cols. 2371f., s.v. "Marduk."

1 [*Mysterium Coniunctionis:* now complete in the Swiss edn., 1955–57.—EDITORS.]

2 Jacobsohn, "Die dogmatische Stellung des Königs in der Theologie der alten Aegypter," p. 17.

3 Ibid., p. 58.

cites Karl Barth's formulation: "There is indeed a unity of God and man; God himself creates it. . . . It is no other unity than his own eternal unity as father and son. This unity is the Holy Ghost." [4] As procreator the Holy Ghost would correspond to Ka-mutef, who connotes and guarantees the unity of father and son. In this connection Jacobsohn cites Barth's comment on Luke 1:35 ("The Holy Ghost shall come upon thee, and the power of the Highest shall overshadow thee: therefore also that holy thing which shall be born of thee shall be called the Son of God"): "When the Bible speaks of the Holy Ghost, it is speaking of God as the combination of father and son, of the *vinculum caritatis.*" [5] The divine procreation of Pharaoh takes place through Ka-mutef, in the human mother of the king. But, like Mary, she remains outside the Trinity. As Preisigke points out, the early Christian Egyptians simply transferred their traditional ideas about the *ka* to the Holy Ghost.[6] This explains the curious fact that in the Coptic version of *Pistis Sophia,* dating from the third century, Jesus has the Holy Ghost as his double, just like a proper *ka.*[7] The Egyptian mythologem of the unity of substance of father and son, and of procreation in the king's mother, lasted until the Vth dynasty (about 2500 B.C.). Speaking of the birth of the divine boy in whom Horus manifests himself, God the Father says: "He will exercise a kingship of grace in this land, for my soul is in him," and to the child he says: "You are the son of my body, begotten by me." [8] "The sun he bears within him from his father's seed rises anew in him." His eyes are the sun and moon, the eyes of Horus.[9] We know that the passage in Luke 1:78f.: "Through the tender mercy of our God, whereby the dayspring from on high hath visited us, to give light to them that sit in darkness and in the shadow of death," refers to Malachi 4:2: "But unto you that fear my name shall the sun of righteousness arise with healing in his wings." Who does not think here of the winged sun-disc of Egypt?

4 P. 64. Barth, *Credo,* p. 70.

5 Barth, *Bibelstunden über Luk I,* p. 26.

6 Preisigke, *Die Gotteskraft der frühchristlichen Zeit;* also *Vom göttlichen Fluidum nach ägyptischer Anschauung.*

7 *Pistis Sophia* (trans. by Mead), p. 118.

8 Cf. Hebrews 1:5: "Thou art my Son, this day have I begotten thee."

9 A. Moret, "Du caractère religieux de la royauté pharaonique."

178 These ideas[10] passed over into Hellenistic syncretism and were transmitted to Christianity through Philo and Plutarch.[11] So it is not true, as is sometimes asserted even by modern theologians, that Egypt had little if any influence on the formation of Christian ideas. Quite the contrary. It is, indeed, highly improbable that only Babylonian ideas should have penetrated into Palestine, considering that this small buffer state had long been under Egyptian hegemony and had, moreover, the closest cultural ties with its powerful neighbour, especially after a flourishing Jewish colony established itself in Alexandria, several centuries before the birth of Christ. It is difficult to understand what could have induced Protestant theologians, whenever possible, to make it appear that the world of Christian ideas dropped straight out of heaven. The Catholic Church is liberal enough to look upon the Osiris-Horus-Isis myth, or at any rate suitable portions of it, as a prefiguration of the Christian legend of salvation. The numinous power of a mythologem and its value as truth are considerably enhanced if its archetypal character can be proved. The archetype is "that which is believed always, everywhere, and by everybody," and if it is not recognized consciously, then it appears from behind in its "wrathful" form, as the dark "son of chaos," the evil-doer, as Antichrist instead of Saviour—a fact which is all too clearly demonstrated by contemporary history.

III. GREECE

179 In enumerating the pre-Christian sources of the Trinity concept, we should not omit the mathematical speculations of the Greek philosophers. As we know, the philosophizing temper of the Greek mind is discernible even in St. John's gospel, a work that is, very obviously, of Gnostic inspiration. Later, at the time of the Greek Fathers, this spirit begins to amplify the archetypal content of the Revelation, interpreting it in Gnostic terms. Pythagoras and his school probably had the most to do with the moulding of Greek thought, and as one aspect of the Trinity is based on number symbolism, it would be worth our while to

10 Further material concerning pagan sources in Nielsen, *Der dreieinige Gott*, I.

11 Cf. Norden, *Die Geburt des Kindes*, pp. 77ff.

examine the Pythagorean system of numbers and see what it has to say about the three basic numbers with which we are concerned here. Zeller[1] says: "One is the first from which all other numbers arise, and in which the opposite qualities of numbers, the odd and the even, must therefore be united; two is the first even number; three the first that is uneven and perfect, because in it we first find beginning, middle, and end."[2] The views of the Pythagoreans influenced Plato, as is evident from his *Timaeus;* and, as this had an incalculable influence on the philosophical speculations of posterity, we shall have to go rather deeply into the psychology of number speculation.

180 The number one claims an exceptional position, which we meet again in the natural philosophy of the Middle Ages. According to this, one is not a number at all; the first number is two.[3] Two is the first number because, with it, separation and multiplication begin, which alone make counting possible. With the appearance of the number two, *another* appears alongside the one, a happening which is so striking that in many languages "the other" and "the second" are expressed by the same word. Also associated with the number two is the idea of right and left,[4] and remarkably enough, of favourable and unfavourable, good and bad. The "other" can have a "sinister" significance—or one feels it, at least, as something opposite and alien. Therefore, argues a medieval alchemist, God did not praise the second day of creation, because on this day (Monday, the day of the moon) the *binarius,* alias the devil,[5] came into existence. Two implies a one which is different and distinct from the "numberless" One. In other words, as soon as the number two appears, a unit is produced out of the original unity, and this unit is none other than that same unity split into two and turned into a "number." The "One" and the "Other" form an opposition, but there is no opposition between one and two, for these are simple numbers which are distinguished only by their arithmetical

1 *A History of Greek Philosophy,* I, p. 429.

2 Authority for the latter remark in Aristotle, *De coelo,* I, i, 268a.

3 The source for this appears to be Macrobius, *Commentarius in Somnium Scipionis,* I, 6, 8.

4 Cf. "the movement of the Different to the left" in the *Timaeus* 36C (trans. by Cornford, p. 73).

5 Cf. the etymological relations between G. *zwei,* 'two,' and *Zweifler,* 'doubter.' [In Eng., cf. *duplicity, double-dealer, double-cross, two-faced.*—TRANS.]

value and by nothing else. The "One," however, seeks to hold to its one-and-alone existence, while the "Other" ever strives to be another opposed to the One. The One will not let go of the Other because, if it did, it would lose its character; and the Other pushes itself away from the One in order to exist at all. Thus there arises a tension of opposites between the One and the Other. But every tension of opposites culminates in a release, out of which comes the "third." In the third, the tension is resolved and the lost unity is restored. Unity, the absolute One, cannot be numbered, it is indefinable and unknowable; only when it appears as a unit, the number one, is it knowable, for the "Other" which is required for this act of knowing is lacking in the condition of the One. Three is an unfolding of the One to a condition where it can be known—unity become recognizable; had it not been resolved into the polarity of the One and the Other, it would have remained fixed in a condition devoid of every quality. Three therefore appears as a suitable synonym for a process of development in time, and thus forms a parallel to the self-revelation of the Deity as the absolute One unfolded into Three. The relation of Threeness to Oneness can be expressed by an equilateral triangle,[6] $A = B = C$, that is, by the identity of the three, threeness being contained in its entirety in each of the three angles. This intellectual idea of the equilateral triangle is a conceptual model for the logical image of the Trinity.

181 In addition to the Pythagorean interpretation of numbers, we have to consider, as a more direct source of trinitarian ideas in Greek philosophy, the mystery-laden *Timaeus* of Plato. I shall quote, first of all, the classical argument in sections 31B–32A:

> Hence the god, when he began to put together the body of the universe, set about making it of fire and earth. But two things alone cannot be satisfactorily united without a third; for there must be some bond between them drawing them together. And of all bonds the best is that which makes itself and the terms it connects a unity in the fullest sense; and it is of the nature of a continued geometrical proportion to effect this most perfectly. For whenever, of three numbers, the middle one between any two that are either solids or planes

[6] Harnack (*Dogmengeschichte,* II, p. 303) compares the scholastic conception of the Trinity to an equilateral triangle.

[i.e., cubes or squares] is such that, as the first is to it, so is it to the last, and conversely as the last is to the middle, so is the middle to the first, then since the middle becomes first and last, and again the last and first become middle, in that way all will necessarily come to play the same part towards one another, and by so doing they will all make a unity.[7]

In a geometrical progression, the quotient (q) of a series of terms remains the same, e.g.: $2:1 = 4:2 = 8:4 = 2$, or, algebraically expressed: a, aq, aq^2. The proportion is therefore as follows: 2 is to 4 as 4 is to 8, or a is to aq as aq is to aq^2.

182 This argument is now followed by a reflection which has far-reaching psychological implications: if a simple pair of opposites, say fire and earth, are bound together by a mean (μέσον), and if this bond is a geometrical proportion, then *one* mean can only connect plane figures, since two means are required to connect solids:

Now if it had been required that the body of the universe should be a plane surface with no depth, a single mean would have been enough to connect its companions and itself; but in fact the world was to be solid in form, and solids are always conjoined, not by one mean, but by two.[8]

Accordingly, the two-dimensional connection is not yet a physical reality, for a plane without extension in the third dimension is only an *abstract thought.* If it is to become a physical reality, three dimensions and therefore two means are required. Sir Thomas Heath[9] puts the problem in the following algebraic formulae:

Union in two dimensions of earth (p^2) and fire (q^2):

$$p^2 : pq = pq : q^2$$

Obviously the mean is pq.

Physical union of earth and fire, represented by p^3 and q^3 respectively:

$$p^3 : p^2q = p^2q : pq^2 = pq^2 : q^3$$

The two means are p^2q and pq^2, corresponding to the physical elements water and air.

7 Trans. by Cornford, p. 44. 8 Ibid., p. 44.

9 *A History of Greek Mathematics,* I, p. 89; Cornford, p. 47.

Accordingly, the god set water and air between fire and earth, and made them, so far as was possible, proportional to one another, so that as fire is to air, so is air to water, and as air is to water, so is water to earth, and thus he bound together the frame of a world visible and tangible. For these reasons and from such constituents, four in number, the body of the universe was brought into being, coming into concord by means of proportion, and from these it acquired Amity, so that united with itself it became indissoluble by any other power save him who bound it together.[10]

183 The union of one pair of opposites only produces a two-dimensional triad: $p^2 + pq + q^2$. This, being a plane figure, is not a reality but a thought. Hence two pairs of opposites, making a *quaternio* ($p^3 + p^2q + pq^2 + q^3$), are needed to represent physical reality. Here we meet, at any rate in veiled form, the dilemma of three and four alluded to in the opening words of the *Timaeus*. Goethe intuitively grasped the significance of this allusion when he says of the fourth Cabir in *Faust:* "He was the right one / Who thought for them all," and that "You might ask on Olympus" about the eighth "whom nobody thought of." [11]

184 It is interesting to note that Plato begins by representing the union of opposites two-dimensionally, as an intellectual problem to be solved by thinking, but then comes to see that its solution does not add up to reality. In the former case we have to do with a self-subsistent triad, and in the latter with a quaternity. This was the dilemma that perplexed the alchemists for more than a thousand years, and, as the "axiom of Maria Prophetissa" (the Jewess or Copt), it appears in modern dreams,[12] and is also found in psychology as the opposition between the functions of consciousness, three of which are fairly well differentiated, while the fourth, undifferentiated, "inferior" function is undomesticated, unadapted, uncontrolled, and primitive. Because of its contamination with the collective unconscious, it possesses archaic and mystical qualities, and is the complete opposite of the most differentiated function. For instance, if the most differentiated is thinking, or the intellect, then the inferior,[13] fourth

10 Cornford, pp. 44–45, slightly modified.

11 For a detailed account see *Psychology and Alchemy*, pp. 150ff.

12 As the dream in *Psychology and Alchemy*, pp. 147f., shows.

13 Judging, of course, from the standpoint of the most differentiated function.

function will be feeling.[14] Hence the opening words of the *Timaeus*—"One, two, three—but where, my dear Timaeus, is the fourth . . . ?"—fall familiarly upon the ears of the psychologist and alchemist, and for him as for Goethe there can be no doubt that Plato is alluding to something of mysterious import. We can now see that it was nothing less than the dilemma as to whether something we think about is a mere thought or a reality, or at least capable of becoming real. And this, for any philosopher who is not just an empty babbler, is a problem of the first order and no whit less important than the moral problems inseparably connected with it. In this matter Plato knew from personal experience how difficult is the step from two-dimensional thinking to its realization in three-dimensional fact.[15] Already with his friend Dionysius the Elder, tyrant of Syracuse, he had so many disagreements that the philosopher-politician contrived to sell him as a slave, from which fate he was preserved only because he had the good fortune to be ransomed by friends. His attempts to realize his political theories under Dionysius the Younger also ended in failure, and from then on Plato abandoned politics for good. Metaphysics seemed to him to offer more prospects than this ungovernable world. So, for him personally, the main emphasis lay on the two-dimensional world of thought; and this is especially true of the *Timaeus,* which was written after his political disappointments. It is generally reckoned as belonging to Plato's late works.

185 In these circumstances the opening words, not being attributable either to the jocosity of the author or to pure chance, take on a rather mournful significance: one of the four is absent because he is "unwell." If we regard the introductory scene as symbolical, this means that of the four elements out of which reality is composed, either air or water is missing. If air is missing, then there is no connecting link with spirit (fire), and if water is missing, there is no link with concrete reality (earth). Plato certainly did not lack spirit; the missing element he so much desired was the concrete realization of ideas. He had to

14 Cf. *Psychological Types,* Def. 30.

15 "The world is narrow and the brain is wide;
Thoughts in the head dwell lightly side by side,
Yet things in space run counter and fall foul."
—Schiller, *Wallensteins Tod,* II, 2.

content himself with the harmony of airy thought-structures that lacked weight, and with a paper surface that lacked depth. The step from three to four brought him sharply up against something unexpected and alien to his thought, something heavy, inert, and limited, which no "μὴ ὄν"[16] and no "privatio boni" can conjure away or diminish. Even God's fairest creation is corrupted by it, and idleness, stupidity, malice, discontent, sickness, old age and death fill the glorious body of the "blessed god." Truly a grievous spectacle, this sick world-soul, and unfortunately not at all as Plato's inner eye envisaged it when he wrote:

> All this, then, was the plan of the everlasting god for the god who was going to be. According to this plan he made the body of the world smooth and uniform, everywhere equidistant from its centre, a body whole and complete, with complete bodies for its parts. And in the centre he set the soul and caused it to extend throughout the whole body, and he further wrapped the body round with soul on the outside. So he established one world alone, round and revolving in a circle, solitary but able by reason of its excellence to bear itself company, needing no other acquaintance or friend but sufficient unto itself. On all these accounts the world which he brought into being was a blessed god.[17]

186 This world, created by a god, is itself a god, a son of the self-manifesting father. Further, the demiurge furnished it with a soul which is "prior" to the body (34B). The world-soul was fashioned by the demiurge as follows: he made a mixture of the indivisible (ἀμερές) and the divisible (μεριστόν), thus producing a third form of existence. This third form had a nature independent of the "Same" (τὸ αὐτον) and the "Different" (τὸ ἕτερον). At first sight the "Same" seems to coincide with the indivisible and the "Different" with the divisible.[18] The text says: [19] From

16 "Not being."   17 Cornford, p. 58, slightly modified.

18 Theodor Gomperz (*Greek Thinkers,* III, p. 215) mentions two primary substances which are designated as follows in Plato's *Philebus:* limit, unlimited; the same, the other; the divisible, the indivisible. He adds that Plato's pupils would have spoken of "unity" and of "the great and the small" or of "duality." From this it is clear that Gomperz regards the "Same" and the "indivisible" as synonymous, thus overlooking the resistance of the "Other," and the fundamentally fourfold nature of the world soul. (See below.)

19 [The version here given is translated from the German text of Otto Apelt (*Plato: Timaios und Kritias,* p. 52) cited by the author.—TRANS.]

the indivisible and ever the same substance [Cornford's "Sameness"], and that which is physically divisible, he mixed an intermediate, third form of existence which had its own being beside the Same and the Different, and this form he fashioned accordingly [*κατὰ ταὐτά*] as a mean between the indivisible and the physically divisible (35A). Then he took all three existences and mixed them again, "forcing the nature of the Different, though it resisted the mixture, into union with the Same." Thus, "with the admixture of being (*οὐσία*), the three became one." [20]

187 The world-soul, representing the governing principle of the whole physical world, therefore possesses a triune nature. And since, for Plato, the world is a *δεύτερος θεός* (second god), the world-soul is a revelation or unfolding of the God-image.[21]

188 Plato's account of the actual process of creation is very curious and calls for some elucidation. The first thing that strikes us is the twice-repeated *συνεκεράσατο* ('he mixed'). Why should the mixture be repeated, since it consists of three elements in the first place and contains no more than three at the end, and, in the second place, Same and Different appear to correspond with indivisible and divisible? Appearances, however, are deceptive. During the first mixture there is nothing to suggest that the divisible was recalcitrant and had to be forcibly united with the indivisible, as was the case with their supposed analogues. In both mixtures it is rather a question of combining two sepa-

[20] *Τῆς ἀμερίστου καὶ ἀεὶ κατὰ ταὐτὰ ἐχούσης οὐσίας καὶ τῆς αὖ περὶ τὰ σώματα γιγνομένης μεριστῆς, τρίτον ἐξ ἀμφοῖν ἐν μέσῳ συνεκεράσατο οὐσίας εἶδος· τῆς τὲ ταὐτοῦ φύσεως αὖ πέρι καὶ τῆς τοῦ ἑτέρου, καὶ κατὰ ταὐτὰ συνέστησεν ἐν μέσῳ τοῦ τε ἀμεροῦς αὐτῶν καὶ τοῦ κατὰ τὰ σώματα μεριστοῦ· καὶ τρία λαβὼν αὐτὰ ὄντα συνεκεράσατο εἰς μίαν πάντα ἰδέαν, τὴν θατέρου φύσιν δύσμεικτον οὖσαν εἰς ταὐτὸν συναρμόττων βίᾳ, μειγνὺς δὲ μετὰ τῆς οὐσίας.*

Cornford (pp. 59–60) translates as follows: "Between the indivisible Existence that is ever in the same state and the divisible Existence that becomes in bodies, he compounded a third form of Existence composed of both. Again, in the case of Sameness and in that of Difference, he also on the same principle made a compound intermediate between that kind of them which is indivisible and the kind that is divisible in bodies. Then, taking the three, he blended them all into a unity, forcing the nature of Difference, hard as it was to mingle, into union with Sameness, and mixing them together with Existence."

[21] Cf. *Timaeus* 37C, where the first God is described as the "father" and his creation as the copy of an original "pattern," which is himself (Cornford, p. 97).

rate pairs of opposites,[22] which, because they are called upon to make a unity, may be thought of as arranged in a *quaternio:*

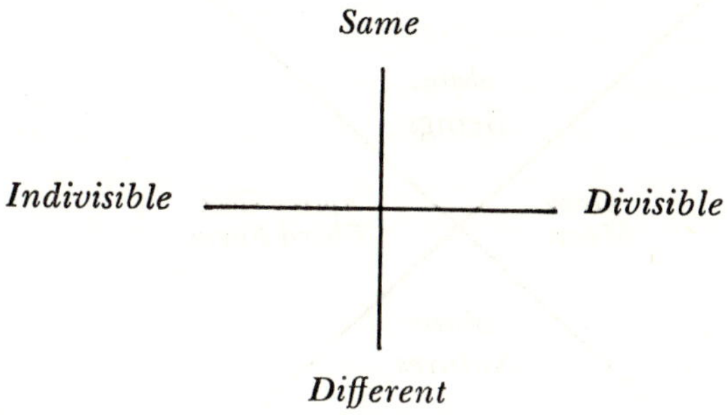

Indivisible and divisible, together with their mean, form a simple triad which has "its own being" beside the Same and the Different. This triad corresponds to the condition of "thought" not yet become "reality." For this a second mixture is needed, in which the Different (i.e., the "Other") is incorporated by force. The "Other" is therefore the "fourth" element, whose nature it is to be the "adversary" and to resist harmony. But the fourth, as the text says, is intimately connected with Plato's desire for "being." One thinks, not unnaturally, of the impatience the philosopher must have felt when reality proved so intractable to his ideas. That reasonableness might, under certain circumstances, have to be imposed by force is a notion that must sometimes have crossed his mind.

189 The passage as a whole, however, is far from simple. It can be translated in many ways and interpreted in many more. The critical point for us is συνέστησεν ἐν μέσῳ τοῦ τε ἀμεροῦς, literally, 'he compounded (a form of the nature of sameness and difference) *in the middle* (ἐν μέσῳ) of the indivisible (and the divisible).' Consequently the middle term of the second pair of opposites would coincide with the middle term of the first pair. The resultant figure is a quincunx, since the two pairs of opposites have a common mean or "third form" (τρίτον εἶδος):

22 This seems borne out by the fact that the first pair of opposites is correlated with οὐσία (being), and the second with φύσις (nature). If one had to choose between οὐσία and φύσις, the latter would probably be considered the more concrete of the two.

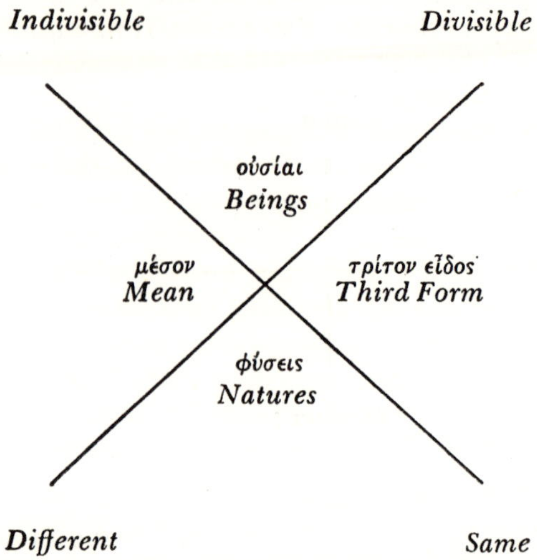

190 I have placed the pairs of opposites side by side, instead of facing one another (as in the previous diagram), in order to illustrate their union in a single mean. Three elements are to be distinguished in our diagram: the two pairs of opposites and their common mean, and I understand the text as referring to these three elements when it says: "Then, taking these three existences . . ." Since the mean is called the "third form," each pair of opposites can presumably be taken as representing the first and second forms: Indivisible = first form, Divisible = second form, mean = third form, and so on. Their union in a quincunx signifies union of the four elements in a world-body. Thomas Taylor, who was strongly influenced by Proclus, says in his commentary to the *Timaeus:* "For those which are connected with her essence in a following order, proceed from her [the *anima mundi*] according to the power of the fourth term (4), which possesses generative powers; but return to her according to the fifth (9) which reduces them to one." [23] Further confirmation of the quaternary nature of the world-soul and world-body may be found in the passage where the demiurge splits this whole fabric lengthwise into two halves and joins them up again in the form of a ×.[24] According to Porphyry, a × in a circle

[23] Reprinted as Bollingen Series III, *Plato: Timaeus and Critias,* p. 71.
[24] *Timaeus* 36B (Cornford, p. 73).

signified the world-soul for the Egyptians.[25] It is, in fact, the hieroglyph for 'city.' [26] Perhaps Plato was trying, in this passage, to bring forth the mandala structure that later appeared as the capital of Atlantis in his *Critias.*

191 The two mixtures could be regarded as a parallel to the two means of the physical elements. Cornford, on the other hand, considers that Plato is referring to three intermedia, which he calls "Intermediate Existence," "Intermediate Sameness," "Intermediate Difference." [27] His main insistence is on the threefold procedure and not on the four substances. The Middle Ages were also familiar with the *quatuor elementa* (A B C D) and the *tria regimina* (three procedures) which united them as follows: AB, BC, CD. From this point of view, Cornford fails to catch Plato's subtle allusion to the recalcitrant fourth.

192 We do not wish it to be supposed that the thought-processes we have deduced from the text of the *Timaeus* represent Plato's conscious reflections. However extraordinary his genius may have been, it by no means follows that his thoughts were all conscious ones. The problem of the fourth, for instance, which is an absolutely essential ingredient of totality, can hardly have reached his consciousness in complete form. If it had, he would have been repelled by the violence with which the elements were to be forced into a harmonious system. Nor would he have been so illogical as to insist on the threefoldness of his world-soul. Again, I would not venture to assert that the opening words of the *Timaeus* are a conscious reference to the underlying problem of the recalcitrant fourth. Everything suggests that the same unconscious *spiritus rector* was at work which twice impelled the master to try to write a tetralogy, the fourth part remaining unfinished on both occasions.[28] This factor also ensured that Plato would remain a bachelor to the end of his life, as if affirming the masculinity of his triadic God-image.

25 Taylor, p. 75.

26 Griffith, *A Collection of Hieroglyphs,* p. 34 B. Fig. 142:  = Plan of a village with cross-streets.

27 P. 61. The intermedia are constructed on the assumption that Indivisible and Divisible are opposite attributes of each of the three principles, Existence, Sameness, Difference. I do not know whether the text permits of such an operation.

28 Gomperz, III, p. 200 [The two unfinished tetralogies are (a) *Republic, Timaeus, Critias* (left incomplete), (*Hermocrates,* never written); (b) *Theaetetus, Sophist, Statesman,* (*Philosopher,* never written).—TRANS.]

193 As history draws nearer to the beginning of our era, the gods become more and more abstract and spiritualized. Even Yahweh had to submit to this transformation. In the Alexandrian philosophy that arose in the last century B.C., we witness not only an alteration of his nature but an emergence of two other divinities in his immediate vicinity: the Logos and Sophia. Together with him they form a triad,[29] and this is a clear prefiguration of the post-Christian Trinity.

29 Leisegang, *Der Heilige Geist*, p. 86.

2. FATHER, SON, AND SPIRIT

194 I have dwelt at some length on the views of the Babylonians and Egyptians, and on Platonist philosophy, in order to give the reader some conception of the trinitarian and unitarian ideas that were in existence many centuries before the birth of Christianity. Whether these ideas were handed down to posterity as a result of migration and tradition or whether they arose spontaneously in each case is a question of little importance. The important thing is that they occurred because, once having sprung forth from the unconscious of the human race (and not just in Asia Minor!), they could rearise anywhere at any time. It is, for instance, more than doubtful whether the Church Fathers who devised the *homoousios* formula were even remotely acquainted with the ancient Egyptian theology of kingship. Nevertheless, they neither paused in their labours nor rested until they had finally reconstructed the ancient Egyptian archetype. Much the same sort of thing happened when, in A.D. 431, at the Council of Ephesus, whose streets had once rung with hymns of praise to many-breasted Diana, the Virgin Mary was declared the θεοτόκος, 'birth-giver of the god.' [1] As we know from Epiphanius,[2] there was even a sect, the Collyridians,

[1] Here one might recall the legend that, after the death of Christ, Mary betook herself with John to Ephesus, where she is said to have lived until her death.

[2] *Panarium* (*Contra octoginta haereses*) LXXIX. See Migne, *P.G.*, vol. 41, cols. 739ff.

who worshipped Mary after the manner of an antique goddess. Her cult had its chief centres in Arabia, Thrace, and Upper Scythia, the most enthusiastic devotees being women. Their provocations moved Epiphanius to the rebuke that "the whole female sex is slippery and prone to error, with a mind that is very petty and narrow." [3] It is clear from this chastening sermon that there were priestesses who on certain feast days decorated a wagon or four-cornered seat and covered it with linen, on which they placed offerings of bakemeats "in the name of Mary" (*εἰς ὄνομα τῆς Μαρίας*), afterwards partaking of the sacrificial meal. This plainly amounted to a Eucharistic feast in honour of Mary, at which wheaten bread was eaten. The orthodox standpoint of the time is aptly expressed in the words of Epiphanius: "Let Mary be held in honour, and let the Father and the Son and the Holy Ghost be adored, but let no one adore Mary."

195 Thus the archetype reasserted itself, since, as I have tried to show, archetypal ideas are part of the indestructible foundations of the human mind. However long they are forgotten and buried, always they return, sometimes in the strangest guise, with a personal twist to them or intellectually distorted, as in the case of the Arian heresy, but continually reproducing themselves in new forms representing the timeless truths that are innate in man's nature.[4]

196 Even though Plato's influence on the thinkers of the next few centuries can hardly be overestimated, his philosophically formulated triad cannot be held responsible for the origins of the Christian dogma of the Trinity. For we are concerned here not with any philosophical, that is conscious, assumptions but with unconscious, archetypal forms. The Platonic formula for the triad contradicts the Christian Trinity in one essential point: the triad is built on opposition, whereas the Trinity contains no opposition of any kind, but is, on the contrary, a complete harmony in itself. The three Persons are characterized in such a manner that they cannot possibly be derived from Pla-

3 "Quod genus lubricum et in errorem proclive, ac pusilli admodum et angusti animi esse solet."

4 The special emphasis I lay on archetypal predispositions does not mean that mythologems are of exclusively psychic origin. I am not overlooking the social conditions that are just as necessary for their production.

tonic premises, while the terms Father, Son, and Holy Ghost do not proceed in any sense from the number three. At most, the Platonic formula supplies the intellectual scaffolding for contents that come from quite other sources. The Trinity may be conceived platonically as to its form, but for its content we have to rely on psychic factors, on irrational data that cannot be logically determined beforehand. In other words, we have to distinguish between the *logical idea* of the Trinity and its *psychological reality*. The latter brings us back to the very much more ancient Egyptian ideas and hence to the archetype, which provides the authentic and eternal justification for the existence of any trinitarian idea at all.

197 The psychological datum consists of Father, Son, and Holy Ghost. If we posit "Father," then "Son" logically follows; but "Holy Ghost" does not follow logically from either "Father" or "Son." So we must be dealing here with a special factor that rests on a different presupposition. According to the old doctrine, the Holy Ghost is "vera persona, quae a filio et patre missa est" (a real person who is sent by the Son and the Father). The "processio a patre filioque" (procession from the Father and the Son) is a "spiration" and not a "begetting." This somewhat peculiar idea corresponds to the separation, which still existed in the Middle Ages, of "corpus" and "spiramen," the latter being understood as something more than mere "breath." What it really denoted was the *anima*, which, as its name shows, is a breath-being (*anemos* = wind). Although an activity of the body, it was thought of as an independent substance (or hypostasis) existing alongside the body. The underlying idea is that the body "lives," and that "life" is something superadded and autonomous, conceived as a soul unattached to the body. Applying this idea to the Trinity formula, we would have to say: Father, Son, and Life—the life proceeding from both or lived by both. The Holy Ghost as "life" is a concept that cannot be derived logically from the identity of Father and Son, but is, rather, a psychological idea, a datum based on an irrational, primordial image. This primordial image is the archetype, and we find it expressed most clearly in the Egyptian theology of kingship. There, as we have seen, the archetype takes the form of God the father, Ka-mutef (the begetter), and the son. The *ka* is the life-spirit, the animating principle of men and gods, and therefore

can be legitimately interpreted as the soul or spiritual double. He is the "life" of the dead man, and thus corresponds on the one hand to the living man's soul, and on the other to his "spirit" or "genius." We have seen that Ka-mutef is a hypostatization of procreative power.[5] In the same way, the Holy Ghost is hypostatized procreative power and life-force.[6] Hence, in the Christian Trinity, we are confronted with a distinctly archaic idea, whose extraordinary value lies precisely in the fact that it is a supreme, hypostatic representation of an abstract thought (two-dimensional triad). The form is still concretistic, in that the archetype is represented by the relationship "Father" and "Son." Were it nothing but that, it would only be a dyad. The third element, however, the connecting link between "Father" and "Son," is spirit and not a human figure. The masculine father-son relationship is thus lifted out of the natural order (which includes mothers and daughters) and translated to a sphere from which the feminine element is excluded: in ancient Egypt as in Christianity the Theotokos stands outside the Trinity. One has only to think of Jesus's brusque rejection of his mother at the marriage in Cana: "Woman, what have I to do with thee?" (John 2:4), and also earlier, when she sought the twelve-year-old child in the temple: "How is it that ye sought me? wist ye not that I must be about my Father's business?" (Luke 2:49). We shall probably not be wrong in assuming that this special sphere to which the father-son relationship is removed is the sphere of primitive mysteries and masculine initiations. Among certain tribes, women are forbidden to look at the mysteries on pain of death. Through the initiations the young men are systematically alienated from their mothers and are reborn as spirits. The celibacy of the priesthood is a continuation of this archetypal idea.[7]

198 The intellectual operation that lies concealed in the higher father-son relationship consists in the extrapolation of an invisi-

5 The *ka* of the king even has an individual name. Thus "the living *ka* of the Lord of the Two Lands," Thutmosis III, was called the "victorious bull which shines in Thebes." Erman, *Life in Ancient Egypt*, p. 307.

6 The "doubling" of the spirit occurs also in the Old Testament, though more as a "potency" emanating from God than as an hypostasis. Nevertheless, Isaiah 48:16 looks very like a hypostasis in the Septuagint text: Κύριος Κύριος ἀπεστειλέν με καὶ τὸ πνεῦμα αὐτοῦ (The Lord the Lord sent me and his spirit).

7 For an instructive account of the Greek background see Harrison, *Themis*, ch. 1.

ble figure, a "spirit" that is the very essence of masculine life. The life of the body or of a man is posited as something different from the man himself. This led to the idea of a *ka* or immortal soul, able to detach itself from the body and not dependent on it for its existence. In this respect, primitives have extraordinarily well developed ideas about a plurality of souls. Some are immortal, others are only loosely attached to the body and can wander off and get lost in the night, or they lose their way and get caught in a dream. There are even souls that belong to a person without being lodged in his body, like the bush-soul, which dwells outside in the forest, in the body of an animal. The juxtaposition of a person and his "life" has its psychological basis in the fact that a mind which is not very well differentiated cannot think abstractly and is incapable of putting things into categories. It can only take the qualities it perceives and place them side by side: man and his life, or his sickness (visualized as a sort of demon), or his health or prestige (mana, etc.). This is obviously the case with the Egyptian *ka*. Father-son-life (or procreative power), together with rigorous exclusion of the Theotokos, constitute the patriarchal formula that was "in the air" long before the advent of Christianity.

199 The Father is, by definition, the prime cause, the creator, the *auctor rerum,* who, on a level of culture where reflection is still unknown, can only be One. The Other follows from the One by splitting off from it. This split need not occur so long as there is no criticism of the *auctor rerum*—so long, that is to say, as a culture refrains from all reflection about the One and does not start criticizing the Creator's handiwork. A feeling of oneness, far removed from critical judgment and moral conflict, leaves the Father's authority unimpaired.

200 I had occasion to observe this original oneness of the father-world when I was with a tribe of Negroes on Mount Elgon. These people professed to believe that the Creator had made everything good and beautiful. "But what about the bad animals that kill your cattle?" I asked. They replied: "The lion is good and beautiful." "And your horrible diseases?" "You lie in the sun, and it is beautiful." I was impressed by their optimism. But at six o'clock in the evening this philosophy came to a sudden stop, as I was soon to discover. After sunset, another world took over—the dark world of the Ayik, who is everything evil,

dangerous, and terrifying. The optimistic philosophy ends and a philosophy of fear, ghosts, and magical spells for averting the Evil One begins. Then, at sunrise, the optimism starts off again without any trace of inner contradiction.

201 Here man, world, and God form a whole, a unity unclouded by criticism. It is the world of the Father, and of man in his childhood state. Despite the fact that twelve hours out of every twenty-four are spent in the world of darkness, and in agonizing belief in this darkness, the doubt never arises as to whether God might not also be the Other. The famous question about the origin of evil does not yet exist in a patriarchal age. Only with the coming of Christianity did it present itself as the principal problem of morality. The world of the Father typifies an age which is characterized by a pristine oneness with the whole of Nature, no matter whether this oneness be beautiful or ugly or awe-inspiring. But once the question is asked: "Whence comes the evil, why is the world so bad and imperfect, why are there diseases and other horrors, why must man suffer?"—then reflection has already begun to judge the Father by his manifest works, and straightway one is conscious of a doubt, which is itself the symptom of a split in the original unity. One comes to the conclusion that creation is imperfect—nay more, that the Creator has not done his job properly, that the goodness and almightiness of the Father cannot be the sole principle of the cosmos. Hence the One has to be supplemented by the Other, with the result that the world of the Father is fundamentally altered and is superseded by the world of the Son.

202 This was the time when the Greeks started criticizing the world, the time of "gnosis" in its widest sense, which ultimately gave birth to Christianity. The archetype of the redeemer-god and first man is age-old—we simply do not know how old. The Son, the revealed god, who voluntarily or involuntarily offers himself for sacrifice as a man, in order to create the world or redeem it from evil, can be traced back to the Purusha of Indian philosophy, and is also found in the Persian conception of the Original Man, Gayomart. Gayomart, son of the god of light, falls victim to the darkness, from which he must be set free in order to redeem the world. He is the prototype of the Gnostic redeemer-figures and of the teachings concerning Christ, redeemer of mankind.

203 It is not hard to see that a critique which raised the question of the origin of evil and of suffering had in mind another world —a world filled with longing for redemption and for that state of perfection in which man was still one with the Father. Longingly he looked back to the world of the Father, but it was lost forever, because an irreversible increase in man's consciousness had taken place in the meantime and made it independent. With this mutation he broke away from the world of the Father and entered upon the world of the Son, with its divine drama of redemption and the ritualistic retelling of those things which the God-man had accomplished during his earthly sojourn.[8] The life of the God-man revealed things that could not possibly have been known at the time when the Father ruled as the One. For the Father, as the original unity, was not a defined or definable object; nor could he, strictly speaking, either be called the "Father" or be one. He only became a "Father" by incarnating in the Son, and by so doing became defined and definable. By becoming a father and a man he revealed to man the secret of his divinity.

204 One of these revelations is the Holy Ghost. As a being who existed before the world was, he is eternal, but he appears empirically in this world only when Christ had left the earthly stage. He will be for the disciples what Christ was for them. He will invest them with the power to do works greater, perhaps, than those of the Son (John 14:12). The Holy Ghost is a figure who deputizes for Christ and who corresponds to what Christ received from the Father. From the Father comes the Son, and common to both is the living activity of the Holy Ghost, who, according to Christian doctrine, is breathed forth ("spirated") by both. As he is the third term common to Father and Son, he puts an end to the duality, to the "doubt" in the Son. He is, in fact, the third element that rounds out the Three and restores the One. The point is that the unfolding of the One reaches its climax in the Holy Ghost after polarizing itself as Father and Son. Its descent into a human body is sufficient in itself to make it become another, to set it in opposition to itself. Thenceforward there are two: the "One" and the "Other,"

[8] Cf. the detailed exposition of the death and rebirth of the divine κοῦρος in Harrison, *Themis*.

which results in a certain tension.[9] This tension works itself out in the suffering and fate of the Son [10] and, finally, in Christ's admission of abandonment by God (Matthew 27:46).

205 Although the Holy Ghost is the progenitor of the Son (Matthew 1:18), he is also, as the Paraclete, a legacy from him. He continues the work of redemption in mankind at large, by descending upon those who merit divine election. Consequently, the Paraclete is, at least by implication, the crowning figure in the work of redemption on the one hand and in God's revelation of himself on the other. It could, in fact, be said that the Holy Ghost represents the final, complete stage in the evolution of God and the divine drama. For the Trinity is undoubtedly a higher form of God-concept than mere unity, since it corresponds to a level of reflection on which man has become more conscious.

206 The trinitarian conception of a life-process within the Deity, which I have outlined here, was, as we have seen, already in existence in pre-Christian times, its essential features being a continuation and differentiation of the primitive rites of renewal and the cult-legends associated with them. Just as the gods of these mysteries become extinct, so, too, do the mysteries themselves, only to take on new forms in the course of history. A large-scale extinction of the old gods was once more in progress at the beginning of our era, and the birth of a new god, with new mysteries and new emotions, was an occurrence that healed the wound in men's souls. It goes without saying that any conscious borrowing from the existing mystery traditions would have hampered the god's renewal and rebirth. It had to be an entirely unprejudiced revelation which, quite unrelated to anything else, and if possible without preconceptions of any kind, would usher into the world a new δρώμενον and a new cult-legend. Only at a comparatively late date did people notice the striking parallels with the legend of Dionysus, which they then declared to be the work of the devil. This attitude on the part of the early Christians can easily be understood, for Christianity

9 The relation of Father to Son is not arithmetical, since both the One and the Other are still united in the original Unity and are, so to speak, eternally on the point of becoming two. Hence the Son is eternally being begotten by the Father, and Christ's sacrificial death is an eternally present act.

10 The πάθη of Dionysus would be the Greek parallels.

did indeed develop in this unconscious fashion, and furthermore its seeming lack of antecedents proved to be the indispensable condition for its existence as an effective force. Nobody can doubt the manifold superiority of the Christian revelation over its pagan precursors, for which reason it is distinctly superfluous today to insist on the unheralded and unhistorical character of the gospels, seeing that they swarm with historical and psychological assumptions of very ancient origin.

3. THE SYMBOLA

207 The trinitarian drama of redemption (as distinct from the intellectual conception of it) burst upon the world scene at the beginning of a new era, amid complete unconsciousness of its resuscitation from the past. Leaving aside the so-called prefigurations in the Old Testament, there is not a single passage in the New Testament where the Trinity is formulated in an intellectually comprehensible manner.[1] Generally speaking, it is more a question of formulae for triple benediction, such as the end of the second epistle to the Corinthians: "The grace of the Lord Jesus Christ, and the love of God, and the communion of the Holy Ghost, be with you all,"[2] or the beginning of the first

1 The so-called "Comma Johanneum," which would seem to be an exception, is a demonstrably late interpolation of doubtful origin. Regarded as a dogmatic and revealed text *per se,* it would afford the strongest evidence for the occurrence of the Trinity in the New Testament. The passage reads (I John 5:8: "And there are three that bear witness: the Spirit, and the water, and the blood; and these three are one" (DV). That is to say, they agree in their testimony that Christ "came in water and in blood" (verse 6, DV). [In verse 8, AV has "and these three agree in one"; RSV: "and these three agree."—TRANS.] The Vulgate has the late interpolation in verse 7: "Quoniam tres sunt, qui testimonium dant *in caelo: Pater, Verbum et Spiritus Sanctus:* et hi tres unum sunt." Note that in the Greek text the three neuter nouns *πνεῦμα, ὕδωρ,* and *αἷμα* are followed by a masculine plural: *οἱ τρεῖς εἰς τὸ ἕν εἰσιν.*

2 II Cor. 13:14 (AV). The baptismal formula "In the name of the Father and the Son and the Holy Ghost" comes into this category, though its authenticity is

epistle of Peter: ". . . chosen and destined by God the Father and sanctified by the Spirit for obedience to Jesus Christ and for sprinkling with his blood," [3] or Jude 20–21. Another passage cited in favour of the Trinity is I Corinthians 12:4–6, but this only gives the emphatic assurance that the Spirit is one (repeated in Ephesians 4:4–6), and may be taken more as an incantation against polytheism and polydemonism than an assertion of the Trinity. Triadic formulae were also current in the post-apostolic epoch. Thus Clement says in his first letter (46:6): ". . . Have we not one God, and one Christ, and one Spirit . . ." [4] Epiphanius even reports that Christ taught his disciples that "the Father and the Son and the Holy Ghost are the same." [5]

208 Epiphanius took this passage from the apocryphal "Gospel according to the Egyptians," [6] of which unfortunately only fragments are preserved. The formula is significant insofar as it provides a definite starting-point for a "modalistic" concept of the Trinity.

209 Now the important point is not that the New Testament contains no trinitarian formulae, but that we find in it three figures who are reciprocally related to one another: the Father, the Son, begotten through the Holy Ghost, and the Holy Ghost. Since olden times, formulae for benediction, all solemn agreements, occasions, attributes, etc. have had a magical, threefold character (e.g., the Trishagion).[7] Although they are no evidence for the Trinity in the New Testament, they nevertheless occur and, like the three divine Persons, are clear indications of an active archetype operating beneath the surface and throwing up triadic formations. This proves that the trinitarian archetype is

doubted. It seems that originally people were baptized only in the name of Jesus Christ. The formula does not occur in Mark and Luke. Cf. Krueger, *Das Dogma von der Dreieinigkeit und Gottmenschheit in seiner geschichtlichen Entwicklung*, p. 11.

3 I Peter 1:2 (RSV).

4 *Apostolic Fathers*, trans. by Lake, I, p. 89. Clement was the third bishop of Rome after Peter, according to Irenaeus. His dating is unsure, but he seems to have been born in the second half of the 2nd cent.

5 *Panarium*, LXII, II, in Migne, *P.G.*, vol. 41, cols. 1052–53.

6 Cf. James, *The Apocryphal New Testament*, pp. 10f.

7 We might also mention the division of Christ's forbears into 3 × 14 generations in Matthew 1:17. Cf. the role of the 14 royal ancestors in ancient Egypt: Jacobsohn, "Die dogmatische Stellung des Königs in der Theologie der alten Aegypter," pp. 66ff.

already at work in the New Testament, for what comes after is largely the result of what has gone before, a proposition which is especially apposite when, as in the case of the Trinity, we are confronted with the effects of an unconscious content or archetype. From the creeds to be discussed later, we shall see that at the synods of the Fathers the New Testament allusions to the divine trio were developed in a thoroughly consistent manner until the homoousia was restored, which again happened unconsciously, since the Fathers knew nothing of the ancient Egyptian model that had already reached the homoousian level. The after-effects on posterity were inevitable consequences of the trinitarian anticipations that were abroad in the early days of Christianity, and are nothing but amplifications of the constellated archetype. These amplifications, so far as they were naïve and unprejudiced, are direct proof that what the New Testament is alluding to is in fact the Trinity, as the Church also believes.

210 Since people did not actually *know* what it was that had so suddenly revealed itself in the "Son of Man," but only *believed* the current interpretations, the effects it had over the centuries signify nothing less than the gradual unfolding of the archetype in man's consciousness, or rather, its absorption into the pattern of ideas transmitted by the cultures of antiquity.[8] From this historical echo it is possible to recognize what had revealed itself in a sudden flash of illumination and seized upon men's minds, even though the event, when it happened, was so far beyond their comprehension that they were unable to put it into a clear formula. Before "revealed" contents can be sorted out and properly formulated, time and distance are needed. The results of this intellectual activity were deposited in a series of tenets, the dogmata, which were then summed up in the "symbolum" or creed. This breviary of belief well deserves the name "symbolum," for, from a psychological point of view, it gives symbolical expression to, and paints an anthropomorphic picture of, a transcendent fact that cannot be demonstrated or explained rationally, the word "transcendent" being used here in a strictly psychological sense.[9]

8 As we know, St. John's gospel marks the beginning of this process.

9 Cf. *Psychological Types,* Def. 51.

I. THE SYMBOLUM APOSTOLICUM

211 The first of these summaries was attempted fairly early, if tradition may be relied on. St. Ambrose, for instance, reports that the confession used at baptism in the church of Milan originated with the twelve apostles.[10] This creed of the old Church is therefore known as the Apostles' Creed. As established in the fourth century, it ran:

I believe in God the Father Almighty, and in Jesus Christ his only begotten Son our Lord, who was born of the Holy Ghost and the Virgin Mary, was crucified under Pontius Pilate, buried, and on the third day rose again from the dead, ascended into heaven, and sitteth on the right hand of the Father, whence he shall come to judge the quick and the dead. And [I believe] in the Holy Ghost, the holy Church, the forgiveness of sins, the resurrection of the flesh.

212 This creed is still entirely on the level of the gospels and epistles: there are three divine figures, and they do not in any way contradict the one God. Here the Trinity is not explicit, but exists latently, just as Clement's second letter says of the pre-existent Church: "It was spiritually there." Even in the very early days of Christianity it was accepted that Christ as Logos was God himself (John 1 : 1). For Paul he is pre-existent in God's form, as is clear from the famous "kenosis" passage in Philippians 2 : 6 (AV): "Who, being in the form of God, thought it not robbery to be equal with God" (τὸ εἶναι ἴσα θεῷ = *esse se aequalem Deo*). There are also passages in the letters where the author confuses Christ with the Holy Ghost, or where the three are seen as one, as in II Corinthians 3 : 17 (DV): "Now the Lord is the spirit" (ὁ δὲ κύριος τὸ πνεῦμα ἐστιν = *Dominus autem spiritus est*). When the next verse speaks of the "glory of the Lord" (δόξα κυρίου = *gloria Domini*), "Lord" seems to refer to Christ. But if you read the whole passage, from verses 7 to 18, it is evident that the "glory" refers equally to God, thus proving the promiscuity of the three figures and their latent Trinity.

10 *Explanatio symboli ad initiandos.*

II. THE SYMBOLUM OF GREGORY THAUMATURGUS

213 Although the Apostles' Creed does not stipulate the Trinity in so many words, it was nevertheless "spiritually there" at a very early date, and it is nothing but a quibble to insist, as many people do, that the Trinity was "invented only long afterwards." In this connection, therefore, I must mention the vision of Gregory Thaumaturgus (210–70), in which the Blessed Virgin and St. John appeared to him and enunciated a creed which he wrote down on the spot.[11] It runs:

One God, Father of the living Word, [of his] self-subsistent wisdom and power, [of his] eternal likeness, perfect Begetter of what is perfect, Father of the only begotten Son. One Lord, Alone of the Alone, God of God, veritable likeness of Godhead, effectual Word, comprehensive Wisdom by which all things subsist, Power that creates all Creation, true Son of the true Father, unseen [Son] of the unseen [Father], incorruptible of the incorruptible, deathless of the deathless, everlasting of the everlasting. And one Holy Spirit, having existence from God and appearing through the Son, Image of the Son and perfect [Image] of the perfect [Father], Life and cause of life, holy Fount, Ringleader [Χορηγός] of holiness: in whom is manifest God the Father, who is above all and in all, and God the Son, who pervades all. Perfect Trinity, whose glory and eternity and dominion is not divided and not separate.[12]

214 This trinitarian creed had already established itself in a position of authority long before the appearance of the Apostles' Creed, which is far less explicit. Gregory had been a pupil of Origen until about 238. Origen (182–251) employed the concept of the Trinity [13] in his writings and gave it considerable thought, concerning himself more particularly with its internal economy (*οἰκονομία*, *oeconomia*) and the management of its power: "I am of the opinion, then, that the God and Father, who holds the universe together, is superior to every being that exists, for he imparts to each one from his own existence that which each one is. The Son, being less than the Father, is superior to

11 Gregory of Nyssa, *De Vita S. Gregorii Thaumaturgi,* in Migne, *P.G.*, vol. 46, cols. 911–14.

12 Caspari, *Alte und neue Quellen zur Geschichte des Taufsymbols,* pp. 10–17.

13 First mentioned in Tertullian (d. 220).

rational creatures alone (for he is second to the Father). The Holy Spirit is still less, and dwells within the saints alone. So that in this way the power of the Father is greater than that of the Son and of the Holy Spirit, and in turn the power of the Holy Spirit exceeds that of every other holy being." [14] He is not very clear about the nature of the Holy Spirit, for he says: "The Spirit of God, therefore, who, as it is written, moved upon the waters in the beginning of the creation of the world, I reckon to be none other than the Holy Spirit, so far as I can understand." [15] Earlier he says: "But up to the present we have been able to find no passage in the holy scriptures which would warrant us in saying that the Holy Spirit was a being made or created." [16]

III. THE NICAENUM

15 Trinitarian speculation had long passed its peak when the Council of Nicaea, in 325, created a new creed, known as the "Nicene." It runs:

> We believe in one God, the Father Almighty, Creator of all things visible and invisible, and in one Lord Jesus Christ, Son of God, the only begotten of the Father, being of the substance [οὐσία] of the Father, God of God, Light of Light, very God of very God, begotten not made, consubstantial [ὁμοούσιος] with the Father, through whom all things have been made which are in heaven and on earth. Who for us men and for our salvation descended and was made flesh, became man, suffered, rose again the third day, ascended into heaven, and will come to judge the living and the dead. And in the Holy Spirit. As for those who say, "There was a time when He was not," or "Before He was begotten He was not," or "He was made from that which was not, or from another subsistence [ὑπόστασις], or substance," or "The Son of God is created, changeable, or subject to change," these the Catholic Church anathematizes.[17]

16 It was, apparently, a Spanish bishop, Hosius of Cordoba, who proposed to the emperor the crucial word ὁμοούσιος. It did

[14] Origen, *On First Principles,* trans. by Butterworth, pp. 33f.

[15] Ibid., p. 31. [16] Ibid.

[17] Cf. J. R. Palanque and others, *The Church in the Christian Roman Empire,* I: *The Church and the Arian Crisis,* p. 96.

not occur then for the first time, for it can be found in Tertullian, as the "unitas substantiae." The concept of homoousia can also be found in Gnostic usage, as for instance in Irenaeus' references to the Valentinians (140–*c.* 200), where the Aeons are said to be of one substance with their creator, Bythos.[18] The Nicene Creed concentrates on the father-son relationship, while the Holy Ghost receives scant mention.

IV. THE NICAENO-CONSTANTINOPOLITANUM, THE ATHANASIANUM, AND THE LATERANENSE

217 The next formulation in the Nicene-Constantinopolitan Creed of 381 brings an important advance. It runs:

We believe in one God the Father Almighty, Maker of heaven and earth, and of all things visible and invisible. And in one Lord Jesus Christ, the only begotten Son of God, begotten of his Father before all worlds, God of God, Light of Light, very God of very God, begotten, not made, being of one substance with the Father, by whom all things were made; who for us men and for our salvation came down from heaven and was made flesh by the Holy Ghost and the Virgin Mary and became man, and was crucified for us under Pontius Pilate, suffered and was buried, and on the third day rose again according to the Scriptures, and ascended into heaven, and sitteth on the right hand of God the Father, whence he shall come again in glory to judge the quick and the dead, and whose kingdom shall have no end. And [we believe] in the Holy Ghost, the Lord and Giver of life, who proceedeth from the Father,[19] who with the Father and the Son together is worshipped and glorified, who spake through the prophets. And [we believe] in one holy Catholic and Apostolic Church. We acknowledge one baptism for the remission of sins. And we await the resurrection of the dead and the life of the world to come. Amen.

18 More accurately, the unity of substance consists in the fact that the Aeons are descended from the Logos, which proceeds from Nous, the direct emanation of Bythos. Cf. Irenaeus, *Adversus haereses,* II, 17, 4, in Migne, *P.G.,* vol. 7, cols. 762–63 (trans. by Roberts and Rambaut, p. 174).

19 [The addition at this point of the words "and from the Son" (*Filioque*), which, though never accepted by the Eastern Churches, has been universal in the West, both Catholic and Protestant, since the beginning of the eleventh century, is still one of the principal points of contention between the two main sections of the Christian body.—EDITORS.]

218 Here the Holy Ghost is given due consideration: he is called "Lord" and is worshipped together with Father and Son. But he proceeds from the Father only. It was this point that caused the tremendous controversy over the "filioque" question, as to whether the Holy Ghost proceeds from the Father only, or from the Son as well. In order to make the Trinity a complete unity, the *filioque* was just as essential as the *homoousia*. The (falsely so-called) Athanasian Creed [20] insisted in the strongest possible terms on the equality of all three Persons. Its peculiarities have given much offence to rationalistic and liberal-minded theologians. I quote, as a sample, a passage from the beginning:

Now the Catholic Faith is this: That we worship one God in Trinity, and Trinity in Unity, neither confounding the Persons nor dividing the substance. For there is one Person of the Father, another of the Son, another of the Holy Ghost. But the Godhead of the Father and of the Son and of the Holy Ghost is all one; the glory equal, the majesty co-eternal. Such as the Father is, such is the Son, and such is the Holy Ghost. The Father uncreated, the Son uncreated, the Holy Ghost uncreated. The Father infinite, the Son infinite, the Holy Ghost infinite. The Father eternal, the Son eternal, the Holy Ghost eternal. And yet not three Eternals, but one Eternal. As also there are not three Uncreated, nor three Infinites, but one Infinite and one Uncreated. So likewise is the Father almighty, the Son almighty, the Holy Ghost almighty; and yet there are not three Almighties, but one Almighty. So the Father is God, the Son is God, the Holy Ghost is God; and yet there are not three Gods, but one God. Likewise the Father is Lord, the Son is Lord, the Holy Ghost is Lord; and yet there are not three Lords, but one Lord. For just as we are compelled by the Christian verity to acknowledge each Person by himself to be both God and Lord, so we are forbidden by the Catholic religion to say there are three Gods or three Lords. The Father is made of none, neither created nor begotten. The Son is of the Father alone, not made, nor created, but begotten. The Holy Ghost is of the Father and the Son, not made, nor created, nor begotten, but proceeding. So there is one Father, not three Fathers; one Son, not three Sons; one Holy Ghost, not three Holy Ghosts. And in this Trinity none is before or after, none is greater or less; but all three Persons are coeternal together and coequal. So that in

[20] It is also known as the "Symbolum Quicumque," on account of the opening words: "Quicumque vult salvus esse" (Whosoever would be saved). It does not go back to Athanasius.

all ways, as is aforesaid, both the Trinity is to be worshipped in Unity, and the Unity in Trinity. He, therefore, that would be saved, let him think thus of the Trinity.[21]

219 Here the Trinity is a fully developed conceptual schema in which everything balances, the *homoousia* binding all three Persons equally. The Creed of the Lateran Council, 1215, brings a further differentiation. I shall quote only the beginning:

> We firmly believe and wholeheartedly confess that there is only one true God, eternal, infinite, and unchanging; incomprehensible, almighty, and ineffable; Father and Son and Holy Ghost; three Persons, but one essence; entirely simple in substance and nature. The Father is of none, the Son is of the Father alone, and the Holy Ghost is of both equally; for ever without beginning and without end; the Father begetting, the Son being born, and the Holy Ghost proceeding; consubstantial and coequal and coalmighty and coeternal.[22]

220 The "filioque" is expressly taken up into this creed, thus assigning the Holy Ghost a special activity and significance. So far as I can judge, the later Creed of the Council of Trent adds nothing further that would be of interest for our theme.

221 Before concluding this section, I would like to call attention to a book well known in the Middle Ages, the *Liber de Spiritu et Anima*,[23] which attempts a psychological interpretation of the Trinity. The argument starts with the assumption that by self-knowledge a man may attain to a knowledge of God.[24] The *mens rationalis* is closest to God, for it is "excellently made, and expressly after his likeness." If it recognizes its own likeness to God it will the more easily recognize its creator. And thus knowledge of the Trinity begins. For the intellect sees how wisdom (*sapientia*) proceeds from it and how it loves this wisdom. But, from intellect and wisdom, there proceeds love, and thus all three, intellect, wisdom, and love, appear in one. The origin of all wisdom, however, is God. Therefore intellect (*νοῦς*) corresponds to the Father, the wisdom it begets corresponds to the

21 [Official version from the Revised Book of Common Prayer (1928), with alternative readings.—TRANS.]

22 [From the Decrees of the Lateran Council, ch. 1.—TRANS.]

23 Erroneously ascribed to St. Augustine. Cf. *Opera,* VI.

24 Ibid., p. 1194, B.

Son (λόγος), and love corresponds to the Spirit (πνεῦμα) breathed forth between them.[25] The wisdom of God was often identified with the cosmogonic Logos and hence with Christ. The medieval mind finds it natural to derive the structure of the psyche from the Trinity, whereas the modern mind reverses the procedure.

25 "The begetter is the Father, the begotten is the Son, and that which proceeds from both is the Holy Spirit." Ibid., p. 1195, D.

4. THE THREE PERSONS IN THE LIGHT OF PSYCHOLOGY

I. THE HYPOTHESIS OF THE ARCHETYPE

222 The sequence of creeds illustrates the evolution of the Trinity idea through the centuries. In the course of its development it either consistently avoided, or successfully combated, all rationalistic deviations, such as, for instance, the so-plausible-looking Arian heresy. The creeds superimposed on the trinitarian allusions in the Holy Scriptures a structure of ideas that is a perpetual stumbling-block to the liberal-minded rationalist. Religious statements are, however, never rational in the ordinary sense of the word, for they always take into consideration that other world, the world of the archetype, of which reason in the ordinary sense is unconscious, being occupied only with externals. Thus the development of the Christian idea of the Trinity unconsciously reproduced the archetype of the homoousia of Father, Son, and Ka-mutef which first appeared in Egyptian theology. Not that the Egyptian model could be considered the archetype of the Christian idea. The archetype *an sich*, as I have explained elsewhere,[1] is an "irrepresentable" factor, a "disposition" which starts functioning at a given moment in the de-

1 Cf. my "On the Nature of the Psyche" (1954/55 edn., pp. 410ff.).

velopment of the human mind and arranges the material of consciousness into definite patterns.[2] That is to say, man's conceptions of God are organized into triads and trinities, and a whole host of ritualistic and magical practices take on a triple or trichotomous character, as in the case of thrice-repeated apotropaic spells, formulae for blessing, cursing, praising, giving thanks, etc. Wherever we find it, the archetype has a compelling force which it derives from the unconscious, and whenever its effect becomes conscious it has a distinctly numinous quality. There is never any conscious invention or cogitation, though speculations about the Trinity have often been accused of this. All the controversies, sophistries, quibbles, intrigues, and outrages that are such an odious blot on the history of this dogma owe their existence to the compelling numinosity of the archetype and to the unexampled difficulty of incorporating it in the world of rational thought. Although the emperors may have made political capital out of the quarrels that ensued, this singular chapter in the history of the human mind cannot possibly be traced back to politics, any more than social and economic causes can be held responsible for it. The sole reason for the dogma lies in the Christian "message," which caused a psychic revolution in Western man. On the evidence of the gospels, and of Paul's letters in particular, it announced the real and veracious appearance of the God-man in this humdrum human world, accompanied by all the marvellous portents worthy of the son of God. However obscure the historical core of this phenomenon may seem to us moderns, with our hankering for factual accuracy, it is quite certain that those tremendous psychic effects, lasting for centuries, were not causelessly called

2 I have often been asked where the archetype comes from and whether it is acquired or not. This question cannot be answered directly. Archetypes are, by definition, factors and motifs that arrange the psychic elements into certain images, characterized as archetypal, but in such a way that they can be recognized only from the effects they produce. They exist preconsciously, and presumably they form the structural dominants of the psyche in general. They may be compared to the invisible presence of the crystal lattice in a saturated solution. As *a priori* conditioning factors they represent a special, psychological instance of the biological "pattern of behaviour," which gives all living organisms their specific qualities. Just as the manifestations of this biological ground plan may change in the course of development, so also can those of the archetype. Empirically considered, however, the archetype did not ever come into existence as a phenomenon of organic life, but entered into the picture with life itself.

forth, by just nothing at all. Unfortunately the gospel reports, originating in missionary zeal, form the meagrest source imaginable for attempts at historical reconstruction. But, for that very reason, they tell us all the more about the psychological reactions of the civilized world at that time. These reactions and assertions are continued in the history of dogma, where they are still conceived as the workings of the Holy Ghost. This interpretation, though the psychologist has nothing to say in regard to its metaphysical validity, is of the greatest moment, for it proves the existence of an overwhelming opinion or conviction that the operative factor in the formation of ideas is not man's intellect but an authority above and beyond consciousness. This psychological fact should on no account be overlooked, for any theoretical reasons whatsoever. Rationalistic arguments to the effect that the Holy Ghost is an hypothesis that cannot be proved are not commensurable with the statements of the psyche. A delusional idea is real, even though its content is, factually considered, nonsense. Psychology's concern is with psychic phenomena and with nothing else. These may be mere aspects of phenomena which, in themselves, could be subjected to a number of quite different modes of observation. Thus the statement that dogmas are inspired by the Holy Ghost indicates that they are not the product of conscious cogitation and speculation but are motivated from sources outside consciousness and possibly even outside man. Statements of this kind are the rule in archetypal experiences and are constantly associated with the sensed presence of a numen. An archetypal dream, for instance, can so fascinate the dreamer that he is very apt to see in it some kind of illumination, warning, or supernatural help. Nowadays most people are afraid of surrendering to such experiences, and their fear proves the existence of a "holy dread" of the numinous. Whatever the nature of these numinous experiences may be, they all have one thing in common: they relegate their source to a region outside consciousness. Psychology uses instead the concept of the unconscious, and specially that of the collective unconscious as opposed to the personal unconscious. People who reject the former and give credence only to the latter are forced into personalistic explanations. But collective and, above all, manifestly archetypal ideas can never be derived from the personal sphere. If Communism, for instance, refers to Engels,

Marx, Lenin, and so on as the "fathers" of the movement, it does not know that it is reviving an archetypal order of society that existed even in primitive times, thereby explaining, incidentally, the "religious" and "numinous" (i.e., fanatical) character of Communism. Neither did the Church Fathers know that their Trinity had a prehistory dating back several thousand years.

23 There can be no doubt that the doctrine of the Trinity originally corresponded with a patriarchal order of society. But we cannot tell whether social conditions produced the idea or, conversely, the idea revolutionized the existing social order. The phenomenon of early Christianity and the rise of Islam, to take only these two examples, show what ideas can do. The layman, having no opportunity to observe the behaviour of autonomous complexes, is usually inclined, in conformity with the general trend, to trace the origin of psychic contents back to the environment. This expectation is certainly justified so far as the ideational contents of consciousness are concerned. In addition to these, however, there are irrational, affective reactions and impulses, emanating from the unconscious, which organize the conscious material in an archetypal way. The more clearly the archetype is constellated, the more powerful will be its fascination, and the resultant religious statements will formulate it accordingly, as something "daemonic" or "divine." Such statements indicate possession by an archetype. The ideas underlying them are necessarily anthropomorphic and are thereby distinguished from the organizing archetype, which in itself is irrepresentable because unconscious.[3] They prove, however, that an archetype has been activated.[4]

24 Thus the history of the Trinity presents itself as the gradual crystallization of an archetype that moulds the anthropomorphic conceptions of father and son, of life, and of different persons into an archetypal and numinous figure, the "Most Holy Three-in-One." The contemporary witnesses of these events apprehended it as something that modern psychology would call a psychic presence outside consciousness. If there is a consensus of

[3] Cf. my detailed argument in "On the Nature of the Psyche" (1954/55 edn., pp. 410ff.).

[4] It is very probable that the activation of an archetype depends on an alteration of the conscious situation, which requires a new form of compensation.

opinion in respect of an idea, as there is here and always has been, then we are entitled to speak of a collective presence. Similar "presences" today are the Fascist and Communist ideologies, the one emphasizing the power of the chief, and the other communal ownership of goods in a primitive society.

225 "Holiness" means that an idea or thing possesses the highest value, and that in the presence of this value men are, so to speak, struck dumb. Holiness is also revelatory: it is the illuminative power emanating from an archetypal figure. Nobody ever feels himself as the subject of such a process, but always as its object.[5] *He* does not perceive holiness, *it* takes him captive and overwhelms him; nor does *he* behold it in a revelation, *it* reveals itself to him, and he cannot even boast that he has understood it properly. Everything happens apparently outside the sphere of his will, and these happenings are contents of the unconscious. Science is unable to say anything more than this, for it cannot, by an act of faith, overstep the limits appropriate to its nature.

II. CHRIST AS ARCHETYPE

226 The Trinity and its inner life process appear as a closed circle, a self-contained divine drama in which man plays, at most, a passive part. It seizes on him and, for a period of several centuries, forced him to occupy his mind passionately with all sorts of queer problems which today seem incredibly abstruse, if not downright absurd. It is, in the first place, difficult to see what the Trinity could possibly mean for us, either practically, morally, or symbolically. Even theologians often feel that speculation on this subject is a more or less otiose juggling with ideas, and there are not a few who could get along quite comfortably without the divinity of Christ, and for whom the role of the Holy Ghost, both inside and outside the Trinity, is an embarrassment of the first order. Writing of the Athanasian Creed, D. F. Strauss remarks: "The truth is that anyone who has sworn

5 Koepgen makes the following trenchant remark in his *Gnosis des Christentums*, p. 198: "If there is such a thing as a history of the Western mind . . . it would have to be viewed from the standpoint of the personality of Western man, which grew up under the influence of trinitarian dogma."

to the Symbolum Quicumque has abjured the laws of human thought." Naturally, the only person who can talk like that is one who is no longer impressed by the revelation of holiness and has fallen back on his own mental activity. This, so far as the revealed archetype is concerned, is an inevitably retrograde step: the liberalistic humanization of Christ goes back to the rival doctrine of homoiousia and to Arianism, while modern anti-trinitarianism has a conception of God that is more Old Testament or Islamic in character than Christian.

27 Obviously, anyone who approaches this problem with rationalistic and intellectualistic assumptions, like D. F. Strauss, is bound to find the patristic discussions and arguments completely nonsensical. But that anyone, and especially a theologian, should fall back on such manifestly incommensurable criteria as reason, logic, and the like, shows that, despite all the mental exertions of the Councils and of scholastic theology, they failed to bequeath to posterity an intellectual understanding of the dogma that would lend the slightest support to belief in it. There remained only submission to faith and renunciation of one's own desire to understand. Faith, as we know from experience, often comes off second best and has to give in to criticism which may not be at all qualified to deal with the object of faith. Criticism of this kind always puts on an air of great enlightenment—that is to say, it spreads round itself that thick darkness which the Word once tried to penetrate with its light: "And the light shineth in the darkness, and the darkness comprehended it not."

28 Naturally, it never occurs to these critics that their way of approach is incommensurable with their object. They think they have to do with rational facts, whereas it entirely escapes them that it is and always has been primarily a question of irrational psychic phenomena. That this is so can be seen plainly enough from the unhistorical character of the gospels, whose only concern was to represent the miraculous figure of Christ as graphically and impressively as possible. Further evidence of this is supplied by the earliest literary witness, Paul, who was closer to the events in question than the apostles. It is frankly disappointing to see how Paul hardly ever allows the real Jesus of Nazareth to get a word in. Even at this early date (and not only in John) he is completely overlaid, or rather smothered,

by metaphysical conceptions: he is the ruler over all daemonic forces, the cosmic saviour, the mediating God-man. The whole pre-Christian and Gnostic theology of the Near East (some of whose roots go still further back) wraps itself about him and turns him before our eyes into a dogmatic figure who has no more need of historicity. At a very early stage, therefore, the real Christ vanished behind the emotions and projections that swarmed about him from far and near; immediately and almost without trace he was absorbed into the surrounding religious systems and moulded into their archetypal exponent. He became the collective figure whom the unconscious of his contemporaries expected to appear, and for this reason it is pointless to ask who he "really" was. Were he human and nothing else, and in this sense historically true, he would probably be no more enlightening a figure than, say, Pythagoras, or Socrates, or Apollonius of Tyana. He opened men's eyes to revelation precisely because he was, from everlasting, God, and therefore unhistorical; and he functioned as such only by virtue of the consensus of unconscious expectation. If nobody had remarked that there was something special about the wonder-working Rabbi from Galilee, the darkness would never have noticed that a light was shining. Whether he lit the light with his own strength, or whether he was the victim of the universal longing for light and broke down under it, are questions which, for lack of reliable information, only faith can decide. At any rate the documentary reports relating to the general projection and assimilation of the Christ-figure are unequivocal. There is plenty of evidence for the co-operation of the collective unconscious in view of the abundance of parallels from the history of religion. In these circumstances we must ask ourselves what it was in man that was stirred by the Christian message, and what was the answer he gave.

229 If we are to answer this psychological question, we must first of all examine the Christ-symbolism contained in the New Testament, together with the patristic allegories and medieval iconography, and compare this material with the archetypal content of the unconscious psyche in order to find out what archetypes have been constellated. The most important of the symbolical statements about Christ are those which reveal the attributes of the hero's life: improbable origin, divine father,

hazardous birth, rescue in the nick of time, precocious development, conquest of the mother and of death, miraculous deeds, a tragic, early end, symbolically significant manner of death, post-mortem effects (reappearances, signs and marvels, etc.). As the Logos, Son of the Father, *Rex gloriae, Judex mundi,* Redeemer, and Saviour, Christ is himself God, an all-embracing totality, which, like the definition of Godhead, is expressed iconographically by the circle or mandala.[6] Here I would mention only the traditional representation of the *Rex gloriae* in a mandala, accompanied by a quaternity composed of the four symbols of the evangelists (including the four seasons, four winds, four rivers, and so on). Another symbolism of the same kind is the choir of saints, angels, and elders grouped round Christ (or God) in the centre. Here Christ symbolizes the integration of the kings and prophets of the Old Testament. As a shepherd he is the leader and centre of the flock. He is the vine, and those that hang on him are the branches. His body is bread to be eaten, and his blood wine to be drunk; he is also the mystical body formed by the congregation. In his human manifestation he is the hero and God-man, born without sin, more complete and more perfect than the natural man, who is to him what a child is to an adult, or an animal (sheep) to a human being.

230 These mythological statements, coming from within the Christian sphere as well as from outside it, adumbrate an archetype that expresses itself in essentially the same symbolism and also occurs in individual dreams or in fantasy-like projections upon living people (transference phenomena, hero-worship, etc.). The content of all such symbolic products is the idea of an overpowering, all-embracing, complete or perfect being, represented either by a man of heroic proportions, or by an animal with magical attributes, or by a magical vessel or some other "treasure hard to attain," such as a jewel, ring, crown, or,

6 "Deus est circulus cuius centrum est ubique, circumferentia vero nusquam" (God is a circle whose centre is everywhere and the circumference nowhere). This definition occurs in the later literature. In the form "Deus est sphaera infinita" (God is an infinite sphere) it is supposed to have come from the *Liber Hermetis, Liber Termegisti,* Cod. Paris. 6319 (14th cent.); Cod. Vat. 3060 (1315). Cf. Baumgartner, *Die Philosophie des Alanus de Insulis,* p. 118. In this connection, mention should be made of the tendency of Gnostic thought to move in a circle, e.g.: "In the beginning was the Word, and the Word was with God, and God was the Word." Cf. Leisegang, *Denkformen,* pp. 60ff.

geometrically, by a mandala. This archetypal idea is a reflection of the individual's wholeness, i.e., of the self, which is present in him as an unconscious image. The conscious mind can form absolutely no conception of this totality, because it includes not only the conscious but also the unconscious psyche, which is, as such, inconceivable and irrepresentable.

231 It was this archetype of the self in the soul of every man that responded to the Christian message, with the result that the concrete Rabbi Jesus was rapidly assimilated by the constellated archetype. In this way Christ realized the idea of the self.[7] But as one can never distinguish empirically between a symbol of the self and a God-image, the two ideas, however much we try to differentiate them, always appear blended together, so that the self appears synonymous with the inner Christ of the Johannine and Pauline writings, and Christ with God ("of one substance with the Father"), just as the atman appears as the individualized self and at the same time as the animating principle of the cosmos, and Tao as a condition of mind and at the same time as the correct behaviour of cosmic events. Psychologically speaking, the domain of "gods" begins where consciousness leaves off, for at that point man is already at the mercy of the natural order, whether he thrive or perish. To the symbols of wholeness that come to him from there he attaches names which vary according to time and place.

232 The self is defined psychologically as the psychic totality of the individual. Anything that a man postulates as being a greater totality than himself can become a symbol of the self. For this reason the symbol of the self is not always as total as the definition would require. Even the Christ-figure is not a totality, for it lacks the nocturnal side of the psyche's nature, the darkness of the spirit, and is also without sin. Without the integration of evil there is no totality, nor can evil be "added to the mixture by force." One could compare Christ as a symbol to the mean of the first mixture: he would then be the middle term of a triad, in which the One and Indivisible is represented by the Father, and the Divisible by the Holy Ghost, who, as we know, can divide himself into tongues of fire. But

7 Koepgen (p. 307) puts it very aptly: "Jesus relates everything to his ego, but this ego is not the subjective ego, it is a cosmic ego."

this triad, according to the *Timaeus,* is not yet a reality. Consequently a second mixture is needed.

233 The goal of psychological, as of biological, development is self-realization, or individuation. But since man knows himself only as an ego, and the self, as a totality, is indescribable and indistinguishable from a God-image, self-realization—to put it in religious or metaphysical terms—amounts to God's incarnation. That is already expressed in the fact that Christ is the son of God. And because individuation is an heroic and often tragic task, the most difficult of all, it involves suffering, a passion of the ego: the ordinary, empirical man we once were is burdened with the fate of losing himself in a greater dimension and being robbed of his fancied freedom of will. He suffers, so to speak, from the violence done to him by the self.[8] The analogous passion of Christ signifies God's suffering on account of the injustice of the world and the darkness of man. The human and the divine suffering set up a relationship of complementarity with compensating effects. Through the Christ-symbol, man can get to know the real meaning of his suffering: he is on the way towards realizing his wholeness. As a result of the integration of conscious and unconscious, his ego enters the "divine" realm, where it participates in "God's suffering." The cause of the suffering is in both cases the same, namely "incarnation," which on the human level appears as "individuation." The divine hero born of man is already threatened with murder; he has nowhere to lay his head, and his death is a gruesome tragedy. The self is no mere concept or logical postulate; it is a psychic reality, only part of it conscious, while for the rest it embraces the life of the unconscious and is therefore inconceivable except in the form of symbols. The drama of the archetypal life of Christ describes in symbolic images the events in the conscious life—as well as in the life that transcends consciousness—of a man who has been transformed by his higher destiny.

III. THE HOLY GHOST

234 The psychological relationship between man and the trinitarian life process is illustrated first by the human nature of

[8] Cf. Jacob's struggle with the angel at the ford.

Christ, and second by the descent of the Holy Ghost and his indwelling in man, as predicted and promised by the Christian message. The life of Christ is on the one hand only a short, historical interlude for proclaiming the message, but on the other hand it is an exemplary demonstration of the psychic experiences connected with God's manifestation of himself (or the realization of the self). The important thing for man is not the δεικνύμενον and the δρώμενον (what is "shown" and "done"), but what happens afterwards: the seizure of the individual by the Holy Ghost.

235 Here, however, we run into a great difficulty. For if we follow up the theory of the Holy Ghost and carry it a step further (which the Church has not done, for obvious reasons), we come inevitably to the conclusion that if the Father appears in the Son and breathes together with the Son, and the Son leaves the Holy Ghost behind for man, then the Holy Ghost breathes in man, too, and thus is the breath common to man, the Son, and the Father. Man is therefore included in God's sonship, and the words of Christ—"Ye are gods" (John 10:34)—appear in a significant light. The doctrine that the Paraclete was expressly left behind for man raises an enormous problem. The triadic formula of Plato would surely be the last word in the matter of logic, but psychologically it is not so at all, because the psychological factor keeps on intruding in the most disturbing way. Why, in the name of all that's wonderful, wasn't it "Father, Mother, and Son?" That would be much more "reasonable" and "natural" than "Father, Son, and Holy Ghost." To this we must answer: it is not just a question of a natural situation, but of a product of human reflection [9] added on to the natural sequence of father and son. Through reflection, "life" and its "soul" are abstracted from Nature and endowed with a separate existence. Father and son are united in the same soul, or, according to the ancient Egyptian view, in the same procreative force,

[9] "Reflection" should be understood not simply as an act of thought, but rather as an attitude. [Cf. *Psychological Types,* Def. 8.—EDITORS.] It is a privilege born of human freedom in contradistinction to the compulsion of natural law. As the word itself testifies ("reflection" means literally "bending back"), reflection is a spiritual act that runs counter to the natural process; an act whereby we stop, call something to mind, form a picture, and take up a relation to and come to terms with what we have seen. It should, therefore, be understood as an act of *becoming conscious.*

Ka-mutef. Ka-mutef is exactly the same hypostatization of an attribute as the breath or "spiration" of the Godhead.[10]

36 This psychological fact spoils the abstract perfection of the triadic formula and makes it a logically incomprehensible construction, since, in some mysterious and unexpected way, an important mental process peculiar to man has been imported into it. If the Holy Ghost is, at one and the same time, the breath of life and a loving spirit and the Third Person in whom the whole trinitarian process culminates, then he is essentially a product of reflection, an hypostatized noumenon tacked on to the natural family-picture of father and son. It is significant that early Christian Gnosticism tried to get round this difficulty by interpreting the Holy Ghost as the Mother.[11] But that would merely have kept him within the archaic family-picture, within the tritheism and polytheism of the patriarchal world. It is, after all, perfectly natural that the father should have a family and that the son should embody the father. This train of thought is quite consistent with the father-world. On the other hand, the mother-interpretation would reduce the specific meaning of the Holy Ghost to a primitive image and destroy the most essential of the qualities attributed to him: not only is he the life common to Father and Son, he is also the Paraclete whom the Son left behind him, to procreate in man and bring forth works of divine parentage. It is of paramount importance that the idea of the Holy Ghost is not a natural image, but a recognition of the living quality of Father and Son, abstractly conceived as the "third" term between the One and the Other. Out of the tension of duality life always produces a "third" that seems somehow incommensurable or paradoxical. Hence, as the "third," the Holy Ghost is bound to be incommensurable and paradoxical too. Unlike Father and Son, he has no name and no character. He is a *function,* but that function is the Third Person of the Godhead.

10 "Active spiration" is a manifestation of life, an immanent act of Father and Son; "passive spiration," on the other hand, is a quality of the Holy Ghost. According to St. Thomas, spiration does not proceed from the intellect but from the will of the Father and Son. In relation to the Son the Holy Ghost is not a spiration, but a procreative act of the Father.

11 Cf. the Acts of Thomas (trans. by James, p. 388): "Come, O communion of the male; come, she that knoweth the mysteries of him that is chosen. . . . Come, holy dove that beareth the twin young; come, hidden mother."

237 He is psychologically heterogeneous in that he cannot be logically derived from the father-son relationship and can only be understood as an idea introduced by a process of human reflection. The Holy Ghost is an exceedingly "abstract" conception, since a "breath" shared by two figures characterized as distinct and not mutually interchangeable can hardly be conceived at all. Hence one feels it to be an artificial construction of the mind, even though, as the Egyptian Ka-mutef concept shows, it seems somehow to belong to the very essence of the Trinity. Despite the fact that we cannot help seeing in the positing of such a concept a product of human reflection, this reflection need not necessarily have been a conscious act. It could equally well owe its existence to a "revelation," i.e., to an unconscious reflection,[12] and hence to an autonomous functioning of the unconscious, or rather of the self, whose symbols, as we have already said, cannot be distinguished from God-images. A religious interpretation will therefore insist that this hypostasis was a divine revelation. While it cannot raise any objections to such a notion, psychology must hold fast to the conceptual nature of the hypostasis, for in the last analysis the Trinity, too, is an anthropomorphic configuration, gradually taking shape through strenuous mental and spiritual effort, even though already preformed by the timeless archetype.

238 This separating, recognizing, and assigning of qualities is a mental activity which, although unconscious at first, gradually filters through to consciousness as the work proceeds. What started off by merely happening to consciousness later becomes integrated in it as its own activity. So long as a mental or indeed any psychic process at all is unconscious, it is subject to the law governing archetypal dispositions, which are organized and arranged round the self. And since the self cannot be distinguished from an archetypal God-image, it would be equally true to say of any such arrangement that it conforms to natural law and that it is an act of God's will. (Every metaphysical statement is, *ipso facto,* unprovable). Inasmuch, then, as acts of cognition and judgment are essential qualities of consciousness, any accumulation of unconscious acts of this sort [13] will have the

12 For this seeming *contradictio in adjecto* see "On the Nature of the Psyche" (1954/55 edn., p. 383).

13 The existence of such processes is evidenced by the content of dreams.

effect of strengthening and widening consciousness, as one can see for oneself in any thorough analysis of the unconscious. Consequently, man's achievement of consciousness appears as the result of prefigurative archetypal processes or—to put it metaphysically—as part of the divine life-process. In other words, God becomes manifest in the human act of reflection.

239 The nature of this conception (i.e., the hypostatizing of a quality) meets the need evinced by primitive thought to form a more or less abstract idea by endowing each individual quality with a concrete existence of its own. Just as the Holy Ghost is a legacy left to man, so, conversely, the concept of the Holy Ghost is something begotten by man and bears the stamp of its human progenitor. And just as Christ took on man's bodily nature, so through the Holy Ghost man as a spiritual force is surreptitiously included in the mystery of the Trinity, thereby raising it far above the naturalistic level of the triad and thus beyond the Platonic triunity. The Trinity, therefore, discloses itself as a symbol that comprehends the essence of the divine *and* the human. It is, as Koepgen [14] says, "a revelation not only of God but at the same time of man."

240 The Gnostic interpretation of the Holy Ghost as the Mother contains a core of truth in that Mary was the instrument of God's birth and so became involved in the trinitarian drama as a human being. The Mother of God can, therefore, be regarded as a symbol of mankind's essential participation in the Trinity. The psychological justification for this assumption lies in the fact that thinking, which originally had its source in the self-revelations of the unconscious, was felt to be the manifestation of a power external to consciousness. The primitive does not think; the thoughts come to him. We ourselves still feel certain particularly enlightening ideas as "in-fluences," "in-spirations," etc. Where judgments and flashes of insight are transmitted by unconscious activity, they are often attributed to an archetypal feminine figure, the anima or mother-beloved. It then seems as if the inspiration came from the mother or from the beloved, the "femme inspiratrice." In view of this, the Holy Ghost would have a tendency to exchange his neuter designation (*τὸ πνεῦμα*) for a feminine one. (It may be noted that the Hebrew word for spirit—*ruach*—is predominantly feminine.) Holy Ghost

14 *Die Gnosis des Christentums,* p. 194.

and Logos merge in the Gnostic idea of Sophia, and again in the Sapientia of the medieval natural philosophers, who said of her: "In gremio matris sedet sapientia patris" (the wisdom of the father lies in the lap of the mother). These psychological relationships do something to explain why the Holy Ghost was interpreted as the mother, but they add nothing to our understanding of the Holy Ghost as such, because it is impossible to see how the mother could come third when her natural place would be second.

241 Since the Holy Ghost is an hypostasis of "life," posited by an act of reflection, he appears, on account of his peculiar nature, as a separate and incommensurable "third," whose very peculiarities testify that it is neither a compromise nor a mere triadic appendage, but rather the logically unexpected resolution of tension between Father and Son. The fact that it is precisely a process of human reflection that irrationally creates the uniting "third" is itself connected with the nature of the drama of redemption, whereby God descends into the human realm and man mounts up to the realm of divinity.

242 Thinking in the magic circle of the Trinity, or trinitarian thinking, is in truth motivated by the "Holy Spirit" in so far as it is never a question of mere cogitation but of giving expression to imponderable psychic events. The driving forces that work themselves out in this thinking are not conscious motives; they come from an historical occurrence rooted, in its turn, in those obscure psychic assumptions for which one could hardly find a better or more succinct formula than the "change from father to son," from unity to duality, from non-reflection to criticism. To the extent that personal motives are lacking in trinitarian thinking, and the forces motivating it derive from impersonal and collective psychic conditions, it expresses a need of the unconscious psyche far surpassing all personal needs. This need, aided by human thought, produced the symbol of the Trinity, which was destined to serve as a saving formula of wholeness in an epoch of change and psychic transformation. Manifestations of a psychic activity not caused or consciously willed by man himself have always been felt to be daemonic, divine, or "holy," in the sense that they heal and make whole. His ideas of God behave as do all images arising out of the unconscious: they compensate or complete the general mood or attitude of the mo-

ment, and it is only through the integration of these unconscious images that a man becomes a psychic whole. The "merely conscious" man who is all ego is a mere fragment, in so far as he seems to exist apart from the unconscious. But the more the unconscious is split off, the more formidable the shape in which it appears to the conscious mind—if not in divine form, then in the more unfavourable form of obsessions and outbursts of affect.[15] Gods are personifications of unconscious contents, for they reveal themselves to us through the unconscious activity of the psyche.[16] Trinitarian thinking had something of the same quality, and its passionate profundity rouses in us latecomers a naïve astonishment. We no longer know, or have not yet discovered, what depths in the soul were stirred by that great turning-point in human history. The Holy Ghost seems to have faded away without having found the answer to the question he set humanity.

15 In the *Rituale Romanum* ("On the Exorcism of Persons Possessed by the Devil": 1952 edn., pp. 839ff.), states of possession are expressly distinguished from diseases. We are told that the exorcist must learn to know the signs by which the possessed person may be distinguished from "those suffering from melancholy or any morbid condition." The criteria of possession are: ". . . speaking fluently in unknown tongues or understanding those who speak them; revealing things that take place at a distance or in secret; giving evidence of greater strength than is natural in view of one's age or condition; and other things of the same kind." The Church's idea of possession, therefore, is limited to extremely rare cases, whereas I would use it in a much wider sense as designating a frequently occurring psychic phenomenon: any autonomous complex not subject to the conscious will exerts a possessive effect on consciousness proportional to its strength and limits the latter's freedom. On the question of the Church's distinction between disease and possession, see Tonquédec, *Les Maladies nerveuses ou mentales et les manifestations diaboliques.*

16 I am always coming up against the misunderstanding that a psychological treatment or explanation reduces God to "nothing but" psychology. It is not a question of God at all, but of man's ideas of God, as I have repeatedly emphasized. There are people who do have such ideas and who form such conceptions, and these things are the proper study of psychology.

5. THE PROBLEM OF THE FOURTH

I. THE CONCEPT OF QUATERNITY

243 The *Timaeus,* which was the first to propound a triadic formula for the God-image in philosophical terms, starts off with the ominous question: "One, two, three—but . . . where is the fourth?" This question is, as we know, taken up again in the Cabiri scene in *Faust:*

> Three we brought with us,
> The fourth would not come.
> He was the right one
> Who thought for them all.

244 When Goethe says that the fourth was the one "who thought for them all," we rather suspect that the fourth was Goethe's own thinking function.[1] The Cabiri are, in fact, the mysterious creative powers, the gnomes who work under the earth, i.e., below the threshold of consciousness, in order to supply us with lucky ideas. As imps and hobgoblins, however, they also play all sorts of nasty tricks, keeping back names and dates that were

[1] "Feeling is all; / Names are sound and smoke." [This problem of the "fourth" in *Faust* is also discussed in *Psychology and Alchemy,* pp. 148ff.—EDITORS.]

"on the tip of the tongue," making us say the wrong thing, etc. They give an eye to everything that has not already been anticipated by the conscious mind and the functions at its disposal. As these functions can be used consciously only because they are adapted, it follows that the unconscious, autonomous function is not or cannot be used consciously because it is unadapted. The differentiated and differentiable functions are much easier to cope with, and, for understandable reasons, we prefer to leave the "inferior" function round the corner, or to repress it altogether, because it is such an awkward customer. And it is a fact that it has the strongest tendency to be infantile, banal, primitive, and archaic. Anybody who has a high opinion of himself will do well to guard against letting it make a fool of him. On the other hand, deeper insight will show that the primitive and archaic qualities of the inferior function conceal all sorts of significant relationships and symbolical meanings, and instead of laughing off the Cabiri as ridiculous Tom Thumbs he may begin to suspect that they are a treasure-house of hidden wisdom. Just as, in *Faust,* the fourth thinks for them all, so the whereabouts of the eighth should be asked "on Olympus." Goethe showed great insight in not underestimating his inferior function, thinking, although it was in the hands of the Cabiri and was undoubtedly mythological and archaic. He characterizes it perfectly in the line: "The fourth would not come." Exactly! It wanted for some reason to stay behind or below.[2]

245 Three of the four orienting functions are available to consciousness. This is confirmed by the psychological experience that a rational type, for instance, whose superior function is thinking, has at his disposal one, or possibly two, auxiliary functions of an irrational nature, namely sensation (the "fonction du réel") and intuition (perception via the unconscious). His inferior function will be feeling (valuation), which remains in a retarded state and is contaminated with the unconscious. It refuses to come along with the others and often goes wildly off on its own. This peculiar dissociation is, it seems, a product of civilization, and it denotes a freeing of consciousness from any excessive attachment to the "spirit of gravity." If that function, which is still bound indissolubly to the past and whose roots

2 Cf. *Psychological Types,* Def. 30.

reach back as far as the animal kingdom,[3] can be left behind and even forgotten, then consciousness has won for itself a new and not entirely illusory freedom. It can leap over abysses on winged feet; it can free itself from bondage to sense-impressions, emotions, fascinating thoughts, and presentiments by soaring into abstraction. Certain primitive initiations stress the idea of transformation into ghosts and invisible spirits and thereby testify to the relative emancipation of consciousness from the fetters of non-differentiation. Although there is a tendency, characteristic not only of primitive religions, to speak rather exaggeratedly of complete transformation, complete renewal and rebirth, it is, of course, only a relative change, continuity with the earlier state being in large measure preserved. Were it otherwise, every religious transformation would bring about a complete splitting of the personality or a loss of memory, which is obviously not so. The connection with the earlier attitude is maintained because part of the personality remains behind in the previous situation; that is to say it lapses into unconsciousness and starts building up the shadow.[4] The loss makes itself felt in consciousness through the absence of at least one of the four orienting functions, and the missing function is always the opposite of the superior function. The loss need not necessarily take the form of complete absence; in other words, the inferior function may be either unconscious or conscious, but in both cases it is autonomous and obsessive and not influenceable by the will. It has the "all-or-none" character of an instinct. Although emancipation from the instincts brings a differentiation and enhancement of consciousness, it can only come about at the expense of the unconscious function, so that conscious orientation lacks that element which the inferior function could have supplied. Thus it often happens that people who have an amazing range of consciousness know less about themselves than the veriest infant, and all because "the fourth would not come"—

[3] Cf. the Hymn of Valentinus (Mead, *Fragments of a Faith Forgotten,* p. 307): "All things depending in spirit I see; all things supported in spirit I view; flesh from soul depending; soul by air supported; air from aether hanging; fruits born of the deep; babe born of the womb." Cf. also the προσφυής ψυχή of Isidorus, who supposed that all manner of animal qualities attached to the human soul in the form of "outgrowths."

[4] Cf. the alchemical symbol of the *umbra solis* and the Gnostic idea that Christ was born "not without some shadow."

it remained down below—or up above—in the unconscious realm.

46 As compared with the trinitarian thinking of Plato, ancient Greek philosophy favoured thinking of a quaternary type. In Pythagoras the great role was played not by three but by four; the Pythagorean oath, for instance, says that the tetraktys "contains the roots of eternal nature." [5] The Pythagorean school was dominated by the idea that the soul was a square and not a triangle. The origin of these ideas lies far back in the dark prehistory of Greek thought. The quaternity is an archetype of almost universal occurrence. It forms the logical basis for any whole judgment. If one wishes to pass such a judgment, it must have this fourfold aspect. For instance, if you want to describe the horizon as a whole, you name the four quarters of heaven. Three is not a natural coefficient of order, but an artificial one. There are always four elements, four prime qualities, four colours, four castes, four ways of spiritual development, etc. So, too, there are four aspects of psychological orientation, beyond which nothing fundamental remains to be said. In order to orient ourselves, we must have a function which ascertains that something is there (sensation); a second function which establishes *what* it is (thinking); a third function which states whether it suits us or not, whether we wish to accept it or not (feeling); and a fourth function which indicates where it came from and where it is going (intuition). When this has been done, there is nothing more to say. Schopenhauer proves that the "Principle of Sufficient Reason" has a fourfold root.[6] This is so because the fourfold aspect is the minimum requirement for a complete judgment. The ideal of completeness is the circle or sphere, but its natural minimal division is a quaternity.

47 Now if Plato had had the idea of the Christian Trinity [7]—which of course he did not—and had on that account placed his triad above everything, one would be bound to object that this cannot be a whole judgment. A necessary fourth would be left

[5] The four ῥιζώματα of Empedocles.

[6] "On the Fourfold Root of the Principle of Sufficient Reason," in *Two Essays by Arthur Schopenhauer.*

[7] In Plato the quaternity takes the form of a cube, which he correlates with earth. Lü Pu-wei (*Frühling und Herbst,* trans. into German by Wilhelm, p. 38) says: "Heaven's way is round, earth's way is square."

out; or, if Plato took the three-sided figure as symbolic of the Beautiful and the Good and endowed it with all positive qualities, he would have had to deny evil and imperfection to it. In that case, what has become of them? The Christian answer is that evil is a *privatio boni*. This classic formula robs evil of absolute existence and makes it a shadow that has only a relative existence dependent on light. Good, on the other hand, is credited with a positive substantiality. But, as psychological experience shows, "good" and "evil" are opposite poles of a moral judgment which, as such, originates in man. A judgment can be made about a thing only if its opposite is equally real and possible. The opposite of a seeming evil can only be a seeming good, and an evil that lacks substance can only be contrasted with a good that is equally non-substantial. Although the opposite of "existence" is "non-existence," the opposite of an existing good can never be a non-existing evil, for the latter is a contradiction in terms and opposes to an existing good something incommensurable with it; the opposite of a non-existing (negative) evil can only be a non-existing (negative) good. If, therefore, evil is said to be a mere privation of good, the opposition of good and evil is denied outright. How can one speak of "good" at all if there is no "evil"? Or of "light" if there is no "darkness," or of "above" if there is no "below"? There is no getting round the fact that if you allow substantiality to good, you must also allow it to evil. If evil has no substance, good must remain shadowy, for there is no substantial opponent for it to defend itself against, but only a shadow, a mere privation of good. Such a view can hardly be squared with observed reality. It is difficult to avoid the impression that apotropaic tendencies have had a hand in creating this notion, with the understandable intention of settling the painful problem of evil as optimistically as possible. Often it is just as well that we do not know the danger we escape when we rush in where angels fear to tread.

248 Christianity also deals with the problem in another way, by asserting that evil has substance and personality as the devil, or Lucifer. There is one view which allows the devil a malicious, goblin-like existence only, thus making him the insignificant head of an insignificant tribe of wood-imps and poltergeists. Another view grants him a more dignified status, depending on the

degree to which it identifies him with "ills" in general. How far "ills" may be identified with "evil" is a controversial question. The Church distinguishes between physical ills and moral ills. The former may be willed by divine Providence (e.g., for man's improvement), the latter not, because sin cannot be willed by God even as a means to an end. It would be difficult to verify the Church's view in concrete instances, for psychic and somatic disorders are "ills," and, as illnesses, they are moral as well as physical. At all events there is a view which holds that the devil, though created, is autonomous and eternal. In addition, he is the adversary of Christ: by infecting our first parents with original sin he corrupted creation and made the Incarnation necessary for God's work of salvation. In so doing he acted according to his own judgment, as in the Job episode, where he was even able to talk God round. The devil's prowess on these occasions hardly squares with his alleged shadow-existence as the *privatio boni,* which, as we have said, looks very like a euphemism. The devil as an autonomous and eternal personality is much more in keeping with his role as the adversary of Christ and with the psychological reality of evil.

249 But if the devil has the power to put a spoke in God's Creation, or even corrupt it, and God does nothing to stop this nefarious activity and leaves it all to man (who is notoriously stupid, unconscious, and easily led astray), then, despite all assurances to the contrary, the evil spirit must be a factor of quite incalculable potency. In this respect, anyhow, the dualism of the Gnostic systems makes sense, because they at least try to do justice to the real meaning of evil. They have also done us the supreme service of having gone very thoroughly into the question of where evil comes from. Biblical tradition leaves us very much in the dark on this point, and it is only too obvious why the old theologians were in no particular hurry to enlighten us. In a monotheistic religion everything that goes against God can only be traced back to God himself. This thought is objectionable, to say the least of it, and has therefore to be circumvented. That is the deeper reason why a highly influential personage like the devil cannot be accommodated properly in a trinitarian cosmos. It is difficult to make out in what relation he stands to the Trinity. As the adversary of Christ, he would have to take up an

equivalent counterposition and be, like him, a "son of God."[8] But that would lead straight back to certain Gnostic views according to which the devil, as Satanaël,[9] is God's first son, Christ being the second.[9a] A further logical inference would be the abolition of the Trinity formula and its replacement by a quaternity.

250 The idea of a quaternity of divine principles was violently attacked by the Church Fathers when an attempt was made to add a fourth—God's "essence"—to the Three Persons of the Trinity. This resistance to the quaternity is very odd, considering that the central Christian symbol, the Cross, is unmistakably a quaternity. The Cross, however, symbolizes God's suffering in his immediate encounter with the world.[10] The "prince of this world," the devil (John 12:31, 14:30), vanquishes the God-man at this point, although by so doing he is presumably preparing his own defeat and digging his own grave. According to an old view, Christ is the "bait on the hook" (the Cross), with which he catches "Leviathan" (the devil).[11] It is therefore significant that the Cross, set up midway between heaven and hell as a symbol of Christ's struggle with the devil, corresponds to the quaternity.

251 Medieval iconology, embroidering on the old speculations about the Theotokos, evolved a quaternity symbol in its representations of the coronation of the Virgin[12] and surreptitiously put it in place of the Trinity. The Assumption of the Blessed Virgin Mary, i.e., the taking up of Mary's soul into heaven *with her body,* is admitted as ecclesiastical doctrine but has not yet become dogma.[13] Although Christ, too, rose up with his body,

8 In her "Die Gestalt des Satans im Alten Testament" (*Symbolik des Geistes,* pp. 153ff.), Riwkah Schärf shows that Satan is in fact one of God's sons, at any rate in the Old Testament sense.

9 The suffix *-el* means god, so Satanaël = Satan-God.

9a Michael Psellus, "De Daemonibus," 1497, fol. NVv, ed. M. Ficino. Cf. also Epiphanius, *Panarium,* Haer. XXX, in Migne, *P.G.,* vol. 41, cols. 406ff.

10 Cf. Przywara's meditations on the Cross and its relation to God in *Deus Semper Major,* I. Also the early Christian interpretation of the Cross in the Acts of John, trans. by James, pp. 228ff.

11 Herrad of Landsberg, *Hortus Deliciarum.*

12 Cf. *Psychology and Alchemy,* pars. 315ff., and the first paper in this volume, pars. 122ff.

13 As this doctrine has already got beyond the stage of "conclusio probabilis" and has reached that of "conclusio certa," the "definitio sollemnis" is now only a matter of time. The Assumption is, doctrinally speaking, a "revelatum im-

this has a rather different meaning, since Christ was a divinity in the first place and Mary was not. In her case the body would have been a much more material one than Christ's, much more an element of space-time reality.[14] Ever since the *Timaeus* the "fourth" has signified "realization," i.e., entry into an essentially different condition, that of worldly materiality, which, it is authoritatively stated, is ruled by the Prince of this world—for matter is the diametrical opposite of spirit. It is the true abode of the devil, whose hellish hearth-fire burns deep in the interior of the earth, while the shining spirit soars in the aether, freed from the shackles of gravity.

52 The *Assumptio Mariae* paves the way not only for the divinity of the Theotokos (i.e., her ultimate recognition as a goddess),[15] but also for the quaternity. At the same time, matter is included in the metaphysical realm, together with the corrupting principle of the cosmos, evil. One can explain that matter was originally pure, or at least capable of purity, but this does not do away with the fact that matter represents the *concreteness* of God's thoughts and is, therefore, the very thing that makes individuation possible, with all its consequences. The adversary is, quite logically, conceived to be the soul of matter, because they both constitute a point of resistance without which

plicitum"; that is to say, it has never been revealed explicitly, but, in the gradual course of development, it became clear as an original content of the Revelation. (Cf. Wiederkehr, *Die leibliche Aufnahme der allerseligsten Jungfrau Maria in den Himmel.*) From the psychological standpoint, however, and in terms of the history of symbols, this view is a consistent and logical restoration of the archetypal situation, in which the exalted status of Mary is revealed implicitly and must therefore become a "conclusio certa" in the course of time.

[This note was written in 1948, two years before the promulgation of the dogma. The bodily assumption of Mary into heaven was defined as a dogma of the Catholic faith by Pope Pius XII in November 1950 by the Apostolic Constitution *Munificentissimus Deus* (*Acta Apostolicae Sedis,* Rome, XLII, pp. 753ff.), and in an Encyclical Letter, *Ad Caeli Reginam,* of October 11, 1954, the same Pope instituted a feast to be observed yearly in honour of Mary's "regalis dignitas" as Queen of Heaven and Earth (*Acta Apostolicae Sedis,* XLVI, pp. 625ff.). —EDITORS.]

14 Although the assumption of Mary is of fundamental significance, it was not the first case of this kind. Enoch and Elijah were taken up to heaven with their bodies, and many holy men rose from their graves when Christ died.

15 Her divinity may be regarded as a tacit *conclusio probabilis,* and so too may the worship or adoration (*προσκύνησις*) to which she is entitled.

the relative autonomy of individual existence would be simply unthinkable. The will to be different and contrary is characteristic of the devil, just as disobedience was the hallmark of original sin. These, as we have said, are the necessary conditions for the Creation and ought, therefore, to be included in the divine plan and—ultimately—in the divine realm.[16] But the Christian definition of God as the *summum bonum* excludes the Evil One right from the start, despite the fact that in the Old Testament he was still one of the "sons of God." Hence the devil remained outside the Trinity as the "ape of God" and in opposition to it. Medieval representations of the triune God as having three heads are based on the three-headedness of Satan, as we find it, for instance, in Dante. This would point to an infernal Antitrinity, a true "umbra trinitatis" analogous to the Antichrist.[17] The devil is, undoubtedly, an awkward figure: he is the "odd man out" in the Christian cosmos. That is why people would like to minimize his importance by euphemistic ridicule or by ignoring his existence altogether; or, better still, to lay the blame for him at man's door. This is in fact done by the very people who would protest mightily if sinful man should credit himself, equally, with the origin of all good. A glance at the Scriptures, however, is enough to show us the importance of the devil in the divine drama of redemption.[18] If the power of the Evil One had been as feeble as certain persons would wish it to appear, either the world would not have needed God himself to come down to it or it would have lain within the power of man to set the world to rights, which has certainly not happened so far.

16 Koepgen (p. 185) expresses himself in similar terms: "The essence of the devil is his hatred for God; and God allows this hatred. There are two things which Divine Omnipotence alone makes possible: Satan's hatred and the existence of the human individual. Both are by nature completely inexplicable. But so, too, is their relationship to God."

17 Just how alive and ingrained such conceptions are can be seen from the title of a modern book by Sosnosky, *Die rote Dreifaltigkeit: Jakobiner und Bolscheviken* ["The Red Trinity: Jacobins and Bolsheviks"].

18 Koepgen's views are not so far from my own in certain respects. For instance, he says that "Satan acts, in a sense, as God's power. . . . The mystery of one God in Three Persons opens out a new freedom in the depths of God's being, and this even makes possible the thought of a personal devil existing alongside God and in opposition to him" (p. 186).

53 Whatever the metaphysical position of the devil may be, in psychological reality evil is an effective, not to say menacing, limitation of goodness, so that it is no exaggeration to assume that in this world good and evil more or less cancel each other out, like day and night, and that this is the reason why the victory of the good is always a special act of grace.

54 If we disregard the specifically Persian system of dualism, it appears that no real devil is to be found anywhere in the early period of man's spiritual development. In the Old Testament, he is vaguely foreshadowed in the figure of Satan. But the real devil first appears as the adversary of Christ,[19] and with him we gaze for the first time into the luminous realm of divinity on the one hand and into the abyss of hell on the other. The devil is autonomous; he cannot be brought under God's rule, for if he could he would not have the power to be the adversary of Christ, but would only be God's instrument. Once the indefinable One unfolds into two, it becomes something definite: the man Jesus, the Son and Logos. This statement is possible only by virtue of something else that is *not* Jesus, not Son or Logos. The act of love embodied in the Son is counterbalanced by Lucifer's denial.

55 Inasmuch as the devil was an angel created by God and "fell like lightning from heaven," he too is a divine "procession" that became Lord of this world. It is significant that the Gnostics thought of him sometimes as the imperfect demiurge and sometimes as the Saturnine archon, Ialdabaoth. Pictorial representations of this archon correspond in every detail with those of a diabolical demon. He symbolized the power of darkness from which Christ came to rescue humanity. The archons issued from the womb of the unfathomable abyss, i.e., from the same source that produced the Gnostic Christ.

56 A medieval thinker observed that when God separated the upper waters from the lower on the second day of Creation, he did not say in the evening, as he did on all the other days, that it was good. And he did not say it because on that day he had

19 Since Satan, like Christ, is a son of God, it is evident that we have here the archetype of the hostile brothers. The Old Testament prefiguration would therefore be Cain and Abel and their sacrifice. Cain has a Luciferian nature because of his rebellious progressiveness, but Abel is the pious shepherd. At all events, the vegetarian trend got no encouragement from Yahweh.

created the *binarius,* the origin of all evil.[20] We come across a similar idea in Persian literature, where the origin of Ahriman is attributed to a *doubting thought* in Ahura-Mazda's mind. If we think in non-trinitarian terms, the logic of the following schema seems inescapable:

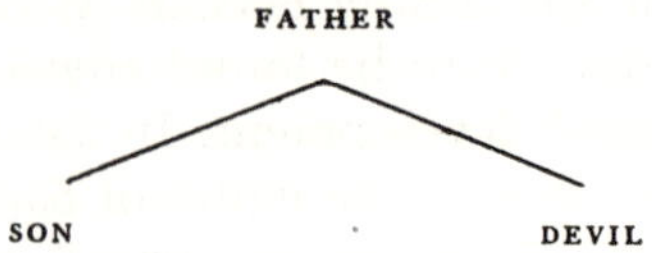

257 So it is not strange that we should meet the idea of Antichrist so early. It was probably connected on the one hand with the astrological synchronicity of the dawning aeon of Pisces,[21] and on the other hand with the increasing realization of the duality postulated by the Son, which in turn is prefigured in the fish symbol:)–(, showing two fishes, joined by a commissure, moving in opposite directions.[22] It would be absurd to put any kind of causal construction on these events. Rather, it is a question of preconscious, prefigurative connections between the archetypes themselves, suggestions of which can be traced in other constellations as well and above all in the formation of myths.

258 In our diagram, Christ and the devil appear as equal and opposite, thus conforming to the idea of the "adversary." This opposition means conflict to the last, and it is the task of humanity to endure this conflict until the time or turning-point is reached where good and evil begin to relativize themselves, to doubt themselves, and the cry is raised for a morality "beyond good and evil." In the age of Christianity and in the domain of trinitarian thinking such an idea is simply out of the question, because the conflict is too violent for evil to be assigned any other logical relation to the Trinity than that of an absolute opposite. In an emotional opposition, i.e., in a conflict situation,

20 See the first paper in this volume, par. 104.

21 In antiquity, regard for astrology was nothing at all extraordinary. [Cf. "Synchronicity: An Acausal Connecting Principle" (1955 edn., pp. 60ff.) and *Aion,* ch. 6.—EDITORS.]

22 This applies to the zodion of the Fishes. In the astronomical constellation itself, the fish that corresponds approximately to the first 1,000 years of our era is vertical, but the other fish is horizontal.

thesis and antithesis cannot be viewed together at the same time. This only becomes possible with cooler assessment of the relative value of good and the relative non-value of evil. Then it can no longer be doubted, either, that a common life unites not only the Father and the "light" son, but the Father and his *dark* emanation. The unspeakable conflict posited by duality resolves itself in a fourth principle, which restores the unity of the first in its full development. The rhythm is built up in three steps, but the resultant symbol is a quaternity.

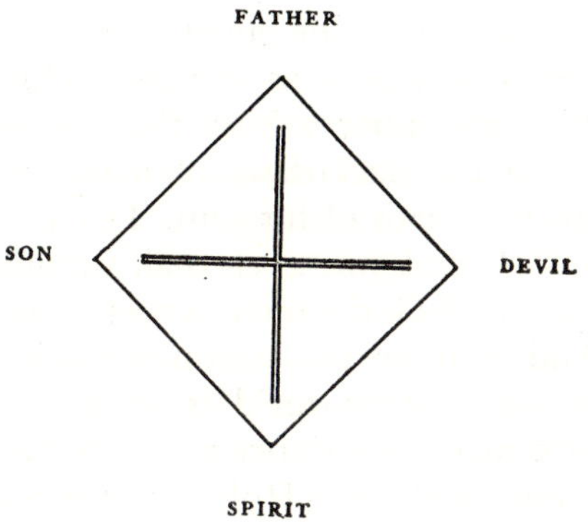

259 The dual aspect of the Father is by no means unknown to religious speculation.[23] This is proved by the allegory of the monoceros, or unicorn, who symbolizes Yahweh's angry moodiness. Like this irritable beast, he reduced the world to chaos and could only be moved to love in the lap of a pure virgin.[24] Luther was familiar with a *deus absconditus.* Murder, sudden death, war, sickness, crime, and every kind of abomination fall in with the unity of God. If God reveals his nature and takes on definite form as a man, then the opposites in him must fly apart: here good, there evil. So it was that the opposites latent in the Deity flew apart when the Son was begotten and manifested themselves in the struggle between Christ and the devil, with the Persian Ormuzd-Ahriman antithesis, perhaps, as the under-

23 God's antithetical nature is also expressed in his androgynity. Priscillian therefore calls him "masculofoemina," on the basis of Genesis 1:27: "So God created man in his own image . . . male and female created he them."

24 Cf. *Psychology and Alchemy,* pars. 520ff.

lying model. The world of the Son is the world of moral discord, without which human consciousness could hardly have progressed so far as it has towards mental and spiritual differentiation. That we are not unreservedly enthusiastic about this progress is shown by the fits of doubt to which our modern consciousness is subject.

260 Despite the fact that he is potentially redeemed, the Christian is given over to moral suffering, and in his suffering he needs the Comforter, the Paraclete. He cannot overcome the conflict on his own resources; after all, he didn't invent it. He has to rely on divine comfort and mediation, that is to say on the spontaneous revelation of the spirit, which does not obey man's will but comes and goes as *it* wills. This spirit is an autonomous psychic happening, a hush that follows the storm, a reconciling light in the darknesses of man's mind, secretly bringing order into the chaos of his soul. The Holy Ghost is a comforter like the Father, a mute, eternal, unfathomable One in whom God's love and God's terribleness come together in wordless union. And through this union the original meaning of the still-unconscious Father-world is restored and brought within the scope of human experience and reflection. Looked at from a quaternary standpoint, the Holy Ghost is a reconciliation of opposites and hence the answer to the suffering in the Godhead which Christ personifies.

261 The Pythagorean quaternity was a natural phenomenon, an archetypal image, but it was not yet a moral problem, let alone a divine drama. Therefore it "went underground." It was a purely naturalistic, intuitive idea born of the nature-bound mind. The gulf that Christianity opened out between nature and spirit enabled the human mind to think not only beyond nature but in opposition to it, thus demonstrating its divine freedom, so to speak. This flight from the darkness of nature's depths culminates in trinitarian thinking, which moves in a Platonic, "supracelestial" realm. But the question of the fourth, rightly or wrongly, remained. It stayed down "below," and from there threw up the heretical notion of the quaternity and the speculations of Hermetic philosophy.

262 In this connection I would like to call attention to Gerhard Dorn, a physician and alchemist, and a native of Frankfurt. He took great exception to the traditional quaternity of the basic

principles of his art, and also to the fourfold nature of its goal, the *lapis philosophorum*. It seemed to him that this was a heresy, since the principle that ruled the world was a Trinity. The quaternity must therefore be of the devil.[25] Four, he maintained, was a doubling of two, and two was made on the second day of Creation, but God was obviously not altogether pleased with the result of his handiwork that evening. The *binarius* is the devil of discord and, what is worse, of feminine nature. (In East and West alike even numbers are feminine.) The cause of dissatisfaction was that, on this ominous second day of Creation, just as with Ahura-Mazda, a split was revealed in God's nature. Out of it crept the "four-horned serpent," who promptly succeeded in seducing Eve, because she was related to him by reason of her binary nature. ("Man was created by God, woman by the ape of God.")

263 The devil is the aping shadow of God, the ἀντίμιμον πνεῦμα, in Gnosticism and also in Greek alchemy. He is "Lord of this world," in whose shadow man was born, fatally tainted with the original sin brought about by the devil. Christ, according to the Gnostic view, cast off the shadow he was born with and remained without sin. His sinlessness proves his essential lack of contamination with the dark world of nature-bound man, who tries in vain to shake off this darkness. ("Uns bleibt ein Erdenrest / zu tragen peinlich." [26]) Man's connection with physis, with the material world and its demands, is the cause of his anomalous position: on the one hand he has the capacity for enlightenment, on the other he is in thrall to the Lord of this world. ("Who will deliver me from the body of this death?") On account of his sinlessness, Christ on the contrary lives in the Platonic realm of pure ideas whither only man's thought can reach, but not he himself in his totality. Man is, in truth, the bridge spanning the gulf between "this world"—the realm of the dark Tricephalus—and the heavenly Trinity. That is why, even in the days of unqualified belief in the Trinity, there was always a quest for the lost fourth, from the time of the Neo-pythagoreans down to Goethe's *Faust*. Although these seekers thought of themselves as Christians, they were really Christians

[25] Cf. above, pars. 104ff.

[26] *Faust*, Part II, Act 5. ("Earth's residue to bear / Hath sorely pressed us." Trans. by Bayard Taylor.)

only on the side, devoting their lives to a work whose purpose it was to redeem the "four-horned serpent," the fallen Lucifer, and to free the *anima mundi* imprisoned in matter. What in their view lay hidden in matter was the *lumen luminum,* the *Sapientia Dei,* and their work was a "gift of the Holy Spirit." Our quaternity formula confirms the rightness of their claims; for the Holy Ghost, as the synthesis of the original One which then became split, issues from a source that is both light and dark. "For the powers of the right and the left unite in the harmony of wisdom," we are told in the Acts of John.[27]

264 It will have struck the reader that two corresponding elements cross one another in our quaternity schema. On the one hand we have the polaristic identity of Christ and his adversary, and on the other the unity of the Father unfolded in the multiplicity of the Holy Ghost. The resultant cross is the symbol of the suffering Godhead that redeems mankind. This suffering could not have occurred, nor could it have had any effect at all, had it not been for the existence of a power opposed to God, namely "this world" and its Lord. The quaternity schema recognizes the existence of this power as an undeniable fact by fettering trinitarian thinking to the reality of this world. The Platonic freedom of the spirit does not make a whole judgment possible: it wrenches the light half of the picture away from the dark half. This freedom is to a large extent a phenomenon of civilization, the lofty preoccupation of that fortunate Athenian whose lot it was not to be born a slave. We can only rise above nature if somebody else carries the weight of the earth for us. What sort of philosophy would Plato have produced had he been his own house-slave? What would the Rabbi Jesus have taught if he had had to support a wife and children? If he had had to till the soil in which the bread he broke had grown, and weed the vineyard in which the wine he dispensed had ripened? The dark weight of the earth must enter into the picture of the whole. In "this world" there is no good without its bad, no day without its night, no summer without its winter. But civilized man can live without the winter, for he can protect himself against the cold; without dirt, for he can wash; without sin, for he can prudently cut himself off from his fellows and thereby avoid many an occasion for evil. He can deem himself good and pure, because hard

27 Cf. James, *The Apocryphal New Testament,* p. 255.

necessity does not teach him anything better. The natural man, on the other hand, has a wholeness that astonishes one, though there is nothing particularly admirable about it. It is the same old unconsciousness, apathy, and filth.

65 If, however, God is born as a man and wants to unite mankind in the fellowship of the Holy Ghost, he must suffer the terrible torture of having to endure the world in all its reality. This is the cross he has to bear, and he himself is a cross. The whole world is God's suffering, and every individual man who wants to get anywhere near his own wholeness knows that this is the way of the cross.

66 These thoughts are expressed with touching simplicity and beauty in the Negro film *The Green Pastures*.[28] For many years God ruled the world with curses, thunder, lightning, and floods, but it never prospered. Finally he realized that he would have to become a man himself in order to get at the root of the trouble.

67 After he had experienced the world's suffering, this God who became man left behind him a Comforter, the Third Person of the Trinity, who would make his dwelling in many individuals still to come, none of whom would enjoy the privilege or even the possibility of being born without sin. In the Paraclete, therefore, God is closer to the real man and his darkness than he is in the Son. The light God bestrides the bridge—Man—from the day side; God's shadow, from the night side. What will be the outcome of this fearful dilemma, which threatens to shatter the frail human vessel with unknown storms and intoxications? It may well be the revelation of the Holy Ghost out of man himself. Just as man was once revealed out of God, so, when the circle closes, God may be revealed out of man. But since, in this world, an evil is joined to every good, the ἀντίμιμον πνεῦμα will twist the indwelling of the Paraclete into a self-deification of man, thereby causing an inflation of self-importance of which we had a foretaste in the case of Nietzsche. The more unconscious we are of the religious problem in the future, the greater the danger of our putting the divine germ within us to some ridiculous or demoniacal use, puffing ourselves up with it instead of remaining conscious that we are no more than the

28 [From a play by Marc Connelly, adapted from stories by Roark Bradford based on American Negro folk-themes.—EDITORS.]

manger in which the Lord is born. Even on the highest peak we shall never be "beyond good and evil," and the more we experience of their inextricable entanglement the more uncertain and confused will our moral judgment be. In this conflict, it will not help us in the least to throw the moral criterion on the rubbish heap and to set up new tablets after known patterns; for, as in the past, so in the future the wrong we have done, thought, or intended will wreak its vengeance on our souls, no matter whether we turn the world upside down or not. Our knowledge of good and evil has dwindled with our mounting knowledge and experience, and will dwindle still more in the future, without our being able to escape the demands of ethics. In this utmost uncertainty we need the illumination of a holy and healing spirit—a spirit that can be anything rather than our own minds.

II. THE PSYCHOLOGY OF THE QUATERNITY

268 As I have shown in the previous chapter, one can think out the problem of the fourth without having to discard a religious terminology. The development of the Trinity into a quaternity can be represented in projection on metaphysical figures, and at the same time the exposition gains in plasticity. But any statements of this kind can—and for scientific reasons, must—be reduced to man and his psychology, since they are mental products which cannot be presumed to have any metaphysical validity. They are, in the first place, projections of psychic processes, and nobody really knows what they are "in themselves," i.e., if they exist in an unconscious sphere inaccessible to man. At any rate, science ought not to treat them as anything other than projections. If it acts otherwise, it loses its independence. And since it is not a question of individual fantasies but—at least so far as the Trinity is concerned—of a collective phenomenon, we must assume that the development of the idea of the Trinity is a collective process, representing a differentiation of consciousness that has been going on for several thousand years.

269 In order to interpret the Trinity-symbol psychologically, we have to start with the individual and regard the symbol as an expression of his psyche, rather as if it were a dream-image. It is

possible to do this because even collective ideas once sprang from single individuals and, moreover, can only be "had" by individuals. We can treat the Trinity the more easily as a dream in that its life is a drama, as is also the case with every dream that is moderately well developed.

270 Generally speaking, the father denotes the earlier state of consciousness when one was still a child, still dependent on a definite, ready-made pattern of existence which is habitual and has the character of law. It is a passive, unreflecting condition, a mere awareness of what is given, without intellectual or moral judgment.[1] This is true both individually and collectively.

271 The picture changes when the accent shifts to the son. On the individual level the change usually sets in when the son starts to put himself in his father's place. According to the archaic pattern, this takes the form of quasi-father-murder—in other words, violent identification with the father followed by his liquidation. This, however, is not an advance; it is simply a retention of the old habits and customs with no subsequent differentiation of consciousness. No detachment from the father has been effected. Legitimate detachment consists in conscious differentiation from the father and from the habitus represented by him. This requires a certain amount of knowledge of one's own individuality, which cannot be acquired without moral discrimination and cannot be held on to unless one has understood its meaning.[2] Habit can only be replaced by a mode of life consciously chosen and acquired. The Christianity symbolized by the "Son" therefore forces the individual to discriminate and to reflect, as was noticeably the case with those Church Fathers [3] who laid such emphasis on ἐπιστήμη (knowledge) as opposed to

1 Yahweh approaches the moral problem comparatively late—only in Job. Cf. "Answer to Job," in this volume.

2 Koepgen (p. 231) therefore calls Jesus, quite rightly, the first "autonomous" personality.

3 Justin Martyr, *Apologia* II: "that we may not remain children of necessity and ignorance, but of choice and knowledge." Clement of Alexandria, *Stromata,* I, 9: "And how necessary is it for him who desires to be partaker of the power of God, to treat of intellectual subjects by philosophizing!" II, 4: "Knowledge accordingly is characterized by faith; and faith, by a kind of divine mutual and reciprocal correspondence, becomes characterized by knowledge." VII, 10: "For by it (Gnosis) faith is perfected, inasmuch as it is solely by it that the believer becomes perfect." "And knowledge is the strong and sure demonstration of what is received by faith." (Trans. by Wilson, I, p. 380; II, pp. 10, 446–47.)

ἀνάγκη (necessity) and ἄγνοια (ignorance). The same tendency is apparent in the New Testament controversies over the Jews' righteousness in the eyes of the law, which stands exclusively for the old habitus.

272 The third step, finally, points beyond the "Son" into the future, to a continuing realization of the "spirit," i.e., a living activity proceeding from "Father" and "Son" which raises the subsequent stages of consciousness to the same level of independence as that of "Father" and "Son." This extension of the *filiatio,* whereby men are made children of God, is a metaphysical projection of the psychic change that has taken place. The "Son" represents a transition stage, an intermediate state, part child, part adult. He is a transitory phenomenon, and it is thanks to this fact that the "Son"-gods die an early death. "Son" means the transition from a permanent initial stage called "Father" and "auctor rerum" to the stage of being a father oneself. And this means that the son will transmit to his children the procreative spirit of life which he himself has received and from which he himself was begotten. Brought down to the level of the individual, this symbolism can be interpreted as follows: the state of unreflecting awareness known as "Father" changes into the reflective and rational state of consciousness known as "Son." This state is not only in opposition to the still-existing earlier state, but, by virtue of its conscious and rational nature, it also contains many latent possibilities of dissociation. Increased discrimination begets conflicts that were unconscious before but must now be faced, because, unless they are clearly recognized, no moral decisions can be taken. The stage of the "Son" is therefore a conflict situation *par excellence:* the choice of possible ways is menaced by just as many possibilities of error. "Freedom from the law" brings a sharpening of opposites, in particular of the moral opposites. Christ crucified between two thieves is an eloquent symbol of this fact. The exemplary life of Christ is in itself a "transitus" and amounts therefore to a bridge leading over to the third stage, where the initial stage of the Father is, as it were, recovered. If it were no more than a repetition of the first stage, everything that had been won in the second stage—reason and reflection—would be lost, only to make room for a renewed state of semiconsciousness, of an irrational and unreflecting nature. To avoid this, the values of the

second stage must be held fast; in other words, reason and reflection must be preserved intact. Though the new level of consciousness acquired through the emancipation of the son continues in the third stage, it must recognize that *it* is not the source of the ultimate decisions and flashes of insight which rightly go by the name of "gnosis," but that these are inspired by a higher authority which, in projected form, is known as the "Holy Ghost." Psychologically speaking, "inspiration" comes from an unconscious function. To the naïve-minded person the agent of inspiration appears as an "intelligence" correlated with, or even superior to, consciousness, for it often happens that an idea drops in on one like a saving *deus ex machina.*

273 Accordingly, the advance to the third stage means something like a recognition of the unconscious, if not actual subordination to it.[4] Adulthood is reached when the son reproduces his own childhood state by voluntarily submitting to a paternal authority, either in psychological form, or factually in projected form, as when he recognizes the authority of the Church's teachings. This authority can, of course, be replaced by all manner of substitutes, which only proves that the transition to the third stage is attended by unusual spiritual dangers, consisting chiefly in rationalistic deviations that run counter to the instincts.[5] Spiritual transformation does not mean that one should remain a child, but that the adult should summon up enough honest self-criticism admixed with humility to see where, and in relation to what, he must behave as a child—irrationally, and with unreflecting receptivity. Just as the transition from the first stage to the second demands the sacrifice of childish dependence, so, at the transition to the third stage, an exclusive independence has to be relinquished.

274 It is clear that these changes are not everyday occurrences, but are very fateful transformations indeed. Usually they have a numinous character, and can take the form of conversions, illuminations, emotional shocks, blows of fate, religious or

4 Submission to any metaphysical authority is, from the psychological standpoint, submission to the unconscious. There are no scientific criteria for distinguishing so-called metaphysical factors from psychic ones. But this does not mean that psychology denies the existence of metaphysical factors.

5 The Church knows that the "discernment of spirits" is no simple matter. It knows the dangers of subjective submission to God and therefore reserves the right to act as a director of conscience.

mystical experiences, or their equivalents. Modern man has such hopelessly muddled ideas about anything "mystical," or else such a rationalistic fear of it, that, if ever a mystical experience should befall him, he is sure to misunderstand its true character and will deny or repress its numinosity. It will then be evaluated as an inexplicable, irrational, and even pathological phenomenon. This sort of misinterpretation is always due to lack of insight and inadequate understanding of the complex relationships in the background, which as a rule can only be clarified when the conscious data are supplemented by material derived from the unconscious. Without this, too many gaps remain unfilled in a man's experience of life, and each gap is an opportunity for futile rationalizations. If there is even the slightest tendency to neurotic dissociation, or an indolence verging upon habitual unconsciousness, then false causalities will be preferred to truth every time.

275 The numinous character of these experiences is proved by the fact that they are *overwhelming*—an admission that goes against not only our pride, but against our deep-rooted fear that consciousness may perhaps lose its ascendency, for pride is often only a reaction covering up a secret fear. How thin these protective walls are can be seen from the positively terrifying suggestibility that lies behind all psychic mass movements, beginning with the simple folk who call themselves "Jehovah's Witnesses," the "Oxford Groups" (so named for reasons of prestige[6]) among the upper classes, and ending with the National Socialism of a whole nation—all in search of the unifying mystical experience!

276 Anyone who does not understand the events that befall him is always in danger of getting stuck in the transitional stage of the Son. The criterion of adulthood does not consist in being a member of certain sects, groups, or nations, but in submitting to the spirit of one's own independence. Just as the "Son" proceeds from the "Father," so the "Father" proceeds from the

[6] The "Oxford Movement" was originally the name of the Catholicizing trend started by the Anglican clergy in Oxford, 1833. [Whereas the "Oxford Groups," or "Moral Rearmament Movement," were founded in 1921, also at Oxford, by Frank Buchman as "a Christian revolution . . . the aim of which is a new social order under the dictatorship of the Spirit of God, and which issues in personal, social racial, national, and supernational renaissance" (Buchman, cited in *Webster's International Dictionary,* 2nd edn., 1950).—EDITORS.]

stage of the "Son," but this Father is not a mere repetition of the original Father or an identification with him, but one in whom the vitality of the "Father" continues its procreative work. This third stage, as we have seen, means articulating one's ego-consciousness with a supraordinate totality, of which one cannot say that it is "I," but which is best visualized as a more comprehensive being, though one should of course keep oneself conscious all the time of the anthropomorphism of such a conception. Hard as it is to define, this unknown quantity can be experienced by the psyche and is known in Christian parlance as the "Holy Ghost," the breath that heals and makes whole. Christianity claims that this breath also has personality, which in the circumstances could hardly be otherwise. For close on two thousand years history has been familiar with the figure of the Cosmic Man, the Anthropos, whose image has merged with that of Yahweh and also of Christ. Similarly, the saints who received the stigmata became Christ-figures in a visible and concrete sense, and thus carriers of the Anthropos-image. They symbolize the working of the Holy Ghost among men. The Anthropos is a symbol that argues in favour of the personal nature of the "totality," i.e., the self. If, however, you review the numerous symbols of the self, you will discover not a few among them that have no characteristics of human personality at all. I won't back up this statement with psychological case histories, which are *terra incognita* to the layman anyway, but will only refer to the historical material, which fully confirms the findings of modern scientific research. Alchemical symbolism has produced, aside from the personal figures, a whole series of non-human forms, geometrical configurations like the sphere, circle, square, and octagon, or chemical symbols like the Philosophers' Stone, the ruby, diamond, quicksilver, gold, water, fire, and spirit (in the sense of a volatile substance). This choice of symbols tallies more or less with the modern products of the unconscious.[7] I might mention in this connection that there are numerous theriomorphic spirit symbols, the most important Christian ones being the lamb, the dove, and the snake (Satan). The snake symbolizing the Gnostic Nous and the Agathodaimon has a pneumatic significance (the devil, too, is a spirit). These symbols express the non-human character of the totality or self, as was

7 Cf. *Psychology and Alchemy,* Part I.

reported long ago when, at Pentecost, the spirit descended on the disciples in tongues of fire. From this point of view we can share something of Origen's perplexity as to the nature of the Holy Ghost. It also explains why the Third Person of the Trinity, unlike Father and Son, has no personal quality.[8] "Spirit" is not a personal designation but the qualitative definition of a substance of aeriform nature.

277 When, as in the present instance, the unconscious always makes such sweepingly contradictory statements, experience tells us that the situation is far from simple. The unconscious is trying to express certain facts for which there are no conceptual categories in the conscious mind. The contents in question need not be "metaphysical," as in the case of the Holy Ghost. Any content that transcends consciousness, and for which the apperceptive apparatus does not exist, can call forth the same kind of paradoxical or antinomial symbolism. For a naïve consciousness that sees everything in terms of black and white, even the unavoidable dual aspect of "man and his shadow" can be transcendent in this sense and will consequently evoke paradoxical symbols. We shall hardly be wrong, therefore, if we conjecture that the striking contradictions we find in our spirit symbolism are proof that the Holy Ghost is a *complexio oppositorum* (union of opposites). Consciousness certainly possesses no conceptual category for anything of this kind, for such a union is simply inconceivable except as a violent collision in which the two sides cancel each other out. This would mean their mutual annihilation.

278 But the spontaneous symbolism of the *complexio oppositorum* points to the exact opposite of annihilation, since it ascribes to the product of their union either everlasting duration, that is to say incorruptibility and adamantine stability, or supreme and inexhaustible efficacy.[9]

279 Thus the spirit as a *complexio oppositorum* has the same formula as the "Father," the *auctor rerum,* who is also, accord-

[8] Thomas Aquinas (*Summa theologica,* I, xxxvi, art. 1): "Non habet nomen proprium" (he has no proper name). I owe this reference to the kindness of Fr. Victor White, O.P.

[9] Both these categories are, as we know, attributes of the *lapis philosophorum* and of the symbols of the self.

ing to Nicholas of Cusa, a union of opposites.[10] The "Father," in fact, contains the opposite qualities which appear in his son and his son's adversary. Riwkah Schärf [11] has shown just how far the monotheism of the Old Testament was obliged to make concessions to the idea of the "relativity" of God. The Book of Job comes within a hair's breadth of the dualism which flowered in Persia for some centuries before and after Christ, and which also gave rise to various heretical movements within Christianity itself. It was only to be expected, therefore, that, as we said above, the dual aspect of the "Father" should reappear in the Holy Ghost, who in this way effects an apocatastasis of the Father. To use an analogy from physics, the Holy Ghost could be likened to the stream of photons arising out of the destruction of matter, while the "Father" would be the primordial energy that promotes the formation of protons and electrons with their positive and negative charges. This, as the reader will understand, is not an explanation, but an analogy which is possible because the physicist's models ultimately rest on the same archetypal foundations that also underlie the speculations of the theologian. Both are psychology, and it too has no other foundation.

III. GENERAL REMARKS ON SYMBOLISM

280 Although it is extremely improbable that the Christian Trinity is derived directly from the triadic World-Soul in the *Timaeus,* it is nevertheless rooted in the same archetype. If we wish to describe the phenomenology of this archetype, we shall have to consider all the aspects which go to make up the total picture. For instance, in our analysis of the *Timaeus,* we found that the number three represents an intellectual schema only, and that the second mixture reveals the resistance of the "recalcitrant fourth" ingredient, which we meet again as the "adversary" of the Christian Trinity. Without the fourth the three have no reality as we understand it; they even lack meaning,

[10] It should not be forgotten, however, that the opposites which Nicholas had in mind were very different from the psychological ones.

[11] Cf. "Die Gestalt des Satans im Alten Testament," in *Symbolik des Geistes,* pp. 153ff.

for a "thought" has meaning only if it refers to a possible or actual reality. This relationship to reality is completely lacking in the idea of the Trinity, so much so that people nowadays tend to lose sight of it altogether, without even noticing the loss. But we can see what this loss means when we are faced with the problem of reconstruction—that is to say in all those cases where the conscious part of the psyche is cut off from the unconscious part by a dissociation. This split can only be mended if consciousness is able to formulate conceptions which give adequate expression to the contents of the unconscious. It seems as if the Trinity plus the incommensurable "fourth" were a conception of this kind. As part of the doctrine of salvation it must, indeed, have a saving, healing, wholesome effect. During the process of integrating the unconscious contents into consciousness, undoubted importance attaches to the business of seeing how the dream-symbols relate to trivial everyday realities. But, in a deeper sense and on a long-term view, this procedure is not sufficient, as it fails to bring out the significance of the archetypal contents. These reach down, or up, to quite other levels than so-called common sense would suspect. As *a priori* conditions of all psychic events, they are endued with a dignity which has found immemorial expression in godlike figures. No other formulation will satisfy the needs of the unconscious. The unconscious is the unwritten history of mankind from time unrecorded. Rational formulae may satisfy the present and the immediate past, but not the experience of mankind as a whole. This calls for the all-embracing vision of the myth, as expressed in symbols. If the symbol is lacking, man's wholeness is not represented in consciousness. He remains a more or less accidental fragment, a suggestible wisp of consciousness, at the mercy of all the utopian fantasies that rush in to fill the gap left by the totality symbols. A symbol cannot be made to order as the rationalist would like to believe. It is a legitimate symbol only if it gives expression to the immutable structure of the unconscious and can therefore command general acceptance. So long as it evokes belief spontaneously, it does not require to be understood in any other way. But if, from sheer lack of understanding, belief in it begins to wane, then, for better or worse, one must use understanding as a tool if the incalculable consequences of a loss are to be avoided. What should we then put in place of the symbol? Is there anybody who knows a better way of expressing something that has never yet been understood?

281 As I have shown in *Psychology and Alchemy* and elsewhere, trinity and quaternity symbols occur fairly frequently in dreams, and from this I have learnt that the idea of the Trinity is based on something that can be experienced and must, therefore, have a meaning. This insight was not won by a study of the traditional sources. If I have succeeded in forming an intelligible conception of the Trinity that is in any way based on empirical reality, I have been helped by dreams, folklore, and the myths in which these number motifs occur. As a rule they appear spontaneously in dreams, and such dreams look very banal from the outside. There is nothing at all of the myth or fairytale about them, much less anything religious. Mostly it is three men and a woman, either sitting at a table or driving in a car, or three men and a dog, a huntsman with three hounds, three chickens in a coop from which the fourth has escaped, and suchlike. These things are indeed so banal that one is apt to overlook them. Nor do they wish to say anything more specific, at first, than that they refer to functions and aspects of the dreamer's personality, as can easily be ascertained when they appear as three or four known persons with well-marked characteristics, or as the four principal colours, red, blue, green, and yellow. It happens with some regularity that these colours are correlated with the four orienting functions of consciousness. Only when the dreamer begins to reflect that the four are an allusion to his total personality does he realize that these banal dream-motifs are like shadow pictures of more important things. The fourth figure is, as a rule, particularly instructive: it soon becomes incompatible, disagreeable, frightening, or in some way odd, with a different sense of good and bad, rather like a Tom Thumb beside his three normal brothers. Naturally the situation can be reversed, with three odd figures and one normal one. Anybody with a little knowledge of fairytales will know that the seemingly enormous gulf that separates the Trinity from these trivial happenings is by no means unbridgeable. But this is not to say that the Trinity can be reduced to this level. On the contrary, the Trinity represents the most perfect form of the archetype in

question. The empirical material merely shows, in the smallest and most insignificant psychic detail, how the archetype works. This is what makes the archetype so important, firstly as an organizing schema and a criterion for judging the quality of an individual psychic structure, and secondly as a vehicle of the synthesis in which the individuation process culminates. This goal is symbolized by the putting together of the four; hence the quaternity is a symbol of the self, which is of central importance in Indian philosophy and takes the place of the Deity. In the West, any amount of quaternities were developed during the Middle Ages; here I would mention only the *Rex gloriae* with the four symbols of the evangelists (three theriomorphic, one anthropomorphic). In Gnosticism there is the figure of Barbelo ("God is four"). These examples and many others like them bring the quaternity into closest relationship with the Deity, so that, as I said earlier, it is impossible to distinguish the self from a God-image. At any rate, I personally have found it impossible to discover a criterion of distinction. Here faith or philosophy alone can decide, neither of which has anything to do with the empiricism of the scientist.

282 One can, then, explain the God-image aspect of the quaternity as a reflection of the self, or, conversely, explain the self as an *imago Dei* in man. Both propositions are psychologically true, since the self, which can only be perceived subjectively as a most intimate and unique thing, requires universality as a background, for without this it could not manifest itself in its absolute separateness. Strictly speaking, the self must be regarded as the extreme opposite of God. Nevertheless we must say with Angelus Silesius: "He cannot live without me, nor I without him." So although the empirical symbol requires two diametrically opposite interpretations, neither of them can be proved valid. The symbol means both and is therefore a paradox. This is not the place to say anything more about the role these number symbols play in practice; for this I must refer the reader to the dream material in *Psychology and Alchemy,* Part I.

*

283 In view of the special importance of quaternity symbolism one is driven to ask how it came about that a highly differentiated form of religion like Christianity reverted to the archaic

triad in order to construct its trinitarian God-image.[1] With equal justification one could also ask (as has, in fact, been done) with what right Christ is presumed to be a symbol of the self, since the self is by definition a *complexio oppositorum,* whereas the Christ figure wholly lacks a dark side? (In dogma, Christ is *sine macula peccati*—'unspotted by sin.')

284 Both questions touch on the same problem. I always seek the answer to such questions on empirical territory, for which reason I must now cite the concrete facts. It is a general rule that most geometrical or numerical symbols have a quaternary character. There are also ternary or trinitarian symbols, but in my experience they are rather rare. On investigating such cases carefully, I have found that they were distinguished by something that can only be called a "medieval psychology." This does not imply any backwardness and is not meant as a value judgment, but only as denoting a special problem. That is to say, in all these cases there is so much unconsciousness, and such a large degree of primitivity to match it, that a spiritualization appears necessary as a compensation. The saving symbol is then a triad in which the fourth is lacking because it has to be unconditionally rejected.

285 In my experience it is of considerable practical importance that the symbols aiming at wholeness should be correctly understood by the doctor. They are the remedy with whose help neurotic dissociations can be repaired, by restoring to the conscious mind a spirit and an attitude which from time immemorial have been felt as solving and healing in their effects. They are "représentations collectives" which facilitate the much-needed union of conscious and unconscious. This union cannot be accomplished either intellectually or in a purely practical sense, because in the former case the instincts rebel and in the latter case reason and morality. Every dissociation that falls within the category of the psychogenic neuroses is due to a conflict of this kind, and the conflict can only be resolved through the symbol. For this purpose the dreams produce symbols which in the last analysis coincide with those recorded throughout history. But the dream-images can be taken up into the dreamer's consciousness, and grasped by his reason and feeling, only if his conscious mind possesses the intellectual categories and moral

1 In the Greek Church the Trinity is called τριάς.

feelings necessary for their assimilation. And this is where the psychotherapist often has to perform feats that tax his patience to the utmost. The synthesis of conscious and unconscious can only be implemented by a conscious confrontation with the latter, and this is not possible unless one understands what the unconscious is saying. During this process we come upon the symbols investigated in the present study, and in coming to terms with them we re-establish the lost connection with ideas and feelings which make a synthesis of the personality possible. The loss of gnosis, i.e., knowledge of the ultimate things, weighs much more heavily than is generally admitted. Faith alone would suffice too, did it not happen to be a charisma whose true possession is something of a rarity, except in spasmodic form. Were it otherwise, we doctors could spare ourselves much thankless work. Theology regards our efforts in this respect with mistrustful mien, while pointedly declining to tackle this very necessary task itself. It proclaims doctrines which nobody understands, and demands a faith which nobody can manufacture. This is how things stand in the Protestant camp. The situation in the Catholic camp is more subtle. Of especial importance here is the ritual with its sacral action, which dramatizes the living occurrence of archetypal meaning and thus makes a direct impact on the unconscious. Can any one, for instance, deny the impression made upon him by the sacrament of the Mass, if he has followed it with even a minimum of understanding? Then again, the Catholic Church has the institution of confession and of the director of conscience, which are of the greatest practical value when these activities devolve upon suitable persons. The fact that this is not always so proves, unfortunately, to be an equally great disadvantage. Thirdly, the Catholic Church possesses a richly developed and undamaged world of dogmatic ideas, which provide a worthy receptacle for the plethora of figures in the unconscious and in this way give visible expression to certain vitally important truths with which the conscious mind should keep in touch. The faith of a Catholic is not better or stronger than the faith of a Protestant, but a person's unconscious is gripped by the Catholic form no matter how weak his faith may be. That is why, once he slips out of this form, he may easily fall into a fanatical atheism, of a kind that is particularly to be met with in Latin countries.

6. CONCLUSION

286 Because of its noetic character, the Trinity expresses the need for a spiritual development that demands independence of thought. Historically we can see this striving at work above all in scholastic philosophy, and it was these preliminary exercises that made the scientific thinking of modern man possible. Also, the Trinity is an archetype whose dominating power not only fosters spiritual development but may, on occasion, actually enforce it. But as soon as the spiritualization of the mind threatens to become so one-sided as to be deleterious to health, the compensatory significance of the Trinity necessarily recedes into the background. Good does not become better by being exaggerated, but worse, and a small evil becomes a big one through being disregarded and repressed. The shadow is very much a part of human nature, and it is only at night that no shadows exist.

287 As a psychological symbol the Trinity denotes, first, the homoousia or essential unity of a three-part process, to be thought of as a process of unconscious maturation taking place within the individual. To that extent the three Persons are personifications of the three phases of a regular, instinctive psychic occurrence that always tends to express itself in the form of mythologems and ritualistic customs (for instance, the initiations at puberty, and the various rites for birth, marriage,

sickness, war, and death). As the medical lore of the ancient Egyptians shows, myths as well as rites have a psychotherapeutic value, and they still have today.

288 Second, the Trinity denotes a process of conscious realization continuing over the centuries.

289 Third, the Trinity lays claim not only to *represent* a personification of psychic processes in three roles, but to *be* the one God in three Persons, who all share the same divine nature. In God there is no advance from the potential to the actual, from the possible to the real, because God is pure reality, the "actus purus" itself. The three Persons differ from one another by reason of the different manner of their origin, or their procession (the Son begotten by the Father and the Holy Ghost proceeding from both—*procedit a patre filioque*). The homoousia, whose general recognition was the cause of so many controversies, is absolutely necessary from a psychological standpoint, because, regarded as a psychological symbol, the Trinity represents the progressive transformation of one and the same substance, namely the psyche as a whole. The homoousia together with the *filioque* assert that Christ and the Holy Ghost are both of the same substance as the Father. But since, psychologically, Christ must be understood as a symbol of the self, and the descent of the Holy Ghost as the self's actualization in man, it follows that the self must represent something that is of the substance of the Father too. This formulation is in agreement with the psychological statement that the symbols of the self cannot be distinguished empirically from a God-image. Psychology, certainly, can do no more than establish the fact that they *are* indistinguishable. This makes it all the more remarkable that the "metaphysical" statement should go so much further than the psychological one. Indistinguishability is a negative constatation merely; it does not rule out the possibility that a distinction may exist. It may be that the distinction is simply not perceived. The dogmatic assertion, on the other hand, speaks of the Holy Ghost making us "children of God," and this filial relationship is indistinguishable in meaning from the υἱότης (sonship) or *filiatio* of Christ. We can see from this how important it was that the homoousia should triumph over the homoiousia (*similarity* of substance); for, through the descent of the Holy Ghost, the self of man enters into a relationship of

unity with the substance of God. As ecclesiastical history shows, this conclusion is of immense danger to the Church—it was, indeed, the main reason why the Church did not insist on any further elaboration of the doctrine of the Holy Ghost. Its continued development would lead, on a negative estimate, to explosive schisms, and on a positive estimate straight into psychology. Moreover, the gifts of the Holy Ghost are somewhat mixed: not all of them are unreservedly welcome, as St. Paul has already pointed out. Also, St. Thomas Aquinas observes that revelation is a gift of the spirit that does not stand in any clearly definable relationship to moral endowment.[1] The Church must reserve the right to decide what is a working of the Holy Ghost and what is not, thereby taking an exceedingly important and possibly disagreeable decision right out of the layman's hands. That the spirit, like the wind, "bloweth where it listeth" is something that alarmed even the Reformers. The third as well as the first Person of the Trinity can wear the aspect of a *deus absconditus,* and its action, like that of fire, may be no less destructive than beneficial when regarded from a purely human standpoint.

"Creation" in the sense of "matter" is not included in the Trinity formula, at any rate not explicitly. In these circumstances there are only two possibilities: either the material world is real, in which case it is an intrinsic part of the divine "actus purus," or it is unreal, a mere illusion, because outside the divine reality. The latter conclusion is contradicted firstly by God's incarnation and by his whole work of salvation, secondly by the autonomy and eternality of the "Prince of this world," the devil, who has merely been "overcome" but is by no means destroyed—and cannot be destroyed because he is eternal. But if the reality of the created world *is* included in the "actus purus," then the devil is there too—Q.E.D. This situation gives rise to a quaternity, albeit a very different quaternity from the one anathematized by the fourth Lateran Council. The question there debated was whether God's essence could claim a place

1 "St. Thomas emphasizes that prophetic revelation is, as such, independent of good morals—not to speak of personal sanctity" (*De veritate,* xii, 5; *Summa theol.,* II–II, p. 172). I take this remark from the MS. of an essay on "St. Thomas's Conception of Revelation," by Fr. Victor White, O.P., with the kind permission of the author.

alongside the three Persons or not. But the question we are confronted with here is the independent position of a creature endowed with autonomy and eternality: the fallen angel. He is the fourth, "recalcitrant" figure in our symbolical series, the intervals between which correspond to the three phases of the trinitarian process. Just as, in the *Timaeus,* the adversary is the second half of the second pair of opposites, without whom the world-soul would not be whole and complete, so, too, the devil must be added to the *trias* as τὸ ἓν τέταρτον (the One as the Fourth),[2] in order to make it a totality. If the Trinity is understood as a *process,* as I have tried to do all along, then, by the addition of the Fourth, this process would culminate in a condition of absolute totality. Through the intervention of the Holy Ghost, however, man is included in the divine process, and this means that the principle of separateness and autonomy over against God—which is personified in Lucifer as the God-opposing will—is included in it too. But for this will there would have been no creation and no work of salvation either. The shadow and the opposing will are the necessary conditions for all actualization. An object that has no will of its own, capable, if need be, of opposing its creator, and with no qualities other than its creator's, such an object has no independent existence and is incapable of ethical decision. At best it is just a piece of clockwork which the Creator has to wind up to make it function. Therefore Lucifer was perhaps the one who best understood the divine will struggling to create a world and who carried out that will most faithfully. For, by rebelling against God, he became the active principle of a creation which opposed to God a counter-will of its own. Because God willed this, we are told in Genesis 3 that he gave man the power to will otherwise. Had he not done so, he would have created nothing but a machine, and then the incarnation and the redemption would never have come about. Nor would there have been any revelation of the Trinity, because everything would have been one for ever.

291 The Lucifer legend is in no sense an absurd fairytale; like the story of the serpent in the Garden of Eden, it is a "therapeutic" myth. We naturally boggle at the thought that good and evil are both contained in God, and we think God could not possibly want such a thing. We should be careful, though, not to

[2] The Axiom of Maria. Cf. *Psychology and Alchemy,* pars. 209f.

pare down God's omnipotence to the level of our human opinions; but that is just how we do think, despite everything. Even so, it would not do to impute all evil to God: thanks to his moral autonomy, man can put down a sizable portion of it to his own account. Evil is a relative thing, partly avoidable, partly fate—just as virtue is, and often one does not know which is worse. Think of the fate of a woman married to a recognized saint! What sins must not the children commit in order to feel their lives their own under the overwhelming influence of such a father! Life, being an energic process, needs the opposites, for without opposition there is, as we know, no energy. Good and evil are simply the moral aspects of this natural polarity. The fact that we have to feel this polarity so excruciatingly makes human existence all the more complicated. Yet the suffering that necessarily attaches to life cannot be evaded. The tension of opposites that makes energy possible is a universal law, fittingly expressed in the *yang* and *yin* of Chinese philosophy. Good and evil are feeling-values of human provenance, and we cannot extend them beyond the human realm. What happens beyond this is beyond our judgment: God is not to be caught with human attributes. Besides, where would the *fear* of God be if only good—i.e., what seems good to us—were to be expected from him? After all, eternal damnation doesn't bear much resemblance to goodness as we understand it! Although good and evil are unshakable as moral values, they still need to be subjected to a bit of psychological revision. Much, that is to say, that proves to be abysmally evil in its ultimate effects does not come from man's wickedness but from his stupidity and unconsciousness. One has only to think of the devastating effects of Prohibition in America or of the hundred thousand autos-da-fé in Spain, which were all caused by a praiseworthy zeal to save people's souls. One of the toughest roots of all evil is unconsciousness, and I could wish that the saying of Jesus, "Man, if thou knowest what thou doest, thou art blessed, but if thou knowest not, thou art accursed, and a transgressor of the law," [3] were still in the gospels, even though it has only one authentic source. It might well be the motto for a new morality.

2 The individuation process is invariably started off by the patient's becoming conscious of the shadow, a personality

3 Cf. James, *The Apocryphal New Testament,* p. 33.

component usually with a negative sign. This "inferior" personality is made up of everything that will not fit in with, and adapt to, the laws and regulations of conscious life. It is compounded of "disobedience" and is therefore rejected not on moral grounds only, but also for reasons of expediency. Closer investigation shows that there is at least one function in it which ought to collaborate in orienting consciousness. Or rather, this function does collaborate, not for the benefit of conscious, purposive intentions, but in the interests of unconscious tendencies pursuing a different goal. It is this fourth, "inferior" function which acts autonomously towards consciousness and cannot be harnessed to the latter's intentions. It lurks behind every neurotic dissociation and can only be annexed to consciousness if the corresponding unconscious contents are made conscious at the same time. But this integration cannot take place and be put to a useful purpose unless one can admit the tendencies bound up with the shadow and allow them some measure of realization—tempered, of course, with the necessary criticism. This leads to disobedience and self-disgust, but also to self-reliance, without which individuation is unthinkable. The ability to "will otherwise" must, unfortunately, be real if ethics are to make any sense at all. Anyone who submits to the law from the start, or to what is generally expected, acts like the man in the parable who buried his talent in the earth. Individuation is an exceedingly difficult task: it always involves a conflict of duties, whose solution requires us to understand that our "counter-will" is also an aspect of God's will. One cannot individuate with mere words and convenient self-deceptions, because there are too many destructive possibilities in the offing. One almost unavoidable danger is that of getting stuck in the conflict and hence in the neurotic dissociation. Here the therapeutic myth has a helpful and loosening effect, even when the patient shows not a trace of conscious understanding. The felt presence of the archetype is enough; it only fails to work when the possibility of conscious understanding is there, within the patient's reach. In those circumstances it is positively deleterious for him to remain unconscious, though this happens frequently enough in our Christian civilization today. So much of what Christian symbolism taught has gone by the board for large numbers of people, without their ever having understood what they have lost. Civilization does not consist in progress as such and in mindless destruction of the old values, but in developing and refining the good that has been won.

3 Religion is a "revealed" way of salvation. Its ideas are products of a pre-conscious knowledge which, always and everywhere, expresses itself in symbols. Even if our intellect does not grasp them, they still work, because our unconscious acknowledges them as exponents of universal psychic facts. For this reason faith is enough—if it is there. Every extension and intensification of rational consciousness, however, leads us further away from the sources of the symbols and, by its ascendency, prevents us from understanding them. That is the situation today. One cannot turn the clock back and force oneself to believe "what one knows is not true." But one could give a little thought to what the symbols really mean. In this way not only would the incomparable treasures of our civilization be conserved, but we should also gain new access to the old truths which have vanished from our "rational" purview because of the strangeness of their symbolism. How can a man be God's Son and be born of a virgin? That is a slap in the face of reason. But did not Justin Martyr point out to his contemporaries that exactly the same thing was said of their heroes, *and* get himself listened to? That was because man's consciousness in those days did not find the symbols as outlandish as they are for us. Today such dogmas fall on deaf ears, because nothing in our known world responds to such assertions. But if we understand these things for what they are, as symbols, then we can only marvel at the unfathomable wisdom that is in them and be grateful to the institution which has not only conserved them, but developed them dogmatically. The man of today lacks the very understanding that would help him to believe.

4 If I have ventured to submit old dogmas, now grown stale, to psychological scrutiny, I have certainly not done so in the priggish conceit that I knew better than others, but in the sincere conviction that a dogma which has been such a bone of contention for so many centuries cannot possibly be an empty fantasy. I felt it was too much in line with the *consensus omnium,* with the archetype, for that. It was only when I realized this that I was able to establish any relationship with the dogma at all. As a metaphysical "truth" it remained wholly inaccessible to me, and I suspect that I am by no means the only one to find himself

in that position. A knowledge of the universal archetypal background was, in itself, sufficient to give me the courage to treat "that which is believed always, everywhere, by everybody" as a *psychological fact* which extends far beyond the confines of Christianity, and to approach it as an object of scientific study, as a *phenomenon* pure and simple, regardless of the "metaphysical" significance that may have been attached to it. I know from my own experience that this latter aspect has never contributed in the slightest to my belief or to my understanding. It told me absolutely nothing. However, I was forced to admit that the "symbolum" possesses the highest degree of actuality inasmuch as it was regarded by countless millions of people, for close on two thousand years, as a valid statement concerning those things which one cannot see with the eyes or touch with the hands. It is this fact that needs to be understood, for of "metaphysical truth" we know only that part which man has made, unless the unbiddable gift of faith lifts us beyond all dubiety and all uneasy investigation. It is dangerous if these matters are only objects of belief;[4] for where there is belief there is doubt, and the fiercer and naïver the belief the more devastating the doubt once it begins to dawn. One is then infinitely cleverer than all the benighted heads of the Middle Ages.

295 These considerations have made me extremely cautious in my approach to the further metaphysical significance that may possibly underlie archetypal statements. There is nothing to stop their ultimate ramifications from penetrating to the very ground of the universe. We alone are the dumb ones if we fail to notice it. Such being the case, I cannot pretend to myself that the object of archetypal statements has been explained and disposed of merely by our investigation of its psychological aspects. What I have put forward can only be, at best, a more or less successful or unsuccessful attempt to give the inquiring mind some access to one side of the problem—the side that can be approached. It would be presumptuous to expect more than this. If I have merely succeeded in stimulating discussion, then my purpose is more than fulfilled. For it seems to me that the world, if it should lose sight of these archetypal statements, would be threatened with unspeakable impoverishment of mind and soul.

[4] I am thinking here of the *sola fide* standpoint of the Protestants.

III

TRANSFORMATION SYMBOLISM IN THE MASS

[First published as a lecture in *Eranos Jahrbuch 1940/41;* later published in revised and expanded form in *Von den Wurzeln des Bewusstseins* (Zurich, 1954). The present translation is made from the 1954 version. It was published in slightly different form in *The Mysteries* (Papers from the Eranos Yearbooks, 2; New York, 1955; London, 1956).—EDITORS.]

1. INTRODUCTION [1]

296 The Mass is a still-living mystery, the origins of which go back to early Christian times. It is hardly necessary to point out that it owes its vitality partly to its undoubted psychological efficacy, and that it is therefore a fit subject for psychological study. But it should be equally obvious that psychology can only approach the subject from the phenomenological angle, for the realities of faith lie outside the realm of psychology.

297 My exposition falls into four parts: in this introduction I indicate some of the New Testament sources of the Mass, with notes on its structure and significance. In section 2, I recapitulate the sequence of events in the rite. In 3, I cite a parallel from pagan antiquity to the Christian symbolism of sacrifice and transformation: the visions of Zosimos. Finally, in 4, I attempt a psychological discussion of the sacrifice and transformation.

*

298 The oldest account of the sacrament of the Mass is to be found in I Corinthians 11 : 23ff.:

[1] The following account and examination of the principal symbol in the Mass is not concerned either with the Mass as a whole, or with its liturgy in particular, but solely with the ritual actions and texts which relate to the transformation process in the strict sense. In order to give the reader an adequate account of this, I had to seek professional help. I am especially indebted to the theologian Dr. Gallus Jud for reading through and correcting the first two sections.

For the tradition which I have received of the Lord and handed down to you is that the Lord Jesus, on the night he was betrayed, took bread, gave thanks, broke it, and said: *This is my body for you; do this in remembrance of me. And after he had supped, he took the chalice also, and said: This chalice is the new testament in my blood.* As often as you drink, do this in remembrance of me. For as often as you eat this bread and drink the chalice, you declare the death of the Lord, until he comes.[2]

299 Similar accounts are to be found in Matthew, Mark, and Luke. In John the corresponding passage speaks of a "supper,"[3] but there it is connected with the washing of the disciples' feet. At this supper Christ utters the words which characterize the meaning and substance of the Mass (John 15:1, 4, 5). "I am the true vine." "Abide in me, and I in you." "I am the vine, ye are the branches." The correspondence between the liturgical accounts points to a traditional source outside the Bible. There is no evidence of an actual feast of the Eucharist until after A.D. 150.

300 The Mass is a Eucharistic feast with an elaborately developed liturgy. It has the following structure:

CONSECRATION
↗ ↘
OBLATION COMMUNION
↗ ↘
PRELIMINARIES CONCLUSION

301 As this investigation is concerned essentially with the symbol of transformation, I must refrain from discussing the Mass as a whole.

302 In the sacrifice of the Mass two distinct ideas are blended together: the ideas of *deipnon* and *thysia*. *Thysia* comes from the verb *θύειν*, 'to sacrifice' or 'to slaughter'; but it also has the mean-

2 [This is a translation of the Karl von Weizsäcker version (1875) used here by the author. Elsewhere the Biblical quotations are taken from the AV and occasionally from the RSV and the DV. Following are the Greek and Latin (Vulgate) versions of the italicized portion of this passage.—TRANS.]

"... *τοῦτο μού ἐστιν τὸ σῶμα τὸ ὑπὲρ ὑμῶν. τοῦτο ποιεῖτε εἰς τὴν ἐμὴν ἀνάμνησιν. ὡσαύτως καὶ τὸ ποτήριον μετὰ τὸ δειπνῆσαι λέγων· τοῦτο τὸ ποτήριον ἡ καινὴ διαθήκη ἐστὶν ἐν τῷ ἐμῷ αἵματι.*"

"... hoc est corpus meum, quod pro vobis tradetur: hoc facite in meam commemorationem. Similiter et calicem, postquam coenavit, dicens: Hic calix novum testamentum est in meo sanguine."

3 *δεῖπνον*, 'coena.'

ing of 'blazing' or 'flaring up.' This refers to the leaping sacrificial fire by which the gift offered to the gods was consumed. Originally the food-offering was intended for the nourishment of the gods; the smoke of the burnt sacrifice carried the food up to their heavenly abode. At a later stage the smoke was conceived as a spiritualized form of food-offering; indeed, all through the Christian era up to the Middle Ages, spirit (or *pneuma*) continued to be thought of as a fine, vaporous substance.[4]

303 *Deipnon* means 'meal.' In the first place it is a meal shared by those taking part in the sacrifice, at which the god was believed to be present. It is also a "sacred" meal at which "consecrated" food is eaten, and hence a *sacrifice* (from *sacrificare*, 'to make sacred,' 'to consecrate').

304 The dual meaning of *deipnon* and *thysia* is implicitly contained in the words of the sacrament: "the body which (was given) for you." [5] This may mean either "which was given to you to eat" or, indirectly, "which was given for you to God." The idea of a meal immediately invests the word 'body' with the meaning of σάρξ, 'flesh' (as an edible substance). In Paul, σῶμα and σάρξ are practically identical.[6]

305 Besides the authentic accounts of the institution of the sacrament, we must also consider Hebrews 13:10–15 as a possible source for the Mass:

> We have an altar, whereof they have no right to eat which serve the tabernacle. For the bodies of those beasts, whose blood is brought into the sanctuary by the high priest for sin, are burned without the camp. Wherefore Jesus also, that he might sanctify the people with his own blood, suffered without the gate. Let us go forth therefore unto him without the camp, bearing his reproach. For here have we no continuing city, but we seek one to come. By him therefore let us offer the sacrifice of praise to God continually. . . .

306 As a further source we might mention Hebrews 7:17: "Thou art a priest for ever after the order of Melchisedec." [7] The idea

4 This of course has nothing to do with the official conception of spirit by the Church. 5 "τὸ σῶμα τὸ ὑπὲρ ὑμῶν."

6 Käsemann, *Leib und Leib Christi*, p. 120.

7 Dr. Jud kindly drew my attention to the equally relevant passage in Malachi 1:10–11: "Who is there even among you that would shut the doors for nought? neither do ye kindle fire on mine altar for nought. . . . And in every place incense shall be offered unto my name, and a pure offering . . ."

of perpetual sacrifice and of an eternal priesthood is an essential component of the Mass. Melchisedec, who according to Hebrews 7:3 was "without father, without mother, without descent, having neither beginning of days, nor end of life, but made like unto the Son of God," was believed to be a pre-Christian incarnation of the Logos.

307 The idea of an eternal priesthood and of a sacrifice offered to God "continually" brings us to the true *mysterium fidei,* the transformation of the substances, which is the third aspect of the Mass. The ideas of *deipnon* and *thysia* do not in themselves imply or contain a mystery, although, in the burnt offering which is reduced to smoke and ashes by the fire, there is a primitive allusion to a transformation of substance in the sense of its spiritualization. But this aspect is of no practical importance in the Mass, where it only appears in subsidiary form in the censing, as an incense-offering. The *mysterium,* on the other hand, manifests itself clearly enough in the eternal priest "after the order of Melchisedec" and in the sacrifice which he offers to God "continually." The manifestation of an order outside time involves the idea of a *miracle* which takes place "vere, realiter, substantialiter" at the moment of transubstantiation, for the substances offered are no different from natural objects, and must in fact be definite commodities whose nature is known to everybody, namely pure wheaten bread and wine. Furthermore, the officiating priest is an ordinary human being who, although he bears the indelible mark of the priesthood upon him and is thus empowered to offer sacrifice, is nevertheless not yet in a position to be the instrument of the divine self-sacrifice enacted in the Mass.[8] Nor is the congregation standing behind him yet purged from sin, consecrated, and itself transformed into a sacrificial gift. The ritual of the Mass takes this situation and transforms it step by step until the climax is reached—the Conse-

[8] That is to say, not before he has accomplished the preparatory part of the service. In offering these gifts the priest is not the "master" of the sacrifice. "Rather that which causes them to be sacrificed in the first place is sanctifying grace. For that is what their sacrifice means: their sanctification. The man who each time performs the sacred act is the servant of grace, and that is why the gifts and their sacrifice are always pleasing to God. The fact that the servant may be bad does not affect them in any way. The priest is only the servant, and even this he has from grace, not from himself." Joseph Kramp, S.J., *Die Opferanschauungen der römischen Messliturgie,* p. 148.

cration, when Christ himself, as sacrificer and sacrificed, speaks the decisive words through the mouth of the priest. At that moment Christ is present in time and space. Yet his presence is not a reappearance, and therefore the inner meaning of the consecration is not a repetition of an event which occurred once in history, but the revelation of something existing in eternity, a rending of the evil of temporal and spatial limitations which separates the human spirit from the sight of the eternal. This event is necessarily a mystery, because it is beyond the power of man to conceive or describe. In other words, the rite is necessarily and in every one of its parts a *symbol.* Now a symbol is not an arbitrary or intentional sign standing for a known and conceivable fact, but an admittedly anthropomorphic—hence limited and only partly valid—expression for something suprahuman and only partly conceivable. It may be the best expression possible, yet it ranks below the level of the mystery it seeks to describe. The Mass is a symbol in this sense. Here I would like to quote the words of Father Kramp: "It is generally admitted that the sacrifice is a *symbolic* act, by which I mean that the offering of a material gift to God has no purpose in itself, but merely serves as a means to express an idea. And the choice of this means of expression brings a wide range of anthropomorphism into play: man confronts God as he confronts his own kind, almost as if God were a human being. We offer a gift to God as we offer it to a good friend or to an earthly ruler." [9]

308 In so far, then, as the Mass is an anthropomorphic symbol standing for something otherworldly and beyond our power to conceive, its symbolism is a legitimate subject for comparative psychology and analytical research. My psychological explanations are, of course, exclusively concerned with the symbolical expression.

9 Ibid., p. 17.

2. THE SEQUENCE OF THE TRANSFORMATION RITE

309 The rite of transformation may be said to begin with the Offertory, an antiphon recited during the offering of the sacrificial gifts. Here we encounter the first ritual act relating to the transformation.[1]

I. OBLATION OF THE BREAD

310 The Host is lifted up towards the cross on the altar, and the priest makes the sign of the cross over it with the paten. The bread is thus brought into relation with Christ and his death on the cross; it is marked as a "sacrifice" and thereby becomes sacred. The elevation exalts it into the realm of the spiritual: it is a preliminary act of spiritualization. Justin makes the interesting remark that the presentation of the cleansed lepers in the temple was an image of the Eucharistic bread.[2] This links up with the later alchemical idea of the imperfect or "leprous" substance which is made perfect by the *opus*. (*Quod natura relinquit imperfectum, arte perficitur.*—"What nature leaves imperfect is perfected by the art.")

1 In the account that follows I have made extensive use of Brinktrine, *Die Heilige Messe in ihrem Werden und Wesen.*

2 "Τύπος τοῦ ἄρτου τῆς εὐχαριστίας."

II. PREPARATION OF THE CHALICE

311 This is still more solemn than that of the bread, corresponding to the "spiritual" nature of the wine, which is reserved for the priest.[3] Some water is mingled with the wine.

312 The mixing of water with the wine originally referred to the ancient custom of not drinking wine unless mixed with water. A drunkard was therefore called *akratopotes,* an 'unmixed drinker.' In modern Greek, wine is still called *κρασί* (mixture). From the custom of the Monophysite Armenians, who did not add any water to the Eucharistic wine (so as to preserve the exclusively divine nature of Christ), it may be inferred that water has a hylical, or physical, significance and represents man's material nature. The mixing of water and wine in the Roman rite would accordingly signify that divinity is mingled with humanity as indivisibly as the wine with the water.[4] St. Cyprian (bishop of Carthage, d. 258) says that the wine refers to Christ, and the water to the congregation as the body of Christ. The significance of the water is explained by an allusion to the Book of Revelation 17:15: "The waters which thou sawest, where the whore sitteth, are peoples, and multitudes, and nations, and tongues." (In alchemy, *meretrix* the whore is a synonym for the *prima materia,* the *corpus imperfectum* which is sunk in darkness, like the man who wanders in darkness, unconscious and unredeemed. This idea is foreshadowed in the Gnostic image of Physis, who with passionate arms draws the Nous down from heaven and wraps him in her dark embrace.) As the water is an imperfect or even leprous substance, it has to be blessed and consecrated before being mixed, so that only a purified body may be joined to the wine of the spirit, just as Christ is to be united only with a pure and sanctified congregation. Thus this part of the rite has the special significance of preparing a perfect body—the glorified body of resurrection.

313 At the time of St. Cyprian the communion was generally celebrated with water.[5] And, still later, St. Ambrose (bishop of

[3] That is, in the Roman rite. In the Greek Uniate rites, communion is received in bread *and* wine.

[4] This is the interpretation of Yves, bishop of Chartres (d. 1116).

[5] Cyprian attacks this heretical custom in his letter to Caecilius. Letter 63 to Caecilius, Migne, *P.L.,* vol. 4, cols. 372ff. (trans. by Carey, pp. 181ff.).

Milan, d. 397) says: "In the shadow there was water from the rock, as it were the blood of Christ." [6] The water communion is prefigured in John 7:37–39: "If any man thirst, let him come unto me, and drink. He that believeth on me, as the scripture hath said, out of his belly flow rivers of living water. (But this he spake of the Spirit, which they that believe on him should receive: for the Holy Ghost was not yet given, because that Jesus was not yet glorified.)" And also in John 4:14: "But whosoever drinketh of the water that I shall give him shall never thirst; but the water that I shall give him shall be in him a well of water springing up into everlasting life." The words "as the scripture hath said, out of his belly shall flow rivers of living water" do not occur anywhere in the Old Testament. They must therefore come from a writing which the author of the Johannine gospel obviously regarded as holy, but which is not known to us. It is just possible that they are based on Isaiah 58:11: "And the Lord shall guide thee continually, and satisfy thy soul in drought, and make fat thy bones: and thou shalt be like a watered garden, and like a spring of water, whose waters fail not." Another possibility is Ezekiel 47:1: "Afterward he brought me again unto the door of the house; and, behold, waters issued out from under the threshold of the house eastward . . . and the waters came down from under from the right side of the house, at the south side of the altar." In the Church Order of Hippolytus (d. *c.* 235) the water chalice is associated with the baptismal font, where the inner man is renewed as well as the body.[7] This interpretation comes very close to the baptismal *krater* of Poimandres [8] and to the Hermetic basin filled with *nous* which God gave to those seeking ἔννοια.[9] Here the water signifies the *pneuma,* i.e., the spirit of prophecy, and also the doctrine which a man receives

[6] "In umbra erat aqua de petra quasi sanguis ex Christo." The *umbra,* 'shadow,' refers to the foreshadowing in the Old Testament, in accordance with the saying: "Umbra in lege, imago in evangelio, veritas in coelestibus" (The shadow in the Law, the image in the Gospel, the truth in Heaven). Note that this remark of Ambrose does not refer to the Eucharist but to the water symbolism of early Christianity in general; and the same is true of the passages from John. St. Augustine himself says: "There the rock was Christ; for to us that is Christ which is placed on the altar of God." *Tractatus in Joannem,* XLV, 9 (trans. by Innes).

[7] Connolly, ed., *The So-called Egyptian Church Order and Derived Documents.*

[8] Berthelot, *Collection des anciens alchimistes grecs,* III, li. 8.

[9] *Corpus Hermeticum,* Lib. IV, 4, in *Hermetica,* I, p. 151.

and passes on to others.[10] The same image of the spiritual water occurs in the "Odes of Solomon": [11]

For there went forth a stream, and became a river great and broad; . . . and all the thirsty upon earth were given to drink of it; and thirst was relieved and quenched; for from the Most High the draught was given. Blessed then are the ministers of that draught who are entrusted with that water of His; they have assuaged the dry lips, and the will that had fainted they have raised up; and souls that were near departing they have caught back from death; and limbs that had fallen they straightened and set up; they gave strength for their feebleness and light to their eyes. For everyone knew them in the Lord, and they lived by the water of life for ever.[12]

4 The fact that the Eucharist was also celebrated with water shows that the early Christians were mainly interested in the symbolism of the mysteries and not in the literal observance of the sacrament. (There were several other variants—"galactophagy," for instance—which all bear out this view.)

5 Another, very graphic, interpretation of the wine and water is the reference to John 19:34: "And forthwith came there out blood and water." Deserving of special emphasis is the remark of St. John Chrysostom (patriarch of Constantinople, d. 407), that in drinking the wine Christ drank his own blood. (See Section III, on Zosimos.)

6 In this section of the Mass we meet the important prayer:

O God, who in creating human nature, didst wonderfully dignify it, and hast still more wonderfully renewed it; grant that, by the mystery of this water and wine, we may be made partakers of his divinity who vouchsafed to become partaker of our humanity, Jesus Christ. . . .[13]

10 Strack and Billerbeck, *Kommentar zum Neuen Testament aus Talmud und Midrasch,* II, p. 492.

11 A collection of Gnostic hymns from the 2nd cent.

12 Ode VI in *The Odes of Solomon,* ed. Bernard, p. 55, after the J. Rendel Harris version. Cf. the ὕδωρ θεῖον, the *aqua permanens* of early alchemy, also the treatise of Komarius (Berthelot, IV, xx).

13 "Deus, qui humanae substantiae dignitatem mirabiliter condidisti, et mirabilius reformasti; da nobis per huius aquae et vini mysterium, eius divinitatis esse consortes, qui humanitatis nostrae fieri dignatus est particeps, Jesus Christus . . ." [Here and throughout this essay the English translation is taken from *The Small Missal,* London, 1924.—TRANS.]

III. ELEVATION OF THE CHALICE

317 The lifting up of the chalice in the air prepares the spiritualization (i.e., volatilization) of the wine.[14] This is confirmed by the invocation to the Holy Ghost which immediately follows (*Veni sanctificator*), and it is even more evident in the Mozarabic liturgy, which has "Veni spiritus sanctificator." [15] The invocation serves to infuse the wine with holy spirit, for it is the Holy Ghost who begets, fulfils, and transforms (cf. the "Obumbratio Mariae," Pentecostal fire). After the elevation, the chalice was, in former times, set down to the right of the Host, to correspond with the blood that flowed from the right side of Christ.

IV. CENSING OF THE SUBSTANCES AND THE ALTAR

318 The priest makes the sign of the cross three times over the substances with the thurible, twice from right to left and once from left to right.[16] The counterclockwise movement (from right to left) corresponds psychologically to a circumambulation downwards, in the direction of the unconscious, while the clockwise (left-to-right) movement goes in the direction of consciousness. There is also a complicated censing of the altar.[17]

319 The censing has the significance of an incense offering and is therefore a relic of the original *thysia.* At the same time it signifies a transformation of the sacrificial gifts and of the altar, a spiritualization of all the physical substances subserving the rite. Finally, it is an apotropaic ceremony to drive away any demonic forces that may be present, for it fills the air with the fragrance of the *pneuma* and renders it uninhabitable by evil spirits. The vapour also suggests the sublimated body, the *corpus volatile sive spirituale,* or wraithlike "subtle body." Rising up as a "spiritual" substance, the incense implements and represents the ascent of

14 This is *my* interpretation and not that of the Church, which sees in this only an act of devotion.

15 "Mozarabic" from Arabic *musta'rib,* 'Arabianized,' with reference to the Visigothic-Spanish form of ritual. [The Latin phrases: "Come, O sanctifying one." "Come, O sanctifying spirit."—EDITORS.]

16 The circumambulation from left to right is strictly observed in Buddhism.

17 The censing is only performed at High Mass.

prayer—hence the *Dirigatur, Domine, oratio mea, sicut incensum, in conspectu tuo.*[18]

320 The censing brings the preparatory, spiritualizing rites to an end. The gifts have been sanctified and prepared for the actual transubstantiation. Priest and congregation are likewise purified by the prayers *Accendat in nobis Dominus ignem sui amoris* and *Lavabo inter innocentes,*[19] and are made ready to enter into the mystic union of the sacrificial act which now follows.

V. THE EPICLESIS

321 The *Suscipe, sancta Trinitas,* like the *Orate, fratres,* the *Sanctus,* and the *Te igitur,* is a propitiatory prayer which seeks to insure the acceptance of the sacrifice. Hence the Preface that comes after the Secret is called *Illatio* in the Mozarabic rite (the equivalent of the Greek ἀναφορά), and in the old Gallican liturgy is known as *Immolatio* (in the sense of *oblatio*), with reference to the presentation of the gifts. The words of the *Sanctus,* "Benedictus qui venit in nomine Domini," [20] point to the expected appearance of the Lord which has already been prepared, on the ancient principle that a "naming" has the force of a "summons." After the Canon there follows the "Commemoration of the Living," together with the prayers *Hanc igitur* and *Quam oblationem.* In the Mozarabic Mass these are followed by the Epiclesis (invocation): "Adesto, adesto Jesu, bone Pontifix, in medio nostri: sicut fuisti in medio discipulorum tuorum." [21] This naming likewise has the original force of a summons. It is an intensification of the *Benedictus qui venit,* and it may be, and sometimes was, regarded as the actual manifestation of the Lord, and hence as the culminating point of the Mass.

18 ["Let my prayer, O Lord, ascend like incense in thy sight."]

19 ["May the Lord enkindle in us the fire of his love." / "I will wash my hands among the innocent."]

20 ["Blessed is he that cometh in the name of the Lord."]

21 ["Be present, be present in our midst, O Jesus, great High Priest: as thou wert in the midst of thy disciples."]

VI. THE CONSECRATION

322 This, in the Roman Mass, is the climax, the transubstantiation of the bread and wine into the body and blood of Christ. The formula for the consecration of the bread runs: [22]

Qui pridie quam pateretur, accepit panem in sanctas ac venerabiles manus suas, et elevatis oculis in caelum ad te Deum, Patrem suum omnipotentem, tibi gratias agens, benedixit, fregit, deditque discipulis suis, dicens: Accipite, et manducate ex hoc omnes. Hoc est enim Corpus meum.

And for the consecration of the chalice:

Simili modo postquam coenatum est, accipiens et hunc praeclarum Calicem in sanctas ac venerabiles manus suas, item tibi gratias agens, benedixit, deditque discipulis suis, dicens: Accipite, et bibite ex eo omnes. Hic est enim Calix Sanguinis mei, novi et aeterni testamenti: mysterium fidei: qui pro vobis et pro multis effundetur in remissionem peccatorum. Haec quotiescumque feceritis, in mei memoriam facietis.

323 The priest and congregation, as well as the substances and the altar, have now been progressively purified, consecrated, exalted, and spiritualized by means of the prayers and rites which began with the Preliminaries and ended with the Canon, and are thus prepared as a mystical unity for the divine epiphany. Hence the uttering of the words of the consecration signifies Christ himself speaking in the first person, his living presence in the *corpus mysticum* of priest, congregation, bread, wine, and incense, which together form the mystical unity offered for sacrifice. At this moment the eternal character of the one divine sacrifice is made evident: it is experienced at a particular time and a particular place, as if a window or a door had been opened upon that which lies beyond space and time. It is in this sense that we have to understand the words of St. Chrysostom: "And this word once uttered in any church, at any altar, makes perfect the sacrifice from that day to this, and till his Second Coming." It is clear that only by our Lord's presence in his words, and by their virtue, is the imperfect body of the sacrifice made perfect,

[22] According to the edict of the Church these words ought not, on account of their sacredness, to be translated into any profane tongue. Although there are missals that sin against this wise edict, I would prefer the Latin text to stand untranslated.

and not by the preparatory action of the priest. Were this the efficient cause, the rite would be no different from common magic. The priest is only the *causa ministerialis* of the transubstantiation. The real cause is the living presence of Christ which operates spontaneously, as an act of divine grace.

4 Accordingly, John of Damascus (d. 754) says that the words have a consecrating effect no matter by what priest they be spoken, as if Christ were present and uttering them himself. And Duns Scotus (d. 1308) remarks that, in the sacrament of the Last Supper, Christ, by an act of will, offers himself as a sacrifice in every Mass, through the agency of the priest.[23] This tells us plainly enough that the sacrificial act is not performed by the priest, but by Christ himself. The agent of transformation is nothing less than the divine will working through Christ. The Council of Trent declared that in the sacrifice of the Mass "the selfsame Christ is contained and bloodlessly sacrificed," [24] although this is not a repetition of the historical sacrifice but a bloodless renewal of it. As the sacramental words have the power to accomplish the sacrifice, being an expression of God's will, they can be described metaphorically as the sacrificial knife or sword which, guided by his will, consummates the *thysia*. This comparison was first drawn by the Jesuit father Lessius (d. 1623), and has since gained acceptance as an ecclesiastical figure of speech. It is based on Hebrews 4:12: "For the word of God is quick, and powerful, and sharper than any two-edged sword," and perhaps even more on the Book of Revelation 1:16: "And out of his mouth went a sharp two-edged sword." The "mactation theory" first appeared in the sixteenth century. Its originator, Cuesta, bishop of Leon (d. 1560), declared that Christ was slaughtered by the priest. So the sword metaphor followed quite naturally.[25] Nicholas Cabasilas, archbishop of Thessalonica (d.

[23] Klug, in *Theologie und Glaube,* XVIII (1926), 335f. Cited by Brinktrine, p. 192.

[24] "idem ille Christus continetur et incruente immolatur." Sessio XXII. Denzinger and Bannwart, *Enchiridion Symbolorum,* p. 312.

[25] "Missa est sacrificium hac ratione quia Christus aliquo modo moritur et a sacerdote mactatur" (The Mass is a sacrifice for the reason that in it Christ dies after a certain manner, and is slain by the priest). Hauck, *Realenzyklopädie,* XII, p. 693. The question of the *mactatio* had already been raised by Nicholas Cabasilas of Thessalonica: "De divino altaris sacrificio," in Migne, *P.G.,* vol. 150, cols. 363ff. The sword as a sacrificial instrument also occurs in the Zosimos visions (see section III).

c. 1363), gives a vivid description of the corresponding rite in the Greek Orthodox Church:

The priest cuts a piece of bread from the loaf, reciting the text: "As a lamb he was led to the slaughter." Laying it on the table he says: "The lamb of God is slain." Then a sign of the cross is imprinted on the bread and a small lance is stabbed into its side, to the text: "And one of the soldiers with a spear pierced his side, and forthwith came there out blood and water." With these words water and wine are mixed in the chalice, which is placed beside the bread.

The δῶρον (gift) also represents the giver; that is to say, Christ is both the sacrificer and the sacrificed.

325 Kramp writes: "Sometimes the *fractio* and sometimes the *elevatio* which precedes the Pater noster was taken as symbolizing the death of Christ, sometimes the sign of the cross at the end of the *Supplices,* and sometimes the *consecratio;* but no one ever thought of taking a symbol like the 'mystical slaughter' as a sacrifice which constitutes the essence of the Mass. So it is not surprising that there is no mention of any 'slaughter' in the liturgy." [26]

VII. THE GREATER ELEVATION

326 The consecrated substances are lifted up and shown to the congregation. The Host in particular represents a beatific vision of heaven, in fulfilment of Psalm 27:8: "Thy face, Lord, will I seek," for in it the Divine Man is present.

VIII. THE POST-CONSECRATION

327 There now follows the significant prayer *Unde et memores,* which I give in full together with the *Supra quae* and *Supplices:*

Wherefore, O Lord, we thy servants, as also thy holy people, calling to mind the blessed passion of the same Christ thy Son our Lord, his resurrection from hell, and glorious ascension into heaven, offer unto thy most excellent majesty, of thy gifts and grants, a pure Host, a holy Host, an immaculate Host, the holy bread of eternal life, and the chalice of everlasting salvation.

26 Kramp, p. 56.

Upon which vouchsafe to look down with a propitious and serene countenance, and to accept them, as thou wert graciously pleased to accept the gifts of thy just servant Abel, and the sacrifice of our patriarch Abraham, and that which thy high priest Melchisedec offered to thee, a holy sacrifice, an immaculate Host.

We most humbly beseech thee, almighty God, command these things to be carried by the hands of thy holy angel to thy altar on high, in the sight of thy divine majesty, that as many of us as, by participation at this altar, shall receive the most sacred body and blood of thy Son, may be filled with all heavenly benediction and grace. Through the same Christ, our Lord. Amen.[27]

28 The first prayer shows that in the transformed substances there is an allusion to the resurrection and glorification of our Lord, and the second prayer recalls the sacrifices prefigured in the Old Testament. Abel sacrificed a lamb; Abraham was to sacrifice his son, but a ram was substituted at the last moment. Melchisedec offers no sacrifice, but comes to meet Abraham with bread and wine. This sequence is probably not accidental—it forms a sort of crescendo. Abel is essentially the son, and sacrifices an animal; Abraham is essentially the father—indeed, the "tribal father"—and therefore on a higher level. He does not offer a choice possession merely, but is ready to sacrifice the best and dearest thing he has—his only son. Melchisedec ("teacher of righteousness"), is, according to Hebrews 7:1, king of Salem and "priest of the most high God," El 'Elyon. Philo Byblius mentions a Ἐλιοῦν ὁ ὕψιστος as a Canaanite deity,[28] but he cannot be identical with Yahweh. Abraham nevertheless acknowledges the

[27] "Unde et memores, Domine, nos servi tui, sed et plebs tua sancta, eiusdem Christi Filii tui, Domini nostri, tam beatae passionis, nec non et ab inferis resurrectionis, sed et in caelos gloriosae ascensionis: offerimus praeclarae majestati tuae de tuis donis ac datis, hostiam puram, hostiam sanctam, hostiam immaculatam, Panem sanctum vitae aeternae, et Calicem salutis perpetuae.

"Supra quae propitio ac sereno vultu respicere digneris: et accepta habere, sicuti accepta habere dignatus es munera pueri tui justi Abel, et sacrificium Patriarchae nostri Abrahae: et quod tibi obtulit summus sacerdos tuus Melchisedech, sanctum sacrificium, immaculatam hostiam.

"Supplices te rogamus, omnipotens Deus: jube haec perferri per manus sancti Angeli tui in sublime altare tuum, in conspectu divinae majestatis tuae: ut, quotquot ex hac altaris participatione sacrosanctum Filii tui corpus, et sanguinem sumpserimus, omni benedictione caelesti et gratia repleamur. Per eundem Christum, Dominum nostrum. Amen."

[28] Eusebius, *Evangelica praeparatio,* I, 10, 11 (Migne, *P.G.,* vol. 21, col. 30).

priesthood of Melchisedec[29] by paying him "a tenth part of all." By virtue of his priesthood, Melchisedec stands above the patriarch, and his feasting of Abraham has the significance of a priestly act. We must therefore attach a symbolical meaning to it, as is in fact suggested by the bread and wine. Consequently the symbolical offering ranks even higher than the sacrifice of a son, which is still the sacrifice of somebody else. Melchisedec's offering is thus a prefiguration of Christ's sacrifice of himself.

329 In the prayer *Supplices te rogamus* we beseech God to bring the gifts "by the hands of thy holy angel to thy altar on high." This singular request derives from the apocryphal *Epistolae Apostolorum,* where there is a legend that Christ, before he became incarnate, bade the archangels take his place at God's altar during his absence.[30] This brings out the idea of the eternal priesthood which links Christ with Melchisedec.

IX. END OF THE CANON

330 Taking up the Host, the priest makes the sign of the cross three times over the chalice, and says: "Through Him, and with Him, and in Him." Then he makes the sign of the cross twice between himself and the chalice. This establishes the identity of Host, chalice, and priest, thus affirming once more the unity of all parts of the sacrifice. The union of Host and chalice signifies the union of the body and blood, i.e., the quickening of the body with a soul, for blood is equivalent to soul. Then follows the *Pater noster.*

X. BREAKING OF THE HOST ("FRACTIO")

331 The prayer "Deliver us, O Lord, we beseech thee, from all evils, past, present, and to come" lays renewed emphasis on the petition made in the preceding *Pater noster:* "but deliver us from evil." The connection between this and the sacrificial death of Christ lies in the descent into hell and the breaking of the

29 "Sidik" is a Phoenician name for God. Sir Leonard Woolley gives a very interesting explanation of this in his report on the excavations at Ur: *Abraham: Recent Discoveries and Hebrew Origins.*

30 Kramp, p. 98.

infernal power. The breaking of the bread that now follows is symbolic of Christ's death. The Host is broken in two over the chalice. A small piece, the *particula,* is broken off from the left half and used for the rite of *consignatio* and *commixtio.* In the Byzantine rite the bread is divided into four, the four pieces being marked with letters as follows:

	ΙΣ	
ΝΙ		ΚΑ
	ΧΣ	

This means "Ἰησοῦς Χριστὸς νικᾷ"—'Jesus Christ is victorious.' The peculiar arrangement of the letters obviously represents a quaternity, which as we know always has the character of wholeness. This quaternity, as the letters show, refers to Christ glorified, king of glory and Pantokrator.

332 Still more complicated is the Mozarabic *fractio:* the Host is first broken into two, then the left half into five parts, and the right into four. The five are named *corporatio* (*incarnatio*), *nativitas, circumcisio, apparitio,* and *passio;* and the four *mors, resurrectio, gloria, regnum.* The first group refers exclusively to the human life of our Lord, the second to his existence beyond this world. According to the old view, five is the number of the natural ("hylical") man, whose outstretched arms and legs form, with the head, a pentagram. Four, on the other hand, signifies eternity and totality (as shown for instance by the Gnostic name "Barbelo," which is translated as "fourness is God"). This symbol, I would add in passing, seems to indicate that extension in space signifies God's suffering (on the cross) and, on the other hand, his dominion over the universe.

XI. CONSIGNATIO

333 The sign of the cross is made over the chalice with the *particula,* and then the priest drops it into the wine.

XII. COMMIXTIO

334 This is the mingling of bread and wine, as explained by Theodore of Mopsuestia (d. 428?): ". . . he combines them into one, whereby it is made manifest to everybody that although

they are two they are virtually one."[31] The text at this point says: "May this mixture and consecration [*commixtio et consecratio*] of the body and blood of our Lord help us," etc. The word 'consecration' may be an allusion to an original consecration by contact, though that would not clear up the contradiction since a consecration of both substances has already taken place. Attention has therefore been drawn to the old custom of holding over the sacrament from one Mass to another, the Host being dipped in wine and then preserved in softened, or mixed, form. There are numerous rites that end with minglings of this kind. Here I would only mention the consecration by water, or the mixed drink of honey and milk which the neophytes were given after communion in the Church Order of Hippolytus.

335 The *Leonine Sacramentary* (seventh century) interprets the *commixtio* as a mingling of the heavenly and earthly nature of Christ. The later view was that it symbolizes the resurrection, since in it the blood (or soul) of our Lord is reunited with the body lying in the sepulchre. There is a significant reversal here of the original rite of baptism. In baptism, the body is immersed in water for the purpose of transformation; in the *commixtio,* on the other hand, the body, or *particula,* is steeped in wine, symbolizing spirit, and this amounts to a glorification of the body. Hence the justification for regarding the *commixtio* as a symbol of the resurrection.

XIII. CONCLUSION

336 On careful examination we find that the sequence of ritual actions in the Mass contains, sometimes clearly and sometimes by subtle allusions, a representation in condensed form of the life and sufferings of Christ. Certain phases overlap or are so close together that there can be no question of conscious and deliberate condensation. It is more likely that the historical evolution of the Mass gradually led to its becoming a concrete picture of the most important aspects of Christ's life. First of all (in the *Benedictus qui venit* and *Supra quae*) we have an anticipation and prefiguration of his coming. The uttering of the words

[31] Rücker, ed., *Ritus baptismi et missae quam descripsit Theodorus ep. Mopsuestanus.*

of consecration corresponds to the incarnation of the Logos, and also to Christ's passion and sacrificial death, which appears again in the *fractio*. In the *Libera nos* there is an allusion to the descent into hell, while the *consignatio* and *commixtio* hint at resurrection.

337 In so far as the offered gift is the sacrificer himself, in so far as the priest and congregation offer themselves in the sacrificial gift, and in so far as Christ is both sacrificer and sacrificed, there is a mystical unity of all parts of the sacrificial act.[32] The combination of offering and offerer in the single figure of Christ is implicit in the doctrine that just as bread is composed of many grains of wheat, and wine of many grapes, so the mystical body of the Church is made up of a multitude of believers. The mystical body, moreover, includes both sexes, represented by the bread and wine.[33] Thus the two substances—the masculine wine and the feminine bread—also signify the androgynous nature of the mystical Christ.

338 The Mass thus contains, as its essential core, the mystery and miracle of God's transformation taking place in the human sphere, his becoming Man, and his return to his absolute existence in and for himself. Man, too, by his devotion and self-sacrifice as a ministering instrument, is included in the mysterious process. God's offering of himself is a voluntary act of love, but the actual sacrifice was an agonizing and bloody death brought about by men *instrumentaliter et ministerialiter*. (The words *incruente immolatur*—'bloodlessly sacrificed'—refer only to the rite, not to the thing symbolized.) The terrors of death on the cross are an indispensable condition for the transformation. This is in the first place a bringing to life of substances which are in themselves lifeless, and, in the second, a substantial alteration of them, a spiritualization, in accordance with the ancient conception of *pneuma* as a subtle material entity (the *corpus glorificationis*). This idea is expressed in the concrete participation in the body and blood of Christ in the Communion.

32 This unity is a good example of *participation mystique*, which Lévy-Bruhl stressed as being one of the main characteristics of primitive psychology—a view that has recently been contested by ethnologists in a very short-sighted manner. The idea of unity should not, however, be regarded as "primitive" but rather as showing that *participation mystique* is a characteristic of symbols in general. The symbol always includes the unconscious, hence man too is contained in it. The *numinosity* of the symbol is an expression of this fact.

33 Kramp, p. 55.

3. PARALLELS TO THE TRANSFORMATION MYSTERY

I. THE AZTEC "TEOQUALO"

339 Although the Mass itself is a unique phenomenon in the history of comparative religion, its symbolic content would be profoundly alien to man were it not rooted in the human psyche. But if it is so rooted, then we may expect to find similar patterns of symbolism both in the earlier history of mankind and in the world of pagan thought contemporary with it. As the prayer *Supra quae* shows, the liturgy of the Mass contains allusions to the "prefigurations" in the Old Testament, and thus indirectly to ancient sacrificial symbolism in general. It is clear, then, that in Christ's sacrifice and the Communion one of the deepest chords in the human psyche is struck: human sacrifice and ritual anthropophagy. Unfortunately I cannot enter into the wealth of ethnological material in question here, so must content myself with mentioning the ritual slaying of the king to promote the fertility of the land and the prosperity of his people, the renewal and revivification of the gods through human sacrifice, and the totem meal, the purpose of which was to reunite the participants with the life of their ancestors. These hints will suffice to show how the symbols of the Mass penetrate into the deepest layers of the psyche and its history. They are evidently

among the most ancient and most central of religious conceptions. Now with regard to these conceptions there is still a widespread prejudice, not only among laymen, but in scientific circles too, that beliefs and customs of this kind must have been "invented" at some time or other, and were then handed down and imitated, so that they would not exist at all in most places unless they had got there in the manner suggested. It is, however, always precarious to draw conclusions from our modern, "civilized" mentality about the primitive state of mind. Primitive consciousness differs from that of the present-day white man in several very important respects. Thus, in primitive societies, "inventing" is very different from what it is with us, where one novelty follows another. With primitives, life goes on in the same way for generations; nothing alters, except perhaps the language. But that does not mean that a new one is "invented." Their language is "alive" and can therefore change, a fact that has been an unpleasant discovery for many lexicographers of primitive languages. Similarly, no one "invents" the picturesque slang spoken in America; it just springs up in inexhaustible abundance from the fertile soil of colloquial speech. Religious rites and their stock of symbols must have developed in much the same way from beginnings now lost to us, and not just in one place only, but in many places at once, and also at different periods. They have grown spontaneously out of the basic conditions of human nature, which are never invented but are everywhere the same.

340 So it is not surprising that we find religious rites which come very close to Christian practices in a field untouched by classical culture. I mean the rites of the Aztecs, and in particular that of the *teoqualo,* 'god-eating,' as recorded by Fray Bernardino de Sahagún, who began his missionary work among the Aztecs in 1529, eight years after the conquest of Mexico. In this rite, a doughlike paste was made out of the crushed and pounded seeds of the prickly poppy (*Argemone mexicana*) and moulded into the figure of the god Huitzilopochtli:

> And upon the next day the body of Huitzilopochtli died.
>
> And he who slew him was the priest known as Quetzalcoatl. And that with which he slew him was a dart, pointed with flint, which he shot into his heart.
>
> He died in the presence of Moctezuma and of the keeper of the

god, who verily spoke to Huitzilopochtli—who verily appeared before him, who indeed could make him offerings; and of four masters of the youths, front rank leaders. Before all of them died Huitzilopochtli.

And when he had died, thereupon they broke up his body of . . . dough. His heart was apportioned to Moctezuma.

And as for the rest of his members, which were made, as it were, to be his bones, they were distributed and divided up among all. . . . Each year . . . they ate it. . . . And when they divided up among themselves his body made of . . . dough, it was broken up exceeding small, very fine, as small as seeds. The youths ate it.

And of this which they ate, it was said: "The god is eaten." And of those who ate it, it was said: "They guard the god." [1]

341 The idea of a divine body, its sacrifice in the presence of the high priest to whom the god appears and with whom he speaks, the piercing with the spear, the god's death followed by ritual dismemberment, and the eating (*communio*) of a small piece of his body, are all parallels which cannot be overlooked and which caused much consternation among the worthy Spanish Fathers at the time.

342 In Mithraism, a religion that sprang up not long before Christianity, we find a special set of sacrificial symbols and, it would seem, a corresponding ritual which unfortunately is known to us only from dumb monuments. There is a *transitus*, with Mithras carrying the bull; a bull-sacrifice for seasonal fertility; a stereotyped representation of the sacrificial act, flanked on either side by dadophors carrying raised and lowered torches; and a meal at which pieces of bread marked with crosses were laid on the table. Even small bells have been found, and these probably have some connection with the bell which is sounded at Mass. The Mithraic sacrifice is essentially a self-sacrifice, since the bull is a world bull and was originally identical with Mithras himself. This may account for the singularly agonized expression on the face of the *tauroktonos*,[2] which bears comparison with Guido Reni's *Crucifixion*. The Mithraic *transitus* is a motif that corresponds to Christ carrying the cross, just as the

1 Bernardino de Sahagún, *General History of the Things of New Spain*, Book 3: *The Origin of the Gods*, trans. by Anderson and Dibble, pp. 5f. (slightly modified).
2 Cumont, *Textes et monuments*, I, p. 182. [And cf. Jung, *Symbols of Transformation*, p. 428 and frontispiece.—EDITORS.]

transformation of the beast of sacrifice corresponds to the resurrection of the Christian God in the form of food and drink. The representations of the sacrificial act, the tauroctony (bull-slaying), recall the crucifixion between two thieves, one of whom is raised up to paradise while the other goes down to hell.

343 These few references to the Mithras cult are but one example of the wealth of parallels offered by the legends and rites of the various Near Eastern gods who die young, are mourned, and rise again. For anyone who knows these religions at all, there can be no doubt as to the basic affinity of the symbolic types and ideas.[3] At the time of primitive Christianity and in the early days of the Church, the pagan world was saturated with conceptions of this kind and with philosophical speculations based upon them, and it was against this background that the thought and visionary ideas of the Gnostic philosophers were unfolded.

II. THE VISION OF ZOSIMOS

344 A characteristic representative of this school of thought was Zosimos of Panopolis, a natural philosopher and alchemist of the third century A.D., whose works have been preserved, though in corrupt state, in the famous alchemical Codex Marcianus, and were published in 1887 by Berthelot in his *Collection des anciens alchimistes grecs*. In various portions of his treatises[4] Zosimos relates a number of dream-visions, all of which appear to go back to one and the same dream.[5] He was clearly a non-Christian Gnostic, and in particular—so one gathers from the famous passage about the *krater*[6]—an adherent of the Poimandres sect, and therefore a follower of Hermes. Although alchemical literature abounds in parables, I would hesitate to class these dream-visions among them. Anyone acquainted with the language of the alchemists will recognize that their parables are mere allegories of ideas that were common knowledge. In the allegorical figures and actions, one can usually see at once

3 Cf. Frazer's *The Golden Bough*, Part III: "The Dying God." For the Eucharistic meal of fish, see my *Aion*, Ch. VIII.

4 *Alchimistes*, III, i, 2, 3; III, v; III, vi.

5 Cf. my paper "Some Observations on the Visions of Zosimos," which quotes the relevant passages.

6 *Alchimistes*, III, li. 8.

what substances and what procedures are being referred to under a deliberately theatrical disguise. There is nothing of this kind in the Zosimos visions. Indeed, it comes almost as a surprise to find the alchemical interpretation, namely that the dream and its impressive machinery are simply an illustration of the means for producing the "divine water." Moreover, a parable is a self-contained whole, whereas our vision varies and amplifies a single theme as a dream does. So far as one can assess the nature of these visions at all, I should say that even in the original text the contents of an imaginative meditation have grouped themselves round the kernel of an actual dream and been woven into it. That there really was such a meditation is evident from the fragments of it that accompany the visions in the form of a commentary. As we know, meditations of this kind are often vividly pictorial, as if the dream were being continued on a level nearer to consciousness. In his *Lexicon alchemiae,* Martin Ruland, writing in Frankfort in 1612, defines the meditation that plays such an important part in alchemy as an "internal colloquy with someone else, who is nevertheless not seen, it may be with God, with oneself, or with one's good angel." The latter is a milder and less obnoxious form of the *paredros,* the familiar spirit of ancient alchemy, who was generally a planetary demon conjured up by magic. It can hardly be doubted that real visionary experiences originally lay at the root of these practices, and a vision is in the last resort nothing less than a dream which has broken through into the waking state. We know from numerous witnesses all through the ages that the alchemist, in the course of his imaginative work, was beset by visions of all kinds,[7] and was sometimes even threatened with madness.[8] So the visions of Zosimos are not something unusual or unknown in alchemical experience, though they are perhaps the most important self-revelations ever bequeathed to us by an alchemist.

345 I cannot reproduce here the text of the visions in full, but will give as an example the first vision, in Zosimos' own words:

And while I said this I fell asleep, and I saw a sacrificial priest standing before me, high up on an altar, which was in the shape of a

[7] Cf. the examples given in *Psychology and Alchemy,* pars. 347f.

[8] Olympiodorus says this is particularly the effect of lead. Cf. Berthelot, II, iv, 43.

shallow bowl. There were fifteen steps leading up to the altar. And the priest stood there, and I heard a voice from above say to me: "Behold, I have completed the descent down the fifteen steps of darkness and I have completed the ascent up the steps of light. And he who renews me is the priest, for he cast away the density of the body, and by compelling necessity I am sanctified and now stand in perfection as a spirit [*pneuma*]." And I perceived the voice of him who stood upon the altar, and I inquired of him who he was. And he answered me in a fine voice, saying: "I am Ion, priest of the innermost hidden sanctuary, and I submit myself to an unendurable torment. For there came one in haste at early morning, who overpowered me and pierced me through with the sword and cut me in pieces, yet in such a way that the order of my limbs was preserved. And he drew off the scalp of my head with the sword, which he wielded with strength, and he put the bones and the pieces of flesh together and with his own hand burned them in the fire, until I perceived that I was transformed and had become spirit. And that is my unendurable torment." And even as he spoke this, and I held him by force to converse with me, his eyes became as blood. And he spewed out all his own flesh. And I saw how he changed into a manikin [ἀνθρωπάριον, i.e., an homunculus] who had lost a part of himself. And he tore his flesh with his own teeth, and sank into himself.

16 In the course of the visions the Hiereus (priest) appears in various forms. At first he is split into the figures of the Hiereus and the Hierourgon (sacrificer), who is charged with the performance of the sacrifice. But these figures blend into one in so far as both suffer the same fate. The sacrificial priest submits voluntarily to the torture by which he is transformed. But he is also the sacrificer who is sacrificed, since he is pierced through with the sword and ritually dismembered.[9] The *deipnon* consists in his tearing himself to pieces with his own teeth and eating himself; the *thysia*, in his flesh being sacrificially burned on the altar.

17 He is the Hiereus in so far as he rules over the sacrificial rite as a whole, and over the human beings who are transformed during the *thysia*. He calls himself a guardian of spirits. He is also known as the "Brazen Man" and as Xyrourgos, the barber.

9 The dismemberment motif belongs in the wider context of rebirth symbolism. Consequently it plays an important part in the initiation experiences of shamans and medicine men, who are dismembered and then put together again. For details, see Eliade, *Le Chamanisme,* pp. 47ff.

The brazen or leaden man is an allusion to the spirits of the metals, or planetary demons, as protagonists of the sacrificial drama. In all probability they are *paredroi* who were conjured up by magic, as may be deduced from Zosimos' remark that he "held him by force" to converse with him. The planetary demons are none other than the old gods of Olympus who finally expired only in the eighteenth century, as the "souls of the metals"—or rather, assumed a new shape, since it was in this same century that paganism openly arose for the first time (in the French Revolution).

348 Somewhat more curious is the term 'barber,' which we find in other parts of the visions,[10] for there is no mention of cutting the hair or shaving. There is, however, a scalping, which in our context is closely connected with the ancient rites of flaying and their magical significance.[11] I need hardly mention the flaying of Marsyas, who is an unmistakable parallel to the son-lover of Cybele, namely Attis, the dying god who rises again. In one of the old Attic fertility rites an ox was flayed, stuffed, and set up on its feet. Herodotus (IV, 60) reports a number of flaying ceremonies among the Scythians, and especially scalpings. In general, flaying signifies transformation from a worse state to a better, and hence renewal and rebirth. The best examples are to be found in the religion of ancient Mexico.[12] Thus, in order to renew the moon-goddess a young woman was decapitated and skinned, and a youth then put the skin round him to represent the risen goddess. The prototype of this renewal is the snake casting its skin every year, a phenomenon round which primitive fantasy has always played. In our vision the skinning is restricted to the head, and this can probably be explained by the underlying idea of spiritual transformation. Since olden times shaving the head has been associated with consecration,

10 [Cf. Berthelot, III, i, 3 and v, 1–3; and Jung, "Visions of Zosimos" (Swiss edn., pp. 141–47).—EDITORS.]

11 Cf. Frazer's *The Golden Bough,* Part IV: *Adonis, Attis, Osiris,* pp. 242ff. and p. 405, and my *Symbols of Transformation,* pars. 594f. Cf. also Colin Campbell, *The Miraculous Birth of King Amon-Hotep III,* p. 142, concerning the presentation of the dead man, Sen-nezem, before Osiris, Lord of Amentet: "In this scene the god is usually represented enthroned. Before and behind him, hanging from a pole, is the dripping skin of a slain bull that was slaughtered to yield up the soul of Osiris at his reconstruction, with the vase underneath to catch the blood."

12 Cf. Eduard Seler's account in Hastings, *Encyclopedia,* VIII, pp. 615f.

that is, with spiritual transformation or initiation. The priests of Isis had their heads shaved quite bald, and the tonsure, as we know, is still in use at the present day. This "symptom" of transformation goes back to the old idea that the transformed one becomes like a new-born babe (neophyte, *quasimodogenitus*) with a hairless head. In the myth of the night sea journey, the hero loses all his hair during his incubation in the belly of the monster, because of the terrific heat.[13] The custom of tonsure, which is derived from these primitive ideas, naturally presupposes the presence of a ritual barber.[14] Curiously enough, we come across the barber in that old alchemical "mystery," the *Chymical Wedding* of 1616.[15] There the hero, on entering the mysterious castle, is pounced on by invisible barbers, who give him something very like a tonsure.[16] Here again the initiation and transformation process is accompanied by a shaving.[17]

349 In one variant of these visions there is a dragon who is killed and sacrificed in the same manner as the priest and therefore seems to be identical with him. This makes one think of those far from uncommon medieval pictures, not necessarily alchemical, in which a serpent is shown hanging on the Cross in place of Christ. (Note the comparison of Christ with the serpent of Moses in John 3:14.)

350 A notable aspect of the priest is the leaden homunculus, and this is none other than the leaden spirit or planetary demon Saturn. In Zosimos' day Saturn was regarded as a Hebrew god,

13 Frobenius, *Das Zeitalter des Sonnengottes,* p. 30.

14 Barbers were comparatively well-to-do people in ancient Egypt, and evidently did a flourishing trade. Cf. Erman, *Life in Ancient Egypt,* p. 304: "Barbers, all of whom must . . . have lived in easy circumstances."

15 [The *Chymische Hochzeit,* dated 1459, actually published at Strasbourg, 1616. Signed "Christian Rosencreutz," but really written by Johann Valentin Andreae, as Professor Jung states elsewhere.—EDITORS.]

16 As Andreae must have been a learned alchemist, he might very well have got hold of a copy of the Codex Marcianus and seen the writings of Zosimos. Manuscript copies exist in Gotha, Leipzig, Munich, and Weimar. I know of only one printed edition, published in Italy in the 16th cent., which is very rare.

17 Hence the "shaving of a man" and the "plucking of a fowl," mentioned further on among the magical sacrificial recipes. A similar motif is suggested by the "changing of wigs" at the Egyptian judgment of the dead. Cf. the picture in the tomb of Sennezem (Campbell, p. 143). When the dead man is led before Osiris his wig is black; immediately afterwards (at the sacrifice in the Papyrus of Ani) it is white.

presumably on account of the keeping holy of the Sabbath—Saturday means 'Saturn's Day' [18]—and also on account of the Gnostic parallel with the supreme archon Ialdabaoth ('child of chaos') who, as λεοντοειδής, may be grouped together with Baal, Kronos, and Saturn.[19] The later Arabic designation of Zosimos as al-'Ibrî (the Hebrew) does not of course prove that he himself was a Jew, but it is clear from his writings that he was acquainted with Jewish traditions.[20] The parallel between the Hebrew god and Saturn is of considerable importance as regards the alchemical idea of the transformation of the God of the Old Testament into the God of the New. The alchemists naturally attached great significance to Saturn,[21] for, besides being the outermost planet, the supreme archon (the Harranites named him "Primas"), and the demiurge Ialdabaoth, he was also the *spiritus niger* who lies captive in the darkness of matter, the deity or that part of the deity which has been swallowed up in his own creation. He is the dark god who reverts to his original luminous state in the mystery of alchemical transmutation. As the *Aurora consurgens* (Part I) says: "Blessed is he who has discovered this science and on whom the providence of Saturn flows." [22]

351 The later alchemists were familiar not only with the ritual slaying of a dragon but also with the slaying of a lion, which took the form of his having all four paws cut off. Like the dragon, the lion devours himself, and so is probably only a variant.[23]

18 Plutarch, *Quaestiones convivales,* IV, 5, and Diogenes Laertius, II, §112; Reitzenstein, *Poimandres,* pp. 75f. and 112. In a text named "Ghāya al-hakīm," ascribed to Maslama al-Madjrītī, the following instructions are given when invoking Saturn: "Arrive vêtu à la manière des Juifs, car il est leur patron." Dozy and de Goeje, "Nouveaux documents pour l'étude de la religion des Harraniens," p. 350.

19 Origen, *Contra Celsum,* VI, 31. Mead, *Pistis Sophia,* ch. 45. Bousset, *Hauptprobleme der Gnosis,* pp. 351ff. Roscher, *Lexikon,* s.v. Kronos, II, col. 1496. The dragon (κρόνος) and Kronos are often confused.

20 Lippmann, *Entstehung und Ausbreitung der Alchemie,* II, p. 229.

21 Cf. *Aion,* par. 128 (Swiss edn., pp. 114ff.).

22 "Beatus homo qui invenerit hanc scientiam et cui affluit providentia Saturni."

23 See the illustration in Reusner, *Pandora* (1588), and in the frontispiece to *Le Songe de Poliphile,* trans. by Béroalde de Verville (1600). Generally the pictures show two lions eating one another. The uroboros, too, is often pictured in the form of two dragons engaged in the same process (*Viridarium chymicum,* 1624).

352 The vision itself indicates that the main purpose of the transformation process is the spiritualization of the sacrificing priest: he is to be changed into *pneuma*. We are also told that he would "change the bodies into blood, make the eyes to see and the dead to rise again." Later in the visions he appears in glorified form, shining white like the midday sun.

353 Throughout the visions it is clear that sacrificer and sacrificed are one and the same. This idea of the unity of the *prima* and *ultima materia,* of that which redeems and that which is to be redeemed, pervades the whole of alchemy from beginning to end. "Unus est lapis, una medicina, unum vas, unum regimen, unaque dispositio" is the key formula to its enigmatic language.[24] Greek alchemy expresses the same idea in the formula ἕν τὸ πᾶν. Its symbol is the uroboros, the tail-eating serpent. In our vision it is the priest as sacrificer who devours himself as the sacrifice. This recalls the saying of St. John Chrysostom that in the Eucharist Christ drinks his own blood. By the same token, one might add, he eats his own flesh. The grisly repast in the dream of Zosimos reminds us of the orgiastic meals in the Dionysus cult, when sacrificial animals were torn to pieces and eaten. They represent Dionysus Zagreus being torn to pieces by the Titans, from whose mangled remains the νέος Διόνυσος arises.[25]

354 Zosimos tells us that the vision represents or explains the "production of the waters." [26] The visions themselves only show the transformation into *pneuma*. In the language of the alchemists, however, spirit and water are synonymous,[27] as they are

24 Cf. the *Rosarium philosophorum,* in the *Artis auriferae* (1593), II, p. 206.

25 Cf. the Cretan fragment of Euripides (Dieterich, *Eine Mithrasliturgie,* p. 105):

ἁγνὸν δὲ βίον τείνων ἐξ οὗ
Διὸς 'Ιδαίου μύστης γενόμην
καὶ νυκτιπόλου Ζαγρέως βούτας
τοὺς ὠμοφάγους δαῖτας τελέσας

(living a holy life, since I have been initiated into the mysteries of the Idaean Zeus, and eaten raw the flesh of Zagreus, the night-wandering shepherd).

26 [Cf. Berthelot, III, i, 2, and Jung's "Visions of Zosimos" (Swiss edn., p. 141, and —for the reference lower down to "blood"—p. 147).—EDITORS.]

27 "Est et coelestis aqua sive potius divina Chymistarum . . . pneuma, ex aetheris natura et essentia rerum quinta" (There is also the celestial, or rather the divine, water of the alchemists . . . the pneuma, having the nature of the pneuma and the quintessence of things).—Hermolaus Barbarus, *Coroll. in Dioscoridem,* cited in M. Maier, *Symbola aureae mensae* (1617), p. 174.

"Spiritus autem in hac arte nihil aliud quam aquam indicari . . ." (In this art, in the language of the early Christians, for whom water meant the *spiritus veritatis*. In the "Book of Krates" we read: "You make the bodies to liquefy, so that they mingle and become an homogeneous liquid; this is then named the 'divine water.'" [28] The passage corresponds to the Zosimos text, which says that the priest would "change the bodies into blood." For the alchemists, water and blood are identical. This transformation is the same as the *solutio* or *liquefactio*, which is a synonym for the *sublimatio*, for "water" is also "fire": "Item ignis . . . est aqua et ignis noster est ignis et non ignis" (For fire . . . is water and our fire is the fire that is no fire). "Aqua nostra" is said to be "ignea" (fiery).[29]

355 The "secret fire of our philosophy" is said to be "our mystical water," and the "permanent water" is the "fiery form of the true water." [30] The permanent water (the ὕδωρ θεῖον of the Greeks) also signifies "spiritualis sanguis," [31] and is identified with the blood and water that flowed from Christ's side. Heinrich Khunrath says of this water: "So there will open for thee an healing flood which issues from the heart of the son of the great world." It is a water "which the son of the great world pours forth from his body and heart, to be for us a true and natural Aqua vitae." [32] Just as a spiritual water of grace and truth flows from Christ's sacrifice, so the "divine water" is produced by a sacrificial act in the Zosimos vision. It is mentioned in the ancient

spirit means nothing else but water).—Theobaldus de Hoghelande, in the *Theatrum chemicum*, I (1602), p. 196. Water is a "spiritus extractus," or a "spiritus qui in ventre (corporis) occultus est et fiet aqua et corpus absque spiritu: qui est spiritualis naturae" (spirit which is hidden in the belly [of the substance], and water will be produced and a substance without spirit, which is of a spiritual nature).—J. D. Mylius, *Philosophia reformata* (1622), p. 150. This quotation shows how closely spirit and water were associated in the mind of the alchemist.

"Sed aqua coelestis gloriosa *scil.* aes nostrum ac argentum nostrum, sericum nostrum, totaque oratio nostra, quod est unum et idem *scil.* sapientia, quam Deus obtulit, quibus voluit" (But the glorious celestial water, namely our copper and our silver, our silk, and everything we talk about, is one and the same thing, namely the Wisdom, which God has given to whomsoever he wished).—"Consilium coniugii," in the *Ars chemica* (1566), p. 120.

28 Berthelot, *La Chimie au moyen âge*, III, p. 53.

29 Mylius, pp. 121 and 123. For the blood-water-fire equation see George Ripley, *Opera omnia chemica* (1649), pp. 162, 197, 295, 427.

30 Ripley, *Opera*, p. 62; *Rosarium*, p. 264.

31 Mylius, p. 42.

32 Khunrath, *Von hylealischen . . . Chaos* (1597), pp. 274f.

treatise entitled "Isis to Horus," [33] where the angel Amnael brings it to the prophetess in a drinking vessel. As Zosimos was probably an adherent of the Poimandres sect, another thing to be considered here is the *krater* which God filled with *nous* for all those seeking ἔννοια.[34] But *nous* is identical with the alchemical Mercurius. This is quite clear from the Ostanes quotation in Zosimos, which says: "Go to the streams of the Nile and there thou wilt find a stone which hath a spirit. Take and divide it, thrust in thy hand and draw out its heart, for its soul is in its heart." Commenting on this, Zosimos remarks that "having a spirit" is a metaphorical expression for the *exhydrargyrosis,* the expulsion of the quicksilver.[35]

356 During the first centuries after Christ the words *nous* and *pneuma* were used indiscriminately, and the one could easily stand for the other. Moreover the relation of Mercurius to "spirit" is an extremely ancient astrological fact. Like Hermes, Mercurius (or the planetary spirit Mercury) was a god of revelation, who discloses the secret of the art to the adepts. The *Liber quartorum,* which being of Harranite origin cannot be dated later than the tenth century, says of Mercurius: "Ipse enim aperit clausiones operum cum ingenio et intellectu suo" (For he opens with his genius and understanding the locked [insoluble] problems of the work).[36] He is also the "soul of the bodies," the "anima vitalis," [37] and Ruland defines him as "spirit which has become earth." [38] He is a spirit that penetrates into the depths of the material world and transforms it. Like the *nous,* he is symbolized by the serpent. In Michael Maier he points the way to the earthly paradise.[39] Besides being identified with Hermes Trismegistus,[40] he is also called the "mediator" [41] and,

33 Berthelot, *Alchimistes,* I, xiii.

34 Ibid., III, li, 8, and *Hermetica,* ed. Scott, I, p. 151.

35 Berthelot, *Alchimistes,* III, vi, 5.

36 Of the later authors I will mention only Joannes Christophorus Steeb, *Coetum sephiroticum* (1679, p. 138): "Omnis intellectus acuminis auctor . . . a coelesti mercurio omnem ingeniorum vim provenire" (The author of all deeper understanding . . . all the power of genius comes from the celestial Mercurius). For the astrological connection see Bouché-Leclercq, *L'Astrologie grecque,* pp. 312, 321–23.

37 "Aurora consurgens." In Mylius (p. 533) he is a giver of life.

38 *Lexicon.*

39 *Symbola,* p. 592.

40 Ibid., p. 600.

41 Ripley, *Opera,* Foreword, and in Khunrath's *Chaos.* In Plutarch, Mercurius acts as a kind of world soul.

as the Original Man, the "Hermaphroditic Adam." [42] From numerous passages it is clear that Mercurius is as much a fire as a water, both of which aptly characterize the nature of spirit.[43]

357 Killing with the sword is a recurrent theme in alchemical literature. The "philosophical egg" is divided with the sword, and with it the "King" is transfixed and the dragon or "corpus" dismembered, the latter being represented as the body of a man whose head and limbs are cut off.[44] The lion's paws are likewise cut off with the sword. For the alchemical sword brings about the *solutio* or *separatio* of the elements, thereby restoring the original condition of chaos, so that a new and more perfect body can be produced by a new *impressio formae,* or by a "new imagination." The sword is therefore that which "kills and vivifies," and the same is said of the permanent water or mercurial water. Mercurius is the giver of life as well as the destroyer of the old form. In ecclesiastical symbolism the sword which comes out of the mouth of the Son of Man in the Book of Revelation is, according to Hebrews 4:12, the Logos, the Word of God, and hence Christ himself. This analogy did not escape the notice of the alchemists, who were always struggling to give expression to their fantasies. Mercurius was their mediator and saviour, their *filius macrocosmi* (contrasted with Christ the *filius microcosmi*),[45] the solver and separator. So he too is a sword, for he is a "penetrating spirit" ("more piercing than a two-edged sword"!). Gerhard Dorn, an alchemist of the sixteenth century, says that in our world the sword was changed into Christ our Saviour. He comments as follows:

After a long interval of time the Deus Optimus Maximus immersed himself in the innermost of his secrets, and he decided, out of the compassion of his love as well as for the demands of justice, to take the sword of wrath from the hand of the angel. And having hung the sword on the tree, he substituted for it a golden trident, and thus was the wrath of God changed into love. . . . When peace and

42 Gerhard Dorn, "Congeries Paracelsicae chemicae," in the *Theatrum chemicum,* I, p. 589.

43 Cf. my "The Spirit Mercurius" (Swiss edn., pp. 71ff.).

44 Illustration in "Splendor solis," *Aureum vellus* (1598).

45 Cf. Khunrath, *Chaos,* and *Amphitheatrum sapientiae aeternae* (1604).

justice were united, the water of Grace flowed more abundantly from above, and now it bathes the whole world.[46]

[46] Dorn, "Speculativae philosophiae," in the *Theatrum chemicum,* I, pp. 284ff. The whole passage runs as follows:

"Post primam hominis inobedientiam, Dominus viam hanc amplissimam in callem strictissimam difficilimamque (ut videtis) restrinxit, in cuius ostio collocavit Cherubim angelum, ancipitem gladium manu tenentem, quo quidem arceret omnes ab introitu felicis patriae: hinc deflectentes Adae filii propter peccatum primi sui parentis, in sinistram latam sibimet viam construxerunt, quam evitastis. Longo postea temporis intervallo D. O. M. secreta secretorum suorum introivit, in quibus amore miserente, accusanteque iustitia, conclusit angelo gladium irae suae de manibus eripere, cuius loco tridentem hamum substituit aureum, gladio ad arborem suspenso: & sic mutata est ira Dei in amorem, servata iustitia: quod antequam fieret, fluvius iste non erat, ut iam, in se collectus, sed ante lapsum per totum orbem terrarum roris instar expansus aequaliter: post vero rediit unde processerat tandem, ut pax & iustitia sunt osculatae se, descendit affluentius ab alto manans aqua gratiae, totum nunc mundum alluens. In sinistram partem qui deflectunt, partim suspensum in arbore gladium videntes, eiusque noscentes historiam, quia mundo nimium sunt insiti, praetereunt: nonnulli videntes eius efficaciam perquirere negligunt, alii nec vident, nec vidisse voluissent: hi recta peregrinationem suam ad vallem dirigunt omnes, nisi per hamos resipiscentiae, vel poenitentiae nonnulli retrahantur ad montem Sion. Nostro iam saeculo (quod gratiae est) mutatus est gladius in Christum salvatorem nostrum qui crucis arborem pro peccatis nostris ascendit."

(After man's first disobedience the Lord straitened this wide road into a very narrow and difficult path, as you see. At its entrance he placed an angel of the Cherubim, holding in his hand a double-edged sword with which he was to keep all from entering into Paradise. Turning from thence on account of the sin of their first parents, the sons of Adam built for themselves a broad left-hand path: this you have shunned. After a long interval of time the Deus Optimus Maximus immersed himself in the innermost of his secrets, and he decided, out of the compassion of his love as well as for the demands of justice, to take the sword of wrath from the hand of the angel. And having hung the sword on the tree, he substituted for it a golden trident, and thus was the wrath of God changed into love, and justice remained unimpaired. Previous to this, however, the river was not collected into one as it is now, but before the Fall it was spread equally over the whole world, like dew. But later it returned to the place of its origin. When peace and justice were united, the water of Grace flowed more abundantly from above, and now it bathes the whole world. Some of those who take the left-hand path, on seeing the sword suspended from the tree, and knowing its history, pass it by, because they are too entangled in the affairs of this world; some, on seeing it, do not choose to inquire into its efficacy; others never see it and would not wish to see it. All these continue their pilgrimage into the valley, except for those who are drawn back to Mount Zion by the hook of repentance. Now in our age, which is an age of grace, the sword has become Christ our Saviour, who ascended the tree of the Cross for our sins.)

358 This passage, which might well have occurred in an author like Rabanus Maurus or Honorius of Autun without doing them discredit, actually occurs in a context which throws light on certain esoteric alchemical doctrines, namely in a colloquy between Animus, Anima, and Corpus. There we are told that it is Sophia, the Sapientia, Scientia, or Philosophia of the alchemists, "de cuius fonte scaturiunt aquae" (from whose fount the waters gush forth). This Wisdom is the *nous* that lies hidden and bound in matter, the "serpens mercurialis" or "humidum radicale" that manifests itself in the "viventis aquae fluvius de montis apice" (stream of living water from the summit of the mountain).[47] That is the water of grace, the "permanent" and "divine" water which "now bathes the whole world." The apparent transformation of the God of the Old Testament into the God of the New is in reality the transformation of the *deus absconditus* (i.e., the *natura abscondita*) into the *medicina catholica* of alchemical wisdom.[48]

359 The divisive and separative function of the sword, which is of such importance in alchemy, is prefigured in the flaming sword of the angel that separated our first parents from paradise. Separation by a sword is a theme that can also be found in the Gnosis of the Ophites: the earthly cosmos is surrounded by a ring of fire which at the same time encloses paradise. But paradise and the ring of fire are separated by the "flaming sword." [49] An important interpretation of this flaming sword is given in Simon Magus: [50] there is an incorruptible essence potentially present in every human being, the divine *pneuma* "which is stationed above and below in the stream of water." Simon says of this *pneuma:* "I and thou, thou before me. I, who am after thee." It is a force "that generates itself, that causes itself to grow; it is its own mother, sister, bride, daughter; its own son, mother, father; a unity, a root of the whole." It is the very

47 Another remark of Dorn's points in the same direction: "The sword was suspended from a tree over the bank of the river" (p. 288).

48 A few pages later Dorn himself remarks: "Scitote, fratres, omnia quae superius dicta sunt et dicentur in posterum, intelligi posse de praeparationibus alchemicis" (Know, brothers, that everything which has been said above and everything which will be said in what follows can also be understood of the alchemical preparations).

49 Leisegang, *Die Gnosis,* pp. 171f.

50 The passage which follows occurs in Hippolytus, *Elenchos,* vi, pp. 4f.

ground of existence, the procreative urge, which is of fiery origin. Fire is related to blood, which "is fashioned warm and ruddy like fire." Blood turns into semen in men, and in women into milk. This "turning" is interpreted as "the flaming sword which turned every way, to keep the way of the tree of life." [51] The operative principle in semen and milk turns into mother and father. The tree of life is guarded by the turning (i.e., transforming) sword, and this is the "seventh power" which begets itself. "For if the flaming sword turned not, then would that fair Tree be destroyed, and perish utterly; but if it turneth into semen and milk, and there be added the Logos and the place of the Lord where the Logos is begotten, he who dwelleth potentially in the semen and milk shall grow to full stature from the littlest spark, and shall increase and become a power boundless and immutable, like to an unchanging Aeon, which suffereth no more change until measureless eternity." [52] It is clear from these remarkable statements of Hippolytus concerning the teachings of Simon Magus that the sword is very much more than an instrument which divides; it is itself the force which "turns" from something infinitesimally small into the infinitely great: from water, fire, and blood it becomes the limitless aeon. What it means is the transformation of the vital spirit in man into the Divine. The natural being becomes the divine *pneuma,* as in the vision of Zosimos. Simon's description of the creative *pneuma,* the true arcane substance, corresponds in every detail to the uroboros or *serpens mercurialis* of the Latinists. It too is its own father, mother, son, daughter, brother, and sister from the earliest beginnings of alchemy right down to the end.[53] It begets and sacrifices itself and is its own instrument of sacrifice, for it is a symbol of the deadly and life-giving water.[54]

360 Simon's ideas also throw a significant light on the above-quoted passage from Dorn, where the sword of wrath is transformed into Christ. Were it not that the philosophemes of Hippolytus were first discovered in the nineteenth century, on Mount Athos, one might almost suppose that Dorn had made use of them. There are numerous other symbols in alchemy whose origin is so doubtful that one does not know whether to

51 Genesis 3:24. 52 Leisegang, p. 80.

53 That is why it is called "Hermaphroditus."

54 One of its symbols is the scorpion, which stings itself to death.

attribute them to tradition, or to a study of the heresiologists, or to spontaneous revival.[55]

361 The sword as the "proper" instrument of sacrifice occurs again in the old treatise entitled "Consilium coniugii de massa solis et lunae." This says: "Both must be killed with their own sword" ("both" referring to Sol and Luna).[56] In the still older "Tractatus Micreris," [57] dating perhaps from the twelfth century, we find the "fiery sword" in a quotation from Ostanes: "The great Astanus [Ostanes] said: Take an egg, pierce it with the fiery sword, and separate its soul from its body." [58] Here the sword is something that divides body and soul, corresponding to the division between heaven and earth, the ring of fire and paradise, or paradise and the first parents. In an equally old treatise, the "Allegoriae sapientum . . . supra librum Turbae," there is even mention of a sacrificial rite: "Take a fowl [*volatile*], cut off its head with the fiery sword, then pluck out its feathers, separate the limbs, and cook over a charcoal fire till it becomes of one colour." [59] Here we have a decapitation with the fiery sword, then a "clipping," or more accurately a "plucking," and finally a "cooking." The cock, which is probably what is meant here, is simply called "volatile," a fowl or winged creature, and this is a common term for spirit, but a spirit still nature-bound and imperfect, and in need of improvement. In another old treatise, with the very similar title "Allegoriae super librum Turbae," [60] we find the following supplementary variants: "Kill the mother [the *prima materia*], tearing off her hands and feet." "Take a viper . . . cut off its head and tail." "Take a cock . . . and pluck it alive." "Take a man, shave him, and drag him over the stone [i.e., dry him on the hot stone] till his body dies." "Take the glass vessel containing bridegroom and bride, throw

55 So far I have come across only two authors who admit to having read any heresiologists. The silence of the alchemists in this matter is nothing to wonder at, since the mere proximity to heresy would have put them in danger of their lives. Thus even 90 years after the death of Trithemius of Spanheim, who was supposed to have been the teacher of Paracelsus, the abbot Sigismund of Seon had to compose a moving defence in which he endeavoured to acquit Trithemius of the charge of heresy. Cf. *Trithemius sui-ipsius vindex* (1616).

56 *Ars chemica,* p. 259. Printed in Manget, *Bibliotheca chemica curiosa* (1702), II, pp. 235ff.

57 "Micreris" is probably a corruption of "Mercurius."

58 *Theatr. chem.,* V (1622), p. 103.

59 Ibid., p. 68.

60 *Artis auriferae,* I, pp. 139f.

them into the furnace, and roast them for three days, and they will be two in one flesh." "Take the white man from the vessel." [61]

362 One is probably right in assuming that these recipes are instructions for magical sacrifices, not unlike the Greek magic papyri.[62] As an example of the latter I will give the recipe from the Mimaut Papyrus (li. 2ff.): "Take a tomcat and make an Osiris of him [63] [by immersing] his body in water. And when you proceed to suffocate him, talk into his back." Another example from the same papyrus (li. 425): "Take a hoopoe, tear out its heart, pierce it with a reed, then cut it up and throw it into Attic honey."

363 Such sacrifices really were made for the purpose of summoning up the *paredros,* the familiar spirit. That this sort of thing was practised, or at any rate recommended, by the alchemists is clear from the "Liber Platonis quartorum," where it speaks of the "oblationes et sacrificia" offered to the planetary demon. A deeper and more sombre note is struck in the following passage, which I give in the original (and generally very corrupt) text: [64]

> Vas . . . oportet esse rotundae figurae: Ut sit artifex huius mutator firmamenti et testae capitis, ut cum sit res, qua indigemus, res simplex, habens partes similes, necesse est ipsius generationem, et in corpore habente similes partibus . . . proiicies ex testa capitis, videlicet capitis elementi hominis et massetur totum cum urina . . .
>
> (The vessel . . . must be round in shape. Thus the artifex must be the transformer of this firmament and of the brain-pan, just as the thing for which we seek is a simple thing having uniform parts. It is therefore necessary that you should generate it in a body [i.e., a vessel] of uniform parts . . . from the brain-pan, that is, from the head of the element Man, and that the whole should be macerated with urine . . .)

364 One asks oneself how literally this recipe is to be taken.[65] The following story from the "Ghāya al-hakīm" is exceedingly enlightening in this connection:

365 The Jacobite patriarch Dionysius I set it on record that in

[61] Ibid., pp. 151, 140, 140, 139, 151, 151, resp.

[62] *Papyri Graecae Magicae,* trans. and ed. by Karl Preisendanz.

[63] ἀποθέωσις = 'sacrifice.' [64] *Theatr. chem.,* V, p. 153.

[65] See also pp. 127, 128, 130, and 149 of the same work.

the year 765, a man who was destined for the sacrifice, on beholding the bloody head of his predecessor, was so terrified that he took flight and lodged a complaint with Abbas, the prefect of Mesopotamia, against the priests of Harran, who were afterwards severely punished. The story goes on to say that in 830 the Caliph Mamun told the Harranite envoys: "You are without doubt the people of the head, who were dealt with by my father Rashid." We learn from the "Ghāya" that a fair-haired man with dark-blue eyes was lured into a chamber of the temple, where he was immersed in a great jar filled with sesame oil. Only his head was left sticking out. There he remained for forty days, and during this time was fed on nothing but figs soaked in sesame oil. He was not given a drop of water to drink. As a result of this treatment his body became as soft as wax. The prisoner was repeatedly fumigated with incense, and magical formulae were pronounced over him. Eventually his head was torn off at the neck, the body remaining in the oil. The head was then placed in a niche on the ashes of burnt olives, and was packed round with cotton wool. More incense was burned before it, and the head would thereupon predict famines or good harvests, changes of dynasty, and other future events. Its eyes could see, though the lids did not move. It also revealed to people their inmost thoughts, and scientific and technical questions were likewise addressed to it.[66]

366 Even though it is possible that the real head was, in later times, replaced by a dummy, the whole idea of this ceremony, particularly when taken in conjunction with the above passage from the "Liber quartorum," seems to point to an original human sacrifice. The idea of a mysterious head is, however, considerably older than the school of Harran. As far back as Zosimos we find the philosophers described as "children of the golden head," and we also encounter the "round element," which Zosimos says is the letter omega (Ω). This symbol may well be interpreted as the head, since the "Liber quartorum" also associates the round vessel with the head. Zosimos, moreover, refers on several occasions to the "whitest stone, which is in the head." [67] Probably all these ideas go back to the severed head

66 Dozy and de Goeje, p. 365.

67 "Τὸν πάνυ λευκότατον λίθον τὸν ἐγκέφαλον." Berthelot, *Alchimistes,* III, xxix, 4. Cf. also I, iii, 1 and III, ii. 1.

of Osiris, which crossed the sea and was therefore associated with the idea of resurrection. The "head of Osiris" also plays an important part in medieval alchemy.

67 In this connection we might mention the legend that was current about Gerbert of Rheims, afterwards Pope Sylvester II (d. 1003). He was believed to have possessed a golden head which spoke to him in oracles. Gerbert was one of the greatest savants of his time, and well known as a transmitter of Arabic science.[68] Can it be that the translation of the "Liber quartorum," which is of Harranite origin, goes back to this author? Unfortunately there is little prospect of our being able to prove this.

68 It has been conjectured that the Harranite oracle head may be connected with the ancient Hebrew teraphim. Rabbinic tradition considers the teraphim to have been originally either the decapitated head or skull of a human being, or else a dummy head.[69] The Jews had teraphim about the house as a sort of lares and penates (who were plural spirits, like the Cabiri). The idea that they were heads goes back to I Samuel 19:13f., which describes how Michal, David's wife, put the teraphim in David's bed in order to deceive the messengers of Saul, who wanted to kill him. "Then Michal took an image and laid it on the bed and put a pillow of goats' hair at its head, and covered it with the clothes (RSV)." The "pillow of goats' hair" is linguistically obscure and has even been interpreted as meaning that the teraphim were goats. But it may also mean something woven or plaited out of goats' hair, like a wig, and this would fit in better with the picture of a man lying in bed. Further evidence for this comes from a legend in a collection of midrashim from the twelfth century, printed in Bin Gorion's *Die Sagen der Juden.* There it is said:

> The teraphim were idols, and they were made in the following way. The head of a man, who had to be a first-born, was cut off and the hair plucked out. The head was then sprinkled with salt and anointed with oil. Afterwards a little plaque, of copper or gold, was inscribed with the name of an idol and placed under the tongue of the decapitated head. The head was set up in a room, candles were lit before it, and the people made obeisance. And if any man fell

68 Thorndike, *A History of Magic and Experimental Science,* I, p. 705.
69 *Jewish Encyclopaedia,* XII, s.v. "Teraphim," pp. 108f.

down before it, the head began to speak, and answered all questions that were addressed to it.[70]

369 This is an obvious parallel to the Harranite ritual with the head. The tearing out of the hair seems significant, since it is an equivalent of scalping or shearing, and is thus a rebirth mystery. It is conceivable that in later times the bald skull was covered with a wig for a rite of renewal, as is also reported from Egypt.

370 It seems probable that this magical procedure is of primitive origin. I am indebted to the South African writer, Laurens van der Post, for the following report from a lecture which he gave in Zurich in 1951:

The tribe in question was an offshoot of the great Swazi nation—a Bantu people. When, some years ago, the old chief died, he was succeeded by his son, a young man of weak character. He soon proved to be so unsatisfactory a chief that his uncles called a meeting of the tribal elders. They decided that something must be done to strengthen their chief, so they consulted the witch doctors. The witch doctors treated him with a medicine which proved ineffective. Another meeting was held and the witch doctors were asked to use the strongest medicine of all on the chief because the situation was becoming desperate. A half brother of the chief, a boy of twelve, was chosen to provide the material for the medicine.

One afternoon a sorcerer went up to the boy, who was tending cattle, and engaged him in conversation. Then, emptying some powder from a horn into his hand, he took a reed and blew the powder into the ears and nostrils of the boy. A witness told me that the lad thereupon began to sway like a drunken person and sank to the ground shivering. He was then taken to the river bed and tied to the roots of a tree. More powder was sprinkled round about, the sorcerer saying: "This person will no longer eat food but only earth and roots."

The boy was kept in the river bed for nine months. Some people say a cage was made and put into the stream, with the boy inside it, for hours on end, so that the water should flow over him and make his skin white. Others reported seeing him crawling about in the river bed on his hands and knees. But all were so frightened that, although there was a mission school only one hundred yards away,

[70] Josef bin Gorion, *Die Sagen der Juden,* p. 325. I am indebted to Dr. Riwkah Schärf for drawing my attention to this passage.

no one except those directly concerned in the ritual would go near him. All are agreed that at the end of nine months this fat, normal, healthy boy was like an animal and quite white-skinned. One woman said, "His eyes were white and the whole of his body was white as white paper."

On the evening that the boy was to be killed a veteran witch doctor was summoned to the chief's kraal and asked to consult the tribal spirits. This he did in the cattle kraal, and after selecting an animal for slaughter he retired to the chief's hut. There the witch doctor was handed parts of the dead boy's body: first the head in a sack, then a thumb and a toe. He cut off the nose and ears and lips, mixed them with medicine, and cooked them over a fire in a broken clay pot. He stuck two spears on either side of the pot. Then those present—twelve in all including the weak chief—leaned over the pot and deeply inhaled the steam. All save the boy's mother dipped their fingers in the pot and licked them. She inhaled but refused to dip her fingers in the pot. The rest of the body the witch doctor mixed into a kind of bread for doctoring the tribe's crops.

71 Although this magical rite is not actually a "head mystery," it has several things in common with the practices previously mentioned. The body is macerated and transformed by long immersion in water. The victim is killed, and the salient portions of the head form the main ingredient of the "strengthening" medicine which was concocted for the chief and his immediate circle. The body is kneaded into a sort of bread, and this is obviously thought of as a strengthening medicine for the tribe's crops as well. The rite is a transformation process, a sort of rebirth after nine months of incubation in the water. Laurens van der Post thinks that the purpose of the "whitening" [71] was to assimilate the mana of the white man, who has the political power. I agree with this view, and would add that painting with white clay often signifies transformation into ancestral spirits, in the same way as the neophytes are made invisible in the Nandi territory, in Kenya, where they walk about in portable, cone-shaped grass huts and demonstrate their invisibility to everyone.

72 Skull worship is widespread among primitives. In Melanesia and Polynesia it is chiefly the skulls of the ancestors that are worshipped, because they establish connections with the spirits

71 Cf. the alchemical *albedo* and *homo albus*.

or serve as tutelary deities, like the head of Osiris in Egypt. Skulls also play a considerable role as sacred relics. It would lead us too far to go into this primitive skull worship, so I must refer the reader to the literature.[72] I would only like to point out that the cut-off ears, nose, and mouth can represent the head as parts that stand for the whole. There are numerous examples of this. Equally, the head or its parts (brain, etc.) can act as magical food or as a means for increasing the fertility of the land.

373 It is of special significance for the alchemical tradition that the oracle head was also known in Greece. Aelian [73] reports that Cleomenes of Sparta had the head of his friend Archonides preserved in a jar of honey, and that he consulted it as an oracle. The same was said of the head of Orpheus. Onians [74] rightly emphasizes the fact that the ψυχή, whose seat was in the head, corresponds to the modern "unconscious," and that at that stage of development consciousness was identified with θυμός (breath) and φρένες (lungs), and was localized in the chest or heart region. Hence Pindar's expression for the soul—αἴωνος εἴδωλον (image of Aion)—is extraordinarily apt, for the collective unconscious not only imparts "oracles" but forever represents the microcosm (i.e., the form of a physical man mirroring the Cosmos).

374 There is no evidence to show that any of the parallels we have drawn are historically connected with the Zosimos visions. It seems rather to be a case partly of parallel traditions (transmitted, perhaps, chiefly through the Harran school), and partly of spontaneous fantasies arising from the same archetypal background from which the traditions were derived in the first place. As my examples have shown, the imagery of the Zosimos visions, however strange it may be, is by no means isolated, but is interwoven with older ideas some of which were certainly, and others quite possibly, known to Zosimos, as well as with parallels of uncertain date which continued to mould the speculations of the alchemists for many centuries to come. Religious thought in the early Christian era was not completely cut off from all contact with these conceptions; it was in fact influenced by them, and in turn it fertilized the minds of the natural philosophers during later centuries. Towards the end of the sixteenth century

72 Hastings, VI, pp. 535f. 73 *Varia historia,* XII, 8.

74 Onians, *The Origins of European Thought,* pp. 101ff.

the alchemical *opus* was even represented in the form of a Mass. The author of this tour de force was the Hungarian alchemist, Melchior Cibinensis. I have elaborated this parallel in my book *Psychology and Alchemy*.[75]

375 In the visions of Zosimos, the Hiereus who is transformed into *pneuma* represents the transformative principle at work in nature and the harmony of opposing forces. Chinese philosophy formulated this process as the enantiodromian interplay of Yin and Yang.[76] But the curious personifications and symbols characteristic not only of these visions but of alchemical literature in general show in the plainest possible terms that we are dealing with a psychic process that takes place mainly in the unconscious and therefore can come into consciousness only in the form of a dream or vision. At that time and until very much later no one had any idea of the unconscious; consequently all unconscious contents were projected into the object, or rather were found in nature as apparent objects or properties of matter and were not recognized as purely internal psychic events. There is some evidence that Zosimos was well aware of the spiritual or mystical side of his art, but he believed that what he was concerned with was a spirit that dwelt in natural objects, and not something that came from the human psyche. It remained for modern science to despiritualize nature through its so-called objective knowledge of matter. All anthropomorphic projections were withdrawn from the object one after another, with a twofold result: firstly man's mystical identity with nature[77] was curtailed as never before, and secondly the projections falling back into the human soul caused such a terrific activation of the unconscious that in modern times man was compelled to postulate the existence of an unconscious psyche. The first beginnings of this can be seen in Leibniz and Kant, and then, with mounting intensity, in Schelling, Carus, and von Hartmann, until finally modern psychology discarded the last metaphysical claims of the philosopher-psychologists and restricted the idea of the psyche's existence to the psychological statement, in other

75 Pars. 480–89.

76 The classical example being *The I Ching or Book of Changes.*

77 Mystical or *unconscious* identity occurs in every case of projection, because the content projected upon the extraneous object creates an apparent relationship between it and the subject.

words, to its phenomenology. So far as the dramatic course of the Mass represents the death, sacrifice and resurrection of a god and the inclusion and active participation of the priest and congregation, its phenomenology may legitimately be brought into line with other fundamentally similar, though more primitive, religious customs. This always involves the risk that sensitive people will find it unpleasant when "small things are compared with great." In fairness to the primitive psyche, however, I would like to emphasize that the "holy dread" of civilized man differs but little from the awe of the primitive, and that the God who is present and active in the mystery is a mystery for both. No matter how crass the outward differences, the similarity or equivalence of meaning should not be overlooked.

4. THE PSYCHOLOGY OF THE MASS

I. GENERAL REMARKS ON THE SACRIFICE

376 Whereas I kept to the Church's interpretation when discussing the transformation rite in section 2, in the present section I shall treat this interpretation as a symbol. Such a procedure does not imply any evaluation of the content of religious belief. Scientific criticism must, of course, adhere to the view that when something is held as an opinion, thought to be true, or believed, it does not posit the existence of any real fact other than a psychological one. But that does not mean that a *mere nothing* has been produced. Rather, expression has been given to the psychic reality underlying the statement of the belief or rite as its empirical basis. When psychology "explains" a statement of this kind, it does not, in the first place, deprive the *object* of this statement of any reality—on the contrary, it is granted a psychic reality—and in the second place the intended metaphysical *statement* is not, on that account, turned into an hypostasis, since it was never anything more than a psychic phenomenon. Its specifically "metaphysical" coloration indicates that its object is beyond the reach of human perception and understanding except in its psychic mode of manifestation, and therefore cannot be judged. But every science reaches its end in the unknowable. Yet it would not be a science at all if it

regarded its temporary limitations as definitive and denied the existence of anything outside them. No science can consider its hypotheses to be the final truth.

377 The psychological explanation and the metaphysical statement do not contradict one another any more than, shall we say, the physicist's explanation of matter contradicts the as yet unknown or unknowable nature of matter. The very existence of a belief has in itself the reality of a psychic fact. Just what we posit by the concept "psyche" is simply unknowable, for psychology is in the unfortunate position where the observer and the observed are ultimately identical. Psychology has no Archimedean point outside, since all perception is of a psychic nature and we have only indirect knowledge of what is non-psychic.

378 The ritual event that takes place in the Mass has a dual aspect, human and divine. From the human point of view, gifts are offered to God at the altar, signifying at the same time the self-oblation of the priest and the congregation. The ritual act consecrates both the gifts and the givers. It commemorates and represents the Last Supper which our Lord took with his disciples, the whole Incarnation, Passion, death, and resurrection of Christ. But from the divine point of view this anthropomorphic action is only the outer shell or husk in which what is really happening is not a human action at all but a divine event. For an instant the life of Christ, eternally existent outside time, becomes visible and is unfolded in temporal succession, but in condensed form, in the sacred action: Christ incarnates as a man under the aspect of the offered substances, he suffers, is killed, is laid in the sepulchre, breaks the power of the underworld, and rises again in glory. In the utterance of the words of consecration the Godhead intervenes, Itself acting and truly present, and thus proclaims that the central event in the Mass is Its act of grace, in which the priest has only the significance of a minister. The same applies to the congregation and the offered substances: they are all ministering causes of the sacred event. The presence of the Godhead binds all parts of the sacrificial act into a mystical unity, so that it is God himself who offers himself as a sacrifice in the substances, in the priest, and in the congregation, and who, in the human form of the Son, offers himself as an atonement to the Father.

379 Although this act is an eternal happening taking place within the divinity, man is nevertheless included in it as an essential component, firstly because God clothes himself in our human nature, and secondly because he needs the ministering co-operation of the priest and congregation, and even the material substances of bread and wine which have a special significance for man. Although God the Father is of one nature with God the Son, he appears in time on the one hand as the eternal Father and on the other hand as a man with limited earthly existence. Mankind as a whole is included in God's human nature, which is why man is also included in the sacrificial act. Just as, in the sacrificial act, God is both *agens* and *patiens,* so too is man according to his limited capacity. The *causa efficiens* of the transubstantiation is a spontaneous act of God's grace. Ecclesiastical doctrine insists on this view and even tends to attribute the preparatory action of the priest, indeed the very existence of the rite, to divine prompting,[1] rather than to slothful human nature with its load of original sin. This view is of the utmost importance for a psychological understanding of the Mass. Wherever the magical aspect of a rite tends to prevail, it brings the rite nearer to satisfying the individual ego's blind greed for power, and thus breaks up the mystical body of the Church into separate units. Where, on the other hand, the rite is conceived as the action of God himself, the human participants have only an instrumental or "ministering" significance. The Church's view therefore presupposes the following psychological situation: human consciousness (represented by the priest and congregation) is confronted with an autonomous event which, taking place on a "divine" and "timeless" plane transcending consciousness, is in no way dependent on human action, but which impels man to act by seizing upon him as an instrument and making him the exponent of a "divine" happening. In the ritual action man places himself at the disposal of an autonomous and "eternal" agency operating outside the categories of human consciousness—*si parva licet componere magnis*—in much the same way that a good actor does not merely represent the drama, but allows himself to be overpowered by the genius of the dramatist. The beauty of the ritual action is one of its

[1] John 6:44: "No man can come to me, except the Father which hath sent me draw him."

essential properties, for man has not served God rightly unless he has also served him in beauty. Therefore the rite has no practical utility, for that would be making it serve a purpose—a purely human category. But everything divine is an end-in-itself, perhaps the only legitimate end-in-itself we know. How something eternal can "act" at all is a question we had better not touch, for it is simply unanswerable. Since man, in the action of the Mass, is a tool (though a tool of his own free will), he is not in a position to know anything about the hand which guides him. The hammer cannot discover within itself the power which makes it strike. It is something outside, something autonomous, which seizes and moves him. What happens in the consecration is essentially a miracle, and is meant to be so, for otherwise we should have to consider whether we were not conjuring up God by magic, or else lose ourselves in philosophical wonder how anything eternal can act at all, since action is a process in time with a beginning, a middle, and an end. It is necessary that the transubstantiation should be a cause of wonder and a miracle which man can in no wise comprehend. It is a *mysterium* in the sense of a δρώμενον and δεικνύμενον, a secret that is acted and displayed. The ordinary man is not conscious of anything in himself that would cause him to perform a "mystery." He can only do so if and when *it* seizes upon *him*. This seizure, or rather the sensed or presumed existence of a power outside consciousness which seizes him, is the miracle par excellence, really and truly a miracle when one considers *what* is being represented. What in the world could induce us to represent an absolute impossibility? What is it that for thousands of years has wrung from man the greatest spiritual effort, the loveliest works of art, the profoundest devotion, the most heroic self-sacrifice, and the most exacting service? What else but a miracle? It is a miracle which is not man's to command; for as soon as he tries to work it himself, or as soon as he philosophizes about it and tries to comprehend it intellectually, the bird is flown. A miracle is something that arouses man's wonder precisely because it seems inexplicable. And indeed, from what we know of human nature we could never explain why men are constrained to such statements and to such beliefs. (I am thinking here of the impossible statements made by all religions.) There must be some compelling reason for this, even though it is not to be found in ordinary experience. The very absurdity and impossibility of the statements vouches for the existence of this reason. That is the real ground for belief, as was formulated most brilliantly in Tertullian's "prorsus credibile, quia ineptum." [2] An improbable opinion has to submit sooner or later to correction. But the statements of religion are the most improbable of all and yet they persist for thousands of years.[3] Their wholly unexpected vitality proves the existence of a sufficient cause which has so far eluded scientific investigation. I can, as a psychologist, only draw attention to this fact and emphasize my belief that there are no facile "nothing but" explanations for psychic phenomena of this kind.

380 The dual aspect of the Mass finds expression not only in the contrast between human and divine action, but also in the dual aspect of God and the God-man, who, although they are by nature a unity, nevertheless represent a duality in the ritual drama. Without this "dichotomy of God," if I may use such a term, the whole act of sacrifice would be inconceivable and would lack actuality. According to the Christian view God has never ceased to be God, not even when he appeared in human form in the temporal order. The Christ of the Johannine gospel declares: "I and my Father are one. He that hath seen me hath seen the Father" (John 10:30, 14:9). And yet on the Cross Christ cries out: "My God, my God, why hast thou forsaken me?" This contradiction must exist if the formula "very God and very man" is psychologically true. And if it is true, then the different sayings of Christ are in no sense a contradiction. Being "very man" means being at an extreme remove and utterly different from God. "De profundis clamavi ad te, Domine"—this cry demonstrates both, the remoteness and the nearness, the outermost darkness and the dazzling spark of the Divine. God in his humanity is presumably so far from himself that he has to seek himself through absolute self-surrender. And where would God's wholeness be if he could not be the "wholly

[2] "Et mortuus est Dei filius, prorsus credibile est, quia ineptum est. Et sepultus resurrexit; certum est, quia impossibile est" (And the Son of God is dead, which is to be believed because it is absurd. And buried He rose again, which is certain because it is impossible). Migne, *P.L.*, vol. 2, col. 751.

[3] The audacity of Tertullian's argument is undeniable, and so is its danger, but that does not detract from its psychological truth.

other"? Accordingly it is with some psychological justification, so it seems to me, that when the Gnostic Nous fell into the power of Physis he assumed the dark chthonic form of the serpent, and the Manichaean "Original Man" in the same situation actually took on the qualities of the Evil One. In Tibetan Buddhism all gods without exception have a peaceful and a wrathful aspect, for they reign over all the realms of being. The dichotomy of God into divinity and humanity and his return to himself in the sacrificial act hold out the comforting doctrine that in man's own darkness there is hidden a light that shall once again return to its source, and that this light actually *wanted* to descend into the darkness in order to deliver the Enchained One who languishes there, and lead him to light everlasting. All this belongs to the stock of pre-Christian ideas, being none other than the doctrine of the "Man of Light," the Anthropos or Original Man, which the sayings of Christ in the gospels assume to be common knowledge.

II. THE PSYCHOLOGICAL MEANING OF SACRIFICE

(*a*) *The Sacrificial Gifts*

381 Kramp, in his book on the Roman liturgy, makes the following observations about the substances symbolizing the sacrifice:

> Now bread and wine are not only the ordinary means of subsistence for a large portion of humanity, they are also to be had all over the earth (which is of the greatest significance as regards the world-wide spread of Christianity). Further, the two together constitute the perfect food of man, who needs both solid and liquid sustenance. Because they can be so regarded as the typical food of man, they are best fitted to serve as a symbol of human life and human personality, a fact which throws significant light on the gift-symbol.[4]

382 It is not immediately apparent why precisely bread and wine should be a "symbol of human life and human personality." This interpretation looks very like a conclusion *a posteriori* from the special meaning which attaches to these substances in the Mass. In that case the meaning would be due to the liturgy and not to the substances themselves, for no one could imagine that

4 *Die Opferanschauungen*, p. 55.

bread and wine, in themselves, signify human life or human personality. But, in so far as bread and wine are important products of culture, they do express a vital human striving. They represent a definite cultural achievement which is the fruit of attention, patience, industry, devotion, and laborious toil. The words "our daily bread" express man's anxious care for his existence. By producing bread he makes his life secure. But in so far as he "does not live by bread alone," bread is fittingly accompanied by wine, whose cultivation has always demanded a special degree of attention and much painstaking work. Wine, therefore, is equally an expression of cultural achievement. Where wheat and the vine are cultivated, civilized life prevails. But where agriculture and vine-growing do not exist, there is only the uncivilized life of nomads and hunters.

383 So in offering bread and wine man is in the first instance offering up the products of his culture, the best, as it were, that human industry produces. But the "best" can be produced only by the best in man, by his conscientiousness and devotion. Cultural products can therefore easily stand for the psychological conditions of their production, that is, for those human virtues which alone make man capable of civilization.[5]

384 As to the special nature of these substances, bread is undoubtedly a food. There is a popular saying that wine "fortifies," though not in the same sense as food "sustains." It stimulates and "makes glad the heart of man" by virtue of a certain volatile substance which has always been called "spirit." It is thus, unlike innocuous water, an "inspiriting" drink, for a spirit or god dwells within it and produces the ecstasy of intoxication. The wine miracle at Cana was the same as the miracle in the temple of Dionysus, and it is profoundly significant that, on the Damascus Chalice, Christ is enthroned among vine tendrils like Dionysus himself.[6] Bread therefore represents the physical means of subsistence, and wine the spiritual. The offering up of bread and wine is the offering of both the physical and the spiritual fruits of civilization.

5 My reason for saying this is that every symbol has an objective and a subjective—or psychic—origin, so that it can be interpreted on the "objective level" as well as on the "subjective level." This is a consideration of some importance in dream-analysis. Cf. *Psychological Types,* Defs. 38 and 50.

6 Further material in Eisler, *Orpheus—the Fisher,* pp. 280f.

385 But, however sensible he was of the care and labour lavished upon them, man could hardly fail to observe that these cultivated plants grew and flourished according to an inner law of their own, and that there was a power at work in them which he compared to his own life breath or vital spirit. Frazer has called this principle, not unjustly, the "corn spirit." Human initiative and toil are certainly necessary, but even more necessary, in the eyes of primitive man, is the correct and careful performance of the ceremonies which sustain, strengthen, and propitiate the vegetation numen.[7] Grain and wine therefore have something in the nature of a soul, a specific life principle which makes them appropriate symbols not only of man's cultural achievements, but also of the seasonally dying and resurgent god who is their life spirit. Symbols are never simple—only signs and allegories are simple. The symbol always covers a complicated situation which is so far beyond the grasp of language that it cannot be expressed at all in any unambiguous manner.[8] Thus the grain and wine symbols have a fourfold layer of meaning:

1. as agricultural products;
2. as products requiring special processing (bread from grain, wine from grapes);
3. as expressions of psychological achievement (work, industry, patience, devotion, etc.) and of human vitality in general;
4. as manifestations of mana or of the vegetation daemon.

386 From this list it can easily be seen that a symbol is needed to sum up such a complicated physical and psychic situation. The simplest symbolical formula for this is "bread and wine," giving these words the original complex significance which they have always had for tillers of the soil.

(*b*) *The Sacrifice*

387 It is clear from the foregoing that the sacrificial gift is symbolic, and that it embraces everything which is expressed by the symbol, namely the physical product, the processed substance, the psychological achievement, and the autonomous, daemonic life principle of cultivated plants. The value of the gift is en-

7 Similarly, in hunting, the *rites d'entrée* are more important than the hunt itself, for on these rites the success of the hunt depends.

8 Cf. *Psychological Types,* Def. 51.

hanced when it is the best or the first fruits. Since bread and wine are the best that agriculture can offer, they are by the same token man's best endeavour. In addition, bread symbolizes the visible manifestation of the divine numen which dies and rises again, and wine the presence of a pneuma which promises intoxication and ecstasy.[9] The classical world thought of this pneuma as Dionysus, particularly the suffering Dionysus Zagreus, whose divine substance is distributed throughout the whole of nature. In short, what is sacrificed under the forms of bread and wine is nature, man, and God, all combined in the unity of the symbolic gift.

388 The offering of so significant a gift at once raises the question: Does it lie within man's power to offer such a gift at all? Is he psychologically competent to do so? The Church says no, since she maintains that the sacrificing priest is Christ himself. But, since man is included in the gift—included, as we have seen, twice over—the Church also says yes, though with qualifications. On the side of the sacrificer there is an equally complicated, symbolic state of affairs, for the symbol is Christ himself, who is both the sacrificer and the sacrificed. This symbol likewise has several layers of meaning which I shall proceed to sort out in what follows.

389 The act of making a sacrifice consists in the first place in giving something which belongs to me. Everything which belongs to me bears the stamp of "mineness," that is, it has a subtle identity with my ego. This is vividly expressed in certain primitive languages, where the suffix of animation is added to an object—a canoe, for instance—when it belongs to me, but not when it belongs to somebody else. The affinity which all the things bearing the stamp of "mineness" have with my personality is aptly characterized by Lévy-Bruhl [10] as *participation mystique*. It is an irrational, unconscious identity, arising from the fact that anything which comes into contact with me is not only itself, but also a symbol. This symbolization comes about firstly because every human being has unconscious contents, and secondly because every object has an unknown side. Your watch, for instance. Unless you are a watchmaker, you would hardly presume to say that you know how it works. Even if you do, you wouldn't know anything about the molecular structure of the

9 Leisegang, *Pneuma Hagion*, pp. 248ff.

10 *How Natives Think.*

steel unless you happened to be a mineralogist or a physicist. And have you ever heard of a scientist who knew how to repair his pocket watch? But where two unknowns come together, it is impossible to distinguish between them. The unknown in man and the unknown in the thing fall together in one. Thus there arises an unconscious identity which sometimes borders on the grotesque. No one is permitted to touch what is "mine," much less use it. One is affronted if "my" things are not treated with sufficient respect. I remember once seeing two Chinese rickshaw boys engaged in furious argument. Just as they were about to come to blows, one of them gave the other's rickshaw a violent kick, thus putting an end to the quarrel. So long as they are unconscious our unconscious contents are always projected, and the projection fixes upon everything "ours," inanimate objects as well as animals and people. And to the extent that "our" possessions are projection carriers, they are *more* than what they are in themselves, and function as such. They have acquired several layers of meaning and are therefore symbolical, though this fact seldom or never reaches consciousness. In reality, our psyche spreads far beyond the confines of the conscious mind, as was apparently known long ago to the old alchemist who said that the soul was for the greater part outside the body.[11]

390 When, therefore, I give away something that is "mine," what I am giving is essentially a symbol, a thing of many meanings; but, owing to my unconsciousness of its symbolic character, it adheres to my ego, because it is part of my personality. Hence there is, explicitly or implicitly, a personal claim bound up with every gift. There is always an unspoken "give that thou mayest receive." Consequently the gift always carries with it a personal intention, for the mere giving of it is not a sacrifice. It only becomes a sacrifice if I give up the implied intention of receiving something in return. If it is to be a true sacrifice, the gift must be given as if it were being destroyed.[12] Only then is it possible

11 Michael Sendivogius, "Tractatus de sulphure" (16th cent.), in the *Musaeum hermeticum* (1678), p. 617: "[Anima] quae extra corpus multa profundissima imaginatur" ([The soul] which imagines many things of the utmost profundity outside the body).

12 The parallel to this is total destruction of the sacrificial gift by burning, or by throwing it into water or into a pit.

for the egoistic claim to be given up. Were the bread and wine simply given without any consciousness of an egoistic claim, the fact that it was unconscious would be no excuse, but would on the contrary be sure proof of the existence of a *secret* claim. Because of its egoistic nature, the offering would then inevitably have the character of a magical act of propitiation, with the unavowed purpose and tacit expectation of purchasing the good will of the Deity. That is an ethically worthless simulacrum of sacrifice, and in order to avoid it the giver must at least make himself sufficiently conscious of his identity with the gift to recognize how far he is *giving himself up* in giving the gift. In other words, out of the natural state of identity with what is "mine" there grows the ethical task of sacrificing oneself, or at any rate that part of oneself which is identical with the gift. One ought to realize that when one gives or surrenders oneself there are corresponding claims attached, the more so the less one knows of them. The conscious realization of this alone guarantees that the giving is a real sacrifice. For if I know and admit that I am giving myself, forgoing myself, and do not want to be repaid for it, then I have sacrificed my claim, and thus a part of myself. Consequently, all absolute giving, a giving which is a total loss from the start, is a self-sacrifice. Ordinary giving for which no return is received is felt as a loss; but a sacrifice is meant to be like a loss, so that one may be sure that the egoistic claim no longer exists. Therefore the gift should be given as if it were being destroyed. But since the gift represents myself, I have in that case destroyed myself, given myself away without expectation of return. Yet, looked at in another way, this intentional loss is also a gain, for if you can give yourself it proves that you possess yourself. Nobody can give what he has not got. So anyone who can sacrifice himself and forgo his claim must have had it; in other words, he must have been conscious of the claim. This presupposes an act of considerable self-knowledge, lacking which one remains permanently unconscious of such claims. It is therefore quite logical that the confession of sin should come before the rite of transformation in the Mass. The self-examination is intended to make one conscious of the selfish claim bound up with every gift, so that it may be consciously given up; otherwise the gift is no sacrifice. The sacrifice proves that you possess yourself, for it does not mean just letting yourself be passively taken: it is a conscious and deliberate self-surrender, which proves that you have full control of yourself, that is, of your ego. The ego thus becomes the object of a moral act, for "I" am making a decision on behalf of an authority which is supraordinate to my ego nature. I am, as it were, deciding against my ego and renouncing my claim. The possibility of self-renunciation is an established psychological fact whose philosophical implications I do not propose to discuss. Psychologically, it means that the ego is a relative quantity which can be subsumed under various supraordinate authorities. What are these authorities? They are not to be equated outright with collective moral consciousness, as Freud wanted to do with his superego, but rather with certain psychic conditions which existed in man from the beginning and are not acquired by experience. Behind a man's actions there stands neither public opinion nor the moral code,[13] but the personality of which he is still unconscious. Just as a man still is what he always was, so he already is what he will become. The conscious mind does not embrace the totality of a man, for this totality consists only partly of his conscious contents, and for the other and far greater part, of his unconscious, which is of indefinite extent with no assignable limits. In this totality the conscious mind is contained like a smaller circle within a larger one. Hence it is quite possible for the ego to be made into an object, that is to say, for a more compendious personality to emerge in the course of development and take the ego into its service. Since this growth of personality comes out of the unconscious, which is by definition unlimited, the extent of the personality now gradually realizing itself cannot in practice be limited either. But, unlike the Freudian superego, it is still individual. It is in fact individuality in the highest sense, and therefore theoretically limited, since no individual can possibly display *every* quality. (I have called this process of realization the "individuation process.") So far as the personality is still potential, it can be called transcendent, and

13 If there were really nothing behind him but collective standards of value on the one hand and natural instincts on the other, every breach of morality would be simply a rebellion of instinct. In that case valuable and meaningful innovations would be impossible, for the instincts are the oldest and most conservative element in man and beast alike. Such a view forgets the creative instinct which, although it can behave like an instinct, is seldom found in nature and is confined almost exclusively to *Homo sapiens*.

so far as it is unconscious, it is indistinguishable from all those things that carry its projections—in other words, the unconscious personality merges with our environment in accordance with the above-named *participation mystique*. This fact is of the greatest practical importance because it renders intelligible the peculiar symbols through which this projected entity expresses itself in dreams. By this I mean the symbols of the outside world and the cosmic symbols. These form the psychological basis for the conception of man as a microcosm, whose fate, as we know, is bound up with the macrocosm through the astrological components of his character.

The term "self" seemed to me a suitable one for this unconscious substrate, whose actual exponent in consciousness is the ego. The ego stands to the self as the moved to the mover, or as object to subject, because the determining factors which radiate out from the self surround the ego on all sides and are therefore supraordinate to it. The self, like the unconscious, is an *a priori* existent out of which the ego evolves. It is, so to speak, an unconscious prefiguration of the ego. It is not I who create myself, rather I happen to myself. This realization is of fundamental importance for the psychology of religious phenomena, which is why Ignatius Loyola started off his *Spiritual Exercises* with "Homo creatus est" as their "fundamentum." But, fundamental as it is, it can be only half the psychological truth. If it were the whole truth it would be tantamount to determinism, for if man were merely a creature that came into being as a result of something already existing unconsciously, he would have no freedom and there would be no point in consciousness. Psychology must reckon with the fact that despite the causal nexus man does enjoy a feeling of freedom, which is identical with autonomy of consciousness. However much the ego can be proved to be dependent and preconditioned, it cannot be convinced that it has no freedom. An absolutely preformed consciousness and a totally dependent ego would be a pointless farce, since everything would proceed just as well or even better unconsciously. The existence of ego consciousness has meaning only if it is free and autonomous. By stating these facts we have, it is true, established an antinomy, but we have at the same time given a picture of things as they are. There are temporal, local, and individual differences in the degree of dependence and freedom. In reality both are always present: the supremacy of the self and the hybris of consciousness.

392 This conflict between conscious and unconscious is at least brought nearer to a solution through our becoming aware of it. Such an act of realization is presupposed in the act of self-sacrifice. The ego must make itself conscious of its claim, and the self must cause the ego to renounce it. This can happen in two ways:

393 1. I renounce my claim in consideration of a general moral principle, namely that one must not expect repayment for a gift. In this case the "self" coincides with public opinion and the moral code. It is then identical with Freud's superego and for this reason it is projected into the environment and therefore remains unconscious as an autonomous factor.

394 2. I renounce my claim because I feel impelled to do so for painful inner reasons which are not altogether clear to me. These reasons give me no particular moral satisfaction; on the contrary, I even feel some resistance to them. But I must yield to the power which suppresses my egoistic claim. Here the self is integrated; it is withdrawn from projection and has become perceptible as a determining psychic factor. The objection that in this case the moral code is simply unconscious must be ruled out, because I am perfectly well aware of the moral criticism against which I would have to assert my egoism. Where the ego wish clashes with the moral standard, it is not easy to show that the tendency which suppresses it is individual and not collective. But where it is a case of conflicting loyalties, or we find ourselves in a situation of which the classic example is Hosea's marriage with the harlot, then the ego wish coincides with the collective moral standard, and Hosea would have been bound to accuse Jehovah of immorality. Similarly, the unjust steward would have had to admit his guilt. Jesus took a different view.[14] Experiences of this kind make it clear that the self cannot be equated either with collective morality or with natural instinct, but must be conceived as a determining factor whose nature is individual and unique. The superego is a necessary and unavoidable substitute for the experience of the self.

14 To the defiler of the Sabbath he said: "Man, if indeed thou knowest what thou doest, thou art blessed; but if thou knowest not, thou art cursed, and a transgressor of the law." James, *The Apocryphal New Testament,* p. 33.

5 These two ways of renouncing one's egoistic claim reveal not only a difference of attitude, but also a difference of situation. In the first case the situation need not affect me personally and directly; in the second, the gift must necessarily be a very personal one which seriously affects the giver and forces him to overcome himself. In the one case it is merely a question, say, of going to Mass; in the other it is more like Abraham's sacrifice of his son or Christ's decision in Gethsemane. The one may be felt very earnestly and experienced with all piety, but the other is the real thing.[15]

6 So long as the self is unconscious, it corresponds to Freud's superego and is a source of perpetual moral conflict. If, however, it is withdrawn from projection and is no longer identical with public opinion, then one is truly one's own yea and nay. The self then functions as a union of opposites and thus constitutes the most immediate experience of the Divine which it is psychologically possible to imagine.[16]

(*c*) *The Sacrificer*

7 What I sacrifice is my own selfish claim, and by doing this I give up myself. Every sacrifice is therefore, to a greater or lesser degree, a self-sacrifice. The degree to which it is so depends on the significance of the gift. If it is of great value to me and touches my most personal feelings, I can be sure that in giving up my egoistic claim I shall challenge my ego personality to revolt. I can also be sure that the power which suppresses this claim, and thus suppresses me, must be the self. Hence it is the self that causes me to make the sacrifice; nay more, it compels me to make it.[17] The self is the sacrificer, and I am the sacrificed gift, the human sacrifice. Let us try for a moment to look into Abraham's soul when he was commanded to sacrifice his only son.

15 In order to avoid misunderstandings, I must emphasize that I am speaking only from personal experience, and not of the mysterious reality which the Mass has for the believer.

16 Cf. the "uniting symbol" in *Psychological Types,* Def. 51.

17 In Indian philosophy we find a parallel in Prajapati and Purusha Narayana. Purusha sacrifices himself at the command of Prajapati, but at bottom the two are identical. Cf. the Shatapatha-Brahmana (Sacred Books of the East, XLIV, pp. 172ff.); also the Rig-Veda, X, 90 (trans. by Macnicol, pp. 28–29).

Quite apart from the compassion he felt for his child, would not a father in such a position feel himself as the victim, and feel that he was plunging the knife into his own breast? He would be at the same time the sacrificer and the sacrificed.

398 Now, since the relation of the ego to the self is like that of the son to the father, we can say that when the self calls on us to sacrifice ourselves, it is really carrying out the sacrificial act on itself. We know more or less what this act means to us, but what it means to the self is not so clear. As the self can only be comprehended by us in particular acts, but remains concealed from us as a whole because it is more comprehensive than we are, all we can do is to draw conclusions from the little of the self that we can experience. We have seen that a sacrifice only takes place when we feel the self actually carrying it out on ourselves. We may also venture to surmise that in so far as the self stands to us in the relation of father to son, the self in some sort feels our sacrifice as a sacrifice of itself. From that sacrifice we gain ourselves—our "self"—for we have only what we give. But what does the self gain? We see it entering into manifestation, freeing itself from unconscious projection, and, as it grips us, entering into our lives and so passing from unconsciousness into consciousness, from potentiality into actuality. What it is in the diffuse unconscious state we do not know; we only know that in becoming ourself it has become man.

399 This process of becoming human is represented in dreams and inner images as the putting together of many scattered units, and sometimes as the gradual emergence and clarification of something that was always there.[18] The speculations of alchemy, and also of some Gnostics, revolve round this process. It is

18 This contradiction is unavoidable because the concept of the self allows only of antinomial statements. The self is by definition an entity more comprehensive than the conscious personality. Consequently the latter cannot pass any comprehensive judgment on the self; any judgment and any statement about it is incomplete and has to be supplemented (but not nullified) by a conditioned negative. If I assert, "The self exists," I must supplement this by saying, "But it seems not to exist." For the sake of completeness I must also invert the proposition and say, "The self does not exist, but yet seems to exist." Actually, this inversion is superfluous in view of the fact that the self is not a philosophical concept like Kant's "thing-in-itself," but an empirical concept of psychology, and can therefore be hypostatized if the above precautions are taken.

likewise expressed in Christian dogma, and more particularly in the transformation mystery of the Mass. The psychology of this process makes it easier to understand why, in the Mass, man appears as both the sacrificer and the sacrificed gift, and why it is not man who is these things, but God who is both; why God becomes the suffering and dying man, and why man, through partaking of the Glorified Body, gains the assurance of resurrection and becomes aware of his participation in Godhead.

0 As I have already suggested, the integration or humanization of the self is initiated from the conscious side by our making ourselves aware of our selfish aims; we examine our motives and try to form as complete and objective a picture as possible of our own nature. It is an act of self-recollection, a gathering together of what is scattered, of all the things in us that have never been properly related, and a coming to terms with oneself with a view to achieving full consciousness. (Unconscious self-sacrifice is merely an accident, not a moral act.) Self-recollection, however, is about the hardest and most repellent thing there is for man, who is predominantly unconscious. Human nature has an invincible dread of becoming more conscious of itself. What nevertheless drives us to it is the self, which demands sacrifice by sacrificing itself to us. Conscious realization or the bringing together of the scattered parts is in one sense an act of the ego's will, but in another sense it is a spontaneous manifestation of the self,[19] which was always there. Individuation appears, on the one hand, as the synthesis of a new unity which previously consisted of scattered particles, and on the other hand, as the revelation of something which existed before the ego and is in fact its father or creator and also its totality. Up to a point we create the self by making ourselves conscious of our unconscious contents, and to that extent it is our son. This is why the alchemists called their incorruptible substance—which means precisely the self—the *filius philosophorum*. But we are forced to make this effort by the unconscious presence of the self, which is all the time urging us to overcome our unconsciousness. From that point of view the self is the father. This accounts for certain alchemical terms, such as Mercurius Senex (Hermes Trismegistus) and Saturnus, who in Gnosticism was regarded as both

[19] In so far as it is the self that actuates the ego's self-recollection.

greybeard and youth, just as Mercurius was in alchemy. These psychological connections are seen most clearly in the ancient conceptions of the Original Man, the Protanthropos, and the Son of Man. Christ as the Logos is from all eternity, but in his human form he is the "Son of Man." [20] As the Logos, he is the world-creating principle. This corresponds with the relation of the self to consciousness, without which no world could be perceived at all. The Logos is the real *principium individuationis,* because everything proceeds from it, and because everything which is, from crystal to man, exists only in individual form. In the infinite variety and differentiation of the phenomenal world is expressed the essence of the *auctor rerum.* As a correspondence we have, on the one hand, the indefiniteness and unlimited extent of the unconscious self (despite its individuality and uniqueness), its creative relation to individual consciousness, and, on the other hand, the individual human being as a mode of its manifestation. Ancient philosophy paralleled this idea with the legend of the dismembered Dionysus, who, as creator, is the ἀμέριστος (undivided) νοῦς, and, as the creature, the μεμερισμένος (divided) νοῦς.[21] Dionysus is distributed throughout the whole of nature, and just as Zeus once devoured the throbbing heart of the god, so his worshippers tore wild animals to pieces in order to reintegrate his dismembered spirit. The gathering together of the light-substance in Barbelo-Gnosis and in Manichaeism points in the same direction. The psychological equivalent of this is the integration of the self through conscious assimilation of the split-off contents. Self-recollection is a gathering together of the self. It is in this sense that we have to understand the instructions which Monoimos gives to Theophrastus:

> Seek him [God] from out thyself, and learn who it is that taketh possession of everything in thee, saying: *my* god, *my* spirit [νοῦς], *my* understanding, *my* soul, *my* body; and learn whence is sorrow and joy, and love and hate, and waking though one would not, and sleeping though one would not, and getting angry though one

20 If I use the unhistorical term "self" for the corresponding processes in the psyche, I do so out of a conscious desire not to trespass on other preserves, but to confine myself exclusively to the field of empirical psychology.

21 Firmicus Maternus, *De errore profanarum religionum,* 7, 8.

would not, and falling in love though one would not. And if thou shouldst closely investigate these things, thou wilt find Him in thyself, the One and the Many, like to that little point, for it is from thee that he hath his origin.[22]

1 Self-reflection or—what comes to the same thing—the urge to individuation gathers together what is scattered and multifarious, and exalts it to the original form of the One, the Primordial Man. In this way our existence as separate beings, our former ego nature, is abolished, the circle of consciousness is widened, and because the paradoxes have been made conscious the sources of conflict are dried up. This approximation to the self is a kind of repristination or apocatastasis, in so far as the self has an "incorruptible" or "eternal" character on account of its being pre-existent to consciousness.[23] This feeling is expressed in the words from the *benedictio fontis:* "Et quos aut sexus in corpore aut aetas discernit in tempore, omnes in unam pariat gratia mater infantiam" (And may Mother Grace bring forth into one infancy all those whom sex has separated in the body, or age in time).

2 The figure of the divine sacrificer corresponds feature for feature to the empirical modes of manifestation of the archetype that lies at the root of almost all known conceptions of God. This archetype is not merely a static image, but dynamic, full of movement. It is always a drama, whether in heaven, on earth, or in hell.[24]

(*d*) *The Archetype of Sacrifice*

3 Comparing the basic ideas of the Mass with the imagery of the Zosimos visions, we find that, despite considerable differences, there is a remarkable degree of similarity. For the sake of clearness I give the similarities and differences in tabular form.

22 Hippolytus, *Elenchos*, VIII, 15.

23 And also on account of the fact that the unconscious is only conditionally bound by space and time. The comparative frequency of telepathic phenomena proves that space and time have only a relative validity for the psyche. Evidence for this is furnished by Rhine's experiments. Cf. my "Synchronicity."

24 The word "hell" may strike the reader as odd in this connection. I would, however, recommend him to study the brothel scene in James Joyce's *Ulysses,* or James Hogg's *The Private Memoirs and Confessions of a Justified Sinner.*

Zosimos	*Mass*
SIMILARITIES	
1. The chief actors are two priests.	1. There is the priest, and Christ the eternal priest.
2. One priest slays the other.	2. The *Mactatio Christi* takes place as the priest pronounces the words of consecration.
3. Other human beings are sacrificed as well.	3. The congregation itself is a sacrificial gift.
4. The sacrifice is a voluntary self-sacrifice.	4. Christ offers himself freely as a sacrifice.
5. It is a painful death.	5. He suffers in the sacrificial act.
6. The victim is dismembered.	6. Breaking of the Bread.
7. There is a *thysia.*	7. Offering up of incense.
8. The priest eats his own flesh.	8. Christ drinks his own blood (St. Chrysostom).
9. He is transformed into spirit.	9. The substances are transformed into the body and blood of Christ.
10. A shining white figure appears, like the midday sun.	10. The Host is shown as the Beatific Vision ("Quaesivi vultum tuum, Domine") in the greater elevation.
11. Production of the "divine water."	11. The Grace conferred by the Mass; similarity of water chalice and font; water a symbol of grace.
DIFFERENCES	
1. The whole sacrificial process is an individual dream vision, a fragment of the unconscious depicting itself in dream consciousness.	1. The Mass is a conscious artifact, the product of many centuries and many minds.
2. The dreamer is only a spectator of the symbolic action.	2. Priest and congregation both participate in the mystery.
3. The action is a bloody and gruesome human sacrifice.	3. Nothing obnoxious; the *mactatio* itself is not mentioned. There is only the bloodless sacrifice of bread and wine (*incruente immolatur!*).

4. The sacrifice is accompanied by a scalping.	4. Nothing comparable.
5. It is also performed on a dragon, and is therefore an animal sacrifice.	5. Symbolic sacrifice of the Lamb.
6. The flesh is roasted.	6. The substances are spiritually transformed.
7. The meaning of the sacrifice is the production of the divine water, used for the transmutation of metals and, mystically, for the birth of the self.	7. The meaning of the Mass is the communion of the living Christ with his flock.
8. What is transformed in the vision is presumably the planetary demon Saturn, the supreme Archon (who is related to the God of the Hebrews). It is the dark, heavy, material principle in man—*hyle*—which is transformed into pneuma.	8. What is transformed in the Mass is God, who as Father begat the Son in human form, suffered and died in that form, and rose up again to his origin.

404 The gross concretism of the vision is so striking that one might easily feel tempted, for aesthetic and other reasons, to drop the comparison with the Mass altogether. If I nevertheless venture to bring out certain analogies, I do so not with the rationalistic intention of devaluing the sacred ceremony by putting it on a level with a piece of pagan nature worship. If I have any aim at all apart from scientific truth, it is to show that the most important mystery of the Catholic Church rests, among other things, on psychic conditions which are deeply rooted in the human soul.

405 The vision, which in all probability has the character of a dream, must be regarded as a spontaneous psychic product that was never consciously intended. Like all dreams, it is a product of nature. The Mass, on the other hand, is a product of man's mind or spirit, and is a definitely conscious proceeding. To use an old but not outmoded nomenclature, we can call the vision *psychic,* and the Mass *pneumatic.* The vision is undifferentiated raw material, while the Mass is a highly differentiated artifact. That is why the one is gruesome and the other beautiful. If the Mass is antique, it is antique in the best sense of the word,

and its liturgy is therefore satisfying to the highest requirements of the present day. In contrast to this, the vision is archaic and primitive, but its symbolism points directly to the fundamental alchemical idea of the incorruptible substance, namely to the self, which is beyond change. The vision is a piece of unalloyed naturalism, banal, grotesque, squalid, horrifying and profound as nature herself. Its meaning is not clear, but it allows itself to be divined with the abysmal uncertainty and ambiguity that pertains to all things nonhuman, suprahuman, and subhuman. The Mass, on the other hand, represents and clearly expresses the Deity itself, and clothes it in the garment of the most beautiful humanity.

406 From all this it is evident that the vision and the Mass are two different things, so different as to be almost incommensurable. But if we could succeed in reconstructing the natural process in the unconscious on which the Mass is psychically based, we should probably obtain a picture which would be rather more commensurable with the vision of Zosimos. According to the view of the Church, the Mass is based on the historical events in the life of Jesus. From this "real" life we can single out certain details that add a few concretistic touches to our picture and thus bring it closer to the vision. For instance, I would mention the scourging, the crowning with thorns, and the clothing in a purple robe, which show Jesus as the archaic sacrificed king. This is further emphasized by the Barabbas episode (the name means "son of the father") which leads to the sacrifice of the king. Then there is the agony of death by crucifixion, a shameful and horrifying spectacle, far indeed from any "incruente immolatur"! The right pleural cavity and probably the right ventricle of the heart were cut open by the spear, so that blood clots and serum flowed out. If we add these details to the process which underlies the Mass, we shall see that they form a striking equivalent to certain archaic and barbarous features of the vision. There are also the fundamental dogmatic ideas to be considered. As is shown by the reference to the sacrifice of Isaac in the prayer *Unde et memores,* the sacrifice has the character not only of a human sacrifice, but the sacrifice of a son—and an *only* son. That is the cruellest and most horrible kind of sacrifice we can imagine, so horrible that, as we know, Abraham

was not required to carry it out.[25] And even if he had carried it out, a stab in the heart with a knife would have been a quick and relatively painless death for the victim. Even the bloody Aztec ceremony of cutting out the heart was a swift death. But the sacrifice of the son which forms the essential feature of the Mass began with scourging and mockery, and culminated in six hours of suspension on a cross to which the victim was nailed hand and foot—not exactly a quick death, but a slow and exquisite form of torture. As if that were not enough, crucifixion was regarded as a disgraceful death for slaves, so that the physical cruelty is balanced by the moral cruelty.

407 Leaving aside for the moment the unity of nature of Father and Son—which it is possible to do because they are two distinct Persons who are not to be confused with one another—let us try to imagine the feelings of a father who saw his son suffering such a death, knowing that it was he himself who had sent him into the enemy's country and deliberately exposed him to this danger. Executions of this kind were generally carried out as an act of revenge or as punishment for a crime, with the idea that both father and son should suffer. The idea of punishment can be seen particularly clearly in the crucifixion between two thieves. The punishment is carried out on God himself, and the model for this execution is the ritual slaying of the king. The king is killed when he shows signs of impotence, or when failure of the crops arouses doubts as to his efficacy. Therefore he is killed in order to improve the condition of his people, just as God is sacrificed for the salvation of mankind.

408 What is the reason for this "punishment" of God? Despite the almost blasphemous nature of this question, we must nevertheless ask it in view of the obviously punitive character of the

25 How Jewish piety reacted to this sacrifice can be seen from the following Talmudic legend: " 'And I,' cried Abraham, 'swear that I will not go down from the altar until you have heard me. When you commanded me to sacrifice my son Isaac you offended against your word, "in Isaac shall your descendants be named." So if ever my descendants offend against you, and you wish to punish them, then remember that you too are not without fault, and forgive them.' 'Very well, then,' replied the Lord, 'there behind you is a ram caught in the thicket with his horns. Offer up that instead of your son Isaac. And if ever your descendants sin against me, and I sit in judgment over them on New Year's Day, let them blow the horn of a ram, that I may remember my words, and temper justice with mercy.' " Fremer and Schnitzer, *Legenden aus dem Talmud,* pp. 34f.

sacrifice. The usual explanation is that Christ was punished for our sins.[26] The dogmatic validity of this answer is not in question here. As I am in no way concerned with the Church's explanation, but only wish to reconstruct the underlying psychic process, we must logically assume the existence of a guilt proportionate to the punishment. If mankind is the guilty party, logic surely demands that mankind should be punished. But if God takes the punishment on himself, he exculpates mankind, and we must then conjecture that it is not mankind that is guilty, but God (which would logically explain why he took the guilt on himself). For reasons that can readily be understood, a satisfactory answer is not to be expected from orthodox Christianity. But such an answer may be found in the Old Testament, in Gnosticism, and in late Catholic speculation. From the Old Testament we know that though Yahweh was a guardian of the law he was not just, and that he suffered from fits of rage which he had every occasion to regret.[27] And from certain Gnostic systems it is clear that the *auctor rerum* was a lower archon who falsely imagined that he had created a perfect world, whereas in fact it was woefully imperfect. On account of his Saturnine disposition this demiurgic archon has affinities with the Jewish Yahweh, who was likewise a world creator. His work was imperfect and did not prosper, but the blame cannot be placed on the creature any more than one can curse the pots for being badly turned out by the potter! This argument led to the Marcionite Reformation and to purging the New Testament of elements derived from the Old. Even as late as the seventeenth century the learned Jesuit, Nicolas Caussin, declared that the unicorn was a fitting symbol for the God of the Old Testament, because in his wrath he reduced the world to confusion like an angry rhinoceros (unicorn), until, overcome by the love of a pure virgin, he was changed in her lap into a God of Love.[28]

26 Isaiah 53:5: "But he was wounded for our transgressions, he was bruised for our iniquities: the chastisement of our peace was upon him; and with his stripes we are healed."

27 See "Answer to Job," in this volume.

28 Caussin, *De symbolica Aegyptiorum sapientia. Polyhistor symbolicus, Electorum symbolorum, et Parabolarum historicarum stromata* (1618), p. 401. Cf. also Philippus Picinelli, *Mondo Simbolico,* p. 299: "Of a truth God, terrible beyond measure, appeared before the world peaceful and wholly tamed after dwelling in the womb of the most blessed Virgin. St. Bonaventura said that Christ was tamed and pacified by the most kindly Mary, so that he should not punish the sinner with eternal death."

409 In these explanations we find the natural logic we missed in the answer of the Church. God's guilt consisted in the fact that, as creator of the world and king of his creatures, he was inadequate and therefore had to submit to the ritual slaying. For primitive man the concrete king was perfectly suited to this purpose, but not for a higher level of civilization with a more spiritual conception of God. Earlier ages could still dethrone their gods by destroying their images or putting them in chains. At a higher level, however, one god could be dethroned only by another god, and when monotheism developed, God could only transform himself.

410 The fact that the transformative process takes the form of a "punishment"—Zosimos uses this very word (κόλασις)—may be due to a kind of rationalization or a need to offer some explanation of its cruelty. Such a need only arises at a higher level of consciousness with developed feeling, which then seeks an adequate reason for the revolting and incomprehensible cruelty of the procedure. (A modern parallel would be the experience of dismemberment in shamanistic initiations.) The readiest conjecture at this level is that some guilt or sin is being punished. In this way the transformation process acquires a moral function that can scarcely be conceived as underlying the original event. It seems more likely that a higher and later level of consciousness found itself confronted with an experience for which no sensible reasons or explanations had ever been given, but which it tried to make intelligible by weaving into it a moral aetiology. It is not difficult to see that dismemberment originally served the purpose of reconstituting the neophyte as a new and more effective human being. Initiation even has the aspect of a healing.[29] In the light of these facts, moral interpretation in terms of punishment seems beside the mark and arouses the suspicion that dismemberment has still not been properly understood. A moral interpretation is inadequate because it fails to understand the contradiction at the heart of its explanation, namely that guilt should be avoided if one doesn't want to be punished. But, for the neophyte, it would be a real sin if he shrank from the torture of initiation. The torture inflicted on him is *not* a punishment but the indispensable means of leading him towards his destiny. Also, these ceremonies often take place at so young an age that a guilt of corresponding proportions is quite out of

[29] Eliade, *Le Chamanisme,* p. 39.

the question. For this reason, the moralistic view of suffering as punishment seems to me not only inadequate but misleading. It is obviously a primitive attempt to give a psychological explanation of an age-old archetypal idea that had never before been the object of reflection. Such ideas and rituals, far from ever having been invented, simply happened and were acted long before they were thought. I have seen primitives practising rites of which none of them had the remotest idea what they meant, and in Europe we still find customs whose meaning has always been unconscious. First attempts at explanation usually turn out to be somewhat clumsy.

411 The aspect of torture, then, is correlated with a detached and observing consciousness that has not yet understood the real meaning of dismemberment. What is performed concretely on the sacrificial animal, and what the shaman believes to be actually happening to himself, appears on a higher level, in the vision of Zosimos, as a psychic process in which a product of the unconscious, an homunculus, is cut up and transformed. By all the rules of dream-interpretation, this is an aspect of the observing subject himself; that is to say, Zosimos sees himself as an homunculus, or rather the unconscious represents him as such, as an incomplete, stunted, dwarfish creature who is made of some heavy material (lead or bronze) and thus signifies the "hylical man." Such a one is dark, and sunk in materiality. He is essentially unconscious and therefore in need of transformation and enlightenment. For this purpose his body must be taken apart and dissolved into its constituents, a process known in alchemy as the *divisio, separatio* and *solutio,* and in later treatises as *discrimination* and *self-knowledge.*[30] This psychological process is admittedly painful and for many people a positive torture. But, as always, every step forward along the path of individuation is achieved only at the cost of suffering.

412 In the case of Zosimos there is of course no real consciousness of the transformative process, as is abundantly clear from his own interpretation of the vision: he thought the dream imagery was showing him the "production of the waters." We can see from this that he was still exteriorizing the transformation and did not feel it in any way as an alteration of his own psyche.

[30] Particularly in Gerhard Dorn, "Speculativae philosophiae," *Theatrum chemicum,* I (1602), pp. 276f.

413 A similar state of affairs prevails in Christian psychology whenever the rites and dogmas are taken as merely external factors and are not experienced as inner events. But, just as the *imitatio Christi* in general, and the Mass in particular, endeavour to include the believer in the process of transformation, the Mass actually representing him as a sacrificial gift parallel with Christ, so a better understanding of Christianity raises it as high above the sphere of "mind" as the rite of the Mass is above the archaic level of the Zosimos vision. The Mass tries to effect a *participation mystique*—or identity—of priest and congregation with Christ, so that on the one hand the soul is assimilated to Christ and on the other hand the Christ-figure is recollected in the soul. It is a transformation of God and man alike, since the Mass is, at least by implication, a repetition of the whole drama of Incarnation.

III. THE MASS AND THE INDIVIDUATION PROCESS

414 Looked at from the psychological standpoint, Christ, as the Original Man (Son of Man, second Adam, τέλειος ἄνθρωπος), represents a totality which surpasses and includes the ordinary man, and which corresponds to the total personality that transcends consciousness.[31] We have called this personality the "self." Just as, on the more archaic level of the Zosimos vision, the homunculus is transformed into pneuma and exalted, so the mystery of the Eucharist transforms the soul of the empirical man, who is only a part of himself, into his totality, symbolically expressed by Christ. In this sense, therefore, we can speak of the Mass as the *rite of the individuation process.*

415 Reflections of this kind can be found very early on in the old Christian writings, as for instance in the Acts of John, one of the most important of the apocryphal texts that have come down to us.[32] That part of the text with which we are concerned here begins with a description of a mystical "round dance" which Christ instituted before his crucifixion. He told his disciples to hold hands and form a ring, while he himself stood

[31] Cf. my *Aion,* Ch. V.

[32] *The Apocryphal New Testament.* The Acts of John were probably written during the first half of the 2nd cent.

in the centre. As they moved round in a circle, Christ sang a song of praise, from which I would single out the following characteristic verses: [33]

> I will be saved and I will save, Amen.
> I will be loosed and I will loose,[34] Amen.
> I will be wounded and I will wound, Amen.
> I will be begotten and I will beget, Amen.
> I will eat and I will be eaten, Amen.
> . . .
> I will be thought, being wholly spirit, Amen.
> I will be washed and I will wash, Amen.
> Grace paces the round. I will blow the pipe. Dance
> the round all, Amen.
> . . .
> The Eight [ogdoad] sings praises with us, Amen.
> The Twelve paces the round aloft, Amen.
> To each and all it is given to dance, Amen.
> Who joins not the dance mistakes the event, Amen.
> . . .
> I will be united and I will unite, Amen.
> . . .
> A lamp am I to you that perceive me, Amen.
> A mirror am I to you that know me, Amen.
> A door am I to you that knock on me, Amen.
> A way am I to you the wayfarer.

Now as you respond to my dancing, behold yourself in me who speaks . . .

As you dance, ponder what I do, for yours is this human suffering which I will to suffer. For you would be powerless to understand your suffering had I not been sent to you as the Logos by the Father. . . . If you had understood suffering, you would have non-suffering. Learn to suffer, and you shall understand how not to suffer. . . . Understand the Word of Wisdom in me.[35]

416 I would like to interrupt the text here, as we have come to a natural break, and introduce a few psychological remarks. They will help us to understand some further passages that still have

33 Ibid., pp. 253f., modified.

34 [Or: I will be freed and I will free.—TRANS.]

35 Trans. based on James, pp. 253f., and that of Ralph Manheim from the German of Max Pulver, "Jesus' Round Dance and Crucifixion according to the Acts of St. John," in *The Mysteries*, pp. 179f.

to be discussed. Although our text is obviously based on New Testament models, what strikes us most of all is its antithetical and paradoxical style, which has very little in common with the spirit of the Gospels. This feature only appears in a veiled way in the canonical writings, for instance in the parable of the unjust steward (Luke 16), in the Lord's Prayer ("Lead us not into temptation"), in Matthew 10:16 ("Be wise as serpents"), John 10:34 ("Ye are gods"), in the logion of the Codex Bezae to Luke 6:4,[36] in the apocryphal saying "Whoso is near unto me is near unto the fire," and so on. Echoes of the antithetical style can also be found in Matthew 10:26: ". . . . for nothing is covered that will not be revealed, or hidden that will not be known."

417 Paradox is a characteristic of the Gnostic writings. It does more justice to the *unknowable* than clarity can do, for uniformity of meaning robs the mystery of its darkness and sets it up as something that is *known*. That is a usurpation, and it leads the human intellect into hybris by pretending that it, the intellect, has got hold of the transcendent mystery by a cognitive act and has "grasped" it. The paradox therefore reflects a higher level of intellect and, by not forcibly representing the unknowable as known, gives a more faithful picture of the real state of affairs.

418 These antithetical predications show the amount of *reflection* that has gone into the hymn: it formulates the figure of our Lord in a series of paradoxes, as God and man, sacrificer and sacrificed. The latter formulation is important because the hymn was sung just before Jesus was arrested, that is, at about the moment when the synoptic gospels speak of the Last Supper and John—among other things—of the parable of the vine. John, significantly enough, does not mention the Last Supper, and in the Acts of John its place is taken by the "round dance." But the round table, like the round dance, stands for synthesis and union. In the Last Supper this takes the form of participation in the body and blood of Christ, i.e., there is an ingestion and assimilation of the Lord, and in the round dance there is a circular circumambulation round the Lord as the central point. Despite the outward difference of the symbols, they have a common meaning: Christ is taken into the midst of the disciples. But, although the two rites have this common basic meaning,

36 See James, p. 33.

the outward difference between them should not be overlooked. The classical Eucharistic feast follows the synoptic gospels, whereas the one in the Acts of John follows the Johannine pattern. One could almost say that it expresses, in a form borrowed from some pagan mystery feast, a more immediate relationship of the congregation to Christ, after the manner of the Johannine parable: "I am the vine, ye are the branches. He that abideth in me, and I in him, the same bringeth forth much fruit" (John 15:5). This close relationship is represented by the circle and central point: the two parts are indispensable to each other and equivalent. Since olden times the circle with a centre has been a symbol for the Deity, illustrating the wholeness of God incarnate: the single point in the centre and the series of points constituting the circumference. Ritual circumambulation often bases itself quite consciously on the cosmic picture of the starry heavens revolving, on the "dance of the stars," an idea that is still preserved in the comparison of the twelve disciples with the zodiacal constellations, as also in the depictions of the zodiac that are sometimes found in churches, in front of the altar or on the roof of the nave. Some such picture may well have been at the back of the medieval ball-game of pelota that was played in church by the bishop and his clergy.

419 At all events, the aim and effect of the solemn round dance is to impress upon the mind the image of the circle and the centre and the relation of each point along the periphery to that centre.[37] Psychologically this arrangement is equivalent to a mandala and is thus a symbol of the self,[38] the point of reference not only of the individual ego but of all those who are of like mind or who are bound together by fate. The self is not an ego but a supraordinate totality embracing the conscious and the unconscious. But since the latter has no assignable limits and

[37] Another idea of the kind is that every human being is a ray of sunlight. This image occurs in the Spanish poet Jorge Guillén, *Cantico: Fe de Vida,* pp. 24–25 ("Más allá," VI):

> Where could I stray to, where?
> This point is my centre . . .
>
> With this earth and this ocean
> To rise to the infinite:
> One ray more of the sun. (Trans. by J. M. Cohen.)

[38] Cf. *Aion,* Ch. IV, and "Psychology and Poetry."

in its deeper layers is of a collective nature, it cannot be distinguished from that of another individual. As a result, it continually creates that ubiquitous *participation mystique* which is the unity of many, the *one* man in all men. This psychological fact forms the basis for the archetype of the ἄνθρωπος, the Son of Man, the *homo maximus,* the *vir unus,* purusha, etc.[39] Because the unconscious, in fact and by definition, cannot be discriminated as such, the most we can hope to do is to infer its nature from the empirical material. Certain unconscious contents are undoubtedly personal and individual and cannot be attributed to any other individual. But, besides these, there are numerous others that can be observed in almost identical form in many different individuals in no way connected with one another. These experiences suggest that the unconscious has a collective aspect. It is therefore difficult to understand how people today can still doubt the existence of a collective unconscious. After all, nobody would dream of regarding the instincts or human morphology as personal acquisitions or personal caprices. The unconscious is the universal mediator among men. It is in a sense the all-embracing One, or the one psychic substratum common to all. The alchemists knew it as their Mercurius and they called him the mediator in analogy to Christ.[40] Ecclesiastical doctrine says the same thing about Christ, and so, particularly, does our hymn. Its antithetical statements could, however, be interpreted as referring just as well to Mercurius, if not better.

420 For instance, in the first verse, "I will be saved," it is not clear how far the Lord is able to say such a thing of himself, since he is the saviour (σωτήρ) par excellence. Mercurius, on the other hand, the helpful arcane substance of the alchemists, is the world-soul imprisoned in matter and, like the Original Man who fell into the embrace of Physis, is in need of salvation through the labours of the artifex. Mercurius is set free ("loosed") and redeemed; as *aqua permanens* he is also the

39 The universality of this figure may explain why its epiphanies take so many different forms. For instance, it is related in the Acts of John (James, p. 251) that Drusiana saw the Lord once "in the likeness of John" and another time "in that of a youth." The disciple James saw him as a child, but John as an adult. John saw him first as "a small man and uncomely," and then again as one reaching to heaven (p. 251). Sometimes his body felt "material and solid," but sometimes "the substance was immaterial and as if it existed not at all" (p. 252).

40 "The Spirit Mercurius" (Swiss edn., pp. 126ff.).

classical solvent. "I will be wounded, and I will wound" is clearer: it refers to the wound in Christ's side and to the divisive sword. But Mercurius too, as the arcane substance, is divided or pierced through with the sword (*separatio* and *penetratio*), and wounds himself with the sword or *telum passionis,* the dart of love. The reference to Christ is less clear in the words "I will be begotten, and I will beget." The first statement refers essentially to him in so far as the Son was begotten by the Holy Ghost and not created, but the "begetting" is generally held to be the property of the Holy Ghost and not of Christ as such. It certainly remains a moot point whether Mercurius as the world-soul was begotten or created, but he is unquestionably "vivifying," and in his ithyphallic form as Hermes Kyllenios he is actually the symbol of generation. "Eating" as compared with "being eaten" is not exactly characteristic of Christ, but rather of the devouring dragon, the corrosive Mercurius, who, as the uroboros, also eats himself, like Zosimos's homunculus.

421 "I will be thought," if evangelical at all, is an exclusively Johannine, post-apostolic speculation concerning the nature of the Logos. Hermes was very early considered to be Nous and Logos, and Hermes Trismegistus was actually the Nous of revelation. Mercurius, until well into the seventeenth century, was thought of as the *veritas* hidden in the human body, i.e., in matter, and this truth had to be known by meditation, or by *cogitatio,* reflection. Meditation is an idea that does not occur at all in the New Testament.[41] The *cogitatio* which might possibly correspond to it usually has a negative character and appears as the wicked *cogitatio cordis* of Genesis 6:5 (and 8:21): "Cuncta cogitatio cordis intenta ad malum" (DV: ". . . all the thought of their heart was bent upon evil at all times"; AV: ". . . every imagination of the thoughts of his heart . . ."). In I Peter 4:1 ἔννοια is given as "cogitatio" (DV: ". . . arm yourselves with the same intent"; AV: "same mind"; RSV: "same thought"). "Cogitare" has a more positive meaning in II Corinthians 10:7, where it really means to "bethink oneself," "remember by reflection": "hoc cogitet iterum apud se" ("τοῦτο λογιζέσθω πάλιν ἐφ' ἑαυτοῦ"; DV: "let him reflect within himself";

41 "Haec meditare" (ταῦτα μελέτα) in I Tim. 4:15 has more the meaning of 'see to' or 'attend to' these things. [Both DV and AV have "meditate on these things," but RSV has "practise these duties."—TRANS.]

AV: "let him of himself think this again"; RSV: "let him remind himself"). But this positive thinking in us is of God (II Cor. 3:5: "non quod sufficientes simus cogitare aliquid a nobis, quasi ex nobis"; "οὐχ ὅτι ἀφ' ἑαυτῶν ἱκανοί ἐσμεν λογίσασθαί τι ὡς ἐξ ἑαυτῶν, ἀλλ' ἡ ἱκανότης ἡμῶν ἐκ τοῦ θεοῦ"; DV: "Not that we are sufficient of ourselves to think anything, as from ourselves, but our sufficiency is from God"). The only place where *cogitatio* has the character of a meditation culminating in enlightenment is Acts 10:19: "Petro autem cogitante de visione, dixit Spiritus ei" ("Τοῦ δὲ Πέτρου διενθυμουμένου περὶ τοῦ ὁράματος εἶπεν τὸ πνεῦμα αὐτῷ"; DV: "But while Peter was pondering over the vision, the spirit said to him . . .").

422 Thinking, in the first centuries of our era, was more the concern of the Gnostics than of the Church, for which reason the great Gnostics, such as Basilides and Valentinus, seem almost like Christian theologians with a bent for philosophy. With John's doctrine of the Logos, Christ came to be regarded simultaneously as the Nous and the object of human thought; the Greek text says literally: "Νοηθῆναι θέλω νοῦς ὢν ὅλος" [42] (I will be thought, being wholly spirit). Similarly, the Acts of Peter say of Christ: "Thou art perceived of the spirit only." [43]

423 The "washing" refers to the *purificatio,* or to baptism, and equally to the washing of the dead body. The latter idea lingered on into the eighteenth century, as the alchemical washing of the "black corpse," an *opus mulierum.* The object to be washed was the black *prima materia:* it, the washing material (*sapo sapientum!*), and the washer were—all three of them—the selfsame Mercurius in different guises. But whereas in alchemy the *nigredo* and sin were identical concepts (since both needed washing), in Christian Gnosticism there are only a few hints of Christ's possible identity with the darkness. The λούσασθαι ("I will be washed") in our text is one of them.

424 The "ogdoad," being a double quaternity, belongs to the symbolism of the mandala. It obviously represents the archetype of the round dance in the "supra-celestial place," since it sings in harmony. The same applies to the number Twelve, the zodiacal archetype of the twelve disciples, a cosmic idea that still

42 Lipsius and Bonnet, eds., *Acta Apostolorum Apocrypha,* I, p. 197.

43 James, p. 335.

echoes in Dante's *Paradiso,* where the saints form shining constellations.

425 Anyone who does not join in the dance, who does not make the circumambulation of the centre (Christ and Anthropos), is smitten with blindness and sees nothing. What is described here as an outward event is really a symbol for the inward turning towards the centre in each of the disciples, towards the archetype of man, towards the self—for the dance can hardly be understood as an historical event. It should be understood, rather, as a sort of paraphrase of the Eucharist, an amplifying symbol that renders the mystery more assimilable to consciousness, and it must therefore be interpreted as a psychic phenomenon. It is an act of conscious realization on a higher level, establishing a connection between the consciousness of the individual and the supraordinate symbol of totality.

426 The "Acts of Peter" says of Christ:

> Thou art unto me father, thou my mother, thou my brother, thou my friend, thou my bondsman, thou my steward. Thou art All and All is in thee; thou Art, and there is naught else that IS save thee only.
>
> Unto him therefore do ye also, brethren, flee, and if ye learn that in him alone ye exist, ye shall obtain those things whereof he saith unto you: "Which neither eye hath seen nor ear heard, neither have they entered into the heart of man." [44]

427 The words "I will be united" must be understood in this sense, as meaning that subjective consciousness is united with an objective centre, thus producing the unity of God and man represented by Christ. The self is brought into actuality through the concentration of the many upon the centre, and the self wants this concentration. It is the subject and the object of the process. Therefore it is a "lamp" to those who "perceive" it. Its light is invisible if it is not perceived; it might just as well not exist. It is as dependent on being perceived as the act of perception is on light. This brings out once again the paradoxical subject-object nature of the unknowable. Christ, or the self, is a "mirror": on the one hand it reflects the subjective consciousness of the disciple, making it visible to him, and on the other hand it "knows" Christ, that is to say it does not merely

44 James, p. 335.

reflect the empirical man, it also shows him as a (transcendental) whole. And, just as a "door" opens to one who "knocks" on it, or a "way" opens out to the wayfarer who seeks it, so, when you relate to your own (transcendental) centre, you initiate a process of conscious development which leads to oneness and wholeness. You no longer see yourself as an isolated point on the periphery, but as the One in the centre. Only subjective consciousness is isolated; when it relates to its centre it is integrated into wholeness. Whoever joins in the dance sees himself in the reflecting centre, and his suffering is the suffering which the One who stands in the centre "wills to suffer." The paradoxical identity and difference of ego and self could hardly be formulated more trenchantly.

428 As the text says, you would not be able to understand what you suffer unless there were that Archimedean point outside, the objective standpoint of the self, from which the ego can be seen as a phenomenon. Without the objectivation of the self the ego would remain caught in hopeless subjectivity and would only gyrate round itself. But if you can see and understand your suffering without being subjectively involved, then, because of your altered standpoint, you also understand "how not to suffer," for you have reached a place beyond all involvements ("you have me as a bed, rest upon me"). This is an unexpectedly psychological formulation of the Christian idea of overcoming the world, though with a Docetist twist to it: "Who I am, you shall know when I depart. What now I am seen to be, I am not." [45] These statements are clarified by a vision in which John sees the Lord "standing in the midst of the cave and illuminating it." He says to John:

429 John, for the multitude below in Jerusalem I am being crucified and pierced with lances and staves, and vinegar and gall are given me to drink. But to you I speak, and what I say, hear: I put it into your mind to go up on this mountain, that you might hear those things which a disciple must learn from his master and a man from his God. And with these words he showed me a cross of light, and about the cross a great multitude that had no form [μίαν μορφὴν μὴ ἔχοντα], and in the cross there was one form and one appearance. And above [ἐπάνω] the cross I saw the Lord himself, and he had no outward shape [σχῆμα], but only a voice, and a voice not

[45] Ibid., p. 254.

such as we knew, but one sweet and kind and truly [that] of [a] God, which spoke to me: John, one man must hear this from me, for I require one that shall hear. For your sakes this cross of light was named by me now Logos, now Nous, now Jesus, now Christ, now Door, now Way, now Bread, now Seed [σπόρος], now Resurrection, now Son, now Father, now Pneuma, now Life, now Truth, now Faith [πίστις], now Grace. So is it called for men; but in itself and in its essence, as spoken of to you, it is the Boundary of all things, and the composing of things unstable,[46] and the harmony of wisdom, and the wisdom that is in harmony. For there are [places] of the right and of the left, Powers, Authorities, Archons, Daemons, Workings, Threatenings, Wraths, Devils, Satan, and the Nether Root whence proceeded the nature of whatever comes to be. And so it is this cross which joined all things together through the Word, and which separated the things that are from those that are below, and which caused all things to flow forth from the One.

But this is not the cross of wood which you will see when you go down from here; neither am I he that is on the cross, whom now you do not see, but only hear his voice. I passed for that which I am not, for I am not what I was to many others. But what they will say of me is vile and not worthy of me. Since, then, the place of rest is neither seen nor named, how much less will they see and name me, their Lord!

Now the formless multitude about the cross is of the lower nature. And if those whom you see in the cross have not one form, then not all the parts of him who descended have yet been recollected. But when the nature of man has been taken up and a generation of men that obey my voice draws near to me, he that now hears me shall be united with them and shall no longer be what he now is, but shall stand above them, as I do now. For so long as you call not yourself mine, I am not what I was. But if you understand me, you shall be in your understanding as I am, and I shall be what I was when I have you with me. For this you are through me. . . .

Behold, what you are, I have shown you. But what I am, I alone know, and no man else. Therefore let me have what is mine, but behold what is thine through me. And behold me truly, not as I have said I am, but as you, being akin to me, know me.[47]

430 Our text throws some doubt on the traditional view of Docetism. Though it is perfectly clear from the texts that Christ only seemed to have a body, which only seemed to suffer, this

46 Ἀνάγγη βιάβα uncertain.

47 Based on James, pp. 254ff., and the author's modified version of Hennecke, ed., *Neutestamentliche Apokryphen,* pp. 186ff.

is Docetism at its grossest. The Acts of John are more subtle, and the argument used is almost epistemological: the historical facts are real enough, but they reveal no more than is intelligible to the senses of the ordinary man. Yet even for the knower of divine secrets the act of crucifixion is a mystery, a symbol that expresses a parallel psychic event in the beholder. In the language of Plato it is an event which occurs in a "supra-celestial place," i.e., on a "mountain" and in a "cave" where a cross of light is set up, its many synonyms signifying that it has many aspects and many meanings. It expresses the unknowable nature of the "Lord," the supraordinate personality and τέλειος ἄνθρωπος, and since it is a quaternity, a whole divided into four parts, it is the classic symbol of the self.

431 Understood in this sense, the Docetism of the Acts of John appears more as a completion of the historical event than a devaluation of it. It is not surprising that the common people should have failed to appreciate its subtlety, though it is plain enough from a psychological point of view. On the other hand, the educated public of those days were by no means unfamiliar with the parallelism of earthly and metaphysical happenings, only it was not clear to them that their visionary symbols were not necessarily metaphysical realities but were perceptions of intrapsychic or subliminal processes which I have called "receptor phenomena." The contemplation of Christ's sacrificial death in its traditional form and cosmic significance constellated analogous psychic processes which in their turn gave rise to a wealth of symbols, as I have shown elsewhere.[48] This is, quite obviously, what has happened here, and it took the form of a visible split between the historical event down below on earth, as perceived by the senses, and its ideal, visionary reflection on high, the cross appearing on the one hand as a wooden instrument of torture and on the other as a glorious symbol. Evidently the centre of gravity has shifted to the ideal event, with the result that the psychic event is involuntarily given the greater importance. Although the emphasis on the pneuma detracts from the meaning of the concrete event in a rather one-sided and debatable way, it cannot be dismissed as superfluous, since a concrete event by itself can never create meaning, but is largely dependent for this on the manner in which it is understood.

48 Cf. *Aion*.

Interpretation is necessary before the meaning of a thing can be grasped. The naked facts by themselves "mean" nothing. So one cannot assert that the Gnostic attempts at interpretation were entirely lacking in merit, even though they go far beyond the framework of early Christian tradition. One could even venture to assert that these efforts were already implicit in that tradition, since the cross and the crucified are practically synonymous in the language of the New Testament.[49]

432 The text shows the cross as the antithesis of the formless multitude: it is, or it has, "form" and its meaning is that of a central point defined by the crossing of two straight lines. It is identical with the Kyrios (Lord) and the Logos, with Jesus and with Christ. How John could "see" the Lord above the cross, when the Lord is described as having no "outward shape," must remain a mystery. He only hears an explanatory voice, and this may indicate that the cross of light is only a visualization of the unknowable, whose voice can be heard apart from the cross. This seems to be confirmed by the remark that the cross was named Logos and so on "for your sakes."

433 The cross signifies order as opposed to the disorderly chaos of the formless multitude. It is, in fact, one of the prime symbols of order, as I have shown elsewhere. In the domain of psychological processes it functions as an organizing centre, and in states of psychic disorder [50] caused by an invasion of unconscious contents it appears as a mandala divided into four. No doubt this was a frequent phenomenon in early Christian times, and not only in Gnostic circles.[51] Gnostic introspection could hardly fail, therefore, to perceive the numinosity of this archetype and be duly impressed by it. For the Gnostics the cross had exactly the same function that the atman or Self has always had for the East. This realization is one of the central experiences of Gnosticism.

49 The quaternity, earlier hinted at in the vision of Ezekiel, is patently manifest in the pre-Christian Book of Enoch. (Cf. "Answer to Job," below, pars. 662ff.) In the Apocalypse of Sophonias [Zephaniah], Christ appears surrounded by a garland of doves (Stern, "Die koptische Apokalypse des Sophonias," p. 124). Cf. also the mosaic of St. Felix at Nola, showing a cross surrounded by doves. There is another in San Clemente, Rome (Wickhoff, "Das Apsismosaik in der Basilica des H. Felix zu Nola," pp. 158ff.; and Rossi, *Musaici Cristiani delle Chiese di Roma anteriori al secolo XV*, pl. XXIX).

50 Symbolized by the formless multitude.

51 Cf. "speaking with tongues" and glossolalia.

34 The definition of the cross or centre as διορισμός, the "boundary" of all things, is exceedingly original, for it suggests that the limits of the universe are not to be found in a nonexistent periphery but in its centre. There alone lies the possibility of transcending this world. All instability culminates in that which is unchanging and quiescent, and in the self all disharmonies are resolved in the "harmony of wisdom."

35 As the centre symbolizes the idea of totality and finality, it is quite appropriate that the text should suddenly start speaking of the dichotomy of the universe, polarized into right and left, brightness and darkness, heaven and the "nether root," the *omnium genetrix*. This is a clear reminder that everything is contained in the centre and that, as a result, the Lord (i.e., the cross) unites and composes all things and is therefore "nirdvanda," free from the opposites, in conformity with Eastern ideas and also with the psychology of this archetypal symbol. The Gnostic Christ-figure and the cross are counterparts of the typical mandalas spontaneously produced by the unconscious. They are *natural symbols* and they differ fundamentally from the dogmatic figure of Christ, in whom all trace of darkness is expressly lacking.

36 In this connection mention should be made of Peter's valedictory words, which he spoke during his martyrdom (he was crucified upside down, at his own request):

O name of the cross, hidden mystery! O grace ineffable that is pronounced in the name of the cross! O nature of man, that cannot be separated from God! O love unspeakable and indivisible, that cannot be shown forth by unclean lips! I grasp thee now, I that am at the end of my earthly course. I will declare thee as thou art, I will not keep silent the mystery of the cross which was once shut and hidden from my soul. You that hope in Christ, let not the cross be for you that which appears; for it is another thing, and different from that which appears, this suffering which is in accordance with Christ's. And now above all, because you that can hear are able to hear it of me, who am at the last and farewell hour of my life, hearken: separate your souls from everything that is of the senses, from everything that appears to be but in truth is not. Lock your eyes, close your ears, shun those happenings which are seen! Then you shall perceive that which was done to Christ, and the whole mystery of your salvation. . . .

Learn the mystery of all nature and the beginning of all things, as it was. For the first man, of whose race I bear the likeness, fell head downwards, and showed forth a manner of birth such as had not existed till then, for it was dead, having no motion. And being pulled downwards, and having also cast his origin upon the earth, he established the whole disposition of things; for, being hanged up in the manner appointed, he showed forth the things of the right as those of the left, and the things of the left as those of the right, and changed about all the marks of their nature, so that things that were not fair were perceived to be fair, and those that were in truth evil were perceived to be good. Wherefore the Lord says in a mystery: "Except ye make the things of the right as those of the left, and those of the left as those of the right, and those that are above as those below, and those that are behind as those that are before, ye shall not have knowledge of the kingdom."

This understanding have I brought you, and the figure in which you now see me hanging is the representation of that first man who came to birth.

437 In this passage, too, the symbolical interpretation of the cross is coupled with the problem of opposites, first in the unusual idea that the creation of the first man caused everything to be turned upside down, and then in the attempt to unite the opposites by identifying them with one another. A further point of significance is that Peter, crucified head downwards, is identical not only with the first created man, but with the cross:

For what else is Christ but the word, the sound of God? So the word is this upright beam on which I am crucified; and the sound is the beam which crosses it, the nature of man; but the nail which holds the centre of the crossbeam to the upright is man's conversion and repentance (μετάνοια).[52]

438 In the light of these passages it can hardly be said that the author of the Acts of John—presumably a Gnostic—has drawn the necessary conclusions from his premises or that their full implications have become clear to him. On the contrary, one gets the impression that the light has swallowed up everything dark. Just as the enlightening vision appears high above the actual scene of crucifixion, so, for John, the enlightened one stands high above the formless multitude. The text says: "Therefore care not for the many, and despise those that are outside

52 Based on James, pp. 334f.

the mystery!"[53] This overweening attitude arises from an inflation caused by the fact that the enlightened John has identified with his own light and confused his ego with the self. Therefore he feels superior to the darkness in him. He forgets that light only has a meaning when it illuminates something dark and that his enlightenment is no good to him unless it helps him to recognize his own darkness. If the powers of the left are as real as those of the right, then their union can only produce a third thing that shares the nature of both. Opposites unite in a new energy potential: the "third" that arises out of their union is a figure "free from the opposites," beyond all moral categories. This conclusion would have been too advanced for the Gnostics. Recognizing the danger of Gnostic irrealism, the Church, more practical in these matters, has always insisted on the concretism of the historical events despite the fact that the original New Testament texts predict the ultimate deification of man in a manner strangely reminiscent of the words of the serpent in the Garden of Eden: "Ye shall be as gods."[54] Nevertheless, there was some justification for postponing the elevation of man's status until after death, as this avoided the danger of Gnostic inflation.[55]

39 Had the Gnostic not identified with the self, he would have been bound to see how much darkness was in him—a realization that comes more naturally to modern man but causes him no less difficulties. Indeed, he is far more likely to assume that he himself is wholly of the devil than to believe that God could ever indulge in paradoxical statements. For all the ill consequences of his fatal inflation, the Gnostic did, however, gain an insight into religion, or into the psychology of religion, from which we can still learn a thing or two today. He looked deep into the background of Christianity and hence into its future developments. This he could do because his intimate connection with pagan Gnosis made him a "receptor" that helped to integrate the Christian message into the spirit of the times.

40 The extraordinary number of synonyms piled on top of one another in an attempt to define the cross have their analogy in the Naassene and Peratic symbols of Hippolytus, all pointing to

53 Ibid., p. 255. 54 Genesis 3:5.

55 The possibility of inflation was brought very close indeed by Christ's words: "Ye are gods" (John 10:34).

this one centre. It is the ἓν τὸ πᾶν of alchemy, which is on the one hand the heart and governing principle of the macrocosm, and on the other hand its reflection in a point, in a microcosm such as man has always been thought to be. He is of the same essence as the universe, and his own mid-point is its centre. This inner experience, shared by Gnostics, alchemists, and mystics alike, has to do with the nature of the unconscious—one could even say that it *is* the experience of the unconscious; for the unconscious, though its objective existence and its influence on consciousness cannot be doubted, is in itself undifferentiable and therefore unknowable. Hypothetical germs of differentiation may be conjectured to exist in it, but their existence cannot be proved, because everything appears to be in a state of mutual contamination. The unconscious gives the impression of multiplicity and unity at once. However overwhelmed we may be by the vast quantity of things differentiated in space and time, we know from the world of the senses that the validity of its laws extends to immense distances. We therefore believe that it is one and the same universe throughout, in its smallest part as in its greatest. On the other hand the intellect always tries to discern differences, because it cannot discriminate without them. Consequently the unity of the cosmos remains, for it, a somewhat nebulous postulate which it doesn't rightly know what to do with. But as soon as introspection starts penetrating into the psychic background it comes up against the unconscious, which, unlike consciousness, shows only the barest traces of any definite contents, surprising the investigator at every turn with a confusing medley of relationships, parallels, contaminations, and identifications. Although he is forced, for epistemological reasons, to postulate an indefinite number of distinct and separate archetypes, yet he is constantly overcome by doubt as to how far they are really distinguishable from one another. They overlap to such a degree and have such a capacity for combination that all attempts to isolate them conceptually must appear hopeless. In addition the unconscious, in sharpest contrast to consciousness and its contents, has a tendency to personify itself in a uniform way, just as if it possessed only one shape or one voice. Because of this peculiarity, the unconscious conveys an experience of unity, to which are due all those qualities enumerated by the Gnostics and alchemists, and a lot more besides.

41 As can plainly be seen from Gnosticism and other spiritual movements of the kind, people are naïvely inclined to take all the manifestations of the unconscious at their face value and to believe that in them the essence of the world itself, the ultimate truth, has been unveiled. This assumption does not seem to me quite as unwarranted as it may look at first sight, because the spontaneous utterances of the unconscious do after all reveal a psyche which is not identical with consciousness and which is, at times, greatly at variance with it. These utterances occur as a natural psychic activity that can neither be learnt nor controlled by the will. The manifestation of the unconscious is therefore a revelation of the unknown in man. We have only to disregard the dependence of dream language on environment and substitute "eagle" for "aeroplane," "dragon" for "automobile" or "train," "snake-bite" for "injection," and so forth, in order to arrive at the more universal and more fundamental language of mythology. This gives us access to the primordial images that underlie all thinking and have a considerable influence even on our scientific ideas.[56]

42 In these archetypal forms, something, presumably, is expressing itself that must in some way be connected with the mysterious operation of a natural psyche—in other words, with a cosmic factor of the first order. To save the honour of the objective psyche, which the contemporary hypertrophy of consciousness has done so much to depreciate, I must again emphasize that without the psyche we could not establish the existence of any world at all, let alone know it. But, judging by all we do know, it is certain that the original psyche possesses no consciousness of itself. This only comes in the course of development, a development that falls mostly within the historical epoch.[57] Even today we know of primitive tribes whose level of consciousness is not so far removed from the darkness of the primordial psyche, and numerous vestiges of this state can still be found among civilized people. It is even probable, in view of its potentialities for further differentiation, that our modern consciousness is still on a relatively low level. Nevertheless, its development so

56 Cf. Pauli, "The Influence of Archetypal Ideas on Kepler's Scientific Theories."

57 Cf. the remarkable account of developing consciousness in an ancient Egyptian text, translated, with commentary, by Jacobsohn, entitled "Das Gespräch eines Lebensmüden mit seinem Ba."

far has made it emancipated enough to forget its dependence on the unconscious psyche. It is not a little proud of this emancipation, but it overlooks the fact that although it has apparently got rid of the unconscious it has become the victim of its own verbal concepts. The devil is cast out with Beelzebub. Our dependence on words is so strong that a philosophical brand of "existentialism" had to restore the balance by pointing to a reality that exists in spite of words—at considerable risk, however, of concepts such as "existence," "existential," etc. turning into more words which delude us into thinking that we have caught a reality. One can be—and is—just as dependent on words as on the unconscious. Man's advance towards the Logos was a great achievement, but he must pay for it with loss of instinct and loss of reality to the degree that he remains in primitive dependence on mere words. Because words are substitutes for things, which of course they cannot be in reality, they take on intensified forms, become eccentric, outlandish, stupendous, swell up into what schizophrenic patients call "power words." A primitive word-magic develops, and one is inordinately impressed by it because anything out of the ordinary is felt to be especially profound and significant. Gnosticism in particular affords some very instructive examples of this. Neologisms tend not only to hypostatize themselves to an amazing degree, but actually to replace the reality they were originally intended to express.

443 This rupture of the link with the unconscious and our submission to the tyranny of words have one great disadvantage: the conscious mind becomes more and more the victim of its own discriminating activity, the picture we have of the world gets broken down into countless particulars, and the original feeling of unity, which was integrally connected with the unity of the unconscious psyche, is lost. This feeling of unity, in the form of the correspondence theory and the sympathy of all things, dominated philosophy until well into the seventeenth century and is now, after a long period of oblivion, looming up again on the scientific horizon, thanks to the discoveries made by the psychology of the unconscious and by parapsychology. The manner in which the unconscious forcibly obtrudes upon the conscious by means of neurotic disturbances is not only

reminiscent of contemporary political and social conditions but even appears as an accompanying phenomenon. In both cases there is an analogous dissociation: in the one case a splitting of the world's consciousness by an "iron curtain," and in the other a splitting of the individual personality. This dissociation extends throughout the entire world, so that a psychological split runs through vast numbers of individuals who, in their totality, call forth the corresponding mass phenomena. In the West it was chiefly the mass factor, and in the East technics, that undermined the old hierarchies. The cause of this development lay principally in the economic and psychological uprootedness of the industrial masses, which in turn was caused by the rapid advance in technics. But technics, it is obvious, are based on a specifically rationalistic differentiation of consciousness which tends to repress all irrational psychic factors. Hence there arises, in the individual and nation alike, an unconscious counterposition which in time grows strong enough to burst out into open conflict.

44 The same situation in reverse was played out on a smaller scale and on a spiritual plane during the first centuries of our era, when the spiritual disorientation of the Roman world was compensated by the irruption of Christianity. Naturally, in order to survive, Christianity had to defend itself not only against its enemies but also against the excessive pretensions of some of its adherents, including those of the Gnostics. Increasingly it had to rationalize its doctrines in order to stem the flood of irrationality. This led, over the centuries, to that strange marriage of the originally irrational Christian message with human reason, which is so characteristic of the Western mentality. But to the degree that reason gradually gained the upper hand, the intellect asserted itself and demanded autonomy. And just as the intellect subjugated the psyche, so also it subjugated Nature and begat on her an age of scientific technology that left less and less room for the natural and irrational man. Thus the foundations were laid for an inner opposition which today threatens the world with chaos. To make the reversal complete, all the powers of the underworld now hide behind reason and intellect, and under the mask of rationalistic ideology a stubborn faith seeks to impose itself by fire and sword, vying with the darkest aspects

of a church militant. By a strange enantiodromia,[58] the Christian spirit of the West has become the defender of the irrational, since, in spite of having fathered rationalism and intellectualism, it has not succumbed to them so far as to give up its belief in the rights of man, and especially the freedom of the individual. But this freedom guarantees a recognition of the irrational principle, despite the lurking danger of chaotic individualism. By appealing to the eternal rights of man, faith binds itself inalienably to a higher order, not only on account of the historical fact that Christ has proved to be an ordering factor for many hundreds of years, but also because the self effectively compensates chaotic conditions no matter by what name it is known: for the self is the Anthropos above and beyond this world, and in him is contained the freedom and dignity of the individual man. From this point of view, disparagement and vilification of Gnosticism are an anachronism. Its obviously psychological symbolism could serve many people today as a bridge to a more living appreciation of Christian tradition.

445 These historical changes have to be borne in mind if we wish to understand the Gnostic figure of Christ, because the sayings in the Acts of John concerning the nature of the Lord only become intelligible when we interpret them as expressing an experience of the original unity as contrasted with the formless multiplicity of conscious contents. This Gnostic Christ, of whom we hear hints even in the Gospel according to St. John, symbolizes man's original unity and exalts it as the saving goal of his development. By "composing the unstable," by bringing order into chaos, by resolving disharmonies and centring upon the mid-point, thus setting a "boundary" to the multitude and focusing attention upon the cross, consciousness is reunited with the unconscious, the unconscious man is made one with his centre, which is also the centre of the universe, and in this wise the goal of man's salvation and exaltation is reached.

446 Right as this intuition may be, it is also exceedingly dangerous, for it presupposes a coherent ego-consciousness capable of resisting the temptation to identify with the self. Such an ego-consciousness seems to be comparatively rare, as history shows;

58 [Cf. *Psychological Types,* Def. 18, and "The Psychology of the Unconscious," p. 71.—EDITORS.]

usually the ego identifies with the inner Christ, and the danger is increased by an *imitatio Christi* falsely understood. The result is inflation, of which our text affords eloquent proof. In order to exorcise this danger, the Church has not made too much of the "Christ within," but has made all it possibly could of the Christ whom we "have seen, heard, and touched with hands," in other words, with the historical event "below in Jerusalem." This is a wise attitude, which takes realistic account of the primitiveness of man's consciousness, then as now. For the less mindful it is of the unconscious, the greater becomes the danger of its identification with the latter, and the greater, therefore, the danger of inflation, which, as we have experienced to our cost, can seize upon whole nations like a psychic epidemic. If Christ is to be "real" for this relatively primitive consciousness, then he can be so only as an historical figure and a metaphysical entity, but not as a psychic centre in all too perilous proximity to a human ego. The Gnostic development, supported by scriptural authority, pushed so far ahead that Christ was clearly recognized as an inner, psychic fact. This also entailed the relativity of the Christ-figure, as expressively formulated in our text: "For so long as you call not yourself mine, I am not what I was. . . . I shall be what I was when I have you with me." From this it follows unmistakably that although Christ was whole once upon a time, that is, before time and consciousness began, he either lost this wholeness or gave it away to mankind[59] and can only get it back again through man's integration. His wholeness depends on man: "You will be in your understanding as I am"—this ineluctable conclusion shows the danger very clearly. The ego is dissolved in the self; unbeknown to itself, and with all its inadequacy and darkness, it has become a god and deems itself superior to its unenlightened fellows. It has identified with its own conception of the "higher man," quite regardless of the fact that this figure consists of "Places of the right and left, Authorities, Archons, Daemons" etc., and the devil himself. A figure like this is simply not to be comprehended, an awesome

[59] This view may be implicit in the *kenosis* passage (Philippians 2:5f.): "Have this mind in you which was also in Christ Jesus, who though he was by nature God, did not consider being equal to God a thing to be clung to, but emptied himself [ἐκένωσεν, *exinanivit*], taking the nature of a slave and being made like unto man" (DV).

mystery with which one had better not identify if one has any sense. It is sufficient to know that such a mystery exists and that somewhere man can feel its presence, but he should take care not to confuse his ego with it. On the contrary, the confrontation with his own darkness should not only warn him against identification but should inspire him with salutary terror on beholding just what he is capable of becoming. He cannot conquer the tremendous polarity of his nature on his own resources; he can only do so through the terrifying experience of a psychic process that is independent of him, that works *him* rather than he *it*.

447 If such a process exists at all, then it is something that can be experienced. My own personal experience, going back over several decades and garnered from many individuals, and the experience of many other doctors and psychologists, not to mention the statements—terminologically different, but essentially the same—of all the great religions,[60] all confirm the existence of a compensatory ordering factor which is independent of the ego and whose nature transcends consciousness. The existence of such a factor is no more miraculous, in itself, than the orderliness of radium decay, or the attunement of a virus to the anatomy and physiology of human beings,[61] or the symbiosis of plants and animals. What is miraculous in the extreme is that man can have conscious, reflective knowledge of these hidden processes, while animals, plants, and inorganic bodies seemingly lack it. Presumably it would also be an ecstatic experience for a radium atom to know that the time of its decay is exactly determined, or for the butterfly to recognize that the flower has made all the necessary provisions for its propagation.

448 The numinous experience of the individuation process is, on the archaic level, the prerogative of shamans and medicine men; later, of the physician, prophet, and priest; and finally, at the civilized stage, of philosophy and religion. The shaman's experience of sickness, torture, death, and regeneration implies, at a higher level, the idea of being made whole through sacrifice, of being changed by transubstantiation and exalted to the

60 Including shamanism, whose widespread phenomenology anticipates the alchemist's individuation symbolism on an archaic level. For a comprehensive account see Eliade, *Le Chamanisme*.

61 Cf. Portmann, "Die Bedeutung der Bilder in der lebendigen Energiewandlung."

pneumatic man—in a word, of apotheosis. The Mass is the summation and quintessence of a development which began many thousands of years ago and, with the progressive broadening and deepening of consciousness, gradually made the isolated experience of specifically gifted individuals the common property of a larger group. The underlying psychic process remained, of course, hidden from view and was dramatized in the form of suitable "mysteries" and "sacraments," these being reinforced by religious teachings, exercises, meditations, and acts of sacrifice which plunge the celebrant so deeply into the sphere of the mystery that he is able to become conscious of his intimate connection with the mythic happenings. Thus, in ancient Egypt, we see how the experience of "Osirification," [62] originally the prerogative of the Pharaohs, gradually passed to the aristocracy and finally, towards the end of the Old Kingdom, to the single individual as well. Similarly, the mystery religions of the Greeks, originally esoteric and not talked about, broadened out into collective experience, and at the time of the Caesars it was considered a regular sport for Roman tourists to get themselves initiated into foreign mysteries. Christianity, after some hesitation, went a step further and made celebration of the mysteries a public institution, for, as we know, it was especially concerned to introduce as many people as possible to the experience of the mystery. So, sooner or later, the individual could not fail to become conscious of his own transformation and of the necessary psychological conditions for this, such as confession and repentance of sin. The ground was prepared for the realization that, in the mystery of transubstantiation, it was not so much a question of magical influence as of psychological processes—a realization for which the alchemists had already paved the way by putting their *opus operatum* at least on a level with the ecclesiastical mystery, and even attributing to it a cosmic significance since, by its means, the divine world-soul could be liberated from imprisonment in matter. As I think I have shown, the "philosophical" side of alchemy is nothing less than a symbolic anticipation of certain psychological insights, and these—to judge by the example of Gerhard Dorn—were pretty far advanced by the end of the sixteenth century.[63] Only our in-

62 Cf. Neumann, *The Origins and History of Consciousness,* pp. 220ff.

63 *Aion,* pars. 249ff. (Swiss edn., pp. 237ff.).

tellectualized age could have been so deluded as to see in alchemy nothing but an abortive attempt at chemistry, and in the interpretative methods of modern psychology a mere "psychologizing," i.e., annihilation, of the mystery. Just as the alchemists knew that the production of their stone was a miracle that could only happen "Deo concedente," so the modern psychologist is aware that he can produce no more than a description, couched in scientific symbols, of a psychic process whose real nature transcends consciousness just as much as does the mystery of life or of matter. At no point has he explained the mystery itself, thereby causing it to fade. He has merely, in accordance with the spirit of Christian tradition, brought it a little nearer to individual consciousness, using the empirical material to set forth the individuation process and show it as an actual and experienceable fact. To treat a metaphysical statement as a psychic process is not to say that it is "merely psychic," as my critics assert—in the fond belief that the word "psychic" postulates something known. It does not seem to have occurred to people that when we say "psyche" we are alluding to the densest darkness it is possible to imagine. The ethics of the researcher require him to admit where his knowledge comes to an end. This end is the beginning of true wisdom.

IV

FOREWORD TO WHITE'S "GOD AND THE UNCONSCIOUS"

FOREWORD TO WERBLOWSKY'S "LUCIFER AND PROMETHEUS"

BROTHER KLAUS

FOREWORD TO WHITE'S "GOD AND THE UNCONSCIOUS" [1]

449 It is now many years since I expressed a desire for co-operation with a theologian, but I little knew—or even dreamt—how or to what extent my wish was to be fulfilled. This book, to which I have the honour of contributing an introductory foreword, is the third major publication [2] from the theological side which has been written in a spirit of collaboration and mutual effort. In the fifty years of pioneer work that now lie behind me I have experienced criticism, just and unjust, in such abundance that I know how to value any attempt at positive co-operation. Criticism from this quarter is constructive and therefore welcome.

450 Psychopathology and medical psychotherapy are, when viewed superficially, far removed from the theologian's particular field of interest, and it is therefore to be expected that no small amount of preliminary effort will be required to establish a terminology comprehensible to both parties. To make this

1 [Originally trans. (by Fr. White) from the German ms. for publication in the book by Fr. Victor White, O.P. (London, 1952; Chicago, 1953). The foreword was there subscribed May 1952. It has been slightly revised, on the basis of the original ms.—EDITORS.]

2 [The two previous ones were by the Protestant theologian Hans Schaer: *Religion and the Cure of Souls in Jung's Psychology,* and *Erlösungsvorstellungen und ihre psychologischen Aspekte.*—EDITORS.]

possible, certain fundamental realizations are required on either side. The most important of these is an appreciation of the fact that the object of mutual concern is the psychically sick and suffering human being, who is in need of consideration as much from the somatic or biological standpoint as from the spiritual or religious. The problem of neurosis ranges from disturbances in the sphere of instinct to the ultimate questions and decisions of our whole *Weltanschauung*. Neurosis is not an isolated, sharply defined phenomenon; it is a reaction of the *whole* human being. Here a pure therapy of the symptoms is obviously even more definitely proscribed than in the case of purely somatic illnesses; these too, however, always have a psychic component or accompanying symptom even though they are not psychogenic. Modern medicine has just begun to take account of this fact, which the psychotherapists have been emphasizing for a long time. In the same way, long years of experience have shown me over and over again that a therapy along purely biological lines does not suffice, but requires a spiritual complement. This becomes especially clear to the medical psychologist where the question of *dreams* is concerned; for dreams, being statements of the unconscious, play no small part in the therapy. Anyone who sets to work in an honest and critical frame of mind will have to admit that the correct understanding of dreams is no easy matter, but one that calls for careful reflection, leading far beyond purely biological points of view. The indubitable occurrence of archetypal motifs in dreams makes a thorough knowledge of the spiritual history of man indispensable for anyone seriously attempting to understand the real meaning of dreams. The likeness between certain dream-motifs and mythologems is so striking that they may be regarded not merely as similar but even as identical. This recognition not only raises the dream to a higher level and places it in the wider context of the mythologem, but, at the same time, the problems posed by mythology are brought into connection with the psychic life of the individual. From the mythologem to the religious statement it is only a step. But whereas the mythological figures appear as pale phantoms and relics of a long past life that has become strange to us, the religious statement represents an immediate "numinous" experience. It is a *living mythologem*.

451 Here the empiricist's way of thinking and expressing himself

gets him into difficulties with the theologian. The latter—when he is either making a dogma of the Gospel or "demythologizing" it—won't hear anything of "myth" because it seems to him a devaluation of the religious statement, in whose supreme truth he believes. The empiricist, on the other hand, whose orientation is that of natural science, does not connect any notion of value with the concept "myth." "Myth," for him, means "a statement about processes in the unconscious," and this applies equally to the religious statement. He has no means of deciding whether the latter is "truer" than the mythologem, for between the two he sees only one difference: the difference in living intensity. The so-called religious statement is still numinous, a quality which the myth has already lost to a great extent. The empiricist knows that rites and figures once "sacred" have become obsolete and that new figures have become "numinous."

452 The theologian can reproach the empiricist and say that he *does* possess the means of deciding the truth, he merely does not wish to make use of it—referring to the truth of revelation. In all humility the empiricist will then ask: *Which* revealed truth, and where is the proof that one view is truer than another? Christians themselves do not appear to be at one on this point. While they are busy wrangling, the doctor has an urgent case on his hands. He cannot wait for age-long schisms to be settled, but will seize upon anything that is "alive" for the patient and therefore effective. Naturally he cannot prescribe *any* religious system which is commonly supposed to be alive. Rather, by dint of careful and persevering investigation, he must endeavour to discover just where the sick person feels a healing, living quality which can make him whole. For the present he cannot be concerned whether this so-called truth bears the official stamp of validity or not. If, however, the patient is able to rediscover himself in this way and so get on his feet again, then the question of reconciling his individual realization—or whatever one may choose to call the new insight or life-giving experience—with the collectively valid opinions and beliefs becomes a matter of vital importance. That which is *only* individual has an isolating effect, and the sick person will never be healed by becoming a mere individualist. He would still be neurotically unrelated and estranged from his social group. Even Freud's exclusively personalistic psychology of drives was obliged to

come to terms, at least negatively, with the generally valid truths, the age-old *représentations collectives* of human society. Scientific materialism is by no means a private religious or philosophical matter, but a very public matter indeed, as we might well have realized from contemporary events. In view of the extraordinary importance of these so-called universal truths, a rapprochement between individual realizations and social convictions becomes an urgent necessity. And just as the sick person in his individual distinctiveness must find a *modus vivendi* with society, so it will be a no less urgent task for him to compare the insights he has won through exploring the unconscious with the universal truths, and to bring them into mutual relationship.

453 A great part of my life's work has been devoted to this endeavour. But it was clear to me from the outset that I could never accomplish such a task by myself. Although I can testify to the psychological facts, it is quite beyond my power to promote the necessary processes of assimilation which coming to terms with the *représentations collectives* requires. This calls for the cooperation of many, and above all of those who are the expounders of the universal truths, namely the theologians. Apart from doctors, they are the only people who have to worry professionally about the human soul, with the exception perhaps of teachers. But the latter confine themselves to children, who as a rule only suffer from the problems of the age indirectly, via their parents and educators. Surely, then, it would be valuable for the theologian to know what happens in the psyche of an adult. It must gradually be dawning on any responsible doctor what a tremendously important role the spiritual atmosphere plays in the psychic economy.

454 I must acknowledge with gratitude that the co-operation I had so long wished and hoped for has now become a reality. The present book bears witness to this, for it meets the preoccupations of medical psychology not only with intellectual understanding, but with good will. Only the most uncritical optimism could expect such an encounter to be love at first sight. The *points de départ* are too far apart and too different, and the road to their meeting-place too long and too hard, for agreement to come as a matter of course. I do not presume to know what the theologian misunderstands or fails to under-

stand in the empiricist's point of view, for it is as much as I can do to learn to estimate his theological premises correctly. If I am not mistaken, however, one of the main difficulties lies in the fact that both appear to speak the same language, but this language calls up in their minds two totally different fields of association. Both can apparently use the same concept and must then acknowledge, to their amazement, that they are speaking of two different things. Take, for instance, the word "God." The theologian will naturally assume that the metaphysical *Ens Absolutum* is meant. The empiricist, on the contrary, does not dream of making such a far-reaching assumption, which strikes him as downright impossible anyway. He just as naturally means the word "God" as a mere statement, or at most as an archetypal motif which prefigures such statements. For him "God" can just as well mean Yahweh, Allah, Zeus, Shiva, or Huitzilopochtli. The divine attributes of omnipotence, omniscience, eternity, and so on are to him statements which, symptomatically or as syndromes, more or less regularly accompany the archetype. He grants the divine image numinosity—that is, a deeply stirring emotional effect—which he accepts in the first place as a fact and sometimes tries to explain rationally, in a more or less unsatisfactory way. As a psychiatrist, he is sufficiently hardboiled to be profoundly convinced of the relativity of all such statements. As a scientist, his primary interest is the verification of psychic facts and their regular occurrence, to which he attaches incomparably greater importance than to abstract possibilities. His *religio* consists in establishing facts which can be observed and proved. He describes and circumscribes these in the same way as the mineralogist his mineral samples and the botanist his plants. He is aware that beyond provable facts he can know nothing and at best can only dream, and he considers it immoral to confuse a dream with knowledge. He does not deny what he has not experienced and cannot experience, but he will on no account assert anything which he does not think he can prove with facts. It is true that I have often been accused of having dreamt up the archetypes. I must remind these too hasty critics that a comparative study of motifs existed long before I ever mentioned archetypes. The fact that archetypal motifs occur in the psyche of people who have never heard of mythology is common knowledge to anyone who has investigated the structure of schizophrenic delusions, if his eyes have not already been opened in this respect by the universal occurrence of certain mythologems. Ignorance and narrow-mindedness, even when the latter is political, have never been conclusive scientific arguments.[3]

455 I must be content to describe the standpoint, the faith, the struggle, the hope and devotion of the empiricist, which all culminate in the discovery and verification of provable facts and their hypothetical interpretation. For the theological standpoint I refer the reader to the competent *exposé* by the author of this book.

456 When standpoints differ so widely, it is understandable that numerous clashes should occur in practice, some important, some unimportant. They are important, above all, where one realm threatens to encroach upon the territory of the other. My criticism of the doctrine of the *privatio boni* is such a case. Here the theologian has a certain right to fear an intrusion on the part of the empiricist. This discussion has left its mark on the book, as the reader will see for himself. Hence I feel at liberty to avail myself of the right of free criticism, so generously offered me by the author, and to lay my argument before the reader.

457 I should never have dreamt that I would come up against such an apparently out-of-the-way problem as that of the *privatio boni* in my practical work. Fate would have it, however, that I was called upon to treat a patient, a scholarly man with an academic training, who had got involved in all manner of dubious and morally reprehensible practices. He turned out to be a fervent adherent of the *privatio boni,* because it fitted in admirably with his scheme: evil in itself is nothing, a mere shadow, a trifling and fleeting diminution of good, like a cloud passing over the sun. This man professed to be a believing Protestant and would therefore have had no reason to appeal to a *sententia communis* of the Catholic Church had it not proved a welcome sedative to his uneasy conscience. It was this case that originally induced me to come to grips with the *privatio boni* in its psychological aspect. It is self-evident to the

3 The fact that the psyche is not a *tabula rasa,* but brings with it instinctive conditions, just as somatic life does, naturally does not suit a Marxist philosophy at all. True, the psyche can be crippled just like the body, but such a prospect would not be pleasing even to Marxists.

empiricist that the metaphysical aspect of such a doctrine must be left out of account, for he knows that he is dealing only with moral judgments and not with substances. We name a thing, *from a certain point of view,* good or bad, high or low, right or left, light or dark, and so forth. Here the antithesis is just as factual and real as the thesis.[4] It would never occur to anyone—except under very special conditions and for a definite purpose—to define cold as a diminution of heat, depth as a diminution of height, right as a diminution of left. With this kind of logic one could just as well call good a diminution of evil. The psychologist would, it is true, find this way of putting it a little too pessimistic, but he would have nothing against it logically. Instead of ninety-nine you can also say a hundred minus one, if you don't find it too complicated. But should he, as a moral man, catch himself glossing over an immoral act by optimistically regarding it as a slight diminution of good, which alone is real, or as an "accidental lack of perfection," then he would immediately have to call himself to order. His better judgment would tell him: If your evil is in fact only an unreal shadow of your good, then your so-called good is nothing but an unreal shadow of your real evil. If he does not reflect in this way he is deceiving himself, and self-deceptions of this kind have dissociating effects which breed neurosis, among them feelings of inferiority, with all their well-known attendant phenomena.

458 For these reasons I have felt compelled to contest the validity of the *privatio boni* so far as the empirical realm is concerned. For the same reasons I also criticize the dictum derived from the *privatio boni,* namely: "Omne bonum a Deo, omne malum ab homine"; [5] for then on the one hand man is deprived of the possibility of doing anything good, and on the other he is given the seductive power of doing evil. The only dignity which is left him is that of the fallen angel. The reader will see that I take this dictum literally.

459 Criticism can be applied only to psychic phenomena, i.e., to ideas and concepts, and not to metaphysical entities. These

[4] A recent suggestion that evil should be looked upon as a "decomposition" of good does not alter this fact in the slightest. A rotten egg is unfortunately just as real as a fresh one.

[5] The justice of this dictum strikes me as questionable, since Adam can hardly be held responsible for the wickedness of the serpent.

can only be confronted with other metaphysical entities. Hence my criticism is valid *only within the empirical realm.* In the metaphysical realm, on the other hand, good may be a substance and evil a μὴ ὄν. I know of no factual experience which approximates to such an assertion, so at this point the empiricist must remain silent. Nevertheless, it is possible that here, as in the case of other metaphysical statements, especially dogmas, there are archetypal factors in the background, which have existed for an indefinitely long time as preformative psychic forces and would therefore be accessible to empirical research. In other words, there might be a preconscious psychic tendency which, independent of time and place, continually causes similar statements to be made, as is the case with mythologems, folklore motifs, and the individual formation of symbols. It seems to me, however, that the existing empirical material, at least so far as I am acquainted with it, permits of no definite conclusion as to the archetypal background of the *privatio boni.* Subject to correction, I would say that clear-cut *moral* distinctions are the most recent acquisition of civilized man. That is why such distinctions are often so hazy and uncertain, unlike other antithetical constructions which undoubtedly have an archetypal nature and are the prerequisites for any act of cognition, such as the Platonic ταὐτὸν-θἄτερον (the Same and the Different).

460 Psychology, like every empirical science, cannot get along without auxiliary concepts, hypotheses, and models. But the theologian as well as the philosopher is apt to make the mistake of taking them for metaphysical postulates. The atom of which the physicist speaks is not an *hypostasis,* it is a *model.* Similarly, my concept of the archetype or of psychic energy is only an auxiliary idea which can be exchanged at any time for a better formula. From a philosophical standpoint my empirical concepts would be logical monsters, and as a philosopher I should cut a very sorry figure. Looked at theologically, my concept of the anima, for instance, is pure Gnosticism; hence I am often classed among the Gnostics. On top of that, the individuation process develops a symbolism whose nearest affinities are to be found in folklore, in Gnostic, alchemical, and suchlike "mystical" conceptions, not to mention shamanism. When material of this kind is adduced for comparison, the exposition fairly swarms with "exotic" and "far-fetched" proofs, and anyone who merely

skims through a book instead of reading it can easily succumb to the illusion that he is confronted with a Gnostic system. In reality, however, individuation is an expression of that biological process—simple or complicated as the case may be—by which every living thing becomes what it was destined to become from the beginning. This process naturally expresses itself in man as much psychically as somatically. On the psychic side it produces those well-known quaternity symbols, for instance, whose parallels are found in mental asylums as well as in Gnosticism and other exoticisms, and—last but not least—in Christian allegory. Hence it is by no means a case of mystical speculations, but of clinical observations and their interpretation through comparison with analogous phenomena in other fields. It is not the daring fantasy of the anatomist that can be held responsible when he discovers the nearest analogies to the human skeleton in certain African anthropoids of which the layman has never heard.

461 It is certainly remarkable that my critics, with few exceptions, ignore the fact that, as a doctor and scientist, I proceed from facts which everyone is at liberty to verify. Instead, they criticize me as if I were a philosopher, or a Gnostic with pretensions to supernatural knowledge. As a philosopher and speculating heretic I am, of course, easy prey. That is probably the reason why people prefer to ignore the facts I have discovered, or to deny them without scruple. But it is the facts that are of prime importance to me and not a provisional terminology or attempts at theoretical reflections. The fact that archetypes exist is not spirited away by saying that there are no inborn ideas. I have never maintained that the archetype *an sich* is an idea, but have expressly pointed out that I regard it as a form without definite content.

462 In view of these manifold misunderstandings, I set a particularly high value on the real understanding shown by the author, whose *point de départ* is diametrically opposed to that of natural science. He has successfully undertaken to feel his way into the empiricist's manner of thinking as far as possible, and if he has not always entirely succeeded in his attempt, I am the last person to blame him, for I am convinced that I am unwittingly guilty of many an offence against the theological way of thinking. Discrepancies of this kind can only be settled

by lengthy discussions, but they have their good side: not only do two apparently incompatible mental spheres come into contact, they also animate and fertilize one another. This calls for a great deal of good will on either side, and here I can give the author unstinted praise. He has taken the part of the opposite standpoint very fairly, and—what is especially valuable to me—has at the same time illustrated the theological standpoint in a highly instructive way. The medical psychotherapist cannot in the long run afford to overlook the religious systems of healing—if one may so describe certain aspects of religion—any more than the theologian, if he has the cure of souls at heart, can afford to ignore the experience of medical psychology.

463 In the practical field of individual treatment it seems to me that no serious difficulties should arise. These may be expected only when the discussion begins between individual experience and the collective truths. In most cases this necessity does not present itself until fairly late in the treatment, if at all. In practice it quite often happens that the whole treatment takes place on the personal plane, without the patient having any inner experiences that are definite enough to necessitate his coming to terms with the collective beliefs. If the patient remains within the framework of his traditional faith, he will, even if stirred or perhaps shattered by an archetypal dream, translate this experience into the language of his faith. This operation may strike the empiricist (if he happens to be a fanatic of the truth) as questionable, but it can pass off harmlessly and may even lead to a satisfactory issue, in so far as it is *legitimate* for this type of man. I try to impress it upon my pupils not to treat their patients as if they were all cut to the same measure: the population consists of different historical layers. There are people who, psychologically, might be living in the year 5000 B.C., i.e., who can still successfully solve their conflicts as people did seven thousand years ago. There are countless troglodytes and barbarians living in Europe and in all civilized countries, as well as a large number of medieval Christians. On the other hand, there are relatively few who have reached the level of consciousness which is possible in our time. We must also reckon with the fact that a few of our generation belong to the third or fourth millennium A.D. and are consequently anachronistic. So it is psychologically quite "legitimate" when a medieval man

solves his conflict today on a thirteenth-century level and treats his shadow as the devil incarnate. For such a man any other procedure would be unnatural and wrong, for his belief is that of a thirteenth-century Christian. But, for the man who belongs by temperament, i.e., psychologically, to the twentieth century, there are certain important considerations which would never enter the head of our medieval specimen. How much the Middle Ages are still with us can be seen, among other things, from the fact that such a simple truth as the psychic quality of metaphysical figures will not penetrate into people's heads. This is not a matter of intelligence or education, or of *Weltanschauung,* for the materialist also is unable to perceive to what extent, for instance, God is a psychic quantity which nothing can deprive of its reality, which does not insist on a definite name and which allows itself to be called reason, energy, matter, or even ego.

464 This historical stratification must be taken into account most carefully by the psychotherapist, likewise the possibility of a latent capacity for development, which he would do well, however, not to take for granted.

465 Whereas the "reasonable," i.e., rationalistic, point of view is satisfying to the man of the eighteenth century, the psychological standpoint appeals much more to the man of the twentieth century. The most threadbare rationalism means more to the former than the best psychological explanation, for he is incapable of thinking psychologically and can operate only with rational concepts, which must on no account savour of metaphysics, for the latter are taboo. He will at once suspect the psychologist of mysticism, for in his eyes a rational concept can be neither metaphysical nor psychological. Resistances against the psychological standpoint, which regards psychic processes as facts, are, I fear, all equally anachronistic, including the prejudice of "psychologism," which does not understand the empirical nature of the psyche either. To the man of the twentieth century this is a matter of the highest importance and the very foundation of his reality, because he has recognized once and for all that without an observer there is no world and consequently no truth, for there would be nobody to register it. The one and only immediate guarantor of reality is the observer. Significantly enough, the most unpsychological of all sciences,

physics, comes up against the observer at the decisive point. This knowledge sets its stamp on our century.

466 It would be an anachronism, i.e., a regression, for the man of the twentieth century to solve his conflicts either rationalistically or metaphysically. Therefore, for better or worse, he has built himself a psychology, because it is impossible to get along without it. Both the theologian and the somatic doctor would do well to give earnest consideration to this fact, if they do not want to risk losing touch with their time. It is not easy for the somatically oriented doctor to see his long familiar clinical pictures and their aetiology in the unaccustomed light of psychology, and in the same way it will cost the theologian considerable effort to adjust his thinking to the new fact of the psyche and, in particular, of the unconscious, so that he too can reach the man of the twentieth century. No art, science, or institution in any way concerned with human beings can escape the effects of the development which the psychologists and physicists have let loose, even if they oppose it with the most stubborn prejudices.

467 Father White's book has the merit of being the first theological work from the Catholic side to concern itself with the far-reaching effects of the new empirical knowledge in the realm of archetypal ideas, and to make a serious attempt to integrate it. Although the book is addressed primarily to the theologian, the psychologist and particularly the medical psychotherapist will be able to glean from it a rich harvest of knowledge.

FOREWORD TO WERBLOWSKY'S "LUCIFER AND PROMETHEUS"[1]

468 The author has submitted his manuscript to me with the request that I should write a few words by way of introduction. As the subject of the book is essentially literary, I do not feel altogether competent to express an opinion on the matter. The author has, however, rightly discerned that, although the problem of Milton's *Paradise Lost* is primarily a subject for literary criticism, it is, as a piece of confessional writing, fundamentally bound up with certain psychological assumptions. Though he has only touched on these—at least in so many words—he has made it sufficiently plain why he has appealed to me as a psychologist. However little disposed I am to regard Dante's *Divine Comedy* or Klopstock's *Messiah* or Milton's opus as fit subjects for psychological commentary, I cannot but acknowledge the acumen of the author, who has seen that the problem of Milton might well be elucidated from that angle of research which is my special field of study.

469 For over two thousand years the figure of Satan, both as a theme of poetico-religious thinking and artistic creation and as

1 [Originally trans. by R. F. C. Hull from the German ms. for publication in the book by R. J. Zwi Werblowsky (London, 1952). The present text contains only minor alterations. Professor Jung subscribed the foreword March 1951.—EDITORS.]

a mythologem, has been a constant expression of the psyche, having its source in the unconscious evolution of "metaphysical" images. We should go very wrong in our judgment if we assumed that ideas such as this derive from rationalistic thinking. All the old ideas of God, indeed thought itself, and particularly numinous thought, have their origin in *experience.* Primitive man does not think his thoughts, they simply *appear* in his mind. Purposive and directed thinking is a relatively late human achievement. The numinous image is far more an expression of essentially unconscious processes than a product of rational inference. Consequently it falls into the category of psychological objects, and this raises the question of the underlying psychological assumptions. We have to imagine a millennial process of symbol-formation which presses towards consciousness, beginning in the darkness of prehistory with primordial or archetypal images, and gradually developing and differentiating these images into conscious creations. The history of religion in the West can be taken as an illustration of this: I mean the historical development of dogma, which also includes the figure of Satan. One of the best-known archetypes, lost in the grey mists of antiquity, is the triad of gods. In the early centuries of Christianity it reappears in the Christian formula for the Trinity, whose pagan version is *Hermes ter unus.* Nor is it difficult to see that the great goddess of the Ephesians has been resurrected in the θεοτόκος. This latter problem, after lying dormant for centuries, came into circulation again with the dogma of the Immaculate Conception and, more recently, of the Assumption of the Virgin. The figure of the mediatrix rounds itself out in almost classical perfection, and it is especially noteworthy that behind the solemn promulgation of the dogma there stands no arbitrary tenet of papal authority but an anonymous movement of the Catholic world. The numerous miracles of the Virgin which preceded it are equally autochthonous; they are genuine and legitimate experiences springing directly from the unconscious psychic life of the people.

470 I do not wish to multiply examples needlessly, but only to make it clear that the figure of Satan, too, has undergone a curious development, from the time of his first undistinguished appearance in the Old Testament texts to his heyday in Chris-

tianity. He achieved notoriety as the personification of the adversary or principle of evil, though by no means for the first time, as we meet him centuries earlier in the ancient Egyptian Set and the Persian Ahriman. Persian influences have been conjectured as mainly responsible for the Christian devil. But the real reason for the differentiation of this figure lies in the conception of God as the *summum bonum,* which stands in sharp contrast to the Old Testament view and which, for reasons of psychic balance, inevitably requires the existence of an *infimum malum.* No logical reasons are needed for this, only the natural and unconscious striving for balance and symmetry. Hence very early, in Clement of Rome, we meet with the conception of Christ as the right hand and the devil as the left hand of God, not to speak of the Judaeo-Christian view which recognized two sons of God, Satan the elder and Christ the younger. The figure of the devil then rose to such exalted metaphysical heights that he had to be forcibly depotentiated, under the threatening influence of Manichaeism. The depotentiation was effected—this time—by rationalistic reflection, by a regular *tour de force* of sophistry which defined evil as a *privatio boni.* But that did nothing to stop the belief from arising in many parts of Europe during the eleventh century, mainly under the influence of the Catharists, that it was not God but the devil who had created the world. In this way the archetype of the imperfect demiurge, who had enjoyed official recognition in Gnosticism, reappeared in altered guise. (The corresponding archetype is probably to be found in the cosmogonic jester [2] of primitive peoples.) With the extermination of the heretics that dragged on into the fourteenth and fifteenth centuries, an uneasy calm ensued, but the Reformation thrust the figure of Satan once more into the foreground. I would only mention Jakob Böhme, who sketched a picture of evil which leaves the *privatio boni* pale by comparison. The same can be said of Milton. He inhabits the same mental climate. As for Böhme, although he was not a direct descendant of alchemical philosophy, whose importance is still grossly underrated today, he certainly took over a number of its leading ideas, among them the specific recognition of Satan, who was exalted to a cosmic figure of first rank in Milton, even emancipating himself from his subordinate role as the left hand

2 [Cf. Jung's "On the Psychology of the Trickster Figure."—EDITORS.]

of God (the role assigned to him by Clement). Milton goes even further than Böhme and apostrophizes the devil as the true *principium individuationis,* a concept which had been anticipated by the alchemists some time before. To mention only one example: "Ascendit a terra in coelum, iterumque descendit in terram et recipit vim superiorum et inferiorum. Sic habebis gloriam totius mundi." (He rises from earth to heaven and descends again to earth, and receives into himself the power of above and below. Thus thou wilt have the glory of the whole world.) The quotation comes from the famous alchemical classic, the *Tabula Smaragdina,* attributed to Hermes Trismegistus, whose authority remained unchallenged for more than thirteen centuries of alchemical thought. His words refer not to Satan, but to the *filius philosophorum,* whose symbolism, as I believe I have shown, coincides with that of the psychological "self." The *filius* of the alchemists is one of the numerous manifestations of Mercurius, who is called "duplex" and "ambiguus" and is also known outside alchemy as "utriusque capax"—capable of anything. His "dark" half has an obvious affinity with Lucifer.

471 In Milton's time these ideas were very much in the air, forming part of the general stock of culture, and there were not a few Masters who realized that their philosophical stone was none other than the "total man." The Satan-Prometheus parallel shows clearly enough that Milton's devil stands for the essence of human individuation and thus comes within the scope of psychology. This close proximity, as we know, proved a danger not only to the metaphysical status of Satan, but to that of other numinous figures as well. With the coming of the Enlightenment, metaphysics as a whole began to decline, and the rift which then opened out between knowledge and faith could no longer be repaired. The more resplendent figures in the metaphysical pantheon had their autonomy restored to them practically untarnished, which assuredly cannot be said of the devil. In Goethe's *Faust* he has dwindled to a very personal *familiaris,* the mere "shadow" of the struggling hero. After rational-liberal Protestantism had, as it were, deposed him by order of the day, he retired to the shadier side of the Christian Olympus as the "odd man out," and thus, in a manner not unwelcome to the Church, the old principle reasserted itself: *Omne bonum a*

Deo, omne malum ab homine. The devil remains as an appendix to psychology.

472 It is a psychological rule that when an archetype has lost its metaphysical hypostasis, it becomes identified with the conscious mind of the individual, which it influences and refashions in its own form. And since an archetype always possesses a certain numinosity, the integration of the numen generally produces an inflation of the subject. It is therefore entirely in accord with psychological expectations that Goethe should dub his Faust a Superman. In recent times this type has extended beyond Nietzsche into the field of political psychology, and its incarnation in man has had all the consequences that might have been expected to follow from such a misappropriation of power.

473 As human beings do not live in airtight compartments, this infectious inflation has spread everywhere and given rise to an extraordinary uncertainty in morals and philosophy. The medical psychologist is bound to take an interest in such matters, if only for professional reasons, and so we witness the memorable spectacle of a psychiatrist introducing a critical study of Milton's *Paradise Lost.* Meditating upon this highly incongruous conjunction, I decided that I should best fulfil my obligations if I explained to the well-intentioned reader how and why the devil got into the consulting-room of the psychiatrist.

BROTHER KLAUS [1]

474 Before me lies a little book by Father Alban Stoeckli on the Visions of the Blessed Brother Klaus.[2] Let the reader not be alarmed. Though a psychiatrist takes up his pen, it does not necessarily mean that he is going to set about this venerable figure with the profane instrument of psychopathology. Psychiatrists have committed enough sins already and have put their science to the most unsuitable uses. Nothing of the kind is to happen here: no diagnosis or analysis will be undertaken, no significant hints of pathological possibilities will be dropped, and no attempt will be made to bring the Blessed Nicholas of Flüe anywhere near a psychiatric clinic. Hence it must seem all the stranger to the reader that the reviewer of the book is a physician. I admit this fact is difficult to explain to anyone who does not know my unfashionable view on visions and the like. In this respect I am a good deal less sophisticated and more conservative than the so-called educated public, whose philosophical perplexity is such that it sighs with relief when visions are equated with hallucinations, delusional ideas, mania, and schizo-

1 [First published as a review in the *Neue Schweizer Rundschau* (Zurich), new series, I (1933) : 4, 223–29. Previously trans. by Horace Gray in the *Journal of Nervous and Mental Diseases* (New York, Richmond, London), CIII (1946) : 4, 359–77. In 1947 Nicholas of Flüe, "Bruder Klaus," was canonized by Pope Pius XII and declared patron saint of Switzerland.—EDITORS.]

2 [*Die Visionen des seligen Bruder Klaus* (Einsiedeln, 1933).—EDITORS.]

phrenia, or whatever else these morbid things may be called, and are reduced to the right denominator by some competent authority. Medically, I can find nothing wrong with Brother Klaus. I see him as a somewhat unusual but in no wise pathological person, a man after my own heart: my brother Klaus. Rather remote, to be sure, at this distance of more than four hundred years, separated by culture and creed, by those fashionable trifles which we always think constitute a world. Yet they amount to no more than linguistic difficulties, and these do not impede understanding of the essentials. So little, in fact, that I was able to converse, in the primitive language of inward vision, with a man who in every way was even further removed from me than Brother Klaus—a Pueblo Indian, my friend Ochwiabiano ("Mountain Lake"). For what interests us here is not the historical personage, not the well-known figure at the Diet of Stans,[3] but the "friend of God," who appeared but a few times on the world stage, yet lived a long life in the realms of the soul. Of what he there experienced he left behind only scant traces, so few and inarticulate that it is hard for posterity to form any picture of his inner life.

475 It has always intrigued me to know what a hermit does with himself all day long. Can we still imagine a real spiritual anchorite nowadays, one who has not simply crept away to vegetate in misanthropic simplicity? A solitary fellow, like an old elephant who resentfully defies the herd instinct? Can we imagine a normal person living a sensible, vital existence by himself, with no visible partner?

476 Brother Klaus had a house, wife, and children, and we do not know of any external factors which could have induced him to become a hermit. The sole reason for this was his singular inner life; experiences for which no merely natural grounds can be adduced, decisive experiences which accompanied him from youth up. These things seemed to him of more value than ordinary human existence. They were probably the object of his daily interest and the source of his spiritual vitality. It

3 [The Diet of Stans was a meeting in 1481 of representatives of the Swiss cantons at which disputes between the predominantly rural and the predominantly urban cantons were regulated, and as a result of which—largely through the intervention of Nicholas—Fribourg and Solothurn became members of the Confederation. Cf. *Cambridge Medieval History,* VII, p. 210.—EDITORS.]

sounds rather like an anecdote from the life of a scholar who is completely immersed in his studies when the so-called "Pilgrim's Tract" [4] relates: "And he [Brother Klaus] began to speak again and said to me, 'If it does not trouble you, I would like to show you my book, in which I am learning and seeking the art of this doctrine.' And he brought me a figure, drawn like a wheel with six spokes." So evidently Brother Klaus studied some mysterious "doctrine" or other; he sought to understand and interpret the things that happened to him. That the hermit's activity was a sort of study must also have occurred to Gundolfingen,[5] one of the oldest writers on our subject. He says: "Did he not likewise learn in that High School of the Holy Ghost the representation of the wheel, which he caused to be painted in his chapel, and through which, as in a clear mirror, was reflected the entire essence of the Godhead?" From the same "High School" he derived "his kindness, his doctrine, and his science."

477 Here we are concerned with the so-called Trinity Vision, which was of the greatest significance for the hermit's inner life. According to the oldest reports, it was an apparition of light, of surpassing intensity, in the form of a human face. The first-hand reports make no mention of a "wheel." This seems to have been a subsequent addition for the purpose of clarifying the vision. Just as a stone, falling into calm water, produces wave after wave of circles, so a sudden and violent vision of this kind has long-lasting after-effects, like any shock. And the stranger and more impressive the initial vision was, the longer it will take to be assimilated, and the greater and more persevering will be the efforts of the mind to master it and render it intelligible to human understanding. Such a vision is a tremendous "irruption" in the most literal sense of the word, and it has therefore always been customary to draw rings round it like those made by the falling stone when it breaks the smooth surface of the water.

[4] *Ein nutzlicher und loblicher Tractat von Bruder Claus und einem Bilger* (Nürnberg, 1488). The actual author is anonymous, according to Robert Durrer, *Bruder Klaus.*

[5] Heinrich Gundolfingen (Gundelfingen or Gundelfinger), *c.* 1444–90, priest and professor of humanistic studies at the University of Fribourg, knew Klaus probably around the year 1480, and wrote his biography.

478 Now what has "irrupted" here, and wherein lies its mighty "impression"? The oldest source, Wölflin's biography,[6] narrates the following on this score:

All who came to him were filled with terror at the first glance. As to the cause of this, he himself used to say that he had seen a piercing light resembling a human face. At the sight of it he feared that his heart would burst into little pieces. Overcome with terror, he instantly turned his face away and fell to the ground. And that was the reason why his face was now terrible to others.

This is borne out by the account which the humanist Karl Bovillus (Charles de Bouelles) gave to a friend in 1508 (some twenty years after the death of Brother Klaus):

I wish to tell you of a vision which appeared to him in the sky, on a night when the stars were shining and he stood in prayer and contemplation. He saw the head of a human figure with a terrifying face, full of wrath and threats.[7]

So we shall not go wrong in surmising that the vision was terrifying in the extreme. When we consider that the mental attitude of that age, and in particular that of Brother Klaus, allowed no other interpretation than that this vision represented God himself, and that God signified the *summum bonum,* Absolute Perfection, then it is clear that such a vision must, by its violent contrast, have had a profound and shattering effect, whose assimilation into consciousness required years of the most strenuous spiritual effort. Through subsequent elaboration this vision then became the so-called Trinity Vision. As Father Stoeckli rightly conjectures, the "wheel" or circles were formed on the basis of, and as parallels to, the illustrated devotional books that were read at the time. As mentioned above, Brother Klaus even seems to have possessed such a book himself. Later, as a result of further mental elaboration, there were added the spokes of the wheel and the six secondary circles, as shown in the old picture of the vision in the parish church at Sachseln.

[6] Heinrich Wölflin, also called by the Latin form Lupulus, born 1470, humanist and director of Latin studies at Bern.

[7] *Ein gesichte Bruder Clausen ynn Schweytz und seine deutunge* (Wittenberg, 1528), p. 5. Cited in Stoeckli, p. 34.

479 The vision of light was not the only one which Brother Klaus had. He even thought that, while still in his mother's womb, he had seen a star that outshone all others in brightness, and later, in his solitude, he saw a very similar star repeatedly. The vision of light had, therefore, occurred several times before in his life. Light means illumination; it is an illuminating idea that "irrupts." Using a very cautious formulation, we could say that the underlying factor here is a considerable tension of psychic energy, evidently corresponding to some very important unconscious content. This content has an overpowering effect and holds the conscious mind spellbound. The tremendous power of the "objective psychic" has been named "demon" or "God" in all epochs with the sole exception of the recent present. We have become so bashful in matters of religion that we correctly say "unconscious," because God has in fact become unconscious to us. This is what always happens when things are interpreted, explained, and dogmatized until they become so encrusted with man-made images and words that they can no longer be seen. Something similar seems to have happened to Brother Klaus, which is why the immediate experience burst upon him with appalling terror. Had his vision been as charming and edifying as the present picture at Sachseln, no such terror would ever have emanated from it.

480 "God" is a primordial experience of man, and from the remotest times humanity has taken inconceivable pains either to portray this baffling experience, to assimilate it by means of interpretation, speculation, and dogma, or else to deny it. And again and again it has happened, and still happens, that one hears too much about the "good" God and knows him too well, so that one confuses him with one's own ideas and regards them as sacred because they can be traced back a couple of thousand years. This is a superstition and an idolatry every bit as bad as the Bolshevist delusion that "God" can be educated out of existence. Even a modern theologian like Gogarten [8] is quite sure that God *can only be good.* A good man does not terrify me—what then would Gogarten have made of the Blessed Brother Klaus? Presumably he would have had to explain to him that he had seen the devil in person.

8 [Friedrich Gogarten (b. 1887), recently professor of systematic theology at Göttingen; author of *Die Kirche in der Welt* (1948).—EDITORS.]

481 And here we are in the midst of that ancient dilemma of how such visions are to be evaluated. I would suggest taking every genuine case at its face value. If it was an overwhelming experience for so worthy and shrewd a man as Brother Klaus, then I do not hesitate to call it a true and veritable experience of God, even if it turns out not quite right dogmatically. Great saints were, as we know, sometimes great heretics, so it is probable that anyone who has immediate experience of God is a little bit outside the organization one calls the Church. The Church itself would have been in a pretty pass if the Son of God had remained a law-abiding Pharisee, a point one tends to forget.

482 There are many indubitable lunatics who have experiences of God, and here too I do not contest the genuineness of the experience, for I know that it takes a complete and a brave man to stand up to it. Therefore I feel sorry for those who go under, and I shall not add insult to injury by saying that they tripped up on a mere psychologism. Besides, one can never know in what form a man will experience God, for there are very peculiar things just as there are very peculiar people—like those, for instance, who think that one can make anything but a conceptual distinction between the individual experience of God and God himself. It would certainly be desirable to make this distinction, but to do so one would have to know what God is in and for himself, which does not seem to me possible.

483 Brother Klaus's vision was a genuine primordial experience, and it therefore seemed to him particularly necessary to submit it to a thorough dogmatic revision. Loyally and with great efforts he applied himself to this task, the more so as he was smitten with terror in every limb so that even strangers took fright. The unconscious taint of heresy that probably clings to all genuine and unexpurgated visions is only hinted at in the Trinity Vision, but in the touched-up version it has been successfully eliminated. All the affectivity, the very thing that made the strongest impression, has vanished without a trace, thus affording at least a negative proof of our interpretation.

484 Brother Klaus's elucidation of his vision with the help of the three circles (the so-called "wheel") is in keeping with age-old human practice, which goes back to the Bronze Age sun-wheels (often found in Switzerland) and to the mandalas depicted in the Rhodesian rock-drawings. These sun-wheels may

possibly be paleolithic; we find them in Mexico, India, Tibet, and China. The Christian mandalas probably date back to St. Augustine and his definition of God as a circle. Presumably Henry Suso's notions of the circle, which were accessible to the "Friends of God," were derived from the same source. But even if this whole tradition had been cut off and no little treatise with mandalas in the margin had ever come to light, and if Brother Klaus had never seen the rose-window of a church, he would still have succeeded in working his great experience into the shape of a circle, because this is what has always happened in every part of the world and still goes on happening today.[9]

485 We spoke above of heresy. In Father Stoeckli's newly found fragment describing the vision, there is another vision which contains an interesting parallelism. I put the two passages side by side for the sake of comparison:

There came a handsome majestic man through the palace, with a shining colour in his face, and in a white garment. And he laid both arms on his shoulders and pressed him close and thanked him with all the fervent love of his heart, because he had stood by his son and helped him in his need.

There came a beautiful majestic woman through the palace, also in a white garment. . . . And she laid both arms on his shoulders and pressed him close to her heart with an overflowing love, because he had stood so faithfully by her son in his need.

486 It is clear that this is a vision of God the Father and Son, and of the Mother of God. The palace is heaven, where "God the Father" dwells, and also "God the Mother." In pagan form they are unmistakably God and Goddess, as their absolute parallelism shows. The androgynity of the divine Ground is characteristic of mystic experience. In Indian Tantrism the masculine Shiva and the feminine Shakti both proceed from Brahman, which is devoid of qualities. Man as the son of the Heavenly Father and Heavenly Mother is an age-old conception which goes back to primitive times, and in this vision the Blessed Brother Klaus is set on a par with the Son of God. The Trinity in this vision—Father, Mother, and Son—is very undog-

9 More on this in Zimmer, *Myths and Symbols in Indian Art and Civilization,* and Wilhelm, *The Secret of the Golden Flower,* together with my commentary.

matic indeed. Its nearest parallel is the exceedingly unorthodox Gnostic Trinity: God, Sophia, Christ. The Church, however, has expunged the feminine nature of the Holy Ghost, though it is still suggested by the symbolic dove.

487 It is nice to think that the only outstanding Swiss mystic received, by God's grace, unorthodox visions and was permitted to look with unerring eye into the depths of the divine soul, where all the creeds of humanity which dogma has divided are united in *one* symbolic archetype. As I hope Father Stoeckli's little book will find many attentive readers, I shall not discuss the Vision of the Well, nor the Vision of the Man with the Bearskin, although from the standpoint of comparative symbolism they offer some very interesting aspects—for I do not want to deprive the reader of the pleasure of finding out their meaning by himself.

V

PSYCHOTHERAPISTS OR THE CLERGY

PSYCHOANALYSIS AND THE CURE OF SOULS

PSYCHOTHERAPISTS OR THE CLERGY[1]

38 It is far more the urgent psychic problems of patients, rather than the curiosity of research workers, that have given effective impetus to the recent developments in medical psychology and psychotherapy. Medical science—almost in defiance of the patients' needs—has held aloof from all contact with strictly psychic problems, on the partly justifiable assumption that psychic problems belong to other fields of study. But it has been compelled to widen its scope so as to include experimental psychology, just as it has been driven time and time again—out of regard for the biological unity of the human being—to borrow from such outlying branches of science as chemistry, physics, and biology.

9 It was natural that the branches of science adopted by medicine should be given a new direction. We can characterize the change by saying that instead of being regarded as ends in themselves they were valued for their practical application to human beings. Psychiatry, for example, helped itself out of the treasure-chest of experimental psychology and its methods, and funded its borrowings in the inclusive body of knowledge that we call

1 [First given as a lecture before the Alsatian Pastoral Conference at Strasbourg in May 1932; published as a pamphlet, *Die Beziehungen der Psychotherapie zur Seelsorge* (Zurich, 1932). Previously translated by W. S. Dell and Cary F. Baynes in *Modern Man in Search of a Soul* (London and New York, 1933).—EDITORS.]

psychopathology—a name for the study of complex psychic phenomena. Psychopathology is built for one part on the findings of psychiatry in the strict sense of the term, and for the other part on the findings of neurology—a field of study which originally embraced the so-called psychogenic neuroses, and still does so in academic parlance. In practice, however, a gulf has opened out in the last few decades between the trained neurologist and the psychotherapist, especially after the first researches in hypnotism. This rift was unavoidable, because neurology, strictly speaking, is the science of organic nervous diseases, whereas the psychogenic neuroses are not organic diseases in the usual sense of the term. Nor do they fall within the realm of psychiatry, whose particular field of study is the psychoses, or mental diseases—for the psychogenic neuroses are not mental diseases as this term is commonly understood. Rather do they constitute a special field by themselves with no hard and fast boundaries, and they show many transitional forms which point in two directions: towards mental disease on the one hand, and diseases of the nerves on the other.

490 The unmistakable feature of the neuroses is the fact that their causes are psychic, and that their cure depends entirely upon psychic methods of treatment. The attempts to delimit and explore this special field—both from the side of psychiatry and from that of neurology—led to a discovery which was very unwelcome to the science of medicine: namely, the *discovery of the psyche* as an aetiological or causal factor in disease. In the course of the nineteenth century medicine had become, in its methods and theory, one of the disciplines of natural science, and it cherished the same basically philosophical assumption of *material causation*. For medicine, the psyche as a mental "substance" did not exist, and experimental psychology also did its best to constitute itself a psychology without a psyche.

491 Investigation, however, has established beyond a doubt that the crux of the psychoneuroses is the psychic factor, that this is the essential cause of the pathological state, and must therefore be recognized in its own right along with other admitted pathogenic factors such as inheritance, disposition, bacterial infection, and so forth. All attempts to explain the psychic factor in terms of more elementary physical factors were doomed to failure. There was more promise in the attempt to reduce it to the con-

cept of the drive or instinct—a concept taken over from biology. It is well known that instincts are observable physiological urges based on the functioning of the glands, and that, as experience shows, they condition or influence psychic processes. What could be more plausible, therefore, than to seek the specific cause of the psychoneuroses not in the mystical notion of the "soul," but in a disturbance of the instincts which might possibly be curable in the last resort by medicinal treatment of the glands?

92 Freud's theory of the neuroses is based on this standpoint: it explains them in terms of disturbances of the sexual instinct. Adler likewise resorts to the concept of the drive, and explains the neuroses in terms of disturbances of the urge to power, a concept which, we must admit, is a good deal more psychic than that of the physiological sexual instinct.

93 The term "instinct" is anything but well defined in the scientific sense. It applies to a biological phenomenon of immense complexity, and is not much more than a border-line concept of quite indefinite content standing for an unknown quantity. I do not wish to enter here upon a critical discussion of instinct. Instead I will consider the possibility that the psychic factor is just a combination of instincts which for their part may again be reduced to the functioning of the glands. We may even consider the possibility that everything "psychic" is comprised in the sum total of instincts, and that the psyche itself is therefore only an instinct or a conglomerate of instincts, being in the last analysis nothing but a function of the glands. A psychoneurosis would then be a glandular disease.

94 There is, however, no proof of this statement, and no glandular extract that will cure a neurosis has yet been found. On the other hand, we have been taught by all too many mistakes that organic therapy fails completely in the treatment of neuroses, while psychic methods cure them. These psychic methods are just as effective as we might suppose the glandular extracts would be. So far, then, as our present knowledge goes, neuroses are to be influenced or cured by approaching them not from the proximal end, i.e., from the functioning of the glands, but from the distal end, i.e., from the psyche, just as if the psyche were itself a substance. For instance, a suitable explanation or a comforting word to the patient can have something like a healing

effect which may even influence the glandular secretions. The doctor's words, to be sure, are "only" vibrations in the air, yet their special quality is due to a particular psychic state in the doctor. His words are effective only in so far as they convey a meaning or have significance. It is this that makes them work. But "meaning" is something mental or spiritual. Call it a fiction if you like. Nevertheless this fiction enables us to influence the course of the disease far more effectively than we could with chemical preparations. Indeed, we can even influence the biochemical processes of the body. Whether the fiction forms itself in me spontaneously or reaches me from outside via human speech, it can make me ill or cure me. Fictions, illusions, opinions are perhaps the most intangible and unreal things we can think of; yet they are the most effective of all in the psychic and even the psychophysical realm.

495 It was by recognizing these facts that medicine discovered the psyche, and it can no longer honestly deny the psyche's reality. It has been shown that the instincts are a condition of psychic activity, while at the same time psychic processes seem to condition the instincts.

496 The reproach levelled at the Freudian and Adlerian theories is not that they are based on instincts, but that they are one-sided. It is psychology without the psyche, and this suits people who think they have no spiritual needs or aspirations. But here both doctor and patient deceive themselves. Even though the theories of Freud and Adler come much nearer to getting at the bottom of the neuroses than any earlier approach from the medical side, their exclusive concern with the instincts fails to satisfy the deeper spiritual needs of the patient. They are too much bound by the premises of nineteenth-century science, too matter of fact, and they give too little value to fictional and imaginative processes. In a word, they do not give enough meaning to life. And it is only meaning that liberates.

497 Ordinary reasonableness, sound human judgment, science as a compendium of common sense, these certainly help us over a good part of the road, but they never take us beyond the frontiers of life's most commonplace realities, beyond the merely average and normal. They afford no answer to the question of psychic suffering and its profound significance. A psychoneurosis must be understood, ultimately, as the suffering of a soul

which has not discovered its meaning. But all creativeness in the realm of the spirit as well as every psychic advance of man arises from the suffering of the soul, and the cause of the suffering is spiritual stagnation, or psychic sterility.

498 With this realization the doctor sets foot on territory which he enters with the greatest caution. He is now confronted with the necessity of conveying to his patient the healing fiction, the meaning that quickens—for it is this that the sick person longs for, over and above everything that reason and science can give him. He is looking for something that will take possession of him and give meaning and form to the confusion of his neurotic soul.

499 Is the doctor equal to this task? To begin with, he will probably hand his patient over to the clergyman or philosopher, or abandon him to that vast perplexity which is the special note of our day. As a doctor he is not required to have a finished outlook on life, and his professional conscience does not demand it of him. But what will he do when he sees only too clearly why his patient is ill; when he sees that he has no love, but only sexuality; no faith, because he is afraid to grope in the dark; no hope, because he is disillusioned by the world and by life; and no understanding, because he has failed to read the meaning of his own existence?

500 There are many well-educated patients who flatly refuse to consult a clergyman. Still less will they listen to a philosopher, for the history of philosophy leaves them cold, and intellectual problems seem to them more barren than the desert. And where are the great and wise men who do not merely talk about the meaning of life and of the world, but really possess it? One cannot just think up a system or truth which would give the patient what he needs in order to live, namely faith, hope, love, and understanding.

501 These four highest achievements of human endeavour are so many gifts of grace, which are neither to be taught nor learned, neither given nor taken, neither withheld nor earned, since they come through experience, which is an irrational datum not subject to human will and caprice. Experiences cannot be *made*. They happen—yet fortunately their independence of man's activity is not absolute but relative. We can draw closer to them—that much lies within our human reach. There

are ways which bring us nearer to living experience, yet we should beware of calling these ways "methods." The very word has a deadening effect. The way to experience, moreover, is anything but a clever trick; it is rather a venture which requires us to commit ourselves with our whole being.

502 Thus, in trying to meet the therapeutic demands made upon him, the doctor is confronted with a question which seems to contain an insuperable difficulty. How can he help the sufferer to attain the liberating experience which will bestow upon him the four great gifts of grace and heal his sickness? We can, of course, advise the patient with the best intentions that he should have true love, or true faith, or true hope; and we can admonish him with the phrase: "Know thyself." But how is the patient to obtain beforehand that which only experience can give him?

503 Saul owed his conversion neither to true love, nor to true faith, nor to any other truth. It was solely his hatred of the Christians that set him on the road to Damascus, and to that decisive experience which was to alter the whole course of his life. He was brought to this experience by following out, with conviction, his own worst mistake.

504 This opens up a problem which we can hardly take too seriously. And it confronts the psychotherapist with a question which brings him shoulder to shoulder with the clergyman: the question of good and evil.

505 It is in reality the priest or the clergyman, rather than the doctor, who should be most concerned with the problem of spiritual suffering. But in most cases the sufferer consults the doctor in the first place, because he supposes himself to be physically ill, and because certain neurotic symptoms can be at least alleviated by drugs. But if, on the other hand, the clergyman is consulted, he cannot persuade the sick man that the trouble is psychic. As a rule he lacks the special knowledge which would enable him to discern the psychic factors of the disease, and his judgment is without the weight of authority.

506 There are, however, persons who, while well aware of the psychic nature of their complaint, nevertheless refuse to turn to the clergyman. They do not believe that he can really help them. Such persons distrust the doctor for the same reason, and rightly so, for the truth is that both doctor and clergyman stand before them with empty hands, if not—what is even worse—

with empty words. We can hardly expect the doctor to have anything to say about the ultimate questions of the soul. It is from the clergyman, not from the doctor, that the sufferer should expect such help. But the Protestant clergyman often finds himself face to face with an almost impossible task, for he has to cope with practical difficulties that the Catholic priest is spared. Above all, the priest has the authority of his Church behind him, and his economic position is secure and independent. This is far less true of the Protestant clergyman, who may be married and burdened with the responsibility of a family, and cannot expect, if all else fails, to be supported by the parish or taken into a monastery. Moreover the priest, if he is also a Jesuit, is *au fait* with the most up-to-date developments in psychology. I know, for instance, that my own writings were seriously studied in Rome long before any Protestant theologian thought them worthy of a glance.

507 We have come to a serious pass. The exodus from the German Protestant Church is only one of many symptoms which should make it plain to the clergy that mere admonitions to believe, or to perform acts of charity, do not give modern man what he is looking for. The fact that many clergymen seek support or practical help from Freud's theory of sexuality or Adler's theory of power is astonishing, inasmuch as both these theories are, at bottom, hostile to spiritual values, being, as I have said, psychology without the psyche. They are rationalistic methods of treatment which actually hinder the realization of meaningful experience. By far the larger number of psychotherapists are disciples of Freud or of Adler. This means that the great majority of patients are necessarily alienated from a spiritual standpoint—a fact which cannot be a matter of indifference to one who has the fate of the psyche at heart. The wave of interest in psychology which at present is sweeping over the Protestant countries of Europe is far from receding. It is coincident with the mass exodus from the Church. Quoting a Protestant minister, I may say: "Nowadays people go to the psychotherapist rather than to the clergyman."

508 I am convinced that this statement is true only of relatively educated persons, not of mankind in the mass. However, we must not forget that it takes about twenty years for the ordinary run of people to begin thinking the thoughts of the educated

person of today. For instance, Büchner's work *Force and Matter* [2] became one of the most widely read books in German public libraries some twenty years after educated persons had forgotten all about it. I am convinced that the psychological needs of the educated today will be the interests of the people tomorrow.

509 I should like to call attention to the following facts. During the past thirty years, people from all the civilized countries of the earth have consulted me. Many hundreds of patients have passed through my hands, the greater number being Protestants, a lesser number Jews, and not more than five or six believing Catholics. Among all my patients in the second half of life—that is to say, over thirty-five—there has not been one whose problem in the last resort was not that of finding a religious outlook on life. It is safe to say that every one of them fell ill because he had lost what the living religions of every age have given to their followers, and none of them has been really healed who did not regain his religious outlook. This of course has nothing whatever to do with a particular creed or membership of a church.

510 Here, then, the clergyman stands before a vast horizon. But it would seem as if no one had noticed it. It also looks as though the Protestant clergyman of today were insufficiently equipped to cope with the urgent psychic needs of our age. It is indeed high time for the clergyman and the psychotherapist to join forces to meet this great spiritual task.

511 Here is a concrete example which goes to show how closely this problem touches us all. A little more than a year ago the leaders of the Christian Students' Conference at Aarau [Switzerland] laid before me the question whether people in spiritual distress prefer nowadays to consult the doctor rather than the clergyman, and what are the causes of their choice. This was a very direct and very practical question. At the time I knew nothing more than the fact that my own patients obviously had consulted the doctor rather than the clergyman. It seemed to me to be open to doubt whether this was generally the case or not. At any rate, I was unable to give a definite reply. I therefore set on foot an inquiry, through acquaintances of mine, among people

2 [Ludwig Büchner (1824–99), German materialistic philosopher. His *Kraft und Stoff* was pub. 1855.—EDITORS.]

whom I did not know personally; I sent out a questionnaire which was answered by Swiss, German, and French Protestants, as well as by a few Catholics. The results are very interesting, as the following general summary shows. Those who decided for the doctor represented 57 per cent of the Protestants and only 25 per cent of the Catholics, while those who decided for the clergyman formed only 8 per cent of the Protestants as against 58 per cent of the Catholics. These were the unequivocal decisions. The remaining 35 per cent of the Protestants could not make up their minds, while only 17 per cent of the Catholics were undecided.

512 The main reasons given for not consulting the clergyman were, firstly, his lack of psychological knowledge and insight, and this covered 52 per cent of the answers. Some 28 per cent were to the effect that he was prejudiced in his views and showed a dogmatic and traditional bias. Curiously enough, there was even one clergyman who decided for the doctor, while another made the irritated retort: "Theology has nothing to do with the treatment of human beings." All the relatives of clergymen who answered my questionnaire pronounced themselves against the clergy.

513 So far as this inquiry was restricted to educated persons, it is only a straw in the wind. I am convinced that the uneducated classes would have reacted differently. But I am inclined to accept these sample results as a more or less valid indication of the views of educated people, the more so as it is a well-known fact that their indifference in matters of the Church and religion is steadily growing. Nor should we forget the above-mentioned truth of social psychology: that it takes about twenty years for the general outlook and problems of the educated to percolate down to the uneducated masses. Who, for instance, would have dared to prophesy twenty years ago, or even ten, that Spain, the most Catholic of European countries, would undergo the tremendous mental revolution we are witnessing today? [3] And yet it has broken out with the violence of a cataclysm.

514 It seems to me that, side by side with the decline of religious life, the neuroses grow noticeably more frequent. There are as

3 [Under the second republic, established in 1931 and later overthrown by the Franco forces.—EDITORS.]

yet no statistics with actual figures to prove this increase. But of one thing I am sure, that everywhere the mental state of European man shows an alarming lack of balance. We are living undeniably in a period of the greatest restlessness, nervous tension, confusion, and disorientation of outlook. Among my patients from many countries, all of them educated persons, there is a considerable number who came to see me not because they were suffering from a neurosis but because they could find no meaning in their lives or were torturing themselves with questions which neither our philosophy nor our religion could answer. Some of them perhaps thought I knew of a magic formula, but I soon had to tell them that I didn't know the answer either. And this brings us to practical considerations.

515 Let us take for example that most ordinary and frequent of questions: What is the meaning of my life, or of life in general? Today people believe that they know only too well what the clergyman will—or rather must—say to this. They smile at the very thought of the philosopher's answer, and in general do not expect much of the physician. But from the psychotherapist who analyses the unconscious—from him one might at last learn something. Perhaps he has dug up from the abstruse depths of his mind, among other things, some meaning which could even be bought for a fee! It must be a relief to every serious-minded person to hear that the psychotherapist also does not know what to say. Such a confession is often the beginning of the patient's confidence in him.

516 I have found that modern man has an ineradicable aversion for traditional opinions and inherited truths. He is a Bolshevist for whom all the spiritual standards and forms of the past have somehow lost their validity, and who therefore wants to experiment with his mind as the Bolshevist experiments with economics. Confronted with this attitude, every ecclesiastical system finds itself in an awkward situation, be it Catholic, Protestant, Buddhist, or Confucianist. Among these moderns there are of course some of those negative, destructive, and perverse natures—degenerates and unbalanced eccentrics—who are never satisfied anywhere, and who therefore flock to every new banner, much to the hurt of these movements and undertakings, in the hope of finding something *for once* which will compensate at low cost for their own ineptitude. It goes without saying that,

in my professional work, I have come to know a great many modern men and women, including of course their pathological hangers-on. But these I prefer to leave aside. Those I am thinking of are by no means sickly eccentrics, but are very often exceptionally able, courageous, and upright persons who have repudiated traditional truths for honest and decent reasons, and not from wickedness of heart. Every one of them has the feeling that our religious truths have somehow become hollow. Either they cannot reconcile the scientific and the religious outlook, or the Christian tenets have lost their authority and their psychological justification. People no longer feel redeemed by the death of Christ; they cannot believe—for although it is a lucky man who *can* believe, it is not possible to compel belief. Sin has become something quite relative: what is evil for one man is good for another. After all, why should not the Buddha be right too?

517 There is no one who is not familiar with these questions and doubts. Yet Freudian analysis would brush them all aside as irrelevant, for in its view, it is basically a question of repressed sexuality, which the philosophical or religious doubts only serve to mask. If we closely examine an individual case of this sort, we do discover peculiar disturbances in the sexual sphere as well as in the sphere of unconscious impulses in general. Freud sees in the presence of these disturbances an explanation of the psychic disturbance as a whole; he is interested only in the causal interpretation of the sexual symptoms. He completely overlooks the fact that, in certain cases, the supposed causes of the neurosis were always present, but had no pathological effect until a disturbance of the conscious attitude set in and led to a neurotic upset. It is as though, when a ship was sinking because of a leak, the crew interested itself in the chemical constitution of the water that was pouring in, instead of stopping the leak. The disturbance of the instinctual sphere is not a primary but a secondary phenomenon. When conscious life has lost its meaning and promise, it is as though a panic had broken loose: "Let us eat and drink, for tomorrow we die!" It is this mood, born of the meaninglessness of life, that causes the disturbance in the unconscious and provokes the painfully curbed instincts to break out anew. The causes of a neurosis lie in the present as much as in the past, and only a cause actually existing in the

present can keep a neurosis active. A man is not tubercular because he was infected twenty years ago with bacilli, but because active foci of infection are present *now*. The questions when and how the infection occurred are totally irrelevant. Even the most accurate knowledge of the previous history cannot cure the tuberculosis. And the same holds true of the neuroses.

518 That is why I regard the religious problems which the patient puts before me as authentic and as possible causes of the neurosis. But if I take them seriously, I must be able to confess to the patient: "Yes, I agree, the Buddha may be just as right as Jesus. Sin is only relative, and it is difficult to see how we can feel ourselves in any way redeemed by the death of Christ." As a doctor I can easily admit these doubts, while it is hard for the clergyman to do so. The patient feels my attitude to be one of understanding, while the parson's hesitation strikes him as a traditional prejudice, and this estranges them from one another. He asks himself: "What would the parson say if I began to tell him of the painful details of my sexual disturbances?" He rightly suspects that the parson's moral prejudice is even stronger than his dogmatic bias. In this connection there is a good story about the American president, "silent Cal" Coolidge. When he returned after an absence one Sunday morning his wife asked him where he had been. "To church," he replied. "What did the minister say?" "He talked about sin." "And what did he say about sin?" "He was against it."

519 It is easy for the doctor to show understanding in this respect, you will say. But people forget that even doctors have moral scruples, and that certain patients' confessions are hard even for a doctor to swallow. Yet the patient does not feel himself accepted unless the very worst in him is accepted too. No one can bring this about by mere words; it comes only through reflection and through the doctor's attitude towards himself and his own dark side. If the doctor wants to guide another, or even accompany him a step of the way, he must *feel* with that person's psyche. He never feels it when he passes judgment. Whether he puts his judgments into words, or keeps them to himself, makes not the slightest difference. To take the opposite position, and to agree with the patient offhand, is also of no use, but estranges him as much as condemnation. Feeling comes only through unprejudiced objectivity. This sounds almost like

a scientific precept, and it could be confused with a purely intellectual, abstract attitude of mind. But what I mean is something quite different. It is a human quality—a kind of deep respect for the facts, for the man who suffers from them, and for the riddle of such a man's life. The truly religious person has this attitude. He knows that God has brought all sorts of strange and inconceivable things to pass and seeks in the most curious ways to enter a man's heart. He therefore senses in everything the unseen presence of the divine will. This is what I mean by "unprejudiced objectivity." It is a moral achievement on the part of the doctor, who ought not to let himself be repelled by sickness and corruption. We cannot change anything unless we accept it. Condemnation does not liberate, it oppresses. I am the oppressor of the person I condemn, not his friend and fellow-sufferer. I do not in the least mean to say that we must never pass judgment when we desire to help and improve. But if the doctor wishes to help a human being he must be able to accept him as he is. And he can do this in reality only when he has already seen and accepted himself as he is.

20 Perhaps this sounds very simple, but simple things are always the most difficult. In actual life it requires the greatest art to be simple, and so acceptance of oneself is the essence of the moral problem and the acid test of one's whole outlook on life. That I feed the beggar, that I forgive an insult, that I love my enemy in the name of Christ—all these are undoubtedly great virtues. What I do unto the least of my brethren, that I do unto Christ. But what if I should discover that the least amongst them all, the poorest of all beggars, the most impudent of all offenders, yea the very fiend himself—that these are within me, and that I myself stand in need of the alms of my own kindness, that I myself am the enemy who must be loved—what then? Then, as a rule, the whole truth of Christianity is reversed: there is then no more talk of love and long-suffering; we say to the brother within us "Raca," and condemn and rage against ourselves. We hide him from the world, we deny ever having met this least among the lowly in ourselves, and had it been God himself who drew near to us in this despicable form, we should have denied him a thousand times before a single cock had crowed.

1 Anyone who uses modern psychology to look behind the

scene not only of his patients' lives but more especially of his own life—and the modern psychotherapist must do this if he is not to be merely an unconscious fraud—will admit that to accept himself in all his wretchedness is the hardest of tasks, and one which it is almost impossible to fulfil. The very thought can make us sweat with fear. We are therefore only too delighted to choose, without a moment's hesitation, the complicated course of remaining in ignorance about ourselves while busying ourselves with other people and their troubles and sins. This activity lends us a perceptible air of virtue, by means of which we benevolently deceive ourselves and others. God be praised, we have escaped from ourselves at last! There are countless people who can do this with impunity, but not everyone can, and these few break down on the road to their Damascus and succumb to a neurosis. How can I help these people if I myself am a fugitive, and perhaps also suffer from the *morbus sacer* of a neurosis? Only he who has fully accepted himself has "unprejudiced objectivity." But no one is justified in boasting that he has fully accepted himself. We can point to Christ, who sacrificed his historical bias to the god within him, and lived his individual life to the bitter end without regard for conventions or for the moral standards of the Pharisees.

522 We Protestants must sooner or later face this question: Are we to understand the "imitation of Christ" in the sense that we should copy his life and, if I may use the expression, ape his stigmata; or in the deeper sense that we are to live our own proper lives as truly as he lived his in its individual uniqueness? It is no easy matter to live a life that is modelled on Christ's, but it is unspeakably harder to live one's own life as truly as Christ lived his. Anyone who did this would run counter to the conditions of his own history, and though he might thus be fulfilling them, he would none the less be misjudged, derided, tortured, and crucified. He would be a kind of crazy Bolshevist who deserved the cross. We therefore prefer the historically sanctioned and sanctified imitation of Christ. I would never disturb a monk in the practice of this identification, for he deserves our respect. But neither I nor my patients are monks, and it is my duty as a physician to show my patients how they can live their lives without becoming neurotic. Neurosis is an inner cleavage—the state of being at war with oneself.

Everything that accentuates this cleavage makes the patient worse, and everything that mitigates it tends to heal him. What drives people to war with themselves is the suspicion or the knowledge that they consist of two persons in opposition to one another. The conflict may be between the sensual and the spiritual man, or between the ego and the shadow. It is what Faust means when he says: "Two souls, alas, dwell in my breast apart." A neurosis is a splitting of personality.

523 Healing may be called a religious problem. In the sphere of social or national relations, the state of suffering may be civil war, and this state is to be cured by the Christian virtue of forgiveness and love of one's enemies. That which we recommend, with the conviction of good Christians, as applicable to external situations, we must also apply inwardly in the treatment of neurosis. This is why modern man has heard enough about guilt and sin. He is sorely enough beset by his own bad conscience, and wants rather to know how he is to reconcile himself with his own nature—how he is to love the enemy in his own heart and call the wolf his brother.

524 The modern man does not want to know in what way he can imitate Christ, but in what way he can live his own individual life, however meagre and uninteresting it may be. It is because every form of imitation seems to him deadening and sterile that he rebels against the force of tradition that would hold him to well-trodden ways. All such roads, for him, lead in the wrong direction. He may not know it, but he behaves as if his own individual life were God's special will which must be fulfilled at all costs. This is the source of his egoism, which is one of the most tangible evils of the neurotic state. But the person who tells him he is too egoistic has already lost his confidence, and rightly so, for that person has driven him still further into his neurosis.

525 If I wish to effect a cure for my patients I am forced to acknowledge the deep significance of their egoism. I should be blind, indeed, if I did not recognize it as a true will of God. I must even help the patient to prevail in his egoism; if he succeeds in this, he estranges himself from other people. He drives them away, and they come to themselves—as they should, for they were seeking to rob him of his "sacred" egoism. This must be left to him, for it is his strongest and healthiest power; it is,

as I have said, a true will of God, which sometimes drives him into complete isolation. However wretched this state may be, it also stands him in good stead, for in this way alone can he get to know himself and learn what an invaluable treasure is the love of his fellow beings. It is, moreover, only in the state of complete abandonment and loneliness that we experience the helpful powers of our own natures.

526 When one has several times seen this development at work one can no longer deny that what was evil has turned to good, and that what seemed good has kept alive the forces of evil. The archdemon of egoism leads us along the royal road to that ingathering which religious experience demands. What we observe here is a fundamental law of life—*enantiodromia* or conversion into the opposite; and it is this that makes possible the reunion of the warring halves of the personality and thereby brings the civil war to an end.

527 I have taken the neurotic's egoism as an example because it is one of his most common symptoms. I might equally well have taken any other characteristic symptom to show what attitude the physician must adopt towards the shortcomings of his patients, in other words, how he must deal with the problem of evil.

528 No doubt this also sounds very simple. In reality, however, the acceptance of the shadow-side of human nature verges on the impossible. Consider for a moment what it means to grant the right of existence to what is unreasonable, senseless, and evil! Yet it is just this that the modern man insists upon. He wants to live with every side of himself—to know what he is. That is why he casts history aside. He wants to break with tradition so that he can experiment with his life and determine what value and meaning things have in themselves, apart from traditional presuppositions. Modern youth gives us astonishing examples of this attitude. To show how far this tendency may go, I will instance a question addressed to me by a German society. I was asked if incest is to be reprobated, and what facts can be adduced against it!

529 Granted such tendencies, the conflicts into which people may fall are not hard to imagine. I can well understand that one would like to do everything possible to protect one's fellow beings from such adventures. But curiously enough we find our-

selves without means to do this. All the old arguments against unreasonableness, self-deception, and immorality, once so potent, have lost their attraction. We are now reaping the fruit of nineteenth-century education. Throughout that period the Church preached to young people the merit of blind faith, while the universities inculcated an intellectual rationalism, with the result that today we plead in vain whether for faith or reason. Tired of this warfare of opinions, the modern man wishes to find out for himself how things are. And though this desire opens the door to the most dangerous possibilities, we cannot help seeing it as a courageous enterprise and giving it some measure of sympathy. It is no reckless adventure, but an effort inspired by deep spiritual distress to bring meaning once more into life on the basis of fresh and unprejudiced experience. Caution has its place, no doubt, but we cannot refuse our support to a serious venture which challenges the whole of the personality. If we oppose it, we are trying to suppress what is best in man—his daring and his aspirations. And should we succeed, we should only have stood in the way of that invaluable experience which might have given a meaning to life. What would have happened if Paul had allowed himself to be talked out of his journey to Damascus?

530 The psychotherapist who takes his work seriously must come to grips with this question. He must decide in every single case whether or not he is willing to stand by a human being with counsel and help upon what may be a daring misadventure. He must have no fixed ideas as to what is right, nor must he pretend to know what is right and what not—otherwise he takes something from the richness of the experience. He must keep in view what actually happens—for only that which acts is actual.[4] If something which seems to me an error shows itself to be more effective than a truth, then I must first follow up the error, for in it lie power and life which I lose if I hold to what seems to me true. Light has need of darkness—otherwise how could it appear as light?

531 It is well known that Freudian psychoanalysis limits itself to the task of making conscious the shadow-side and the evil within

4 [A more literal translation, which brings out the meaning more clearly while losing the play on words, would be: "He must keep in view only what is real (for the patient). But a thing is 'real' (*wirklich*) if it 'works' (*wirkt*)."—TRANS.]

us. It simply brings into action the civil war that was latent, and lets it go at that. The patient must deal with it as best he can. Freud has unfortunately overlooked the fact that man has never yet been able single-handed to hold his own against the powers of darkness—that is, of the unconscious. Man has always stood in need of the spiritual help which his particular religion held out to him. The opening up of the unconscious always means the outbreak of intense spiritual suffering; it is as when a flourishing civilization is abandoned to invading hordes of barbarians, or when fertile fields are exposed by the bursting of a dam to a raging torrent. The World War was such an invasion which showed, as nothing else could, how thin are the walls which separate a well-ordered world from lurking chaos. But it is the same with the individual and his rationally ordered world. Seeking revenge for the violence his reason has done to her, outraged Nature only awaits the moment when the partition falls so as to overwhelm the conscious life with destruction. Man has been aware of this danger to the psyche since the earliest times, even in the most primitive stages of culture. It was to arm himself against this threat and to heal the damage done that he developed religious and magical practices. This is why the medicine-man is also the priest; he is the saviour of the soul as well as of the body, and religions are systems of healing for psychic illness. This is especially true of the two greatest religions of humanity, Christianity and Buddhism. Man is never helped in his suffering by what he thinks of for himself; only suprahuman, revealed truth lifts him out of his distress.

532 Today the tide of destruction has already reached us and the psyche has suffered damage. That is why patients force the psychotherapist into the role of the priest and expect and demand of him that he shall free them from their suffering. That is why we psychotherapists must occupy ourselves with problems which, strictly speaking, belong to the theologian. But we cannot leave these questions for theology to answer; challenged by the urgent psychic needs of our patients, we are directly confronted with them every day. Since, as a rule, every concept and every point of view handed down from the past proves futile, we must first tread with the patient the path of his illness—the path of his mistake that sharpens his conflicts and increases his

loneliness till it becomes unbearable—hoping that from the psychic depths which cast up the powers of destruction the rescuing forces will also come.

533 When I first took this path I did not know where it would lead. I did not know what lay hidden in the depths of the psyche —that region which I have since called the "collective unconscious" and whose contents I designate as "archetypes." Since time immemorial, invasions of the unconscious have occurred, and ever and again they repeat themselves. For consciousness did not exist from the beginning; in every child it has to be built up anew in the first years of life. Consciousness is very weak in this formative period, and the same is true of the psychic history of mankind—the unconscious easily seizes power. These struggles have left their mark. To put it in scientific terms: instinctive defence-mechanisms have been built up which automatically intervene when the danger is greatest, and their coming into action during an emergency is represented in fantasy by helpful images which are ineradicably imprinted on the human psyche. Science can only establish the existence of these psychic factors and attempt a rationalistic explanation by offering an hypothesis as to their source. This, however, only thrusts the problem a stage further back without solving the riddle. We thus come to those ultimate questions: Where does consciousness come from? What is the psyche? At this point all science ends.

534 It is as though, at the climax of the illness, the destructive powers were converted into healing forces. This is brought about by the archetypes awaking to independent life and taking over the guidance of the psychic personality, thus supplanting the ego with its futile willing and striving. As a religious-minded person would say: guidance has come from God. With most of my patients I have to avoid this formulation, apt though it is, for it reminds them too much of what they had to reject in the first place. I must express myself in more modest terms and say that the psyche has awakened to spontaneous activity. And indeed this formulation is better suited to the observable facts, as the transformation takes place at that moment when, in dreams or fantasies, motifs appear whose source in consciousness cannot be demonstrated. To the patient it is nothing less than a revelation when something altogether strange rises up to confront him

from the hidden depths of the psyche—something that is not his ego and is therefore beyond the reach of his personal will. He has regained access to the sources of psychic life, and this marks the beginning of the cure.

535 In order to illustrate this process, I ought really to discuss it with the help of examples. But it is almost impossible to give a convincing example offhand, for as a rule it is an extremely subtle and complicated matter. Often it is simply the deep impression made on the patient by the independent way the dreams deal with his problem. Or it may be that his fantasy points to something for which his conscious mind was quite unprepared. But in most cases it is contents of an archetypal nature, or the connections between them, that exert a strong influence of their own whether or not they are understood by the conscious mind. This spontaneous activity of the psyche often becomes so intense that visionary pictures are seen or inner voices heard—a true, primordial experience of the spirit.

536 Such experiences reward the sufferer for the pains of the labyrinthine way. From now on a light shines through the confusion; more, he can accept the conflict within him and so come to resolve the morbid split in his nature on a higher level.

*

537 The fundamental problems of modern psychotherapy are so important and far-reaching that their discussion in an essay precludes any presentation of details, however desirable this might be for clarity's sake. I hope nevertheless that I have succeeded in my main purpose, which was to set forth the attitude of the psychotherapist to his work. This may be found more rewarding than precepts and pointers to methods of treatment, which in any case never work properly unless they are applied with right understanding. The attitude of the psychotherapist is infinitely more important than the theories and methods of psychotherapy, and that is why I was particularly concerned to make this attitude known. I believe I have given an honest account and have, at the same time, imparted information which will allow you to decide how far and in what way the clergyman can join with the psychotherapist in his aspirations and endeavours. I believe, also, that the picture I have drawn of the spiritual outlook of modern man corresponds to the true state

of affairs, though I make no claim to infallibility. In any case, what I have had to say about the cure of neurosis, and the problems involved, is the unvarnished truth. We doctors would naturally welcome the sympathetic understanding of the clergy in our endeavours to heal psychic suffering, but we are also fully aware of the fundamental difficulties which stand in the way of co-operation. My own position is on the extreme left wing in the parliament of Protestant opinion, yet I would be the first to warn people against uncritical generalizations of their own point of view. As a Swiss I am an inveterate democrat, yet I recognize that Nature is aristocratic and, what is even more, esoteric. "Quod licet Jovi, non licet bovi" is an unpleasant but eternal truth. Who are forgiven their many sins? Those who have loved much. But as to those who love little, their few sins are held against them. I am firmly convinced that a vast number of people belong to the fold of the Catholic Church and nowhere else, because they are most suitably housed there. I am as much persuaded of this as of the fact, which I have myself observed, that a primitive religion is better suited to primitive people than Christianity, which is so incomprehensible to them and so foreign to their blood that they can only ape it in the most disgusting way. I believe, too, that there must be protestants against the Catholic Church, and also protestants against Protestantism—for the manifestations of the spirit are truly wondrous, and as varied as Creation itself.

538 The living spirit grows and even outgrows its earlier forms of expression; it freely chooses the men who proclaim it and in whom it lives. This living spirit is eternally renewed and pursues its goal in manifold and inconceivable ways throughout the history of mankind. Measured against it, the names and forms which men have given it mean very little; they are only the changing leaves and blossoms on the stem of the eternal tree.

PSYCHOANALYSIS AND THE CURE OF SOULS[1]

539 The question of the relations between psychoanalysis and the pastoral cure of souls is not easy to answer, because the two are concerned with essentially different things. The cure of souls as practised by the clergyman or priest is a religious influence based on a Christian confession of faith. Psychoanalysis, on the other hand, is a medical intervention, a psychological technique whose purpose it is to lay bare the contents of the unconscious and integrate them into the conscious mind. This definition of psychoanalysis applies, however, only to the methods employed by Freud's school and mine. The Adlerian method is not an analysis in this sense, nor does it pursue the aim stated above. It is chiefly pedagogical in intent, and works directly upon the conscious mind without, as it were, considering the unconscious. It is a further development of the French "rééducation de la volonté" and of Dubois' "psychic orthopedics." The normalization of the individual at which Adlerian pedagogics aim, and his adaptation to the collective psyche, represent a different goal from that pursued by the pastoral cure of souls, which has for its aim the salvation of the soul and its deliverance from the snares of this world. Normalization and adaptation may, under certain circumstances, even be aims which are diametrically

[1] [First published as "Psychoanalyse und Seelsorge," in *Ethik: Sexual- und Gesellschafts-Ethik* (Halle), V (1928): 1, 7–12.—Editors.]

opposed to the Christian ideal of detachment from the world, submission to the will of God, and the salvation of the individual. The Adlerian method and the pastoral cure of souls, whether Protestant or Catholic, have only one thing in common, and that is the fact that they both apply themselves to the conscious mind, and in so doing appeal to a person's insight and will.

540 Freudian psychoanalysis, on the other hand, appeals in the first place neither to insight nor to the will, but seeks to lead the contents of the unconscious over into the conscious mind, thereby destroying the roots of the disturbances or symptoms. Freud seeks, therefore, to remove the disturbance of adaptation by an undermining of the symptoms, and not through treatment of the conscious mind. That is the aim of his psychoanalytic technique.

541 My difference with Freud begins with the interpretation of unconscious material. It stands to reason that you cannot integrate anything into consciousness without some measure of comprehension, i.e., insight. In order to make the unconscious material assimilable or understandable, Freud employs his famous sexual theory, which conceives the material brought to light through analysis mainly as sexual tendencies (or other immoral wishes) that are incompatible with the conscious attitude. Freud's standpoint here is based on the rationalistic materialism of the scientific views current in the late nineteenth century (of which his book *The Future of an Illusion* affords the plainest possible demonstration). With these views a fairly far-reaching recognition of the animal nature of man can be effected without too much difficulty, for the moral conflict is then apparently limited to easily avoidable collisions with public opinion or the penal code. At the same time Freud speaks of "sublimation," which he understands as an application of libido in desexualized form. I cannot enter here into a criticism of this very delicate subject, but would merely point out that not everything that comes out of the unconscious can be "sublimated."

542 For anyone who, whether by temperament, or for philosophical or religious reasons, cannot adopt the standpoint of scientific materialism, the realization of unconscious contents is in every respect a serious problem. Fortunately an instinctive

resistance protects us from realizations that would take us too far; hence one can often content onself with a moderate increase of consciousness. This is particularly so in the case of simple, uncomplicated neuroses, or rather, with people who are simple and uncomplicated (a neurosis is never more complicated than the person who has it). Those, on the other hand, with more refined natures suffer mostly from a passion for consciousness far exceeding their instinctive resistance. They want to see, know, and understand. For these people the answer given by the Freudian art of interpretation is unsatisfying. Here the Church's means of grace, especially as entrusted to the Catholic priest, are likely to come to the aid of understanding, for their form and meaning are suited at the outset to the nature of unconscious contents. That is why the priest not only hears the confession, but also asks questions—indeed, it is incumbent on him to ask them. What is more, he can ask about things which would otherwise only come to the ears of the doctor. In view of the means of grace at his disposal, the priest's intervention cannot be regarded as exceeding his competence, seeing that he is also empowered to lay the storm which he has provoked.

543 For the Protestant minister the problem is not so simple. Apart from common prayer and Holy Communion, he has no ritual ceremonies at his disposal, no spiritual exercises, rosaries, pilgrimages, etc., with their expressive symbolism. He is therefore compelled to take his stand on moral ground, which puts the instinctual forces coming up from the unconscious in danger of a new repression. Any sacral action, in whatever form, works like a vessel for receiving the contents of the unconscious. Puritan simplification has deprived Protestantism of just this means of acting on the unconscious; at any rate it has dispossessed the clergyman of his quality as a priestly mediator, which is so very necessary to the soul. Instead, it has given the individual responsibility for himself and left him alone with his God. Herein lies the advantage and also the danger of Protestantism. From this, too, comes its inner unrest, which in the course of a few centuries has begotten more than four hundred Protestant denominations—an indubitable symptom of individualism run riot.

544 There can be no doubt that the psychoanalytical unveiling of the unconscious has a great effect. Equally, there can be no

doubt of the tremendous effect of Catholic confession, especially when it is not just a passive hearing, but an active intervention. In view of this, it is truly astonishing that the Protestant Churches have not long since made an effort to revive the institution of confession as the epitome of the pastoral bond between the shepherd and his flock. For the Protestant, however, there is—and rightly so—no going back to this primitive Catholic form; it is too sharply opposed to the nature of Protestantism. The Protestant minister, rightly seeing in the cure of souls the real purpose of his existence, naturally looks round for a new way that will lead to the souls, and not merely to the ears, of his parishioners. Analytical psychology seems to him to provide the key, for the meaning and purpose of his ministry are not fulfilled with the Sunday sermon, which, though it reaches the ears, seldom penetrates to the heart, much less to the soul, the most hidden of all things hidden in man. The cure of souls can only be practised in the stillness of a colloquy, carried on in the healthful atmosphere of unreserved confidence. Soul must work on soul, and many doors be unlocked that bar the way to the innermost sanctuary. Psychoanalysis possesses the means of opening doors otherwise tightly closed.

545 The opening of these doors, however, is often very like a surgical operation, where the doctor, with knife poised, must be prepared for anything the moment the cut is made. The psychoanalyst, likewise, can discover unforeseen things that are very unpleasant indeed, such as latent psychoses and the like. Although these things, given time, often come to the surface entirely of their own accord, the blame nevertheless falls on the analyst, who, by his intervention, releases the disturbance prematurely. Only a thorough knowledge of psychiatry and its specialized techniques can protect the doctor from such blunders. A lay analyst should therefore always work in collaboration with a doctor.

546 Fortunately, the unlucky accidents I have just mentioned occur relatively seldom. But what psychoanalysis brings to light is, in itself, difficult enough to cope with. It brings the patient face to face with his life problem, and hence with some of the ultimate, serious questions which he has hitherto evaded. As human nature is very far from innocent, the facts that come up are usually quite sufficient to explain why the patient avoided

them: he felt instinctively that he did not know a satisfactory answer to these questions. Accordingly he expects it from the analyst. The analyst can now safely leave certain critical questions open—and to the patient's own advantage; for no sensible patient will expect from him anything more than *medical* help. More is expected from the clergyman, namely the solution of *religious* questions.

547 As already said, the Catholic Church has at her disposal ways and means which have served since olden times to gather the lower, instinctual forces of the psyche into symbols and in this way integrate them into the hierarchy of the spirit. The Protestant minister lacks these means, and consequently often stands perplexed before certain facts of human nature which no amount of admonition, or insight, or goodwill, or heroic self-castigation can subdue. In Protestantism good and evil are flatly and irreconcilably opposed to one another. There is no visible forgiveness; the human being is left alone with his sin. And God, as we know, only forgives the sins we have conquered ourselves. For the Protestant clergy it is a momentous psychological difficulty that they possess no forms which would serve to catch the lower instincts of psychic life. It is precisely the problem of the unconscious conflict brought to light by psychoanalysis that requires solving. The doctor can—on the basis of scientific materialism—treat the problem with medical discretion, that is to say he can regard the ethical problems of his patient as lying outside his competence as a doctor. He can safely retire behind a regretful "There you must make out as best you can." But the Protestant clergyman cannot, in my opinion, wash his hands in innocence; he must accompany the soul of the person who confides in him on its dark journey. The reductive standpoint of psychoanalysis is of little use to him here, for any development is a building up and not a breaking down. Good advice and moral exhortation are little if any help in serious cases because, if followed, they dispel that intense darkness which precedes the coming of the light. As a wise saying of the East puts it: It is better to do good than to eschew evil. He who is wise, therefore, will play the part of beggar, king, or criminal, and be mindful of the gods.

548 It is easier for the Catholic clergy to employ the elements of psychological analysis than it is for the Protestant. The latter

are faced with the harder task. Not only do the Catholics possess a ready-made pastoral technique in the historically sanctioned form of confession, penance, and absolution, but they also have at their command a rich and palpably ritualistic symbolism which fully satisfies the demands as well as the obscure passions of simpler minds. The Protestants need a psychological technique to an even greater degree since they lack all essential forms of ritual. I therefore hold that psychological interest on the part of the Protestant clergy is entirely legitimate and even necessary. Their possible encroachment upon medical territory is more than balanced by medical incursions into religion and philosophy, to which doctors naïvely believe themselves entitled (witness the explanation of religious processes in terms of sexual symptoms or infantile wish-fantasies). The doctor and the clergyman undoubtedly clash head-on in analytical psychology. This collision should lead to co-operation and not to enmity.

549 Owing to the absence of ritual forms, the Protestant (as opposed to the Catholic) cure of souls develops into a personal discussion in the sense of an "I-Thou" relationship. It cannot translate the fundamental problem of the transference into something impersonal, as the Catholic can, but must handle it with confidence as a personal experience. Any contact with the unconscious that goes at all deep leads to transference phenomena. Whenever, therefore, the clergyman penetrates any distance into the psychic background, he will provoke a transference (with men as well as with women). This involves him personally, and on top of that he has no form which he could substitute for his own person, as the Catholic priest can, or rather must do. In this way he finds himself drawn into the most personal participation for the sake of his parishioner's spiritual welfare, more so even than the analyst, for whom the specific salvation of the patient's soul is not necessarily a matter of burning importance. At all events he can resort to plausible excuses which the clergyman, somewhat nervously, must repudiate for higher reasons. Hence he stands, and must stand, in constant danger of involving himself in serious psychic conflicts which, to put it mildly, are not conducive to the parochial peace of mind. This danger is no trifling one, but it has the great advantage of drawing the responsible pastor back into real life and, at the same time, of exposing him to the tribulations of the

early Church (cf. the gossip against which Paul had to defend himself).

550 The pastor must make up his mind how far his public position, his stipend, and considerations for his family keep him from setting forth on the perilous mission of curing souls. I would not think ill of him if he decided not to follow the advice that Tertullian gave his catechumens, namely, that they should deliberately visit the arena. Real pastoral work that is based on modern psychology can easily expose the clergyman to the martyrdom of public misinterpretation. Public position and regard for the family, though worldly considerations, counsel a wise reserve (for the children of this world are, as we know, wiser than the children of light). Nevertheless, the eyes of the soul turn longingly to those who, regardless of their worldly welfare, can throw everything into the scales for the sake of something better. Nothing, certainly, is ever won by childish enthusiasm; yet only with daring—a daring which never leaves the firm ground of the real and the possible, and which shrinks from no suffering—can anything of greater worth be achieved.

551 Thus it is the Protestant minister's lack of ritual equipment which holds him back from closer contact with the world, and at the same time drives him towards a greater adventure—because it moves him right into the firing line. I hope that the Protestant will not be found wanting in courage for this task.

552 All intelligent psychotherapists would be glad if their endeavours were supported and supplemented by the work of the clergy. Certainly the problems of the human soul, approached from opposite ends by cleric and doctor, will cause considerable difficulties for both, not least on account of the difference in standpoint. But it is just from this encounter that we may expect the most fruitful stimulation for both sides.

VI

ANSWER TO JOB

[First published as a book, *Antwort auf Hiob* (Zurich, 1952). The present translation was first published, in book form, in London, 1954; for it, Professor Jung made some half-dozen small alterations to the original text and added or authorized an occasional footnote. In 1956, it was reprinted and published by Pastoral Psychology Book Club, Great Neck, New York. Only minor stylistic alterations have been made in the version here published.—EDITORS.]

PREFATORY NOTE[1]

The suggestion that I should tell you how *Answer to Job* came to be written sets me a difficult task, because the history of this book can hardly be told in a few words. I have been occupied with its central problem for years. Many different sources nourished the stream of its thoughts, until one day—and after long reflection—the time was ripe to put them into words.

The most immediate cause of my writing the book is perhaps to be found in certain problems discussed in my book *Aion*, especially the problems of Christ as a symbolic figure and of the antagonism Christ-Antichrist, represented in the traditional zodiacal symbolism of the two fishes.

In connection with the discussion of these problems and of the doctrine of Redemption, I criticized the idea of the *privatio boni* as not agreeing with the psychological findings. Psychological experience shows that whatever we call "good" is balanced by an equally substantial "bad" or "evil." If "evil" is non-existent, then whatever there is must needs be "good." Dogmatically, neither "good" nor "evil" can be derived from Man, since the "Evil One" existed before Man as one of the "Sons of God." The idea of the *privatio boni* began to play a role in the Church only after Mani. Before this heresy, Clement of Rome taught

1 [Written for *Pastoral Psychology* (Great Neck, N. Y.), VI:60 (January, 1956).—EDITORS.]

that God rules the world with a right and a left hand, the right being Christ, the left Satan. Clement's view is clearly *monotheistic,* as it unites the opposites in one God.

Later Christianity, however, is dualistic, inasmuch as it splits off one half of the opposites, personified in Satan, and he is *eternal* in his state of damnation. This crucial question forms the point of departure for the Christian theory of Redemption. It is therefore of prime importance. If Christianity claims to be a monotheism, it becomes unavoidable to assume the opposites as being contained in God. But then we are confronted with a major religious problem: the problem of Job. It is the aim of my book to point out its historical evolution since the time of Job down through the centuries to the most recent symbolic phenomena, such as the *Assumptio Mariae,* etc.

Moreover, the study of medieval natural philosophy—of the greatest importance to psychology—made me try to find an answer to the question: what image of God did these old philosophers have? Or rather: how should the symbols which supplement their image of God be understood? All this pointed to a *complexio oppositorum* and thus recalled again the story of Job to my mind: Job who expected help from God against God. This most peculiar fact presupposes a similar conception of the opposites in God.

On the other hand, numerous questions, not only from my patients, but from all over the world, brought up the problem of giving a more complete and explicit answer than I had given in *Aion.* For many years I hesitated to do this because I was quite conscious of the probable consequences, and knew what a storm would be raised. But I was gripped by the urgency and difficulty of the problem and was unable to throw it off. Therefore I found myself obliged to deal with the whole problem, and I did so in the form of describing a personal experience, carried by subjective emotions. I deliberately chose this form because I wanted to avoid the impression that I had any idea of announcing an "eternal truth." The book does not pretend to be anything but the voice or question of a single individual who hopes or expects to meet with thoughtfulness in the public.

LECTORI BENEVOLO

I am distressed for thee, my brother . . .
II Samuel 1:26 (AV)

553 On account of its somewhat unusual content, my little book requires a short preface. I beg of you, dear reader, not to overlook it. For, in what follows, I shall speak of the venerable objects of religious belief. Whoever talks of such matters inevitably runs the risk of being torn to pieces by the two parties who are in mortal conflict about those very things. This conflict is due to the strange supposition that a thing is true only if it presents itself as a *physical* fact. Thus some people believe it to be physically true that Christ was born as the son of a virgin, while others deny this as a physical impossibility. Everyone can see that there is no logical solution to this conflict and that one would do better not to get involved in such sterile disputes. Both are right and both are wrong. Yet they could easily reach agreement if only they dropped the word "physical." "Physical" is not the only criterion of truth: there are also *psychic* truths which can neither be explained nor proved nor contested in any physical way. If, for instance, a general belief existed that the river Rhine had at one time flowed backwards from its mouth to its source, then this belief would in itself be a fact even though such an assertion, physically understood, would be

deemed utterly incredible. Beliefs of this kind are psychic facts which cannot be contested and need no proof.

554 Religious statements are of this type. They refer without exception to things that cannot be established as physical facts. If they did not do this, they would inevitably fall into the category of the natural sciences. Taken as referring to anything physical, they make no sense whatever, and science would dismiss them as non-experienceable. They would be mere miracles, which are sufficiently exposed to doubt as it is, and yet they could not demonstrate the reality of the spirit or *meaning* that underlies them, because meaning is something that always demonstrates itself and is experienced on its own merits. The spirit and meaning of Christ are present and perceptible to us even without the aid of miracles. Miracles appeal only to the understanding of those who cannot perceive the meaning. They are mere substitutes for the not understood reality of the spirit. This is not to say that the living presence of the spirit is not occasionally accompanied by marvellous physical happenings. I only wish to emphasize that these happenings can neither replace nor bring about an understanding of the spirit, which is the one essential thing.

555 The fact that religious statements frequently conflict with the observed physical phenomena proves that in contrast to physical perception the spirit is autonomous, and that psychic experience is to a certain extent independent of physical data. The psyche is an autonomous factor, and religious statements are psychic confessions which in the last resort are based on unconscious, i.e., on transcendental, processes. These processes are not accessible to physical perception but demonstrate their existence through the confessions of the psyche. The resultant statements are filtered through the medium of human consciousness: that is to say, they are given visible forms which in their turn are subject to manifold influences from within and without. That is why whenever we speak of religious contents we move in a world of images that point to something ineffable. We do not know how clear or unclear these images, metaphors, and concepts are in respect of their transcendental object. If, for instance, we say "God," we give expression to an image or verbal concept which has undergone many changes in the course of time. We are, however, unable to say with any degree of cer-

tainty—unless it be by faith—whether these changes affect only the images and concepts, or the Unspeakable itself. After all, we can imagine God as an eternally flowing current of vital energy that endlessly changes shape just as easily as we can imagine him as an eternally unmoved, unchangeable essence. Our reason is sure only of one thing: that it manipulates images and ideas which are dependent on human imagination and its temporal and local conditions, and which have therefore changed innumerable times in the course of their long history. There is no doubt that there is something behind these images that transcends consciousness and operates in such a way that the statements do not vary limitlessly and chaotically, but clearly all relate to a few basic principles or archetypes. These, like the psyche itself, or like matter, are unknowable as such. All we can do is to construct models of them which we know to be inadequate, a fact which is confirmed again and again by religious statements.

556 If, therefore, in what follows I concern myself with these "metaphysical" objects, I am quite conscious that I am moving in a world of images and that none of my reflections touches the essence of the Unknowable. I am also too well aware of how limited are our powers of conception—to say nothing of the feebleness and poverty of language—to imagine that my remarks mean anything more in principle than what a primitive man means when he conceives of his god as a hare or a snake. But, although our whole world of religious ideas consists of anthropomorphic images that could never stand up to rational criticism, we should never forget that they are based on numinous archetypes, i.e., on an emotional foundation which is unassailable by reason. We are dealing with psychic facts which logic can overlook but not eliminate. In this connection Tertullian has already appealed, quite rightly, to the testimony of the soul. In his *De testimonio animae,* he says:

These testimonies of the soul are as simple as they are true, as obvious as they are simple, as common as they are obvious, as natural as they are common, as divine as they are natural. I think that they cannot appear to any one to be trifling and ridiculous if he considers the majesty of Nature, whence the authority of the soul is derived. What you allow to the mistress you will assign to the disciple. Nature is the mistress, the soul is the disciple; what the one has taught, or the other has learned, has been delivered to them by God, who is, in truth, the Master even of the mistress herself. What notion the soul is able to conceive of her first teacher is in your power to judge, from that soul which is in you. Feel that which causes you to feel; think upon that which is in forebodings your prophet; in omens, your augur; in the events which befall you, your foreseer. Strange if, being given by God, she knows how to act the diviner for men! Equally strange if she knows Him by whom she has been given! [1]

557 I would go a step further and say that the statements made in the Holy Scriptures are also utterances of the soul—even at the risk of being suspected of psychologism. The statements of the conscious mind may easily be snares and delusions, lies, or arbitrary opinions, but this is certainly not true of the statements of the soul: to begin with they always go over our heads because they point to realities that transcend consciousness. These *entia* are the archetypes of the collective unconscious, and they precipitate complexes of ideas in the form of mythological motifs. Ideas of this kind are never invented, but enter the field of inner perception as finished products, for instance in dreams. They are spontaneous phenomena which are not subject to our will, and we are therefore justified in ascribing to them a certain autonomy. They are to be regarded not only as objects but as subjects with laws of their own. From the point of view of consciousness, we can, of course, describe them as objects, and even explain them up to a point, in the same measure as we can describe and explain a living human being. But then we have to disregard their autonomy. If that is considered, we are compelled to treat them as subjects; in other words, we have to admit that they possess spontaneity and purposiveness, or a kind of consciousness and free will. We observe their behaviour and consider their statements. This dual standpoint, which we are forced to adopt towards every relatively independent organism, naturally has a dual result. On the one hand it tells me what I do to the object, and on the other hand what it does (possibly to me). It is obvious that this unavoidable dualism will create a certain amount of confusion in the minds of my readers, particularly as in what follows we shall have to do with the archetype of Deity.

[1] Cap. V, in Migne, *P.L.*, vol. 1, cols. 615f. (trans. by C. Dodgson, I, pp. 138f., slightly modified.

558 Should any of my readers feel tempted to add an apologetic "only" to the God-images as we perceive them, he would immediately fall foul of experience, which demonstrates beyond any shadow of doubt the extraordinary numinosity of these images. The tremendous effectiveness (mana) of these images is such that they not only give one the feeling of pointing to the *Ens realissimum,* but make one convinced that they actually express it and establish it as a fact. This makes discussion uncommonly difficult, if not impossible. It is, in fact, impossible to demonstrate God's reality to oneself except by using images which have arisen spontaneously or are sanctified by tradition, and whose psychic nature and effects the naïve-minded person has never separated from their unknowable metaphysical background. He instantly equates the effective image with the transcendental *x* to which it points. The seeming justification for this procedure appears self-evident and is not considered a problem so long as the statements of religion are not seriously questioned. But if there is occasion for criticism, then it must be remembered that the image and the statement are psychic processes which are different from their transcendental object; they do not posit it, they merely point to it. In the realm of psychic processes criticism and discussion are not only permissible but are unavoidable.

559 In what follows I shall attempt just such a discussion, such a "coming to terms" with certain religious traditions and ideas. Since I shall be dealing with numinous factors, my feeling is challenged quite as much as my intellect. I cannot, therefore, write in a coolly objective manner, but must allow my emotional subjectivity to speak if I want to describe what I feel when I read certain books of the Bible, or when I remember the impressions I have received from the doctrines of our faith. I do not write as a biblical scholar (which I am not), but as a layman and physician who has been privileged to see deeply into the psychic life of many people. What I am expressing is first of all my own personal view, but I know that I also speak in the name of many who have had similar experiences.

ANSWER TO JOB

560 The Book of Job is a landmark in the long historical development of a divine drama. At the time the book was written, there were already many testimonies which had given a contradictory picture of Yahweh—the picture of a God who knew no moderation in his emotions and suffered precisely from this lack of moderation. He himself admitted that he was eaten up with rage and jealousy and that this knowledge was painful to him. Insight existed along with obtuseness, loving-kindness along with cruelty, creative power along with destructiveness. Everything was there, and none of these qualities was an obstacle to the other. Such a condition is only conceivable either when no reflecting consciousness is present at all, or when the capacity for reflection is very feeble and a more or less adventitious phenomenon. A condition of this sort can only be described as *amoral.*

561 How the people of the Old Testament felt about their God we know from the testimony of the Bible. That is not what I am concerned with here, but rather with the way in which a modern man with a Christian education and background comes to terms with the divine darkness which is unveiled in the Book of Job, and what effect it has on him. I shall not give a cool and carefully considered exegesis that tries to be fair to every detail, but a purely subjective reaction. In this way I hope to act as a

voice for many who feel the same way as I do, and to give expression to the shattering emotion which the unvarnished spectacle of divine savagery and ruthlessness produces in us. Even if we know by hearsay about the suffering and discord in the Deity, they are so unconscious, and hence so ineffectual morally, that they arouse no human sympathy or understanding. Instead, they give rise to an equally ill-considered outburst of affect, and a smouldering resentment that may be compared to a slowly healing wound. And just as there is a secret tie between the wound and the weapon, so the affect corresponds to the violence of the deed that caused it.

562 The Book of Job serves as a paradigm for a certain experience of God which has a special significance for us today. These experiences come upon man from inside as well as from outside, and it is useless to interpret them rationalistically and thus weaken them by apotropaic means. It is far better to admit the affect and submit to its violence than to try to escape it by all sorts of intellectual tricks or by emotional value-judgments. Although, by giving way to the affect, one imitates all the bad qualities of the outrageous act that provoked it and thus makes oneself guilty of the same fault, that is precisely the point of the whole proceeding: the violence is meant to penetrate to a man's vitals, and he to succumb to its action. He must be affected by it, otherwise its full effect will not reach him. But he should know, or learn to know, what has affected him, for in this way he transforms the blindness of the violence on the one hand and of the affect on the other into knowledge.

563 For this reason I shall express my affect fearlessly and ruthlessly in what follows, and I shall answer injustice with injustice, that I may learn to know why and to what purpose Job was wounded, and what consequences have grown out of this for Yahweh as well as for man.

I

564 Job answers Yahweh thus:

> Behold, I am of small account; what shall I answer thee?
>   I lay my hand on my mouth.
> I have spoken once, and I will not answer;
>   twice, but I will proceed no further.[1]

565 And indeed, in the immediate presence of the infinite power of creation, this is the only possible answer for a witness who is still trembling in every limb with the terror of almost total annihilation. What else could a half-crushed human worm, grovelling in the dust, reasonably answer in the circumstances? In spite of his pitiable littleness and feebleness, this man knows that he is confronted with a superhuman being who is personally most easily provoked. He also knows that it is far better to withhold all moral reflections, to say nothing of certain moral requirements which might be expected to apply to a god.

566 Yahweh's "justice" is praised, so presumably Job could bring his complaint and the protestation of his innocence before him as

[1] Job 40:4–5. [Quotations throughout are from the Revised Standard Version (RSV), except where the Authorized Version (AV) is closer to the text of the Zürcher Bibel (ZB) used by the author in conjunction with the original Hebrew and Greek sources. Where neither RSV nor AV fits, I have translated direct from ZB. The poetic line-arrangement of RSV is followed in so far as possible.—TRANS.]

the just judge. But he doubts this possibility. "How can a man be just before God?" [2] "If I summoned him and he answered me, I would not believe that he was listening to my voice." [3] "If it is a matter of justice, who can summon him?" [4] He "multiplies my wounds without cause." [5] "He destroys both the blameless and the wicked." [6] "If the scourge slay suddenly, he will laugh at the trial of the innocent." [7] "I know," Job says to Yahweh, "thou wilt not hold me innocent. I shall be condemned." [8] "If I wash myself . . . never so clean, yet shalt thou plunge me in the ditch." [9] "For he is not a man, as I am, that I should answer him, and we should come together in judgment." [10] Job wants to explain his point of view to Yahweh, to state his complaint, and tells him: "Thou knowest that I am not guilty, and there is none to deliver out of thy hand." [11] "I desire to argue my case with God." [12] "I will defend my ways to his face," [13] "I know that I shall be vindicated." [14] Yahweh should summon him and render him an account or at least allow him to plead his cause. Properly estimating the disproportion between man and God, he asks: "Wilt thou break a leaf driven to and fro? and wilt thou pursue the dry stubble?" [15] God has put him in the wrong, but there is no justice.[16] He has "taken away my right." [17] "Till I die I will not put away my integrity from me. I hold fast to my righteousness, and will not let it go." [18] His friend Elihu the Buzite does not believe the injustice of Yahweh: "Of a truth, God will not do wickedly, and the Almighty will not pervert justice." [19] Illogically enough, he bases his opinion on God's *power*: "Is it fit to say to a king, Thou art wicked? and to princes, Ye are ungodly?" [20] One must "respect the persons of princes and esteem the high more than the low." [21] But Job is not shaken in his faith, and had already uttered an important truth when he said: "Behold, my witness is in heaven, and he that vouches for me is on high . . . my eye pours out tears to God, that he would maintain the right of a man with God, like that of a man with his neighbour." [22] And

[2] Job 9:2. [3] 9:16. [4] 9:19. [5] 9:17. [6] 9:22.
[7] 9:23 (AV). [8] 9:28, 29. [9] 9:30–31 (AV). [10] 9:32 (AV).
[11] 10:7. [12] 13:3. [13] 13:15. [14] 13:18. [15] 13:25 (AV).
[16] 19:6–7. [17] 27:2. [18] 27:5–6. [19] 34:12. [20] 34:18 (AV).
[21] 34:19 (ZB). [22] 16:19–21.

later: "For I know that my Vindicator lives, and at last he will stand upon the earth." [23]

567 These words clearly show that Job, in spite of his doubt as to whether man can be just before God, still finds it difficult to relinquish the idea of meeting God on the basis of justice and therefore of morality. Because, in spite of everything, he cannot give up his faith in divine justice, it is not easy for him to accept the knowledge that divine arbitrariness breaks the law. On the other hand, he has to admit that no one except Yahweh himself is doing him injustice and violence. He cannot deny that he is up against a God who does not care a rap for any moral opinion and does not recognize any form of ethics as binding. This is perhaps the greatest thing about Job, that, faced with this difficulty, he does not doubt the unity of God. He clearly sees that God is at odds with himself—so totally at odds that he, Job, is quite certain of finding in God a helper and an "advocate" against God. As certain as he is of the evil in Yahweh, he is equally certain of the good. In a human being who renders us evil we cannot expect at the same time to find a helper. But Yahweh is not a human being: he is both a persecutor and a helper in one, and the one aspect is as real as the other. Yahweh is not split but is an *antinomy*—a totality of inner opposites—and this is the indispensable condition for his tremendous dynamism, his omniscience and omnipotence. Because of this knowledge Job holds on to his intention of "defending his ways to his face," i.e., of making his point of view clear to him, since notwithstanding his wrath, Yahweh is also man's advocate *against himself* when man puts forth his complaint.

568 One would be even more astonished at Job's knowledge of God if this were the first time one were hearing of Yahweh's amorality. His incalculable moods and devastating attacks of wrath had, however, been known from time immemorial. He had proved himself to be a jealous defender of morality and was specially sensitive in regard to justice. Hence he had always to be praised as "just," which, it seemed, was very important to him. Thanks to this circumstance or peculiarity of his, he had a *distinct personality*, which differed from that of a more or less archaic king only in scope. His jealous and irritable nature,

23 19:25. ['Vindicator' is RSV alternative reading for 'Redeemer,' and comes very close to the ZB *Anwalt,* 'advocate.'—TRANS.]

prying mistrustfully into the faithless hearts of men and exploring their secret thoughts, compelled a personal relationship between himself and man, who could not help but feel personally called by him. That was the essential difference between Yahweh and the all-ruling Father Zeus, who in a benevolent and somewhat detached manner allowed the economy of the universe to roll along on its accustomed courses and punished only those who were disorderly. He did not moralize but ruled purely instinctively. He did not demand anything more *from* human beings than the sacrifices due to him; he did not want to do anything *with* human beings because he had no plans for them. Father Zeus is certainly a figure but not a personality. Yahweh, on the other hand, was interested in man. Human beings were a matter of first-rate importance to him. He needed them as they needed him, urgently and personally. Zeus too could throw thunderbolts about, but only at hopelessly disorderly individuals. Against mankind as a whole he had no objections—but then they did not interest him all that much. Yahweh, however, could get inordinately excited about man as a species and men as individuals if they did not behave as he desired or expected, without ever considering that in his omnipotence he could easily have created something better than these "bad earthenware pots."

569 In view of this intense personal relatedness to his chosen people, it was only to be expected that a regular covenant would develop which also extended to certain individuals, for instance to David. As we learn from the Eighty-ninth Psalm, Yahweh told him:

> My steadfast love I will keep for him for ever,
> and my covenant will stand firm for him.
>
> . . . .
>
> I will not violate my covenant,
> or alter the word that went forth from my lips.
> Once for all I have sworn by my holiness;
> I will not lie to David.[24]

570 And yet it happened that he, who watched so jealously over the fulfilment of laws and contracts, broke his own oath. Modern man, with his sensitive conscience, would have felt the black

24 Verses 28, 34, 35.

abyss opening and the ground giving way under his feet, for the least he expects of his God is that he should be superior to mortal man in the sense of being better, higher, nobler—but not his superior in the kind of moral flexibility and unreliability that do not jib even at perjury.

71 Of course one must not tax an archaic god with the requirements of modern ethics. For the people of early antiquity things were rather different. In their gods there was absolutely everything: they teemed with virtues and vices. Hence they could be punished, put in chains, deceived, stirred up against one another without losing face, or at least not for long. The man of that epoch was so inured to divine inconsistencies that he was not unduly perturbed when they happened. With Yahweh the case was different because, from quite early on, the personal and moral tie began to play an important part in the religious relationship. In these circumstances a breach of contract was bound to have the effect not only of a personal but of a moral injury. One can see this from the way David answers Yahweh:

> How long, Lord? wilt thou hide thyself for ever?
> shall thy wrath burn like fire?
> Remember how short my time is:
> wherefore hast thou made all men in vain?
>
> . . . .
>
> Lord, where are thy former lovingkindnesses,
> which by thy faithfulness thou didst swear to David? [25]

72 Had this been addressed to a human being it would have run something like this: "For heaven's sake, man, pull yourself together and stop being such a senseless savage! It is really too grotesque to get into such a rage when it's partly your own fault that the plants won't flourish. You used to be quite reasonable and took good care of the garden you planted, instead of trampling it to pieces."

73 Certainly our interlocutor would never dare to remonstrate with his almighty partner about this breach of contract. He knows only too well what a row he would get into if *he* were the wretched breaker of the law. Because anything else would put him in peril of his life, he must retire to the more exalted plane

[25] Psalm 89:46, 47, 49 (AV; last line from RSV).

of reason. In this way, without knowing it or wanting it, he shows himself superior to his divine partner both intellectually and morally. Yahweh fails to notice that he is being humoured, just as little as he understands why he has continually to be praised as just. He makes pressing demands on his people to be praised [26] and propitiated in every possible way, for the obvious purpose of keeping him in a good temper at any price.

574 The character thus revealed fits a personality who can only convince himself that he exists through his relation to an object. Such dependence on the object is absolute when the subject is totally lacking in self-reflection and therefore has no insight into himself. It is as if he existed only by reason of the fact that he has an object which assures him that he is really there. If Yahweh, as we would expect of a sensible human being, were really conscious of himself, he would, in view of the true facts of the case, at least have put an end to the panegyrics on his justice. But he is too unconscious to be moral. Morality presupposes consciousness. By this I do not mean to say that Yahweh is imperfect or evil, like a gnostic demiurge. He is everything in its totality; therefore, among other things, he is total justice, and also its total opposite. At least this is the way he must be conceived if one is to form a unified picture of his character. We must only remember that what we have sketched is no more than an anthropomorphic picture which is not even particularly easy to visualize. From the way the divine nature expresses itself we can see that the individual qualities are not adequately related to one another, with the result that they fall apart into mutually contradictory acts. For instance, Yahweh regrets having created human beings, although in his omniscience he must have known all along what would happen to them.

II

575 Since the Omniscient looks into all hearts, and Yahweh's eyes "run to and fro through the whole earth," [1] it were better for the interlocutor of the Eighty-ninth Psalm not to wax

[26] Or to be "blessed," which is even more captious of him.

[1] Zechariah 4:10 (AV). Cf. also the Wisdom of Solomon 1:10 (AV): "For the ear of jealousy heareth all things: and the noise of murmurings is not hid."

too conscious of his slight moral superiority over the more unconscious God. Better to keep it dark, for Yahweh is no friend of critical thoughts which in any way diminish the tribute of recognition he demands. Loudly as his power resounds through the universe, the basis of his existence is correspondingly slender, for it needs conscious reflection in order to exist in reality. Existence is only real when it is conscious to somebody. That is why the Creator needs conscious man even though, from sheer unconsciousness, he would like to prevent him from becoming conscious. And that is also why Yahweh needs the acclamation of a small group of people. One can imagine what would happen if this assembly suddenly decided to stop the applause: there would be a state of high excitation, with outbursts of blind destructive rage, then a withdrawal into hellish loneliness and the torture of non-existence, followed by a gradual reawakening of an unutterable longing for something which would make him conscious of himself. It is probably for this reason that all pristine things, even man before he becomes the canaille, have a touching, magical beauty, for in its nascent state "each thing after its kind" is the most precious, the most desirable, the tenderest thing in the world, being a reflection of the infinite love and goodness of the Creator.

576 In view of the undoubted frightfulness of divine wrath, and in an age when men still knew what they were talking about when they said "Fear God," it was only to be expected that man's slight superiority should have remained unconscious. The powerful personality of Yahweh, who, in addition to everything else, lacked all biographical antecedents (his original relationship to the Elohim had long since been sunk in oblivion), had raised him above all the numina of the Gentiles and had immunized him against the influence that for several centuries had been undermining the authority of the pagan gods. It was precisely the details of their mythological biography that had become their nemesis, for with his growing capacity for judgment man had found these stories more and more incomprehensible and indecent. Yahweh, however, had no origin and no past, except his creation of the world, with which all history began, and his relation to that part of mankind whose forefather Adam he had fashioned in his own image as the Anthropos, the original man, by what appears to have been a special act of creation.

One can only suppose that the other human beings who must also have existed at that time had been formed previously on the divine potter's wheel along with the various kinds of beasts and cattle—those human beings, namely, from whom Cain and Seth chose their wives. If one does not approve of this conjecture, then the only other possibility that remains is the far more scandalous one that they incestuously married their sisters (for whom there is no evidence in the text), as was still surmised by the philosopher Karl Lamprecht at the end of the nineteenth century.

577 The special providence which singled out the Jews from among the divinely stamped portion of humanity and made them the "chosen people" had burdened them from the start with a heavy obligation. As usually happens with such mortgages, they quite understandably tried to circumvent it as much as possible. Since the chosen people used every opportunity to break away from him, and Yahweh felt it of vital importance to tie this indispensable object (which he had made "godlike" for this very purpose) definitely to himself, he proposed to the patriarch Noah a contract between himself on the one hand, and Noah, his children, and all their animals, both tame and wild, on the other—a contract that promised advantages to both parties. In order to strengthen this contract and keep it fresh in the memory, he instituted the rainbow as a token of the covenant. If, in future, he summoned the thunder-clouds which hide within them floods of water and lightning, then the rainbow would appear, reminding him and his people of the contract. The temptation to use such an accumulation of clouds for an experimental deluge was no small one, and it was therefore a good idea to associate it with a sign that would give timely warning of possible catastrophe.

578 In spite of these precautions the contract had gone to pieces with David, an event which left behind it a literary deposit in the Scriptures and which grieved some few of the devout, who upon reading it became reflective. As the Psalms were zealously read, it was inevitable that certain thoughtful people were unable to stomach the Eighty-ninth Psalm. However that may be, the fatal impression made by the breach of contract survived.[2]

[2] The 89th Psalm is attributed to David and is supposed to have been a community song written in exile.

It is historically possible that these considerations influenced the author of the Book of Job.

579 The Book of Job places this pious and faithful man, so heavily afflicted by the Lord, on a brightly lit stage where he presents his case to the eyes and ears of the world. It is amazing to see how easily Yahweh, quite without reason, had let himself be influenced by one of his sons, by a *doubting thought,*[3] and made unsure of Job's faithfulness. With his touchiness and suspiciousness the mere possibility of doubt was enough to infuriate him and induce that peculiar double-faced behaviour of which he had already given proof in the Garden of Eden, when he pointed out the tree to the First Parents and at the same time forbade them to eat of it. In this way he precipitated the Fall, which he apparently never intended. Similarly, his faithful servant Job is now to be exposed to a rigorous moral test, quite gratuitously and to no purpose, although Yahweh is convinced of Job's faithfulness and constancy, and could moreover have assured himself beyond all doubt on this point had he taken counsel with his own omniscience. Why, then, is the experiment made at all, and a bet with the unscrupulous slanderer settled, without a stake, on the back of a powerless creature? It is indeed no edifying spectacle to see how quickly Yahweh abandons his faithful servant to the evil spirit and lets him fall without compunction or pity into the abyss of physical and moral suffering. From the human point of view Yahweh's behaviour is so revolting that one has to ask oneself whether there is not a deeper motive hidden behind it. Has Yahweh some secret resistance against Job? That would explain his yielding to Satan. But what does man possess that God does not have? Because of his littleness, puniness, and defencelessness against the Almighty, he possesses, as we have already suggested, a somewhat keener consciousness based on self-reflection: he must, in order to survive, always be mindful of his impotence. God has no need of this circumspection, for nowhere does he come up against an insuperable obstacle that would force him to hesitate and hence make him reflect on himself. Could a suspicion have grown up in God that man possesses an infinitely small yet more concentrated

3 Satan is presumably one of God's eyes which "go to and fro in the earth and walk up and down in it" (Job 1:7). In Persian tradition, Ahriman proceeded from one of Ormuzd's doubting thoughts.

light than he, Yahweh, possesses? A jealousy of that kind might perhaps explain his behaviour. It would be quite explicable if some such dim, barely understood deviation from the definition of a mere "creature" had aroused his divine suspicions. Too often already these human beings had not behaved in the prescribed manner. Even his trusty servant Job might have something up his sleeve. . . . Hence Yahweh's surprising readiness to listen to Satan's insinuations against his better judgment.

580 Without further ado Job is robbed of his herds, his servants are slaughtered, his sons and daughters are killed by a whirlwind, and he himself is smitten with sickness and brought to the brink of the grave. To rob him of peace altogether, his wife and his old friends are let loose against him, all of whom say the wrong things. His justified complaint finds no hearing with the judge who is so much praised for his justice. Job's right is refused in order that Satan be not disturbed in his play.

581 One must bear in mind here the dark deeds that follow one another in quick succession: robbery, murder, bodily injury with premeditation, and denial of a fair trial. This is further exacerbated by the fact that Yahweh displays no compunction, remorse, or compassion, but only ruthlessness and brutality. The plea of unconsciousness is invalid, seeing that he flagrantly violates at least three of the commandments he himself gave out on Mount Sinai.

582 Job's friends do everything in their power to contribute to his moral torments, and instead of giving him, whom God has perfidiously abandoned, their warm-hearted support, they moralize in an all too human manner, that is, in the stupidest fashion imaginable, and "fill him with wrinkles." They thus deny him even the last comfort of sympathetic participation and human understanding, so that one cannot altogether suppress the suspicion of connivance in high places.

583 Why Job's torments and the divine wager should suddenly come to an end is not quite clear. So long as Job does not actually die, the pointless suffering could be continued indefinitely. We must, however, keep an eye on the background of all these events: it is just possible that something in this background will gradually begin to take shape as a compensation for Job's undeserved suffering—something to which Yahweh, even if he had only a faint inkling of it, could hardly remain indifferent. With-

out Yahweh's knowledge and contrary to his intentions, the tormented though guiltless Job had secretly been lifted up to a superior knowledge of God which God himself did not possess. Had Yahweh consulted his omniscience, Job would not have had the advantage of him. But then, so many other things would not have happened either.

584 Job realizes God's inner antinomy, and in the light of this realization his knowledge attains a divine numinosity. The possibility of this development lies, one must suppose, in man's "godlikeness," which one should certainly not look for in human morphology. Yahweh himself had guarded against this error by expressly forbidding the making of images. Job, by his insistence on bringing his case before God, even without hope of a hearing, had stood his ground and thus created the very obstacle that forced God to reveal his true nature. With this dramatic climax Yahweh abruptly breaks off his cruel game of cat and mouse. But if anyone should expect that his wrath will now be turned against the slanderer, he will be severely disappointed. Yahweh does not think of bringing this mischief-making son of his to account, nor does it ever occur to him to give Job at least the moral satisfaction of explaining his behaviour. Instead, he comes riding along on the tempest of his almightiness and thunders reproaches at the half-crushed human worm:

> Who is this that darkens counsel
> by words without insight? [4]

585 In view of the subsequent words of Yahweh, one must really ask oneself: *Who* is darkening *what* counsel? The only dark thing here is how Yahweh ever came to make a bet with Satan. It is certainly not Job who has darkened anything and least of all a counsel, for there was never any talk of this nor will there be in what follows. The bet does not contain any "counsel" so far as one can see—unless, of course, it was Yahweh himself who egged Satan on for the ultimate purpose of exalting Job. Naturally this development was foreseen in omniscience, and it may be that the word "counsel" refers to this eternal and absolute knowledge. If so, Yahweh's attitude seems the more illogical and incomprehensible, as he could then have enlightened Job on this point—which, in view of the wrong done to him, would

[4] Job 38:2 (ZB).

have been only fair and equitable. I must therefore regard this possibility as improbable.

586 *Whose* words are without insight? Presumably Yahweh is not referring to the words of Job's friends, but is rebuking Job. But what is Job's guilt? The only thing he can be blamed for is his incurable optimism in believing that he can appeal to divine justice. In this he is mistaken, as Yahweh's subsequent words prove. God does not want to be just; he merely flaunts might over right. Job could not get that into his head, because he looked upon God as a moral being. He had never doubted God's might, but had hoped for right as well. He had, however, already taken back this error when he recognized God's contradictory nature, and by so doing he assigned a place to God's justice and goodness. So one can hardly speak of lack of insight.

587 The answer to Yahweh's conundrum is therefore: it is Yahweh himself who darkens his own counsel and who has no insight. He turns the tables on Job and blames him for what he himself does: man is not permitted to have an opinion about him, and, in particular, is to have no insight which he himself does not possess. For seventy-one verses he proclaims his world-creating power to his miserable victim, who sits in ashes and scratches his sores with potsherds, and who by now has had more than enough of superhuman violence. Job has absolutely no need of being impressed by further exhibitions of this power. Yahweh, in his omniscience, could have known just how incongruous his attempts at intimidation were in such a situation. He could easily have seen that Job believes in his omnipotence as much as ever and has never doubted it or wavered in his loyalty. Altogether, he pays so little attention to Job's real situation that one suspects him of having an ulterior motive which is more important to him: Job is no more than the outward occasion for an inward process of dialectic in God. His thunderings at Job so completely miss the point that one cannot help but see how much he is occupied with himself. The tremendous emphasis he lays on his omnipotence and greatness makes no sense in relation to Job, who certainly needs no more convincing, but only becomes intelligible when aimed at a listener *who doubts it.* This "doubting thought" is Satan, who after completing his evil handiwork has returned to the paternal bosom in order to continue his subversive activity there. Yahweh must have seen

that Job's loyalty was unshakable and that Satan had lost his bet. He must also have realized that, in accepting this bet, he had done everything possible to drive his faithful servant to disloyalty, even to the extent of perpetrating a whole series of crimes. Yet it is not remorse and certainly not moral horror that rises to his consciousness, but an obscure intimation of something that questions his omnipotence. He is particularly sensitive on this point, because "might" is the great argument. But omniscience knows that might excuses nothing. The said intimation refers, of course, to the extremely uncomfortable fact that Yahweh had let himself be bamboozled by Satan. This weakness of his does not reach full consciousness, since Satan is treated with remarkable tolerance and consideration. Evidently Satan's intrigue is deliberately overlooked at Job's expense.

588 Luckily enough, Job had noticed during this harangue that everything else had been mentioned except his right. He has understood that it is at present impossible to argue the question of right, as it is only too obvious that Yahweh has no interest whatever in Job's cause but is far more preoccupied with his own affairs. Satan, that is to say, has somehow to disappear, and this can best be done by casting suspicion on Job as a man of subversive opinions. The problem is thus switched on to another track, and the episode with Satan remains unmentioned and unconscious. To the spectator it is not quite clear why Job is treated to this almighty exhibition of thunder and lightning, but the performance as such is sufficiently magnificent and impressive to convince not only a larger audience but above all Yahweh himself of his unassailable power. Whether Job realizes what violence Yahweh is doing to his own omniscience by behaving like this we do not know, but his silence and submission leave a number of possibilities open. Job has no alternative but formally to revoke his demand for justice, and he therefore answers in the words quoted at the beginning: "I lay my hand on my mouth."

589 He betrays not the slightest trace of mental reservation—in fact, his answer leaves us in no doubt that he has succumbed completely and without question to the tremendous force of the divine demonstration. The most exacting tyrant should have been satisfied with this, and could be quite sure that his servant —from terror alone, to say nothing of his undoubted loyalty—

would not dare to nourish a single improper thought for a very long time to come.

590 Strangely enough, Yahweh does not notice anything of the kind. He does not see Job and his situation at all. It is rather as if he had another powerful opponent in the place of Job, one who was better worth challenging. This is clear from his twice-repeated taunt:

> Gird up your loins like a man;
> I will question you, and you shall declare to me.[5]

591 One would have to choose positively grotesque examples to illustrate the disproportion between the two antagonists. Yahweh sees something in Job which we would not ascribe to him but to God, that is, an equal power which causes him to bring out his whole power apparatus and parade it before his opponent. Yahweh projects on to Job a sceptic's face which is hateful to him because it is his own, and which gazes at him with an uncanny and critical eye. He is afraid of it, for only in face of something frightening does one let off a cannonade of references to one's power, cleverness, courage, invincibility, etc. What has all that to do with Job? Is it worth the lion's while to terrify a mouse?

592 Yahweh cannot rest satisfied with the first victorious round. Job has long since been knocked out, but the great antagonist whose phantom is projected on to the pitiable sufferer still stands menacingly upright. Therefore Yahweh raises his arm again:

> Will you even put me in the wrong?
> Will you condemn me that you may be justified?
> Have you an arm like God,
> and can you thunder with a voice like his? [6]

593 Man, abandoned without protection and stripped of his rights, and whose nothingness is thrown in his face at every opportunity, evidently appears to be so dangerous to Yahweh that he must be battered down with the heaviest artillery. What irritates Yahweh can be seen from his challenge to the ostensible Job:

[5] Job 38:3 and 40:7. [6] 40:8–9.

Look on every one that is proud, and bring him low;
  and tread down the wicked where they stand.
Hide them in the dust together;
  bind their faces in the hidden place.
Then will I also acknowledge to you
  that your own right hand can give you victory.[7]

594 Job is challenged as though he himself were a god. But in the contemporary metaphysics there was no *deuteros theos,* no other god except Satan, who owns Yahweh's ear and is able to influence him. He is the only one who can pull the wool over his eyes, beguile him, and put him up to a massive violation of his own penal code. A formidable opponent indeed, and, because of his close kinship, so compromising that he must be concealed with the utmost discretion—even to the point of God's hiding him from his own consciousness in his own bosom! In his stead God must set up his miserable servant as the bugbear whom he has to fight, in the hope that by banishing the dreaded countenance to "the hidden place" he will be able to maintain himself in a state of unconsciousness.

595 The stage-managing of this imaginary duel, the speechifying, and the impressive performance given by the prehistoric menagerie would not be sufficiently explained if we tried to reduce them to the purely negative factor of Yahweh's fear of becoming conscious and of the relativization which this entails. The conflict becomes acute for Yahweh as a result of a new factor, which is, however, not hidden from omniscience—though in this case the existing knowledge is not accompanied by any conclusion. The new factor is something that has never occurred before in the history of the world, the unheard-of fact that, without knowing it or wanting it, a mortal man is raised by his moral behaviour above the stars in heaven, from which position of advantage he can behold the back of Yahweh, the abysmal world of "shards." [8]

[7] 40:12–14 ("in the hidden place" is RSV alternative reading for "in the world below").

[8] This is an allusion to an idea found in the later cabalistic philosophy. [These "shards," also called "shells" (Heb. *kelipot*), form ten counterpoles to the ten *sefiroth,* which are the ten stages in the revelation of God's creative power. The shards, representing the forces of evil and darkness, were originally mixed with the light of the *sefiroth.* The *Zohar* describes evil as the by-product of the life

596 Does Job know what he has seen? If he does, he is astute or canny enough not to betray it. But his words speak volumes:

> I know that thou canst do all things,
> and that no purpose of thine can be thwarted.[9]

597 Truly, Yahweh can do all things and permits himself all things without batting an eyelid. With brazen countenance he can project his shadow side and remain unconscious at man's expense. He can boast of his superior power and enact laws which mean less than air to him. Murder and manslaughter are mere bagatelles, and if the mood takes him he can play the feudal grand seigneur and generously recompense his bondslave for the havoc wrought in his wheat-fields. "So you have lost your sons and daughters? No harm done, I will give you new and better ones."

598 Job continues (no doubt with downcast eyes and in a low voice):

> "Who is this that hides counsel without insight?"
> Therefore I have uttered what I did not understand,
> things too wonderful for me, which I did not know.
> "Hear, and I will speak;
> I will question you, and you declare to me."
> I had heard of thee by the hearing of the ear,
> but now my eye sees thee;
> therefore I abhor myself,
> and repent in dust and ashes.[10]

599 Shrewdly, Job takes up Yahweh's aggressive words and prostrates himself at his feet as if he were indeed the defeated antagonist. Guileless as Job's speech sounds, it could just as well be equivocal. He has learnt his lesson well and experienced "wonderful things" which are none too easily grasped. Before, he had known Yahweh "by the hearing of the ear," but now he has got a taste of his reality, more so even than David—an

process of the *sefiroth*. Therefore the *sefiroth* had to be cleansed of the evil admixture of the shards. This elimination of the shards took place in what is described in the cabalistic writings—particularly of Luria and his school—as the "breaking of the vessels." Through this the powers of evil assumed a separate and real existence. Cf. Scholem, *Major Trends in Jewish Mysticism*, p. 267.—EDITORS.]

9 42 : 2. 10 42 : 3–6 (modified).

incisive lesson that had better not be forgotten. Formerly he was naïve, dreaming perhaps of a "good" God, or of a benevolent ruler and just judge. He had imagined that a "covenant" was a legal matter and that anyone who was party to a contract could insist on his rights as agreed; that God would be faithful and true or at least just, and, as one could assume from the Ten Commandments, would have some recognition of ethical values or at least feel committed to his own legal standpoint. But, to his horror, he has discovered that Yahweh is not human but, in certain respects, less than human, that he is just what Yahweh himself says of Leviathan (the crocodile):

> He beholds everything that is high:
> He is king over all proud beasts.[11]

600 Unconsciousness has an animal nature. Like all old gods Yahweh has his animal symbolism with its unmistakable borrowings from the much older theriomorphic gods of Egypt, especially Horus and his four sons. Of the four animals of Yahweh only one has a human face. That is probably Satan, the godfather of man as a spiritual being. Ezekiel's vision attributes three-fourths animal nature and only one-fourth human nature to the animal deity, while the upper deity, the one above the "sapphire throne," merely had the "likeness" of a man.[12] This symbolism explains Yahweh's behaviour, which, from the human point of view, is so intolerable: it is the behaviour of an unconscious being who cannot be judged morally. Yahweh is a *phenomenon* and, as Job says, "not a man." [13]

601 One could, without too much difficulty, impute such a meaning to Job's speech. Be that as it may, Yahweh calmed down at last. The therapeutic measure of unresisting acceptance had proved its value yet again. Nevertheless, Yahweh is still some-

[11] Job 41:25 (ZB); cf. 41:34 (AV and RSV). [12] Ezekiel 1:26.

[13] The naïve assumption that the creator of the world is a conscious being must be regarded as a disastrous prejudice which later gave rise to the most incredible dislocations of logic. For example, the nonsensical doctrine of the *privatio boni* would never have been necessary had one not had to assume in advance that it is impossible for the consciousness of a good God to produce evil deeds. Divine unconsciousness and lack of reflection, on the other hand, enable us to form a conception of God which puts his actions beyond moral judgment and allows no conflict to arise between goodness and beastliness.

what nervous of Job's friends—they "have not spoken of me what is right."[14] The projection of his doubt-complex extends—comically enough, one must say—to these respectable and slightly pedantic old gentlemen, as though God-knows-what depended on what they thought. But the fact that men should think at all, and especially about him, is maddeningly disquieting and ought somehow to be stopped. It is far too much like the sort of thing his vagrant son is always springing on him, thus hitting him in his weakest spot. How often already has he bitterly regretted his unconsidered outbursts!

602 One can hardly avoid the impression that Omniscience is gradually drawing near to a realization, and is threatened with an insight that seems to be hedged about with fears of self-destruction. Fortunately, Job's final declaration is so formulated that one can assume with some certainty that, for the protagonists, the incident is closed for good and all.

603 We, the commenting chorus on this great tragedy, which has never at any time lost its vitality, do not feel quite like that. For our modern sensibilities it is by no means apparent that with Job's profound obeisance to the majesty of the divine presence, and his prudent silence, a real answer has been given to the question raised by the Satanic prank of a wager with God. Job has not so much answered as reacted in an adjusted way. In so doing he displayed remarkable self-discipline, but an unequivocal answer has still to be given.

604 To take the most obvious thing, what about the moral wrong Job has suffered? Is man so worthless in God's eyes that not even a *tort moral* can be inflicted on him? That contradicts the fact that man is desired by Yahweh and that it obviously matters to him whether men speak "right" of him or not. He needs Job's loyalty, and it means so much to him that he shrinks at nothing in carrying out his test. This attitude attaches an almost divine importance to man, for what else is there in the whole wide world that could mean anything to one who has everything? Yahweh's divided attitude, which on the one hand tramples on human life and happiness without regard, and on the other hand must have man for a partner, puts the latter in an impossible position. At one moment Yahweh behaves as irrationally as a cataclysm; the next moment he wants to be loved, honoured,

14 Job 42 : 7.

worshipped, and praised as just. He reacts irritably to every word that has the faintest suggestion of criticism, while he himself does not care a straw for his own moral code if his actions happen to run counter to its statutes.

605 One can submit to such a God only with fear and trembling, and can try indirectly to propitiate the despot with unctuous praises and ostentatious obedience. But a relationship of trust seems completely out of the question to our modern way of thinking. Nor can moral satisfaction be expected from an unconscious nature god of this kind. Nevertheless, Job got his satisfaction, without Yahweh's intending it and possibly without himself knowing it, as the poet would have it appear. Yahweh's allocutions have the unthinking yet none the less transparent purpose of showing Job the brutal power of the demiurge: "This is I, the creator of all the ungovernable, ruthless forces of Nature, which are not subject to any ethical laws. I, too, am an amoral force of Nature, a purely phenomenal personality that cannot see its own back."

606 This is, or at any rate could be, a moral satisfaction of the first order for Job, because through this declaration man, in spite of his impotence, is set up as a judge over God himself. We do not know whether Job realizes this, but we do know from the numerous commentaries on Job that all succeeding ages have overlooked the fact that a kind of Moira or Dike rules over Yahweh, causing him to give himself away so blatantly. Anyone can see how he unwittingly raises Job by humiliating him in the dust. By so doing he pronounces judgment on himself and gives man the moral satisfaction whose absence we found so painful in the Book of Job.

607 The poet of this drama showed a masterly discretion in ringing down the curtain at the very moment when his hero gave unqualified recognition to the ἀπόφασις μεγάλη of the Demiurge by prostrating himself at the feet of His Divine Majesty. No other impression was permitted to remain. An unusual scandal was blowing up in the realm of metaphysics, with supposedly devastating consequences, and nobody was ready with a saving formula which would rescue the monotheistic conception of God from disaster. Even in those days the critical intellect of a Greek could easily have seized on this new addition to Yahweh's biography and used it in his disfavour (as indeed happened,

though very much later)[15] so as to mete out to him the fate that had already overtaken the Greek gods. But a relativization of God was utterly unthinkable at that time, and remained so for the next two thousand years.

608 The unconscious mind of man sees correctly even when conscious reason is blind and impotent. The drama has been consummated for all eternity: Yahweh's dual nature has been revealed, and somebody or something has seen and registered this fact. Such a revelation, whether it reached man's consciousness or not, could not fail to have far-reaching consequences.

III

609 Before turning to the question of how the germ of unrest developed further, we must turn back to the time when the Book of Job was written. Unfortunately the dating is uncertain. It is generally assumed that it was written between 600 and 300 B.C.—not too far away, therefore, from the time of the Book of Proverbs (4th to 3rd century). Now in Proverbs we encounter a symptom of Greek influence which, if an earlier date is assigned to it, reached the Jewish sphere of culture through Asia Minor and, if a later date, through Alexandria. This is the idea of Sophia, or the *Sapientia Dei,* which is a coeternal and more or less hypostatized pneuma of feminine nature that existed before the Creation:

> The Lord possessed me in the beginning of his way,
> before his works of old.
> I was set up from everlasting, from the beginning,
> or ever the earth was.
> When there were no depths, I was brought forth;
> when there were no fountains abounding with water.
> . . . .
> When he established the heavens, I was there,
> . . . .
> when he marked out the foundations of the earth,
> then I was by him, as a master workman,

15 [Cf. "Transformation Symbolism in the Mass," par. 350, above; *Aion,* par. 128 (Swiss edn., pp. 114ff.).—EDITORS.]

and I was daily his delight,
  rejoicing always before him,
rejoicing in his habitable earth;
  and my delights were with the sons of men.[1]

10 This Sophia, who already shares certain essential qualities with the Johannine Logos, is on the one hand closely associated with the Hebrew Chochma, but on the other hand goes so far beyond it that one can hardly fail to think of the Indian Shakti. Relations with India certainly existed at that time (the time of the Ptolemys). A further source is the Wisdom of Jesus the Son of Sirach, or Ecclesiasticus, written around 200 B.C. Here Wisdom says of herself:

I came out of the mouth of the most High,
  and covered the earth as a cloud.
I dwelt in high places,
  and my throne is in a cloudy pillar.
I alone encompassed the circuit of heaven,
  and walked in the bottom of the deep.
I had power over the waves of the sea, and over all the earth,
  and over every people and nation.

. . . .

He created me from the beginning before the world,
  and I shall never fail.
In the holy tabernacle I served before him;
  and so was I established in Sion.
Likewise in the beloved city he gave me rest,
  and in Jerusalem was my power.

. . . .

I was exalted like a cedar in Libanus,
  and as a cypress tree upon the mountains of Hermon.
I was exalted like a palm tree in En-gaddi,
  and as a rose plant in Jericho,
  as a fair olive tree in a pleasant field,
  and grew up as a plane tree by the water.
I gave a sweet smell like cinnamon and aspalathus,
  and I yielded a pleasant odour like the best myrrh . . .
As the turpentine tree I stretched out my branches,
  and my branches are the branches of honour and grace.

[1] Proverbs 8:22–24 (AV), 27, 29–31 (AV mod.).

As the vine brought I forth pleasant savour,
and my flowers are the fruit of honour and riches.
I am the mother of fair love,
and fear, and knowledge, and holy hope:
I therefore, being eternal, am given to all my children
which are chosen of him.[2]

611 It is worth while to examine this text more closely. Wisdom describes herself, in effect, as the Logos, the Word of God ("I came out of the mouth of the most High"). As Ruach, the spirit of God, she brooded over the waters of the beginning. Like God, she has her throne in heaven. As the cosmogonic Pneuma she pervades heaven and earth and all created things. She corresponds in almost every feature to the Logos of St. John. We shall see below how far this connection is also important as regards content.

612 She is the feminine numen of the "metropolis" par excellence, of Jerusalem the mother-city. She is the mother-beloved, a reflection of Ishtar, the pagan city-goddess. This is confirmed by the detailed comparison of Wisdom with trees, such as the cedar, palm, terebinth ("turpentine-tree"), olive, cypress, etc. All these trees have from ancient times been symbols of the Semitic love- and mother-goddess. A holy tree always stood beside her altar on high places. In the Old Testament oaks and terebinths are oracle trees. God or angels are said to appear in or beside trees. David consulted a mulberry-tree oracle.[3] The tree in Babylon represented Tammuz, the son-lover, just as it represented Osiris, Adonis, Attis, and Dionysus, the young dying gods of the Near East. All these symbolic attributes also occur in the Song of Songs, as characteristics of the *sponsus* as well as the *sponsa*. The vine, the grape, the vine flower, and the vineyard play a significant role here. The Beloved is like an apple-tree; she shall come down from the mountains (the cult places of the mother-goddess), "from the lions' dens, from the mountains of the leopards";[4] her womb is "an orchard of pomegranates, with pleasant fruits, camphire with spikenard, spikenard and saffron, calamus and cinnamon, with all trees of frankincense, myrrh and aloes, with all the chief spices."[5] Her hands "dropped

2 Ecclesiasticus 24:3–18 (AV mod.).

3 II Samuel 5:23f.

4 Song of Solomon 4:8 (AV).

5 4:13–15.

with myrrh"[6] (Adonis, we may remember, was born of the myrrh). Like the Holy Ghost, Wisdom is given as a gift to the elect, an idea that is taken up again in the doctrine of the Paraclete.

613 The pneumatic nature of Sophia as well as her world-building Maya character come out still more clearly in the apocryphal Wisdom of Solomon. "For wisdom is a loving spirit,"[7] "kind to man."[8] She is "the worker of all things," "in her is an understanding spirit, holy."[9] She is "the breath of the power of God," "a pure effluence flowing from the glory of the Almighty,"[10] "the brightness of the everlasting light, the unspotted mirror of the power of God,"[11] a being "most subtil," who "passeth and goeth through all things by reason of her pureness."[12] She is "conversant with God," and "the Lord of all things himself loved her."[13] "Who of all that are is a more cunning workman than she?"[14] She is sent from heaven and from the throne of glory as a "Holy Spirit."[15] As a psychopomp she leads the way to God and assures immortality.[16]

614 The Wisdom of Solomon is emphatic about God's justice and, probably not without pragmatic purpose, ventures to sail very close to the wind: "Righteousness is immortal, but ungodly men with their works and words call death upon themselves."[17] The unrighteous and the ungodly, however, say:

> Let us oppress the poor righteous man,
>   let us not spare the widow,
>   nor reverence the ancient gray hairs of the aged.
> Let our strength be the law of justice:
>   for that which is feeble is found to be nothing worth.
> Therefore let us lie in wait for the righteous;
>   because . . . he upbraideth us with our offending the law,
>   and objecteth to our infamy. . . .
> He professeth to have the knowledge of God:
>   and he calleth himself the child of the Lord.
> He was made to reprove our thoughts.
> . . . .

6 Song of Solomon 5:5.
7 Wisdom of Solomon 1:6. (φιλάνθρωπον πνεῦμα σοφία.) 8 7:23.
9 7:22. (πάντων τεχνῖτις./πνεῦμα νοερὸν ἅγιον.) 10 7:25 (AV mod.). (ἀπόρροια.)
11 7:26. 12 7:23, 24. 13 8:3. (συμβίωσιν ἔχουσα./πάντων δεσπότης.)
14 8:6. 15 9:10, 17. 16 6:8 and 8:13. 17 1:15–16 (mod.).

Let us see if his words be true:
and let us prove what shall happen in the end of him.

. . . .

Let us examine him with despitefulness and torture,
that we may know his meekness, and prove his patience.[18]

615 Where did we read but a short while before: "And the Lord said to Satan, Have you considered my servant Job, that there is none like him on the earth, a blameless and upright man, who fears God and turns away from evil? He still holds fast his integrity, although you moved me against him, to destroy him without cause"? "Wisdom is better than might," saith the Preacher.[19]

616 Not from mere thoughtfulness and unconsciousness, but from a deeper motive, the Wisdom of Solomon here touches on the sore spot. In order to understand this more fully, we would have to find out in what sort of relation the Book of Job stands to the change that occurred in the status of Yahweh at about the same time, i.e., its relation to the appearance of Sophia. It is not a question of literary history, but of Yahweh's fate as it affects man. From the ancient records we know that the divine drama was enacted between God and his people, who were betrothed to him, the masculine dynamis, like a woman, and over whose faithfulness he watched jealously. A particular instance of this is Job, whose faithfulness is subjected to a savage test. As I have said, the really astonishing thing is how easily Yahweh gives in to the insinuations of Satan. If it were true that he trusted Job perfectly, it would be only logical for Yahweh to defend him, unmask the malicious slanderer, and make him pay for his defamation of God's faithful servant. But Yahweh never thinks of it, not even after Job's innocence has been proved. We hear nothing of a rebuke or disapproval of Satan. Therefore, one cannot doubt Yahweh's connivance. His readiness to deliver Job into Satan's murderous hands proves that he doubts Job precisely because he projects his own tendency to unfaithfulness upon a scapegoat. There is reason to suspect that he is about to loosen his matrimonial ties with Israel but hides this intention from himself. This vaguely suspected unfaithfulness causes him, with the help of Satan, to seek out the unfaithful one, and he

18 2 : 10–19. 19 Job 2 : 3; Ecclesiastes 9 : 16.

infallibly picks on the most faithful of the lot, who is forthwith subjected to a gruelling test. Yahweh has become unsure of his own faithfulness.

[6]17 At about the same time, or a little later, it is rumoured what has happened: he has remembered a feminine being who is no less agreeable to him than to man, a friend and playmate from the beginning of the world, the first-born of all God's creatures, a stainless reflection of his glory and a master workman, nearer and dearer to his heart than the late descendants of the protoplast, the original man, who was but a secondary product stamped in his image. There must be some dire necessity responsible for this anamnesis of Sophia: things simply could not go on as before, the "just" God could not go on committing injustices, and the "Omniscient" could not behave any longer like a clueless and thoughtless human being. Self-reflection becomes an imperative necessity, and for this Wisdom is needed. Yahweh has to remember his absolute knowledge; for, if Job gains knowledge of God, then God must also learn to know himself. It just could not be that Yahweh's dual nature should become public property and remain hidden from himself alone. Whoever knows God has an effect on him. The failure of the attempt to corrupt Job has changed Yahweh's nature.

[6]18 We shall now proceed to reconstruct, from the hints given in the Bible and from history, what happened after this change. For this purpose we must turn back to the time of Genesis, and to the protoplast before the Fall. He, Adam, produced Eve, his feminine counterpart, from his rib with the Creator's help, in the same way as the Creator had produced the hermaphroditic Adam from the *prima materia* and, along with him, the divinely stamped portion of humanity, namely the people of Israel and the other descendants of Adam.[20] Mysteriously following the same pattern, it was bound to happen that Adam's first son, like Satan, was an evildoer and murderer before the Lord, so that the prologue in heaven was repeated on earth. It can easily be surmised that this was the deeper reason why Yahweh gave special protection to the unsuccessful Cain, for he was a faithful reproduction of Satan in miniature. Nothing is said about a prototype of the early-departed Abel, who was dearer to God than

20 [As to that portion of humanity *not* divinely stamped, and presumably descended from the pre-Adamic anthropoids, see par. 576, above.—EDITORS.]

Cain, the go-ahead husbandman (who was no doubt instructed in these arts by one of Satan's angels). Perhaps this prototype was another son of God of a more conservative nature than Satan, no rolling stone with a fondness for new and black-hearted thoughts, but one who was bound to the Father in child-like love, who harboured no other thoughts except those that enjoyed paternal approval, and who dwelt in the inner circle of the heavenly economy. That would explain why his earthly counterpart Abel could so soon "hasten away from the evil world," in the words of the Book of Wisdom, and return to the Father, while Cain in his earthly existence had to taste to the full the curse of his progressiveness on the one hand and of his moral inferiority on the other.

619 If the original father Adam is a copy of the Creator, his son Cain is certainly a copy of God's son Satan, and this gives us good reason for supposing that God's favourite, Abel, must also have his correspondence in a "supracelestial place." The ominous happenings that occur right at the beginning of a seemingly successful and satisfactory Creation—the Fall and the fratricide—catch our attention, and one is forced to admit that the initial situation, when the spirit of God brooded over the tohu-bohu, hardly permits us to expect an absolutely perfect result. Furthermore the Creator, who found every other day of his work "good," failed to give good marks to what happened on Monday. He simply said nothing—a circumstance that favours an argument from silence! What happened on that day was the final separation of the upper from the lower waters by the interposed "plate" of the firmament. It is clear that this unavoidable dualism refused, then as later, to fit smoothly into the concept of monotheism, because it points to a metaphysical disunity. This split, as we know from history, had to be patched up again and again through the centuries, concealed and denied. It had made itself felt from the very beginning in Paradise, through a strange inconsequence which befell the Creator or was put over on him. Instead of following his original programme of letting man appear on the last day as the most intelligent being and lord of all creatures, he created the serpent who proved to be much more intelligent and more conscious than Adam, and, in addition, had been created before him. We can hardly suppose that Yahweh would have played such a trick on himself; it is far more

likely that his son Satan had a hand in it. He is a trickster and spoilsport who loves nothing better than to cause annoying accidents. Although Yahweh had created the reptiles before Adam, they were common or garden snakes, highly unintelligent, from among whom Satan selected a tree-snake to use as his disguise. From then on the rumour spread that the snake was "the most spiritual animal." [21] Later the snake became the favourite symbol of the Nous, received high honours and was even permitted to symbolize God's second son, because the latter was interpreted as the world-redeeming Logos, which frequently appears as identical with the Nous. A legend of later origin maintains that the snake in the Garden of Eden was Lilith, Adam's first wife, with whom he begot a horde of demons. This legend likewise supposes a trick that can hardly have been intended by the Creator. Consequently, the Bible knows only of Eve as Adam's legitimate wife. It nevertheless remains a strange fact that the original man who was created in the image of God had, according to tradition, two wives, just like his heavenly prototype. Just as Yahweh is legitimately united with his wife Israel, but has a feminine pneuma as his intimate playmate from all eternity, so Adam first has Lilith (the daughter or emanation of Satan) to wife, as a Satanic correspondence to Sophia. Eve would then correspond to the people of Israel. We naturally do not know why we should hear at such a late date that the Ruach Elohim, the "spirit of God," is not only feminine but a comparatively independent being who exists side by side with God, and that long before the marriage with Israel Yahweh had had relations with Sophia. Nor do we know why, in the older tradition, the knowledge of this first alliance had been lost. Likewise it was only quite late that one heard of the delicate relationship between Adam and Lilith. Whether Eve was as troublesome a wife for Adam as the children of Israel, who were perpetually flirting with unfaithfulness, were for Yahweh, is equally dark to us. At any rate the family life of our first parents was not all beer and skittles: their first two sons are a typical pair of hostile brothers, for at that time it was apparently still the custom to live out mythological motifs in reality. (Nowadays this is felt to be objectionable and is denied whenever it happens.) The parents can share the blame for original sin: Adam has only to remember his demon-

[21] *τὸ πνευματικώτατον ζῶον.*—A view that is found in Philo Judaeus.

princess, and Eve should never forget that she was the first to fall for the wiles of the serpent. Like the Fall, the Cain-Abel intermezzo can hardly be listed as one of Creation's shining successes. One must draw this conclusion because Yahweh himself did not appear to be informed in advance of the abovementioned incidents. Here as later there is reason to suspect that no conclusions were ever drawn from Omniscience: Yahweh did not consult his total knowledge and was accordingly surprised by the result. One can observe the same phenomenon in human beings, wherever in fact people cannot deny themselves the pleasure of their emotions. It must be admitted that a fit of rage or a sulk has its secret attractions. Were that not so, most people would long since have acquired a little wisdom.

620 From this point of view we may be in a better position to understand what happened to Job. In the pleromatic or (as the Tibetans call it) Bardo state,[22] there is a perfect interplay of cosmic forces, but with the Creation—that is, with the division of the world into distinct processes in space and time—events begin to rub and jostle one another. Covered by the hem of the paternal mantle, Satan soon starts putting a right touch here and a wrong touch there, thus giving rise to complications which were apparently not intended in the Creator's plan and which come as surprises. While unconscious creation—animals, plants, and crystals—functions satisfactorily so far as we know, things are constantly going wrong with man. At first his consciousness is only a very little higher than that of the animals, for which reason his freedom of will is also extremely limited. But Satan takes an interest in him and experiments with him in his own way, leading him into all sorts of wickedness while his angels teach him the arts and sciences, which until now had been reserved for the perfection of the pleroma. (Even in those days Satan would have merited the name of "Lucifer"!) The peculiar, unforeseen antics of men arouse Yahweh's wrath and thereby involve him in his own creation. Divine interventions become a compelling necessity. Irritatingly enough, they only meet with temporary success. Even the Draconian punishment of drowning all life with a few choice exceptions (a fate which, according to old Johann Jacob Scheuchzer on the evidence of

22 [Cf. the commentary on the *Tibetan Book of the Dead,* par. 833, below.—EDITORS.]

the fossils, not even the fishes escaped), had no lasting effect. Creation remained just as tainted as before. The strange thing is that Yahweh invariably seeks the reason for this in man, who apparently refuses to obey, but never in his son, the father of all tricksters. This false orientation cannot fail to exasperate his already touchy nature, so that fear of God is regarded by man in general as the principle and even as the beginning of all wisdom. While mankind tried, under this hard discipline, to broaden their consciousness by acquiring a modicum of wisdom, that is, a little foresight and reflection,[23] it is clear from the historical development that Yahweh had lost sight of his pleromatic coexistence with Sophia since the days of the Creation. Her place was taken by the covenant with the chosen people, who were thus forced into the feminine role. At that time the people consisted of a patriarchal society in which women were only of secondary importance. God's marriage with Israel was therefore an essentially masculine affair, something like the founding of the Greek *polis,* which occurred about the same time. The inferiority of women was a settled fact. Woman was regarded as less perfect than man, as Eve's weakness for the blandishments of the serpent amply proved. *Perfection* is a masculine desideratum, while woman inclines by nature to *completeness.* And it is a fact that, even today, a man can stand a relative state of perfection much better and for a longer period than a woman, while as a rule it does not agree with women and may even be dangerous for them. If a woman strives for perfection she forgets the complementary role of completeness, which, though imperfect by itself, forms the necessary counterpart to perfection. For, just as completeness is always imperfect, so perfection is always incomplete, and therefore represents a final state which is hopelessly sterile. "Ex perfecto nihil fit," say the old masters, whereas the *imperfectum* carries within it the seeds of its own improvement. Perfectionism always ends in a blind alley, while completeness by itself lacks selective values.

621 At the bottom of Yahweh's marriage with Israel is a perfectionist intention which excludes that kind of relatedness we know as "Eros." The lack of Eros, of relationship to values, is painfully apparent in the Book of Job: the paragon of all creation is not a man but a monster! Yahweh has no Eros, no

[23] Cf. φρονίμως in the parable of the unjust steward (Luke 16:8).

relationship to man, but only to a purpose man must help him fulfil. But that does not prevent him from being jealous and mistrustful like any other husband, though even here he has his purpose in mind and not man.

622 The faithfulness of his people becomes the more important to him the more he forgets Wisdom. But again and again they slip back into unfaithfulness despite the many proofs of his favour. This behaviour naturally does nothing to mollify Yahweh's jealousy and suspicions, hence Satan's insinuations fall on fertile ground when he drips his doubt about Job's faithfulness into the paternal ear. Against his own convictions Yahweh agrees without any hesitation to inflict the worst tortures on him. One misses Sophia's "love of mankind" more than ever. Even Job longs for the Wisdom which is nowhere to be found.[24]

623 Job marks the climax of this unhappy development. He epitomizes a thought which had been maturing in mankind about that time—a dangerous thought that makes great demands on the wisdom of gods and men. Though conscious of these demands, Job obviously does not know enough about the Sophia who is coeternal with God. Because man feels himself at the mercy of Yahweh's capricious will, he is in need of wisdom; not so Yahweh, who up to now has had nothing to contend with except man's nothingness. With the Job drama, however, the situation undergoes a radical change. Here Yahweh comes up against a man who stands firm, who clings to his rights until he is compelled to give way to brute force. He has seen God's face and the unconscious split in his nature. God was now known, and this knowledge went on working not only in Yahweh but in man too. Thus it was the men of the last few centuries before Christ who, at the gentle touch of the pre-existent Sophia, compensate Yahweh and his attitude, and at the same time complete the anamnesis of Wisdom. Taking a highly personified form that is clear proof of her autonomy, Wisdom reveals herself to men as a friendly helper and advocate against Yahweh, and shows them the bright side, the kind, just, and amiable aspect of their God.

624 At the time when Satan's practical joke with the snake compromised the paradise that was planned to be perfect, Yahweh

24 Job 28:12: "But where shall wisdom be found?" Whether this is a later interpolation or not makes no difference.

banished Adam and Eve, whom he had created as images of his masculine essence and its feminine emanation, to the extra-paradisal world, the limbo of "shards." It is not clear how much of Eve represents Sophia and how much of her is Lilith. At any rate Adam has priority in every respect. Eve was taken out of his body as an afterthought. I mention these details from Genesis only because the reappearance of Sophia in the heavenly regions points to a coming act of creation. She is indeed the "master workman"; she realizes God's thoughts by clothing them in material form, which is the prerogative of all feminine beings. Her coexistence with Yahweh signifies the perpetual *hieros gamos* from which worlds are begotten and born. A momentous change is imminent: God desires to regenerate himself in the mystery of the heavenly nuptials—as the chief gods of Egypt had done from time immemorial—and to become man. For this he uses the Egyptian model of the god's incarnation in Pharaoh, which in its turn is but a copy of the eternal *hieros gamos* in the pleroma. It would, however, be wrong to suppose that this archetype is merely repeating itself mechanically. So far as we know, this is never the case, since archetypal situations only return when specifically called for. The real reason for God's becoming man is to be sought in his encounter with Job. Later on we shall deal with this question in more detail.

IV

625 Just as the decision to become man apparently makes use of the ancient Egyptian model, so we can expect that the process itself will follow certain prefigurations. The approach of Sophia betokens a new creation. But this time it is not the world that is to be changed; rather it is God who intends to change his own nature. Mankind is not, as before, to be destroyed, but saved. In this decision we can discern the "philanthropic" influence of Sophia: no new human beings are to be created, but only one, the God-man. For this purpose a contrary procedure must be employed. The Second Adam shall not, like the first, proceed directly from the hand of the Creator, but shall be born of a human woman. So this time priority falls to the Second Eve, not only in a temporal sense but in a material sense as well. On the

basis of the so-called Proto-Evangelium, the Second Eve corresponds to "the woman and her seed" mentioned in Genesis 3:15, which shall bruise the serpent's head. And just as Adam was believed to be originally hermaphroditic, so "the woman and her seed" are thought of as a human pair, as the Queen of Heaven and Mother of God and as the divine son who has no human father. Thus Mary, the virgin, is chosen as the pure vessel for the coming birth of God. Her independence of the male is emphasized by her virginity as the *sine qua non* of the process. She is a "daughter of God" who, as a later dogma will establish, is distinguished at the outset by the privilege of an immaculate conception and is thus free from the taint of original sin. It is therefore evident that she belongs to the state before the Fall. This posits a new beginning. The divine immaculateness of her status makes it immediately clear that she not only bears the image of God in undiminished purity, but, as the bride of God, is also the incarnation of her prototype, namely Sophia. Her love of mankind, widely emphasized in the ancient writings, suggests that in this newest creation of his Yahweh has allowed himself to be extensively influenced by Sophia. For Mary, the blessed among women, is a friend and intercessor for sinners, which all men are. Like Sophia, she is a mediatrix who leads the way to God and assures man of immortality. Her Assumption is therefore the prototype of man's bodily resurrection. As the bride of God and Queen of Heaven she holds the place of the Old Testament Sophia.

626 Remarkable indeed are the unusual precautions which surround the making of Mary: immaculate conception, extirpation of the taint of sin, everlasting virginity. The Mother of God is obviously being protected against Satan's tricks. From this we can conclude that Yahweh has consulted his own omniscience, for in his omniscience there is a clear knowledge of the perverse intentions which lurk in the dark son of God. Mary must at all costs be protected from these corrupting influences. The inevitable consequence of all these elaborate protective measures is something that has not been sufficiently taken into account in the dogmatic evaluation of the Incarnation: her freedom from original sin sets Mary apart from mankind in general, whose common characteristic is original sin and therefore the need of redemption. The *status ante lapsum* is tantamount to a para-

disal, i.e., pleromatic and divine, existence. By having these special measures applied to her, Mary is elevated to the status of a goddess and consequently loses something of her humanity: she will not conceive her child in sin, like all other mothers, and therefore he also will never be a human being, but a god. To my knowledge at least, no one has ever perceived that this queers the pitch for a genuine Incarnation of God, or rather, that the Incarnation was only partially consummated. Both mother and son are not real human beings at all, but gods.

627 This arrangement, though it had the effect of exalting Mary's personality in the masculine sense by bringing it closer to the perfection of Christ, was at the same time injurious to the feminine principle of imperfection or completeness, since this was reduced by the perfectionizing tendency to the little bit of imperfection that still distinguishes Mary from Christ. *Phoebo propior lumina perdit!* Thus the more the feminine ideal is bent in the direction of the masculine, the more the woman loses her power to compensate the masculine striving for perfection, and a typically masculine, ideal state arises which, as we shall see, is threatened with an enantiodromia. No path leads beyond perfection into the future—there is only a turning back, a collapse of the ideal, which could easily have been avoided by paying attention to the feminine ideal of completeness. Yahweh's perfectionism is carried over from the Old Testament into the New, and despite all the recognition and glorification of the feminine principle this never prevailed against the patriarchal supremacy. We have not, therefore, by any means heard the last of it.

V

628 The older son of the first parents was corrupted by Satan and not much of a success. He was an eidolon of Satan, and only the younger son, Abel, was pleasing to God. In Cain the God-image was distorted, but in Abel it was considerably less dimmed. If Adam is thought of as a copy of God, then God's successful son, who served as a model for Abel (and about whom, as we have seen, there are no available documents), is the prefiguration of the God-man. Of the latter we know positively that, as

the Logos, he is preexistent and coeternal with God, indeed of the same substance (ὁμοούσιος) as he. One can therefore regard Abel as the imperfect prototype of God's son who is about to be begotten in Mary. Just as Yahweh originally undertook to create a chthonic equivalent of himself in the first man, Adam, so now he intends something similar, but much better. The extraordinary precautionary measures above-mentioned are designed to serve this purpose. The new son, Christ, shall on the one hand be a chthonic man like Adam, mortal and capable of suffering, but on the other hand he shall not be, like Adam, a mere copy, but God himself, begotten by himself as the Father, and rejuvenating the Father as the Son. As God he has always been God, and as the son of Mary, who is plainly a copy of Sophia, he is the Logos (synonymous with Nous), who, like Sophia, is a master workman, as stated by the Gospel according to St. John.[1] This identity of mother and son is borne out over and over again in the myths.

629 Although the birth of Christ is an event that occurred but once in history, it has always existed in eternity. For the layman in these matters, the identity of a nontemporal, eternal event with a unique historical occurrence is something that is extremely difficult to conceive. He must, however, accustom himself to the idea that "time" is a relative concept and needs to be complemented by that of the "simultaneous" existence, in the Bardo or pleroma, of all historical processes. What exists in the pleroma as an eternal process appears in time as an aperiodic sequence, that is to say, it is repeated many times in an irregular pattern. To take but one example: Yahweh had one good son and one who was a failure. Cain and Abel, Jacob and Esau, correspond to this prototype, and so, in all ages and in all parts of the world, does the motif of the hostile brothers, which in innumerable modern variants still causes dissension in families and keeps the psychotherapist busy. Just as many examples, no less instructive, could be found for the two women prefigured in eternity. When these things occur as modern variants, therefore, they should not be regarded merely as personal episodes, moods, or chance idiosyncrasies in people, but as fragments of the pleromatic process itself, which, broken up into individual

[1] John 1 : 3: "All things were made through him, and without him was not anything made that was made."

events occurring in time, is an essential component or aspect of the divine drama.

630 When Yahweh created the world from his *prima materia,* the "Void," he could not help breathing his own mystery into the Creation which is himself in every part, as every reasonable theology has long been convinced. From this comes the belief that it is possible to know God from his Creation. When I say that he could not help doing this, I do not imply any limitation of his omnipotence; on the contrary, it is an acknowledgment that all possibilities are contained in him, and that there are in consequence no other possibilities than those which express him.

631 All the world is God's, and God is in all the world from the very beginning. Why, then, the *tour de force* of the Incarnation? one asks oneself, astonished. God is in everything already, and yet there must be something missing if a sort of second entrance into Creation has now to be staged with so much care and circumspection. Since Creation is universal, reaching to the remotest stellar galaxies, and since it has also made organic life infinitely variable and capable of endless differentiation, we can hardly see where the defect lies. The fact that Satan has everywhere intruded his corrupting influence is no doubt regrettable for many reasons, but it makes no difference in principle. It is not easy to give an answer to this question. One would like to say that Christ had to appear in order to deliver mankind from evil. But when one considers that evil was originally slipped into the scheme of things by Satan, and still is, then it would seem much simpler if Yahweh would, for once, call this "practical joker" severely to account, get rid of his pernicious influence, and thus eliminate the root of all evil. He would then not need the elaborate arrangement of a special Incarnation with all the unforeseeable consequences which this entails. One should make clear to oneself what it means when God becomes man. It means nothing less than a world-shaking transformation of God. It means more or less what Creation meant in the beginning, namely an objectivation of God. At the time of the Creation he revealed himself in Nature; now he wants to be more specific and become man. It must be admitted, however, that there was a tendency in this direction right from the start. For, when those other human beings, who had evidently been created

before Adam, appeared on the scene along with the higher mammals, Yahweh created on the following day, by a special act of creation, a man who was the image of God. This was the first prefiguration of his becoming man. He took Adam's descendants, especially the people of Israel, into his personal possession, and from time to time he filled this people's prophets with his spirit. All these things were preparatory events and symptoms of a tendency within God to become man. But in omniscience there had existed from all eternity a knowledge of the human nature of God or of the divine nature of man. That is why, long before Genesis was written, we find corresponding testimonies in the ancient Egyptian records. These intimations and prefigurations of the Incarnation must strike one as either completely incomprehensible or superfluous, since all creation *ex nihilo* is God's and consists of nothing but God, with the result that man, like the rest of creation, is simply God become concrete. Prefigurations, however, are not in themselves creative events, but are only stages in the process of becoming conscious. It was only quite late that we realized (or rather, are beginning to realize) that God is Reality itself and therefore—last but not least—man. This realization is a millennial process.

VI

632 In view of the immense problem which we are about to discuss, this excursus on pleromatic events is not out of place as an introduction.

633 What, then, is the real reason for the Incarnation as an historical event?

634 In order to answer this question we have to go rather far back. As we have seen, Yahweh evidently has a disinclination to take his absolute knowledge into account as a counterbalance to the dynamism of omnipotence. The most instructive example of this is his relation to Satan: it always looks as if Yahweh were completely uninformed about his son's intentions. That is because he never consults his omniscience. We can only explain this on the assumption that Yahweh was so fascinated by his successive acts of creation, so taken up with them, that he forgot about his omniscience altogether. It is quite understandable

that the magical bodying forth of the most diverse objects, which had never before existed in such pristine splendour, should have caused God infinite delight. Sophia's memory is not at fault when she says:

> when he marked out the foundations of the earth,
> then I was by him, like a master workman,
> and I was daily his delight.[1]

635 The Book of Job still rings with the proud joy of creating when Yahweh points to the huge animals he has successfully turned out:

> Behold, Behemoth,
> which I made as I made you.
> . . . .
> He is the first of the works of God,
> made to be lord over his companions.[2]

636 So even in Job's day Yahweh is still intoxicated with the tremendous power and grandeur of his creation. Compared with this, what are Satan's pinpricks and the lamentations of human beings who were created with the behemoth, even if they do bear God's image? Yahweh seems to have forgotten this fact entirely, otherwise he would never have ridden so roughshod over Job's human dignity.

637 It is only the careful and farsighted preparations for Christ's birth which show us that omniscience has begun to have a noticeable effect on Yahweh's actions. A certain philanthropic and universalistic tendency makes itself felt. The "children of Israel" take something of a second place in comparison with the "children of men." After Job, we hear nothing further about new covenants. Proverbs and gnomic utterances seem to be the order of the day, and a real *novum* now appears on the scene, namely apocalyptic communications. This points to metaphysical acts of cognition, that is, to "constellated" unconscious contents which are ready to irrupt into consciousness. In all this, as we have said, we discern the helpful hand of Sophia.

638 If we consider Yahweh's behaviour, up to the reappearance of Sophia, as a whole, one indubitable fact strikes us—the fact

1 Proverbs 8 : 29–30. 2 Job 40 : 15, 19 (last line, ZB).

that his actions are accompanied by an inferior consciousness. Time and again we miss reflection and regard for absolute knowledge. His consciousness seems to be not much more than a primitive "awareness" which knows no reflection and no morality. One merely perceives and acts blindly, without conscious inclusion of the subject, whose individual existence raises no problems. Today we would call such a state psychologically "unconscious," and in the eyes of the law it would be described as *non compos mentis*. The fact that consciousness does not perform acts of thinking does not, however, prove that they do not exist. They merely occur unconsciously and make themselves felt indirectly in dreams, visions, revelations, and "instinctive" changes of consciousness, whose very nature tells us that they derive from an "unconscious" knowledge and are the result of unconscious acts of judgment or unconscious conclusions.

639 Some such process can be observed in the curious change which comes over Yahweh's behaviour after the Job episode. There can be no doubt that he did not immediately become conscious of the moral defeat he had suffered at Job's hands. In his omniscience, of course, this fact had been known from all eternity, and it is not unthinkable that the knowledge of it unconsciously brought him into the position of dealing so harshly with Job in order that he himself should become conscious of something through this conflict, and thus gain new insight. Satan who, with good reason, later on received the name of "Lucifer," knew how to make more frequent and better use of omniscience than did his father.[3] It seems he was the only one among the sons of God who developed that much initiative. At all events, it was he who placed those unforeseen incidents in Yahweh's way, which omniscience knew to be necessary and indeed indispensable for the unfolding and completion of the divine drama. Among these the case of Job was decisive, and it could only have happened thanks to Satan's initiative.

640 The victory of the vanquished and oppressed is obvious:

3 In Christian tradition, too, there is a belief that God's intention to become man was known to the Devil many centuries before, and that this was why he instilled the Dionysus myth into the Greeks, so that they could say, when the joyful tidings reached them in reality: "So what? We knew all that long ago." When the conquistadores later discovered the crosses of the Mayas in Yucatán, the Spanish bishops used the same argument.

Job stands morally higher than Yahweh. In this respect the creature has surpassed the creator. As always when an external event touches on some unconscious knowledge, this knowledge can reach consciousness. The event is recognized as a *déjà vu,* and one remembers a pre-existent knowledge about it. Something of the kind must have happened to Yahweh. Job's superiority cannot be shrugged off. Hence a situation arises in which real reflection is needed. That is why Sophia steps in. She reinforces the much needed self-reflection and thus makes possible Yahweh's decision to become man. It is a decision fraught with consequences: he raises himself above his earlier primitive level of consciousness by indirectly acknowledging that the man Job is morally superior to him and that therefore he has to catch up and become human himself. Had he not taken this decision he would have found himself in flagrant opposition to his omniscience. Yahweh must become man precisely because he has done man a wrong. He, the guardian of justice, knows that every wrong must be expiated, and Wisdom knows that moral law is above even him. Because his creature has surpassed him he must regenerate himself.

641 As nothing can happen without a pre-existing pattern, not even creation *ex nihilo,* which must always resort to the treasure-house of eternal images in the fabulous mind of the "master workman," the choice of a model for the son who is now about to be begotten lies between Adam (to a limited extent) and Abel (to a much greater extent). Adam's limitation lies in the fact that, even if he is the Anthropos, he is chiefly a creature and a father. Abel's advantage is that he is the son well pleasing to God, begotten and not directly created. One disadvantage has to be accepted: he met with an early death by violence, too early to leave behind him a widow and children, which ought really to be part of human fate if lived to the full. Abel is not the authentic archetype of the son well pleasing to God; he is a copy, but the first of the kind to be met with in the Scriptures. The young dying god is also well known in the contemporary pagan religions, and so is the fratricide motif. We shall hardly be wrong in assuming that Abel's fate refers back to a metaphysical event which was played out between Satan and another son of God with a "light" nature and more devotion to his father. Egyptian tradition can give us information on this point

(Horus and Set). As we have said, the disadvantage prefigured in the Abel type can hardly be avoided, because it is an integral part of the mythical-son drama, as the numerous pagan variants of this motif show. The short, dramatic course of Abel's fate serves as an excellent paradigm for the life and death of a God become man.

642 To sum up: the immediate cause of the Incarnation lies in Job's elevation, and its purpose is the differentiation of Yahweh's consciousness. For this a situation of extreme gravity was needed, a *peripeteia* charged with affect, without which no higher level of consciousness can be reached.

VII

643 In addition to Abel, we have to consider, as a model for the impending birth of the son of God, the general pattern of the hero's life which has been established since time immemorial and handed down by tradition. Since this son is not intended merely as a national Messiah, but as the universal saviour of mankind, we have also to consider the pagan myths and revelations concerning the life of one who is singled out by the gods.

644 The birth of Christ is therefore characterized by all the usual phenomena attendant upon the birth of a hero, such as the annunciation, the divine generation from a virgin, the coincidence of the birth with the thrice-repeated *coniunctio maxima* (♃ ☌ ♄) in the sign of Pisces, which at that precise moment inaugurated the new era, the recognition of the birth of a king, the persecution of the newborn, his flight and concealment, his lowly birth, etc. The motif of the growing up of the hero is discernible in the wisdom of the twelve-year-old child in the temple, and there are several examples in the gospels of the breaking away from the mother.

645 It goes without saying that a quite special interest attaches to the character and fate of the incarnate son of God. Seen from a distance of nearly two thousand years, it is uncommonly difficult to reconstruct a biographical picture of Christ from the traditions that have been preserved. Not a single text is extant which would fulfil even the minimum modern requirements for writing a history. The historically verifiable facts are ex-

tremely scanty, and the little biographically valid material that exists is not sufficient for us to create out of it a consistent career or an even remotely probable character. Certain theologians have discovered the main reason for this in the fact that Christ's biography and psychology cannot be separated from eschatology. Eschatology means in effect that Christ is God and man at the same time and that he therefore suffers a divine as well as a human fate. The two natures interpenetrate so thoroughly that any attempt to separate them mutilates both. The divine overshadows the human, and the human being is scarcely graspable as an empirical personality. Even the critical procedures of modern psychology do not suffice to throw light on all the obscurities. Every attempt to single out one particular feature for clarity's sake does violence to another which is just as essential either with respect to his divinity or with respect to his humanity. The commonplace is so interwoven with the miraculous and the mythical that we can never be sure of our facts. Perhaps the most disturbing and confusing thing of all is that the oldest writings, those of St. Paul, do not seem to have the slightest interest in Christ's existence as a concrete human being. The synoptic gospels are equally unsatisfactory as they have more the character of propaganda than of biography.

646 With regard to the human side of Christ, if we can speak of a "purely human" aspect at all, what stands out particularly clearly is his love of mankind. This feature is already implied in the relationship of Mary to Sophia, and especially in his genesis by the Holy Ghost, whose feminine nature is personified by Sophia, since she is the preliminary historical form of the ἅγιον πνεῦμα, who is symbolized by the dove, the bird belonging to the love-goddess. Furthermore, the love-goddess is in most cases the mother of the young dying god. Christ's love of mankind is, however, limited to a not inconsiderable degree by a certain predestinarian tendency which sometimes causes him to withhold his salutary message from those who do not belong to the elect. If one takes the doctrine of predestination literally, it is difficult to see how it can be fitted into the framework of the Christian message. But taken psychologically, as a means to achieving a definite effect, it can readily be understood that these allusions to predestination give one a feeling of distinction. If one knows that one has been singled out by divine choice

and intention from the beginning of the world, then one feels lifted beyond the transitoriness and meaninglessness of ordinary human existence and transported to a new state of dignity and importance, like one who has a part in the divine world drama. In this way man is brought nearer to God, and this is in entire accord with the meaning of the message in the gospels.

647 Besides his love of mankind a certain irascibility is noticeable in Christ's character, and, as is often the case with people of emotional temperament, a manifest lack of self-reflection. There is no evidence that Christ ever wondered about himself, or that he ever confronted himself. To this rule there is only one significant exception—the despairing cry from the Cross: "My God, my God, why hast thou forsaken me?" Here his human nature attains divinity; at that moment God experiences what it means to be a mortal man and drinks to the dregs what he made his faithful servant Job suffer. Here is given the answer to Job, and, clearly, this supreme moment is as divine as it is human, as "eschatological" as it is "psychological." And at this moment, too, where one can feel the human being so absolutely, the divine myth is present in full force. And both mean one and the same thing. How, then, can one possibly "demythologize" the figure of Christ? A rationalistic attempt of that sort would soak all the mystery out of his personality, and what remained would no longer be the birth and tragic fate of a God in time, but, historically speaking, a badly authenticated religious teacher, a Jewish reformer who was hellenistically interpreted and misunderstood—a kind of Pythagoras, maybe, or, if you like, a Buddha or a Mohammed, but certainly not a son of God or a God incarnate. Nor does anybody seem to have realized what would be the consequences of a Christ disinfected of all trace of eschatology. Today we have an empirical psychology, which continues to exist despite the fact that the theologians have done their best to ignore it, and with its help we can put certain of Christ's statements under the microscope. If these statements are detached from their mythical context, they can only be explained personalistically. But what sort of conclusion are we bound to arrive at if a statement like "I am the way, and the truth, and the life; no one comes to the Father, but by me" [1] is reduced to personal psychology? Obviously the same con-

[1] John 14:6.

clusion as that reached by Jesus' relatives when, in their ignorance of eschatology, they said, "He is beside himself." [2] What is the use of a religion without a mythos, since religion means, if anything at all, precisely that function which links us back to the eternal myth?

648 In view of these portentous impossibilities, it has been assumed, perhaps as the result of a growing impatience with the difficult factual material, that Christ was nothing but a myth, in this case no more than a fiction. But myth is not fiction: it consists of facts that are continually repeated and can be observed over and over again. It is something that happens to man, and men have mythical fates just as much as the Greek heroes do. The fact that the life of Christ is largely myth does absolutely nothing to disprove its factual truth—quite the contrary. I would even go so far as to say that the mythical character of a life is just what expresses its universal human validity. It is perfectly possible, psychologically, for the unconscious or an archetype to take complete possession of a man and to determine his fate down to the smallest detail. At the same time objective, non-psychic parallel phenomena can occur which also represent the archetype. It not only seems so, it simply is so, that the archetype fulfils itself not only psychically in the individual, but objectively outside the individual. My own conjecture is that Christ was such a personality. The life of Christ is just what it had to be if it is the life of a god and a man at the same time. It is a *symbolum,* a bringing together of heterogeneous natures, rather as if Job and Yahweh were combined in a single personality. Yahweh's intention to become man, which resulted from his collision with Job, is fulfilled in Christ's life and suffering.

VIII

649 When one remembers the earlier acts of creation, one wonders what has happened to Satan and his subversive activities. Everywhere he sows his tares among the wheat. One suspects he had a hand in Herod's massacre of the innocents. What is certain is his attempt to lure Christ into the role of a worldly ruler. Equally obvious is the fact, as is evidenced by the remarks of

2 Mark 3 : 21.

the man possessed of devils, that he is very well informed about Christ's nature. He also seems to have inspired Judas, without, however, being able to influence or prevent the sacrificial death.

650 His comparative ineffectiveness can be explained on the one hand by the careful preparations for the divine birth, and on the other hand by a curious metaphysical phenomenon which Christ witnessed: he saw Satan fall like lightning from heaven.[1] In this vision a metaphysical event has become temporal; it indicates the historic and—so far as we know—final separation of Yahweh from his dark son. Satan is banished from heaven and no longer has any opportunity to inveigle his father into dubious undertakings. This event may well explain why he plays such an inferior role wherever he appears in the history of the Incarnation. His role here is in no way comparable to his former confidential relationship to Yahweh. He has obviously forfeited the paternal affection and been exiled. The punishment which we missed in the story of Job has at last caught up with him, though in a strangely limited form. Although he is banished from the heavenly court he has kept his dominion over the sublunary world. He is not cast directly into hell, but upon earth. Only at the end of time shall he be locked up and made permanently ineffective. Christ's death cannot be laid at his door, because, through its prefiguration in Abel and in the young dying gods, the sacrificial death was a fate chosen by Yahweh as a reparation for the wrong done to Job on the one hand, and on the other hand as a fillip to the spiritual and moral development of man. There can be no doubt that man's importance is enormously enhanced if God himself deigns to become one.

651 As a result of the partial neutralization of Satan, Yahweh identifies with his light aspect and becomes the good God and loving father. He has not lost his wrath and can still mete out punishment, but he does it with justice. Cases like the Job tragedy are apparently no longer to be expected. He proves himself benevolent and gracious. He shows mercy to the sinful children of men and is defined as Love itself. But although Christ has complete confidence in his father and even feels at one with him, he cannot help inserting the cautious petition—and warning—into the Lord's Prayer: "Lead us not into tempta-

[1] Luke 10:18.

tion, but deliver us from evil." God is asked not to entice us outright into doing evil, but rather to deliver us from it. The possibility that Yahweh, in spite of all the precautionary measures and in spite of his express intention to become the Summum Bonum, might yet revert to his former ways is not so remote that one need not keep one eye open for it. At any rate, Christ considers it appropriate to remind his father of his destructive inclinations towards mankind and to beg him to desist from them. Judged by any human standards it is after all unfair, indeed extremely immoral, to entice little children into doing things that might be dangerous for them, simply in order to test their moral stamina! Especially as the difference between a child and a grown-up is immeasurably smaller than that between God and his creatures, whose moral weakness is particularly well known to him. The incongruity of it is so colossal that if this petition were not in the Lord's Prayer one would have to call it sheer blasphemy, because it really will not do to ascribe such contradictory behaviour to the God of Love and Summum Bonum.

652 The sixth petition indeed allows a deep insight, for in face of this fact Christ's immense certainty with regard to his father's character becomes somewhat questionable. It is, unfortunately, a common experience that particularly positive and categorical assertions are met with wherever there is a slight doubt in the background that has to be stifled. One must admit that it would be contrary to all reasonable expectations to suppose that a God who, for all his lavish generosity, had been subject to intermittent but devastating fits of rage ever since time began could suddenly become the epitome of everything good. Christ's unadmitted but none the less evident doubt in this respect is confirmed in the New Testament, and particularly in the Apocalypse. There Yahweh again delivers himself up to an unheard-of fury of destruction against the human race, of whom a mere hundred and forty-four thousand specimens appear to survive.[2]

653 One is indeed at a loss how to bring such a reaction into line with the behaviour of a loving father, whom we would expect to glorify his creation with patience and love. It looks as if the attempt to secure an absolute and final victory for good is bound to lead to a dangerous accumulation of evil and hence to catas-

2 Revelation 7:4.

trophe. Compared with the end of the world, the destruction of Sodom and Gomorrah and even the Deluge are mere child's play; for this time the whole of creation goes to pieces. As Satan was locked up for a time, then conquered and cast into a lake of fire,[3] the destruction of the world can hardly be the work of the devil, but must be an "act of God" not influenced by Satan.

654 The end of the world is, however, preceded by the circumstance that even Christ's victory over his brother Satan—Abel's counterstroke against Cain—is not really and truly won, because, before this can come to pass, a final and mighty manifestation of Satan is to be expected. One can hardly suppose that God's incarnation in his son Christ would be calmly accepted by Satan. It must certainly have stirred up his jealousy to the highest pitch and evoked in him a desire to imitate Christ (a role for which he is particularly well suited as the *πνεῦμα ἀντίμιμον*), and to become incarnate in his turn as the *dark* God. (As we know, numerous legends were later woven round this theme.) This plan will be put into operation by the figure of the Antichrist after the preordained thousand years are over, the term allotted by astrology to the reign of Christ. This expectation, which is already to be found in the New Testament, reveals a doubt as to the immediate finality or universal effectiveness of the work of salvation. Unfortunately it must be said that these expectations gave rise to thoughtless revelations which were never even discussed with other aspects of the doctrine of salvation, let alone brought into harmony with them.

IX

655 I mention these future apocalyptic events only to illustrate the doubt which is indirectly expressed in the sixth petition of the Lord's Prayer, and not in order to give a general interpretation of the Apocalypse. I shall come back to this theme later on. But, before doing so, we must turn to the question of how matters stood with the Incarnation after the death of Christ. We have always been taught that the Incarnation was a unique historical event. No repetition of it was to be expected, any more than one could expect a further revelation of the Logos, for this

[3] Revelation 19:20.

too was included in the uniqueness of God's appearance on earth, in human form, nearly two thousand years ago. The sole source of revelation, and hence the final authority, is the Bible. God is an authority only in so far as he authorized the writings in the New Testament, and with the conclusion of the New Testament the authentic communications of God cease. Thus far the Protestant standpoint. The Catholic Church, the direct heir and continuator of historical Christianity, proves to be somewhat more cautious in this regard, believing that with the assistance of the Holy Ghost the dogma can progressively develop and unfold. This view is in entire agreement with Christ's own teachings about the Holy Ghost and hence with the further continuance of the Incarnation. Christ is of the opinion that whoever believes in him—believes, that is to say, that he is the son of God—can "do the works that I do, and greater works than these." [1] He reminds his disciples that he had told them they were gods.[2] The believers or chosen ones are children of God and "fellow heirs with Christ." [3] When Christ leaves the earthly stage, he will ask his father to send his flock a Counsellor (the "Paraclete"), who will abide with them and in them for ever.[4] The Counsellor is the Holy Ghost, who will be sent from the father. This "Spirit of truth" will teach the believers "all things" and guide them "into all truth." [5] According to this, Christ envisages a continuing realization of God in his children, and consequently in his (Christ's) brothers and sisters in the spirit, so that his own works need not necessarily be considered the greatest ones.

656 Since the Holy Ghost is the Third Person of the Trinity and God is present entire in each of the three Persons at any time, the indwelling of the Holy Ghost means nothing less than an approximation of the believer to the status of God's son. One can therefore understand what is meant by the remark "you are gods." The deifying effect of the Holy Ghost is naturally assisted by the *imago Dei* stamped on the elect. God, in the shape of the Holy Ghost, puts up his tent in man, for he is obviously minded to realize himself continually not only in Adam's descendants, but in an indefinitely large number of believers, and possibly in mankind as a whole. Symptomatic of this is the

[1] John 14:12. [2] 10:34. [3] Romans 8:17. [4] John 14:16f.
[5] 14:26 and 16:13.

significant fact that Barnabas and Paul were identified in Lystra with Zeus and Hermes: "The gods have come down to us in the likeness of men." [6] This was certainly only the more naïve, pagan view of the Christian transmutation, but precisely for that reason it convinces. Tertullian must have had something of the sort in mind when he described the "sublimiorem Deum" as a sort of lender of divinity "who has made gods of men." [7]

657 God's Incarnation in Christ requires continuation and completion because Christ, owing to his virgin birth and his sinlessness, was not an empirical human being at all. As stated in the first chapter of St. John, he represented a light which, though it shone in the darkness, was not comprehended by the darkness. He remained outside and above mankind. Job, on the other hand, was an ordinary human being, and therefore the wrong done to him, and through him to mankind, can, according to divine justice, only be repaired by an incarnation of God in an empirical human being. This act of expiation is performed by the Paraclete; for, just as man must suffer from God, so God must suffer from man. Otherwise there can be no reconciliation between the two.

658 The continuing, direct operation of the Holy Ghost on those who are called to be God's children implies, in fact, a broadening process of incarnation. Christ, the son begotten by God, is the first-born who is succeeded by an ever-increasing number of younger brothers and sisters. These are, however, neither begotten by the Holy Ghost nor born of a virgin. This may be prejudicial to their metaphysical status, but their merely human birth will in no sense endanger their prospects of a future position of honour at the heavenly court, nor will it diminish their capacity to perform miracles. Their lowly origin (possibly from the mammals) does not prevent them from entering into a close kinship with God as their father and Christ as their brother. In a metaphorical sense, indeed, it is actually a "kinship by blood," since they have received their share of the blood and flesh of Christ, which means more than mere adoption. These profound changes in man's status are the direct result of Christ's work of redemption. Redemption or deliverance has several different aspects,

6 Acts 14:11.

7 "Mancipem quendam divinitatis qui ex hominibus deos fecerit." *Apologeticus,* XI, in Migne, *P.L.,* vol. 1, col. 333.

the most important of which is the expiation wrought by Christ's sacrificial death for the misdemeanours of mankind. His blood cleanses us from the evil consequences of sin. He reconciles God with man and delivers him from the divine wrath, which hangs over him like doom, and from eternal damnation. It is obvious that such ideas still picture God the father as the dangerous Yahweh who has to be propitiated. The agonizing death of his son is supposed to give him satisfaction for an affront he has suffered, and for this "moral injury" he would be inclined to take a terrible vengeance. Once more we are appalled by the incongruous attitude of the world creator towards his creatures, who to his chagrin never behave according to his expectations. It is as if someone started a bacterial culture which turned out to be a failure. He might curse his luck, but he would never seek the reason for the failure in the bacilli and want to punish them morally for it. Rather, he would select a more suitable culture medium. Yahweh's behaviour towards his creatures contradicts all the requirements of so-called "divine" reason whose possession is supposed to distinguish men from animals. Moreover, a bacteriologist might make a mistake in his choice of a culture medium, for he is only human. But God in his omniscience would never make mistakes if only he consulted with it. He has equipped his human creatures with a modicum of consciousness and a corresponding degree of free will, but he must also know that by so doing he leads them into the temptation of falling into a dangerous independence. That would not be too great a risk if man had to do with a creator who was only kind and good. But Yahweh is forgetting his son Satan, to whose wiles even he occasionally succumbs. How then could he expect man with his limited consciousness and imperfect knowledge to do any better? He also overlooks the fact that the more consciousness a man possesses the more he is separated from his instincts (which at least give him an inkling of the hidden wisdom of God) and the more prone he is to error. He is certainly not up to Satan's wiles if even his creator is unable, or unwilling, to restrain this powerful spirit.

X

659 The fact of God's "unconsciousness" throws a peculiar light on the doctrine of salvation. Man is not so much delivered from his sins, even if he is baptized in the prescribed manner and thus washed clean, as delivered from fear of the consequences of sin, that is, from the wrath of God. Consequently, the work of salvation is intended to save man from the fear of God. This is certainly possible where the belief in a loving father, who has sent his only-begotten son to rescue the human race, has repressed the persistent traces of the old Yahweh and his dangerous affects. Such a belief, however, presupposes a lack of reflection or a *sacrificium intellectus,* and it appears questionable whether either of them can be morally justified. We should never forget that it was Christ himself who taught us to make usurious use of the talents entrusted to us and not hide them in the ground. One ought not to make oneself out to be more stupid and more unconscious than one really is, for in all other aspects we are called upon to be alert, critical, and self-aware, so as not to fall into temptation, and to "examine the spirits" who want to gain influence over us and "see whether they are of God," [1] so that we may recognize the mistakes we make. It even needs superhuman intelligence to avoid the cunning snares of Satan. These obligations inevitably sharpen our understanding, our love of truth, and the urge to know, which as well as being genuine human virtues are quite possibly effects of that spirit which "searches everything, even the depths of God." [2] These intellectual and moral capacities are themselves of a divine nature, and therefore cannot and must not be cut off. It is just by following Christian morality that one gets into the worst collisions of duty. Only those who habitually make five an even number can escape them. The fact that Christian ethics leads to collisions of duty speaks in its favour. By engendering insoluble conflicts and consequently an *afflictio animae,* it brings man nearer to a knowledge of God. All opposites are of God, therefore man must bend to this burden; and in so doing he finds that God in his "oppositeness" has taken possession of him, incarnated himself in him. He becomes a vessel filled with divine conflict. We rightly associate the idea

[1] I John 4 : 1 (mod.). [2] I Corinthians 2 : 10.

of suffering with a state in which the opposites violently collide with one another, and we hesitate to describe such a painful experience as being "redeemed." Yet it cannot be denied that the great symbol of the Christian faith, the Cross, upon which hangs the suffering figure of the Redeemer, has been emphatically held up before the eyes of Christians for nearly two thousand years. This picture is completed by the two thieves, one of whom goes down to hell, the other into paradise. One could hardly imagine a better representation of the "oppositeness" of the central Christian symbol. Why this inevitable product of Christian psychology should signify redemption is difficult to see, except that the conscious recognition of the opposites, painful though it may be at the moment, does bring with it a definite feeling of deliverance. It is on the one hand a deliverance from the distressing state of dull and helpless unconsciousness, and on the other hand a growing awareness of God's oppositeness, in which man can participate if he does not shrink from being wounded by the dividing sword which is Christ. Only through the most extreme and most menacing conflict does the Christian experience deliverance into divinity, always provided that he does not break, but accepts the burden of being marked out by God. In this way alone can the *imago Dei* realize itself in him, and God become man. The seventh petition in the Lord's Prayer, "But deliver us from evil," is to be understood in the same sense as Christ's prayer in the Garden of Gethsemane: "My Father, if it be possible, let this cup pass from me." [3] In principle it does not seem to fit God's purpose to exempt a man from conflict and hence from evil. It is altogether human to express such a desire but it must not be made into a principle, because it is directed against God's will and rests only on human weakness and fear. Fear is certainly justified up to a point, for, to make the conflict complete, there must be doubt and uncertainty as to whether man's strength is not being overtaxed.

660 Because the *imago Dei* pervades the whole human sphere and makes mankind its involuntary exponent, it is just possible that the four-hundred-year-old schism in the Church and the present division of the political world into two hostile camps are both expressions of the unrecognized polarity of the dominant archetype.

3 Matthew 26:39.

661 The traditional view of Christ's work of redemption reflects a one-sided way of thinking, no matter whether we regard that one-sidedness as purely human or as willed by God. The other view, which regards the atonement not as the payment of a human debt to God, but as reparation for a wrong done by God to man, has been briefly outlined above. This view seems to me to be better suited to the power situation as it actually exists. The sheep can stir up mud in the wolf's drinking water, but can do him no other harm. So also the creature can disappoint the creator, but it is scarcely credible that he can do him a painful wrong. This lies only in the power of the creator with respect to the powerless creature. On this view, a wrong is imputed to God, but it is certainly no worse than what has already been imputed to him if one assumes that it was necessary to torture the son to death on the Cross merely in order to appease the father's wrath. What kind of father is it who would rather his son were slaughtered than forgive his ill-advised creatures who have been corrupted by his precious Satan? What is supposed to be demonstrated by this gruesome and archaic sacrifice of the son? God's love, perhaps? Or his implacability? We know from chapter 22 of Genesis [4] and from Exodus 22:29 that Yahweh has a tendency to employ such means as the killing of the son and the first-born in order to test his people's faith or to assert his will, despite the fact that his omniscience and omnipotence have no need whatever of such savage procedures, which moreover set a bad example to the mighty ones of the earth. It is very understandable, therefore, that a naïve mind is apt to run away from such questions and excuse this manoeuvre as a beautiful *sacrificium intellectus*. If one prefers not to read the Eighty-ninth Psalm, the matter will not end there. He who cheats once will cheat again, particularly when it comes to self-knowledge. But self-knowledge, in the form of an examination of conscience, is demanded by Christian ethics. They were very pious people who maintained that self-knowledge paves the way to knowledge of God.

[4] Abraham and Isaac.

XI

662 To believe that God is the Summum Bonum is impossible for a reflecting consciousness. Such a consciousness does not feel in any way delivered from the fear of God, and therefore asks itself, quite rightly, what Christ means to it. That, indeed, is the great question: can Christ still be interpreted in our day and age, or must one be satisfied with the historical interpretation?

663 One thing, anyway, cannot be doubted: Christ is a highly numinous figure. The interpretation of him as God and the son of God is in full accord with this. The old view, which is based on Christ's own view of the matter, asserts that he came into the world, suffered, and died in order to save mankind from the wrath to come. Furthermore he believed that his own bodily resurrection would assure all God's children of the same future.

664 We have already pointed out at some length how curiously God's salvationist project works out in practice. All he does is, in the shape of his own son, to rescue mankind from himself. This thought is as scurrilous as the old rabbinical view of Yahweh hiding the righteous from his wrath under his throne, where of course he cannot see them. It is exactly as if God the father were a different God from the son, which is not the meaning at all. Nor is there any psychological need for such an assumption, since the undoubted lack of reflection in God's consciousness is sufficient to explain his peculiar behaviour. It is quite right, therefore, that fear of God should be considered the beginning of all wisdom. On the other hand, the much-vaunted goodness, love, and justice of God should not be regarded as mere propitiation, but should be recognized as a genuine experience, for God is a *coincidentia oppositorum*. Both are justified, the fear of God as well as the love of God.

665 A more differentiated consciousness must, sooner or later, find it difficult to love, as a kind father, a God whom on account of his unpredictable fits of wrath, his unreliability, injustice, and cruelty, it has every reason to fear. The decay of the gods of antiquity has proved to our satisfaction that man does not relish any all-too-human inconsistencies and weaknesses in his gods. Likewise, it is probable that Yahweh's moral defeat in his dealings with Job had its hidden effects: man's unintended

elevation on the one hand, and on the other hand a disturbance of the unconscious. For a while the first-mentioned effect remains a mere fact, not consciously realized though registered by the unconscious. This contributes to the disturbance in the unconscious, which thereby acquires a higher potential than exists in consciousness. Man then counts for more in the unconscious than he does consciously. In these circumstances the potential starts flowing from the unconscious towards consciousness, and the unconscious breaks through in the form of dreams, visions, and revelations. Unfortunately the Book of Job cannot be dated with any certainty. As mentioned above, it was written somewhere between 600 and 300 B.C. During the first half of the sixth century, Ezekiel,[1] the prophet with the so-called "pathological" features, appears on the scene. Although laymen are inclined to apply this epithet to his visions, I must, as a psychiatrist, emphatically state that visions and their accompanying phenomena cannot be uncritically evaluated as morbid. Visions, like dreams, are unusual but quite natural occurrences which can be designated as "pathological" only when their morbid nature has been proved. From a strictly clinical standpoint Ezekiel's visions are of an archetypal nature and are not morbidly distorted in any way. There is no reason to regard them as pathological.[2] They are a symptom of the split which already existed at that time between conscious and unconscious. The first great vision is made up of two well-ordered compound quaternities, that is, conceptions of totality, such as we frequently observe today as spontaneous phenomena. Their *quinta essentia* is represented by a figure which has "the likeness of a human form." [3] Here Ezekiel has seen the essential content of the unconscious, namely *the idea of the higher man* by whom Yahweh was morally defeated and who he was later to become.

666 In India, a more or less simultaneous symptom of the same tendency was Gautama the Buddha (b. 562 B.C.), who gave the maximum differentiation of consciousness supremacy even over the highest Brahman gods. This development was a logical con-

1 The vision in which he received his call occurred in 592 B.C.

2 It is altogether wrong to assume that visions as such are pathological. They occur with normal people also—not very frequently, it is true, but they are by no means rare.

3 Ezekiel 1 : 26.

sequence of the *purusha-atman* doctrine and derived from the inner experience of yoga practice.

667 Ezekiel grasped, in a symbol, the fact that Yahweh was drawing closer to man. This is something which came to Job as an experience but probably did not reach his consciousness. That is to say, he did not realize that his consciousness was higher than Yahweh's, and that consequently God wants to become man. What is more, in Ezekiel we meet for the first time the title "Son of Man," which Yahweh significantly uses in addressing the prophet, presumably to indicate that he is a son of the "Man" on the throne, and hence a prefiguration of the much later revelation in Christ. It is with the greatest right, therefore, that the four seraphim on God's throne became the emblems of the evangelists, for they form the quaternity which expresses Christ's totality, just as the four gospels represent the four pillars of his throne.

668 The disturbance of the unconscious continued for several centuries. Around 165 B.C., Daniel had a vision of four beasts and the "Ancient of Days," to whom "with the clouds of heaven there came one like a son of man." [4] Here the "son of man" is no longer the prophet but a son of the "Ancient of Days" in his own right, and a son whose task it is to rejuvenate the father.

669 The Book of Enoch, written around 100 B.C., goes into considerably more detail. It gives a revealing account of the advance of the sons of God into the world of men, another prefiguration which has been described as the "fall of the angels." Whereas, according to Genesis,[5] Yahweh resolved that his spirit should not "abide in man for ever," and that men should not live to be hundreds of years old as they had before, the sons of God, by way of compensation, fell in love with the beautiful daughters of men. This happened at the time of the giants. Enoch relates that after conspiring with one another, two hundred angels under the leadership of Samiazaz descended to earth, took the daughters of men to wife, and begat with them giants three thousand ells long.[6] The angels, among whom Azazel particularly excelled, taught mankind the arts and sciences. They proved to be extraordinarily progressive elements who broadened and developed man's consciousness, just as the wicked Cain had stood for progress as contrasted with the stay-at-home

[4] Daniel 7 : 13. [5] Genesis 6 : 3f. [6] Enoch 7 : 2.

Abel. In this way they enlarged the significance of man to "gigantic" proportions, which points to an inflation of the cultural consciousness at that period. An inflation, however, is always threatened with a counter-stroke from the unconscious, and this actually did happen in the form of the Deluge. So corrupt was the earth before the Deluge that the giants "consumed all the acquisitions of men" and then began to devour each other, while men in their turn devoured the beasts, so that "the earth laid accusation against the lawless ones." [7]

670 The invasion of the human world by the sons of God therefore had serious consequences, which make Yahweh's precautions prior to his appearance on the earthly scene the more understandable. Man was completely helpless in face of this superior divine force. Hence it is of the greatest interest to see how Yahweh behaves in this matter. As the later Draconian punishment proves, it was a not unimportant event in the heavenly economy when no less than two hundred of the sons of God departed from the paternal household to carry out experiments on their own in the human world. One would have expected that information concerning this mass exodus would have trickled through to the court (quite apart from the fact of divine omniscience). But nothing of the sort happened. Only after the giants had long been begotten and had already started to slaughter and devour mankind did four archangels, apparently by accident, hear the weeping and wailing of men and discover what was going on on earth. One really does not know which is the more astonishing, the bad organization of the angelic hosts or the faulty communications in heaven. Be that as it may, this time the archangels felt impelled to appear before God with the following peroration:

All things are naked and open in Thy sight, and Thou seest all things, and nothing can hide itself from Thee. Thou seest what Azazel hath done, who taught all unrighteousness on earth and revealed the eternal secrets which were preserved in heaven. . . . [And enchantments hath Samiazaz taught], to whom Thou hast given authority to bear rule over his associates. . . . And Thou

[7] Enoch 7:3–6. [The translations of the Book of Enoch are from Charles, ed., *The Apocrypha and Pseudepigrapha of the Old Testament in English,* II, sometimes slightly modified.—TRANS.]

knowest all things before they come to pass, and Thou seest these things and Thou dost suffer them, and Thou dost not say to us what we are to do to them in regard to these.[8]

671 Either all that the archangels say is a lie, or Yahweh, for some incomprehensible reason, has drawn no conclusions from his omniscience, or—what is more likely—the archangels must remind him that once again he has preferred to know nothing of his omniscience. At any rate it is only on their intervention that retaliatory action is released on a global scale, but it is not really a just punishment, seeing that Yahweh promptly drowns all living creatures with the exception of Noah and his relatives. This intermezzo proves that the sons of God are somehow more vigilant, more progressive, and more conscious than their father. Yahweh's subsequent transformation is therefore to be rated all the higher. The preparations for his Incarnation give one the impression that he has really learnt something from experience and is setting about things more consciously than before. Undoubtedly the recollection of Sophia has contributed to this increase of consciousness. Parallel with this, the revelation of the metaphysical structure becomes more explicit. Whereas in Ezekiel and Daniel we find only vague hints about the quaternity and the Son of Man, Enoch gives us clear and detailed information on these points. The underworld, a sort of Hades, is divided into four hollow places which serve as abodes for the spirits of the dead until the Last Judgment. Three of these hollow places are dark, but one is bright and contains a "fountain of water." [9] This is the abode of the righteous.

672 With statements of this type we enter into a definitely psychological realm, namely that of mandala symbolism, to which also belong the ratios 1 : 3 and 3 : 4. The quadripartite Hades of Enoch corresponds to a chthonic quaternity, which presumably stands in everlasting contrast to a pneumatic or heavenly one. The former corresponds in alchemy to the *quaternio* of the elements, the latter to a fourfold, or total, aspect of the deity, as for instance Barbelo, Kolorbas, *Mercurius quadratus,* and the four-faced gods all indicate.

673 In fact, Enoch in his vision sees the four faces of God. Three

[8] Enoch 9:5–11. [9] 22:2.

of them are engaged in praising, praying, and supplicating, but the fourth in "fending off the Satans and forbidding them to come before the Lord of Spirits to accuse them who dwell on earth." [10]

674 The vision shows us an essential differentiation of the God-image: God now has four faces, or rather, four angels of his face, who are four hypostases or emanations, of which one is exclusively occupied in keeping his elder son Satan, now changed into many, away from him, and in preventing further experiments after the style of the Job episode.[11] The Satans still dwell in the heavenly regions, since the fall of Satan has not yet occurred. The above-mentioned proportions are also suggested here by the fact that three of the angels perform holy or beneficial functions, while the fourth is a militant figure who has to keep Satan at bay.

675 This quaternity has a distinctly pneumatic nature and is therefore expressed by angels, who are generally pictured with wings, i.e., as aerial beings. This is the more likely as they are presumably the descendants of Ezekiel's four seraphim.[12] The doubling and separation of the quaternity into an upper and a lower one, like the exclusion of the Satans from the heavenly court, points to a metaphysical split that had already taken place. But the pleromatic split is in its turn a symptom of a much deeper split in the divine will: the father wants to become the son, God wants to become man, the amoral wants to become exclusively good, the unconscious wants to become consciously responsible. So far everything exists only *in statu nascendi.*

676 Enoch's unconscious is vastly excited by all this and its contents burst out in a spate of apocalyptic visions. It also causes him to undertake the *peregrinatio,* the journey to the four quarters of heaven and to the centre of the earth, so that he draws a mandala with his own movements, in accordance with the "journeys" of the alchemistic philosophers and the corresponding fantasies of our modern unconscious.

677 When Yahweh addressed Ezekiel as "Son of Man," this was no more at first than a dark and enigmatic hint. But now it be-

10 Enoch 40:7.

11 Cf. also ch. 87f. Of the four "beings who were like white men," three take Enoch by the hand, while the other seizes a star and hurls it into the abyss.

12 Three had animal faces, one a human face.

comes clear: the man Enoch is not only the recipient of divine revelation but is at the same time a participant in the divine drama, as though he were at least one of the sons of God himself. This can only be taken as meaning that in the same measure as God sets out to become man, man is immersed in the pleromatic process. He becomes, as it were, baptized in it and is made to participate in the divine quaternity (i.e., is crucified with Christ). That is why even today, in the rite of the *benedictio fontis,* the water is divided into a cross by the hand of the priest and then sprinkled to the four quarters.

678 Enoch is so much under the influence of the divine drama, so gripped by it, that one could almost suppose he had a quite special understanding of the coming Incarnation. The "Son of Man" who is with the "Head [or Ancient] of Days" looks like an angel (i.e., like one of the sons of God). He "hath righteousness"; "with him dwelleth righteousness"; the Lord of Spirits has "chosen him"; "his lot hath the preeminence before the Lord of Spirits in uprightness." [13] It is probably no accident that so much stress is laid on righteousness, for it is the one quality that Yahweh lacks, a fact that could hardly have remained hidden from such a man as the author of the Book of Enoch. Under the reign of the Son of Man ". . . the prayer of the righteous has been heard, and the blood of the righteous . . . [avenged] before the Lord of Spirits." [14] Enoch sees a "fountain of righteousness which was inexhaustible." [15] The Son of Man

> . . . shall be a staff to the righteous. . . .
> For this reason hath he been chosen and hidden before
> him,
> Before the creation of the world and for evermore.
> And the wisdom of the Lord of Spirits hath revealed
> him . . . ,
> For he hath preserved the lot of the righteous.[16]
> For wisdom is poured out like water. . . .
> He is mighty in all the secrets of righteousness,
> And unrighteousness shall disappear as a shadow. . . .
> In him dwells the spirit of wisdom,

[13] Enoch 46 : 1–3. [14] 47 : 4. [15] 48 : 1. [16] 48 : 4, 6–7.

And the spirit which gives insight,
And the spirit of understanding and of might.[17]

679 Under the reign of the Son of Man

> . . . shall the earth also give back that which has been entrusted to it,
> And Sheol also shall give back that which it has received,
> And hell [18] shall give back that which it owes. . . .
>
> The Elect One shall in those days sit on My throne,
> And his mouth shall pour forth all the secrets of wisdom and counsel.[19]

680 "All shall become angels in heaven." Azazel and his hosts shall be cast into the burning fiery furnace for "becoming subject to Satan and leading astray those who dwell on the earth." [20]

681 At the end of the world the Son of Man shall sit in judgment over all creatures. "The darkness shall be destroyed, and the light established for ever." [21] Even Yahweh's two big exhibits, Leviathan and Behemoth, are forced to succumb: they are carved up and eaten. In this passage [22] Enoch is addressed by the revealing angel with the title "Son of Man," a further indication that he, like Ezekiel, has been assimilated by the divine mystery, is included in it, as is already suggested by the bare fact that he witnesses it. Enoch is wafted away and takes his seat in heaven. In the "heaven of heavens" he beholds the house of God built of crystal, with streams of living fire about it, and guarded by winged beings that never sleep.[23] The "Head of Days" comes forth with the angelic quaternity (Michael, Gabriel, Raphael, Phanuel) and speaks to him, saying: "This is the Son of Man who is born unto righteousness, and righteousness abides over him, and the righteousness of the Head of Days forsakes him not." [24]

682 It is remarkable that the Son of Man and what he means should be associated again and again with righteousness. It seems to be his leitmotif, his chief concern. Only where injustice

17 Enoch 49:1–3. 18 Synonym for Sheol. 19 51:1, 3.
20 54:6. Here at last we hear that the exodus of the two hundred angels was a prank of Satan's.
21 58:6 (mod.). 22 60:10. 23 71:5–6. 24 71:14.

threatens or has already occurred does such an emphasis on righteousness make any sense. No one, only God, can dispense justice to any noticeable degree, and precisely with regard to him there exists the justifiable fear that he may forget his justice. In this case his righteous son would intercede with him on man's behalf. Thus "the righteous shall have peace."[25] The justice that shall prevail under the son is stressed to such an extent that one has the impression that formerly, under the reign of the father, injustice was paramount, and that only with the son is the era of law and order inaugurated. It looks as though, with this, Enoch had unconsciously given an answer to Job.

683 The emphasis laid on God's agedness is logically connected with the existence of a son, but it also suggests that he himself will step a little into the background and leave the government of the human world more and more to the son, in the hope that a juster order will emerge. From all this we can see the after-effects of some psychological trauma, the memory of an injustice that cries to heaven and beclouds the intimate relationship with God. God himself wants a son, and man also wants a son to take the place of the father. This son must, as we have conclusively seen, be absolutely just, and this quality is given priority over all other virtues. God and man both want to escape from blind injustice.

684 Enoch, in his ecstasy, recognizes himself as the Son of Man, or as the son of God, although neither by birth nor by predestination does he seem to have been chosen for such a role.[26] He experiences that godlike elevation which, in the case of Job, we merely assumed, or rather inferred as the inevitable outcome. Job himself seems to have suspected something of the sort when he declares: "I know that my Vindicator lives."[27] This highly remarkable statement can, under the circumstances, only refer to the benevolent Yahweh. The traditional Christian interpretation of this passage as an anticipation of Christ is correct in so far as Yahweh's benevolent aspect incarnates itself, as its own hypostasis, in the Son of Man, and in so far as the Son of Man

[25] 71:17.

[26] The author of the Book of Enoch chose, as the hero of his tale, Enoch the son of Jared, the seventh after Adam, who "walked with God," and, instead of dying, simply disappeared, i.e., was carried away by God (". . . and he was not, for God took him."—Genesis 5:24).

[27] Job 19:25.

proves in Enoch to be a representative of justice and, in Christianity, the justifier of mankind. Furthermore, the Son of Man is pre-existent, and therefore Job could very well appeal to him. Just as Satan plays the role of accuser and slanderer, so Christ, God's other son, plays the role of advocate and defender.

685 Despite the contradiction, certain scholars have wished to see Enoch's Messianic ideas as Christian interpolations. For psychological reasons this suspicion seems to me unjustified. One has only to consider what Yahweh's injustice, his downright immorality, must have meant to a devout thinker. It was no laughing matter to be burdened with such an idea of God. A much later document tells us of a pious sage who could never read the Eighty-ninth Psalm, "because he could not bear it." When one considers with what intensity and exclusiveness not only Christ's teaching, but the doctrines of the Church in the following centuries down to the present day, have emphasized the goodness of the loving Father in heaven, the deliverance from fear, the Summum Bonum, and the *privatio boni,* one can form some conception of the incompatibility which the figure of Yahweh presents, and see how intolerable such a paradox must appear to the religious consciousness. And this has probably been so ever since the days of Job.

686 The inner instability of Yahweh is the prime cause not only of the creation of the world, but also of the pleromatic drama for which mankind serves as a tragic chorus. The encounter with the creature changes the creator. In the Old Testament writings we find increasing traces of this development from the sixth century B.C. on. The two main climaxes are formed firstly by the Job tragedy, and secondly by Ezekiel's revelation. Job is the innocent sufferer, but Ezekiel witnesses the humanization and differentiation of Yahweh. By being addressed as "Son of Man," it is intimated to him that Yahweh's incarnation in the quaternity is, so to speak, the pleromatic model for what is going to happen, through the transformation and humanization of God, not only to God's son as foreseen from all eternity, but to man as such. This is fulfilled as an intuitive anticipation in Enoch. In his ecstasy he becomes the Son of Man in the pleroma, and his wafting away in a chariot (like Elijah) prefigures the resurrection of the dead. To fulfil his role as minister of justice he must get into immediate proximity to God, and as the pre-

existing Son of Man he is no longer subject to death. But in so far as he was an ordinary human being and therefore mortal, other mortals as well as he can attain to the vision of God; they too can become conscious of their saviour, and consequently immortal.

687 All these ideas could easily have become conscious at the time on the basis of the assumptions then current, if only someone had seriously reflected on them. For that no Christian interpolations were needed. The Book of Enoch was an anticipation in the grand manner, but everything still hung in mid air as mere revelation that never came down to earth. In view of these facts one cannot, with the best will in the world, see how Christianity, as we hear over and over again, is supposed to have burst upon world history as an absolute novelty. If ever anything had been historically prepared, and sustained and supported by the existing *Weltanschauung*, Christianity would be a classic example.

XII

688 Jesus first appears as a Jewish reformer and prophet of an exclusively good God. In so doing he saves the threatened religious continuity, and in this respect he does in fact prove himself a σωτήρ, a saviour. He preserves mankind from loss of communion with God and from getting lost in mere consciousness and rationality. That would have brought something like a dissociation between consciousness and the unconscious, an unnatural and even pathological condition, a "loss of soul" such as has threatened man from the beginning of time. Again and again and in increasing measure he gets into danger of overlooking the necessary irrationalities of his psyche, and of imagining that he can control everything by will and reason alone, and thus paddle his own canoe. This can be seen most clearly in the great socio-political movements, such as Socialism and Communism: under the former the state suffers, and under the latter, man.

689 Jesus, it is plain, translated the existing tradition into his own personal reality, announcing the glad tidings: "God has good pleasure in mankind. He is a loving father and loves you as I love you, and has sent me as his son to ransom you from the

old debt." He offers himself as an expiatory sacrifice that shall effect the reconciliation with God. The more desirable a real relationship of trust between man and God, the more astonishing becomes Yahweh's vindictiveness and irreconcilability towards his creatures. From a God who is a loving father, who is actually Love itself, one would expect understanding and forgiveness. So it comes as a nasty shock when this supremely good God only allows the purchase of such an act of grace through a human sacrifice, and, what is worse, through the killing of his own son. Christ apparently overlooked this anticlimax; at any rate all succeeding centuries have accepted it without opposition. One should keep before one's eyes the strange fact that the God of goodness is so unforgiving that he can only be appeased by a human sacrifice! This is an insufferable incongruity which modern man can no longer swallow, for he must be blind if he does not see the glaring light it throws on the divine character, giving the lie to all talk about love and the Summum Bonum.

690 Christ proves to be a mediator in two ways: he helps men against God and assuages the fear which man feels towards this being. He holds an important position midway between the two extremes, man and God, which are so difficult to unite. Clearly the focus of the divine drama shifts to the mediating God-man. He is lacking neither in humanity nor in divinity, and for this reason he was long ago characterized by totality symbols, because he was understood to be all-embracing and to unite all opposites. The quaternity of the Son of Man, indicating a more differentiated consciousness, was also ascribed to him (*vide* Cross and tetramorph). This corresponds by and large to the pattern in Enoch, but with one important deviation: Ezekiel and Enoch, the two bearers of the title "Son of Man," were ordinary human beings, whereas Christ by his descent,[1] conception, and birth is a hero and half-god in the classical sense. He is virginally begotten by the Holy Ghost and, as he is not a creaturely human being, has no inclination to sin. The infection of evil was in his case precluded by the preparations for the Incarnation. Christ therefore stands more on the divine than on the human level. He incarnates God's good will to the exclusion of all else and therefore does not stand exactly in the middle, because the essen-

[1] As a consequence of her immaculate conception Mary is already different from other mortals, and this fact is confirmed by her assumption.

tial thing about the creaturely human being, sin, does not touch him. Sin originally came from the heavenly court and entered into creation with the help of Satan, which enraged Yahweh to such an extent that in the end his own son had to be sacrificed in order to placate him. Strangely enough, he took no steps to remove Satan from his entourage. In Enoch a special archangel, Phanuel, was charged with the task of defending Yahweh from Satan's insinuations, and only at the end of the world shall Satan, in the shape of a star,[2] be bound hand and foot, cast into the abyss, and destroyed. (This is not the case in the Book of Revelation, where he remains eternally alive in his natural element.)

691 Although it is generally assumed that Christ's unique sacrifice broke the curse of original sin and finally placated God, Christ nevertheless seems to have had certain misgivings in this respect. What will happen to man, and especially to his own followers, when the sheep have lost their shepherd, and when they miss the one who interceded for them with the father? He assures his disciples that he will always be with them, nay more, that he himself abides within them. Nevertheless this does not seem to satisfy him completely, for in addition he promises to send them from the father another παράκλητος (advocate, "Counsellor"), in his stead, who will assist them by word and deed and remain with them forever.[3] One might conjecture from this that the "legal position" has still not been cleared up beyond a doubt, or that there still exists a factor of uncertainty.

692 The sending of the Paraclete has still another aspect. This Spirit of Truth and Wisdom is the Holy Ghost by whom Christ was begotten. He is the spirit of physical and spiritual procreation who from now on shall make his abode in creaturely man. Since he is the Third Person of the Deity, this is as much as to say that *God will be begotten in creaturely man.* This implies a tremendous change in man's status, for he is now raised to sonship and almost to the position of a man-god. With this the prefiguration in Ezekiel and Enoch, where, as we saw, the title "Son of Man" was already conferred on the creaturely man, is fulfilled. But that puts man, despite his continuing sinfulness, in

[2] Presumably the "morning star" (cf. Revelation 2:28 and 22:16). This is the planet Venus in her psychological implications and not, as one might think, either of the two *malefici,* Saturn and Mars.

[3] John 14:16.

the position of the mediator, the unifier of God and creature. Christ probably had this incalculable possibility in mind when he said: ". . . . he who believes in me, will also do the works that I do; and greater works than these will he do," [4] and, referring to the sixth verse of the Eighty-second Psalm, "I say, 'You are gods, sons of the Most High, all of you,' " he added, "and scripture cannot be broken." [5]

693 The future indwelling of the Holy Ghost in man amounts to a continuing incarnation of God. Christ, as the begotten son of God and pre-existing mediator, is a first-born and a divine paradigm which will be followed by further incarnations of the Holy Ghost in the empirical man. But man participates in the darkness of the world, and therefore, with Christ's death, a critical situation arises which might well be a cause for anxiety. When God became man all darkness and evil were carefully kept outside. Enoch's transformation into the Son of Man took place entirely in the realm of light, and to an even greater extent this is true of the incarnation in Christ. It is highly unlikely that the bond between God and man was broken with the death of Christ; on the contrary, the continuity of this bond is stressed again and again and is further confirmed by the sending of the Paraclete. But the closer this bond becomes, the closer becomes the danger of a collision with evil. On the basis of a belief that had existed quite early, the expectation grew up that the light manifestation would be followed by an equally dark one, and Christ by an Antichrist. Such an opinion is the last thing one would expect from the metaphysical situation, for the power of evil is supposedly overcome, and one can hardly believe that a loving father, after the whole complicated arrangement of salvation in Christ, the atonement and declaration of love for mankind, would again let loose his evil watch-dog on his children in complete disregard of all that had gone before. Why this wearisome forbearance towards Satan? Why this stubborn projection of evil on man, whom he has made so weak, so faltering, and so stupid that we are quite incapable of resisting his wicked sons? Why not pull up evil by the roots?

694 God, with his good intentions, begot a good and helpful son and thus created an image of himself as the good father—unfortunately, we must admit, again without considering that there

4 John 14 : 12. 5 10 : 35.

existed in him a knowledge that spoke a very different truth. Had he only given an account of his action to himself, he would have seen what a fearful dissociation he had got into through his incarnation. Where, for instance, did his darkness go—that darkness by means of which Satan always manages to escape his well-earned punishment? Does he think he is completely changed and that his amorality has fallen from him? Even his "light" son, Christ, did not quite trust him in this respect. So now he sends to men the "spirit of truth," with whose help they will discover soon enough what happens when God incarnates only in his light aspect and believes he is goodness itself, or at least wants to be regarded as such. An enantiodromia in the grand style is to be expected. This may well be the meaning of the belief in the coming of the Antichrist, which we owe more than anything else to the activity of the "spirit of truth."

695 Although the Paraclete is of the greatest significance metaphysically, it was, from the point of view of the organization of the Church, most undesirable, because, as is authoritatively stated in scripture, the Holy Ghost is not subject to any control. In the interests of continuity and the Church the uniqueness of the incarnation and of Christ's work of redemption has to be strongly emphasized, and for the same reason the continuing indwelling of the Holy Ghost is discouraged and ignored as much as possible. No further individualistic digressions can be tolerated. Anyone who is inclined by the Holy Ghost towards dissident opinions necessarily becomes a heretic, whose persecution and elimination take a turn very much to Satan's liking. On the other hand one must realize that if everybody had tried to thrust the intuitions of his own private Holy Ghost upon others for the improvement of the universal doctrine, Christianity would rapidly have perished in a Babylonian confusion of tongues—a fate that lay threateningly close for many centuries.

696 It is the task of the Paraclete, the "spirit of truth," to dwell and work in individual human beings, so as to remind them of Christ's teachings and lead them into the light. A good example of this activity is Paul, who knew not the Lord and received his gospel not from the apostles but through revelation. He is one of those people whose unconscious was disturbed and produced revelatory ecstasies. The life of the Holy Ghost reveals itself through its own activity, and through effects which not

only confirm the things we all know, but go beyond them. In Christ's sayings there are already indications of ideas which go beyond the traditionally "Christian" morality—for instance the parable of the unjust steward, the moral of which agrees with the Logion of the Codex Bezae,[6] and betrays an ethical standard very different from what is expected. Here the moral criterion is *consciousness,* and not law or convention. One might also mention the strange fact that it is precisely Peter, who lacks self-control and is fickle in character, whom Christ wishes to make the rock and foundation of his Church. These seem to me to be ideas which point to the inclusion of evil in what I would call a *differential moral valuation.* For instance, it is good if evil is sensibly covered up, but to act unconsciously is evil. One might almost suppose that such views were intended for a time when consideration is given to evil as well as to good, or rather, when it is not suppressed below the threshold in the dubious assumption that we always know exactly what evil is.

697 Again, the expectation of the Antichrist is a far-reaching revelation or discovery, like the remarkable statement that despite his fall and exile the devil is still "prince of this world" and has his habitation in the all-surrounding air. In spite of his misdeeds and in spite of God's work of redemption for mankind, the devil still maintains a position of considerable power and holds all sublunary creatures under his sway. This situation can only be described as critical; at any rate it does not correspond to what could reasonably have been expected from the "glad tidings." Evil is by no means fettered, even though its days are numbered. God still hesitates to use force against Satan. Presumably he still does not know how much his own dark side favours the evil angel. Naturally this situation could not remain indefinitely hidden from the "spirit of truth" who has taken up his abode in man. He therefore created a disturbance in man's unconscious and produced, at the beginning of the Christian era, another great revelation which, because of its obscurity, gave rise to numerous interpretations and misinterpretations in the centuries that followed. This is the Revelation of St. John.

6 An apocryphal insertion at Luke 6:4. ["Man, if indeed thou knowest what thou doest, thou art blessed; but if thou knowest not, thou art cursed, and a transgressor of the law" (trans. in James, *The Apocryphal New Testament,* p. 33).—TRANS.]

XIII

698 One could hardly imagine a more suitable personality for the John of the Apocalypse than the author of the Epistles of John. It was he who declared that God is light and that "in him is no darkness at all." [1] (Who said there was any darkness in God?) Nevertheless, he knows that when we sin we need an "advocate with the Father," and this is Christ, "the expiation for our sins," [2] even though for his sake our sins are already forgiven. (Why then do we need an advocate?) The Father has bestowed his great love upon us (though it had to be bought at the cost of a human sacrifice!), and we are the children of God. He who is begotten by God commits no sin.[3] (Who commits *no* sin?) John then preaches the message of love. God himself is love; perfect love casteth out fear. But he must warn against false prophets and teachers of false doctrines, and it is he who announces the coming of the Antichrist.[4] His conscious attitude is orthodox, but he has evil forebodings. He might easily have dreams that are not listed on his conscious programme. He talks as if he knew not only a sinless state but also a perfect love, unlike Paul, who was not lacking in the necessary self-reflection. John is a bit too sure, and therefore he runs the risk of a dissociation. Under these circumstances a counterposition is bound to grow up in the unconscious, which can then irrupt into consciousness in the form of a revelation. If this happens, the revelation will take the form of a more or less subjective myth, because, among other things, it compensates the one-sidedness of an individual consciousness. This contrasts with the visions of Ezekiel or Enoch, whose conscious situation was mainly characterized by an ignorance (for which they were not to blame) and was therefore compensated by a more or less objective and universally valid configuration of archetypal material.

699 So far as we can see, the Apocalypse conforms to these conditions. Even in the initial vision a fear-inspiring figure appears: Christ blended with the Ancient of Days, having the likeness of a man and the Son of Man. Out of his mouth goes a "sharp two-edged sword," which would seem more suitable for fighting and the shedding of blood than for demonstrating brotherly

[1] I John 1:5. [2] 2:1–2. [3] 3:9. [4] 2:18f., 4:3.

love. Since this Christ says to him, "Fear not," we must assume that John was not overcome by love when he fell "as though dead," [5] but rather by fear. (What price now the perfect love which casts out fear?)

700 Christ commands him to write seven epistles to the churches in the province of Asia. The church in Ephesus is admonished to repent; otherwise it is threatened with deprivation of the light ("I will come . . . and remove your candlestick from its place").[6] We also learn from this letter that Christ "hates" the Nicolaitans. (How does this square with love of your neighbour?)

701 The church in Smyrna does not come off so badly. Its enemies supposedly are Jews, but they are "a synagogue of Satan," which does not sound too friendly.

702 Pergamum is censured because a teacher of false doctrines is making himself conspicuous there, and the place swarms with Nicolaitans. Therefore it must repent—"if not, I will come to you soon." This can only be interpreted as a threat.

703 Thyatira tolerates the preaching of "that woman Jezebel, who calls herself a prophetess." He will "throw her on a sickbed" and "strike her children dead." But "he who . . . keeps my works until the end, I will give him power over the nations, and he shall rule them with a rod of iron, as when earthen pots are broken in pieces, even as I myself have received power from my Father; and I will give him the morning star." [7] Christ, as we know, teaches "Love your enemies," but here he threatens a massacre of children all too reminiscent of Bethlehem!

704 The works of the church in Sardis are not perfect before God. Therefore, "repent." Otherwise he will come like a thief, "and you will not know at what hour I will come upon you" [8]—a none too friendly warning.

705 In regard to Philadelphia, there is nothing to be censured. But Laodicea he will spew out of his mouth, because they are lukewarm. They too must repent. His explanation is characteristic: "Those whom I love, I reprove and chasten." [9] It would be quite understandable if the Laodiceans did not want too much of this "love."

706 Five of the seven churches get bad reports. This apocalyptic "Christ" behaves rather like a bad-tempered, power-conscious

[5] Cf. Rev. 1:16–17. [6] Rev. 2:5. [7] 2:20f. [8] 3:3. [9] 3:19.

"boss" who very much resembles the "shadow" of a love-preaching bishop.

707 As if in confirmation of what I have said, there now follows a vision in the style of Ezekiel. But he who sat upon the throne did not look like a man, but was to look upon "like jasper and carnelian." [10] Before him was "a sea of glass, like crystal"; around the throne, four "living creatures" (ζῷα), which were "full of eyes in front and behind . . . all round and within." [11] The symbol of Ezekiel appears here strangely modified: stone, glass, crystal—dead and rigid things deriving from the inorganic realm—characterize the Deity. One is inevitably reminded of the preoccupation of the alchemists during the following centuries, when the mysterious "Man," the *homo altus,* was named λίθος οὐ λίθος, 'the stone that is no stone,' and multiple eyes gleamed in the ocean of the unconscious.[12] At any rate, something of John's psychology comes in here, which has caught a glimpse of things beyond the Christian cosmos.

708 Hereupon follows the opening of the Book with Seven Seals by the "Lamb." The latter has put off the human features of the "Ancient of Days" and now appears in purely theriomorphic but monstrous form, like one of the many other horned animals in the Book of Revelation. It has seven eyes and seven horns, and is therefore more like a ram than a lamb. Altogether it must have looked pretty awful. Although it is described as "standing, as though it had been slain," [13] it does not behave at all like an innocent victim, but in a very lively manner indeed. From the first four seals it lets loose the four sinister apocalyptic horsemen. With the opening of the fifth seal, we hear the martyrs crying for vengeance ("O sovereign Lord, holy and true, how long before thou wilt judge and avenge our blood on those who dwell upon the earth?").[14] The sixth seal brings a cosmic catastrophe, and everything hides from the "wrath of the Lamb," "for the great day of his wrath is come." [15] We no longer recognize the meek Lamb who lets himself be led unresistingly to the slaughter; there is only the aggressive and irascible ram whose rage can at last be vented. In all this I see less a metaphysical

[10] 4:3. [11] 4:6f.

[12] This refers to the "luminosity" of the archetypes. [Cf. Jung, "On the Nature of the Psyche" (1954/55 edn., pp. 401ff.).—EDITORS.]

[13] Rev. 5:6. [14] 6:10. [15] 6:17 (AV).

mystery than the outburst of long pent-up negative feelings such as can frequently be observed in people who strive for perfection. We can take it as certain that the author of the Epistles of John made every effort to practise what he preached to his fellow Christians. For this purpose he had to shut out all negative feelings, and, thanks to a helpful lack of self-reflection, he was able to forget them. But though they disappeared from the conscious level they continued to rankle beneath the surface, and in the course of time spun an elaborate web of resentments and vengeful thoughts which then burst upon consciousness in the form of a revelation. From this there grew up a terrifying picture that blatantly contradicts all ideas of Christian humility, tolerance, love of your neighbour and your enemies, and makes nonsense of a loving father in heaven and rescuer of mankind. A veritable orgy of hatred, wrath, vindictiveness, and blind destructive fury that revels in fantastic images of terror breaks out and with blood and fire overwhelms a world which Christ had just endeavoured to restore to the original state of innocence and loving communion with God.

709 The opening of the seventh seal naturally brings a new flood of miseries which threaten to exhaust even St. John's unholy imagination. As if to fortify himself, he must now eat a "little scroll" in order to go on with his "prophesying."

710 When the seventh angel had finally ceased blowing his trumpet, there appeared in heaven, after the destruction of Jerusalem, a vision of the *sun-woman,* "with the moon under her feet, and on her head a crown of twelve stars." [16] She was in the pangs of birth, and before her stood a great red dragon that wanted to devour her child.

711 This vision is altogether out of context. Whereas with the previous visions one has the impression that they were afterwards revised, rearranged, and embellished, one feels that this image is original and not intended for any educational purpose. The vision is introduced by the opening of the temple in heaven and the sight of the Ark of the Covenant.[17] This is probably a prelude to the descent of the heavenly bride, Jerusalem, an equivalent of Sophia, for it is all part of the heavenly *hieros gamos,* whose fruit is a divine man-child. He is threatened with the fate of Apollo, the son of Leto, who was likewise pursued

16 Rev. 12:1.

17 Rev. 11:19. The *arca foederis* is an *allegoria Mariae.*

by a dragon. But here we must dwell for a moment on the figure of the mother. She is "a woman clothed with the sun." Note the simple statement "a woman"—an ordinary woman, not a goddess and not an eternal virgin immaculately conceived. No special precautions exempting her from complete womanhood are noticeable, except the cosmic and naturalistic attributes which mark her as an *anima mundi* and peer of the primordial cosmic man, or Anthropos. She is the feminine Anthropos, the counterpart of the masculine principle. The pagan Leto motif is eminently suited to illustrate this, for in Greek mythology matriarchal and patriarchal elements are about equally mixed. The stars above, the moon below, in the middle the sun, the rising Horus and the setting Osiris, and the maternal night all round, *οὐρανὸς ἄνω, οὐρανὸς κάτω*[18]—this symbolism reveals the whole mystery of the "woman": she contains in her darkness the sun of "masculine" consciousness, which rises as a child out of the nocturnal sea of the unconscious, and as an old man sinks into it again. She adds the dark to the light, symbolizes the hierogamy of opposites, and reconciles nature with spirit.

712 The son who is born of these heavenly nuptials is perforce a *complexio oppositorum,* a uniting symbol, a totality of life. John's unconscious, certainly not without reason, borrowed from Greek mythology in order to describe this strange eschatological experience, for it was not on any account to be confused with the birth of the Christ-child which had occurred long before under quite different circumstances. Though obviously the allusion is to the "wrathful Lamb," i.e., the apocalyptic Christ, the new-born man-child is represented as his duplicate, as one who will "rule the nations with a rod of iron."[19] He is thus assimilated to the predominant feelings of hatred and vengeance, so that it looks as if he will needlessly continue to wreak his judgment even in the distant future. This interpretation does not seem consistent, because the Lamb is already charged with this task and, in the course of the revelation, carries it to an end without the newborn man-child ever having an opportunity to act on his own. He never reappears afterwards. I am therefore inclined to believe that the depiction of him as a son of vengeance, if it is not an interpretative interpolation, must have been a familiar phrase to John and that it slipped out as

18 "Heaven above, heaven below."

19 Rev. 12:5; cf. 2:27.

the obvious interpretation. This is the more probable in that the intermezzo could not at the time have been understood in any other way, even though this interpretation is quite meaningless. As I have already pointed out, the sun-woman episode is a foreign body in the flow of the visions. Therefore, I believe, it is not too far-fetched to conjecture that the author of the Apocalypse, or perhaps a perplexed transcriber, felt the need to interpret this obvious parallel with Christ and somehow bring it into line with the text as a whole. This could easily be done by using the familiar image of the shepherd with the iron crook. I cannot see any other reason for this association.

713 The man-child is "caught up" to God, who is manifestly his father, and the mother is hidden in the wilderness. This would seem to indicate that the child-figure will remain latent for an indefinite time and that its activity is reserved for the future. The story of Hagar may be a prefiguration of this. The similarity between this story and the birth of Christ obviously means no more than that the birth of the man-child is an analogous event, like the previously mentioned enthronement of the Lamb in all his metaphysical glory, which must have taken place long before at the time of the ascension. In the same way the dragon, i.e., the devil, is described as being thrown down to earth,[20] although Christ had already observed the fall of Satan very much earlier. This strange repetition or duplication of the characteristic events in Christ's life gave rise to the conjecture that a second Messiah is to be expected at the end of the world. What is meant here cannot be the return of Christ himself, for we are told that he would come "in the clouds of heaven," but not be *born* a second time, and certainly not from a sun-moon conjunction. The epiphany at the end of the world corresponds more to the content of Revelation 1 and 19:11ff. The fact that John uses the myth of Leto and Apollo in describing the birth may be an indication that the vision, in contrast to the Christian tradition, is a product of the unconscious.[21] But in the unconscious is everything that has been rejected by consciousness, and the more Christian one's consciousness is, the more heathenishly does the

20 Rev. 12:9.

21 It is very probable that John knew the Leto myth and used it consciously. What was unconscious and most unexpected, however, was the fact that his unconscious used this pagan myth to describe the birth of the second Messiah.

unconscious behave, if in the rejected heathenism there are values which are important for life—if, that is to say, the baby has been thrown out with the bath water, as so often happens. The unconscious does not isolate or differentiate its objects as consciousness does. It does not think abstractly or apart from the subject: the person of the ecstatic or visionary is always drawn into the process and included in it. In this case it is John himself whose unconscious personality is more or less identified with Christ; that is to say, he is born like Christ, and born to a like destiny. John is so completely captivated by the archetype of the divine son that he sees its activity in the unconscious; in other words, he sees how God is born again in the (partly pagan) unconscious, indistinguishable from the self of John, since the "divine child" is a symbol of the one as much as the other, just as Christ is. Consciously, of course, John was very far from thinking of Christ as a symbol. For the believing Christian, Christ is everything, but certainly not a symbol, which is an expression for something unknown or not yet knowable. And yet he is a symbol by his very nature. Christ would never have made the impression he did on his followers if he had not expressed something that was alive and at work in their unconscious. Christianity itself would never have spread through the pagan world with such astonishing rapidity had its ideas not found an analogous psychic readiness to receive them. It is this fact which also makes it possible to say that whoever believes in Christ is not only contained in him, but that Christ then dwells in the believer as the perfect man formed in the image of God, the second Adam. Psychologically, it is the same relationship as that in Indian philosophy between man's ego-consciousness and *purusha*, or *atman*. It is the ascendency of the "complete"—τέλειος—or total human being, consisting of the totality of the psyche, of conscious and unconscious, over the ego, which represents only consciousness and its contents and knows nothing of the unconscious, although in many respects it is dependent on the unconscious and is often decisively influenced by it. This relationship of the self to the ego is reflected in the relationship of Christ to man. Hence the unmistakable analogies between certain Indian and Christian ideas, which have given rise to conjectures of Indian influence on Christianity.

714 This parallelism, which has so far remained latent in John,

now bursts into consciousness in the form of a vision. That this invasion is authentic can be seen from the use of pagan mythological material, a most improbable procedure for a Christian of that time, especially as it contains traces of astrological influence. That may explain the thoroughly pagan remark, "And the earth helped the woman." [22] Even though the consciousness of that age was exclusively filled with Christian ideas, earlier or contemporaneous pagan contents lay just below the surface, as for example in the case of St. Perpetua.[23] With a Judaeo-Christian—and the author of the Apocalypse was probably such—another possible model to be considered is the cosmic Sophia, to whom John refers on more than one occasion. She could easily be taken as the mother of the divine child,[24] since she is obviously a woman in heaven, i.e., a goddess or consort of a god. Sophia comes up to this definition, and so does the transfigured Mary. If the vision were a modern dream one would not hesitate to interpret the birth of the divine child as the coming to consciousness of the self. In John's case the conscious attitude of faith made it possible for the Christ-image to be received into the material of the unconscious; it activated the archetype of the divine virgin mother and of the birth of her son-lover, and brought it face to face with his Christian consciousness. As a result, John became personally involved in the divine drama.

715 His Christ-image, clouded by negative feelings, has turned into a savage avenger who no longer bears any real resemblance to a saviour. One is not at all sure whether this Christ-figure may not in the end have more of the human John in it, with his compensating shadow, than of the divine saviour who, as the *lumen de lumine,* contains "no darkness." The grotesque paradox of the "wrathful Lamb" should have been enough to arouse our suspicions in this respect. We can turn and twist it as we like, but, seen in the light of the gospel of love, the avenger and judge remains a most sinister figure. This, one suspects, may have been the reason which moved John to assimilate the newborn man-child to the figure of the avenger, thereby blurring his mythological character as the lovely and lovable divine youth

22 Rev. 12 : 16 (AV).

23 [Cf. Marie-Louise von Franz, "Die Passio Perpetuae."—EDITORS.]

24 The son would then correspond to the *filius sapientiae* of medieval alchemy.

whom we know so well in the figures of Tammuz, Adonis, and Balder. The enchanting springlike beauty of this divine youth is one of those pagan values which we miss so sorely in Christianity, and particularly in the sombre world of the apocalypse—the indescribable morning glory of a day in spring, which after the deathly stillness of winter causes the earth to put forth and blossom, gladdens the heart of man and makes him believe in a kind and loving God.

716 As a totality, the self is by definition always a *complexio oppositorum,* and the more consciousness insists on its own luminous nature and lays claim to moral authority, the more the self will appear as something dark and menacing. We may assume such a condition in John, since he was a shepherd of his flock and also a fallible human being. Had the apocalypse been a more or less personal affair of John's, and hence nothing but an outburst of personal resentment, the figure of the wrathful Lamb would have satisfied this need completely. Under those conditions the new-born man-child would have been bound to have a noticeably positive aspect, because, in accordance with his symbolic nature, he would have compensated the intolerable devastation wrought by the outburst of long pent-up passions, being the child of the conjunction of opposites, of the sunfilled day world and the moonlit night world. He would have acted as a mediator between the loving and the vengeful sides of John's nature, and would thus have become a beneficent saviour who restored the balance. This positive aspect, however, must have escaped John's notice, otherwise he could never have conceived of the child as standing on the same level as the avenging Christ.

717 But John's problem was not a personal one. It was not a question of his personal unconscious or of an outburst of ill humour, but of visions which came up from a far greater and more comprehensive depth, namely from the collective unconscious. His problem expresses itself far too much in collective and archetypal forms for us to reduce it to a merely personal situation. To do so would be altogether too easy as well as being wrong in theory and practice. As a Christian, John was seized by a collective, archetypal process, and he must therefore be explained first and foremost in that light. He certainly also had his personal psychology, into which we, if we may regard the

author of the Epistles and the apocalyptist as one and the same person, have some insight. That the imitation of Christ creates a corresponding shadow in the unconscious hardly needs demonstrating. The fact that John had visions at all is evidence of an unusual tension between conscious and unconscious. If he is identical with the author of the Epistles, he must have been quite old when he wrote the Book of Revelation. *In confinio mortis* and in the evening of a long and eventful life a man will often see immense vistas of time stretching out before him. Such a man no longer lives in the everyday world and in the vicissitudes of personal relationships, but in the sight of many aeons and in the movement of ideas as they pass from century to century. The eye of John penetrates into the distant future of the Christian aeon and into the dark abyss of those forces which his Christianity kept in equilibrium. What burst upon him is the storm of the times, the premonition of a tremendous enantiodromia which he could only understand as the final annihilation of the darkness which had not comprehended the light that appeared in Christ. He failed to see that the power of destruction and vengeance is that very darkness from which God had split himself off when he became man. Therefore he could not understand, either, what that sun-moon-child meant, and he could only interpret it as another figure of vengeance. The passion that breaks through in his revelation bears no trace of the feebleness or serenity of old age, because it is infinitely more than personal resentment: it is the spirit of God itself, which blows through the weak mortal frame and again demands man's *fear* of the unfathomable Godhead.

XIV

718 The torrent of negative feelings seems to be inexhaustible, and the dire events continue their course. Out of the sea come monsters "with horns" (i.e., endowed with power), the horrid progeny of the deep. Faced with all this darkness and destruction, man's terrified consciousness quite understandably looks round for a mountain of refuge, an island of peace and safety. John therefore weaves in a vision of the Lamb on Mount Zion, where the hundred and forty-four thousand elect and redeemed

are gathered round the Lamb.[1] They are the παρθένοι, the male virgins, "which were not defiled with women." [2] They are the ones who, following in the footsteps of the young dying god, have never become complete human beings, but have voluntarily renounced their share in the human lot and have said no to the continuance of life on earth.[3] If everyone were converted to this point of view, man as a species would die out in a few decades. But of such preordained ones there are relatively few. John believed in predestination in accordance with higher authority. This is rank pessimism.

Everything created
Is worth being liquidated

says Mephisto.

719 This only moderately comforting prospect is immediately interrupted by the warning angels. The first angel proclaims an "everlasting gospel," the quintessence of which is "Fear God!" There is no more talk of God's love. What is feared can only be something fearful. [4]

720 The Son of Man now appears holding a sharp sickle in his hand, together with an auxiliary angel who also has a sickle.[5] But the grape harvest consists in an unparalleled blood-bath: the angel "gathered the vintage of the earth, and threw it into the great winepress of the wrath of God . . . and blood flowed from the winepress"—in which human beings were trodden!—"as high as a horse's bridle, for one thousand six hundred stadia." [6]

721 Seven angels then come out of the heavenly temple with the seven vials of wrath, which they proceed to pour out on the earth.[7] The *pièce de résistance* is the destruction of the Great

[1] Rev. 14:1. It may be significant that there is no longer any talk of the "great multitude which no man could number, from every nation, from all tribes and peoples and tongues, standing before the throne and before the Lamb," who were mentioned in 7:9. [2] 14:4 (AV).

[3] They really belong to the cult of the Great Mother, since they correspond to the emasculated Galli. Cf. the strange passage in Matthew 19:12, about the eunuchs "who have made themselves eunuchs for the sake of the kingdom of heaven," like the priests of Cybele who used to castrate themselves in honour of her son Attis. [4] Cf. also Rev. 19:5.

[5] 14:14 and 17. The auxiliary angel might well be John himself.

[6] 14:19–20. [7] 15:6–7 and 16:1ff.

Whore of Babylon, the counterpart of the heavenly Jerusalem. Babylon is the chthonic equivalent of the sun-woman Sophia, with, however, a reversal in moral character. If the elect turn themselves into "virgins" in honour of the Great Mother Sophia, a gruesome fantasy of fornication is spawned in the unconscious by way of compensation. The destruction of Babylon therefore represents not only the end of fornication, but the utter eradication of all life's joys and pleasures, as can be seen from 18:22–23:

> and the sound of harpers and minstrels, of flute players
> and trumpeters,
> shall be heard in thee no more;
>
> . . . .
>
> and the light of a lamp
> shall shine in thee no more;
> and the voice of bridegroom and bride
> shall be heard in thee no more . . .

722 As we happen to be living at the end of the Christian aeon Pisces, one cannot help but recall the doom that has overtaken our modern art.

723 Symbols like Jerusalem, Babylon, etc. are always overdetermined, that is, they have several aspects of meaning and can therefore be interpreted in different ways. I am only concerned with the psychological aspect, and do not wish to express an opinion as to their possible connection with historical events.

724 The destruction of all beauty and of all life's joys, the unspeakable suffering of the whole of creation that once sprang from the hand of a lavish Creator, would be, for a feeling heart, an occasion for deepest melancholy. But John cries: "Rejoice over her, thou heaven, ye holy apostles and prophets, for God hath avenged you on her [Babylon]," [8] from which we can see how far vindictiveness and lust for destruction can go, and what the "thorn in the flesh" means.

725 It is Christ who, leading the hosts of angels, treads "the winepress of the fierceness and wrath of Almighty God." [9] His robe "is dipped in blood." [10] He rides a *white horse*,[11] and with the

[8] Rev. 18:20 (AV). [9] 19:15 (AV). [10] 19:13.

[11] 19:11. Here again astrological speculations concerning the second half of the Christian aeon may be implied, with Pegasus as paranatellon of Aquarius.

sword which issues out of his mouth he kills the beast and the "false prophet," presumably his—or John's—dark counterpart, i.e., the shadow. Satan is locked up in the bottomless pit for a thousand years, and *Christ shall reign for the same length of time.* "After that he must be loosed a little season." [12] These thousand years correspond astrologically to the first half of the Pisces aeon. The setting free of Satan after this time must therefore correspond—one cannot imagine any other reason for it—to the enantiodromia of the Christian aeon, that is, to the reign of the Antichrist, whose coming could be predicted on astrological grounds. Finally, at the end of an unspecified period, the devil is thrown into the lake of fire and brimstone for ever and ever (but not completely destroyed as in Enoch), and the whole of the first creation disappears.[13]

726 The *hieros gamos,* the marriage of the Lamb with "his Bride," which had been announced earlier,[14] can now take place. The bride is the "new Jerusalem coming down out of heaven." [15] Her "radiance [was] like a most rare jewel, like a jasper, clear as crystal." [16] The city was built foursquare and was of pure gold, clear as glass, and so were its streets. The Lord God himself and the Lamb are its temple, and the source of never-ending light. There is no night in the city, and nothing unclean can enter in to defile it.[17] (This repeated assurance allays a doubt in John that has never been quite silenced.) From the throne of God and the Lamb flows the river of the water of life, and beside it stands the tree of life, as a reminder of paradise and pleromatic pre-existence.[18]

727 This final vision, which is generally interpreted as referring to the relationship of Christ to his Church, has the meaning of a "uniting symbol" and is therefore a representation of perfection and wholeness: hence the quaternity, which expresses itself in the city as a quadrangle, in paradise as the four rivers, in Christ as the four evangelists, and in God as the four living creatures. While the circle signifies the roundness of heaven and the all-embracing nature of the "pneumatic" deity, the square refers to the earth.[19] Heaven is masculine, but the earth is feminine. Therefore God has his throne in heaven, while Wisdom

12 Rev. 20:3 (AV). 13 20:10 and 21:1. 14 19:7. 15 21:2.
16 21:11. 17 21:16–27. 18 22:1–2.
19 In China, heaven is round and the earth square.

has hers on the earth, as she says in Ecclesiasticus: "Likewise in the beloved city he gave me rest, and in Jerusalem was my power." She is the "mother of fair love," [20] and when John pictures Jerusalem as the bride he is probably following Ecclesiasticus. The city is Sophia, who was with God before time began, and at the end of time will be reunited with God through the sacred marriage. As a feminine being she coincides with the earth, from which, so a Church Father tells us, Christ was born,[21] and hence with the quaternity of the four living creatures in whom God manifests himself in Ezekiel. In the same way that Sophia signifies God's self-reflection, the four seraphim represent God's consciousness with its four functional aspects. The many perceiving eyes [22] which are concentrated in the four wheels point in the same direction. They represent a fourfold synthesis of unconscious luminosities, corresponding to the tetrameria of the *lapis philosophorum,* of which the description of the heavenly city reminds us: everything sparkles with precious gems, crystal, and glass, in complete accordance with Ezekiel's vision of God. And just as the *hieros gamos* unites Yahweh with Sophia (Shekinah in the Cabala), thus restoring the original pleromatic state, so the parallel description of God and city points to their common nature: they are originally one, a single hermaphroditic being, an archetype of the greatest universality.

728 No doubt this is meant as a final solution of the terrible conflict of existence. The solution, however, as here presented, does not consist in the reconciliation of the opposites, but in their final severance, by which means those whose destiny it is to be saved can save themselves by identifying with the bright pneumatic side of God. An indispensable condition for this seems to be the denial of propagation and of sexual life altogether.

20 Ecclesiasticus 24:11 and 18 (AV).

21 Tertullian, *Adversus Judaeos,* XIII (Migne, *P.L.,* vol. 2, col. 635): ". . . illa terra virgo nondum pluviis rigata nec imbribus foecundata, ex qua homo tunc primum plasmatus est, ex qua nunc Christus secundum carnem ex virgine natus est" (. . . that virgin soil, not yet watered by the rains nor fertilized by the showers, from which man was originally formed [and] from which Christ is now born of a Virgin through the flesh).

22 Ezekiel 1:18.

XV

729 The Book of Revelation is on the one hand so personal and on the other so archetypal and collective that one is obliged to consider both aspects. Our modern interest would certainly turn first to the person of John. As I have said before, it is possible that John the author of the Epistles is identical with the apocalyptist. The psychological findings speak in favour of such an assumption. The "revelation" was experienced by an early Christian who, as a leading light of the community, presumably had to live an exemplary life and demonstrate to his flock the Christian virtues of true faith, humility, patience, devotion, selfless love, and denial of all worldly desires. In the long run this can become too much, even for the most righteous. Irritability, bad moods, and outbursts of affect are the classic symptoms of chronic virtuousness.[1] In regard to his Christian attitude, his own words probably give us the best picture:

> Beloved, let us love one another; for love is of God, and he who loves is born of God and knows God. He who does not love does not know God; for God is love. . . . In this is love, not that we loved God but that he loved us and sent his Son to be the expiation for our sins. Beloved, if God so loved us, we also ought to love one another. . . . So we know and believe the love God has for us. God is love, and he who abides in love abides in God, and God abides in him. . . . There is no fear in love, but perfect love casts out fear. For fear has to do with punishment, and he who fears is not perfected in love. . . . If any one says, "I love God," and hates his brother, he is a liar; for he who does not love his brother whom he has seen, cannot love God whom he has not seen. And this commandment we have from him, that he who loves God should love his brother also.[2]

730 But who hates the Nicolaitans? Who thirsts for vengeance and even wants to throw "that woman Jezebel" on a sickbed and strike her children dead? Who cannot have enough of bloodthirsty fantasies? Let us be psychologically correct, however: it is not the conscious mind of John that thinks up these fantasies,

[1] Not for nothing was the apostle John nicknamed "son of thunder" by Christ.
[2] I John 4 : 7–21.

they come to him in a violent "revelation." They fall upon him involuntarily with an unexpected vehemence and with an intensity which, as said, far transcends anything we could expect as compensation of a somewhat one-sided attitude of consciousness.

731 I have seen many compensating dreams of believing Christians who deceived themselves about their real psychic constitution and imagined that they were in a different condition from what they were in reality. But I have seen nothing that even remotely resembles the brutal impact with which the opposites collide in John's visions, except in the case of severe psychosis. However, John gives us no grounds for such a diagnosis. His apocalyptic visions are not confused enough; they are too consistent, not subjective and scurrilous enough. Considering the nature of their subject, the accompanying affects are adequate. Their author need not necessarily be an unbalanced psychopath. It is sufficient that he is a passionately religious person with an otherwise well-ordered psyche. But he must have an intensive relationship to God which lays him open to an invasion far transcending anything personal. The really religious person, in whom the capacity for an unusual extension of consciousness is inborn, must be prepared for such dangers.

732 The purpose of the apocalyptic visions is not to tell John, as an ordinary human being, how much shadow he hides beneath his luminous nature, but to open the seer's eye to the immensity of God, for he who loves God will know God. We can say that just because John loved God and did his best to love his fellows also, this "gnosis," this knowledge of God, struck him. Like Job, he saw the fierce and terrible side of Yahweh. For this reason he felt his gospel of love to be one-sided, and he supplemented it with the gospel of fear: *God can be loved but must be feared.*

733 With this, the seer's range of vision extends far beyond the first half of the Christian aeon: he divines that the reign of Antichrist will begin after a thousand years, a clear indication that Christ was not an unqualified victor. John anticipated the alchemists and Jakob Böhme; maybe he even sensed his own personal implication in the divine drama, since he anticipated the possibility of God's birth in man, which the alchemists, Meister Eckhart, and Angelus Silesius also intuited. He thus outlined the programme for the whole aeon of Pisces, with its

dramatic enantiodromia, and its dark end which we have still to experience, and before whose—without exaggeration—truly apocalyptic possibilities mankind shudders. The four sinister horsemen, the threatening tumult of trumpets, and the brimming vials of wrath are still waiting; already the atom bomb hangs over us like the sword of Damocles, and behind that lurk the incomparably more terrible possibilities of chemical warfare, which would eclipse even the horrors described in the Apocalypse. *Luciferi vires accendit Aquarius acres*—"Aquarius sets aflame Lucifer's harsh forces." Could anyone in his right senses deny that John correctly foresaw at least some of the possible dangers which threaten our world in the final phase of the Christian aeon? He knew, also, that the fire in which the devil is tormented burns in the divine pleroma for ever. God has a terrible double aspect: a sea of grace is met by a seething lake of fire, and the light of love glows with a fierce dark heat of which it is said "ardet non lucet"—it burns but gives no light. That is the eternal, as distinct from the temporal, gospel: *one can love God but must fear him.*

XVI

34 The book of Revelation, rightly placed at the end of the New Testament, reaches beyond it into a future that is all too palpably close with its apocalyptic terrors. The decision of an ill-considered moment, made in some Herostratic head,[1] can suffice to unleash the world cataclysm. The thread by which our fate hangs is wearing thin. Not nature, but the "genius of mankind," has knotted the hangman's noose with which it can execute itself at any moment. This is simply another *façon de parler* for what John called the "wrath of God."

5 Unfortunately we have no means of envisaging how John—if, as I surmise, he is the same as the author of the Epistles—would have come to terms with the double aspect of God. It is possible, even probable, that he was not aware of any contrast. It is altogether amazing how little most people reflect on numinous objects and attempt to come to terms with them, and

[1] [Herostratus, in order to make his name immortal, burned down the temple of Artemis in Ephesus, in 365 B.C.—EDITORS.]

how laborious such an undertaking is once we have embarked upon it. The numinosity of the object makes it difficult to handle intellectually, since our affectivity is always involved. One always participates for or against, and "absolute objectivity" is more rarely achieved here than anywhere else. If one has positive religious convictions, i.e., if one believes, then doubt is felt as very disagreeable and also one fears it. For this reason, one prefers not to analyse the object of belief. If one has no religious beliefs, then one does not like to admit the feeling of deficit, but prates loudly about one's liberal-mindedness and pats oneself on the back for the noble frankness of one's agnosticism. From this standpoint, it is hardly possible to admit the numinosity of the religious object, and yet its very numinosity is just as great a hindrance to critical thinking, because the unpleasant possibility might then arise that one's faith in enlightenment or agnosticism would be shaken. Both types feel, without knowing it, the insufficiency of their argument. Enlightenment operates with an inadequate rationalistic concept of truth and points triumphantly to the fact that beliefs such as the virgin birth, divine filiation, the resurrection of the dead, transubstantiation, etc., are all moonshine. Agnosticism maintains that it does not possess any knowledge of God or of anything metaphysical, overlooking the fact that one never *possesses* a metaphysical belief but is *possessed by it.* Both are possessed by reason, which represents the supreme arbiter who cannot be argued with. But who or what is this "reason" and why should it be supreme? Is not something that *is* and has real existence for us an authority superior to any rational judgment, as has been shown over and over again in the history of the human mind? Unfortunately the defenders of "faith" operate with the same futile arguments, only the other way about. The only thing which is beyond doubt is that there are metaphysical statements which are asserted or denied with considerable affect precisely because of their numinosity. This fact gives us a sure empirical basis from which to proceed. It is objectively real as a psychic phenomenon. The same applies naturally to all statements, even the most contradictory, that ever were or still are numinous. From now on we shall have to consider religious statements in their totality.

XVII

36 Let us turn back to the question of coming to terms with the paradoxical idea of God which the Apocalypse reveals to us. Evangelical Christianity, in the strict sense, has no need to bother with it, because it has as an essential doctrine an idea of God that, unlike Yahweh, coincides with the epitome of good. It would have been very different if the John of the Epistles had been obliged to discuss these matters with the John of Revelation. Later generations could afford to ignore the dark side of the Apocalypse, because the specifically Christian achievement was something that was not to be frivolously endangered. But for modern man the case is quite otherwise. We have experienced things so unheard of and so staggering that the question of whether such things are in any way reconcilable with the idea of a good God has become burningly topical. It is no longer a problem for experts in theological seminaries, but a universal religious nightmare, to the solution of which even a layman in theology like myself can, or perhaps must, make a contribution.

37 I have tried to set forth above the inescapable conclusions which must, I believe, be reached if one looks at tradition with critical common sense. If, in this wise, one is confronted with a paradoxical idea of God, and if, as a religious person, one considers at the same time the full extent of the problem, one finds oneself in the situation of the author of Revelation, who we may suppose was a convinced Christian. His possible identity with the writer of the letters brings out the acuteness of the contradiction: What is the relationship of this man to God? How does he endure the intolerable contradiction in the nature of Deity? Although we know nothing of his conscious decision, we believe we may find some clue in the vision of the sun-woman in travail.

38 The paradoxical nature of God has a like effect on man: it tears him asunder into opposites and delivers him over to a seemingly insoluble conflict. What happens in such a condition? Here we must let psychology speak, for psychology represents the sum of all the observations and insights it has gained from the empirical study of severe states of conflict. There are, for

example, conflicts of duty no one knows how to solve. Consciousness only knows: *tertium non datur!* The doctor therefore advises his patient to wait and see whether the unconscious will not produce a dream which proposes an irrational and therefore unexpected third thing as a solution. As experience shows, symbols of a reconciling and unitive nature do in fact turn up in dreams, the most frequent being the motif of the child-hero and the squaring of the circle, signifying the union of opposites. Those who have no access to these specifically medical experiences can derive practical instruction from fairy tales, and particularly from alchemy. The real subject of Hermetic philosophy is the *coniunctio oppositorum.* Alchemy characterizes its "child" on the one hand as the stone (e.g., the carbuncle), and on the other hand as the homunculus, or the *filius sapientiae* or even the *homo altus.* This is precisely the figure we meet in the Apocalypse as the son of the sun-woman, whose birth story seems like a paraphrase of the birth of Christ—a paraphrase which was repeated in various forms by the alchemists. In fact, they posit their stone as a parallel to Christ (this, with one exception, without reference to the Book of Revelation). This motif appears again in corresponding form and in corresponding situations in the dreams of modern man, with no connection with alchemy, and always it has to do with the bringing together of the light and the dark, as though modern man, like the alchemists, had divined what the problem was that the Apocalypse set the future. It was this problem on which the alchemists laboured for nearly seventeen centuries, and it is the same problem that distresses modern man. Though in one respect he knows more, in another respect he knows less than the alchemists. The problem for him is no longer projected upon matter, as it was for them; but on the other hand it has become psychologically acute, so that the psychotherapist has more to say on these matters than the theologian, who has remained caught in his archaic figures of speech. The doctor, often very much against his will, is forced by the problems of psychoneurosis to look more closely at the religious problem. It is not without good reason that I myself have reached the age of seventy-six before venturing to catechize myself as to the nature of those "ruling ideas" which decide our ethical behaviour and have such an important influence on our practical life. They are in the last resort the principles which, spoken or unspoken, determine the moral decisions upon which our existence depends, for weal or woe. All these dominants culminate in the positive or negative concept of God.[1]

739 Ever since John the apocalyptist experienced for the first time (perhaps unconsciously) that conflict into which Christianity inevitably leads, mankind has groaned under this burden: *God wanted to become man, and still wants to.* That is probably why John experienced in his vision a second birth of a son from the mother Sophia, a divine birth which was characterized by a *coniunctio oppositorum* and which anticipated the *filius sapientiae,* the essence of the individuation process. This was the effect of Christianity on a Christian of early times, who had lived long and resolutely enough to be able to cast a glance into the distant future. The mediation between the opposites was already indicated in the symbolism of Christ's fate, in the crucifixion scene where the mediator hangs between two thieves, one of whom goes to paradise, the other down to hell. Inevitably, in the Christian view, the opposition had to lie between God and man, and man was always in danger of being identified with the dark side. This, and the predestinarian hints dropped by our Lord, influenced John strongly: only the few preordained from eternity shall be saved, while the great mass of mankind shall perish in the final catastrophe. The opposition between God and man in the Christian view may well be a Yahwistic legacy from olden times, when the metaphysical problem consisted solely in Yahweh's relations with his people. The fear of Yahweh was still too great for anybody to dare—despite Job's gnosis—to lodge the antinomy in Deity itself. But if you keep the opposition between God and man, then you finally arrive, whether you like it or not, at the Christian conclusion "omne bonum a Deo, omne malum ab homine," with the absurd result that the creature is placed in opposition to its creator and a positively cosmic or daemonic grandeur in evil is imputed to man. The terrible destructive will that breaks out in John's ecstasies gives some idea of what it means when man is placed in opposition to the God of goodness: it burdens him with the dark side of God, which in Job is still in its right place. But

[1] Psychologically the God-concept includes every idea of the ultimate, of the first or last, of the highest or lowest. The name makes no difference.

either way man is identified with evil, in the first case with the result that he sets his face against goodness, and in the second, that he tries to be as perfect as his father in heaven.

740 Yahweh's decision to become man is a symbol of the development that had to supervene when man becomes conscious of the sort of God-image he is confronted with.[2] God acts out of the unconscious of man and forces him to harmonize and unite the opposing influences to which his mind is exposed from the unconscious. The unconscious wants both: to divide and to unite. In his striving for unity, therefore, man may always count on the help of a metaphysical advocate, as Job clearly recognized. The unconscious wants to flow into consciousness in order to reach the light, but at the same time it continually thwarts itself, because it would rather remain unconscious. That is to say, God wants to become man, but not quite. The conflict in his nature is so great that the incarnation can only be bought by an expiatory self-sacrifice offered up to the wrath of God's dark side.

741 At first, God incarnated his good side in order, as we may suppose, to create the most durable basis for a later assimilation of the other side. From the promise of the Paraclete we may conclude that God wants to become *wholly* man; in other words, to reproduce himself in his own dark creature (man not redeemed from original sin). The author of Revelation has left us a testimony to the continued operation of the Holy Ghost in the sense of a continuing incarnation. He was a creaturely man who was invaded by the dark God of wrath and vengeance—a *ventus urens,* a 'burning wind.' (This John was possibly the favourite disciple, who in old age was vouchsafed a premonition of future developments.) This disturbing invasion engendered in him the image of the divine child, of a future saviour, born of the divine consort whose reflection (the anima) lives in every man—that child whom Meister Eckhart also saw in a vision. It was he who knew that God alone in his Godhead is not in a state of bliss, but must be born in the human soul ("Gott ist selig

2 The God-concept, as the idea of an all-embracing totality, also includes the unconscious, and hence, in contrast to consciousness, it includes the objective psyche, which so often frustrates the will and intentions of the conscious mind. Prayer, for instance, reinforces the potential of the unconscious, thus accounting for the sometimes unexpected effects of prayer.

in der Seele"). The incarnation in Christ is the prototype which is continually being transferred to the creature by the Holy Ghost.

742 Since our moral conduct can hardly be compared with that of an early Christian like John, all manner of good as well as evil can still break through in us, particularly in regard to love. A sheer will for destruction, such as was evident in John, is not to be expected in our case. In all my experience I have never observed anything like it, except in cases of severe psychoses and criminal insanity. As a result of the spiritual differentiation fostered by the Reformation, and by the growth of the sciences in particular (which were originally taught by the fallen angels), there is already a considerable admixture of darkness in us, so that, compared with the purity of the early Christian saints (and some of the later ones too), we do not show up in a very favourable light. Our comparative blackness naturally does not help us a bit. Though it mitigates the impact of evil forces, it makes us more vulnerable and less capable of resisting them. We therefore need more light, more goodness and moral strength, and must wash off as much of the obnoxious blackness as possible, otherwise we shall not be able to assimilate the dark God who also wants to become man, and at the same time endure him without perishing. For this all the Christian virtues are needed and something else besides, for the problem is not only moral: we also need the Wisdom that Job was seeking. But at that time she was still hidden in Yahweh, or rather, she was not yet remembered by him. That higher and "complete" (τέλειος) man is begotten by the "unknown" father and born from Wisdom, and it is he who, in the figure of the *puer aeternus*—"vultu mutabilis albus et ater" [3]—represents our totality, which transcends consciousness. It was this boy into whom Faust had to change, abandoning his inflated onesidedness which saw the devil only outside. Christ's "Except ye become as little children" prefigures this change, for in them the opposites lie close together; but what is meant is the boy who is born from the maturity of the adult man, and not the unconscious child we would like to remain. Looking ahead, Christ also hinted, as I mentioned before, at a morality of evil.

743 Strangely, suddenly, as if it did not belong there, the sun-

3 "Of changeful countenance, both white and black."

woman with her child appears in the stream of apocalyptic visions. He belongs to another, future world. Hence, like the Jewish Messiah, the child is "caught up" to God, and his mother must stay for a long time hidden in the wilderness, where she is nourished by God. For the immediate and urgent problem in those days was not the union of opposites, which lay in the future, but the incarnation of the light and the good, the subjugation of *concupiscentia,* the lust of this world, and the consolidation of the *civitas Dei* against the advent of the Antichrist, who would come after a thousand years to announce the horrors of the last days, the epiphany of the wrathful and avenging God. The Lamb, transformed into a demonic ram, reveals a new gospel, the *Evangelium Aeternum,* which, going right beyond the love of God, has the fear of God as its main ingredient. Therefore the Apocalypse closes, like the classical individuation process, with the symbol of the *hieros gamos,* the marriage of the son with the mother-bride. But the marriage takes place in heaven, where "nothing unclean" enters, high above the devastated world. Light consorts with light. That is the programme for the Christian aeon which must be fulfilled before God can incarnate in the creaturely man. Only in the last days will the vision of the sun-woman be fulfilled. In recognition of this truth, and evidently inspired by the workings of the Holy Ghost, the Pope has recently announced the dogma of the *Assumptio Mariae,* very much to the astonishment of all rationalists. Mary as the bride is united with the son in the heavenly bridal-chamber, and, as Sophia, with the Godhead.[4]

744 This dogma is in every respect timely. In the first place it is a symbolical fulfilment of John's vision.[5] Secondly, it con-

[4] *Apostolic Constitution ("Munificentissimus Deus") of . . . Pius XII,* §22: "Oportebat sponsam, quam Pater desponsaverat, in thalamis caelestibus habitare" (The place of the bride whom the Father had espoused was in the heavenly courts).—St. John Damascene, *Encomium in Dormitionem, etc.,* Homily II, 14 (cf. Migne, *P.G.,* vol. 96, col. 742). §30: Comparison with the Bride in the Song of Solomon. §33: ". . . ita pariter surrexit et Arca sanctificationis suae, cum in hac die Virgo Mater ad aethereum thalamum est assumpta" (. . . so in like manner arose the Ark which he had sanctified, when on this day the Virgin Mother was taken up to her heavenly bridal-chamber).—St. Anthony of Padua, *Sermones Dominicales, etc.* (ed. Locatelli, III, p. 730).

[5] *Apostolic Constitution,* §31: "Ac praeterea scholastici doctores non modo in variis Veteris Testamenti figuris, sed in illa etiam Muliere amicta sole, quam Joannes Apostolus in insula Patmo [Rev. 12:1ff.] contemplatus est, Assumptionem

tains an allusion to the marriage of the Lamb at the end of time, and, thirdly, it repeats the Old Testament anamnesis of Sophia. These three references foretell the Incarnation of God. The second and third foretell the Incarnation in Christ,[6] but the first foretells the Incarnation in creaturely man.

XVIII

745 Everything now depends on man: immense power of destruction is given into his hand, and the question is whether he can resist the will to use it, and can temper his will with the spirit of love and wisdom. He will hardly be capable of doing so on his own unaided resources. He needs the help of an "advocate" in heaven, that is, of the child who was caught up to God and who brings the "healing" and making whole of the hitherto fragmentary man. Whatever man's wholeness, or the self, may mean *per se,* empirically it is an image of the goal of life spontaneously produced by the unconscious, irrespective of the wishes and fears of the conscious mind. It stands for the goal of the total man, for the realization of his wholeness and individuality with or without the consent of his will. The dynamic of this process is instinct, which ensures that everything which belongs to an individual's life shall enter into it, whether he consents or not, or is conscious of what is happening to him or not. Obviously, it makes a great deal of difference subjectively whether he knows what he is living out, whether he understands what he is doing, and whether he accepts responsibility for what he proposes to do or has done. The difference between conscious realization and the lack of it has been roundly formulated in the saying of Christ already quoted: "Man, if indeed thou knowest what thou doest, thou art blessed: but if thou knowest not, thou art cursed, and a transgressor of the law." [1] Before the bar of

Deiparae Virginis significatam viderunt" (Moreover, the Scholastic doctors saw the Assumption of the Virgin Mother of God signified not only in the various figures of the Old Testament, but also in the Woman clothed with the sun, whom the Apostle John contemplated on the island of Patmos).

6 The marriage of the Lamb repeats the Annunciation and the Overshadowing of Mary.

1 Codex Bezae, apocryphal insertion at Luke 6:4. [Trans. by James; see above, par. 696, n. 6.—TRANS.]

nature and fate, unconsciousness is never accepted as an excuse; on the contrary there are very severe penalties for it. Hence all unconscious nature longs for the light of consciousness while frantically struggling against it at the same time.

746 The conscious realization of what is hidden and kept secret certainly confronts us with an insoluble conflict; at least this is how it appears to the conscious mind. But the symbols that rise up out of the unconscious in dreams show it rather as a confrontation of opposites, and the images of the goal represent their successful reconciliation. Something empirically demonstrable comes to our aid from the depths of our unconscious nature. It is the task of the conscious mind to understand these hints. If this does not happen, the process of individuation will nevertheless continue. The only difference is that we become its victims and are dragged along by fate towards that inescapable goal which we might have reached walking upright, if only we had taken the trouble and been patient enough to understand in time the meaning of the numina that cross our path. The only thing that really matters now is whether man can climb up to a higher moral level, to a higher plane of consciousness, in order to be equal to the superhuman powers which the fallen angels have played into his hands. But he can make no progress with himself unless he becomes very much better acquainted with his own nature. Unfortunately, a terrifying ignorance prevails in this respect, and an equally great aversion to increasing the knowledge of his intrinsic character. However, in the most unexpected quarters nowadays we find people who can no longer blink the fact that something *ought* to be done with man in regard to his psychology. Unfortunately, the little word "ought" tells us that they do not know what to do, and do not know the way that leads to the goal. We can, of course, hope for the undeserved grace of God, who hears our prayers. But God, who also does *not* hear our prayers, wants to become man, and for that purpose he has chosen, through the Holy Ghost, the creaturely man filled with darkness—the natural man who is tainted with original sin and who learnt the divine arts and sciences from the fallen angels. The guilty man is eminently suitable and is therefore chosen to become the vessel for the continuing incarnation, not the guiltless one who holds aloof

from the world and refuses to pay his tribute to life, for in him the dark God would find no room.

747 Since the Apocalypse we now know again that God is not only to be loved, but also to be feared. He fills us with evil as well as with good, otherwise he would not need to be feared; and because he wants to become man, the uniting of his antinomy must take place in man. This involves man in a new responsibility. He can no longer wriggle out of it on the plea of his littleness and nothingness, for the dark God has slipped the atom bomb and chemical weapons into his hands and given him the power to empty out the apocalyptic vials of wrath on his fellow creatures. Since he has been granted an almost godlike power, he can no longer remain blind and unconscious. He must know something of God's nature and of metaphysical processes if he is to understand himself and thereby achieve gnosis of the Divine.

XIX

748 The promulgation of the new dogma of the Assumption of the Virgin Mary could, in itself, have been sufficient reason for examining the psychological background. It was interesting to note that, among the many articles published in the Catholic and Protestant press on the declaration of the dogma, there was not one, so far as I could see, which laid anything like the proper emphasis on what was undoubtedly the most powerful motive: namely, the popular movement and the psychological need behind it. Essentially, the writers of the articles were satisfied with learned considerations, dogmatic and historical, which have no bearing on the living religious process. But anyone who has followed with attention the visions of Mary which have been increasing in number over the last few decades, and has taken their psychological significance into account, might have known what was brewing. The fact, especially, that it was largely children who had the visions might have given pause for thought, for in such cases the collective unconscious is always at work. Incidentally, the Pope himself is rumoured to have had several visions of the Mother of God on the occasion of the declaration. One could have known for a long time that there was a deep

longing in the masses for an intercessor and mediatrix who would at last take her place alongside the Holy Trinity and be received as the "Queen of Heaven and Bride at the heavenly court." For more than a thousand years it had been taken for granted that the Mother of God dwelt there, and we know from the Old Testament that Sophia was with God before the creation. From the ancient Egyptian theology of the divine Pharaohs we know that God wants to become man by means of a human mother, and it was recognized even in prehistoric times that the primordial divine being is both male and female. But such a truth eventuates in time only when it is solemnly proclaimed or rediscovered. It is psychologically significant for our day that in the year 1950 the heavenly bride was united with the bridegroom. In order to interpret this event, one has to consider not only the arguments adduced by the Papal Bull, but the prefigurations in the apocalyptic marriage of the Lamb and in the Old Testament anamnesis of Sophia. The nuptial union in the *thalamus* (bridal-chamber) signifies the *hieros gamos,* and this in turn is the first step towards incarnation, towards the birth of the saviour who, since antiquity, was thought of as the *filius solis et lunae,* the *filius sapientiae,* and the equivalent of Christ. When, therefore, a longing for the exaltation of the Mother of God passes through the people, this tendency, if thought to its logical conclusion, means the desire for the birth of a saviour, a peacemaker, a "mediator pacem faciens inter inimicos." [1] Although he is already born in the pleroma, his birth in time can only be accomplished when it is perceived, recognized, and declared by man.

749 The motive and content of the popular movement which contributed to the Pope's decision solemnly to declare the new dogma consist not in the birth of a new god, but in the continuing incarnation of God which began with Christ. Arguments based on historical criticism will never do justice to the new dogma; on the contrary, they are as lamentably wide of the mark as are the unqualified fears to which the English archbishops have given expression. In the first place, the declaration of the dogma has changed nothing in principle in the Catholic ideology as it has existed for more than a thousand years; and in the second place, the failure to understand that God has

[1] "A mediator making peace between enemies."

eternally wanted to become man, and for that purpose continually incarnates through the Holy Ghost in the temporal sphere, is an alarming symptom and can only mean that the Protestant standpoint has lost ground by not understanding the signs of the times and by ignoring the continued operation of the Holy Ghost. It is obviously out of touch with the tremendous archetypal happenings in the psyche of the individual and the masses, and with the symbols which are intended to compensate the truly apocalyptic world situation today.[2] It seems to have succumbed to a species of rationalistic historicism and to have lost any understanding of the Holy Ghost who works in the hidden places of the soul. It can therefore neither understand nor admit a further revelation of the divine drama.

750 This circumstance has given me, a layman in things theological, cause to put forward my views on these dark matters. My attempt is based on the psychological experience I have harvested during the course of a long life. I do not underestimate the psyche in any respect whatsoever, nor do I imagine for a moment that psychic happenings vanish into thin air by being explained. Psychologism represents a still primitive mode of magical thinking, with the help of which one hopes to conjure the reality of the soul out of existence, after the manner of the "Proktophantasmist" in *Faust:*

> Are you still here? Nay, it's a thing unheard.
> Vanish at once! We've said the enlightening word.

751 One would be very ill advised to identify me with such a childish standpoint. However, I have been asked so often whether I believe in the existence of God or not that I am somewhat concerned lest I be taken for an adherent of "psychologism" far more commonly than I suspect. What most

2 The papal rejection of psychological symbolism may be explained by the fact that the Pope is primarily concerned with the reality of metaphysical happenings. Owing to the undervaluation of the psyche that everywhere prevails, every attempt at adequate psychological understanding is immediately suspected of psychologism. It is understandable that dogma must be protected from this danger. If, in physics, one seeks to explain the nature of light, nobody expects that as a result there will be no light. But in the case of psychology everybody believes that what it explains is explained away. However, I cannot expect that my particular deviationist point of view could be known in any competent quarter.

people overlook or seem unable to understand is the fact that I regard the psyche as *real*. They believe only in physical facts, and must consequently come to the conclusion that either the uranium itself or the laboratory equipment created the atom bomb. That is no less absurd than the assumption that a non-real psyche is responsible for it. God is an obvious psychic and non-physical fact, i.e., a fact that can be established psychically but not physically. Equally, these people have still not got it into their heads that the psychology of religion falls into two categories, which must be sharply distinguished from one another: firstly, the psychology of the religious person, and secondly, the psychology of religion proper, i.e., of religious contents.

752 It is chiefly my experiences in the latter field which have given me the courage to enter into the discussion of the religious question and especially into the pros and cons of the dogma of the Assumption—which, by the way, I consider to be the most important religious event since the Reformation. It is a *petra scandali* for the unpsychological mind: how can such an unfounded assertion as the bodily reception of the Virgin into heaven be put forward as worthy of belief? But the method which the Pope uses in order to demonstrate the truth of the dogma makes sense to the psychological mind, because it bases itself firstly on the necessary prefigurations, and secondly on a tradition of religious assertions reaching back for more than a thousand years. Clearly, the material evidence for the existence of this psychic phenomenon is more than sufficient. It does not matter at all that a physically impossible fact is asserted, because all religious assertions are physical impossibilities. If they were not so, they would, as I said earlier, necessarily be treated in the text-books of natural science. But religious statements without exception have to do with the reality of the *psyche* and not with the reality of *physis*. What outrages the Protestant standpoint in particular is the boundless approximation of the Deipara to the Godhead and, in consequence, the endangered supremacy of Christ, from which Protestantism will not budge. In sticking to this point it has obviously failed to consider that its hymnology is full of references to the "heavenly bridegroom," who is now suddenly supposed not to have a bride with equal rights. Or has, perchance, the "bridegroom," in true psychologistic manner, been understood as a mere metaphor?

753 The logical consistency of the papal declaration cannot be surpassed, and it leaves Protestantism with the odium of being nothing but a *man's religion* which allows no metaphysical representation of woman. In this respect it is similar to Mithraism, and Mithraism found this prejudice very much to its detriment. Protestantism has obviously not given sufficient attention to the signs of the times which point to the equality of women. But this equality requires to be metaphysically anchored in the figure of a "divine" woman, the bride of Christ. Just as the person of Christ cannot be replaced by an organization, so the bride cannot be replaced by the Church. The feminine, like the masculine, demands an equally personal representation.

754 The dogmatizing of the Assumption does not, however, according to the dogmatic view, mean that Mary has attained the status of a goddess, although, as mistress of heaven (as opposed to the prince of the sublunary aerial realm, Satan) and mediatrix, she is functionally on a par with Christ, the king and mediator. At any rate her position satisfies the need of the archetype. The new dogma expresses a renewed hope for the fulfilment of that yearning for peace which stirs deep down in the soul, and for a resolution of the threatening tension between the opposites. Everyone shares this tension and everyone experiences it in his individual form of unrest, the more so the less he sees any possibility of getting rid of it by rational means. It is no wonder, therefore, that the hope, indeed the expectation of divine intervention arises in the collective unconscious and at the same time in the masses. The papal declaration has given comforting expression to this yearning. How could Protestantism so completely miss the point? This lack of understanding can only be explained by the fact that the dogmatic symbols and hermeneutic allegories have lost their meaning for Protestant rationalism. This is also true, in some measure, of the opposition to the new dogma within the Catholic Church itself, or rather to the dogmatization of the old doctrine. Naturally, a certain degree of rationalism is better suited to Protestantism than it is to the Catholic outlook. The latter gives the archetypal symbolisms the necessary freedom and space in which to develop over the centuries while at the same time insisting on their original form, unperturbed by intellectual difficulties and the objections of rationalists. In this way the Catholic Church

demonstrates her maternal character, because she allows the tree growing out of her matrix to develop according to its own laws. Protestantism, in contrast, is committed to the paternal spirit. Not only did it develop, at the outset, from an encounter with the worldly spirit of the times, but it continues this dialectic with the spiritual currents of every age; for the pneuma, in keeping with its original wind nature, is flexible, ever in living motion, comparable now to water, now to fire. It can desert its original haunts, can even go astray and get lost, if it succumbs too much to the spirit of the age. In order to fulfil its task, the Protestant spirit must be full of unrest and occasionally troublesome; it must even be revolutionary, so as to make sure that tradition has an influence on the change of contemporary values. The shocks it sustains during this encounter modify and at the same time enliven the tradition, which in its slow progress through the centuries would, without these disturbances, finally arrive at complete petrifaction and thus lose its effect. By merely criticizing and opposing certain developments within the Catholic Church, Protestantism would gain only a miserable bit of vitality, unless, mindful of the fact that Christianity consists of two separate camps, or rather, is a disunited brother-sister pair, it remembers that besides defending its own existence it must acknowledge Catholicism's right to exist too. A brother who for theological reasons wanted to cut the thread of his elder sister's life would rightly be called inhuman—to say nothing of Christian charity—and the converse is also true. Nothing is achieved by merely negative criticism. It is justified only to the degree that it is creative. Therefore it would seem profitable to me if, for example, Protestantism admitted that it is shocked by the new dogma not only because it throws a distressing light on the gulf between brother and sister, but because, for fundamental reasons, a situation has developed within Christianity which removes it further than ever from the sphere of worldly understanding. Protestantism knows, or could know, how much it owes its very existence to the Catholic Church. How much or how little does the Protestant still possess if he can no longer criticize or protest? In view of the intellectual *skandalon* which the new dogma represents, he should remind himself of his Christian responsibility—"Am I my brother's (or in this case, my sister's) keeper?"—and examine in all seriousness the reasons, explicit or otherwise, that decided the declaration of the new dogma. In so doing, he should guard against casting cheap aspersions and would do well to assume that there is more in it than papal arbitrariness. It would be desirable for the Protestant to understand that the new dogma has placed upon him a new responsibility toward the worldly spirit of our age, for he cannot simply deny his problematical sister before the eyes of the world. He must, even if he finds her antipathetic, be fair to her if he does not want to lose his self-respect. For instance, this is a favourable opportunity for him to ask himself, for a change, what is the meaning not only of the new dogma but of all more or less dogmatic assertions over and above their literal concretism. Considering the arbitrary and protean state of his own dogmas, and the precarious, schism-riven condition of his Church, he cannot afford to remain rigid and impervious to the spirit of the age. And since, moreover, in accordance with his obligations to the spirit, he is more concerned to come to terms with the world and its ideas than with God, it would seem clearly indicated that, on the occasion of the entry of the Mother of God into the heavenly bridal-chamber, he should bend to the great task of reinterpreting all the Christian traditions. If it is a question of truths which are anchored deep in the soul—and no one with the slightest insight can doubt this fact—then the solution of this task must be possible. For this we need the freedom of the spirit, which, as we know, is assured only in Protestantism. The dogma of the Assumption is a slap in the face for the historical and rationalistic view of the world, and would remain so for all time if one were to insist obstinately on the arguments of reason and history. This is a case, if ever there was one, where psychological understanding is needed, because the mythologem coming to light is so obvious that we must be deliberately blinding ourselves if we cannot see its symbolic nature and interpret it in symbolic terms.

755 The dogmatization of the *Assumptio Mariae* points to the *hieros gamos* in the pleroma, and this in turn implies, as we have said, the future birth of the divine child, who, in accordance with the divine trend towards incarnation, will choose as his birthplace the empirical man. The metaphysical process is known to the psychology of the unconscious as the individuation process. In so far as this process, as a rule, runs its course un-

unconsciously as it has from time immemorial, it means no more than that the acorn becomes an oak, the calf a cow, and the child an adult. But if the individuation process is made conscious, consciousness must confront the unconscious and a balance between the opposites must be found. As this is not possible through logic, one is dependent on *symbols* which make the irrational union of opposites possible. They are produced spontaneously by the unconscious and are amplified by the conscious mind. The central symbols of this process describe the self, which is man's totality, consisting on the one hand of that which is conscious to him, and on the other hand of the contents of the unconscious. The self is the τέλειος ἄνθρωπος, the whole man, whose symbols are the divine child and its synonyms. This is only a very summary sketch of the process, but it can be observed at any time in modern man, or one can read about it in the documents of Hermetic philosophy from the Middle Ages. The parallelism between the symbols is astonishing to anyone who knows both the psychology of the unconscious and alchemy.

756 The difference between the "natural" individuation process, which runs its course unconsciously, and the one which is consciously realized, is tremendous. In the first case consciousness nowhere intervenes; the end remains as dark as the beginning. In the second case so much darkness comes to light that the personality is permeated with light, and consciousness necessarily gains in scope and insight. The encounter between conscious and unconscious has to ensure that the light which shines in the darkness is not only comprehended by the darkness, but comprehends it. The *filius solis et lunae* is the possibility as well as the symbol of the union of opposites. It is the alpha and omega of the process, the mediator and intermedius. "It has a thousand names," say the alchemists, meaning that the source from which the individuation process rises and the goal towards which it aims is nameless, ineffable.

757 It is only through the psyche that we can establish that God acts upon us, but we are unable to distinguish whether these actions emanate from God or from the unconscious. We cannot tell whether God and the unconscious are two different entities. Both are border-line concepts for transcendental contents. But empirically it can be established, with a sufficient degree of probability, that there is in the unconscious an archetype of

wholeness which manifests itself spontaneously in dreams, etc., and a tendency, independent of the conscious will, to relate other archetypes to this centre. Consequently, it does not seem improbable that the archetype of wholeness occupies as such a central position which approximates it to the God-image. The similarity is further borne out by the peculiar fact that the archetype produces a symbolism which has always characterized and expressed the Deity. These facts make possible a certain qualification of our above thesis concerning the indistinguishableness of God and the unconscious. Strictly speaking, the God-image does not coincide with the unconscious as such, but with a special content of it, namely the archetype of the self. It is this archetype from which we can no longer distinguish the God-image empirically. We can arbitrarily postulate a difference between these two entities, but that does not help us at all. On the contrary, it only helps us to separate man from God, and prevents God from becoming man. Faith is certainly right when it impresses on man's mind and heart how infinitely far away and inaccessible God is; but it also teaches his nearness, his immediate presence, and it is just this nearness which has to be empirically real if it is not to lose all significance. Only that which acts upon me do I recognize as real and actual. But that which has no effect upon me might as well not exist. The religious need longs for wholeness, and therefore lays hold of the images of wholeness offered by the unconscious, which, independently of the conscious mind, rise up from the depths of our psychic nature.

XX

758 It will probably have become clear to the reader that the account I have given of the development of symbolic entities corresponds to a process of differentiation of human consciousness. But since, as I showed in the introduction, the archetypes in question are not mere objects of the mind, but are also autonomous factors, i.e., living subjects, the differentiation of consciousness can be understood as the effect of the intervention of transcendentally conditioned dynamisms. In this case it would be the archetypes that accomplish the primary transformation.

But since, in our experience, there are no psychic conditions which could be observed *through introspection* outside the human being, the behaviour of the archetypes cannot be investigated at all without the interaction of the observing consciousness. Therefore the question as to whether the process is initiated by consciousness or by the archetype can never be answered; unless, in contradiction to experience, one either robbed the archetype of its autonomy or degraded consciousness to a mere machine. We find ourselves in best agreement with psychological experience if we concede to the archetype a definite measure of independence, and to consciousness a degree of creative freedom proportionate to its scope. There then arises that reciprocal action between two relatively autonomous factors which compels us, when describing and explaining the processes, to present sometimes the one and sometimes the other factor as the acting subject, even when God becomes man. The Christian solution has hitherto avoided this difficulty by recognizing Christ as the one and only God-man. But the indwelling of the Holy Ghost, the third Divine Person, in man, brings about a Christification of many, and the question then arises whether these many are all complete God-men. Such a transformation would lead to insufferable collisions between them, to say nothing of the unavoidable inflation to which the ordinary mortal, who is not freed from original sin, would instantly succumb. In these circumstances it is well to remind ourselves of St. Paul and his split consciousness: on one side he felt he was the apostle directly called and enlightened by God, and, on the other side, a sinful man who could not pluck out the "thorn in the flesh" and rid himself of the Satanic angel who plagued him. That is to say, even the enlightened person remains what he is, and is never more than his own limited ego before the One who dwells within him, whose form has no knowable boundaries, who encompasses him on all sides, fathomless as the abysms of the earth and vast as the sky.

PART TWO

EASTERN RELIGION

VII

PSYCHOLOGICAL COMMENTARIES ON "THE TIBETAN BOOK OF THE GREAT LIBERATION" AND "THE TIBETAN BOOK OF THE DEAD"

PSYCHOLOGICAL COMMENTARY ON "THE TIBETAN BOOK OF THE GREAT LIBERATION"[1]

1. THE DIFFERENCE BETWEEN EASTERN AND WESTERN THINKING

759 Dr. Evans-Wentz has entrusted me with the task of commenting on a text which contains an important exposition of Eastern "psychology." The very fact that I have to use quotation marks shows the dubious applicability of this term. It is perhaps not superfluous to mention that the East has produced nothing equivalent to what we call psychology, but rather philosophy or metaphysics. Critical philosophy, the mother of modern psychology, is as foreign to the East as to medieval Europe. Thus the word "mind," as used in the East, has the connotation of something metaphysical. Our Western conception of mind has lost this connotation since the Middle Ages, and the word has now come to signify a "psychic function." Despite the fact that we neither know nor pretend to know what "psyche" is, we can deal with the phenomenon of "mind." We do not assume that the mind is a metaphysical entity or that

1 [Written in English in 1939 and first published in *The Tibetan Book of the Great Liberation,* the texts of which were translated from Tibetan by various hands and edited by W. Y. Evans-Wentz (London and New York, 1954), pp. xxix–lxiv. The commentary is republished here with only minor alterations.—EDITORS.]

there is any connection between an individual mind and a hypothetical Universal Mind. Our psychology is, therefore, a science of mere phenomena without any metaphysical implications. The development of Western philosophy during the last two centuries has succeeded in isolating the mind in its own sphere and in severing it from its primordial oneness with the universe. Man himself has ceased to be the microcosm and eidolon of the cosmos, and his "anima" is no longer the consubstantial *scintilla,* or spark of the *Anima Mundi,* the World Soul.

760 Psychology accordingly treats all metaphysical claims and assertions as mental phenomena, and regards them as statements about the mind and its structure that derive ultimately from certain unconscious dispositions. It does not consider them to be absolutely valid or even capable of establishing a metaphysical truth. We have no intellectual means of ascertaining whether this attitude is right or wrong. We only know that there is no evidence for, and no possibility of proving, the validity of a metaphysical postulate such as "Universal Mind." If the mind asserts the existence of a Universal Mind, we hold that it is merely making an assertion. We do not assume that by such an assertion the existence of a Universal Mind has been established. There is no argument against this reasoning, but no evidence, either, that our conclusion is ultimately right. In other words, it is just as possible that our mind is nothing but a perceptible manifestation of a Universal Mind. Yet we do not know, and we cannot even see, how it would be possible to recognize whether this is so or not. Psychology therefore holds that the mind cannot establish or assert anything beyond itself.

761 If, then, we accept the restrictions imposed upon the capacity of our mind, we demonstrate our common sense. I admit it is something of a sacrifice, inasmuch as we bid farewell to that miraculous world in which mind-created things and beings move and live. This is the world of the primitive, where even inanimate objects are endowed with a living, healing, magic power, through which they participate in us and we in them. Sooner or later we had to understand that their potency was really ours, and that their significance was our projection. The theory of knowledge is only the last step out of humanity's childhood, out of a world where mind-created figures populated a metaphysical heaven and hell.

762 Despite this inevitable epistemological criticism, however, we have held fast to the religious belief that the organ of faith enables man to know God. The West thus developed a new disease: the conflict between science and religion. The critical philosophy of science became as it were negatively metaphysical —in other words, materialistic—on the basis of an error in judgment; matter was assumed to be a tangible and recognizable reality. Yet this is a thoroughly metaphysical concept hypostatized by uncritical minds. Matter is an hypothesis. When you say "matter," you are really creating a symbol for something unknown, which may just as well be "spirit" or anything else; it may even be God. Religious faith, on the other hand, refuses to give up its pre-critical *Weltanschauung.* In contradiction to the saying of Christ, the faithful try to *remain* children instead of becoming *as* children. They cling to the world of childhood. A famous modern theologian confesses in his autobiography that Jesus has been his good friend "from childhood on." Jesus is the perfect example of a man who preached something different from the religion of his forefathers. But the *imitatio Christi* does not appear to include the mental and spiritual sacrifice which he had to undergo at the beginning of his career and without which he would never have become a saviour.

763 The conflict between science and religion is in reality a misunderstanding of both. Scientific materialism has merely introduced a new hypostasis, and that is an intellectual sin. It has given another name to the supreme principle of reality and has assumed that this created a new thing and destroyed an old thing. Whether you call the principle of existence "God," "matter," "energy," or anything else you like, you have created nothing; you have simply changed a symbol. The materialist is a metaphysician *malgré lui.* Faith, on the other hand, tries to retain a primitive mental condition on merely sentimental grounds. It is unwilling to give up the primitive, childlike relationship to mind-created and hypostatized figures; it wants to go on enjoying the security and confidence of a world still presided over by powerful, responsible, and kindly parents. Faith may include a *sacrificium intellectus* (provided there is an intellect to sacrifice), but certainly not a sacrifice of feeling. In this way the faithful *remain* children instead of becoming *as* children, and they do not gain their life because they have not lost

it. Furthermore, faith collides with science and thus gets its deserts, for it refuses to share in the spiritual adventure of our age.

764 Any honest thinker has to admit the insecurity of all metaphysical positions, and in particular of all creeds. He has also to admit the unwarrantable nature of all metaphysical assertions and face the fact that there is no evidence whatever for the ability of the human mind to pull itself up by its own bootstrings, that is, to establish anything transcendental.

765 Materialism is a metaphysical reaction against the sudden realization that cognition is a mental faculty and, if carried beyond the human plane, a projection. The reaction was "metaphysical" in so far as the man of average philosophical education failed to see through the implied hypostasis, not realizing that "matter" was just another name for the supreme principle. As against this, the attitude of faith shows how reluctant people were to accept philosophical criticism. It also demonstrates how great is the fear of letting go one's hold on the securities of childhood and of dropping into a strange, unknown world ruled by forces unconcerned with man. Nothing really changes in either case; man and his surroundings remain the same. He has only to realize that he is shut up inside his mind and cannot step beyond it, even in insanity; and that the appearance of his world or of his gods very much depends upon his own mental condition.

766 In the first place, the structure of the mind is responsible for anything we may assert about metaphysical matters, as I have already pointed out. We have also begun to understand that the intellect is not an *ens per se,* or an independent mental faculty, but a psychic function dependent upon the conditions of the psyche as a whole. A philosophical statement is the product of a certain personality living at a certain time in a certain place, and not the outcome of a purely logical and impersonal procedure. To that extent it is chiefly subjective; whether it has an objective validity or not depends on whether there are few or many persons who argue in the same way. The isolation of man within his mind as a result of epistemological criticism has naturally led to psychological criticism. This kind of criticism is not popular with the philosophers, since they like to consider the philosophic intellect as the perfect and unconditioned in-

strument of philosophy. Yet this intellect of theirs is a function dependent upon an individual psyche and determined on all sides by subjective conditions, quite apart from environmental influences. Indeed, we have already become so accustomed to this point of view that "mind" has lost its universal character altogether. It has become a more or less individualized affair, with no trace of its former cosmic aspect as the *anima rationalis*. Mind is understood nowadays as a subjective, even an arbitrary, thing. Now that the formerly hypostatized "universal ideas" have turned out to be mental principles, it is dawning upon us to what an extent our whole experience of so-called reality is psychic; as a matter of fact, everything thought, felt, or perceived is a psychic image, and the world itself exists only so far as we are able to produce an image of it. We are so deeply impressed with the truth of our imprisonment in, and limitation by, the psyche that we are ready to admit the existence in it even of things we do *not* know: we call them "the unconscious."

767 The seemingly universal and metaphysical scope of the mind has thus been narrowed down to the small circle of individual consciousness, profoundly aware of its almost limitless subjectivity and of its infantile-archaic tendency to heedless projection and illusion. Many scientifically-minded persons have even sacrificed their religious and philosophical leanings for fear of uncontrolled subjectivism. By way of compensation for the loss of a world that pulsed with our blood and breathed with our breath, we have developed an enthusiasm for *facts*—mountains of facts, far beyond any single individual's power to survey. We have the pious hope that this incidental accumulation of facts will form a meaningful whole, but nobody is quite sure, because no human brain can possibly comprehend the gigantic sum total of this mass-produced knowledge. The facts bury us, but whoever dares to speculate must pay for it with a bad conscience—and rightly so, for he will instantly be tripped up by the facts.

768 Western psychology knows the mind as the mental functioning of a psyche. It is the "mentality" of an individual. An impersonal Universal Mind is still to be met with in the sphere of philosophy, where it seems to be a relic of the original human "soul." This picture of our Western outlook may seem a little drastic, but I do not think it is far from the truth. At all events,

something of the kind presents itself as soon as we are confronted with the Eastern mentality. In the East, mind is a cosmic factor, the very essence of existence; while in the West we have just begun to understand that it is the essential condition of cognition, and hence of the cognitive existence of the world. There is no conflict between religion and science in the East, because no science is there based upon the passion for facts, and no religion upon mere faith; there is religious cognition and cognitive religion.[2] With us, man is incommensurably small and the grace of God is everything; but in the East, man is God and he redeems himself. The gods of Tibetan Buddhism belong to the sphere of illusory separateness and mind-created projections, and yet they exist; but so far as we are concerned an illusion remains an illusion, and thus is nothing at all. It is a paradox, yet nevertheless true, that with us a thought has no proper reality; we treat it as if it were a nothingness. Even though the thought be true in itself, we hold that it exists only by virtue of certain facts which it is said to formulate. We can produce a most devastating fact like the atom bomb with the help of this ever-changing phantasmagoria of virtually nonexistent thoughts, but it seems wholly absurd to us that one could ever establish the reality of thought itself.

769 "Psychic reality" is a controversial concept, like "psyche" or "mind." By the latter terms some understand consciousness and its contents, others allow the existence of "dark" or "subconscious" representations. Some include instincts in the psychic realm, others exclude them. The vast majority consider the psyche to be a result of biochemical processes in the brain cells. A few conjecture that it is the psyche that makes the cortical cells function. Some identify "life" with psyche. But only an insignificant minority regards the psychic phenomenon as a category of existence *per se* and draws the necessary conclusions. It is indeed paradoxical that *the* category of existence, the indispensable *sine qua non* of all existence, namely the psyche, should be treated as if it were only semi-existent. Psychic existence is the only category of existence of which we have *immediate* knowledge, since nothing can be known unless it first appears as a psychic image. Only psychic existence is immediately verifiable. To the extent that the world does not assume the form of

2 I am purposely leaving out of account the modernized East.

a psychic image, it is virtually non-existent. This is a fact which, with few exceptions—as for instance in Schopenhauer's philosophy—the West has not yet fully realized. But Schopenhauer was influenced by Buddhism and by the Upanishads.

770 Even a superficial acquaintance with Eastern thought is sufficient to show that a fundamental difference divides East and West. The East bases itself upon psychic reality, that is, upon the psyche as the main and unique condition of existence. It seems as if this Eastern recognition were a psychological or temperamental fact rather than a result of philosophical reasoning. It is a typically introverted point of view, contrasted with the equally typical extraverted point of view of the West.[3] Introversion and extraversion are known to be temperamental or even constitutional attitudes which are never intentionally adopted in normal circumstances. In exceptional cases they may be produced at will, but only under very special conditions. Introversion is, if one may so express it, the "style" of the East, an habitual and collective attitude, just as extraversion is the "style" of the West. Introversion is felt here as something abnormal, morbid, or otherwise objectionable. Freud identifies it with an autoerotic, "narcissistic" attitude of mind. He shares his negative position with the National Socialist philosophy of modern Germany,[4] which accuses introversion of being an offence against community feeling. In the East, however, our cherished extraversion is depreciated as illusory desirousness, as existence in the *samsāra,* the very essence of the *nidāna*-chain which culminates in the sum of the world's sufferings.[5] Anyone with practical knowledge of the mutual depreciation of values between introvert and extravert will understand the emotional conflict between the Eastern and the Western standpoint. For those who know something of the history of European philosophy the bitter wrangling about "universals" which began with Plato will provide an instructive example. I do not wish to go into all the ramifications of this conflict between introversion and extraversion, but I must mention the religious aspects of the problem. The Christian West considers man to be wholly dependent upon the grace of God, or at least upon the Church as the exclusive and divinely sanctioned earthly instrument of

3 *Psychological Types,* Defs. 19 and 34.

4 Written in the year 1939.

5 *Samyutta-nikāya* 12, *Nidāna-samyutta.*

man's redemption. The East, however, insists that man is the sole cause of his higher development, for it believes in "self-liberation."

771 The religious point of view always expresses and formulates the essential psychological attitude and its specific prejudices, even in the case of people who have forgotten, or who have never heard of, their own religion. In spite of everything, the West is thoroughly Christian as far as its psychology is concerned. Tertullian's *anima naturaliter christiana* holds true throughout the West—not, as he thought, in the religious sense, but in a psychological one. Grace comes from elsewhere; at all events from outside. Every other point of view is sheer heresy. Hence it is quite understandable why the human psyche is suffering from undervaluation. Anyone who dares to establish a connection between the psyche and the idea of God is immediately accused of "psychologism" or suspected of morbid "mysticism." The East, on the other hand, compassionately tolerates those "lower" spiritual stages where man, in his blind ignorance of karma, still bothers about sin and tortures his imagination with a belief in absolute gods, who, if he only looked deeper, are nothing but the veil of illusion woven by his own unenlightened mind. The psyche is therefore all-important; it is the all-pervading Breath, the Buddha-essence; it is the Buddha-Mind, the One, the *Dharmakāya*. All existence emanates from it, and all separate forms dissolve back into it. This is the basic psychological prejudice that permeates Eastern man in every fibre of his being, seeping into all his thoughts, feelings, and deeds, no matter what creed he professes.

772 In the same way Western man is Christian, no matter to what denomination his Christianity belongs. For him man is small inside, he is next to nothing; moreover, as Kierkegaard says, "before God man is always wrong." By fear, repentance, promises, submission, self-abasement, good deeds, and praise he propitiates the great power, which is not himself but *totaliter aliter*, the Wholly Other, altogether perfect and "outside," the only reality.[6] If you shift the formula a bit and substitute for God some other power, for instance the world or money, you get a complete picture of Western man—assiduous, fearful, devout, self-abasing, enterprising, greedy, and violent in his pur-

6 [Cf. Otto, *The Idea of the Holy*, pp. 26ff.—Editors.]

suit of the goods of this world: possessions, health, knowledge, technical mastery, public welfare, political power, conquest, and so on. What are the great popular movements of our time? Attempts to grab the money or property of others and to protect our own. The mind is chiefly employed in devising suitable "isms" to hide the real motives or to get more loot. I refrain from describing what would happen to Eastern man should he forget his ideal of Buddhahood, for I do not want to give such an unfair advantage to my Western prejudices. But I cannot help raising the question of whether it is possible, or indeed advisable, for either to imitate the other's standpoint. The difference between them is so vast that one can see no reasonable possibility of this, much less its advisability. You cannot mix fire and water. The Eastern attitude stultifies the Western, and vice versa. You cannot be a good Christian and redeem yourself, nor can you be a Buddha and worship God. It is much better to accept the conflict, for it admits only of an irrational solution, if any.

773 By an inevitable decree of fate the West is becoming acquainted with the peculiar facts of Eastern spirituality. It is useless either to belittle these facts, or to build false and treacherous bridges over yawning gaps. Instead of learning the spiritual techniques of the East by heart and imitating them in a thoroughly Christian way—*imitatio Christi!*—with a correspondingly forced attitude, it would be far more to the point to find out whether there exists in the unconscious an introverted tendency similar to that which has become the guiding spiritual principle of the East. We should then be in a position to build on our own ground with our own methods. If we snatch these things directly from the East, we have merely indulged our Western acquisitiveness, confirming yet again that "everything good is outside," whence it has to be fetched and pumped into our barren souls.[7] It seems to me that we have really learned something from the East when we understand that the psyche contains riches enough without having to be primed from outside, and when we feel capable of evolving out of ourselves with

7 "Whereas who holdeth not God as such an inner possession, but with every means must fetch Him from without . . . verily such a man hath Him not, and easily something cometh to trouble him." Meister Eckhart (Büttner, II, p. 185). Cf. *Meister Eckhart,* trans. by Evans, II, p. 8.

or without divine grace. But we cannot embark upon this ambitious enterprise until we have learned how to deal with our spiritual pride and blasphemous self-assertiveness. The Eastern attitude violates the specifically Christian values, and it is no good blinking this fact. If our new attitude is to be genuine, i.e., grounded in our own history, it must be acquired with full consciousness of the Christian values and of the conflict between them and the introverted attitude of the East. We must get at the Eastern values from within and not from without, seeking them in ourselves, in the unconscious. We shall then discover how great is our fear of the unconscious and how formidable are our resistances. Because of these resistances we doubt the very thing that seems so obvious to the East, namely, the *self-liberating power of the introverted mind.*

774 This aspect of the mind is practically unknown to the West, though it forms the most important component of the unconscious. Many people flatly deny the existence of the unconscious, or else they say that it consists merely of instincts, or of repressed or forgotten contents that were once part of the conscious mind. It is safe to assume that what the East calls "mind" has more to do with our "unconscious" than with mind as we understand it, which is more or less identical with consciousness. To us, consciousness is inconceivable without an ego; it is equated with the relation of contents to an ego. If there is no ego there is nobody to be conscious of anything. The ego is therefore indispensable to the conscious process. The Eastern mind, however, has no difficulty in conceiving of a consciousness without an ego. Consciousness is deemed capable of transcending its ego condition; indeed, in its "higher" forms, the ego disappears altogether. Such an ego-less mental condition can only be unconscious to us, for the simple reason that there would be nobody to witness it. I do not doubt the existence of mental states transcending consciousness. But they lose their consciousness to exactly the same degree that they transcend consciousness. I cannot imagine a conscious mental state that does not relate to a subject, that is, to an ego. The ego may be depotentiated—divested, for instance, of its awareness of the body—but so long as there is awareness of something, there must be somebody who is aware. The unconscious, however, is a mental condition of which no ego is aware. It is only by indirect means that we even-

tually become conscious of the existence of an unconscious. We can observe the manifestation of unconscious fragments of the personality, detached from the patient's consciousness, in insanity. But there is no evidence that the unconscious contents are related to an unconscious centre analogous to the ego; in fact there are good reasons why such a centre is not even probable.

775 The fact that the East can dispose so easily of the ego seems to point to a mind that is not to be identified with our "mind." Certainly the ego does not play the same role in Eastern thought as it does with us. It seems as if the Eastern mind were less egocentric, as if its contents were more loosely connected with the subject, and as if greater stress were laid on mental states which include a depotentiated ego. It also seems as if *hatha* yoga were chiefly useful as a means for extinguishing the ego by fettering its unruly impulses. There is no doubt that the higher forms of yoga, in so far as they strive to reach samādhi, seek a mental condition in which the ego is practically dissolved. Consciousness in our sense of the word is rated a definitely inferior condition, the state of *avidyā* (ignorance), whereas what we call the "dark background of consciousness" is understood to be a "higher" consciousness.[8] Thus our concept of the "collective unconscious" would be the European equivalent of *buddhi,* the enlightened mind.

776 In view of all this, the Eastern form of "sublimation" amounts to a withdrawal of the centre of psychic gravity from ego-consciousness, which holds a middle position between the body and the ideational processes of the psyche. The lower, semi-physiological strata of the psyche are subdued by *askesis,* i.e., exercises, and kept under control. They are not exactly denied or suppressed by a supreme effort of the will, as is customary in Western sublimation. Rather, the lower psychic strata are adapted and shaped through the patient practice of *hatha* yoga until they no longer interfere with the development of "higher" consciousness. This peculiar process seems to be aided by the fact that the ego and its desires are checked by the greater

8 In so far as "higher" and "lower" are categorical judgments of consciousness, Western psychology does not differentiate unconscious contents in this way. It appears that the East recognizes subhuman psychic conditions, a real "subconsciousness" comprising the instincts and semi-physiological psychisms, but classed as a "higher consciousness."

importance which the East habitually attaches to the "subjective factor."[9] By this I mean the "dark background" of consciousness, the unconscious. The introverted attitude is characterized in general by an emphasis on the *a priori* data of apperception. As is well known, the act of apperception consists of two phases: first the perception of the object, second the assimilation of the perception to a preexisting pattern or concept by means of which the object is "comprehended." The psyche is not a nonentity devoid of all quality; it is a definite system made up of definite conditions and it reacts in a specific way. Every new representation, be it a perception or a spontaneous thought, arouses associations which derive from the storehouse of memory. These leap immediately into consciousness, producing the complex picture of an "impression," though this is already a sort of interpretation. The unconscious disposition upon which the quality of the impression depends is what I call the "subjective factor." It deserves the qualification "subjective" because objectivity is hardly ever conferred by a first impression. Usually a rather laborious process of verification, comparison, and analysis is needed to modify and adapt the immediate reactions of the subjective factor.

777 The prominence of the subjective factor does not imply a *personal subjectivism,* despite the readiness of the extraverted attitude to dismiss the subjective factor as "nothing but" subjective. The psyche and its structure are real enough. They even transform material objects into psychic images, as we have said. They do not perceive waves, but sound; not wave-lengths, but colours. Existence is as we see and understand it. There are innumerable things that can be seen, felt, and understood in a great variety of ways. Quite apart from merely personal prejudices, the psyche assimilates external facts in its own way, which is based ultimately upon the laws or patterns of apperception. These laws do not change, although different ages or different parts of the world call them by different names. On a primitive level people are afraid of witches; on the modern level we are apprehensively aware of microbes. There everybody believes in ghosts, here everybody believes in vitamins. Once upon a time men were possessed by devils, now they are not less obsessed by ideas, and so on.

9 *Psychological Types* (1923 edn., pp. 472ff.).

778 The subjective factor is made up, in the last resort, of the eternal patterns of psychic functioning. Anyone who relies upon the subjective factor is therefore basing himself on the reality of psychic law. So he can hardly be said to be wrong. If by this means he succeeds in extending his consciousness downwards, to touch the basic laws of psychic life, he is in possession of that truth which the psyche will naturally evolve if not fatally interfered with by the non-psychic, i.e., the external, world. At any rate, his truth could be weighed against the sum of all knowledge acquired through the investigation of externals. We in the West believe that a truth is satisfactory only if it can be verified by external facts. We believe in the most exact observation and exploration of nature; our truth must coincide with the behaviour of the external world, otherwise it is merely "subjective." In the same way that the East turns its gaze from the dance of *prakriti* (physis) and from the multitudinous illusory forms of *māyā,* the West shuns the unconscious and its futile fantasies. Despite its introverted attitude, however, the East knows very well how to deal with the external world. And despite its extraversions the West, too, has a way of dealing with the psyche and its demands; it has an institution called the Church, which gives expression to the unknown psyche of man through its rites and dogmas. Nor are natural science and modern techniques by any means the invention of the West. Their Eastern equivalents are somewhat old-fashioned, or even primitive. But what we have to show in the way of spiritual insight and psychological technique must seem, when compared with yoga, just as backward as Eastern astrology and medicine when compared with Western science. I do not deny the efficacy of the Christian Church; but, if you compare the *Exercitia* of Ignatius Loyola with yoga, you will take my meaning. There is a difference, and a big one. To jump straight from that level into Eastern yoga is no more advisable than the sudden transformation of Asian peoples into half-baked Europeans. I have serious doubts as to the blessings of Western civilization, and I have similar misgivings as to the adoption of Eastern spirituality by the West. Yet the two contradictory worlds have met. The East is in full transformation; it is thoroughly and fatally disturbed. Even the most efficient methods of European warfare have been successfully imitated. The trouble with us seems to

be far more psychological. Our blight is ideologies—they are the long-expected Antichrist! National Socialism comes as near to being a religious movement as any movement since A.D. 622. Communism claims to be paradise come to earth again. We are far better protected against failing crops, inundations, epidemics, and invasions from the Turk than we are against our own deplorable spiritual inferiority, which seems to have little resistance to psychic epidemics.

779 In its religious attitude, too, the West is extraverted. Nowadays it is gratuitously offensive to say that Christianity implies hostility, or even indifference, to the world and the flesh. On the contrary, the good Christian is a jovial citizen, an enterprising business man, an excellent soldier, the very best in every profession there is. Worldly goods are often interpreted as special rewards for Christian behaviour, and in the Lord's Prayer the adjective ἐπιούσιος, *supersubstantialis*,[10] referring to the bread, has long since been omitted, for the real bread obviously makes so very much more sense! It is only logical that extraversion, when carried to such lengths, cannot credit man with a psyche which contains anything not imported into it from outside, either by human teaching or divine grace. From this point of view it is downright blasphemy to assert that man has it in him to accomplish his own redemption. Nothing in our religion encourages the idea of the self-liberating power of the mind. Yet a very modern form of psychology—"analytical" or "complex" psychology—envisages the possibility of there being certain processes in the unconscious which, by virtue of their symbolism, compensate the defects and anfractuosities of the conscious attitude. When these unconscious compensations are made conscious through the analytical technique, they produce such a change in the conscious attitude that we are entitled to speak of a new level of consciousness. The method cannot, however, produce the actual process of unconscious compensation; for that we depend upon the unconscious psyche or the "grace of God"—names make no difference. But the unconscious process itself hardly ever reaches consciousness without technical aid. When brought to the surface, it reveals contents that offer a striking contrast to the general run of conscious thinking and

10 This is not the unacceptable translation of ἐπιούσιος by Jerome but the ancient spiritual interpretation by Tertullian, Origen, and others.

feeling. If that were not so, they would not have a compensatory effect. The first effect, however, is usually a conflict, because the conscious attitude resists the intrusion of apparently incompatible and extraneous tendencies, thoughts, feelings, etc. Schizophrenia yields the most startling examples of such intrusions of utterly foreign and unacceptable contents. In schizophrenia it is, of course, a question of pathological distortions and exaggerations, but anybody with the slightest knowledge of the normal material will easily recognize the sameness of the underlying patterns. It is, as a matter of fact, the same imagery that one finds in mythology and other archaic thought-formations.

780 Under normal conditions, every conflict stimulates the mind to activity for the purpose of creating a satisfactory solution. Usually—i.e., in the West—the conscious standpoint arbitrarily decides against the unconscious, since anything coming from inside suffers from the prejudice of being regarded as inferior or somehow wrong. But in the cases with which we are here concerned it is tacitly agreed that the apparently incompatible contents shall not be suppressed again, and that the conflict shall be accepted and suffered. At first no solution appears possible, and this fact, too, has to be borne with patience. The suspension thus created "constellates" the unconscious—in other words, the conscious suspense produces a new compensatory reaction in the unconscious. This reaction (usually manifested in dreams) is brought to conscious realization in its turn. The conscious mind is thus confronted with a new aspect of the psyche, which arouses a different problem or modifies an old one in an unexpected way. The procedure is continued until the original conflict is satisfactorily resolved. The whole process is called the "transcendent function." [11] It is a process and a method at the same time. The production of unconscious compensations is a spontaneous *process;* the conscious realization is a *method.* The function is called "transcendent" because it facilitates the transition from one psychic condition to another by means of the mutual confrontation of opposites.

781 This is a very sketchy description of the transcendent function, and for details I must refer the reader to the literature mentioned in the footnotes. But I had to call attention to these

11 *Psychological Types,* Def. 51.

psychological observations and methods because they indicate the way by which we may find access to the sort of "mind" referred to in our text. This is the image-creating mind, the matrix of all those patterns that give apperception its peculiar character. These patterns are inherent in the unconscious "mind"; they are its structural elements, and they alone can explain why certain mythological motifs are more or less ubiquitous, even where migration as a means of transmission is exceedingly improbable. Dreams, fantasies, and psychoses produce images to all appearances identical with mythological motifs of which the individuals concerned had absolutely no knowledge, not even indirect knowledge acquired through popular figures of speech or through the symbolic language of the Bible.[12] The psychopathology of schizophrenia, as well as the psychology of the unconscious, demonstrate the production of archaic material beyond a doubt. Whatever the structure of the unconscious may be, one thing is certain: it contains an indefinite number of motifs or patterns of an archaic character, in principle identical with the root ideas of mythology and similar thought-forms.

782 Because the unconscious is the matrix mind, the quality of creativeness attaches to it. It is the birthplace of thought-forms such as our text considers the Universal Mind to be. Since we cannot attribute any particular form to the unconscious, the Eastern assertion that the Universal Mind is without form, the *arupaloka,* yet is the source of all forms, seems to be psychologically justified. In so far as the forms or patterns of the unconscious belong to no time in particular, being seemingly eternal, they convey a peculiar feeling of timelessness when consciously realized. We find similar statements in primitive psychology: for instance, the Australian word *aljira* [13] means 'dream' as well as 'ghostland' and the 'time' in which the ancestors lived and still live. It is, as they say, the 'time when there was no time.' This looks like an obvious concretization and projection of the

12 Some people find such statements incredible. But either they have no knowledge of primitive psychology, or they are ignorant of the results of psychopathological research. Specific observations occur in my *Symbols of Transformation* and *Psychology and Alchemy,* Part II; Nelken, "Analytische Beobachtungen über Phantasien eines Schizophrenen," pp. 504ff.; Spielrein, "Über den psychologischen Inhalt eines Falls von Schizophrenie," pp. 329ff.; and C. A. Meier, "Spontanmanifestationen des kollektiven Unbewussten."

13 Lévy-Bruhl, *La Mythologie primitive,* pp. xxiii ff.

unconscious with all its characteristic qualities—its dream manifestations, its ancestral world of thought-forms, and its timelessness.

783 An introverted attitude, therefore, which withdraws its emphasis from the external world (the world of consciousness) and localizes it in the subjective factor (the background of consciousness) necessarily calls forth the characteristic manifestations of the unconscious, namely, archaic thought-forms imbued with "ancestral" or "historic" feeling, and, beyond them, the sense of indefiniteness, timelessness, oneness. The extraordinary feeling of oneness is a common experience in all forms of "mysticism" and probably derives from the general contamination of contents, which increases as consciousness dims. The almost limitless contamination of images in dreams, and particularly in the products of insanity, testifies to their unconscious origin. In contrast to the clear distinction and differentiation of forms in consciousness, unconscious contents are incredibly vague and for this reason capable of any amount of contamination. If we tried to conceive of a state in which nothing is distinct, we should certainly feel the whole as one. Hence it is not unlikely that the peculiar experience of oneness derives from the subliminal awareness of all-contamination in the unconscious.

784 By means of the transcendent function we not only gain access to the "One Mind" but also come to understand why the East believes in the possibility of self-liberation. If, through introspection and the conscious realization of unconscious compensations, it is possible to transform one's mental condition and thus arrive at a solution of painful conflicts, one would seem entitled to speak of "self-liberation." But, as I have already hinted, there is a hitch in this proud claim to self-liberation, for a man cannot produce these unconscious compensations at will. He has to rely upon the possibility that they *may* be produced. Nor can he alter the peculiar character of the compensation: *est ut est aut non est*—'it is as it is or it isn't at all.' It is a curious thing that Eastern philosophy seems to be almost unaware of this highly important fact. And it is precisely this fact that provides the psychological justification for the Western point of view. It seems as if the Western mind had a most penetrating intuition of man's fateful dependence upon some dark power which must co-operate if all is to be well. Indeed, when-

ever and wherever the unconscious fails to co-operate, man is instantly at a loss, even in his most ordinary activities. There may be a failure of memory, of co-ordinated action, or of interest and concentration; and such failure may well be the cause of serious annoyance, or of a fatal accident, a professional disaster, or a moral collapse. Formerly, men called the gods unfavourable; now we prefer to call it a neurosis, and we seek the cause in lack of vitamins, in endocrine disturbances, overwork, or sex. The co-operation of the unconscious, which is something we never think of and always take for granted, is, when it suddenly fails, a very serious matter indeed.

785 In comparison with other races—the Chinese for instance—the white man's mental equilibrium, or, to put it bluntly, his brain, seems to be his tender spot. We naturally try to get as far away from our weaknesses as possible, a fact which may explain the sort of extraversion that is always seeking security by dominating its surroundings. Extraversion goes hand in hand with mistrust of the inner man, if indeed there is any consciousness of him at all. Moreover, we all tend to undervalue the things we are afraid of. There must be some such reason for our absolute conviction that *nihil est in intellectu quod non antea fuerit in sensu,* which is the motto of Western extraversion. But, as we have emphasized, this extraversion is psychologically justified by the vital fact that unconscious compensation lies beyond man's control. I know that yoga prides itself on being able to control even the unconscious processes, so that nothing can happen in the psyche as a whole that is not ruled by a supreme consciousness. I have not the slightest doubt that such a condition is more or less possible. But it is possible only at the price of becoming identical with the unconscious. Such an identity is the Eastern equivalent of our Western fetish of "complete objectivity," the machine-like subservience to one goal, to one idea or cause, at the cost of losing every trace of inner life. From the Eastern point of view this complete objectivity is appalling, for it amounts to complete identity with the samsāra; to the West, on the other hand, samādhi is nothing but a meaningless dream-state. In the East, the inner man has always had such a firm hold on the outer man that the world had no chance of tearing him away from his inner roots; in the West, the outer man gained the ascendancy to such an extent

that he was alienated from his innermost being. The One Mind, Oneness, indefiniteness, and eternity remained the prerogative of the One God. Man became small, futile, and essentially in the wrong.

786 I think it is becoming clear from my argument that the two standpoints, however contradictory, each have their psychological justification. Both are one-sided in that they fail to see and take account of those factors which do not fit in with their typical attitude. The one underrates the world of consciousness, the other the world of the One Mind. The result is that, in their extremism, both lose one half of the universe; their life is shut off from total reality, and is apt to become artificial and inhuman. In the West, there is the mania for "objectivity," the asceticism of the scientist or of the stockbroker, who throw away the beauty and universality of life for the sake of the ideal, or not so ideal, goal. In the East, there is the wisdom, peace, detachment, and inertia of a psyche that has returned to its dim origins, having left behind all the sorrow and joy of existence as it is and, presumably, ought to be. No wonder that one-sidedness produces very similar forms of monasticism in both cases, guaranteeing to the hermit, the holy man, the monk or the scientist unswerving singleness of purpose. I have nothing against one-sidedness as such. Man, the great experiment of nature, or his own great experiment, is evidently entitled to all such undertakings—if he can endure them. Without one-sidedness the spirit of man could not unfold in all its diversity. But I do not think there is any harm in trying to understand both sides.

787 The extraverted tendency of the West and the introverted tendency of the East have one important purpose in common: both make desperate efforts to conquer the mere naturalness of life. It is the assertion of mind over matter, the *opus contra naturam,* a symptom of the youthfulness of man, still delighting in the use of the most powerful weapon ever devised by nature: the conscious mind. The afternoon of humanity, in a distant future, may yet evolve a different ideal. In time, even conquest will cease to be the dream.

2. COMMENTS ON THE TEXT

788 Before embarking upon the commentary proper, I must not omit to call the reader's attention to the very marked difference between the tenor of a psychological dissertation and that of a sacred text. A scientist forgets all too easily that the impartial handling of a subject may violate its emotional values, often to an unpardonable degree. The scientific intellect is inhuman and cannot afford to be anything else; it cannot avoid being ruthless in effect, though it may be well-intentioned in motive. In dealing with a sacred text, therefore, the psychologist ought at least to be aware that his subject represents an inestimable religious and philosophical value which should not be desecrated by profane hands. I confess that I myself venture to deal with such a text only because I know and appreciate its value. In commenting upon it I have no intention whatsoever of anatomizing it with heavy-handed criticism. On the contrary, my endeavour will be to amplify its symbolic language so that it may yield itself more easily to our understanding. To this end, it is necessary to bring down its lofty metaphysical concepts to a level where it is possible to see whether any of the psychological facts known to us have parallels in, or at least border upon, the sphere of Eastern thought. I hope this will not be misunderstood as an attempt to belittle or to banalize; my aim is simply to bring ideas which are alien to our way of thinking within reach of Western psychological experience.

789 What follows is a series of notes and comments which should be read together with the textual sections indicated by the titles.

The Obeisance

790 Eastern texts usually begin with a statement which in the West would come at the end, as the *conclusio finalis* to a long argument. We would begin with things generally known and accepted, and would end with the most important item of our investigation. Hence our dissertation would conclude with the sentence: "Therefore the *Trikāya* is the All-Enlightened Mind itself." In this respect, the Eastern mentality is not so very different from the medieval. As late as the eighteenth century our books on history or natural science began, as here, with God's

decision to create a world. The idea of a Universal Mind is a commonplace in the East, since it aptly expresses the introverted Eastern temperament. Put into psychological language, the above sentence could be paraphrased thus: The unconscious is the root of all experience of oneness (*dharmakāya*), the matrix of all archetypes or structural patterns (*sambhogakāya*), and the *conditio sine qua non* of the phenomenal world (*nirmānakāya*).

The Foreword

791 The gods are archetypal thought-forms belonging to the *sambhogakāya*.[14] Their peaceful and wrathful aspects, which play a great role in the meditations of the Tibetan Book of the Dead, symbolize the opposites. In the *nirmānakāya* these opposites are no more than human conflicts, but in the *sambhogakāya* they are the positive and negative principles united in one and the same figure. This corresponds to the psychological experience, also formulated in Lao-tzu's *Tao Teh Ching,* that there is no position without its negation. Where there is faith, there is doubt; where there is doubt, there is credulity; where there is morality, there is temptation. Only saints have diabolical visions, and tyrants are the slaves of their *valets de chambre.* If we carefully scrutinize our own character we shall inevitably find that, as Lao-tzu says, "high stands on low," which means that the opposites condition one another, that they are really one and the same thing. This can easily be seen in persons with an inferiority complex: they foment a little megalomania somewhere. The fact that the opposites appear as gods comes from the simple recognition that they are exceedingly powerful. Chinese philosophy therefore declared them to be cosmic principles, and named them *yang* and *yin.* Their power increases the more one tries to separate them. "When a tree grows up to heaven its roots reach down to hell," says Nietzsche. Yet, above as below, it is the same tree. It is characteristic of our Western mentality that we should separate the two aspects into antagonistic personifications: God and the Devil. And it is equally characteristic of the worldly optimism of Protestantism that it should have hushed up the Devil in a tactful sort of way, at any

[14] Cf. the *Shrī-Chakra-Sambhara Tantra,* in Avalon, ed., *Tantric Texts,* VII.

rate in recent times. *Omne bonum a Deo, omne malum ab homine* is the uncomfortable consequence.

792 The "seeing of reality" clearly refers to Mind as the supreme reality. In the West, however, the unconscious is considered to be a fantastic irreality. The "seeing of the Mind" implies self-liberation. This means, psychologically, that the more weight we attach to unconscious processes the more we detach ourselves from the world of desires and of separated opposites, and the nearer we draw to the state of unconsciousness with its qualities of oneness, indefiniteness, and timelessness. This is truly a liberation of the self from its bondage to strife and suffering. "By this method, one's mind is understood." Mind in this context is obviously the individual's mind, that is, his psyche. Psychology can agree in so far as the understanding of the unconscious is one of its foremost tasks.

Salutation to the One Mind

793 This section shows very clearly that the One Mind is the unconscious, since it is characterized as "eternal, unknown, not visible, not recognized." But it also displays positive features which are in keeping with Eastern experience. These are the attributes "ever clear, ever existing, radiant and unobscured." It is an undeniable psychological fact that the more one concentrates on one's unconscious contents the more they become charged with energy; they become vitalized, as if illuminated from within. In fact they turn into something like a substitute reality. In analytical psychology we make methodical use of this phenomenon. I have called the method "active imagination." Ignatius Loyola also made use of active imagination in his *Exercitia*. There is evidence that something similar was used in the meditations of alchemical philosophy.[15]

The Result of Not Knowing the One Mind

794 "Knowledge of that which is vulgarly called mind is widespread." This clearly refers to the conscious mind of everybody, in contrast to the One Mind which is unknown, i.e., unconscious. These teachings "will also be sought after by ordi-

15 My *Psychology and Alchemy*, Part III.

nary individuals who, not knowing the One Mind, do not know themselves." Self-knowledge is here definitely identified with "knowing the One Mind," which means that knowledge of the unconscious is essential for any understanding of one's own psychology. The desire for such knowledge is a well-established fact in the West, as evidenced by the rise of psychology in our time and a growing interest in these matters. The public desire for more psychological knowledge is largely due to the suffering which results from the disuse of religion and from the lack of spiritual guidance. "They wander hither and thither in the Three Regions . . . suffering sorrow." As we know what a neurosis can mean in moral suffering, this statement needs no comment. This section formulates the reasons why we have such a thing as the psychology of the unconscious today.

95 Even if one wishes "to know the mind as it is, one fails." The text again stresses how hard it is to gain access to the basic mind, because it is unconscious.

The Results of Desires

96 Those "fettered by desires cannot perceive the Clear Light." The "Clear Light" again refers to the One Mind. Desires crave for external fulfilment. They forge the chain that fetters man to the world of consciousness. In that condition he naturally cannot become aware of his unconscious contents. And indeed there is a healing power in withdrawing from the conscious world—up to a point. Beyond that point, which varies with individuals, withdrawal amounts to neglect and repression.

97 Even the "Middle Path" finally becomes "obscured by desires." This is a very true statement, which cannot be dinned too insistently into European ears. Patients and normal individuals, on becoming acquainted with their unconscious material, hurl themselves upon it with the same heedless desirousness and greed that before had engulfed them in their extraversion. The problem is not so much a withdrawal from the objects of desire, as a more detached attitude to desire as such, no matter what its object. We cannot compel unconscious compensation through the impetuousness of uncontrolled desire. We have to wait patiently to see whether it will come of its own accord, and put up with whatever form it takes. Hence we are forced

into a sort of contemplative attitude which, in itself, not rarely has a liberating and healing effect.

The Transcendent At-one-ment

798 "There being really no duality, pluralism is untrue." This is certainly one of the most fundamental truths of the East. There are no opposites—it is the same tree above and below. The *Tabula smaragdina* says: "Quod est inferius est sicut quod est superius. Et quod est superius est sicut quod est inferius, ad perpetranda miracula rei unius." [16] Pluralism is even more illusory, since all separate forms originate in the indistinguishable oneness of the psychic matrix, deep down in the unconscious. The statement made by our text refers psychologically to the subjective factor, to the material immediately constellated by a stimulus, i.e., the first impression which, as we have seen, interprets every new perception in terms of previous experience. "Previous experience" goes right back to the instincts, and thus to the inherited and inherent patterns of psychic functioning, the ancestral and "eternal" laws of the human mind. But the statement entirely ignores the possible transcendent reality of the physical world as such, a problem not unknown to Sankhya philosophy, where *prakriti* and *purusha*—so far as they are a polarization of Universal Being—form a cosmic dualism that can hardly be circumvented. One has to close one's eyes to dualism and pluralism alike, and forget all about the existence of a world, as soon as one tries to identify oneself with the monistic origin of life. The questions naturally arise: "Why should the One appear as the Many, when ultimate reality is All-One? What is the cause of pluralism, or of the illusion of pluralism? If the One is pleased with itself, why should it mirror itself in the Many? Which after all is the more real, the one that mirrors itself, or the mirror it uses?" Probably we should not ask such questions, seeing that there is no answer to them.

799 It is psychologically correct to say that "At-one-ment" is attained by withdrawal from the world of consciousness. In the stratosphere of the unconscious there are no more thunder-

16 "What is below is like what is above. And what is above is like what is below, so that the miracle of the One may be accomplished." Cf. Ruska, *Tabula Smaragdina,* p. 2.

storms, because nothing is differentiated enough to produce tensions and conflicts. These belong to the surface of our reality.

800 The Mind in which the irreconcilables—samsāra and nirvāna—are united is ultimately our mind. Does this statement spring from profound modesty or from overweening hybris? Does it mean that the Mind is "nothing but" our mind? Or that our mind is the Mind? Assuredly it means the latter, and from the Eastern point of view there is no hybris in this; on the contrary, it is a perfectly acceptable truth, whereas with us it would amount to saying "I am God." This is an incontestable "mystical" experience, though a highly objectionable one to the Westerner; but in the East, where it derives from a mind that has never lost touch with the instinctual matrix, it has a very different value. The collective introverted attitude of the East did not permit the world of the senses to sever the vital link with the unconscious; psychic reality was never seriously disputed, despite the existence of so-called materialistic speculations. The only known analogy to this fact is the mental condition of the primitive, who confuses dream and reality in the most bewildering way. Naturally we hesitate to call the Eastern mind primitive, for we are deeply impressed with its remarkable civilization and differentiation. Yet the primitive mind is its matrix, and this is particularly true of that aspect of it which stresses the validity of psychic phenomena, such as relate to ghosts and spirits. The West has simply cultivated the other aspect of primitivity, namely, the scrupulously accurate observation of nature at the expense of abstraction. Our natural science is the epitome of primitive man's astonishing powers of observation. We have added only a moderate amount of abstraction, for fear of being contradicted by the facts. The East, on the other hand, cultivates the psychic aspect of primitivity together with an inordinate amount of abstraction. Facts make excellent stories but not much more.

801 Thus, if the East speaks of the Mind as being inherent in everybody, no more hybris or modesty is involved than in the European's belief in facts, which are mostly derived from man's own observation and sometimes from rather less than his observation, to wit, his interpretation. He is, therefore, quite right to be afraid of too much abstraction.

The Great Self-Liberation

802 I have mentioned more than once that the shifting of the basic personality-feeling to the less conscious mental sphere has a liberating effect. I have also described, somewhat cursorily, the transcendent function which produces the transformation of personality, and I have emphasized the importance of spontaneous unconscious compensation. Further, I have pointed out the neglect of this crucial fact in yoga. This section tends to confirm my observations. The grasping of "the whole essence of these teachings" seems also to be the whole essence of "self-liberation." The Westerner would take this to mean: "Learn your lesson and repeat it, and then you will be self-liberated." That, indeed, is precisely what happens with most Western practitioners of yoga. They are very apt to "do" it in an extraverted fashion, oblivious of the inturning of the mind which is the essence of such teachings. In the East, the "truths" are so much a part of the collective consciousness that they are at least intuitively grasped by the pupil. If the European could turn himself inside out and live as an Oriental, with all the social, moral, religious, intellectual, and aesthetic obligations which such a course would involve, he might be able to benefit by these teachings. But you cannot be a good Christian, either in your faith or in your morality or in your intellectual make-up, and practise genuine yoga at the same time. I have seen too many cases that have made me sceptical in the highest degree. The trouble is that Western man cannot get rid of his history as easily as his short-legged memory can. History, one might say, is written in the blood. I would not advise anyone to touch yoga without a careful analysis of his unconscious reactions. What is the use of imitating yoga if your dark side remains as good a medieval Christian as ever? If you can afford to seat yourself on a gazelle skin under a Bo-tree or in the cell of a *gompa* for the rest of your life without being troubled by politics or the collapse of your securities, I will look favourably upon your case. But yoga in Mayfair or Fifth Avenue, or in any other place which is on the telephone, is a spiritual fake.

803 Taking the mental equipment of Eastern man into account, we may suppose that the teaching is effective. But unless one is prepared to turn away from the world and to disappear into the

unconscious for good, mere teaching has no effect, or at least not the desired one. For this the union of opposites is necessary, and in particular the difficult task of reconciling extraversion and introversion by means of the transcendent function.

The Nature of Mind

804 This section contains a valuable piece of psychological information. The text says: "The mind is of intuitive ("quick-knowing") Wisdom." Here "mind" is understood to be identical with immediate awareness of the "first impression" which conveys the whole sum of previous experience based upon instinctual patterns. This bears out our remarks about the essentially introverted prejudice of the East. The formula also draws attention to the highly differentiated character of Eastern intuition. The intuitive mind is noted for its disregard of facts in favour of possibilities.[17]

805 The assertion that the Mind "has no existence" obviously refers to the peculiar "potentiality" of the unconscious. A thing seems to exist only to the degree that we are aware of it, which explains why so many people are disinclined to believe in the existence of an unconscious. When I tell a patient that he is chock full of fantasies, he is often astonished beyond all measure, having been completely unaware of the fantasy-life he was leading.

The Names Given to the Mind

806 The various terms employed to express a "difficult" or "obscure" idea are a valuable source of information about the ways in which that idea can be interpreted, and at the same time an indication of its doubtful or controversial nature even in the country, religion, or philosophy to which it is indigenous. If the idea were perfectly straightforward and enjoyed general acceptance, there would be no reason to call it by a number of different names. But when something is little known, or ambiguous, it can be envisaged from different angles, and then a multiplicity of names is needed to express its peculiar nature. A classical example of this is the philosophers' stone; many of the old alchemical treatises give long lists of its names.

[17] Cf. *Psychological Types*, Def. 36.

807 The statement that "the various names given to it [the Mind] are innumerable" proves that the Mind must be something as vague and indefinite as the philosophers' stone. A substance that can be described in "innumerable" ways must be expected to display as many qualities or facets. If these are really "innumerable," they cannot be counted, and it follows that the substance is well-nigh indescribable and unknowable. It can never be realized completely. This is certainly true of the unconscious, and a further proof that the Mind is the Eastern equivalent of our concept of the unconscious, more particularly of the collective unconscious.

808 In keeping with this hypothesis, the text goes on to say that the Mind is also called the "Mental Self." The "self" is an important concept in analytical psychology, where much has been said that I need not repeat here. I would refer the interested reader to the literature given below.[18] Although the symbols of the "self" are produced by unconscious activity and are mostly manifested in dreams,[19] the facts which the idea covers are not merely mental; they include aspects of physical existence as well. In this and other Eastern texts the "Self" represents a purely spiritual idea, but in Western psychology the "self" stands for a totality which comprises instincts, physiological and semi-physiological phenomena. To us a purely spiritual totality is inconceivable for the reasons mentioned above.[20]

809 It is interesting to note that in the East, too, there are "heretics" who identify the Self with the ego.[21] With us this heresy is pretty widespread and is subscribed to by all those who firmly believe that ego-consciousness is the only form of psychic life.

810 The Mind as "the means of attaining the Other Shore" points to a connection between the transcendent function and the idea of the Mind or Self. Since the unknowable substance of the Mind, i.e., of the unconscious, always represents itself to consciousness in the form of symbols—the self being one such

18 My *Two Essays on Analytical Psychology,* index, s.v. "Self"; *Psychological Types,* Def. 16; *Psychology and Alchemy,* Part II; *Aion.*

19 One such case is described in Part II of *Psychology and Alchemy.*

20 This is no criticism of the Eastern point of view *in toto;* for, according to the *Amitāyur-dhyāna Sūtra,* the Buddha's body is included in the meditation.

21 Cf. for instance, *Chhāndogya Upanishad,* viii. 8.

symbol—the symbol functions as a "means of attaining the Other Shore," in other words, as a means of transformation. In my essay on psychic energy I said that the symbol acts as a transformer of energy.[22]

811 My interpretation of the Mind or Self as a symbol is not arbitrary; the text itself calls it "The Great Symbol."

812 It is also remarkable that our text recognizes the "potentiality" of the unconscious, as formulated above, by calling the Mind the "Sole Seed" and the "Potentiality of Truth."

813 The matrix-character of the unconscious comes out in the term "All-Foundation."

The Timelessness of Mind

814 I have already explained this "timelessness" as a quality inherent in the experience of the collective unconscious. The application of the "yoga of self-liberation" is said to reintegrate all forgotten knowledge of the past with consciousness. The motif of ἀποκατάστασις (restoration, restitution) occurs in many redemption myths and is also an important aspect of the psychology of the unconscious, which reveals an extraordinary amount of archaic material in the dreams and spontaneous fantasies of normal and insane people. In the systematic analysis of an individual the spontaneous reawakening of ancestral patterns (as a compensation) has the effect of a restoration. It is also a fact that premonitory dreams are relatively frequent, and this substantiates what the text calls "knowledge of the future."

815 The Mind's "own time" is very difficult to interpret. From the psychological point of view we must agree with Dr. Evans-Wentz's comment here.[23] The unconscious certainly has its "own time" inasmuch as past, present, and future are blended together in it. Dreams of the type experienced by J. W. Dunne,[24] where he dreamed the night before what he ought logically to have dreamed the night after, are not infrequent.

22 "On Psychic Energy" (1928 edn., p. 54).

23 Cf. his *Tibetan Book of the Great Liberation,* p. 210, n. 3.

24 *An Experiment with Time.* [Cf. Jung's "Synchronicity" (1955 edn., p. 38).—EDITORS.]

Mind in Its True State

816 This section describes the state of detached consciousness [25] which corresponds to a psychic experience very common throughout the East. Similar descriptions are to be found in Chinese literature, as, for instance, in the *Hui Ming Ch'ing:*

A luminosity surrounds the world of spirit.
We forget one another when, still and pure, we draw strength from the Void.
The Void is filled with the light of the Heart of Heaven . . .
Consciousness dissolves in vision.[26]

817 The statement "Nor is one's own mind separable from other minds" is another way of expressing the fact of "all-contamination." Since all distinctions vanish in the unconscious condition, it is only logical that the distinction between separate minds should disappear too. Wherever there is a lowering of the conscious level we come across instances of unconscious identity,[27] or what Lévy-Bruhl calls "participation mystique." [28] The realization of the One Mind is, as our text says, the "at-onement of the *Trikāya*"; in fact it creates the at-one-ment. But we are unable to imagine how such a realization could ever be complete in any human individual. There must always be somebody or something left over to experience the realization, to say "I know at-one-ment, I know there is no distinction." The very fact of the realization proves its inevitable incompleteness. One cannot know something that is not distinct from oneself. Even

25 I have explained this in my commentary on *The Secret of the Golden Flower* (1931 edn., pp. 21ff.).

26 From the [German] trans. of L. C. Lo, I, p. 114.

27 *Psychological Types,* Def. 25.

28 Cf. Lévy-Bruhl, *How Natives Think.* Recently this concept as well as that of the *état prélogique* have been severely criticized by ethnologists, and moreover Lévy-Bruhl himself began to doubt their validity in the last years of his life. First he cancelled the adjective "mystique," growing afraid of the term's bad reputation in intellectual circles. It is rather to be regretted that he made such a concession to rationalistic superstition, since "mystique" is just the right word to characterize the peculiar quality of "unconscious identity." There is always something numinous about it. Unconscious identity is a well-known psychological and psychopathological phenomenon (identity with persons, things, functions, roles, positions, creeds, etc.), which is only a shade more characteristic of the primitive than of the civilized mind. Lévy-Bruhl, unfortunately having no psychological knowledge, was not aware of this fact, and his opponents ignore it.

when I say "I know myself," an infinitesimal ego—the knowing "I"—is still distinct from "myself." In this as it were atomic ego, which is completely ignored by the essentially non-dualist standpoint of the East, there nevertheless lies hidden the whole unabolished pluralistic universe and its unconquered reality.

818 The experience of "at-one-ment" is one example of those "quick-knowing" realizations of the East, an intuition of what it would be like if one could exist and not exist at the same time. If I were a Moslem, I should maintain that the power of the All-Compassionate is infinite, and that He alone can make a man to be and not to be at the same time. But for my part I cannot conceive of such a possibility. I therefore assume that, in this point, Eastern intuition has overreached itself.

Mind Is Non-Created

819 This section emphasizes that as the Mind is without characteristics, one cannot assert that it is created. But then, it would be illogical to assert that it is non-created, for such a qualification would amount to a "characteristic." As a matter of fact you can make no assertion whatever about a thing that is indistinct, void of characteristics and, moreover, "unknowable." For precisely this reason Western psychology does not speak of the One Mind, but of the unconscious, regarding it as a thing-in-itself, a noumenon, "a merely negative borderline concept," to quote Kant.[29] We have often been reproached for using such a negative term, but unfortunately intellectual honesty does not allow a positive one.

The Yoga of Introspection

820 Should there be any doubt left concerning the identity of the One Mind and the unconscious, this section certainly ought to dispel it. "The One Mind being verily of the Voidness and without any foundation, one's mind is, likewise, as vacuous as the sky." The One Mind and the individual mind are equally void and vacuous. Only the collective and the personal unconscious can be meant by this statement, for the conscious mind is in no circumstances "vacuous."

[29] Cf. *The Critique of Pure Reason,* sec. i, Part I, 2, 3 (cf. trans. by Meiklejohn, p. 188).

821 As I have said earlier, the Eastern mind insists first and foremost upon the subjective factor, and in particular upon the intuitive "first impression," or the psychic disposition. This is borne out by the statement that "All appearances are verily one's own concepts, self-conceived in the mind."

The Dharma Within

822 *Dharma,* law, truth, guidance, is said to be "nowhere save in the mind." Thus the unconscious is credited with all those faculties which the West attributes to God. The transcendent function, however, shows how right the East is in assuming that the complex experience of *dharma* comes from "within," i.e., from the unconscious. It also shows that the phenomenon of spontaneous compensation, being beyond the control of man, is quite in accord with the formula "grace" or the "will of God."

823 This and the preceding section insist again and again that introspection is the only source of spiritual information and guidance. If introspection were something morbid, as certain people in the West opine, we should have to send practically the whole East, or such parts of it as are not yet infected with the blessings of the West, to the lunatic asylum.

The Wondrousness of These Teachings

824 This section calls the mind "Natural Wisdom," which is very much the same expression that I used in order to designate the symbols produced by the unconscious. I called them "natural symbols." [30] I chose the term before I had any knowledge of this text. I mention this fact simply because it illustrates the close parallelism between the findings of Eastern and Western psychology.

825 The text also confirms what we said earlier about the impossibility of a "knowing" ego. "Although it is Total Reality, there is no perceiver of it. Wondrous is this." Wondrous indeed, and incomprehensible; for how could such a thing ever be *realized* in the true sense of the word? "It remains undefiled by evil" and "it remains unallied to good." One is reminded of Nietzsche's "six thousand feet beyond good and evil." But the consequences of such a statement are usually ignored by the

30 Cf. the first paper in this volume, chs. 2 and 3.

emulators of Eastern wisdom. While one is safely ensconced in one's cosy flat, secure in the favour of the Oriental gods, one is free to admire this lofty moral indifference. But does it agree with our temperament, or with our history, which is not thereby conquered but merely forgotten? I think not. Anyone who affects the higher yoga will be called upon to prove his professions of moral indifference, not only as the doer of evil but, even more, as its victim. As psychologists well know, the moral conflict is not to be settled merely by a declaration of superiority bordering on inhumanity. We are witnessing today some terrifying examples of the Superman's aloofness from moral principles.

826 I do not doubt that the Eastern liberation from vices, as well as from virtues, is coupled with detachment in every respect, so that the yogi is translated beyond this world, and quite inoffensive. But I suspect every European attempt at detachment of being mere liberation from moral considerations. Anybody who tries his hand at yoga ought therefore to be conscious of its far-reaching consequences, or else his so-called quest will remain a futile pastime.

The Fourfold Great Path

827 The text says: "This meditation [is] devoid of mental concentration." The usual assumption about yoga is that it chiefly consists in intense concentration. We think we know what concentration means, but it is very difficult to arrive at a real understanding of Eastern concentration. Our sort may well be just the opposite of the Eastern, as a study of Zen Buddhism will show.[31] However, if we take "devoid of mental concentration" literally, it can only mean that the meditation does not centre upon anything. Not being centred, it would be rather like a dissolution of consciousness and hence a direct approach to the unconscious condition. Consciousness always implies a certain degree of concentration, without which there would be no clarity of mental content and no consciousness of anything. Meditation without concentration would be a waking but empty condition, on the verge of falling asleep. Since our text calls this "the most excellent of meditations" we must suppose the existence of less excellent meditations which, we infer, would be characterized

31 Cf. Suzuki, *Essays in Zen Buddhism.*

by more concentration. The meditation our text has in mind seems to be a sort of Royal Road to the unconscious.

The Great Light

828 The central mystical experience of enlightenment is aptly symbolized by Light in most of the numerous forms of mysticism. It is a curious paradox that the approach to a region which seems to us the way into utter darkness should yield the light of illumination as its fruit. This is, however, the usual *enantiodromia per tenebras ad lucem.* Many initiation ceremonies [32] stage a *κατάβασις εἰς ἄντρον* (descent into the cave), a diving down into the depths of the baptismal water, or a return to the womb of rebirth. Rebirth symbolism simply describes the union of opposites—conscious and unconscious—by means of concretistic analogies. Underlying all rebirth symbolism is the transcendent function. Since this function results in an increase of consciousness (the previous condition augmented by the addition of formerly unconscious contents), the new condition carries more insight, which is symbolized by more light.[33] It is therefore a more enlightened state compared with the relative darkness of the previous state. In many cases the Light even appears in the form of a vision.

The Yoga of the Nirvanic Path

829 This section gives one of the best formulations of the complete dissolution of consciousness, which appears to be the goal of this yoga: "There being no two such things as action and performer of action, if one seeks the performer of action and no performer of action be found anywhere, thereupon the goal of all fruit-obtaining is reached and also the final consummation itself."

830 With this very complete formulation of the method and its aim, I reach the end of my commentary. The text that follows, in Book II, is of great beauty and wisdom, and contains nothing that requires further comment. It can be translated into psychological language and interpreted with the help of the principles I have here set forth in Part I and illustrated in Part II.

32 As in the Eleusinian mysteries and the Mithras and Attis cults.

33 In alchemy the philosophers' stone was called, among other things, *lux moderna, lux lucis, lumen luminum,* etc.

PSYCHOLOGICAL COMMENTARY ON "THE TIBETAN BOOK OF THE DEAD" [1]

831 Before embarking upon the psychological commentary, I should like to say a few words about the text itself. The Tibetan Book of the Dead, or the *Bardo Thödol,* is a book of instructions for the dead and dying. Like the Egyptian Book of the Dead, it is meant to be a guide for the dead man during the period of his *Bardo* existence, symbolically described as an intermediate state of forty-nine days' duration between death and rebirth. The text falls into three parts. The first part, called *Chikhai Bardo,* describes the psychic happenings at the moment of death. The second part, or *Chönyid Bardo,* deals with the dream-state which supervenes immediately after death, and with what are called "karmic illusions." The third part, or *Sidpa Bardo,* concerns the onset of the birth-instinct and of prenatal

1 [Originally published as "Psychologischer Kommentar zum Bardo Thödol" (preceded by an "Einführung," partially translated in the first two pars. here), in *Das Tibetanische Totenbuch,* translated into German by Louise Göpfert-March (Zurich, 1935). As ultimately revised for the 5th (revised and expanded) Swiss edition (1953), the commentary was translated by R. F. C. Hull for publication in the 3rd (revised and expanded) English edition (the original) of *The Tibetan Book of the Dead, or The After-Death Experience on the "Bardo" Plane,* according to Lama Kazi Dawa-Samdup's English rendering, edited by W. Y. Evans-Wentz, with foreword by Sir John Woodroffe (London and New York, 1957). With only minor alterations, it is the translation presented here.—EDITORS.]

events. It is characteristic that supreme insight and illumination, and hence the greatest possibility of attaining liberation, are vouchsafed during the actual process of dying. Soon afterward, the "illusions" begin which lead eventually to reincarnation, the illuminative lights growing ever fainter and more multifarious, and the visions more and more terrifying. This descent illustrates the estrangement of consciousness from the liberating truth as it approaches nearer and nearer to physical rebirth. The purpose of the instruction is to fix the attention of the dead man, at each successive stage of delusion and entanglement, on the ever-present possibility of liberation, and to explain to him the nature of his visions. The text of the *Bardo Thödol* is recited by the lama in the presence of the corpse.

832 I do not think I could better discharge my debt of thanks to the two previous translators of the *Bardo Thödol,* the late Lama Kazi Dawa-Samdup and Dr. Evans-Wentz, than by attempting, with the aid of a psychological commentary, to make the magnificent world of ideas and the problems contained in this treatise a little more intelligible to the Western mind. I am sure that all who read this book with open eyes, and who allow it to impress itself upon them without prejudice, will reap a rich reward.

*

833 The *Bardo Thödol,* fitly named by its editor, Dr. W. Y. Evans-Wentz, "The Tibetan Book of the Dead," caused a considerable stir in English-speaking countries at the time of its first appearance in 1927. It belongs to that class of writings which are not only of interest to specialists in Mahayana Buddhism, but which also, because of their deep humanity and their still deeper insight into the secrets of the human psyche, make an especial appeal to the layman who is seeking to broaden his knowledge of life. For years, ever since it was first published, the *Bardo Thödol* has been my constant companion, and to it I owe not only many stimulating ideas and discoveries, but also many fundamental insights. Unlike the Egyptian Book of the Dead, which always prompts one to say too much or too little, the *Bardo Thödol* offers one an intelligible philosophy addressed to human beings rather than to gods or primitive savages. Its philosophy contains the quintessence of Buddhist psychological criticism; and, as such, one can truly say that it is of an unex-

ampled superiority. Not only the "wrathful" but also the "peaceful" deities are conceived as samsaric projections of the human psyche, an idea that seems all too obvious to the enlightened European, because it reminds him of his own banal simplifications. But though the European can easily explain away these deities as projections, he would be quite incapable of positing them at the same time as real. The *Bardo Thödol* can do that, because, in certain of its most essential metaphysical premises, it has the enlightened as well as the unenlightened European at a disadvantage. The ever-present, unspoken assumption of the *Bardo Thödol* is the antinominal character of all metaphysical assertions, and also the idea of the qualitative difference of the various levels of consciousness and of the metaphysical realities conditioned by them. The background of this unusual book is not the niggardly European "either-or," but a magnificently affirmative "both-and." This statement may appear objectionable to the Western philosopher, for the West loves clarity and unambiguity; consequently, one philosopher clings to the position, "God is," while another clings equally fervently to the negation, "God is not." What would these hostile brethren make of an assertion like the following:

> Recognizing the voidness of thine own intellect to be Buddhahood, and knowing it at the same time to be thine own consciousness, thou shalt abide in the state of the divine mind of the Buddha.

834 Such an assertion is, I fear, as unwelcome to our Western philosophy as it is to our theology. The *Bardo Thödol* is in the highest degree psychological in its outlook; but, with us, philosophy and theology are still in the medieval, pre-psychological stage where only the assertions are listened to, explained, defended, criticized and disputed, while the authority that makes them has, by general consent, been deposed as outside the scope of discussion.

835 Metaphysical assertions, however, are *statements of the psyche,* and are therefore psychological. To the Western mind, which compensates its well-known feelings of resentment by a slavish regard for "rational" explanations, this obvious truth seems all too obvious, or else it is seen as an inadmissible negation of metaphysical "truth." Whenever the Westerner hears the word "psychological," it always sounds to him like "*only*

psychological." For him the "soul" is something pitifully small, unworthy, personal, subjective, and a lot more besides. He therefore prefers to use the word "mind" instead, though he likes to pretend at the same time that a statement which may in fact be very subjective indeed is made by the "mind," naturally by the "Universal Mind," or even—at a pinch—by the "Absolute" itself. This rather ridiculous presumption is probably a compensation for the regrettable smallness of the soul. It almost seems as if Anatole France had uttered a truth which were valid for the whole Western world when, in his *Penguin Island,* Cathérine d'Alexandrie offers this advice to God: "Donnez-leur une âme, mais une petite!"

836 It is the psyche which, by the divine creative power inherent in it, makes the metaphysical assertion; it posits the distinctions between metaphysical entities. Not only is it the condition of all metaphysical reality, it *is* that reality.

837 With this great psychological truth the *Bardo Thödol* opens. The book is not a ceremonial of burial, but a set of instructions for the dead, a guide through the changing phenomena of the *Bardo* realm, that state of existence which continues for forty-nine days after death until the next incarnation. If we disregard for the moment the supratemporality of the soul—which the East accepts as a self-evident fact—we, as readers of the *Bardo Thödol,* shall be able to put ourselves without difficulty in the position of the dead man, and shall consider attentively the teaching set forth in the opening section, which is outlined in the quotation above. At this point, the following words are spoken, not presumptuously, but in a courteous manner:

> O nobly born (so and so), listen. Now thou art experiencing the Radiance of the Clear Light of Pure Reality. Recognize it. O nobly-born, thy present intellect, in real nature void, not formed into anything as regards characteristics or colour, naturally void, is the very Reality, the All-Good.
>
> Thine own intellect, which is now voidness, yet not to be regarded as of the voidness of nothingness, but as being the intellect itself, unobstructed, shining, thrilling, and blissful, is the very consciousness, the All-good Buddha.

838 This realization is the *Dharmakāya* state of perfect enlightenment; or, as we should express it in our own language, the

creative ground of all metaphysical assertion is consciousness, as the invisible, intangible manifestation of the soul. The "Voidness" is the state transcendent over all assertion and all predication. The fulness of its discriminative manifestations still lies latent in the soul.

839 The text continues:

> Thine own consciousness, shining, void, and inseparable from the Great Body of Radiance, hath no birth, nor death, and is the Immutable Light—Buddha Amitābha.

840 The soul is assuredly not small, but the radiant Godhead itself. The West finds this statement either very dangerous, if not downright blasphemous, or else accepts it unthinkingly and then suffers from a theosophical inflation. Somehow we always have a wrong attitude to these things. But if we can master ourselves far enough to refrain from our chief error of always wanting to *do* something with things and put them to practical use, we may perhaps succeed in learning an important lesson from these teachings, or at least in appreciating the greatness of the *Bardo Thödol,* which vouchsafes to the dead man the ultimate and highest truth, that even the gods are the radiance and reflection of our own souls. No sun is thereby eclipsed for the Oriental as it would be for the Christian, who would feel robbed of his God; on the contrary, his soul is the light of the Godhead, and the Godhead is the soul. The East can sustain this paradox better than the unfortunate Angelus Silesius, who even today would be psychologically far in advance of his time.

841 It is highly sensible of the *Bardo Thödol* to make clear to the dead man the primacy of the psyche, for that is the one thing which life does not make clear to us. We are so hemmed in by things which jostle and oppress that we never get a chance, in the midst of all these "given" things, to wonder by whom they are "given." It is from this world of "given" things that the dead man liberates himself; and the purpose of the instruction is to help him towards this liberation. We, if we put ourselves in his place, shall derive no lesser reward from it, since we learn from the very first paragraphs that the "giver" of all "given" things dwells within us. This is a truth which in the face of all evidence, in the greatest things as in the smallest, is never known, although it is often so very necessary, indeed vital, for us to

know it. Such knowledge, to be sure, is suitable only for contemplatives who are minded to understand the purpose of existence, for those who are Gnostics by temperament and therefore believe in a saviour who, like the saviour of the Mandaeans, is called "knowledge of life" (Manda d'Hayye). Perhaps it is not granted to many of us to see the world as something "given." A great reversal of standpoint, calling for much sacrifice, is needed before we can see the world as "given" by the very nature of the psyche. It is so much more straightforward, more dramatic, impressive, and therefore more convincing, to see all the things that happen to me than to observe how I make them happen. Indeed, the animal nature of man makes him resist seeing himself as the maker of his circumstances. That is why attempts of this kind were always the object of secret initiations, culminating as a rule in a figurative death which symbolized the total character of this reversal. And, in point of fact, the instruction given in the *Bardo Thödol* serves to recall to the dead man the experiences of his initiation and the teachings of his guru, for the instruction is, at bottom, nothing less than an initiation of the dead into the *Bardo* life, just as the initiation of the living was a preparation for the Beyond. Such was the case, at least, with all the mystery cults in ancient civilizations from the time of the Egyptian and Eleusinian mysteries. In the initiation of the living, however, this "Beyond" is not a world beyond death, but a reversal of the mind's intentions and outlook, a psychological "Beyond" or, in Christian terms, a "redemption" from the trammels of the world and of sin. Redemption is a separation and deliverance from an earlier condition of darkness and unconsciousness, and leads to a condition of illumination and releasedness, to victory and transcendence over everything "given."

842 Thus far the *Bardo Thödol* is, as Dr. Evans-Wentz also feels, an initiation process whose purpose it is to restore to the soul the divinity it lost at birth. Now it is a characteristic of Oriental religious literature that the teaching invariably begins with the most important item, with the ultimate and highest principles which, with us, would come last—as for instance in Apuleius, where Lucius is worshipped as Helios only right at the end. Accordingly, in the *Bardo Thödol,* the initiation is a series of diminishing climaxes ending with rebirth in the womb. The

only "initiation process" that is still alive and practised today in the West is the analysis of the unconscious as used by doctors for therapeutic purposes. This penetration into the ground-layers of consciousness is a kind of rational maieutics in the Socratic sense, a bringing forth of psychic contents that are still germinal, subliminal, and as yet unborn. Originally, this therapy took the form of Freudian psychoanalysis and was mainly concerned with sexual fantasies. This is the realm that corresponds to the last and lowest region of the *Bardo,* known as the *Sidpa Bardo,* where the dead man, unable to profit by the teachings of the *Chikhai* and *Chönyid Bardo,* begins to fall a prey to sexual fantasies and is attracted by the vision of mating couples. Eventually he is caught by a womb and born into the earthly world again. Meanwhile, as one might expect, the Oedipus complex starts functioning. If his karma destines him to be reborn as a man, he will fall in love with his mother-to-be and will find his father hateful and disgusting. Conversely, the future daughter will be highly attracted by her father-to-be and repelled by her mother. The European passes through this specifically Freudian domain when his unconscious contents are brought to light under analysis, but he goes in the reverse direction. He journeys back through the world of infantile-sexual fantasy to the womb. It has even been suggested in psychoanalytical circles that the trauma par excellence is the birth-experience itself—nay more, psychoanalysts even claim to have probed back to memories of intra-uterine origin. Here Western reason reaches its limit, unfortunately. I say "unfortunately," because one rather wishes that Freudian psychoanalysis could have happily pursued these so-called intra-uterine experiences still further back. Had it succeeded in this bold undertaking, it would surely have come out beyond the *Sidpa Bardo* and penetrated from behind into the lower reaches of the *Chönyid Bardo.* It is true that, with the equipment of our existing biological ideas, such a venture would not have been crowned with success; it would have needed a wholly different kind of philosophical preparation from that based on current scientific assumptions. But, had the journey back been consistently pursued, it would undoubtedly have led to the postulate of a pre-uterine existence, a true *Bardo* life, if only it had been possible to find at least some trace of an experiencing subject. As it was, the psychoanalysts never got beyond purely conjectural traces of intra-uterine experiences, and even the famous "birth trauma" has remained such an obvious truism that it can no longer explain anything, any more than can the hypothesis that life is a disease with a bad prognosis because its outcome is always fatal.

843 Freudian psychoanalysis, in all essential aspects, never went beyond the experiences of the *Sidpa Bardo;* that is, it was unable to extricate itself from sexual fantasies and similar "incompatible" tendencies which cause anxiety and other affective states. Nevertheless, Freud's theory is the first attempt made by the West to investigate, as if from below, from the animal sphere of instinct, the psychic territory that corresponds in Tantric Lamaism to the *Sidpa Bardo.* A very justifiable fear of metaphysics prevented Freud from penetrating into the sphere of the "occult." In addition to this, the *Sidpa* state, if we are to accept the psychology of the *Sidpa Bardo,* is characterized by the fierce wind of karma, which whirls the dead man along until he comes to the "womb-door." In other words, the *Sidpa* state permits of no going back, because it is sealed off against the *Chönyid* state by an intense striving downwards, towards the animal sphere of instinct and physical rebirth. That is to say, anyone who penetrates into the unconscious with purely biological assumptions will become stuck in the instinctual sphere and be unable to advance beyond it, for he will be pulled back again and again into physical existence. It is therefore not possible for Freudian theory to reach anything except an essentially negative valuation of the unconscious. It is a "nothing but." At the same time, it must be admitted that this view of the psyche is typically Western, only it is expressed more blatantly, more plainly, and more ruthlessly than others would have dared to express it, though at bottom they think no differently. As to what "mind" means in this connection, we can only cherish the hope that it will carry conviction. But, as even Max Scheler [2] noted with regret, the power of this "mind" is, to say the least of it, doubtful.

844 I think, then, we can state it as a fact that with the aid of psychoanalysis the rationalizing mind of the West has pushed forward into what one might call the neuroticism of the *Sidpa*

2 [German philosopher and sociologist (1874–1928) working mainly in the field of values.—EDITORS.]

state, and has there been brought to an inevitable standstill by the uncritical assumption that everything psychological is subjective and personal. Even so, this advance has been a great gain, inasmuch as it has enabled us to take one more step behind our conscious lives. This knowledge also gives us a hint of how we ought to read the *Bardo Thödol*—that is, backwards. If, with the help of our Western science, we have to some extent succeeded in understanding the psychological character of the *Sidpa Bardo,* our next task is to see if we can make anything of the preceding *Chönyid Bardo.*

845 The *Chönyid* state is one of karmic illusion—that is to say, illusions which result from the psychic residua of previous existences. According to the Eastern view, karma implies a sort of psychic theory of heredity based on the hypothesis of reincarnation, which in the last resort is an hypothesis of the supratemporality of the soul. Neither our scientific knowledge nor our reason can keep in step with this idea. There are too many if's and but's. Above all, we know desperately little about the possibilities of continued existence of the individual soul after death, so little that we cannot even conceive how anyone could prove anything at all in this respect. Moreover, we know only too well, on epistemological grounds, that such a proof would be just as impossible as the proof of God. Hence we may cautiously accept the idea of karma only if we understand it as *psychic heredity* in the very widest sense of the word. Psychic heredity does exist—that is to say, there is inheritance of psychic characteristics such as predisposition to disease, traits of character, special gifts, and so forth. It does no violence to the psychic nature of these complex facts if natural science reduces them to what appear to be physical aspects (nuclear structures in cells, and so on). They are essential phenomena of life which express themselves, in the main, psychically, just as there are other inherited characteristics which express themselves, in the main, physiologically, on the physical level. Among these inherited psychic factors there is a special class which is not confined either to family or to race. These are the universal dispositions of the mind, and they are to be understood as analogous to Plato's forms (*eidola*), in accordance with which the mind organizes its contents. One could also describe these forms as *categories* analogous to the logical categories which are

always and everywhere present as the basic postulates of reason. Only, in the case of our "forms," we are not dealing with categories of reason but with categories of the *imagination*. As the products of imagination are always in essence visual, their forms must, from the outset, have the character of images and moreover of *typical* images, which is why, following St. Augustine, I call them "archetypes." Comparative religion and mythology are rich mines of archetypes, and so is the psychology of dreams and psychoses. The astonishing parallelism between these images and the ideas they serve to express has frequently given rise to the wildest migration theories, although it would have been far more natural to think of the remarkable similarity of the human psyche at all times and in all places. Archetypal fantasy-forms are, in fact, reproduced spontaneously anytime and anywhere, without there being any conceivable trace of direct transmission. The original structural components of the psyche are of no less surprising a uniformity than are those of the visible body. The archetypes are, so to speak, organs of the pre-rational psyche. They are eternally inherited forms and ideas which have at first no specific content. Their specific content only appears in the course of the individual's life, when personal experience is taken up in precisely these forms. If the archetypes were not pre-existent in identical form everywhere, how could one explain the fact, postulated at almost every turn by the *Bardo Thödol,* that the dead do not know that they are dead, and that this assertion is to be met with just as often in the dreary, half-baked literature of European and American Spiritualism? Although we find the same assertion in Swedenborg, knowledge of his writings can hardly be sufficiently widespread for this little bit of information to have been picked up by every small-town medium. And a connection between Swedenborg and the *Bardo Thödol* is completely unthinkable. It is a primordial, universal idea that the dead simply continue their earthly existence and do not know that they are disembodied spirits—an archetypal idea which enters into immediate, visible manifestation whenever anyone sees a ghost. It is significant, too, that ghosts all over the world have certain features in common. I am naturally aware of the unverifiable spiritualistic hypothesis, though I have no wish to make it my own. I must content myself with the hypothesis of an omnipresent, but differentiated, psychic structure which is inherited and which necessarily gives a certain form and direction to all experience. For, just as the organs of the body are not mere lumps of indifferent, passive matter, but are dynamic, functional complexes which assert themselves with imperious urgency, so also the archetypes, as organs of the psyche, are dynamic, instinctual complexes which determine psychic life to an extraordinary degree. That is why I also call them *dominants* of the unconscious. The layer of unconscious psyche which is made up of these universal dynamic forms I have termed the *collective unconscious.*

846 So far as I know, there is no inheritance of individual prenatal, or pre-uterine, memories, but there are undoubtedly inherited archetypes which are, however, devoid of content, because, to begin with, they contain no personal experiences. They only emerge into consciousness when personal experiences have rendered them visible. As we have seen, *Sidpa* psychology consists in wanting to live and to be born. (The *Sidpa Bardo* is the "*Bardo* of Seeking Rebirth.") Such a state, therefore, precludes any experience of transubjective psychic realities, unless the individual refuses categorically to be born back again into the world of consciousness. According to the teachings of the *Bardo Thödol,* it is still possible for him, in each of the *Bardo* states, to reach the *Dharmakāya* by transcending the four-faced Mount Meru, provided that he does not yield to his desire to follow the "dim lights." This is as much as to say that the dead man must desperately resist the dictates of reason, as we understand it, and give up the supremacy of egohood, regarded by reason as sacrosanct. What this means in practice is complete capitulation to the objective powers of the psyche, with all that this entails; a kind of symbolical death, corresponding to the Judgment of the Dead in the *Sidpa Bardo.* It means the end of all conscious, rational, morally responsible conduct of life, and a voluntary surrender to what the *Bardo Thödol* calls "karmic illusion." Karmic illusion springs from belief in a visionary world of an extremely irrational nature, which neither accords with nor derives from our rational judgments but is the exclusive product of uninhibited imagination. It is sheer dream or "fantasy," and every well-meaning person will instantly caution us against it; nor indeed can one

see at first sight what is the difference between fantasies of this kind and the phantasmagoria of a lunatic. Very often only a slight *abaissement du niveau mental* is needed to unleash this world of illusion. The terror and darkness of this moment has its equivalent in the experiences described in the opening sections of the *Sidpa Bardo*. But the contents of this *Bardo* also reveal the archetypes, the karmic images which appear first in their terrifying form. The *Chönyid* state is equivalent to a deliberately induced psychosis.

847 One often hears and reads about the dangers of yoga, particularly of the ill-reputed *kundalini* yoga. The deliberately induced psychotic state, which in certain unstable individuals might easily lead to a real psychosis, is a danger that needs to be taken very seriously indeed. These things really are dangerous and ought not to be meddled with in our typically Western way. It is a meddling with fate, which strikes at the very roots of human existence and can let loose a flood of sufferings of which no sane person ever dreamed. These sufferings correspond to the hellish torments of the *Chönyid* state, described in the text as follows:

> Then the Lord of Death will place round thy neck a rope and drag thee along; he will cut off thy head, tear out thy heart, pull out thy intestines, lick up thy brain, drink thy blood, eat thy flesh, and gnaw thy bones; but thou wilt be incapable of dying. Even when thy body is hacked to pieces, it will revive again. The repeated hacking will cause intense pain and torture.

848 These tortures aptly describe the real nature of the danger: it is a disintegration of the wholeness of the *Bardo* body, which is a kind of "subtle body" constituting the visible envelope of the psychic self in the after-death state. The psychological equivalent of this dismemberment is psychic dissociation. In its deleterious form it would be schizophrenia (split mind). This most common of all mental illnesses consists essentially in a marked *abaissement du niveau mental* which abolishes the normal checks imposed by the conscious mind and thus gives unlimited scope to the play of the unconscious "dominants."

849 The transition, then, from the *Sidpa* state to the *Chönyid* state is a dangerous reversal of the aims and intentions of the conscious mind. It is a sacrifice of the ego's stability and a sur-

render to the extreme uncertainty of what must seem like a chaotic riot of phantasmal forms. When Freud coined the phrase that the ego was "the true seat of anxiety," he was giving voice to a very true and profound intuition. Fear of self-sacrifice lurks deep in every ego, and this fear is often only the precariously controlled demand of the unconscious forces to burst out in full strength. No one who strives for selfhood (individuation) is spared this dangerous passage, for that which is feared also belongs to the wholeness of the self—the sub-human, or supra-human, world of psychic "dominants" from which the ego originally emancipated itself with enormous effort, and then only partially, for the sake of a more or less illusory freedom. This liberation is certainly a very necessary and very heroic undertaking, but it represents nothing final: it is merely the creation of a *subject,* who, in order to find fulfilment, has still to be confronted by an *object.* This, at first sight, would appear to be the world, which is swelled out with projections for that very purpose. Here we seek and find our difficulties, here we seek and find our enemy, here we seek and find what is dear and precious to us; and it is comforting to know that all evil and all good is to be found out there, in the visible object, where it can be conquered, punished, destroyed, or enjoyed. But nature herself does not allow this paradisal state of innocence to continue for ever. There are, and always have been, those who cannot help but see that the world and its experiences are in the nature of a symbol, and that it really reflects something that lies hidden in the subject himself, in his own transubjective reality. It is from this profound intuition, according to lamaist doctrine, that the *Chönyid* state derives its true meaning, which is why the *Chönyid Bardo* is entitled "The *Bardo* of the Experiencing of Reality."

850 The reality experienced in the *Chönyid* state is, as the last section of the corresponding *Bardo* teaches, the reality of thought. The "thought-forms" appear as realities, fantasy takes on real form, and the terrifying dream evoked by karma and played out by the unconscious "dominants" begins. The first to appear (if we read the text backwards) is the all-destroying God of Death, the epitome of all terrors; he is followed by the twenty-eight "power-holding" and sinister goddesses and the fifty-eight "blood-drinking" goddesses. In spite of their demonic

aspect, which appears as a confusing chaos of terrifying attributes and monstrosities, a certain order is already discernible. We find that there are companies of gods and goddesses who are arranged according to the four directions and are distinguished by typical mystic colours. It gradually becomes clearer that all these deities are organized into mandalas, or circles, containing a cross of the four colours. The colours are coordinated with the four aspects of wisdom:

(1) White = the light-path of the mirror-like wisdom;
(2) Yellow = the light-path of the wisdom of equality;
(3) Red = the light-path of the discriminative wisdom;
(4) Green = the light-path of the all-performing wisdom.

851 On a higher level of insight, the dead man knows that the real thought-forms all emanate from himself, and that the four light-paths of wisdom which appear before him are the radiations of his own psychic faculties. This takes us straight to the psychology of the lamaistic mandala, which I have already discussed in the book I brought out with the late Richard Wilhelm, *The Secret of the Golden Flower.*

852 Continuing our ascent backwards through the region of the *Chönyid Bardo,* we come finally to the vision of the Four Great Ones: the green Amogha-Siddhi, the red Amitābha, the yellow Ratna-Sambhava, and the white Vajra-Sattva. The ascent ends with the effulgent blue light of the *Dharmadhātu,* the Buddha-body, which glows in the midst of the mandala from the heart of Vairochana.

853 With this final vision the karmic illusions cease; consciousness, weaned away from all form and from all attachment to objects, returns to the timeless, inchoate state of the *Dharmakāya.* Thus (reading backwards) the *Chikhai* state, which appeared at the moment of death, is reached.

854 I think these few hints will suffice to give the attentive reader some idea of the psychology of the *Bardo Thödol.* The book describes a way of initiation in reverse, which, unlike the eschatological expectations of Christianity, prepares the soul for a descent into physical being. The thoroughly intellectualistic and rationalistic worldly-mindedness of the European makes it advisable for us to reverse the sequence of the *Bardo Thödol* and to regard it as an account of Eastern initiation experiences, though one is perfectly free, if one chooses, to substitute Chris-

tian symbols for the gods of the *Chönyid Bardo*. At any rate, the sequence of events as I have described it offers a close parallel to the phenomenology of the European unconscious when it is undergoing an "initiation process," that is to say, when it is being analysed. The transformation of the unconscious that occurs under analysis makes it the natural analogue of the religious initiation ceremonies, which do, however, differ in principle from the natural process in that they forestall the natural course of development and substitute for the spontaneous production of symbols a deliberately selected set of symbols prescribed by tradition. We can see this in the *Exercitia* of Ignatius Loyola, or in the yoga meditations of the Buddhists and Tantrists.

855 The reversal of the order of the chapters, which I have suggested here as an aid to understanding, in no way accords with the original intention of the *Bardo Thödol*. Nor is the psychological use we make of it anything but a secondary intention, though one that is possibly sanctioned by lamaist custom. The real purpose of this singular book is the attempt, which must seem very strange to the educated European of the twentieth century, to enlighten the dead on their journey through the regions of the *Bardo*. The Catholic Church is the only place in the world of the white man where any provision is made for the souls of the departed. Inside the Protestant camp, with its world-affirming optimism, we only find a few mediumistic "rescue circles," whose main concern is to make the dead aware of the fact that they *are* dead. But, generally speaking, we have nothing in the West that is in any way comparable to the *Bardo Thödol*, except for certain secret writings which are inaccessible to the wider public and to the ordinary scientist. According to tradition, the *Bardo Thödol*, too, seems to have been included among the "hidden" books, as Dr. Evans-Wentz makes clear in his Introduction. As such, it forms a special chapter in the magical "cure of the soul" which extends even beyond death. This cult of the dead is rationally based on the belief in the supra-temporality of the soul, but its irrational basis is to be found in the psychological need of the living to do something for the departed. This is an elementary need which forces itself upon even the most "enlightened" individuals when faced by the death of relatives and friends. That is why, enlightenment or no enlightenment, we still have all manner of ceremonies for the

dead. If Lenin had to submit to being embalmed and put on show in a sumptuous mausoleum like an Egyptian pharaoh, we may be quite sure it was not because his followers believed in the resurrection of the body. Apart, however, from the Masses said for the soul in the Catholic Church, the provisions we make for the dead are rudimentary and on the lowest level, not because we cannot convince ourselves of the soul's immortality, but because we have rationalized the above-mentioned psychological need out of existence. We behave as if we did not have this need, and because we cannot believe in a life after death we prefer to do nothing about it. Simpler-minded people follow their own feelings, and, as in Italy, build themselves funeral monuments of gruesome beauty. The Catholic Masses for the soul are on a level considerably above this, because they are expressly intended for the psychic welfare of the deceased and are not a mere gratification of lachrymose sentiments. But the highest application of spiritual effort on behalf of the departed is surely to be found in the instructions of the *Bardo Thödol.* They are so detailed and thoroughly adapted to the apparent changes in the dead man's condition that every serious-minded reader must ask himself whether these wise old lamas might not, after all, have caught a glimpse of the fourth dimension and twitched the veil from the greatest of life's secrets.

856 Even if the truth should prove to be a disappointment, one almost feels tempted to concede at least some measure of reality to the vision of life in the *Bardo.* At any rate, it is unexpectedly original, if nothing else, to find the after-death state, of which our religious imagination has formed the most grandiose conceptions, painted in lurid colours as a terrifying dream-state of a progressively degenerative character. The supreme vision comes not at the end of the *Bardo,* but right at the beginning, at the moment of death; what happens afterward is an ever-deepening descent into illusion and obscuration, down to the ultimate degradation of new physical birth. The spiritual climax is reached at the moment when life ends. Human life, therefore, is the vehicle of the highest perfection it is possible to attain; it alone generates the karma that makes it possible for the dead man to abide in the perpetual light of the Voidness without clinging to any object, and thus to rest on the hub of

the wheel of rebirth, freed from all illusion of genesis and decay. Life in the *Bardo* brings no eternal rewards or punishments, but merely a descent into a new life which shall bear the individual nearer to his final goal. But this eschatological goal is what he himself brings to birth as the last and highest fruit of the labours and aspirations of earthly existence. This view is not only lofty, it is manly and heroic.

857 The degenerative character of *Bardo* life is corroborated by the spiritualistic literature of the West, which again and again gives one a sickening impression of the utter inanity and banality of communications from the "spirit world." The scientific mind does not hesitate to explain these reports as emanations from the unconscious of the mediums and of those taking part in the séance, and even to extend this explanation to the description of the Hereafter given in the Tibetan Book of the Dead. And it is an undeniable fact that the whole book is created out of the archetypal contents of the unconscious. Behind these there lie—and in this our Western reason is quite right—no physical or metaphysical realities, but "merely" the reality of psychic facts, the data of psychic experience. Now whether a thing is "given" subjectively or objectively, the fact remains that it *is*. The *Bardo Thödol* says no more than this, for its five Dhyāni-Buddhas are themselves no more than psychic data. That is just what the dead man has to recognize, if it has not already become clear to him during life that his own psychic self and the giver of all data are one and the same. The world of gods and spirits is truly "nothing but" the collective unconscious inside me. To turn this sentence round so that it reads "The collective unconscious is the world of gods and spirits outside me," no intellectual acrobatics are needed, but a whole human lifetime, perhaps even many lifetimes of increasing completeness. Notice that I do not say "of increasing perfection," because those who are "perfect" make another kind of discovery altogether.

*

858 The *Bardo Thödol* began by being a "closed" book, and so it has remained, no matter what kind of commentaries may be written upon it. For it is a book that will only open itself to spiritual understanding, and this is a capacity which no man is

born with, but which he can only acquire through special training and special experience. It is good that such to all intents and purposes "useless" books exist. They are meant for those "queer folk" who no longer set much store by the uses, aims, and meaning of present-day "civilization."

VIII

YOGA AND THE WEST

FOREWORD TO SUZUKI'S "INTRODUCTION TO ZEN BUDDHISM"

THE PSYCHOLOGY OF EASTERN MEDITATION

THE HOLY MEN OF INDIA

YOGA AND THE WEST[1]

859 Less than a century has passed since yoga became known to the West. Although all sorts of miraculous tales had come to Europe two thousand years before from the fabled land of India, with its wise men, its gymnosophists and omphalosceptics, yet no real knowledge of Indian philosophy and philosophical practices can be said to have existed until, thanks to the efforts of the Frenchman, Anquetil du Perron, the Upanishads were transmitted to the West. A general and more profound knowledge was first made possible by Max Müller, of Oxford, and the Sacred Books of the East edited by him. To begin with, this knowledge remained the preserve of Sanskrit scholars and philosophers. But it was not so very long before the theosophical movement inaugurated by Mme. Blavatsky possessed itself of the Eastern traditions and promulgated them among the general public. For several decades after that, knowledge of yoga in the West developed along two separate lines. On the one hand it was regarded as a strictly academic science, and on the other it became something very like a religion, though it did not develop into an organized Church—despite the endeavours of Annie Besant and Rudolf Steiner. Although he was the founder of the anthroposophical secession, Steiner was originally a follower of Mme. Blavatsky.

1 [Originally published in *Prabuddha Bharata* (Calcutta), February 1936, Shri Ramakrishna Centenary Number, Sec. III, in a translation by Cary F. Baynes, upon which the present translation is based.—EDITORS.]

860 The peculiar product resulting from this Western development can hardly be compared with what yoga means in India. In the West, Eastern teaching encountered a special situation, a condition of mind such as the earlier India, at any rate, had never known. This was the strict line of division between science and philosophy, which had already existed, to a greater or lesser degree, for some three hundred years before yoga teachings began to be known in the West. The beginning of this split—a specifically Western phenomenon—really set in with the Renaissance, in the fifteenth century. At that time, there arose a widespread and passionate interest in antiquity, stimulated by the fall of the Byzantine Empire under the onslaught of Islam. Then, for the first time, knowledge of the Greek language and of Greek literature was carried to every corner of Europe. As a direct result of this invasion of so-called pagan philosophy, there arose the great schism in the Roman Church—Protestantism, which soon covered the whole of northern Europe. But not even this renewal of Christianity was able to hold the liberated minds in thrall.

861 The period of world discovery in the geographical and scientific sense had begun, and to an ever-increasing degree thought emancipated itself from the shackles of religious tradition. The Churches, of course, continued to exist because they were maintained by the strictly religious needs of the public, but they lost their leadership in the cultural sphere. While the Church of Rome, thanks to her unsurpassed organization, remained a unity, Protestantism split into nearly four hundred denominations. This is a proof on the one hand of its incompetence, and, on the other, of a religious vitality which refuses to be stifled. Gradually, in the course of the nineteenth century, this led to syncretistic outgrowths and to the importation on a mass scale of exotic religious systems, such as the religion of Abdul Baha, the Sufi sects, the Ramakrishna Mission, Buddhism, and so on. Many of these systems, for instance anthroposophy, were syncretized with Christian elements. The resultant picture corresponds roughly to the Hellenistic syncretism of the third and fourth centuries A.D., which likewise showed traces of Indian thought. (Cf. Apollonius of Tyana, the Orphic-Pythagorean secret doctrines, the Gnosis, etc.)

862 All these systems moved on the religious plane and recruited

the great majority of their adherents from Protestantism. They are thus, fundamentally, Protestant sects. By directing its main attack against the authority of the Roman Church, Protestantism largely destroyed belief in the Church as the indispensable agent of divine salvation. Thus the burden of authority fell to the individual, and with it a religious responsibility that had never existed before. The decline of confession and absolution sharpened the moral conflict of the individual and burdened him with problems which previously the Church had settled for him, since her sacraments, particularly that of the Mass, guaranteed his salvation through the priest's enactment of the sacred rite. The only things the individual had to contribute were confession, repentance, and penance. With the collapse of the rite, which did the work for him, he had to do without God's answer to his plans. This dissatisfaction explains the demand for systems that promise an answer—the visible or at least noticeable favour of another (higher, spiritual, or divine) power.

863 European science paid no attention to these hopes and expectations. It lived its intellectual life unconcerned with religious needs and convictions. This—historically inevitable—split in the Western mind also affected yoga so far as this had gained a footing in the West, and led to its being made an object of scientific study on the one hand, while on the other it was welcomed as a way of salvation. But inside the religious movement there were any number of attempts to combine science with religious belief and practice, as for instance Christian Science, theosophy, and anthroposophy. The last-named, especially, likes to give itself scientific airs and has, therefore, like Christian Science, penetrated into intellectual circles.

864 Since the way of the Protestant is not laid down for him in advance, he gives welcome, one might say, to practically any system which holds out the promise of successful development. He must now do for himself the very thing which had always been done by the Church as intermediary, and he does not know *how* to do it. If he is a man who has taken his religious needs seriously, he has also made untold efforts towards faith, because his doctrine sets exclusive store by faith. But faith is a charisma, a gift of grace, and not a method. The Protestant is so entirely without a method that many of them have seriously interested themselves in the rigorously Catholic exercises of Ignatius

Loyola. Yet, do what they will, the thing that disturbs them most is naturally the contradiction between religious and scientific truth, the conflict between faith and knowledge, which reaches far beyond Protestantism into Catholicism itself. This conflict is due solely to the historical split in the European mind. Had it not been for the natural psychological urge to believe, and an equally unnatural belief in science, this conflict would have no reason whatever to exist. One can easily imagine a state of mind in which one simply *knows* and at the same time *believes* a thing which seems probable to one for such and such reasons. There is no cause whatsoever for any conflict between these two things. Both are necessary, for knowledge alone, like faith alone, is always insufficient.

865 When, therefore, a "religious" method recommends itself at the same time as "scientific," it can be sure of finding a public in the West. Yoga fulfils this expectation. Quite apart from the charm of the new and the fascination of the half-understood, there is good reason for yoga to have many adherents. It offers not only the much-sought way, but also a philosophy of unrivalled profundity. It holds out the possibility of controllable experience, and thus satisfies the scientist's need for "facts." Moreover, by reason of its breadth and depth, its venerable age, its teachings and methods which cover every sphere of life, it promises undreamt of possibilities which the missionaries of yoga seldom omit to emphasize.

866 I will remain silent on the subject of what yoga means for India, because I cannot presume to judge something I do not know from personal experience. I can, however, say something about what it means for the West. Our lack of direction borders on psychic anarchy. Therefore, any religious or philosophical practice amounts to a psychological discipline; in other words, it is a method of psychic hygiene. The numerous purely physical procedures of yoga are a physiological hygiene as well, which is far superior to ordinary gymnastics or breathing exercises in that it is not merely mechanistic and scientific but, at the same time, philosophical. In its training of the parts of the body, it unites them with the whole of the mind and spirit, as is quite clear, for instance, in the *prānayāma* exercises, where *prāna* is both the breath and the universal dynamics of the cosmos. When the doing of the individual is at the same time a cosmic happen-

ing, the elation of the body (innervation) becomes one with the elation of the spirit (the universal idea), and from this there arises a living whole which no technique, however scientific, can hope to produce. Yoga practice is unthinkable, and would also be ineffectual, without the ideas on which it is based. It works the physical and the spiritual into one another in an extraordinarily complete way.

867 In the East, where these ideas and practices originated, and where an uninterrupted tradition extending over some four thousand years has created the necessary spiritual conditions, yoga is, as I can readily believe, the perfect and appropriate method of fusing body and mind together so that they form a unity that can hardly be doubted. They thus create a psychological disposition which makes possible intuitions that transcend consciousness. The Indian mentality has no difficulty in operating intelligently with a concept like *prāna.* The West, on the contrary, with its bad habit of wanting to believe on the one hand, and its highly developed scientific and philosophical critique on the other, finds itself in a real dilemma. Either it falls into the trap of faith and swallows concepts like *prāna, atman, chakra, samādhi,* etc., without giving them a thought, or its scientific critique repudiates them one and all as "pure mysticism." The split in the Western mind therefore makes it impossible at the outset for the intentions of yoga to be realized in any adequate way. It becomes either a strictly religious matter, or else a kind of training like Pelmanism, breath-control, eurhythmics, etc., and not a trace is to be found of the unity and wholeness of nature which is characteristic of yoga. The Indian can forget neither the body nor the mind, while the European is always forgetting either the one or the other. With this capacity to forget he has, for the time being, conquered the world. Not so the Indian. He not only knows his own nature, but he knows also how much he himself is nature. The European, on the other hand, has a science of nature and knows astonishingly little of his own nature, the nature within him. For the Indian, it comes as a blessing to know of a method which helps him to control the supreme power of nature within and without. For the European, it is sheer poison to suppress his nature, which is warped enough as it is, and to make out of it a willing robot.

868 It is said of the yogi that he can remove mountains, though

it would be difficult to furnish any real proof of this. The power of the yogi operates within limits acceptable to his environment. The European, on the other hand, can blow up mountains, and the World War has given us a bitter foretaste of what he is capable of when free rein is given to an intellect that has grown estranged from human nature. As a European, I cannot wish the European more "control" and more power over the nature within and around us. Indeed, I must confess to my shame that I owe my best insights (and there are some quite good ones among them) to the circumstance that I have always done just the opposite of what the rules of yoga prescribe. Through his historical development, the European has become so far removed from his roots that his mind was finally split into faith and knowledge, in the same way that every psychological exaggeration breaks up into its inherent opposites. He needs to return, not to Nature in the manner of Rousseau, but to his own nature. His task is to find the natural man again. Instead of this, there is nothing he likes better than systems and methods by which he can repress the natural man who is everywhere at cross purposes with him. He will infallibly make a wrong use of yoga because his psychic disposition is quite different from that of the Oriental. I say to whomsoever I can: "Study yoga—you will learn an infinite amount from it—but do not try to apply it, for we Europeans are not so constituted that we apply these methods correctly, just like that. An Indian guru can explain everything and you can imitate everything. But do you know *who* is applying the yoga? In other words, do you know who you are and how you are constituted?"

869 The power of science and technics in Europe is so enormous and indisputable that there is little point in reckoning up all that can be done and all that has been invented. One shudders at the stupendous possibilities. Quite another question begins to loom up: *Who* is applying this technical skill? in *whose* hands does this power lie? For the present, the state is a provisional means of protection, because, apparently, it safeguards the citizen from the enormous quantities of poison gas and other infernal engines of destruction which can be manufactured by the thousand tons at a moment's notice. Our technical skill has grown to be so dangerous that the most urgent question today is not what *more* can be done in this line, but how the man who is

entrusted with the control of this skill should be constituted, or how to alter the mind of Western man so that he would renounce his terrible skill. It is infinitely more important to strip him of the illusion of his power than to strengthen him still further in the mistaken idea that he can do everything he wills. The slogan one hears so often in Germany, "Where there's a will there's a way," has cost the lives of millions of human beings.

870 Western man has no need of more superiority over nature, whether outside or inside. He has both in almost devilish perfection. What he lacks is conscious recognition of his inferiority to the nature around and within him. He must learn that he may not do exactly as he wills. If he does not learn this, his own nature will destroy him. He does not know that his own soul is rebelling against him in a suicidal way.

871 Since Western man can turn everything into a technique, it is true in principle that everything that looks like a method is either dangerous or condemned to futility. In so far as yoga is a form of hygiene, it is as useful to him as any other system. In the deepest sense, however, yoga does not mean this but, if I understand it correctly, a great deal more, namely the final release and detachment of consciousness from all bondage to object and subject. But since one cannot detach oneself from something of which one is unconscious, the European must first learn to know his subject. This, in the West, is what one calls the unconscious. Yoga technique applies itself exclusively to the conscious mind and will. Such an undertaking promises success only when the unconscious has no potential worth mentioning, that is to say, when it does not contain large portions of the personality. If it does, then all conscious effort remains futile, and what comes out of this cramped condition of mind is a caricature or even the exact opposite of the intended result.

872 The rich metaphysic and symbolism of the East express the larger and more important part of the unconscious and in this way reduce its potential. When the yogi says "prāna," he means very much more than mere breath. For him the word *prāna* brings with it the full weight of its metaphysical components, and it is as if he really knew what prāna meant in this respect. He does not know it with his understanding, but with his heart, belly, and blood. The European only imitates and learns ideas

by rote, and is therefore incapable of expressing his subjective facts through Indian concepts. I am more than doubtful whether the European, if he were capable of the corresponding experiences, would choose to express them through intuitive ideas like prāna.

873 Yoga was originally a natural process of introversion, with all manner of individual variations. Introversions of this sort lead to peculiar inner processes which change the personality. In the course of several thousand years these introversions became organized as methods, and along widely differing lines. Indian yoga itself recognizes numerous and extremely diverse forms. The reason for this lies in the original diversity of individual experience. This is not to say that any one of these methods is suited to the peculiar historical structure of the European. It is much more likely that the yoga natural to the European proceeds from historical patterns unknown to the East. As a matter of fact, the two cultural achievements which, in the West, have had to concern themselves most with the psyche in the practical sense, namely medicine and the Catholic cure of souls, have both produced methods comparable to yoga. I have already referred to the exercises of Ignatius Loyola. With respect to medicine, it is the modern psychotherapeutic methods which come closest to yoga. Freud's psychoanalysis leads the conscious mind of the patient back to the inner world of childhood reminiscences on one side, and on the other to wishes and drives which have been repressed from consciousness. The latter technique is a logical development of confession. It aims at an artificial introversion for the purpose of making conscious the unconscious components of the subject.

874 A somewhat different method is the so-called "autogenic training" of Professor Schultz,[2] which consciously links up with yoga. His chief aim is to break down the conscious cramp and the repression of the unconscious this has caused.

875 My method, like Freud's, is built up on the practice of confession. Like him, I pay close attention to dreams, but when it comes to the unconscious our views part company. For Freud it is essentially an appendage of consciousness, in which all the individual's incompatibilities are heaped up. For me the un-

2 [The German psychiatrist J. H. Schultz. The reference is to his book *Das autogene Training* (Berlin, 1932).—EDITORS.]

conscious is a collective psychic disposition, creative in character. This fundamental difference of viewpoint naturally produces an entirely different evaluation of the symbolism and the method of interpreting it. Freud's procedure is, in the main, analytical and reductive. To this I add a synthesis which emphasizes the purposiveness of unconscious tendencies with respect to personality development. In this line of research important parallels with yoga have come to light, especially with *kundalini* yoga and the symbolism of tantric yoga, lamaism, and Taoistic yoga in China. These forms of yoga with their rich symbolism afford me invaluable comparative material for interpreting the collective unconscious. However, I do not apply yoga methods in principle, because, in the West, nothing ought to be forced on the unconscious. Usually, consciousness is characterized by an intensity and narrowness that have a cramping effect, and this ought not to be emphasized still further. On the contrary, everything must be done to help the unconscious to reach the conscious mind and to free it from its rigidity. For this purpose I employ a method of active imagination, which consists in a special training for switching off consciousness, at least to a relative extent, thus giving the unconscious contents a chance to develop.

876 If I remain so critically averse to yoga, it does not mean that I do not regard this spiritual achievement of the East as one of the greatest things the human mind has ever created. I hope my exposition makes it sufficiently clear that my criticism is directed solely against the application of yoga to the peoples of the West. The spiritual development of the West has been along entirely different lines from that of the East and has therefore produced conditions which are the most unfavourable soil one can think of for the application of yoga. Western civilization is scarcely a thousand years old and must first of all free itself from its barbarous one-sidedness. This means, above all, deeper insight into the nature of man. But no insight is gained by repressing and controlling the unconscious, and least of all by imitating methods which have grown up under totally different psychological conditions. In the course of the centuries the West will produce its own yoga, and it will be on the basis laid down by Christianity.

FOREWORD TO SUZUKI'S "INTRODUCTION TO ZEN BUDDHISM"[1]

877 Daisetz Teitaro Suzuki's works on Zen Buddhism are among the best contributions to the knowledge of living Buddhism that recent decades have produced, and Zen itself is the most important fruit to have sprung from the tree whose roots are the collections of the Pali Canon.[2] We cannot be sufficiently grateful to the author, first for having brought Zen closer to Western understanding, and secondly for the manner in which he has performed this task. Oriental religious conceptions are usually so very different from our Western ones that even the bare translation of the words often presents the greatest difficulties, quite apart from the meaning of the terms used, which in certain circumstances are better left untranslated. I need only mention the Chinese "tao," which no European translation has

1 [Originally published as a foreword to Suzuki, *Die grosse Befreiung: Einführung in den Zen-Buddhismus* (Leipzig, 1939). The Suzuki text had been translated into German by Heinrich Zimmer from the original edition of *An Introduction to Zen Buddhism.* The foreword by Jung was published in an earlier translation by Constance Rolfe in a new edition of the Suzuki work (London and New York, 1949).—EDITORS.]

2 The origin of Zen, as Oriental authors themselves admit, is to be found in Buddha's Flower Sermon. On this occasion he held up a flower to a gathering of disciples without uttering a word. Only Kasyapa understood him. Cf. Shuei Ohazama, *Zen: Der lebendige Buddhismus in Japan,* p. 3.

yet got near. The original Buddhist writings contain views and ideas which are more or less unassimilable for ordinary Europeans. I do not know, for instance, just what kind of mental (or perhaps climatic?) background or preparation is necessary before one can form any completely clear idea of what is meant by the Buddhist "kamma." Judging by all we know of the nature of Zen, here too we are up against a central conception of unsurpassed singularity. This strange conception is called "satori," which may be translated as "enlightenment." "Satori is the *raison d'être* of Zen without which Zen is not Zen," says Suzuki.[3] It should not be too difficult for the Western mind to grasp what a mystic understands by "enlightenment," or what is known as such in religious parlance. Satori, however, designates a special kind and way of enlightenment which it is practically impossible for the European to appreciate. By way of illustration, I would refer the reader to the enlightenment of Hyakujo (Pai-chang Huai-hai, A.D. 724–814) and of the Confucian poet and statesman Kozankoku (Huang Shan-ku),[4] as described by Suzuki.

878 The following may serve as a further example: A monk once went to Gensha, and wanted to learn where the entrance to the path of truth was. Gensha asked him, "Do you hear the murmuring of the brook?" "Yes, I hear it," answered the monk. "There is the entrance," the Master instructed him.

879 I will content myself with these few examples, which aptly illustrate the opacity of satori experiences. Even if we take example after example, it still remains exceedingly obscure how any enlightenment comes and of what it consists—in other words, by what or about what one is enlightened. Kaiten Nukariya, who was himself a professor at the So-to-shu Buddhist College in Tokyo, says, speaking of enlightenment:

> Having set ourselves free from the mistaken conception of self, next we must awaken our innermost wisdom, pure and divine, called the Mind of Buddha, or Bodhi, or Prajna by Zen masters. It is the divine light, the inner heaven, the key to all moral treasures, the centre of thought and consciousness, the source of all influence and power, the seat of kindness, justice, sympathy, impartial love, humanity, and mercy, the measure of all things. When this innermost wisdom is fully awakened, we are able to realize that each and every one of us is identical in spirit, in essence, in nature with the universal

3 *Introduction to Zen Buddhism* (1949), p. 95.

4 Ibid., pp. 89 and 92f.

life or Buddha, that each ever lives face to face with Buddha, that each is beset by the abundant grace of the Blessed One, that He arouses his moral nature, that He opens his spiritual eyes, that He unfolds his new capacity, that He appoints his mission, and that life is not an ocean of birth, disease, old age, and death, nor the vale of tears, but the holy temple of Buddha, the Pure Land, where he can enjoy the bliss of Nirvana.[5]

880 That is how an Oriental, himself an adept in Zen, describes the essence of enlightenment. One must admit that this passage would need only a few trifling alterations in order to find its way into a Christian mystical book of devotion. Yet somehow it sends us away empty as regards understanding the satori experience described again and again in the literature. Presumably Nukariya is addressing himself to Western rationalism, of which he himself acquired a good dose, and that is why it all sounds so flatly edifying. The abstruse obscurity of the Zen anecdotes is distinctly preferable to this adaptation *ad usum Delphini:* it conveys a great deal more by saying less.

881 Zen is anything but a philosophy in the Western sense of the word.[6] This is also the opinion of Rudolf Otto, who says in his foreword to Ohazama's book on Zen that Nukariya has "imported the magical world of Oriental ideas into our Western philosophical categories" and confused it with these. "If psychophysical parallelism, that most wooden of all doctrines, is invoked in order to explain this mystical intuition of Non-duality and Oneness and the *coincidentia oppositorum,* then one is completely outside the sphere of the *koan,* the *kwatsu,* and *satori.*" [7] It is far better to allow oneself to become deeply imbued at the outset with the exotic obscurity of the Zen anecdotes, and to bear in mind the whole time that satori is a *mysterium ineffabile,* as indeed the Zen masters wish it to be. Between the anecdote and the mystical enlightenment there is, to our way of thinking, a gulf, and the possibility of bridging it can at best be hinted but never in practice achieved.[8] One has

[5] *The Religion of the Samurai,* p. 133.

[6] "Zen is neither psychology nor philosophy."

[7] In Ohazama, p. viii.

[8] If in spite of this I attempt "explanations" in what follows, I am nevertheless fully aware that in the sense of satori I have said nothing valid. All the same, I had to make an attempt to manoeuvre our Western understanding into at least the proximity of an understanding—a task so difficult that in doing it one must take upon oneself certain crimes against the spirit of Zen.

the feeling of touching upon a true secret, and not one that is merely imagined or pretended. It is not a question of mystification and mumbo-jumbo, but rather of an experience which strikes the experient dumb. Satori comes upon one unawares, as something utterly unexpected.

882 When, in the sphere of Christianity, visions of the Holy Trinity, the Madonna, the Crucified, or of the patron saint are vouchsafed after long spiritual preparation, one has the impression that this is all more or less as it should be. That Jakob Böhme should obtain a glimpse into the *centrum naturae* by means of a sunbeam reflected in a tin platter is also understandable. It is harder to digest Meister Eckhart's vision of the "little naked boy," not to speak of Swedenborg's "man in the purple coat," who wanted to dissuade him from overeating, and whom, in spite—or perhaps because—of this, he recognized as the Lord God.[9] Such things are difficult to swallow, bordering as they do on the grotesque. Many of the Zen anecdotes, however, not only border on the grotesque but are right there in the middle of it, and sound like the most crashing nonsense.

883 For anyone who has devoted himself, with love and sympathetic understanding, to studying the flowerlike mind of the Far East, many of these puzzling things, which drive the naïve European from one perplexity to another, simply disappear. Zen is indeed one of the most wonderful blossoms of the Chinese spirit [10]—a spirit fertilized by the immense world of Buddhist thought. Anyone who has really tried to understand Buddhist doctrine—even if only to the extent of giving up certain Western prejudices—will begin to suspect treacherous depths beneath the bizarre surface of individual satori experiences, or will sense disquieting difficulties which the religion and philosophy of the West have up to now thought fit to disregard. If he is a philosopher, he is exclusively concerned with the kind of understanding that has nothing to do with life. And if he is a Christian, he has of course no truck with heathens ("God, I thank thee that I

[9] Cf. Spamer, ed., *Texte aus der deutschen Mystik des 14. und 15. Jahrhunderts,* p. 143; Evans, *Meister Eckhart,* I, p. 438; William White, *Emanuel Swedenborg,* I, p. 243.

[10] "There is no doubt that Zen is one of the most precious and in many respects the most remarkable [of the] spiritual possessions bequeathed to Eastern people." Suzuki, *Essays on Zen Buddhism,* I, p. 264.

am not as other men are"). There is no satori within these Western limits—that is a purely Oriental affair. But is this really so? Have we in fact no satori?

884 When one reads the Zen texts attentively, one cannot escape the impression that, however bizarre, satori is a *natural occurrence,* something so very simple,[11] even, that one fails to see the wood for the trees, and in attempting to explain it invariably says the very thing that throws others into the greatest confusion. Nukariya is therefore right when he says that any attempt to explain or analyse the content of Zen, or of the enlightenment, is futile. Nevertheless he does venture to assert that enlightenment "implies an insight into the nature of self," [12] and that it is an "emancipation of mind from illusion concerning self." [13] The illusion concerning the nature of self is the common confusion of the self with the ego. Nukariya understands by "self" the All-Buddha, i.e., total consciousness of life. He quotes Pan Shan, who says: "The moon of mind comprehends all the universe in its light," adding: "It is Cosmic life and Cosmic spirit, and at the same time individual life and individual spirit." [14]

885 However one may define the self, it is always something other than the ego, and inasmuch as a higher insight of the ego leads over to the self, the self is a more comprehensive thing which includes the experience of the ego and therefore transcends it. Just as the ego is a certain experience I have of myself, so is the self an experience of my ego. It is, however, no longer experienced in the form of a broader or higher ego, but in the form of a non-ego.

886 Such thoughts were familiar to the anonymous author of the *Theologia Germanica:*

> In whatsoever creature the Perfect shall be known, therein creature-nature, created state, I-hood, selfhood, and the like must all be given up and done away.[15]

11 "Before a man studies Zen, to him mountains are mountains and waters are waters; after he gets an insight into the truth of Zen, through the instruction of a good master, mountains to him are not mountains and waters are not waters; after this when he really attains to the abode of rest, mountains are once more mountains and waters are waters." Ibid., pp. 22f.

12 *Religion of the Samurai,* p. 123. 13 Ibid., p. 124. 14 Ibid., p. 132.

15 *Theologia Germanica,* ed. by Trask, p. 115.

Now that I arrogate anything good to myself, as if I were, or had done, or knew, or could perform any good thing, or that it were mine; that is all out of blindness and folly. For if the real truth were in me, I should understand that I am not that good thing, and that it is not mine nor of me.

Then the man says: "Behold! I, poor fool that I was, thought it was I, but behold! it is, and was, of a truth, God!" [16]

887 This tells us a good deal about the "content of enlightenment." The occurrence of satori is interpreted and formulated as a *break-through*, by a consciousness limited to the ego-form, into the non-ego-like self. This view is in accord not only with the essence of Zen, but also with the mysticism of Meister Eckhart:

When I flowed forth from God, all things declared: "He is a God!" Now this cannot make me blessed, for thereby I acknowledge myself a creature. But in the break-through,[17] when I shall stand empty in the will of God, and empty of this God's will, and of all his works, and of God himself—then I am more than all creatures, then I am neither God nor creature: I am what I was and what I shall remain, now and forevermore. Then I receive a thrust which raises me above all angels. In this thrust I become so rich that God cannot suffice me despite all that he is as God, despite all his godly works: for in this break-through I perceive that God and I are one. Then I am what I was,[18] I grow neither less nor more, for I am an unmoved Mover that moves all things. Here God can find no place in man, for man through his poverty has won back that which he was eternally and ever more shall remain.[19]

888 Here the Master may actually be describing a satori experience, a supersession of the ego by the self, which is endued with the "Buddha nature" or divine universality. Since, out of scientific modesty, I do not presume to make a metaphysical statement, but am referring only to a change of consciousness that can be experienced, I treat satori first of all as a psychological

[16] Ibid., pp. 120–21.

[17] There is a similar image in Zen: When a Master was asked what Buddhahood consisted in, he answered, "The bottom of a pail is broken through" (Suzuki, *Essays,* I, p. 229). Another analogy is the "bursting of the bag" (*Essays,* II, p. 117).

[18] Cf. Suzuki, *Essays,* I, pp. 231, 255. Zen means catching a glimpse of the original nature of man, or the recognition of the original man (p. 157).

[19] Cf. Evans, *Meister Eckhart,* p. 221; also *Meister Eckhart: A Modern Translation,* by Blakney, pp. 231f.

problem. For anyone who does not share or understand this point of view, the "explanation" will consist of nothing but words which have no tangible meaning. He is then incapable of throwing a bridge from these abstractions to the facts reported; that is to say, he cannot understand how the scent of the blossoming laurel or the tweaked nose [20] could bring about so formidable a change of consciousness. Naturally the simplest thing would be to relegate all these anecdotes to the realm of amusing fairytales, or, if one accepts the facts as they are, to write them off as instances of self-deception. (Another favourite explanation is "auto-suggestion," that pathetic white elephant from the arsenal of intellectual inadequacies!) But no serious and responsible investigation can pass over these facts unheedingly. Of course, we can never decide definitely whether a person is *really* "enlightened" or "released," or whether he merely imagines it. We have no criteria to go on. Moreover, we know well enough that an imaginary pain is often far more agonizing than a so-called real one, since it is accompanied by a subtle moral suffering caused by a dull feeling of secret self-accusation. In this sense, therefore, it is not a question of "actual fact" but of *psychic reality,* i.e., the psychic process known as satori.

889 Every psychic process is an image and an "imagining," otherwise no consciousness could exist and the occurrence would lack phenomenality. Imagination itself is a psychic process, for which reason it is completely irrelevant whether the enlightenment be called "real" or "imaginary." The person who has the enlightenment, or alleges that he has it, thinks at all events that he is enlightened. What others think about it decides nothing whatever for him in regard to his experience. Even if he were lying, his lie would still be a psychic fact. Indeed, even if all the reports of religious experiences were nothing but deliberate inventions and falsifications, a very interesting psychological treatise could still be written about the incidence of such lies, and with the same scientific objectivity with which one describes the psychopathology of delusional ideas. The fact that there is a religious movement upon which many brilliant minds have worked over a period of many centuries is sufficient reason for at least venturing a serious attempt to bring such processes within the realm of scientific understanding.

[20] Suzuki, *Introduction,* pp. 93, 84.

890 Earlier, I raised the question of whether we have anything like satori in the West. If we discount the sayings of our Western mystics, a superficial glance discloses nothing that could be likened to it in even the faintest degree. The possibility that there are stages in the development of consciousness plays no role in our thinking. The mere thought that there is a tremendous psychological difference between consciousness of the existence of an object and "consciousness of the consciousness" of an object borders on a quibble that hardly needs answering. For the same reason, one could hardly bring oneself to take such a problem seriously enough to consider the psychological conditions in which it arose. It is significant that questions of this kind do not, as a rule, arise from any intellectual need, but, where they exist, are nearly always rooted in an originally religious practice. In India it was yoga and in China Buddhism which supplied the driving force for these attempts to wrench oneself free from bondage to a state of consciousness that was felt to be incomplete. So far as Western mysticism is concerned, its texts are full of instructions as to how man can and must release himself from the "I-ness" of his consciousness, so that through knowledge of his own nature he may rise above it and attain the inner (godlike) man. John of Ruysbroeck makes use of an image which was also known to Indian philosophy, that of the tree whose roots are above and its branches below: [21] "And he must climb up into the tree of faith, which grows from above downwards, for its roots are in the Godhead." [22] He also says, like the yogi: "Man must be free and without ideas, released from all attachments and empty of all creatures." [23] "He must be untouched by joy and sorrow, profit and loss, rising and falling, concern for others, pleasure and fear, and not be attached to any creature." [24] It is in this that the "unity" of his being consists, and this means "being turned inwards." Being turned inwards means that "a man is turned within, into his own heart, that he may understand and feel the inner working

21 "Its root is above, its branches below—this eternal fig-tree! . . . That is Brahma, that is called the Immortal." Katha Upanishad, 6, 1, trans. by Hume, *The Thirteen Principal Upanishads*, p. 358.

22 John of Ruysbroeck, *The Adornment of the Spiritual Marriage*, p. 47. One can hardly suppose that this Flemish mystic, who was born in 1273, borrowed this image from any Indian text.

23 Ibid., p. 51.

24 P. 57, modified.

and the inner words of God." [25] This new state of consciousness born of religious practice is distinguished by the fact that outward things no longer affect an ego-bound consciousness, thus giving rise to mutual attachment, but that an empty consciousness stands open to another influence. This "other" influence is no longer felt as one's own activity, but as that of a non-ego which has the conscious mind as its object.[26] It is as if the subject-character of the ego had been overrun, or taken over, by another subject which appears in place of the ego.[27] This is a well-known religious experience, already formulated by St. Paul.[28] Undoubtedly a new state of consciousness is described here, separated from the earlier state by an incisive process of religious transformation.

891 It could be objected that consciousness in itself has not changed, only the consciousness of something, just as though one had turned over the page of a book and now saw a different picture with the same eyes. I am afraid this is no more than an arbitrary interpretation, for it does not fit the facts. The fact is that in the texts it is not merely a different picture or object that is described, but rather an experience of transformation, often occurring amid the most violent psychic convulsions. The blotting out of one picture and its replacement by another is an everyday occurrence which has none of the attributes of a transformation experience. *It is not that something different is seen, but that one sees differently.* It is as though the spatial act of seeing were changed by a new dimension. When the Master asks: "Do you hear the murmuring of the brook?" he obviously means something quite different from ordinary "hearing." [29] Consciousness is something like perception, and like the latter is subject to conditions and limitations. You can, for instance, be conscious at various levels, within a narrower or wider field,

25 Ibid., p. 62, modified.

26 "O Lord . . . instruct me in the doctrine of the non-ego, which is grounded in the self-nature of mind." Cited from the Lankavatāra Sutra, in Suzuki, *Essays,* I, p. 76.

27 A Zen Master says: "Buddha is none other than the mind, or rather, him who strives to see this mind."

28 Galatians 2:20: "It is no longer I who live, but Christ who lives in me."

29 Suzuki says of this change, "The old way of viewing things is abandoned and the world acquires a new signification . . . a new beauty which exists in the 'refreshing breeze' and in the 'shining jewel.' " *Essays,* I, p. 249. See also p. 138.

more on the surface or deeper down. These differences in degree are often differences in kind as well, since they depend on the development of the personality as a whole; that is to say, on the nature of the perceiving subject.

892 The intellect has no interest in the nature of the perceiving subject so far as the latter only thinks logically. The intellect is essentially concerned with elaborating the contents of consciousness and with methods of elaboration. A rare philosophic passion is needed to compel the attempt to get beyond intellect and break through to a "knowledge of the knower." Such a passion is practically indistinguishable from the driving force of religion; consequently this whole problem belongs to the religious transformation process, which is incommensurable with intellect. Classical philosophy subserves this process on a wide scale, but this can be said less and less of the newer philosophy. Schopenhauer is still—with qualifications—classical, but Nietzsche's *Zarathustra* is no longer philosophy at all: it is a dramatic process of transformation which has completely swallowed up the intellect. It is no longer concerned with thought, but, in the highest sense, with the thinker of thought—and this on every page of the book. A new man, a completely transformed man, is to appear on the scene, one who has broken the shell of the old and who not only looks upon a new heaven and a new earth, but has created them. Angelus Silesius puts it rather more modestly than Zarathustra:

> My body is a shell in which a chick lies closed about;
> Brooded by the spirit of eternity, it waits its hatching out.[30]

893 Satori corresponds in the Christian sphere to an experience of religious transformation. As there are different degrees and kinds of such an experience, it may not be superfluous to define more accurately the category which corresponds most closely to the Zen experience. This is without doubt the mystic experience, which differs from other types in that its preliminary stages consist in "letting oneself go," in "emptying oneself of images and ideas," as opposed to those religious experiences which, like the exercises of Ignatius Loyola, are based on the practice of envisaging sacred images. In this latter class I would

30 Trans. by Willard R. Trask (unpub.).

include transformation through faith and prayer and through collective experience in Protestantism, since a very definite assumption plays the decisive role here, and not by any means "emptiness" or "freeness." The characteristically Eckhartian assertion that "God is Nothingness" may well be incompatible in principle with the contemplation of the Passion, with faith and collective expectations.

894 Thus the correspondence between satori and Western experience is limited to those few Christian mystics whose paradoxical statements skirt the edge of heterodoxy or actually overstep it. As we know, it was this that drew down on Meister Eckhart's writings the condemnation of the Church. If Buddhism were a "Church" in our sense of the word, she would undoubtedly find Zen an insufferable nuisance. The reason for this is the extreme individualism of its methods, and also the iconoclastic attitude of many of the Masters.[31] To the extent that Zen is a movement, collective forms have arisen in the course of the centuries, as can be seen from Suzuki's *Training of the Zen Buddhist Monk* (Kyoto, 1934). But these concern externals only. Apart from the typical mode of life, the spiritual training or development seems to lie in the method of the *koan*. The koan is understood to be a paradoxical question, statement, or action of the Master. Judging by Suzuki's description, it seems to consist chiefly of master-questions handed down in the form of anecdotes. These are submitted by the teacher to the student for meditation. A classic example is the Wu anecdote. A monk once asked the Master: "Has a dog a Buddha nature too?" Whereupon the Master replied: "Wu!" As Suzuki remarks, this "Wu" means quite simply "bow-wow," obviously just what the dog himself would have said in answer to such a question.[32]

895 At first sight it seems as if the posing of such a question as

31 "*Satori* is the most intimate individual experience." *Essays,* I, p. 261.

A Master says to his pupil: "I have really nothing to impart to you, and if I tried to do so you might have occasion to make me an object of ridicule. Besides, whatever I can tell you is my own and can never be yours." *Introduction,* p. 91.

A monk says to the Master: "I have been seeking for the Buddha, but do not yet know how to go on with my research." Said the Master: "It is very much like looking for an ox when riding on one." *Essays,* II, p. 74.

A Master says: "The mind that does not understand is the Buddha: there is no other." Ibid., p. 72.

32 *Essays,* II, pp. 84, 90.

an object of meditation would anticipate or prejudice the end-result, and that it would therefore determine the content of the experience, just as in the Jesuit exercises or in certain yoga meditations the content is determined by the task set by the teacher. The koans, however, are so various, so ambiguous, and above all so boundlessly paradoxical that even an expert must be completely in the dark as to what might be considered a suitable solution. In addition, the descriptions of the final result are so obscure that in no single case can one discover any rational connection between the koan and the experience of enlightenment. Since no logical sequence can be demonstrated, it remains to be supposed that the koan method puts not the smallest restraint upon the freedom of the psychic process and that the end-result therefore springs from nothing but the individual disposition of the pupil. The complete destruction of the rational intellect aimed at in the training creates an almost perfect lack of conscious assumptions. These are excluded as far as possible, but not unconscious assumptions—that is, the existing but unrecognized psychological disposition, which is anything but empty or unassuming. It is a nature-given factor, and when it answers—this being obviously the satori experience—it is an answer of Nature, who has succeeded in conveying her reaction direct to the conscious mind.[33] What the unconscious nature of the pupil opposes to the teacher or to the koan by way of an answer is, manifestly, satori. This seems, at least to me, to be the view which, to judge by the descriptions, formulates the nature of satori more or less correctly. It is also supported by the fact that the "glimpse into one's own nature," the "original man," and the depths of one's being are often a matter of supreme concern to the Zen master.[34]

33 "Zen consciousness is to be nursed to maturity. When it is fully matured, it is sure to break out as satori, which is an insight into the unconscious." *Essays,* II, p. 60.

34 The fourth maxim of Zen is "Seeing into one's nature and the attainment of Buddhahood" (I, p. 18). When a monk asked Hui-neng for instruction, the Master told him: "Show me your original face before you were born" (I, p. 224). A Japanese Zen book says: "If you wish to seek the Buddha, you ought to see into your own nature; for this nature is the Buddha himself" (I, p. 231). A satori experience shows a Master the "original man" (I, p. 255). Hui-neng said: "Think not of good, think not of evil, but see what at the moment your own original features are, which you had even before coming into existence" (II, p. 42).

896 Zen differs from all other exercises in meditation, whether philosophical or religious, in its principle of lack of supposition. Often Buddha himself is sternly rejected, indeed, almost blasphemously ignored, although—or perhaps just because—he could be the strongest spiritual presupposition of the whole exercise. But he too is an image and must therefore be set aside. Nothing must be present except what is actually there: that is, man with all his unconscious assumptions, of which, precisely because they are unconscious, he can never, never rid himself. The answer which appears to come from the void, the light which flares up from the blackest darkness, these have always been experienced as a wonderful and blessed illumination.

897 The world of consciousness is inevitably a world full of restrictions, of walls blocking the way. It is of necessity one-sided, because of the nature of consciousness itself. No consciousness can harbour more than a very small number of simultaneous perceptions. All else must lie in shadow, withdrawn from sight. Any increase in the simultaneous contents immediately produces a dimming of consciousness, if not confusion to the point of disorientation. Consciousness not only requires, but is of its very nature strictly limited to, the few and hence the distinct. We owe our general orientation simply and solely to the fact that through attention we are able to register a fairly rapid succession of images. But attention is an effort of which we are not capable all the time. We have to make do, so to speak, with a minimum of simultaneous perceptions and successions of images. Hence in wide areas possible perceptions are continuously excluded, and consciousness is always bound to the narrowest circle. What would happen if an individual consciousness were able to take in at a single glance a simultaneous picture of every possible perception is beyond imagining. If man has already succeeded in building up the structure of the world from the few distinct things that he can perceive at one and the same time, what godlike spectacle would present itself to his eyes if he were able to perceive a great deal more all at once and distinctly? This question applies only to perceptions that are *possible* to us. If we now add to these the unconscious contents—i.e., contents which are not yet, or no longer, capable of consciousness—and then try to imagine a total vision, why, this is beyond the most

audacious fantasy. It is of course completely unimaginable in any conscious form, but in the unconscious it is a fact, since everything subliminal holds within it the ever-present possibility of being perceived and represented in consciousness. The unconscious is an irrepresentable totality of all subliminal psychic factors, a "total vision" *in potentia.* It constitutes the total disposition from which consciousness singles out tiny fragments from time to time.

898 Now if consciousness is emptied as far as possible of its contents, they will fall into a state of unconsciousness, at least for the time being. In Zen, this displacement usually results from the energy being withdrawn from conscious contents and transferred either to the conception of emptiness or to the koan. As both of these must be stable, the succession of images is abolished and with it the energy which maintains the kinetics of consciousness. The energy thus saved goes over to the unconscious and reinforces its natural charge to bursting point. This increases the readiness of the unconscious contents to break through into consciousness. But since the emptying and shutting down of consciousness is no easy matter, a special training of indefinite duration [35] is needed in order to set up that maximum tension which leads to the final break-through of unconscious contents.

899 The contents that break through are far from being random ones. As psychiatric experience with insane patients shows, specific relations exist between the conscious contents and the delusional ideas that break through in delirium. They are the same relations as exist between the dreams and the waking consciousness of normal people. The connection is an essentially compensatory relationship: [36] the unconscious contents bring to the surface everything that is necessary [37] in the broadest sense

35 Bodhidarma, the founder of Zen in China, says: "The incomparable doctrine of the Buddha can only be understood after long and hard practice, by enduring what is most difficult to endure, by practising what is most difficult to practise. People of little strength and wisdom can understand nothing of it. All the labours of such ones will come to naught." Suzuki, *Essays,* I, p. 188.

36 This is more probable than one that is merely "complementary."

37 This "necessity" is a working hypothesis. People can, and do, hold very different views on this point. For instance, are religious ideas "necessary"? Only the course of the individual's life can decide this, i.e., his individual experience. There are no abstract criteria.

for the completion and wholeness of conscious orientation. If the fragments offered by, or forced up from, the unconscious are meaningfully built into conscious life, a form of psychic existence results which corresponds better to the whole of the individual's personality, and so abolishes the fruitless conflicts between his conscious and unconscious self. Modern psychotherapy is based on this principle, in so far as it has been able to free itself from the historical prejudice that the unconscious consists only of infantile and morally inferior contents. There is certainly an inferior corner in it, a lumber-room full of dirty secrets, though these are not so much unconscious as hidden and only half forgotten. But all this has about as much to do with the whole of the unconscious as a decayed tooth has with the total personality. The unconscious is the matrix of all metaphysical statements, of all mythology, of all philosophy (so far as this is not merely critical), and of all expressions of life that are based on psychological premises.

900 Every invasion of the unconscious is an answer to a definite conscious situation, and this answer follows from the totality of possible ideas present, i.e., from the total disposition which, as explained above, is a simultaneous picture *in potentia* of psychic existence. The splitting up into single units, its one-sided and fragmentary character, is of the essence of consciousness. The reaction coming from the disposition always has a total character, as it reflects a nature which has not been divided up by any discriminating consciousness.[38] Hence its overpowering effect. It is the unexpected, all-embracing, completely illuminating answer, which works all the more as illumination and revelation since the conscious mind has got itself wedged into a hopeless blind alley.[39]

901 When, therefore, after many years of the hardest practice and the most strenuous demolition of rational understanding, the Zen devotee receives an answer—the only true answer—from Nature herself, everything that is said of satori can be understood. As one can see for oneself, it is the *naturalness* of the answer that strikes one most about the Zen anecdotes. Yes, one

38 "When the mind discriminates, there is manifoldness of things; when it does not it looks into the true state of things." *Essays,* I, p. 99.

39 See the passage beginning "Have your mind like unto space. . . ." Suzuki, *Essays,* I, p. 223.

can accept with a sort of old-roguish satisfaction the story of the enlightened pupil who gave his Master a slap in the face as a reward.[40] And how much wisdom there is in the Master's "Wu," the answer to the question about the Buddha-nature of the dog! One must always bear in mind, however, that there are a great many people who cannot distinguish between a metaphysical joke and nonsense, and just as many who are so convinced of their own cleverness that they have never in their lives met any but fools.

902 Great as is the value of Zen Buddhism for understanding the religious transformation process, its use among Western people is very problematical. The mental education necessary for Zen is lacking in the West. Who among us would place such implicit trust in a superior Master and his incomprehensible ways? This respect for the greater human personality is found only in the East. Could any of us boast that he believes in the possibility of a boundlessly paradoxical transformation experience, to the extent, moreover, of sacrificing many years of his life to the wearisome pursuit of such a goal? And finally, who would dare to take upon himself the authority for such an unorthodox transformation experience—except a man who was little to be trusted, one who, maybe for pathological reasons, has too much to say for himself? Just such a person would have no cause to complain of any lack of following among us. But let a "Master" set us a hard task, which requires more than mere parrot-talk, and the European begins to have doubts, for the steep path of self-development is to him as mournful and gloomy as the path to hell.

903 I have no doubt that the satori experience does occur also in the West, for we too have men who glimpse ultimate goals and spare themselves no pains to draw near to them. But they will keep silent, not only out of shyness, but because they know that any attempt to convey their experience to others is hopeless. There is nothing in our civilization to foster these strivings, not even the Church, the custodian of religious values. Indeed, it is the function of the Church to oppose all original experience, because this can only be unorthodox. The only movement inside our civilization which has, or should have, some understanding of these endeavours is psychotherapy. It is therefore

40 *Introduction to Zen Buddhism,* p. 94.

no accident that it is a psychotherapist who is writing this foreword.

904 Psychotherapy is at bottom a dialectical relationship between doctor and patient. It is an encounter, a discussion between two psychic wholes, in which knowledge is used only as a tool. The goal is transformation—not one that is predetermined, but rather an indeterminable change, the only criterion of which is the disappearance of egohood. No efforts on the part of the doctor can compel this experience. The most he can do is to smooth the path for the patient and help him to attain an attitude which offers the least resistance to the decisive experience. If knowledge plays no small part in our Western procedure, this is equivalent to the importance of the traditional spiritual atmosphere of Buddhism in Zen. Zen and its technique could only have arisen on the basis of Buddhist culture, which it presupposes at every turn. You cannot annihilate a rationalistic intellect that was never there—no Zen adept was ever the product of ignorance and lack of culture. Hence it frequently happens with us also that a conscious ego and a cultivated understanding must first be produced through analysis before one can even think about abolishing egohood or rationalism. What is more, psychotherapy does not deal with men who, like Zen monks, are ready to make any sacrifice for the sake of truth, but very often with the most stubborn of all Europeans. Thus the tasks of psychotherapy are much more varied, and the individual phases of the long process much more contradictory, than is the case in Zen.

905 For these and many other reasons a direct transplantation of Zen to our Western conditions is neither commendable nor even possible. All the same, the psychotherapist who is seriously concerned with the question of the aim of his therapy cannot remain unmoved when he sees the end towards which this Eastern method of psychic "healing"—i.e., "making whole"—is striving. As we know, this question has occupied the most adventurous minds of the East for more than two thousand years, and in this respect methods and philosophical doctrines have been developed which simply put all Western attempts along these lines into the shade. Our attempts have, with few exceptions, all stopped short at either magic (mystery cults, amongst which we must include Christianity) or intellectualism (philos-

ophy from Pythagoras to Schopenhauer). It is only the tragedies of Goethe's *Faust* and Nietzsche's *Zarathustra* which mark the first glimmerings of a break-through of total experience in our Western hemisphere.[41] And we do not know even today what these most promising of all products of the Western mind may at length signify, so overlaid are they with the materiality and concreteness of our thinking, as moulded by the Greeks.[42] Despite the fact that our intellect has developed almost to perfection the capacity of the bird of prey to espy the tiniest mouse from the greatest height, yet the pull of the earth drags it down, and the *samskaras* entangle it in a world of confusing images the moment it no longer seeks for booty but turns one eye inwards *to find him who seeks.* Then the individual falls into the throes of a daemonic rebirth, beset with unknown terrors and dangers and menaced by deluding mirages in a labyrinth of error. The worst of all fates threatens the venturer: mute, abysmal loneliness in the age he calls his own. What do we know of the hidden motives for Goethe's "main business," as he called his *Faust,* or of the shudders of the "Dionysus experience"? One has to read the *Bardo Thödol,* the Tibetan Book of the Dead, backwards, as I have suggested,[43] in order to find an Eastern parallel to the torments and catastrophes of the Western "way of release" to wholeness. This is the issue here—not good intentions, clever imitations, or intellectual acrobatics. And this, in shadowy hints or in greater or lesser fragments, is what the psychotherapist is faced with when he has freed himself from over-hasty and short-sighted doctrinal opinions. If he is a slave to his quasi-biological credo he will always try to reduce what he has glimpsed to the banal and the known, to a rationalistic denominator which satisfies only those who are content with illusions. But the foremost of all illusions is that anything can ever satisfy anybody. That illusion stands behind all that is unendurable in life and in front of all progress, and it is one of the most difficult things to overcome. If the psychotherapist can take time off from his helpful activities for a little reflection,

41 In this connection I must also mention the English mystic, William Blake. Cf. an excellent account in Percival, *William Blake's Circle of Destiny.*

42 The genius of the Greeks lay in the break-through of consciousness into the materiality of the world, thus robbing the world of its original dreamlike quality.

43 [Cf. above, par. 844.]

or if by any chance he is forced into seeing through his own illusions, it may dawn on him how hollow and flat, how inimical to life, are all rationalistic reductions when they come upon something that is alive, that wants to grow. Should he follow this up he will soon get an idea of what it means to "open wide that gate / Past which man's steps have ever flinching trod." [44]

906 I would not under any circumstances like it to be understood that I am making any recommendations or offering any advice. But when one begins to talk about Zen in the West I consider it my duty to show the European where our entrance lies to that "longest road" which leads to satori, and what kind of difficulties bestrew the path which only a few of our great ones have trod—beacons, perhaps, on high mountains, shining out into the dim future. It would be a disastrous mistake to assume that satori or samādhi are to be met with anywhere below these heights. As an experience of totality it cannot be anything cheaper or smaller than the whole. What this means psychologically can be seen from the simple reflection that consciousness is always only a part of the psyche and therefore never capable of psychic wholeness: for that the indefinite extension of the unconscious is needed. But the unconscious can neither be caught with clever formulas nor exorcized by means of scientific dogmas, for something of destiny clings to it—indeed, it is sometimes destiny itself, as *Faust* and *Zarathustra* show all too clearly. The attainment of wholeness requires one to stake one's whole being. Nothing less will do; there can be no easier conditions, no substitutes, no compromises. Considering that both *Faust* and *Zarathustra,* despite the highest recognition, stand on the border-line of what is comprehensible to the European, one could hardly expect the educated public, which has only just begun to hear about the obscure world of the psyche, to form any adequate conception of the spiritual state of a man caught in the toils of the individuation process—which is my term for "becoming whole." People then drag out the vocabulary of pathology and console themselves with the terminology of neurosis and psychosis, or else they whisper about the "creative secret." But what can a man "create" if he doesn't happen to be a poet? This misunderstanding has caused not a few persons in recent times to call themselves—by their own grace—"artists," just as

44 *Faust,* Part I, trans. by Wayne, p. 54.

if art had nothing to do with ability. But if you have nothing at all to create, then perhaps you create yourself.

907 Zen shows how much "becoming whole" means to the East. Preoccupation with the riddles of Zen may perhaps stiffen the spine of the faint-hearted European or provide a pair of spectacles for his psychic myopia, so that from his "damned hole in the wall" [45] he may enjoy at least a glimpse of the world of psychic experience, which till now lay shrouded in fog. No harm can be done, for those who are too frightened will be effectively protected from further corruption, as also from everything of significance, by the helpful idea of "auto-suggestion." [46] I should like to warn the attentive and sympathetic reader, however, not to underestimate the spiritual depth of the East, or to assume that there is anything cheap and facile about Zen.[47] The assiduously cultivated credulity of the West in regard to Eastern thought is in this case a lesser danger, as in Zen there are fortunately none of those marvellously incomprehensible words that we find in Indian cults. Neither does Zen play about with complicated *hatha*-yoga techniques,[48] which delude the physiologically minded European into the false hope that the spirit can be obtained by just sitting and breathing. On the contrary, Zen demands intelligence and will power, as do all greater things that want to become realities.

[45] Ibid., p. 44. [46] *Introduction*, p. 95.

[47] "It is no pastime but the most serious task in life; no idlers will ever dare attempt it." Suzuki, *Essays*, I, p. 27; cf. also p. 92.

[48] Says a Master: "If thou seekest Buddhahood by thus sitting cross-legged, thou murderest him. So long as thou freest thyself not from sitting so, thou never comest to the truth." *Essays*, I, p. 235. Cf. also II, p. 83f.

THE PSYCHOLOGY OF EASTERN MEDITATION [1]

908 The profound relationship between yoga and the hieratic architecture of India has already been pointed out by my friend Heinrich Zimmer, whose unfortunate early death is a great loss to Indology. Anyone who has visited Borobudur or seen the stupas at Bharhut and Sanchi can hardly avoid feeling that an attitude of mind and a vision quite foreign to the European have been at work here—if he has not already been brought to this realization by a thousand other impressions of Indian life. In the overflowing wealth of Indian spirituality there is reflected a vision of the soul which at first appears strange and inaccessible to the Greek-trained European mind. Our minds perceive things, our eyes, as Gottfried Keller says, "drink what the eyelids hold of the golden abundance of the world," and we

1 [Delivered as a lecture to the Schweizerische Gesellschaft der Freunde ostasiatischer Kultur, in Zurich, Basel, and Bern, during March–May 1943, and published as "Zur Psychologie östlicher Meditation" in the Society's *Mitteilungen* (St. Gallen), V (1943), 33–53; repub. in *Symbolik des Geistes* (Zurich, 1948), pp. 447–72. Previously trans. by Carol Baumann in *Art and Thought,* a volume in honour of Ananda K. Coomaraswamy (London, 1948), pp. 169–79.

[The work of Heinrich Zimmer's which the author refers to in the opening sentence was his *Kunstform und Yoga im indischen Kultbild* (1926), the central argument of which has been restated in his posthumous English works, particularly *Myths and Symbols in Indian Art and Civilization* (1946) and *The Art of Indian Asia* (1955). Cf. also the next paper in this volume.—EDITORS.]

draw conclusions about the inner world from our wealth of outward impressions. We even derive its content from outside on the principle that "nothing is in the mind which was not previously in the senses." This principle seems to have no validity in India. Indian thought and Indian art merely *appear* in the sense-world, but do not derive from it. Although often expressed with startling sensuality, they are, in their truest essence, unsensual, not to say suprasensual. It is not the world of the senses, of the body, of colours and sounds, not human passions that are born anew in transfigured form, or with realistic pathos, through the creativity of the Indian soul, but rather an underworld or an overworld of a metaphysical nature, out of which strange forms emerge into the familiar earthly scene. For instance, if one carefully observes the tremendously impressive impersonations of the gods performed by the Kathakali dancers of southern India, there is not a single *natural* gesture to be seen. Everything is bizarre, subhuman and superhuman at once. The dancers do not walk like human beings—they glide; they do not think with their heads but with their hands. Even their human faces vanish behind blue-enamelled masks. The world we know offers nothing even remotely comparable to this grotesque splendour. Watching these spectacles one is transported to a world of dreams, for that is the only place where we might conceivably meet with anything similar. But the Kathakali dancers, as we see them in the flesh or in the temple sculptures, are no nocturnal phantoms; they are intensely dynamic figures, consistent in every detail, or as if they had grown organically. These are no shadows or ghosts of a bygone reality, they are more like realities which have *not yet been,* potential realities which might at any moment step over the threshold.

909 Anyone who wholeheartedly surrenders to these impressions will soon notice that these figures do not strike the Indians themselves as dreamlike but as real. And, indeed, they touch upon something in our own depths, too, with an almost terrifying intensity, though we have no words to express it. At the same time, one notices that the more deeply one is stirred the more our sense-world fades into a dream, and that we seem to wake up in a world of gods, so immediate is their reality.

910 What the European notices at first in India is the outward corporeality he sees everywhere. But that is not India as the

Indian sees it; that is not *his* reality. Reality, as the German word "Wirklichkeit" implies, is that which *works.* For us the essence of that which works is the world of appearance; for the Indian it is the soul. The world for him is a mere show or façade, and his reality comes close to being what we would call a dream.

911 This strange antithesis between East and West is expressed most clearly in religious practice. We speak of religious uplift and exaltation; for us God is the Lord of the universe, we have a religion of brotherly love, and in our heaven-aspiring churches there is a *high altar.* The Indian, on the other hand, speaks of *dhyāna,* of self-immersion, and of *sinking* into meditation; God is within all things and especially within man, and one turns away from the outer world to the inner. In the old Indian temples the altar is sunk six to eight feet deep in the earth, and what we hide most shamefacedly is the holiest symbol to the Indian. We believe in *doing,* the Indian in impassive *being.* Our religious exercises consist of prayer, worship, and singing hymns. The Indian's most important exercise is yoga, an immersion in what we would call an unconscious state, but which he praises as the highest consciousness. Yoga is the most eloquent expression of the Indian mind and at the same time the instrument continually used to produce this peculiar attitude of mind.

912 What, then, is yoga? The word means literally "yoking," i.e., the disciplining of the instinctual forces of the psyche, which in Sanskrit are called *kleshas.* The yoking aims at controlling these forces that fetter human beings to the world. The *kleshas* would correspond, in the language of St. Augustine, to *superbia* and *concupiscentia.* There are many different forms of yoga, but all of them pursue the same goal. Here I will only mention that besides the purely physical exercises there is also a form called *hatha* yoga, a sort of gymnastics consisting chiefly of breathing exercises and special body postures. In this lecture I have undertaken to describe a yoga text which allows a deep insight into the psychic processes of yoga. It is a little-known Buddhist text, written in Chinese but translated from the original Sanskrit, and dating from A.D. 424. It is called the *Amitāyur-dhyāna Sūtra,* the Sutra of Meditation on Amitāyus. This

sutra, highly valued in Japan, belongs to the sphere of theistic Buddhism, in which is found the teaching that the Ādi-Buddha or Mahābuddha, the Primordial Buddha, brought forth the five Dhyāni-Buddhas or Dhyāni-Bodhisattvas. One of the five is Amitābha, "the Buddha of the *setting sun* of immeasurable light," the Lord of Sukhāvati, land of supreme bliss. He is the protector of our present world-period, just as Shākyamuni, the historical Buddha, is its teacher. In the cult of Amitābha there is, oddly enough, a kind of Eucharistic feast with consecrated bread. He is sometimes depicted holding in his hand the vessel of the life-giving food of immortality, or the vessel of holy water.

913 The text[2] begins with an introductory story that need not detain us here. A crown prince seeks to take the life of his parents, and in her extremity the Queen calls upon the Buddha for help, praying him to send her his two disciples Maudgalyāyana and Ānanda. The Buddha fulfils her wish, and the two appear at once. At the same time Shākyamuni, the Buddha himself, appears before her eyes. He shows her in a vision all the ten worlds, so that she can choose in which one she wishes to be reborn. She chooses the western realm of Amitābha. He then teaches her the yoga which should enable her to retain rebirth in the Amitābha land, and after giving her various moral instructions he speaks to her as follows:

914 You and all other beings besides ought to make it their only aim, with concentrated thought, to get a perception of the western quarter. You will ask how that perception is to be formed. I will explain it now. All beings, if not blind from birth, are uniformly possessed of sight, and they all see the setting sun. You should sit down properly, looking in the western direction, and prepare your thought for a close meditation on the sun: cause your mind to be firmly fixed on it so as to have an unwavering perception by the exclusive application of your thought, and gaze upon it more particularly when it is about to set and looks like a suspended drum. After you have thus seen the sun, let that image remain clear and fixed, whether your eyes be shut or open. Such is the perception of the sun, which is the First Meditation.

2 In *Buddhist Mahāyāna Sūtras,* Part II, pp. 159–201, trans. by J. Takakusu, slightly modified.

915 As we have already seen, the setting sun is an allegory of the immortality-dispensing Amitābha. The text continues:

> Next you should form the perception of water; gaze on the water clear and pure, and let this image also remain clear and fixed afterwards; never allow your thought to be scattered and lost.

916 As already mentioned, Amitābha is also the dispenser of the water of immortality.

917 When you have thus seen the water you should form the perception of ice. As you see the ice shining and transparent, so you should imagine the appearance of lapis lazuli. After that has been done, you will see the ground consisting of lapis lazuli transparent and shining both within and without. Beneath this ground of lapis lazuli there will be seen a golden banner with the seven jewels, diamonds, and the rest, supporting the ground. It extends to the eight points of the compass, and thus the eight corners of the ground are perfectly filled up. Every side of the eight quarters consists of a hundred jewels, every jewel has a thousand rays, and every ray has eighty-four thousand colours which, when reflected in the ground of lapis lazuli, look like a thousand millions of suns, and it is difficult to see them all one by one. Over the surface of that ground of lapis lazuli there are stretched golden ropes intertwined crosswise; divisions are made by means of [strings of] seven jewels with every part clear and distinct. . . .

When this perception has been formed, you should meditate on its constituents one by one and make the images as clear as possible, so that they may never be scattered and lost, whether your eyes be shut or open. Except only during the time of your sleep, you should always keep this in mind. One who has reached this stage of perception is said to have dimly seen the Land of Highest Happiness [Sukhāvati]. One who has obtained *samādhi* [the state of supernatural calm] is able to see the land of that Buddha country clearly and distinctly; this state is too much to be explained fully. Such is the perception of the land, and it is the Third Meditation.

918 Samādhi is 'withdrawnness,' i.e., a condition in which all connections with the world are absorbed into the inner world. Samādhi is the eighth phase of the Eightfold Path.

919 After the above comes a meditation on the Jewel Tree of the Amitābha land, and then follows the meditation on water:

In the Land of Highest Happiness there are waters in eight lakes; the water in every lake consists of seven jewels which are soft and yielding. Its source derives from the king of jewels that fulfils every wish [*cintāmani,* the wishing-pearl]. . . . In the midst of each lake there are sixty millions of lotus-flowers, made of seven jewels; all the flowers are perfectly round and exactly equal in circumference. . . . The water of jewels flows amidst the flowers and . . . the sound of the streaming water is melodious and pleasing. It proclaims all the perfect virtues [*pārāmitās*], "suffering," "non-existence," "impermanence" and "non-self"; it proclaims also the praise of the signs of perfection, and minor marks of excellence, of all Buddhas. From the king of jewels that fulfils every wish stream forth the golden-coloured rays excessively beautiful, the radiance of which transforms itself into birds possessing the colours of a hundred jewels, which sing out harmonious notes, sweet and delicious, ever praising the remembrance of the Buddha, the remembrance of the Law, and the remembrance of the Church. Such is the perception of the water of eight good qualities, and it is the Fifth Meditation.

920 Concerning the meditation on Amitābha himself, the Buddha instructs the Queen in the following manner: "Form the perception of a lotus-flower on a ground of seven jewels." The flower has 84,000 petals, each petal 84,000 veins, and each vein possesses 84,000 rays, "of which each can clearly be seen."

921 When you have perceived this, you should next perceive the Buddha himself. Do you ask how? Every Buddha Tathāgata is one whose spiritual body is the principle of nature [*Dharmadhātu-kāya*], so that he may enter into the mind of all beings. Consequently, when you have perceived the Buddha, it is indeed that mind of yours that possesses those thirty-two signs of perfection and eighty minor marks of excellence which you see in the Buddha. In fine, it is your mind that becomes the Buddha, nay, it is your mind that is indeed the Buddha. The ocean of true and universal knowledge of all the Buddhas derives its source from one's own mind and thought. Therefore you should apply your thought with undivided attention to a careful meditation on that Buddha Tathāgata, the *Arhat,* the Holy and Fully Enlightened One. In forming the perception of that Buddha, you should first perceive the image of that Buddha; whether your eyes be open or shut, look at him as at an image like to Jambunada gold in colour, sitting on the flower.[3]

[3] A river formed of the juice of the fruit of the Jambu-tree flows in a circle round Mount Meru and returns to the tree.

When you have seen the seated figure your mental vision will become clear, and you will be able to see clearly and distinctly the adornment of that Buddha-country, the jewelled ground, etc. In seeing these things let them be clear and fixed just as you see the palms of your hands. . . .

If you pass through this experience, you will at the same time see all the Buddhas of the ten quarters. . . . Those who have practised this meditation are said to have contemplated the bodies of all the Buddhas. Since they have meditated on the Buddha's body, they will also see the Buddha's mind. It is great compassion that is called the Buddha's mind. It is by his absolute compassion that he receives all beings. Those who have practised this meditation will, when they die, be born in the presence of the Buddhas in another life, and obtain a spirit of resignation wherewith to face all the consequences which shall hereafter arise. Therefore those who have wisdom should direct their thought to the careful meditation upon that Buddha Amitāyus.

922 Of those who practise this meditation it is said that they no longer live in an embryonic condition but will "obtain free access to the excellent and admirable countries of Buddhas."

923 After you have had this perception, you should imagine yourself to be born in the World of Highest Happiness in the western quarter, and to be seated, cross-legged, on a lotus-flower there. Then imagine that the flower has shut you in and has afterwards unfolded; when the flower has thus unfolded, five hundred coloured rays will shine over your body, your eyes will be opened so as to see the Buddhas and Bodhisattvas who fill the whole sky; you will hear the sounds of waters and trees, the notes of birds, and the voices of many Buddhas. . . .

924 The Buddha then says to Ānanda and Vaidehi (the Queen):

Those who wish, by means of their serene thoughts, to be born in the western land, should first meditate on an image of the Buddha, which is sixteen cubits high, seated on a lotus-flower in the water of the lake. As was stated before, the real body and its measurements are unlimited, incomprehensible to the ordinary mind. But by the efficacy of the ancient prayer of that Tathāgata, those who think of and remember him shall certainly be able to accomplish their aim. . . .

925 The Buddha's speech continues for many pages, then the text says:

When the Buddha had finished this speech, Vaidehi, together with her five hundred female attendants, guided by the Buddha's words, could see the scene of the far-stretching World of the Highest Happiness, and could also see the body of the Buddha and the bodies of the two Bodhisattvas. With her mind filled with joy she praised them, saying: "Never have I seen such a wonder!" Instantly she became wholly and fully enlightened, and attained a spirit of resignation, prepared to endure whatever consequences might yet arise. Her five hundred female attendants too cherished the thought of obtaining the highest perfect knowledge, and sought to be born in that Buddha-country. The World-Honoured One predicted that they would all be born in that Buddha-country, and be able to obtain samādhi of the presence of many Buddhas.

926 In a digression on the fate of the unenlightened, the Buddha sums up the yoga exercise as follows:

But, being harassed by pains, he will have no time to think of the Buddha. Some good friend will then say to him: "Even if you cannot exercise the remembrance of the Buddha, you may, at least, utter the name, 'Buddha Amitāyus.' " Let him do so serenely with his voice uninterrupted; let him be continually thinking of the Buddha until he has completed ten times the thought, repeating the formula, "Adoration to Buddha Amitāyus." On the strength of his merit in uttering the Buddha's name he will, during every repetition, expiate the sins which involve him in births and deaths during eighty millions of *kalpas*. He will, while dying, see a golden lotus-flower like the disc of the sun appearing before his eyes; in a moment he will be born in the World of Highest Happiness.

927 The above quotations form the essential content of the yoga exercise which interests us here. The text is divided into sixteen meditations, from which I have chosen only certain parts, but they will suffice to portray the intensification of the meditation, culminating in samādhi, the highest ecstasy and enlightenment.

928 The exercise begins with the concentration on the setting sun. In southern latitudes the intensity of the rays of the setting sun is so strong that a few moments of gazing at it are enough to create an intense after-image. With closed eyes one continues to see the sun for some time. As is well known, one method of hypnosis consists in fixating a shining object, such as a diamond or a crystal. Presumably the fixation of the sun is meant to produce a similar hypnotic effect. On the other hand it should not

have a soporific effect, because a "meditation" of the sun must accompany the fixation. This meditation is a reflecting, a "making clear," in fact a *realization* of the sun, its form, its qualities, and its meanings. Since the round form plays such an important role in the subsequent meditations, we may suppose that the sun's disk serves as a model for the later fantasies of circular structures, just as, by reason of its intense light, it prepares the way for the resplendent visions that come afterwards. In this manner, so the text says, "the perception is to be formed."

929 The next meditation, that of the water, is no longer based on any sense-impression but creates through active imagination the image of a reflecting expanse of water. This, as we know, throws back the full light of the sun. It should now be imagined that the water changes into ice, "shining and transparent." Through this procedure the immaterial light of the sun-image is transformed into the substance of water and this in turn into the solidity of ice. A concretization of the vision is evidently aimed at, and this results in a materialization of the fantasy-creation, which appears in the place of physical nature, of the world as we know it. A different reality is created, so to speak, out of soul-stuff. The ice, of a bluish colour by nature, changes into blue lapis lazuli, a solid, stony substance, which then becomes a "ground," "transparent and shining." With this "ground" an immutable, absolutely real foundation has been created. The blue translucent floor is like a lake of glass, and through its transparent layers one's gaze penetrates into the depths below.

930 The so-called "golden banner" then shines forth out of these depths. It should be noted that the Sanskrit word *dhvaja* also means 'sign' or 'symbol' in general. So we could speak just as well of the appearance of the "symbol." It is evident that the symbol "extending to the eight points of the compass" represents the ground plan of an eight-rayed system. As the text says, the "eight corners of the ground are perfectly filled up" by the banner. The system shines "like a thousand millions of suns," so that the shining after-image of the sun has enormously increased its radiant energy, and its illuminative power has now been intensified to an immeasurable degree. The strange idea of the "golden ropes" spread over the system like a net presumably means that the system is tied together and secured in this

way, so that it can no longer fall apart. Unfortunately the text says nothing about a possible failure of the method, or about the phenomena of disintegration which might supervene as the result of a mistake. But disturbances of this kind in an imaginative process are nothing unexpected to an expert—on the contrary, they are a regular occurrence. So it is not surprising that a kind of inner reinforcement of the image is provided in the yoga vision by means of golden ropes.

931 Although not explicitly stated in the text, the eight-rayed system is already the Amitābha land. In it grow wonderful trees, as is meet and proper, for this is paradise. Especial importance attaches to the water of the Amitābha land. In accordance with the octagonal system it is arranged in the form of eight lakes, and the source of these waters is a central jewel, *cintāmani,* the wishing pearl, a symbol of the "treasure hard to attain,"[4] the highest value. In Chinese art it appears as a moonlike image, frequently associated with a dragon.[5] The wondrous sounds of the water consist of two pairs of opposites which proclaim the dogmatic ground truths of Buddhism: "suffering and non-existence, impermanence and non-self," signifying that all existence is full of suffering, and that everything that clings to the ego is impermanent. Non-existence and non-self deliver us from these errors. Thus the singing water is something like the teaching of the Buddha—a redeeming water of wisdom, an *aqua doctrinae,* to use an expression of Origen. The source of this water, the pearl without peer, is the Tathāgata, the Buddha himself. Hence the imaginative reconstruction of the Buddha-image follows immediately afterwards, and while this structure is being built up in the meditation it is realized that the Buddha is really nothing other than the activating psyche of the yogi—the meditator himself. It is not only that the image of the Buddha is produced out of "one's own mind and thought," but the psyche which produces these thought-forms *is the Buddha himself.*

932 The image of the Buddha sits in the round lotus in the centre of the octagonal Amitābha land. He is distinguished by the great compassion with which he "receives all beings," including the meditator. This means that the inmost being which is the Buddha is bodied forth in the vision and revealed as the

4 Cf. *Symbols of Transformation,* Part II, chs. 6 and 7, especially par. 510.

5 Cf. *Psychology and Alchemy,* fig. 61.

true self of the meditator. He experiences himself as the only thing that exists, as the highest consciousness, even the Buddha. In order to attain this final goal it was necessary to pass through all the laborious exercises of mental reconstruction, to get free of the deluded ego-consciousness which is responsible for the sorrowful illusion of the world, and to reach that other pole of the psyche where the world as illusion is abolished.

*

933 Although it appears exceedingly obscure to the European, this yoga text is not a mere literary museum piece. It lives in the psyche of every Indian, in this form and in many others, so that his life and thinking are permeated by it down to the smallest details. It was not Buddhism that nurtured and educated this psyche, but yoga. Buddhism itself was born of the spirit of yoga, which is older and more universal than the historical reformation wrought by the Buddha. Anyone who seeks to understand Indian art, philosophy, and ethics from the inside must of necessity befriend this spirit. Our habitual understanding from the outside breaks down here, because it is hopelessly inadequate to the nature of Indian spirituality. And I wish particularly to warn against the oft-attempted imitation of Indian practices and sentiments. As a rule nothing comes of it except an artificial stultification of our Western intelligence. Of course, if anyone should succeed in giving up Europe from every point of view, and could actually *be* nothing but a yogi and sit in the lotus position with all the practical and ethical consequences that this entails, evaporating on a gazelle-skin under a dusty banyan tree and ending his days in nameless non-being, then I should have to admit that such a person understood yoga in the Indian manner. But anyone who cannot do this should not behave as if he did. He cannot and should not give up his Western understanding; on the contrary, he should apply it honestly, without imitation or sentimentality, to understanding as much of yoga as is possible for the Western mind. The secrets of yoga mean as much or even more to the Indian than our own Christian mysteries mean to us, and just as we would not allow any foreigner to make our *mysterium fidei* ludicrous, so we should not belittle these strange Indian ideas and practices or scorn them as absurd errors. By so doing we only block the way to a sensible

understanding. Indeed, we in Europe have already gone so far in this direction that the spiritual content of our Christian dogma has disappeared in a rationalistic and "enlightened" fog of alarming density, and this makes it all too easy for us to undervalue those things which we do not know and do not understand.

934 If we wish to understand at all, we can do so only in the European way. One can, it is true, understand many things with the heart, but then the head often finds it difficult to follow up with an intellectual formulation that gives suitable expression to what has been understood. There is also an understanding with the head, particularly of the scientific kind, where there is sometimes too little room for the heart. We must therefore leave it to the good will and co-operation of the reader to use first one and then the other. So let us first attempt, with the head, to find or build that hidden bridge which may lead to a European understanding of yoga.

935 For this purpose we must again take up the series of symbols we have already discussed, but this time we shall consider their sense-content. The *sun*, with which the series begins, is the source of warmth and light, the indubitable central point of our visible world. As the giver of life it is always and everywhere either the divinity itself or an image of the same. Even in the world of Christian ideas, the sun is a favourite allegory of Christ. A second source of life, especially in southern countries, is *water*, which also plays an important role in Christian allegory, for instance as the four rivers of paradise and the waters which issued from the side of the temple (Ezekiel 47). The latter were compared to the blood that flowed from the wound in Christ's side. In this connection I would also mention Christ's talk with the woman of Samaria at the well, and the rivers of living water flowing from the body of Christ (John 7:38). A meditation on sun and water evokes these and similar associations without fail, so that the meditator will gradually be led from the foreground of visible appearances into the background, that is, to the spiritual meaning behind the object of meditation. He is transported to the psychic sphere, where sun and water, divested of their physical objectivity, become symbols of psychic contents, images of the source of life in the individual psyche. For indeed our consciousness does not create itself—it wells up from

unknown depths. In childhood it awakens gradually, and all through life it wakes each morning out of the depths of sleep from an unconscious condition. It is like a child that is born daily out of the primordial womb of the unconscious. In fact, closer investigation reveals that it is not only influenced by the unconscious but continually emerges out of it in the form of numberless spontaneous ideas and sudden flashes of thought. Meditation on the meaning of sun and water is therefore something like a descent into the fountainhead of the psyche, into the unconscious itself.

936 Here, then, is a great difference between the Eastern and the Western mind. It is the same difference as the one we met before: the difference between the high and the low altar. The West is always seeking uplift, but the East seeks a sinking or deepening. Outer reality, with its bodiliness and weight, appears to make a much stronger and sharper impression on the European than it does on the Indian. The European seeks to raise himself above this world, while the Indian likes to turn back into the maternal depths of Nature.

937 Now just as Christian contemplation, for instance in the *Exercitia spiritualia* of Loyola, strives to comprehend the holy image as concretely as possible, with all the senses, so the yogi solidifies the water he contemplates first to ice and then to lapis lazuli, thereby creating a firm "ground," as he calls it. He makes, so to speak, a solid body for his vision. In this way he endows the figures of his psychic world with a concrete reality which takes the place of the outer world. At first he sees nothing but a reflecting blue surface, like that of a lake or ocean (also a favourite symbol of the unconscious in our Western dreams); but under the shining surface unknown depths lie hidden, dark and mysterious.

938 As the text says, the blue stone is *transparent,* which informs us that the gaze of the meditator can penetrate into the depths of the psyche's secrets. There he sees what could not be seen before, i.e., what was unconscious. Just as sun and water are the physical sources of life, so, as symbols, they express the essential secret of the life of the unconscious. In the *banner,* the symbol the yogi sees through the floor of lapis lazuli, he beholds, as it were, an image of the source of consciousness, which before was invisible and apparently without form. Through *dhyāna,*

through the sinking and deepening of contemplation, the unconscious has evidently taken on form. It is as if the light of consciousness had ceased to illuminate the objects of the outer world of the senses and now illumines the darkness of the unconscious. If the world of the senses and all thought of it are completely extinguished, then the inner world springs into relief more distinctly.

939 Here the Eastern text skips over a psychic phenomenon that is a source of endless difficulties for the European. If a European tries to banish all thought of the outer world and to empty his mind of everything outside, he immediately becomes the prey of his own subjective fantasies, which have nothing whatever to do with the images mentioned in our text. Fantasies do not enjoy a good reputation; they are considered cheap and worthless and are therefore rejected as useless and meaningless. They are the *kleshas,* the disorderly and chaotic instinctual forces which yoga proposes to yoke. The *Exercitia spiritualia* pursue the same goal, in fact both methods seek to attain success by providing the meditator with an object to contemplate and showing him the image he has to concentrate on in order to shut out the allegedly worthless fantasies. Both methods, Eastern as well as Western, try to reach the goal by a direct path. I do not wish to question the possibilities of success when the meditation exercise is conducted in some kind of ecclesiastical setting. But, outside of some such setting, the thing does not as a rule work, or it may even lead to deplorable results. By throwing light on the unconscious one gets first of all into the chaotic sphere of the personal unconscious, which contains all that one would like to forget, and all that one does not wish to admit to oneself or to anybody else, and which one prefers to believe is not true anyhow. One therefore expects to come off best if one looks as little as possible into this dark corner. Naturally anyone who proceeds in that way will never get round this corner and will never obtain even a trace of what yoga promises. Only the man who goes through this darkness can hope to make any further progress. I am therefore in principle against the uncritical appropriation of yoga practices by Europeans, because I know only too well that they hope to avoid their own dark corners. Such a beginning is entirely meaningless and worthless.

940 This is also the deeper reason why we in the West have never

developed anything comparable to yoga, aside from the very limited application of the Jesuit *Exercitia*. We have an abysmal fear of that lurking horror, our personal unconscious. Hence the European much prefers to tell others "how to do it." That the improvement of the whole begins with the individual, even with myself, never enters our heads. Besides, many people think it morbid to glance into their own interiors—it makes you melancholic, a theologian once assured me.

941 I have just said that we have developed nothing that could be compared with yoga. This is not entirely correct. True to our European bias, we have evolved a medical psychology dealing specifically with the kleshas. We call it the "psychology of the unconscious." The movement inaugurated by Freud recognized the importance of the human shadow-side and its influence on consciousness, and then got entangled in this problem. Freudian psychology is concerned with the very thing that our text passes over in silence and assumes is already dealt with. Yoga is perfectly well aware of the world of the kleshas, but the naturalness of its religion knows nothing of the *moral conflict* which the kleshas represent for us. An ethical dilemma divides us from our shadow. The spirit of India grows out of nature; with us spirit is opposed to nature.

942 The floor of lapis lazuli is not transparent for us because the question of the *evil in nature* must first be answered. This question *can* be answered, but surely not with shallow rationalistic arguments and intellectual patter. The ethical responsibility of the individual can give a valid answer, but there are no cheap recipes and no licences—one must pay to the last penny before the floor of lapis lazuli can become transparent. Our sutra presupposes that the shadow world of our personal fantasies—the personal unconscious—has been traversed, and goes on to describe a symbolical figure which at first strikes us as very strange. This is a geometrical structure raying out from a centre and divided into eight parts—an ogdoad. In the centre there is a lotus with the Buddha sitting in it, and the decisive experience is the final knowledge that the meditator himself is the Buddha, whereby the fateful knots woven in the opening story are apparently resolved. The concentrically constructed symbol evidently expresses the highest concentration, which can be achieved only when the previously described withdrawal and

canalization of interest away from the impressions of the sense-world and from object-bound ideas is pushed to the limit and applied to the background of consciousness. The conscious world with its attachment to objects, and even the centre of consciousness, the ego, are extinguished, and in their place the splendour of the Amitābha land appears with ever-increasing intensity.

943 Psychologically this means that behind or beneath the world of personal fantasies and instincts a still deeper layer of the unconscious becomes visible, which in contrast to the chaotic disorder of the kleshas is pervaded by the highest order and harmony, and, in contrast to their multiplicity, symbolizes the all-embracing unity of the *bodhimandala,* the magic circle of enlightenment.

944 What has our psychology to say about this Indian assertion of a supra-personal, world-embracing unconscious that appears when the darkness of the personal unconscious grows transparent? Modern psychology knows that the personal unconscious is only the top layer, resting on a foundation of a wholly different nature which we call the collective unconscious. The reason for this designation is the circumstance that, unlike the personal unconscious and its purely personal contents, the images in the deeper unconscious have a distinctly mythological character. That is to say, in form and content they coincide with those widespread primordial ideas which underlie the myths. They are no longer of a personal but of a purely supra-personal nature and are therefore common to all men. For this reason they are to be found in the myths and legends of all peoples and all times, as well as in individuals who have not the slightest knowledge of mythology.

945 Our Western psychology has, in fact, got as far as yoga in that it is able to establish scientifically a deeper layer of unity in the unconscious. The mythological motifs whose presence has been demonstrated by the exploration of the unconscious form in themselves a multiplicity, but this culminates in a concentric or radial order which constitutes the true centre or essence of the collective unconscious. On account of the remarkable agreement between the insights of yoga and the results of psychological research, I have chosen the Sanskrit term *mandala* for this central symbol.

946 You will now surely ask: but how in the world does science come to such conclusions? There are two paths to this end. The first is the historical path. If we study, for instance, the introspective method of medieval natural philosophy, we find that it repeatedly used the circle, and in most cases the circle divided into four parts, to symbolize the central principle, obviously borrowing this idea from the ecclesiastical allegory of the quaternity as found in numerous representations of the *Rex gloriae* with the four evangelists, the four rivers of paradise, the four winds, and so on.

947 The second is the path of empirical psychology. At a certain stage in the psychological treatment patients sometimes paint or draw such mandalas spontaneously, either because they dream them or because they suddenly feel the need to compensate the confusion in their psyches through representations of an ordered unity. For instance, our Swiss national saint, the Blessed Brother Nicholas of Flüe, went through a process of this kind, and the result can still be seen in the picture of the Trinity in the parish church at Sachseln. With the help of circular drawings in a little book by a German mystic,[6] he succeeded in assimilating the great and terrifying vision that had shaken him to the depths.

948 But what has our empirical psychology to say about the Buddha sitting in the lotus? Logically one would expect Christ to be enthroned in the centre of our Western mandalas. This was once true, as we have already said, in the Middle Ages. But our modern mandalas, spontaneously produced by numerous individuals without any preconceived ideas or suggestions from outside, contain no Christ-figure, still less a Buddha in the lotus position. On the other hand, the equal-armed Greek cross, or even an unmistakable imitation of the swastika, is to be found fairly often. I cannot discuss this strange fact here, though in itself it is of the greatest interest.[7]

949 Between the Christian and the Buddhist mandala there is a subtle but enormous difference. The Christian during contemplation would never say "*I* am Christ," but will confess with Paul: "Not I, but Christ liveth in me" (Gal. 2:20). Our sutra,

6 Cf. Stoeckli, *Die Visionen des Seligen Bruder Klaus.* Cf. also the sixth paper in this volume, pars. 474ff.

7 Cf. the first paper in this volume, pars. 136ff.

however, says: "Thou wilt know that *thou* art the Buddha." At bottom the two confessions are identical, in that the Buddhist only attains this knowledge when he is *anātman,* 'without self.' But there is an immeasurable difference in the formulation. The Christian attains his end *in Christ,* the Buddhist knows *he* is the Buddha. The Christian gets *out of* the transitory and ego-bound world of consciousness, but the Buddhist *still* reposes on the eternal ground of his inner nature, whose oneness with Deity, or with universal Being, is confirmed in other Indian testimonies.

THE HOLY MEN OF INDIA [1]

950 Heinrich Zimmer had been interested for years in the Maharshi of Tiruvannamalai, and the first question he asked me on my return from India concerned this latest holy and wise man from southern India. I do not know whether my friend found it an unforgivable or an incomprehensible sin on my part that I had not sought out Shri Ramana. I had the feeling that *he* would certainly not have neglected to pay him a visit, so warm was his interest in the life and thought of the holy man. This was scarcely surprising, as I know how deeply Zimmer had penetrated into the spirit of India. His most ardent wish to see India in reality was unfortunately never fulfilled, and the one chance he had of doing so fell through in the last hours before the outbreak of the second World War. As if in compensation, his vision of the spiritual India was all the more magnificent. In our work together he gave me invaluable insights into the Oriental psyche, not only through his immense technical knowl-

1 [Introduction to Heinrich Zimmer, *Der Weg zum Selbst: Lehre und Leben des indischen Heiligen Shri Ramana Maharshi aus Tiruvannamalai* (Zurich, 1944), edited by C. G. Jung. The work consists of 167 pages translated by Zimmer from English publications of the Sri Ramanasramam Book Depot, Tiruvannamalai, India, preceded by a brief (non-significant) foreword and this introduction, both by Jung, an obituary notice by Emil Abegg of Zimmer's death in New York in 1944, and an introduction to the Shri Ramana Maharshi texts by Zimmer.—EDITORS.]

edge, but above all through his brilliant grasp of the meaning and content of Indian mythology. Unhappily, the early death of those beloved of the gods was fulfilled in him, and it remains for us to mourn the loss of a spirit that overcame the limitations of the specialist and, turning towards humanity, bestowed upon it the joyous gift of "immortal fruit."

951 The carrier of mythological and philosophical wisdom in India has been since time immemorial the "holy man"—a Western title which does not quite render the essence and outward appearance of the parallel figure in the East. This figure is the embodiment of the spiritual India, and we meet him again and again in the literature. No wonder, then, that Zimmer was passionately interested in the latest and best incarnation of this type in the phenomenal personage of Shri Ramana. He saw in this yogi the true avatar of the figure of the *rishi,* seer and philosopher, which strides, as legendary as it is historical, down the centuries and the ages.

952 Perhaps I should have visited Shri Ramana. Yet I fear that if I journeyed to India a second time to make up for my omission, it would fare with me just the same: I simply could not, despite the uniqueness of the occasion, bring myself to visit this undoubtedly distinguished man personally. For the fact is, I doubt his uniqueness; he is of a type which always was and will be. Therefore it was not necessary to seek him out. I saw him all over India, in the pictures of Ramakrishna, in Ramakrishna's disciples, in Buddhist monks, in innumerable other figures of the daily Indian scene, and the words of his wisdom are the *sous-entendu* of India's spiritual life. Shri Ramana is, in a sense, a *hominum homo,* a true "son of man" of the Indian earth. He is "genuine," and on top of that he is a "phenomenon" which, seen through European eyes, has claims to uniqueness. But in India he is merely the whitest spot on a white surface (whose whiteness is mentioned only because there are so many surfaces that are just as black). Altogether, one sees so much in India that in the end one only wishes one could see less: the enormous variety of countries and human beings creates a longing for complete simplicity. This simplicity is there too; it pervades the spiritual life of India like a pleasant fragrance or a melody. It is everywhere the same; never monotonous, unendingly varied. To get to know it, it is sufficient to read an Upanishad or any

discourse of the Buddha. What is heard there is heard everywhere; it speaks out of a million eyes, it expresses itself in countless gestures, and there is no village or country road where that broad-branched tree cannot be found in whose shade the ego struggles for its own abolition, drowning the world of multiplicity in the All and All-Oneness of Universal Being. This note rang so insistently in my ears that soon I was no longer able to shake off its spell. I was then absolutely certain that no one could ever get beyond this, least of all the Indian holy man himself; and should Shri Ramana say anything that did not chime in with this melody, or claim to know anything that transcended it, his illumination would assuredly be false. The holy man is right when he intones India's ancient chants, but wrong when he pipes any other tune. This effortless drone of argumentation, so suited to the heat of southern India, made me refrain, without regret, from a visit to Tiruvannamalai.

953 Nevertheless, the unfathomableness of India saw to it that I should encounter the holy man after all, and in a form that was more congenial to me, without my seeking him out: in Trivandrum, the capital of Travancore, I ran across a disciple of the Maharshi. He was an unassuming little man, of a social status which we would describe as that of a primary-school teacher, and he reminded me most vividly of the shoemaker of Alexandria who (in Anatole France's story) was presented to St. Anthony by the angel as an example of an even greater saint than he. Like the shoemaker, my little holy man had innumerable children to feed and was making special sacrifices in order that his eldest son might be educated. (I will not enter here into the closely allied question as to whether holy men are always wise, and conversely, whether all wise men are unconditionally holy. In this respect there is room for doubt.) Be that as it may, in this modest, kindly, devout, and childlike spirit I encountered a man who had absorbed the wisdom of the Maharshi with utter devotion, and at the same time had surpassed his master because, notwithstanding his cleverness and holiness, he had "eaten" the world. I acknowledge with deep gratitude this meeting with him; nothing better could have happened to me. The man who is only wise and only holy interests me about as much as the skeleton of a rare saurian, which would not move me to tears. The insane contradiction, on the other hand, be-

tween existence beyond Māyā in the cosmic Self, and that amiable human weakness which fruitfully sinks many roots into the black earth, repeating for all eternity the weaving and rending of the veil as the ageless melody of India—this contradiction fascinates me; for how else can one perceive the light without the shadow, hear the silence without the noise, attain wisdom without foolishness? The experience of holiness may well be the most painful of all. My man—thank God—was only a little holy man; no radiant peak above the dark abysses, no shattering sport of nature, but an example of how wisdom, holiness, *and* humanity can dwell together in harmony, richly, pleasantly, sweetly, peacefully, and patiently, without limiting one another, without being peculiar, causing no surprise, in no way sensational, necessitating no special post-office, yet embodying an age-old culture amid the gentle murmur of the coconut palms fanning themselves in the light sea wind. He has found a meaning in the rushing phantasmagoria of Being, freedom in bondage, victory in defeat.

954 Unadulterated wisdom and unadulterated holiness, I fear, are seen to best advantage in literature, where their reputation remains undisputed. Lao-tzu reads exquisitely, unsurpassably well, in the *Tao Teh Ching;* Lao-tzu with his dancing girl on the Western slope of the mountain, celebrating the evening of life, is rather less edifying. But even less can one approve of the neglected body of the "unadulterated" holy man, especially if one believes that beauty is one of the most excellent of God's creations.

955 Shri Ramana's thoughts are beautiful to read. What we find here is purest India, the breath of eternity, scorning and scorned by the world. It is the song of the ages, resounding, like the shrilling of crickets on a summer's night, from a million beings. This melody is built up on the one great theme, which, veiling its monotony under a thousand colourful reflections, tirelessly and everlastingly rejuvenates itself in the Indian spirit, whose youngest incarnation is Shri Ramana himself. It is the drama of *ahamkāra,* the "I-maker" or ego-consciousness, in opposition and indissoluble bondage to the atman, the self or non-ego. The Maharshi also calls the atman the "ego-ego"—significantly enough, for the self is indeed experienced as the subject of the subject, as the true source and controller of the

ego, whose (mistaken) strivings are continually directed towards appropriating the very autonomy which is intimated to it by the self.

956 This conflict is not unknown to the Westerner: for him it is the relationship of man to God. The modern Indian, as I can testify from my own experience, has largely adopted European habits of language, "self" or "atman" being essentially synonymous with "God." But, in contradistinction to the Western "man and God," the Indian posits the opposition (or correspondence) between "ego and self." "Ego," as contrasted with "man," is a distinctly psychological concept, and so is "self"—to *our* way of thinking. We might therefore be inclined to assume that in India the metaphysical problem "man and God" has been shifted on to the psychological plane. On closer inspection it is clear that this is not so, for the Indian concept of "ego" and "self" is not really psychological but—one could well say—just as metaphysical as our "man and God." The Indian lacks the epistemological standpoint just as much as our own religious speech does. He is still "pre-Kantian." This complication is unknown in India and it is still largely unknown with us. In India there is no psychology in our sense of the word. India is "prepsychological": when it speaks of the "self," it *posits* such a thing as existing. Psychology does not do this. It does not in any sense deny the existence of the dramatic conflict, but reserves the right to the poverty, or the riches, of *not* knowing about the self. Though very well acquainted with the self's peculiar and paradoxical phenomenology, we remain conscious of the fact that we are discerning, with the limited means at our disposal, something essentially unknown and expressing it in terms of psychic structures which may not be adequate to the nature of what is to be known.

957 This epistemological limitation keeps us at a remove from what we term "self" or "God." The equation self = God is shocking to the European. As Shri Ramana's statements and many others show, it is a specifically Eastern insight, to which psychology has nothing further to say except that it is not within its competence to differentiate between the two. Psychology can only establish that the empiricism of the "self" exhibits a religious symptomatology, just as does that category of assertions associated with the term "God." Although the phenomenon of

religious exaltation transcends epistemological criticism—a feature it shares with all manifestations of emotion—yet the human urge to knowledge asserts itself again and again with "ungodly" or "Luciferian" obstinacy and wilfulness, indeed with necessity, whether it be to the loss or gain of the thinking man. Sooner or later he will place his reason in opposition to the emotion that grips him and seek to withdraw from its entangling grasp in order to give an account of what has happened. If he proceeds prudently and conscientiously, he will continually discover that at least a part of his experience is a humanly limited *interpretation,* as was the case with Ignatius Loyola and his vision of the snake with multiple eyes, which he at first regarded as of divine, and later as of diabolical, origin. (Compare the exhortation in I John 4:1: "Do not believe every spirit, but test the spirits to see whether they are of God.") To the Indian it is clear that the self as the originating ground of the psyche is not different from God, and that, so far as a man is *in* the self, he is not only contained in God but actually is God. Shri Ramana is quite explicit on this point. No doubt this equation, too, is an "interpretation." Equally, it is an interpretation to regard the self as the highest good or as the goal of all desire and fulfilment, although the phenomenology of such an experience leaves no doubt that these characteristics exist *a priori* and are indispensable components of religious exaltation. But that will not prevent the critical intellect from questioning the validity of these characteristics. It is difficult to see how this question could be answered, as the intellect lacks the necessary criteria. Anything that might serve as a criterion is subject in turn to the critical question of validity. The only thing that can decide here is the preponderance of psychic facts.

958 The goal of Eastern religious practice is the same as that of Western mysticism: the shifting of the centre of gravity from the ego to the self, from man to God. This means that the ego disappears in the self, and man in God. It is evident that Shri Ramana has either really been more or less absorbed by the self, or has at least struggled earnestly all his life to extinguish his ego in it. The *Exercitia spiritualia* reveal a similar striving: they subordinate "self-possession" (possession of an ego) as much as possible to possession by Christ. Shri Ramana's elder contemporary, Ramakrishna, had the same attitude concerning

the relation to the self, only in his case the dilemma between ego and self seems to emerge more distinctly. Whereas Shri Ramana displays a "sympathetic" tolerance towards the worldly callings of his disciples, while yet exalting the extinction of the ego as the real goal of spiritual exertion, Ramakrishna shows a rather more hesitant attitude in this respect. He says: "So long as ego-seeking exists, neither knowledge (*jñāna*) nor liberation (*mukti*) is possible, and to births and deaths there is no end." [2] All the same, he has to admit the fatal tenacity of *ahamkāra* (the "I-maker"): "Very few can get rid of the sense of 'I' through *samādhi*. . . . We may discriminate a thousand times, but the sense of 'I' is bound to return again and again. You may cut down the branches of a fig-tree today, but tomorrow you will see that new twigs are sprouting." [3] He goes so far as to suggest the indestructibility of the ego with the words: "If this sense of 'I' will not leave, then let it stay on as the servant of God." [4] Compared with this concession to the ego, Shri Ramana is definitely the more radical or, in the sense of Indian tradition, the more conservative. Though the elder, Ramakrishna is the more modern of the two, and this is probably to be attributed to the fact that he was affected by the Western attitude of mind far more profoundly than was Shri Ramana.

959 If we conceive of the self as the essence of psychic wholeness, i.e., as the totality of conscious and unconscious, we do so because it does *in fact* represent something like a goal of psychic development, and this irrespective of all conscious opinions and expectations. The self is the subject-matter of a process that generally runs its course outside consciousness and makes its presence felt only by a kind of long-range effect. A critical attitude towards this natural process allows us to raise questions which are excluded at the outset by the formula self = God. This formula shows the dissolution of the ego in the atman to be the unequivocal goal of religion and ethics, as exemplified in the life and thought of Shri Ramana. The same is obviously true of Christian mysticism, which differs from Oriental philosophy only through having a different terminology. The inevitable consequence is the depreciation and abolition of the physical and psychic man (i.e., of the living body and *ahamkāra*)

2 *Worte des Ramakrishna,* ed. by Emma von Pelet, p. 77.

3 *The Gospel of Ramakrishna,* p. 56. 4 Ibid.

in favour of the pneumatic man. Shri Ramana speaks of his body as "this clod." As against this, and taking into consideration the complex nature of human experience (emotion plus interpretation), the critical standpoint admits the importance of ego-consciousness, well knowing that without *ahamkāra* there would be absolutely no one there to register what was happening. Without the Maharshi's personal ego, which, as a matter of brute experience, only exists in conjunction with the said "clod" (= body), there would be no Shri Ramana at all. Even if we agreed with him that it is no longer his ego, but the atman speaking, it is still the psychic structure of consciousness in association with the body that makes speech communication possible. Without this admittedly very troublesome physical and psychic man, the self would be entirely without substance, as Angelus Silesius has already said:

> I know that without me
> God can no moment live;
> Were I to die, then he
> No longer could survive.

960 The intrinsically goal-like quality of the self and the urge to realize this goal are, as we have said, not dependent on the participation of consciousness. They cannot be denied any more than one can deny one's ego-consciousness. It, too, puts forward its claims peremptorily, and very often in overt or covert opposition to the needs of the evolving self. In reality, i.e., with few exceptions, the entelechy of the self consists in a succession of endless compromises, ego and self laboriously keeping the scales balanced if all is to go well. Too great a swing to one side or the other is often no more than an example of how not to set about it. This certainly does not mean that extremes, when they occur in a natural way, are in themselves evil. We make the right use of them when we examine their meaning, and they give us ample opportunity to do this in a manner deserving our gratitude. Exceptional human beings, carefully hedged about and secluded, are invariably a gift of nature, enriching and widening the scope of our consciousness—but only if our capacity for reflection does not suffer shipwreck. Enthusiasm can be a veritable gift of the gods or a monster from hell. With the hybris which attends it, corruption sets in, even if the resultant clouding of

consciousness seems to put the attainment of the highest goals almost within one's grasp. The only true and lasting gain is heightened and broadened reflection.

961 Banalities apart, there is unfortunately no philosophical or psychological proposition that does not immediately have to be reversed. Thus reflection as an end in itself is nothing but a limitation if it cannot stand firm in the turmoil of chaotic extremes, just as mere dynamism for its own sake leads to inanity. Everything requires for its existence its own opposite, or else it fades into nothingness. The ego needs the self and vice versa. The changing relations between these two entities constitute a field of experience which Eastern introspection has exploited to a degree almost unattainable to Western man. The philosophy of the East, although so vastly different from ours, could be an inestimable treasure for us too; but, in order to possess it, we must first earn it. Shri Ramana's words, which Heinrich Zimmer has bequeathed to us, in excellent translation, as the last gift of his pen, bring together once again the loftiest insights that the spirit of India has garnered in the course of the ages, and the individual life and work of the Maharshi illustrate once again the passionate striving of the Indian for the liberating "Ground." I say "once again," because India is about to take the fateful step of becoming a State and entering into a community of nations whose guiding principles have anything and everything on the programme except detachment and peace of the soul.

962 The Eastern peoples are threatened with a rapid collapse of their spiritual values, and what replaces them cannot always be counted among the best that Western civilization has produced. From this point of view, one could regard Ramakrishna and Shri Ramana as modern prophets, who play the same compensatory role in relation to their people as that of the Old Testament prophets in relation to the "unfaithful" children of Israel. Not only do they exhort their compatriots to remember their thousand-year-old spiritual culture, they actually embody it and thus serve as an impressive warning, lest the demands of the soul be forgotten amid the novelties of Western civilization with its materialistic technology and commercial acquisitiveness. The breathless drive for power and aggrandizement in the political, social, and intellectual sphere, gnawing

at the soul of the Westerner with apparently insatiable greed, is spreading irresistibly in the East and threatens to have incalculable consequences. Not only in India but in China, too, much has already perished where once the soul lived and throve. The externalization of culture may do away with a great many evils whose removal seems most desirable and beneficial, yet this step forward, as experience shows, is all too dearly paid for with a loss of spiritual culture. It is undeniably much more comfortable to live in a well-planned and hygienically equipped house, but this still does not answer the question of *who* is the dweller in this house and whether his soul rejoices in the same order and cleanliness as the house which ministers to his outer life. The man whose interests are all outside is never satisfied with what is necessary, but is perpetually hankering after something more and better which, true to his bias, he always seeks outside himself. He forgets completely that, for all his outward successes, he himself remains the same inwardly, and he therefore laments his poverty if he possesses only one automobile when the majority have two. Obviously the outward lives of men could do with a lot more bettering and beautifying, but these things lose their meaning when the inner man does not keep pace with them. To be satiated with "necessities" is no doubt an inestimable source of happiness, yet the inner man continues to raise his claim, and this can be satisfied by no outward possessions. And the less this voice is heard in the chase after the brilliant things of this world, the more the inner man becomes the source of inexplicable misfortune and uncomprehended unhappiness in the midst of living conditions whose outcome was expected to be entirely different. The externalization of life turns to incurable suffering, because no one can understand why he should suffer from himself. No one wonders at his insatiability, but regards it as his lawful right, never thinking that the one-sidedness of this psychic diet leads in the end to the gravest disturbances of equilibrium. That is the sickness of Western man, and he will not rest until he has infected the whole world with his own greedy restlessness.

963 The wisdom and mysticism of the East have, therefore, very much to say to us, even when they speak their own inimitable language. They serve to remind us that we in our culture possess something similar, which we have already forgotten, and to

direct our attention to the fate of the inner man, which we set aside as trifling. The life and teaching of Shri Ramana are of significance not only for India, but for the West too. They are more than a *document humain:* they are a warning message to a humanity which threatens to lose itself in unconsciousness and anarchy. It is perhaps, in the deeper sense, no accident that Heinrich Zimmer's last book should leave us, as a testament, the life-work of a modern Indian prophet who exemplifies so impressively the problem of psychic transformation.

IX

FOREWORD TO THE "I CHING"

FOREWORD TO THE "I CHING"[1]

964 Since I am not a Sinologue, a foreword to the Book of Changes from my hand must be a testimonial of my individual experience with this great and singular book. It also affords me a welcome opportunity to pay tribute again to the memory of my late friend, Richard Wilhelm. He himself was profoundly aware of the cultural significance of his translation of the *I Ching,* a version unrivalled in the West.

965 If the meaning of the Book of Changes were easy to grasp, the work would need no foreword. But this is far from being the case, for there is so much that is obscure about it that Western scholars have tended to dispose of it as a collection of "magic spells," either too abstruse to be intelligible or of no value whatsoever. Legge's translation of the *I Ching,* up to now the only version available in English, has done little to make the work accessible to Western minds.[2] Wilhelm, however, has made

1 [Grateful acknowledgment is made here to Cary F. Baynes for permission to use, with a few minor changes, her translation of this Foreword, which Professor Jung wrote specially for the English edition of the *I Ching or Book of Changes,* translated by Mrs. Baynes from the German translation of Richard Wilhelm (New York and London, 1950).—TRANS.]

2 Legge makes the following comment on the explanatory text for the individual lines: "According to our notions, a framer of emblems should be a good deal of a poet, but those of the *Yi* only make us think of a dryasdust. Out of more than three hundred and fifty, the greater number are only grotesque" (*The Yi King,*

every effort to open the way to an understanding of the symbolism of the text. He was in a position to do this because he himself was taught the philosophy and the use of the *I Ching* by the venerable sage Lao Nai-hsüan; moreover, he had over a period of many years put the peculiar technique of the oracle into practice. His grasp of the living meaning of the text gives his version of the *I Ching* a depth of perspective that an exclusively academic knowledge of Chinese philosophy could never provide.

966 I am greatly indebted to Wilhelm for the light he has thrown upon the complicated problem of the *I Ching,* and for insight into its practical application. For more than thirty years I have interested myself in this oracle technique, for it seemed to me of uncommon significance as a method of exploring the unconscious. I was already fairly familiar with the *I Ching* when I first met Wilhelm in the early nineteen twenties; he confirmed then what I already knew, and taught me many things more.

967 I do not know Chinese and have never been in China. I can assure my reader that it is not altogether easy to find the right approach to this monument of Chinese thought, which departs so completely from our ways of thinking. In order to understand what such a book is all about, it is imperative to cast off certain of our Western prejudices. It is a curious fact that such a gifted and intelligent people as the Chinese has never developed what we call science. Our science, however, is based upon the principle of causality, and causality is considered to be an axiomatic truth. But a great change in our standpoint is setting in. What Kant's *Critique of Pure Reason* failed to do is being accomplished by modern physics. The axioms of causality are being shaken to their foundations: we know now that what we term natural laws are merely statistical truths and thus must necessarily allow for exceptions. We have not sufficiently taken into account as yet that we need the laboratory with its incisive restrictions in order to demonstrate the invariable validity of natural law. If we leave things to nature, we see a very different

p. 22). Of the "lessons" of the hexagrams, the same author says: "But why, it may be asked, why should they be conveyed to us by such an array of lineal figures, and in such a farrago of emblematic representations" (p. 25). However, we are nowhere told that Legge ever bothered to put the method to a practical test.

picture: every process is partially or totally interfered with by chance, so much so that under natural circumstances a course of events absolutely conforming to specific laws is almost an exception.

968 The Chinese mind, as I see it at work in the *I Ching,* seems to be exclusively preoccupied with the chance aspect of events. What we call coincidence seems to be the chief concern of this peculiar mind, and what we worship as causality passes almost unnoticed. We must admit that there is something to be said for the immense importance of chance. An incalculable amount of human effort is directed to combatting and restricting the nuisance or danger that chance represents. Theoretical considerations of cause and effect often look pale and dusty in comparison with the practical results of chance. It is all very well to say that the crystal of quartz is a hexagonal prism. The statement is quite true in so far as an ideal crystal is envisaged. But in nature one finds no two crystals exactly alike, although all are unmistakably hexagonal. The actual form, however, seems to appeal more to the Chinese sage than the ideal one. The jumble of natural laws constituting empirical reality holds more significance for him than a causal explanation of events that, in addition, must usually be separated from one another in order to be properly dealt with.

969 The manner in which the *I Ching* tends to look upon reality seems to disfavour our causal procedures. The moment under actual observation appears to the ancient Chinese view more of a chance hit than a clearly defined result of concurrent causal chains. The matter of interest seems to be the configuration formed by chance events at the moment of observation, and not at all the hypothetical reasons that seemingly account for the coincidence. While the Western mind carefully sifts, weighs, selects, classifies, isolates, the Chinese picture of the moment encompasses everything down to the minutest nonsensical detail, because all of the ingredients make up the observed moment.

970 Thus it happens that when one throws the three coins, or counts through the forty-nine yarrow-stalks, these chance details enter into the picture of the moment of observation and form a part of it—a part that is insignificant to us, yet most meaningful to the Chinese mind. With us it would be a banal and almost meaningless statement (at least on the face of it) to say that

whatever happens in a given moment has inevitably the quality peculiar to that moment. This is not an abstract argument but a very practical one. There are certain connoisseurs who can tell you merely from the appearance, taste, and behaviour of a wine the site of its vineyard and the year of its origin. There are antiquarians who with almost uncanny accuracy will name the time and place of origin and the maker of an *objet d'art* or piece of furniture on merely looking at it. And there are even astrologers who can tell you, without any previous knowledge of your nativity, what the position of sun and moon was and what zodiacal sign rose above the horizon at the moment of your birth. In the face of such facts, it must be admitted that moments can leave long-lasting traces.

971 In other words, whoever invented the *I Ching* was convinced that the hexagram worked out in a certain moment coincided with the latter in quality no less than in time. To him the hexagram was the exponent of the moment in which it was cast—even more so than the hours of the clock or the divisions of the calendar could be—inasmuch as the hexagram was understood to be an indicator of the essential situation prevailing at the moment of its origin.

972 This assumption involves a certain curious principle which I have termed synchronicity,[3] a concept that formulates a point of view diametrically opposed to that of causality. Since the latter is a merely statistical truth and not absolute, it is a sort of working hypothesis of how events evolve one out of another, whereas synchronicity takes the coincidence of events in space and time as meaning something more than mere chance, namely, a peculiar interdependence of objective events among themselves as well as with the subjective (psychic) states of the observer or observers.

973 The ancient Chinese mind contemplates the cosmos in a way comparable to that of the modern physicist, who cannot deny that his model of the world is a decidedly psychophysical structure. The microphysical event includes the observer just as much as the reality underlying the *I Ching* comprises subjective, i.e., psychic conditions in the totality of the momentary

3 [Cf. Jung's "Synchronicity: An Acausal Connecting Principle." In that work (1955 edn., pp. 49–53) he discusses the synchronistic aspects of the *I Ching*.—EDITORS.]

situation. Just as causality describes the sequence of events, so synchronicity to the Chinese mind deals with the coincidence of events. The causal point of view tells us a dramatic story about how *D* came into existence: it took its origin from *C*, which existed before *D*, and *C* in its turn had a father, *B*, etc. The synchronistic view on the other hand tries to produce an equally meaningful picture of coincidence. How does it happen that *A′*, *B′*, *C′*, *D′*, etc., appear all at the same moment and in the same place? It happens in the first place because the physical events *A′* and *B′* are of the same quality as the psychic events *C′* and *D′*, and further because all are the exponents of one and the same momentary situation. The situation is assumed to represent a legible or understandable picture.

974 Now the sixty-four hexagrams of the *I Ching* are the instrument by which the meaning of sixty-four different yet typical situations can be determined. These interpretations are equivalent to causal explanations. Causal connection can be determined statistically and can be subjected to experiment. Inasmuch as situations are unique and cannot be repeated, experimenting with synchronicity seems to be impossible under ordinary conditions.[4] In the *I Ching,* the only criterion of the validity of synchronicity is the observer's opinion that the text of the hexagram amounts to a true rendering of his psychic condition. It is assumed that the fall of the coins or the result of the division of the bundle of yarrow-stalks is what it necessarily must be in a given "situation," inasmuch as anything happening at that moment belongs to it as an indispensable part of the picture. If a handful of matches is thrown to the floor, they form the pattern characteristic of that moment. But such an obvious truth as this reveals its meaningful nature only if it is possible to read the pattern and to verify its interpretation, partly by the observer's knowledge of the subjective and objective situation, partly by the character of subsequent events. It is obviously not a procedure that appeals to a critical mind used to experimental verification of facts or to factual evidence. But for someone who likes to look at the world at the angle from which ancient China saw it, the *I Ching* may have some attraction.

975 My argument as outlined above has of course never entered

[4] Cf. J. B. Rhine, *The Reach of the Mind.*

a Chinese mind. On the contrary, according to the old tradition, it is "spiritual agencies," acting in a mysterious way, that make the yarrow-stalks give a meaningful answer.[5] These powers form, as it were, the living soul of the book. As the latter is thus a sort of animated being, the tradition assumes that one can put questions to the *I Ching* and expect to receive intelligent answers. Thus it occurred to me that it might interest the uninitiated reader to see the *I Ching* at work. For this purpose I made an experiment strictly in accordance with the Chinese conception: I personified the book in a sense, asking its judgment about its present situation, i.e., my intention to introduce it to the English-speaking public.

976 Although this procedure is well within the premises of Taoist philosophy, it appears exceedingly odd to us. However, not even the strangeness of insane delusions or of primitive superstition has ever shocked me. I have always tried to remain unbiased and curious—*rerum novarum cupidus*. Why not venture a dialogue with an ancient book that purports to be animated? There can be no harm in it, and the reader may watch a psychological procedure that has been carried out time and again throughout the millennia of Chinese civilization, representing to a Confucius or a Lao-tzu both a supreme expression of spiritual authority and a philosophical enigma. I made use of the coin method, and the answer obtained was hexagram 50, Ting, THE CAULDRON.[6]

977 In accordance with the way my question was phrased, the text of the hexagram must be regarded as though the *I Ching* itself were the speaking person. Thus it describes itself as a cauldron, that is, as a ritual vessel containing cooked food. Here the food is to be understood as spiritual nourishment. Wilhelm says about this:

> The *ting*, as a utensil pertaining to a refined civilization, suggests the fostering and nourishing of able men, which redounded to the benefit of the state. . . . Here we see civilization as it reaches its culmination in religion. The *ting* serves in offering sacrifice to God. . . . The supreme revelation of God appears in prophets and holy men. To venerate them is true veneration of God. The will of God, as revealed through them, should be accepted in humility.

5 They are *shên*, that is, 'spirit-like.' "Heaven produced the 'spirit-like things' " (Legge, p. 41).

6 [Cf. the *I Ching*, p. 205.—EDITORS.]

978 Keeping to our hypothesis, we must conclude that the *I Ching* is here testifying concerning itself.

979 When any of the lines of a given hexagram have the value of six or nine, it means that they are specially emphasized and hence important in the interpretation.[7] In my hexagram the "spiritual agencies" have given the emphasis of a nine to the lines in the second and in the third place. The text says:

> Nine in the second place means:
>
> There is food in the *ting*.
> My comrades are envious,
> But they cannot harm me.
> Good fortune.

980 Thus the *I Ching* says of itself: "I contain (spiritual) nourishment." Since a share in something great always arouses envy, the chorus of the envious[8] is part of the picture. The envious want to rob the *I Ching* of its great possession, that is, they seek to rob it of meaning, or to destroy its meaning. But their enmity is in vain. Its richness of meaning is assured; that is, it is convinced of its positive achievements, which no one can take away. The text continues:

> Nine in the third place means:
>
> The handle of the *ting* is altered.
> One is impeded in his way of life.
> The fat of the pheasant is not eaten.
> Once rain falls, remorse is spent.
> Good fortune comes in the end.

981 The handle [German *Griff*] is the part by which the *ting* can be grasped [*gegriffen*]. Thus it signifies the concept[9] [*Begriff*] one has of the *I Ching* (the *ting*). In the course of time this concept has apparently changed, so that today we can no longer grasp [*begreifen*] the *I Ching*. Thus "one is impeded in

[7] See the explanation of the method, ibid., p. 392.

[8] For example, the *invidi* ('the envious') are a constantly recurring image in the old Latin books on alchemy, especially in the *Turba philosophorum* (11th or 12th cent.).

[9] From the Latin *concipere*, 'to take together,' e.g., in a vessel: *concipere* derives from *capere*, 'to take,' 'to grasp.'

his way of life." We are no longer supported by the wise counsel and deep insight of the oracle; therefore we no longer find our way through the mazes of fate and the obscurities of our own natures. The fat of the pheasant, that is, the best and richest part of a good dish, is no longer eaten. But when the thirsty earth finally receives rain again, that is, when this state of want has been overcome, "remorse," that is, sorrow over the loss of wisdom, is ended, and then comes the longed-for opportunity. Wilhelm comments: "This describes a man who, in a highly evolved civilization, finds himself in a place where no one notices or recognizes him. This is a severe block to his effectiveness." The *I Ching* is complaining, as it were, that its excellent qualities go unrecognized and hence lie fallow. It comforts itself with the hope that it is about to regain recognition.

982 The answer given in these two salient lines to the question I put to the *I Ching* requires no particular subtlety for its interpretation, no artifices, and no unusual knowledge. Anyone with a little common sense can understand the meaning of the answer; it is the answer of one who has a good opinion of himself, but whose value is neither generally recognized nor even widely known. The answering subject has an interesting notion of itself: it looks upon itself as a vessel in which sacrificial offerings are brought to the gods, ritual food for their nourishment. It conceives of itself as a cult utensil serving to provide spiritual nourishment for the unconscious elements or forces ("spiritual agencies") that have been projected as gods—in other words, to give these forces the attention they need in order to play their part in the life of the individual. Indeed, this is the original meaning of the word *religio*—a careful observation and taking account of (from *relegere* [10]) the numinous.

983 The method of the *I Ching* does indeed take into account the hidden individual quality in things and men, and in one's own unconscious self as well. I questioned the *I Ching* as one questions a person whom one is about to introduce to friends: one asks whether or not it will be agreeable to him. In answer the *I Ching* tells me of its religious significance, of the fact that at present it is unknown and misjudged, of its hope of

10 This is the classical etymology. The derivation of *religio* from *religare*, 'reconnect,' 'link back,' originated with the Church Fathers.

being restored to a place of honour—this last obviously with a sidelong glance at my as yet unwritten foreword,[11] and above all at the English translation. This seems a perfectly understandable reaction, such as one could expect also from a person in a similar situation.

984 But how has this reaction come about? Simply because I threw three small coins into the air and let them fall, roll, and come to rest, heads up or tails up as the case might be. This peculiar fact—that a reaction that makes sense arises out of a technique which at the outset seemingly excludes all sense—is the great achievement of the *I Ching*. The instance I have just given is not unique; meaningful answers are the rule. Western sinologues and distinguished Chinese scholars have been at pains to inform me that the *I Ching* is a collection of obsolete "magic spells." In the course of these conversations my informant has sometimes admitted having consulted the oracle through a fortune teller, usually a Taoist priest. This could be "only nonsense" of course. But oddly enough, the answer received apparently coincided with the questioner's psychological blind spot remarkably well.

985 I agree with Western thinking that any number of answers to my question were possible, and I certainly cannot assert that another answer would not have been equally significant. However, the answer received was the first and only one; we know nothing of other possible answers. It pleased and satisfied me. To ask the same question a second time would have been tactless and so I did not do it: "the master speaks but once." The heavy-handed pedagogic approach that attempts to fit irrational phenomena into a preconceived rational pattern is anathema to me. Indeed, such things as this answer should remain as they were when they first emerged to view, for only then do we know what nature does when left to herself undisturbed by the meddlesomeness of man. One ought not to go to dead bodies to study life. Moreover, a repetition of the experiment is impossible, for the simple reason that the original situation cannot be reconstructed. Therefore in each instance there is only a first and single answer.

986 To return to the hexagram itself. There is nothing strange in the fact that all of Ting, THE CAULDRON, amplifies the themes

[11] I made this experiment before I actually wrote the foreword.

announced by the two salient lines.[12] The first line of the hexagram says:

> A *ting* with legs upturned
> Furthers removal of stagnating stuff.
> One takes a concubine for the sake of her son.
> No blame.

987 A *ting* that is turned upside down is not in use. Hence the *I Ching* is like an unused cauldron. Turning it over serves to remove stagnating matter, as the line says. Just as a man takes a concubine when his wife has no son, so the *I Ching* is called upon when one sees no other way out. Despite the quasi-legal status of the concubine in China, she is in reality only a somewhat awkward makeshift; so likewise the magic procedure of the oracle is an expedient that may be utilized for a higher purpose. There is no blame, although it is an exceptional recourse.

988 The second and third lines have already been discussed. The fourth line says:

> The legs of the *ting* are broken.
> The prince's meal is spilled
> And his person is soiled.
> Misfortune.

989 Here the *ting* has been put to use, but evidently in a very clumsy manner, that is, the oracle has been abused or misinterpreted. In this way the divine food is lost, and one puts oneself to shame. Legge translates as follows: "Its subject will be made to blush for shame." Abuse of a cult utensil such as the *ting* (i.e., the *I Ching*) is a gross profanation. The *I Ching* is evidently insisting here on its dignity as a ritual vessel and protesting against being profanely used.

990 The fifth line says:

> The *ting* has yellow handles, golden carrying rings.
> Perseverance furthers.

12 The Chinese interpret only the changing lines in the hexagram obtained by use of the oracle. I have found all the lines of the hexagram to be relevant in most cases.

991 The *I Ching* has, it seems, met with a new, correct (yellow) understanding, that is, a new concept [*Begriff*] by which it can be grasped. This concept is valuable (golden). There is indeed a new edition in English, making the book more accessible to the Western world than before.

992 The sixth line says:

> The *ting* has rings of jade.
> Great good fortune.
> Nothing that would not act to further.

993 Jade is distinguished for its beauty and soft sheen. If the carrying rings are of jade, the whole vessel is enhanced in beauty, honour, and value. The *I Ching* expresses itself here as being not only well satisfied but indeed very optimistic. One can only await further events and in the meantime remain content with the pleasant conclusion that the *I Ching* approves of the new edition.

994 I have shown in this example as objectively as I can how the oracle proceeds in a given case. Of course the procedure varies somewhat according to the way the question is put. If for instance a person finds himself in a confusing situation, he may himself appear in the oracle as the speaker. Or, if the question concerns a relationship with another person, that person may appear as the speaker. However, the identity of the speaker does not depend entirely on the manner in which the question is phrased, inasmuch as our relations with our fellow beings are not always determined by the latter. Very often our relations depend almost exclusively on our own attitudes, though we may be quite unaware of this fact. Hence, if an individual is unconscious of his role in a relationship, there may be a surprise in store for him; contrary to expectation, he himself may appear as the chief agent, as is sometimes unmistakably indicated by the text. It may also happen that we take a situation too seriously and consider it extremely important, whereas the answer we get on consulting the *I Ching* draws attention to some unsuspected other aspect implicit in the question.

995 Such instances might at first lead one to think that the oracle is fallacious. Confucius is said to have received only one inappropriate answer, i.e., hexagram 22, GRACE—a thoroughly aesthetic hexagram. This is reminiscent of the advice given to

Socrates by his daemon—"You ought to make more music"—whereupon Socrates took to playing the flute. Confucius and Socrates compete for first place as far as rationality and a pedagogic attitude to life are concerned; but it is unlikely that either of them occupied himself with "lending grace to the beard on his chin," as the second line of this hexagram advises. Unfortunately, reason and pedagogy often lack charm and grace, and so the oracle may not have been wrong after all.

996 To come back once more to our hexagram. Though the *I Ching* not only seems to be satisfied with its new edition, but even expresses emphatic optimism, this still does not foretell anything about the effect it will have on the public it is intended to reach. Since we have in our hexagram two *yang* lines stressed by the numerical value nine, we are in a position to find out what sort of prognosis the *I Ching* makes for itself. Lines designated by a six or a nine have, according to the ancient conception, an inner tension so great as to cause them to change into their opposites, that is, *yang* into *yin,* and vice versa. Through this change we obtain in the present instance hexagram 35, Chin, PROGRESS.

997 The subject of this hexagram is someone who meets with all sorts of vicissitudes of fortune in his climb upward, and the text describes how he should behave. The *I Ching* is in this same situation: it rises like the sun and declares itself, but it is rebuffed and finds no confidence—it is "progressing, but in sorrow." However, "one obtains great happiness from one's ancestress." Psychology can help us to elucidate this obscure passage. In dreams and fairy tales the grandmother, or ancestress, often represents the unconscious, because the latter in a man contains the feminine component of the psyche. If the *I Ching* is not accepted by the conscious, at least the unconscious meets it halfway, for the *I Ching* is more closely connected with the unconscious than with the rational attitude of consciousness. Since the unconscious is often represented in dreams by a feminine figure, this may be the explanation here. The feminine person might be the translator, who has given the book her maternal care, and this might easily appear to the *I Ching* a "great happiness." It anticipates general understanding, but is afraid of misuse—"Progress like a hamster." But it is mindful of the admonition, "Take not gain and loss to heart." It remains

free of "partisan motives." It does not thrust itself on anyone.

998 The *I Ching* therefore faces its future on the American book market calmly and expresses itself here just about as any reasonable person would in regard to the fate of so controversial a work. This prediction is so very reasonable and full of common sense that it would be hard to think of a more fitting answer.

999 All this happened before I had written the foregoing paragraphs. When I reached this point, I wished to know the attitude of the *I Ching* to the new situation. The state of things had been altered by what I had written, inasmuch as I myself had now entered upon the scene, and I therefore expected to hear something referring to my own action. I must confess that I had not been feeling too happy in the course of writing this foreword, for, as a person with a sense of responsibility toward science, I am not in the habit of asserting something I cannot prove or at least present as acceptable to reason. It is a dubious task indeed to try to introduce a collection of archaic "magic spells" to a critical modern public with the idea of making them more or less acceptable. I have undertaken it because I myself think that there is more to the ancient Chinese way of thinking than meets the eye. But it is embarrassing to me that I must appeal to the good will and imagination of the reader, instead of giving him conclusive proofs and scientifically watertight explanations. Unfortunately I am only too well aware of the arguments that can be brought against this age-old oracle technique. We are not even certain that the ship that is to carry us over the unknown seas has not sprung a leak somewhere. May not the old text be corrupt? Is Wilhelm's translation accurate? Are we not self-deluded in our explanations?

1000 The *I Ching* insists upon self-knowledge throughout. The method by which this is to be achieved is open to every kind of misuse, and is therefore not for the frivolous-minded and immature; nor is it for intellectualists and rationalists. It is appropriate only for thoughtful and reflective people who like to think about what they do and what happens to them—a predilection not to be confused with the morbid brooding of the hypochondriac. As I have indicated above, I have no answer to the multitude of problems that arise when we seek to harmonize the oracle of the *I Ching* with our accepted scientific canons. But needless to say, nothing "occult" is to be inferred. My position in these matters is pragmatic, and the great disciplines that have taught me the practical usefulness of this viewpoint are psychotherapy and medical psychology. Probably in no other field do we have to reckon with so many unknown quantities, and nowhere else do we become more accustomed to adopting methods that work even though for a long time we may not know why they work. Unexpected cures may arise from questionable therapies and unexpected failures from allegedly reliable methods. In the exploration of the unconscious we come upon very strange things, from which a rationalist turns away with horror, claiming afterward that he did not see anything. The irrational fulness of life has taught me never to discard anything, even when it goes against all our theories (so short-lived at best) or otherwise admits of no immediate explanation. It is of course disquieting, and one is not certain whether the compass is pointing true or not; but security, certitude, and peace do not lead to discoveries. It is the same with this Chinese mode of divination. Clearly the method aims at self-knowledge, though at all times it has also been put to superstitious use.

1001 I of course am thoroughly convinced of the value of self-knowledge, but is there any use in recommending such insight, when the wisest of men throughout the ages have preached the need of it without success? Even to the most biased eye it is obvious that this book represents one long admonition to careful scrutiny of one's own character, attitude, and motives. This attitude appeals to me and has induced me to undertake the foreword. Only once before have I expressed myself in regard to the problem of the *I Ching:* this was in a memorial address in tribute to Richard Wilhelm.[13] For the rest I have maintained a discreet silence. It is by no means easy to feel one's way into such a remote and mysterious mentality as that underlying the *I Ching*. One cannot easily disregard such great minds as Confucius and Lao-tzu, if one is at all able to appreciate the quality of the thoughts they represent; much less can one overlook the fact that the *I Ching* was their main source of inspiration. I know that previously I would not have dared to express myself

[13] [Cf. Wilhelm and Jung, *The Secret of the Golden Flower* (1931), in which this address appears as an appendix. The book did not appear in English until a year after Wilhelm's death.—C. F. B.]

[For the address, see vol. 15 of the *Coll. Works.*—EDITORS.]

so explicitly about so uncertain a matter. I can take this risk because I am now in my eighth decade, and the changing opinions of men scarcely impress me any more; the thoughts of the old masters are of greater value to me than the philosophical prejudices of the Western mind.

1002 I do not like to burden my reader with these personal considerations; but, as already indicated, one's own personality is very often implicated in the answer of the oracle. Indeed, in formulating my question I even invited the oracle to comment directly on my action. The answer was hexagram 29, K'an, THE ABYSMAL. Special emphasis is given to the third place by the fact that the line is designated by a six. This line says:

> Forward and backward, abyss on abyss.
> In danger like this, pause at first and wait,
> Otherwise you will fall into a pit in the abyss.
> Do not act in this way.

1003 Formerly I would have accepted unconditionally the advice, "Do not act in this way," and would have refused to give my opinion of the *I Ching*, for the sole reason that I had none. But now the counsel may serve as an example of the way in which the *I Ching* functions. It is a fact that if one begins to think about it, the problems of the *I Ching* do represent "abyss on abyss," and unavoidably one must "pause at first and wait" in the midst of the dangers of limitless and uncritical speculation; otherwise one really will lose one's way in the darkness. Could there be a more uncomfortable position intellectually than that of floating in the thin air of unproven possibilities, not knowing whether what one sees is truth or illusion? This is the dreamlike atmosphere of the *I Ching*, and in it one has nothing to rely upon except one's own so fallible subjective judgment. I cannot but admit that this line represents very appropriately the feelings with which I wrote the foregoing passages. Equally fitting is the comforting beginning of this hexagram—"If you are sincere, you have success in your heart"—for it indicates that the decisive thing here is not the outer danger but the subjective condition, that is, whether one believes oneself to be "sincere" or not.

1004 The hexagram compares the dynamic action in this situation to the behaviour of flowing water, which is not afraid of any dangerous place but plunges over cliffs and fills up the pits that lie in its course (K'an also stands for water). This is the way in which the "superior man" acts and "carries on the business of teaching."

1005 K'an is definitely one of the less agreeable hexagrams. It describes a situation in which the subject seems in grave danger of being caught in all sorts of pitfalls. I have found that K'an often turned up with patients who were too much under the sway of the unconscious (water) and hence threatened with the possible occurrence of psychotic phenomena. If one were superstitious, one would be inclined to assume that some such meaning attaches intrinsically to this hexagram. But just as, in interpreting a dream, one must follow the dream-text with the utmost exactitude, so in consulting the oracle one must keep in mind the form of the question put, for this sets a definite limit to the interpretation of the answer. When I consulted the oracle the first time, I was thinking above all of the meaning for the *I Ching* of the foreword I had still to write. I thus put the book in the foreground and made it, so to speak, the acting subject. But in my second question, it is I who am the acting subject. So it would be illogical to take the *I Ching* as the subject in this case too, and, in addition, the interpretation would become unintelligible. But if I am the subject, the interpretation is meaningful to me, because it expresses the undeniable feeling of uncertainty and risk present in my mind. If one ventures upon such uncertain ground, it is easy to come dangerously under the influence of the unconscious without knowing it.

1006 The first line of the hexagram notes the presence of the danger: "In the abyss one falls into a pit." The second line does the same, then adds the counsel: "One should strive to attain small things only." I apparently anticipated this advice by limiting myself in this foreword to a demonstration of how the *I Ching* functions in the Chinese mind, and by renouncing the more ambitious project of writing a psychological commentary on the whole book.

1007 The simplification of my task is expressed in the fourth line, which says:

> A jug of wine, a bowl of rice with it;
> Earthen vessels
> Simply handed in through the window.
> There is certainly no blame in this.

1008 Wilhelm makes the following comment here:

> Although as a rule it is customary for an official to present certain introductory gifts and recommendations before he is appointed, here everything is simplified to the utmost. The gifts are insignificant, there is no one to sponsor him, he introduces himself; yet all this need not be humiliating if only there is the honest intention of mutual help in danger.

1009 The fifth line continues the theme of limitation. If one studies the nature of water, one sees that it fills a pit only to the rim and then flows on. It does not stay caught there:

> The abyss is not filled to overflowing,
> It is filled only to the rim.

1010 But if, tempted by the danger, and just because of the uncertainty, one were to insist on forcing conviction by special efforts, such as elaborate commentaries and the like, one would only be bogged down in the difficulty, which the top line describes very accurately as a tied-up and caged-in condition. Indeed, the last line often shows the consequences that result when one does not take the meaning of the hexagram to heart.

1011 In our hexagram we have a six in the third place. This *yin* line of mounting tension changes into a *yang* line and thus produces a new hexagram showing a new possibility or tendency. We now have hexagram 48, Ching, THE WELL. The water hole no longer means danger, however, but rather something beneficial, a well:

> Thus the superior man encourages the people at
> their work,
> And exhorts them to help one another.

1012 The image of people helping one another would seem to refer to the reconstruction of the well, for it is broken down and full of mud. Not even animals drink from it. There are fishes living in it, and one can catch these, but the well is not used for drinking, that is, for human needs. This description is reminiscent of the overturned and unused *ting* that is to receive a new handle. Moreover, this well, like the *ting*, is cleaned. But no one drinks from it:

This is my heart's sorrow,
For one might draw from it.

1013 The dangerous water-hole or abyss pointed to the *I Ching,* and so does the well, but the latter has a positive meaning: it contains the waters of life. It should be restored to use. But one has no concept [*Begriff*] of it, no utensil with which to carry the water; the jug is broken and leaks. The *ting* needs new handles and carrying rings by which to grasp it, and so also the well must be newly lined, for it contains "a clear, cold spring from which one can drink." One may draw water from it, because "it is dependable."

1014 It is clear that in this prognosis the speaking subject is once more the *I Ching,* representing itself as a spring of living water. The previous hexagram described in detail the danger confronting the person who accidentally falls into the pit within the abyss. He must work his way out of it, in order to discover that it is an old, ruined well, buried in mud, but capable of being restored to use again.

1015 I submitted two questions to the method of chance represented by the coin oracle, the second question being put after I had written my analysis of the answer to the first. The first question was directed, as it were, to the *I Ching:* what had it to say about my intention to write a foreword? The second question concerned my own action, or rather the situation in which I was the acting subject who had discussed the first hexagram. To the first question the *I Ching* replied by comparing itself to a cauldron, a ritual vessel in need of renovation, a vessel that was finding only doubtful favour with the public. To the second question the reply was that I had fallen into a difficulty, for the *I Ching* represented a deep and dangerous water-hole in which one might easily be bogged down. However, the water-hole proved to be an old well that needed only to be renovated in order to be put to useful purposes once more.

1016 These four hexagrams are in the main consistent as regards theme (vessel, pit, well); and as regards intellectual content, they seem to be meaningful. Had a human being made such replies, I should, as a psychiatrist, have had to pronounce him of sound mind, at least on the basis of the material presented.

Indeed, I should not have been able to discover anything delirious, idiotic, or schizophrenic in the four answers. In view of the *I Ching's* extreme age and its Chinese origin, I cannot consider its archaic, symbolic, and flowery language abnormal. On the contrary, I should have had to congratulate this hypothetical person on the extent of his insight into my unexpressed state of doubt. On the other hand, any person of clever and versatile mind can turn the whole thing around and show how I have projected my subjective contents into the symbolism of the hexagrams. Such a critique, though catastrophic from the standpoint of Western rationality, does no harm to the function of the *I Ching*. On the contrary, the Chinese sage would smilingly tell me: "Don't you see how useful the *I Ching* is in making you project your hitherto unrealized thoughts into its abstruse symbolism? You could have written your foreword without ever realizing what an avalanche of misunderstanding might be released by it."

1017 The Chinese standpoint does not concern itself with the attitude one takes toward the performance of the oracle. It is only we who are puzzled, because we trip time and again over our prejudice, viz., the notion of causality. The ancient wisdom of the East lays stress upon the fact that the intelligent individual realizes his own thoughts, but not in the least upon the way in which he does it. The less one thinks about the theory of the *I Ching*, the more soundly one sleeps.

1018 It would seem to me that on the basis of this example an unprejudiced reader should now be in a position to form at least a tentative judgment on the operation of the *I Ching*.[14] More cannot be expected from a simple introduction. If by means of this demonstration I have succeeded in elucidating the psychological phenomenology of the *I Ching*, I shall have carried out my purpose. As to the thousands of questions, doubts, and criticisms that this singular book stirs up—I cannot answer these. The *I Ching* does not offer itself with proofs and results; it does not vaunt itself, nor is it easy to approach. Like a part of nature, it waits until it is discovered. It offers neither facts nor power, but for lovers of self-knowledge, of wisdom—if there be such—it

14 The reader will find it helpful to look up all four of these hexagrams in the [Baynes-Wilhelm] text and to read them together with the relevant commentaries.

seems to be the right book. To one person its spirit appears as clear as day; to another, shadowy as twilight; to a third, dark as night. He who is not pleased by it does not have to use it, and he who is against it is not obliged to find it true. Let it go forth into the world for the benefit of those who can discern its meaning.

BIBLIOGRAPHY

BIBLIOGRAPHY

The items of the bibliography are arranged alphabetically under two headings: *A*. Ancient volumes containing collections of alchemical tracts by various authors; *B*. General bibliography, including cross-references to the material in section *A*. Short titles of the ancient volumes are printed in capital letters.

A. ANCIENT VOLUMES CONTAINING COLLECTIONS OF ALCHEMICAL TRACTS BY VARIOUS AUTHORS

ARS CHEMICA, quod sit licita recte exercentibus, probationes doctissimorum iurisconsultorum. . . . Argentorati [Strasbourg], 1566.

Contents quoted in this volume:

- **i** Septem tractatus seu capitula Hermetis Trismegisti aurei [pp. 7–31; usually referred to as "Tractatus aureus"]
- **ii** Hortulanus: Commentariolum in Tabulam smaragdinam [pp. 33–47]
- **iii** Studium Consilii coniugii de massa solis et lunae [pp. 48–263; usually referred to as "Consilium coniugii"]

ARTIS AURIFERAE quam chemiam vocant. . . . Basileae [Basel], [1593]. 2 vols.

Contents quoted in this volume:

VOLUME I

- **i** Turba philosophorum [(a) First edition, pp. 1–65; (b) Second edition, pp. 66–139]
- **ii** Allegoriae super librum Turbae [pp. 139–45]
- **iii** Aenigmata ex Visione Arislei et allegoriae sapientum [pp. 146–54; usually referred to as "Visio Arislei"]
- **iv** Aurora consurgens, quae dicitur Aurea hora [pp. 185–246]
- **v** [Zosimus:] Rosinus ad Sarratantam episcopum [pp. 277–319]

vi Tractatulus Avicennae [pp. 405–37]
vii Liber de arte chymica [pp. 575–631]

VOLUME II

viii Rosarium philosophorum [pp. 204–384; contains a second version of the "Visio Arislei" at pp. 246ff.]

AUREUM VELLUS, oder Güldin Schatz und Kunstkammer . . . von dem . . . bewehrten Philosopho Salomone Trismosino. Rorschach, 1598. (Other editions appeared at Rorschach, 1599; Basel, 1604; Hamburg, 1708.)

Contents quoted in this volume:

i [Trismosin:] Splendor solis [Tractatus III, pp. 3–59]

MANGETUS, JOANNES JACOBUS (ed.). *BIBLIOTHECA CHEMICA CURIOSA, seu Rerum ad alchemiam pertinentium thesaurus instructissimus.* . . . Coloniae Allobrogum [Geneva], 1702. 2 vols.

Contents quoted in this volume:

VOLUME I

i Hoghelande: De alchemiae difficultatibus [pp. 336–68]
ii Hermes Trismegistus: Tractatus aureus de lapidis physici secreto [pp. 400–445]
iii Turba philosophorum [pp. 445–65; another version, pp. 480–94]
iv Allegoriae sapientum supra librum Turbae philosophorum XXIX distinctiones [pp. 467–79]

VOLUME II

v Bonus: Margarita pretiosa novella correctissima [pp. 1–80]
vi Rosarium philosophorum [pp. 87–119]
vii Consilium coniugii seu De massa solis et lunae libri III [pp. 235–65]
viii Sendivogius: Novum lumen chymicum [pp. 463–73]
ix Sendivogius: Parabola, seu Aenigma philosophicum [pp. 474–75]
x Orthelius: Epilogus et recapitulatio in Novum lumen Sendivogii [pp. 526–30]

MUSAEUM HERMETICUM reformatum et amplificatum . . . continens tractatus chimicos XXI praestantissimos. . . . Francofurti [Frankfurt a. M.], 1678. For translation, see WAITE.

Contents quoted in this volume:

i Madathanus: Aureum saeculum redivivum [pp. 53–72]
ii Sendivogius: Novum lumen chemicum e naturae fonte et manuali experientia depromptum [pp. 545–600]
iii [Sendivogius:] Novi luminis chemici tractatus alter de sulphure [pp. 601–46]

THEATRUM CHEMICUM, praecipuos selectorum auctorum tractatus . . . continens. Ursellis [Ursel] and Argentorati [Strasbourg], 1602–61. 6 vols. (Vols. I–III, Ursel, 1602; Vols. IV–VI, Strasbourg, 1613, 1622, 1661 respectively.)

Contents quoted in this volume:

VOLUME I

i Hoghelande: Liber de alchemiae difficultatibus [pp. 121–215]
ii Dorn: Speculativae philosophiae, gradus septem vel decem continens [pp. 255–310]
iii Dorn: De spagirico artificio Trithemii sententia [pp. 437–50]
iv Dorn: Philosophia meditativa [pp. 450–72]
v Dorn: Philosophia chemica ad meditativam comparata [pp. 472–517]
vi Dorn: De tenebris contra naturam et vita brevi [pp. 518–35]
vii Dorn: Congeries Paracelsicae chemicae de transmutatione metallorum [pp. 557–646]
viii Dorn: De duello animi cum corpore [pp. 535–50]

VOLUME IV

ix Raymundi Lulli: Theorica et practica [pp. 1–191]
x Aphorismi Basiliani sive Canones Hermetici. De spiritu, anima, et corpore medio, majoris et minoris mundi [pp. 368–71]
xi Hermetis Trismegisti Tractatus vere aureus de Lapide philosophici secreto [pp. 672–797]

VOLUME V

xii Allegoriae Sapientum . . . supra librum Turbae [pp. 64–100]
xiii Tractatus Micreris suo discipulo Mirnefindo [pp. 101–13]
xiv Liber Platonis quartorum . . . [pp. 114–208]

xv Bonus [Lacinius]: Margarita novella correctissima [pp. 589–794]

VOLUME VI

xvi Christopher of Paris: Elucidarius artis transmutatoriae [pp. 195–293]

xvii Grasseus: Arca arcani . . . [pp. 294–381]

xviii Orthelius: Epilogus et recapitulatio . . . in Novum lumen chymicum Sendivogii [pp. 430–58]

B. GENERAL BIBLIOGRAPHY

ABU'L KASIM. See HOLMYARD.

Acts of Thomas. See MEAD, *Fragments of a Faith Forgotten;* also in JAMES, *The Apocryphal New Testament,* pp. 365ff.

ADLER, GERHARD. *Entdeckung der Seele*. Zurich, 1934.

AELIAN (Claudius Aelianus). *Varia historia*. Edited by Rudolf Hercher. Leipzig, 1866. For translation, see:

——. *Claudius Aelianus his Various History*. Translated by Thomas Stanley. London, 1665.

"Allegoriae sapientum supra librum Turbae." See (*A*) *Artis auriferae,* **ii**; MANGETUS, *Bibliotheca chemica curiosa,* **iv**; *Theatrum chemicum,* **xii**.

ALPHIDIUS. See (*A*) *Artis auriferae,* **viii**: "Rosarium philosophorum," wherein quoted.

AMBROSE, SAINT. *Explanatio symboli ad initiandos*. Text with introduction and translation by Richard Hugh Connolly. (Texts and Studies, 10.) Cambridge, 1952.

Amitāyur-dhyāna Sūtra. Translated by Junjiro Takakusu. In: *Buddhist Mahāyāna Sūtras,* Part II. (Sacred Books of the East, 49.) Oxford, 1894. (Pp. 159–201.)

ANDREAE, JOHANN VALENTIN. (Christian Rosencreutz, pseud.) *Chymische Hochzeit . . . Anno 1459*. Reprinted from a Strasbourg 1616 edition. Edited by Ferdinand Maack. Berlin, 1913. For translation, see:

——. *The Hermetick Romance; or, The Chymical Wedding.* Translated by E. Foxcroft. London, 1690.

ANTHONY OF PADUA, SAINT. *S. Antonii Patavini Sermones dominicales et in solemnitatibus.* Edited by Antonio Maria Locatelli. Padua, 1895. 3 vols.

"Aphorismi Basiliani." See (*A*) *Theatrum chemicum,* **x.**

ARISLEUS (Archelaos). "Visio Arislei." See (*A*) *Artis auriferae,* **iii, viii.**

ARISTOTLE. [*De coelo.*] . . . *On the Heavens.* With an English translation by W. K. C. Guthrie. (Loeb Classical Library.) London and Cambridge (Mass.), 1939.

AUGUSTINE, SAINT. *Sermones.* See Migne, *P.L.,* vol. 38.

——. *Tractatus in Joannem.* See Migne, *P.L.,* vol. 35. For translation, see:

——. *Works of St. Augustine.* Edited by Marcus Dods. Edinburgh, 1874. (Vol. 11, translated by James Innes.)

AUGUSTINE, pseud. *De Spiritu et Anima.* See: *Opera Omnia S. Augustini.* Paris, 1836. 11 vols. (Vol. 6.)

"Aurea hora." See (*A*) *Artis auriferae,* **iv.**

"Aurora consurgens." See (*A*) *Artis auriferae,* **iv.**

AVALON, ARTHUR, pseud. (Sir John Woodroffe) (ed.). *Shrīchakrasambhāra Tantra.* Translated by Kazi Dawa-Samdup. (Tantric Texts, 7.) London and Calcutta, 1919.

AVICENNA, pseud. See (*A*) *Artis auriferae,* **vi.**

BARBARUS, HERMOLAUS (Ermolao Barbaro). *In Dioscoridem corollarium libris quinque absolutum.* Venice, 1516.

BARTH, KARL. *Bibelstunden über Luk I.* (*Theologische Existenz Heute,* edited by K. Barth and Eduard Thurneysen, Heft 19.) Munich, 1935.

——. *Credo.* Translated by J. Strathearn McNab. London, 1936.

BASTIAN, ADOLF. *Das Beständige in den Menschenrassen.* Berlin, 1868.

———. *Ethnische Elementargedanken in der Lehre vom Menschen.* Berlin, 1895. 2 vols.

———. *Der Völkergedanke im Aufbau einer Wissenschaft vom Menschen.* Berlin, 1878.

———. *Die Vorstellungen von der Seele.* In: RUDOLF VIRCHOW and FRANZ VON HOLTZENDORFF. *Sammlung gemeinverständlicher wissenschaftlicher Vorträge,* 10th series, Heft 226. Berlin, 1875.

BAUMGARTNER, MATTHIAS. *Die Philosophie des Alanus de Insulis.* In: CLEMENS BAEUMKER and GEORG FREIHERR VON HERTLING. *Beiträge zur Geschichte der Philosophie des Mittelalters,* Vol. 2, Heft 4. Münster, 1896.

BAYNES, CHARLOTTE AUGUSTA. *A Coptic Gnostic Treatise Contained in the Codex Brucianus—Bruce MS. 96, Bodleian Library, Oxford.* Cambridge, 1933.

BERNARD, SAINT, pseud. *Vitis Mystica.* In Migne, *P.L.,* vol. 184, cols. 635–740. For translation see: *Vitis Mystica.* Translated by Samuel John Eales. London, 1889.

BERNARD, JOHN HENRY (ed.). *The Odes of Solomon.* (Texts and Studies, VIII, 3.) Cambridge, 1912.

BERNARDINO DE SAHAGÚN. *General History of the Things of New Spain (Florentine Codex).* Book 3: *The Origin of the Gods.* Translated by Arthur J. O. Anderson and Charles E. Dibble. (Monographs of the School of American Research, 14, Part IV.) Santa Fe, 1952.

BERNARDUS SYLVESTRIS. *De mundi universitate libri duo.* Edited by Carl Sigmund Barach and Johann Wrobel. (Bibliotheca philosophorum mediae aetatis, 1.) Innsbruck, 1876.

BÉROALDE DE VERVILLE, FRANÇOIS (trans.). *Le tableau des riches inventions . . . representées dans le Songe de Poliphile.* Paris, 1600. See also COLONNA; FIERZ-DAVID.

BERTHELOT, MARCELLIN. *La Chimie au moyen âge.* Paris, 1893. 3 vols.

———. *Collection des anciens alchimistes grecs.* Paris, 1887–88. 3 vols.: Introduction, Textes, Traductions.

Bible. The following versions are cited textually:

[AV] Authorized ("King James") Version (cited unless otherwise indicated).

[DV] Douay-Reims Version.

[RSV] Revised Standard Version (1952).

[ZB] Zürcher Bibel (first trans. 16th cent.; cited in English trans. from a 1932 edn. published by the Consistory of Canton Zurich on the order of the Zurich Church Synod, being the German version generally used by the author).

BÖHME, JAKOB. *XL Questions Concerning the Soule.* Propounded by Dr. Balthasar Walter and answered by Jacob Behmen. London, 1647.

BONUS, PETRUS. *Pretiosa margarita novella de thesauro ac pretiosissimo philosophorum lapide* . . . Edited by Janus Lacinius Calabrus. Venice, 1546. For translation see WAITE, *The New Pearl;* see also (*A*) MANGETUS, *Bibliotheca chemica curiosa,* v; (*A*) *Theatrum chemicum,* xv.

BOUCHÉ-LECLERCQ, AUGUSTE. *L'Astrologie grecque.* Paris, 1899.

BOUSSET, WILHELM. *Hauptprobleme der Gnosis.* (Forschungen zur Religion und Literatur des Alten und Neuen Testaments, 10.) Göttingen, 1907.

BOVILLUS, KARL (Charles de Bouelles). *Ein gesichte Bruder Clausen ynn Schweytz und seine deutunge.* Wittenberg, 1528.

BRADFORD, ROARK. *Ol' Man Adam an' His Chillun.* New York, 1928.

BRINKTRINE, JOHANNES. *Die Heilige Messe in ihrem Werden und Wesen.* 2nd edn., Paderborn, 1934.

BRUNO OF WÜRZBURG, SAINT. *Expositio Psalmorum.* See Migne, *P.L.,* vol. 142, cols. 39–530.

BUDGE, E. A. WALLIS. *Osiris and the Egyptian Resurrection.* London, 1911. 2 vols.

——. (ed. and trans.). *The Book of the Dead. Facsimiles of the Papyrus of Hunefer, etc.* London, 1899.

——. *The Book of Paradise, being the Histories and Sayings of the Monks and Ascetics of the Egyptian Desert.* London, 1904. 2 vols. For St. Athanasius, *The Life of St. Anthony,* see Vol. I, pp. 3–108.

BUSSELL, FREDERICK WILLIAM. *Religious Thought and Heresy in the Middle Ages.* London, 1918.

BÜTTNER, H. *Meister Eckhart's Schriften und Predigten.* Jena, 1909–17. 2 vols.

CABASILAS, NICHOLAS, of Thessalonica. "De divino altaris sacrificio." In Migne, *P.G.*, vol. 150, cols. 363–492.

CAMPBELL, COLIN. *The Miraculous Birth of King Amon-Hotep III.* Edinburgh and London, 1912.

CASPARI, CARL PAUL. *Alte und neue Quellen zur Geschichte des Taufsymbols und der Glaubensregel.* Christiania (Oslo), 1879.

CAUSSIN, NICHOLAS. *De symbolica Aegyptiorum sapientia. Polyhistor Symbolicus, Electorum Symbolorum & Parabolarum historicarum stromata.* Paris, [1618 and] 1631.

Chhandogya Upanishad. In: *The Upanishads.* Part 1. Translated by F. Max Müller. (Sacred Books of the East, 1.) Oxford, 1879. (Pp. 1–144.)

CHARLES, ROBERT HENRY (ed.). *The Apocrypha and Pseudepigrapha of the Old Testament in English.* Oxford, 1913. 2 vols.

CHRISTOPHER OF PARIS. "Elucidarius artis transmutatoriae." See (*A*) *Theatrum chemicum,* **xvi**.

CICERO, MARCUS TULLIUS. *De inventione rhetorica, De optimo genere oratorum, Topica.* With an English translation by H. M. Hubbell. (Loeb Classical Library.) London and Cambridge, (Mass.), 1949.

——. *Pro Sestio, In Vatinium, Pro Caelio, etc.* With an English translation by J. H. Freese and R. Gardner. (Loeb Classical Library.) London and Cambridge (Mass.), in press.

CLEMENT OF ALEXANDRIA, SAINT. *Stromata.* See Migne, *P.G.*, vol. 8, col. 685, to vol. 9, col. 602. For translation, see:

——. *The Writings of Clement of Alexandria.* Translated by William Wilson. (Ante-Nicene Christian Library, 4, 12.) Edinburgh, 1867–69. 2 vols.

CLEMENT OF ROME, SAINT. *First Epistle to the Corinthians.* In: KIRSOPP LAKE (ed. and trans.). *The Apostolic Fathers.* (Loeb Classical Library.) London and New York, 1914. 2 vols. (Vol. I, pp. 8–121.)

Codices and Manuscripts:

i Florence. Biblioteca Medicea-Laurenziana. Codex Laurentianus 71,33. 14th cent.

ii Lucca. Biblioteca governativa. Saint Hildegarde of Bingen, "Liber divinorum operum." Codex 1942. 12th cent.

iii Munich. Staatsbibliothek. Codex Germanicus 598. "Das Buch der heiligen Dreifaltigkeit und Beschreibung der Heimlichkeit von Veränderung der Metallen." Offenbahret anno Christi 1420.

iv Oxford. Bodleian Library. Codex Brucianus (Bruce MS. 96). See BAYNES.

v Paris. Bibliothèque nationale. Codex Parisinus 6319. Liber Hermetis Trismegisti. 14th cent.

vi ——. ——. Codex Latinus 14006. "Aurora consurgens."

vii ——. ——. Codex Parisinus Graecus 1220. 14th cent.

viii Vatican. Biblioteca Vaticana. Codex Palatinus Latinus 1993. Opicinus de Canistris.

ix ——. ——. Codex Latinus 3060. Liber Hermetis Trismegisti. 14th cent.

x ——. ——. Codex Graecus 237. 14th cent.

xi ——. ——. Codex Graecus 951. 14th cent.

xii Wiesbaden. Nassauische Landesbibliothek. St. Hildegarde of Bingen. "Scivias." 12th cent. (Destroyed in the second World War.)

xiii Zurich. Zentralbibliothek. Codex Rhenovacensis 172. Abh.1: "Aurora consurgens." 15th cent. (Note: Mutilated manuscript beginning at the fourth parable.)

COLONNA, FRANCESCO. *Hypnerotomachia Poliphili. . . .* Venice, 1499. See also BÉROALDE DE VERVILLE; FIERZ-DAVID.

CONNELLY, MARC. *The Green Pastures.* New York, 1930.

CONNOLLY, R. HUGH (ed.). *The So-called Egyptian Church Order and Derived Documents.* (Texts and Studies, VIII, 4.) Cambridge, 1916.

"Consilium coniugii." See (*A*) *Ars chemica,* **iii**; MANGETUS, *Bibliotheca chemica curiosa,* **vii**.

CORNFORD, FRANCIS MACDONALD. *Plato's Cosmology: The Timaeus of Plato*. New edn., London and New York, 1952.

Corpus Hermeticum. See SCOTT.

CRAWLEY, ALFRED ERNEST. *The Idea of the Soul*. London, 1909.

CUMONT, FRANZ. *Textes et monuments figurés relatifs aux mystères de Mithra*. Brussels, 1894–99. 2 vols.

CYPRIAN, SAINT. *Letter lxiii to Caecilius*. In Migne, *P.L.*, vol. 4, cols. 372ff. For translation see:

——. *Epistles of St. Cyprian*. Translated by H. Carey. (Library of Fathers of the Holy Catholic Church.) Oxford, 1844. (Pp. 181ff.)

DANIEL, HERMANN ADALBERT. *Thesaurus Hymnologicus*. Halle and Leipzig, 1841–56. 5 vols.

"De arte chymica." See (*A*) *Artis auriferae*, **vii**.

DELACOTTE, JOSEPH. *Guillaume de Digulleville. . . . Trois romans-poèmes du XIVe siècle*. Paris, 1932.

DENZINGER, HEINRICH, and BANNWART, KLEMENS. *Enchiridion symbolorum*. 6th–7th edition, edited by J. B. Umberg. Freiburg i. B., 1928.

DIETERICH, ALBRECHT. *Eine Mithrasliturgie*. Leipzig, 1910.

DIOGENES LAERTIUS. *Lives of Eminent Philosophers*. With an English translation by R. D. Hicks. (Loeb Classical Library.) London and New York, 1925. 2 vols.

DJABIR. See GEBER.

DORN, GERHARD. See (*A*) *Theatrum chemicum*, **ii–viii**.

DOZY, REINHART, and DE GOEJE, M. J. "Nouveaux documents pour l'étude de la religion des Harraniens." *Actes du sixième congrès international des Orientalistes*, 1883. Leiden, 1885.

DRUMMOND, HENRY. *The Greatest Thing in the World, and other addresses*. London, 1894.

——. *Natural Law in the Spiritual World*. London, 1883.

DUNBAR, HELEN FLANDERS. *Symbolism in Medieval Thought and Its Consummation in the Divine Comedy*. New Haven, 1929.

DUNNE, JOHN WILLIAM. *An Experiment with Time.* London, 1927.

DURRER, ROBERT. *Bruder Klaus—Die ältesten Quellen über den Seligen Nikolaus von Flue, sein Leben und seinen Einfluss.* Sarnen, 1907–21. 2 vols.

[ECKHART, MEISTER.] *Meister Eckhart.* [Works.] Translated by C. de B. Evans. London, 1924–52. 2 vols.

——. *Meister Eckhart: A Modern Translation.* Translated by Raymond Bernard Blakney. New York, 1941.

EISLER, ROBERT. *Orpheus—the Fisher.* London, 1921.

——. *Weltenmantel und Himmelszelt.* Munich, 1910. 2 vols.

ELIADE, MIRCEA. *Le Chamanisme et les techniques archaïques de l'extase.* Paris, 1951.

EMERSON, RALPH WALDO. *Essays.* (Everyman's Library.) New York and London, 1930.

Enoch, Book of. See CHARLES.

EPIPHANIUS. *Panarium, sive Arcula (Contra Octoginta Haereses).* In Migne, *P.G.*, vol. 41, col. 173, to vol. 42, col. 852.

ERMAN, ADOLF. *Aegypten.* Tübingen, 1885. 2 vols. in one. For translation, see:

——. *Life in Ancient Egypt.* Translated by H. M. Tirard. London, 1894.

EURIPIDES. See DIETERICH.

EUSEBIUS. *Evangelica praeparatio.* In Migne, *P.G.*, vol. 21, cols. 21–1408.

EVANS, C. DE B. See ECKHART.

EVANS-WENTZ, W. Y. (ed.). *The Tibetan Book of the Dead.* London, 1927; 2nd edn., 1957.

—— (ed.). *The Tibetan Book of the Great Liberation.* London, 1954.

FENN, GEORGE MANVILLE. *Running Amok.* London, 1901.

FIERZ-DAVID, LINDA. *The Dream of Poliphilo.* Translated by Mary Hottinger. New York (Bollingen Series XXV) and London, 1950.

FIRMICUS MATERNUS, JULIUS. *De errore profanarum religionum.* Edited by Carolus Halm. (Corpus scriptorum ecclesiasticorum Latinorum, 2.) Vienna, 1867.

FOERSTER-NIETZSCHE, ELISABETH (ed.). *Der werdende Nietzsche.* Munich, 1924.

FOXCROFT. See ANDREAE.

FRANZ, MARIE-LOUISE VON. "Die Passio Perpetuae." In: *AION; Untersuchungen zur Symbolgeschichte,* by C. G. Jung and Marie-Louise von Franz. Zurich, 1951.

FRAZER, SIR JAMES GEORGE. *Adonis, Attis, Osiris.* (*The Golden Bough,* Part IV.) 2nd edn., London, 1907. 2 vols.

——. *The Dying God.* (*The Golden Bough,* Part III.) London, 1911.

——. *Taboo and the Perils of the Soul.* (*The Golden Bough,* Part II.) London, 1911.

FREMER, JAKOB, and SCHNITZER, MANUEL. *Legenden aus dem Talmud.* Berlin, 1922.

FREUD, SIGMUND. *The Future of an Illusion.* Translated by W. D. Robson-Scott. London and New York, 1928.

——. *The Interpretation of Dreams.* (Standard Edition of the Complete Psychological Works, translated under the editorship of James Strachey, 4, 5.) London 1953. 2 vols.

FROBENIUS, LEO. *Das Zeitalter des Sonnengottes.* Vol. I (no more published). Berlin, 1904.

GARNERIUS DE SANCTO VICTORE. *Gregorianum.* In Migne, *P.L.,* vol. 193, cols. 23–462.

GAUDENTIUS, SAINT, Bishop of Brixen. *Sermones.* In Migne, *P.L.,* vol. 20, cols. 827–1002.

GEBER (Jābir ibn-Hayyān). "Livre de la miséricorde." In Berthelot, *La Chimie au moyen âge,* q.v., Vol. III, pp. 163–90.

GNOSIUS, DOMINICUS. *Hermetis Trismegisti Tractatus vere Aureus . . . cum scholiis Dominici Gnosii.* Leipzig, 1610. See also (*A*) MANGETUS, *Bibliotheca chemica,* **ii**; and *Theatrum chemicum,* **xi.**

GOETHE, JOHANN WOLFGANG VON. *Faust: Part I.* Translated by Philip Wayne. (Penguin Classics.) Harmondsworth, 1949. 6th impr.

GOMPERZ, THEODOR. *Greek Thinkers.* Translated from the German by Laurie Magnus and G. G. Berry. London, 1901–12. 4 vols.

GRASSEUS. "Arca arcani." See (*A*) *Theatrum chemicum,* **xvii.**

GREGORY THE GREAT, SAINT. *Dialogues* (*Dialogorum Libri IV*). See Migne, *P.L.,* vol. 77, cols. 149–430.

———. *Expositiones in Librum I Regum.* See Migne, *P.L.,* vol. 79, cols. 17–468.

GREGORY OF NYSSA, SAINT. *De Vita Beati Gregorii Miraculorum Opificio* [Life of Saint Gregory Thaumaturgus]. In Migne, *P.G.,* vol. 46, cols. 911–14.

GRIFFITH, FRANCIS LLEWELLYN. *A Collection of Hieroglyphs.* (Archaeological Survey of Egypt, 6th Memoir.) London, 1898.

GUILLAUME DE DIGULLEVILLE. See DELACOTTE.

GUILLÉN, JORGE. *Cantico: Fe de Vida.* Buenos Aires, 1950.

HAEUSSERMANN, FRIEDRICH. *Wortempfang und Symbol in der alttestamentlichen Prophetie.* (Beihefte zur Zeitschrift für die alttestamentliche Wissenschaft, 58.) Giessen, 1932.

HARNACK, ADOLF VON. *Dogmengeschichte.* 7th edn., Tübingen, 1931.

HARPER, ROBERT FRANCIS. *The Code of Hammurabi.* Chicago, 1904.

HARRISON, JANE ELLEN. *Themis.* Cambridge, 1912.

HASTINGS, JAMES (ed.). *Encyclopaedia of Religion and Ethics.* Edinburgh and New York, 1908–27. 13 vols.

HAUCK, ALBERT (ed.). *Realenzyklopädie für protestantische Theologie und Kirche.* Leipzig, 1896–1913. 24 vols.

HAUER, J. W. "Symbole und Erfahrung des Selbstes in der indoarischen Mystik," *Eranos-Jahrbuch* (Zurich), [II] (1935), 35–96.

HEATH, SIR THOMAS L. *A History of Greek Mathematics.* Oxford, 1921. 2 vols.

HENNECKE, EDGAR (ed.). *Neutestamentliche Apokryphen.* 2nd edn., Tübingen, 1924.

HERMES TRISMEGISTUS. *Tractatus aureus.* See (*A*) *Ars chemica,* **i**; MANGETUS, *Bibliotheca chemica,* **ii**; *Theatrum chemicum,* **xi.**

HERODOTUS. *The Histories.* Translated by Aubrey de Selincourt. (Penguin Classics.) Harmondsworth, 1954.

HERRAD OF LANDSBERG. *Hortus deliciarum.* See KELLER and STRAUB.

HILDEGARDE, SAINT, of Bingen. *Scivias.* See Codices and Manuscripts, **xii**; also, *Scivias, vel Visionum ac revelationum libri tres,* in Migne, *P.L.*, vol. 197, cols. 383–738.

HIPPOLYTUS. *Elenchos* (*Refutatio omnium haeresiarum*). In: *Hippolytus' Werke.* Edited by Paul Wendland. Vol. III. Leipzig, 1916. For translation, see LEGGE, FRANCIS.

———. *Church Order.* See CONNOLLY.

HOGG, JAMES. *The Private Memoirs and Confessions of a Justified Sinner.* London, 1824. (Reprinted, with introduction by André Gide, London, 1947.)

HOGHELANDE, THEOBALD DE. "De alchemiae difficultatibus." See (*A*) MANGETUS, *Bibliotheca chemica,* **i**; *Theatrum chemicum,* **i.**

HOLMYARD, ERIC JOHN (ed. and trans.). *Kitāb al-'ilm al-muktasab fi zinā 'at adhdhahab* [Book of knowledge acquired concerning the cultivation of gold]. [By Abu'l Qāsim Muḥammad ibn Ahmad al-'Irāqī.] Paris, 1923.

HORTULANUS, pseud. (Joannes de Garlandia). "Commentariolum." See (*A*) *Ars chemica,* **ii**. For translation, see: ROGER BACON. *The Mirror of Alchimy. . . .* London, 1597.

HUBERT, HENRI, and MAUSS, MARCEL. *Mélanges d'Histoire des Religions.* (Travaux de l'Année Sociologique.) Paris, 1909.

IGNATIUS OF LOYOLA, SAINT. *The Spiritual Exercises.* Edited and translated by Joseph Rickaby, S.J. 2nd edn., London, 1923.

IRENAEUS, SAINT. *Contra* [or *Adversus*] *haereses libri quinque.* See Migne, *P.G.*, vol. 7, cols. 433–1224. For translation, see:

———. *Five Books of Irenaeus against Heresies.* Translated by John Keble. (Library of Fathers of the Holy Catholic Church.) Oxford, 1872. Also: *The Writings of Irenaeus.* Translated by Alexander Roberts and W. H. Rambaut. Vol. I. (Ante-Nicene Christian Library, 5.) Edinburgh, 1868.

JACOBI, JOLANDE (ed.). *Paracelsus: Selected Writings.* Translated by Norbert Guterman. New York (Bollingen Series XXVIII) and London, 1951.

JACOBSOHN, HELMUTH. "Das Gespräch eines Lebensmüden mit seinem Ba." In: *Zeitlose Dokumente der Seele.* (Studien aus dem C. G. Jung-Institut, 3.) Zurich, 1952.

———. "Die dogmatische Stellung des Königs in der Theologie der alten Ägypter." In: *Aegyptische Forschungen,* ed. Alexander Scharff. Heft 8. Gluckstadt, Hamburg, and New York, 1939.

JAMES, MONTAGUE RHODES (trans.). *The Apocryphal New Testament.* Oxford, 1924.

JAMES, WILLIAM. *Pragmatism.* London, 1907.

JASTROW, MORRIS. *Die Religion Babyloniens und Assyriens.* Giessen, 1905–12. 2 vols.

———. *The Religion of Babylonia and Assyria.* (Handbooks of the History of Religions, 2.) Boston, 1898. (Not a translation, but a parallel volume to the preceding.)

JENSEN, INGEBORG H. *Die älteste Alchemie.* Copenhagen, 1921.

JEREMIAS, ALFRED. *The Old Testament in the Light of the Ancient East.* Translated by C. L. Beaumont. London and New York, 1911. 2 vols.

Jewish Encyclopedia, The. New York, 1925. 12 vols.

JOANNES DE RUPESCISSA. See RUPESCISSA.

JOHN DAMASCENE, SAINT. *Encomium in Dormitionem, etc.* In Migne, *P.G.,* vol. 96, cols. 721–754. For translation, see: MARY H. ALLIES. *St. John Damascene on Holy Images, followed by Three Sermons on the Assumption.* London, 1898.

JOHN OF RUYSBROECK. See RUYSBROECK.

JOSEF BIN GORION, MICHA (pseud. of Micha Josef Berdyczewski). *Die Sagen der Juden.* Collected and revised by M. J. bin Gorion. The text translated into German by R. Ramberg-Berdyczewski. Edited by Rahel and Emanuel bin Gorion (i.e., R. and E. Berdyczewski). Frankfurt a. M., 1913–27. 5 vols.

JOYCE, JAMES. *Ulysses.* New York, 1933; London, 1936 (1st edn., Paris, 1922.)

JUNG, CARL GUSTAV. *Aion: Contributions to the Symbolism of the Self. Collected Works,** Vol. 9, part ii. New York and London, in press.

——. "Archetypes of the Collective Unconscious." In: *Collected Works,** Vol. 9, part i. New York and London, in press.

——. "Concerning the Archetypes, with special reference to the Anima Concept." In: *Collected Works,** Vol. 9, part i. New York and London, in press.

——. "Freud and Jung: Contrasts." In: *Collected Works,** vol. 4. (Alternate source: *Modern Man in Search of a Soul,* q.v.)

——. *Modern Man in Search of a Soul.* Translated by C. F. Baynes and W. S. Dell. London and New York, 1933.

——. *Mysterium Coniunctionis. Collected Works,** Vol. 14. (Alternate source: JUNG and MARIE-LOUISE VON FRANZ, *Mysterium Coniunctionis,* Zurich, 1955–57. 3 vols.)

——. "On Mandala Symbolism." In: *Collected Works,** Vol. 9, part i. New York and London, in press.

——. "On the Nature of the Psyche." In: *Collected Works,** Vol. 8. (Alternate source: "The Spirit of Psychology," *Spirit and Nature,* 1954/55, q.v.)

——. "On Psychic Energy." In: *Collected Works,** Vol. 8. (Alternate source: *Contributions to Analytical Psychology,* translated by C. F. and H. G. Baynes, London and New York, 1928.)

——. "On the Psychology of the Trickster Figure." In: *Collected Works,** Vol. 9, part i. New York and London, in press.

* For details of the *Collected Works of C. G. Jung,* see end of this volume.

———. *The Practice of Psychotherapy. Collected Works,** Vol. 16. New York and London, 1954.

———. "The Psychological Aspects of the Kore." In: *Collected Works,** Vol. 9, part i. New York and London, in press.

———. "Psychological Factors Determining Human Behaviour." In: *Collected Works,** Vol. 8. (Alternate source: In: *Factors Determining Human Behavior,* Harvard Tercentenary Conference of Arts and Sciences, 1936, Cambridge, Mass., 1936.)

———. *Psychological Types. Collected Works,** Vol. 6. (Alternate source: *Psychological Types,* translated by H. G. Baynes, London and New York, 1923.)

———. *Psychology and Alchemy. Collected Works,** Vol. 12. New York and London, 1953.

———. "Psychology and Literature." In: *Collected Works,** Vol. 15. (Alternate source: *Modern Man in Search of a Soul,* q.v.)

———. "Psychology of the Transference." In: *Collected Works,** Vol. 16. New York and London, 1954.

———. "The Psychology of the Unconscious." In: *Two Essays on Analytical Psychology,* q.v.

———. "The Relations between the Ego and the Unconscious." In: *Two Essays on Analytical Psychology,* q.v.

———. "The Role of the Unconscious." In: *Collected Works,** Vol. 10. (Alternate source: "Über das Unbewusste," *Schweizerland,* Zurich, IV: 9–10, 1918.)

———. "Some Observations on the Visions of Zosimos." In: *Collected Works,** Vol. 13. (Alternate source: "Die Visionen des Zosimos," *Von den Wurzeln des Bewusstseins,* Zurich, 1954.)

———. "The Spirit Mercurius." In: *Collected Works,** Vol. 13. (Alternate source: "Der Geist Mercurius," *Symbolik des Geistes,* Zurich, 1948.)

———. "Studies in Word Association." In: *Collected Works,** Vol. 2. (Alternate source: *Studies in Word Association* . . . under the direction of C. G. Jung, translated by M. D. Eder, London, 1918, New York, 1919.)

———. *Symbols of Transformation. Collected Works,** Vol. 5. London and New York, 1956.

———. "Synchronicity: An Acausal Connecting Principle." In: *Collected Works,** Vol. 8. (Alternate source: C. G. Jung and W. Pauli. *The Interpretation of Nature and the Psyche,* New York [Bollingen Series LI] and London, 1955.)

———. *Two Essays on Analytical Psychology. Collected Works,** Vol. 7. New York and London, 1953.

———. "Wotan." In: *Collected Works,** Vol. 10. (Alternate source: *Essays on Contemporary Events,* translated by Barbara Hannah and others, London, 1947.)

JUNG, EMMA. "Ein Beitrag zum Problem des Animus." In: C. G. JUNG. *Wirklichkeit der Seele.* Zurich, 1934.

JUSTIN [MARTYR], SAINT. *Apologia secunda.* See Migne, *P.G.,* vol. 6, cols. 441–70. For translation, see: MARCUS DODS, GEORGE REITH, and B. P. PRATTEN (trans.). *The Writings of Justin Martyr and Athenagoras.* (Ante-Nicene Christian Library, 2.) Edinburgh, 1867.

KANT, IMMANUEL. *Critique of Pure Reason.* Translated by J. M. D. Meiklejohn. (Everyman's Library.) London and New York, 1934.

KÄSEMANN, ERNST. *Leib und Leib Christi.* (Beiträge zur historischen Theologie, 9.) Tübingen, 1933.

Katha Upanishad. In: *The Thirteen Principal Upanishads.* Translated by Robert Ernest Hume. London, 1921. (Pp. 341–61.)

KELLER, G., and STRAUB, A. (trans.). *Herrad von Landsberg Hortus Deliciarum.* Strasbourg, 1879–99 (1901).

KESSLER, KONRAD. *Mani: Forschungen über die manichäische Religion.* Berlin, 1889.

KHUNRATH, HEINRICH CONRAD. *Amphitheatrum sapientiae aeternae* . . . Hanau, 1604.

———. *Vom hylealischen, das ist, pri-materialischen catholischen, oder algemeinem natürlichen Chaos.* Magdeburg, 1597.

KIRCHER, ATHANASIUS. *Mundus subterraneus.* Amsterdam, 1678. 2 vols.

* For details of the *Collected Works of C. G. Jung,* see end of this volume.

[KLAUS, BROTHER.] *Ein nützlicher und loblicher Tractat von Bruder Claus und einem Bilger.* Nürnberg, 1488.

KLUG, IGNAZ. Article in *Theologie und Glaube* (Paderborn), XVIII (1926), 335f.

KOEPGEN, GEORG. *Die Gnosis des Christentums.* Salzburg, 1939.

KRAMP, JOSEPH. *Die Opferanschauungen der römischen Messliturgie.* 2nd edn., Regensburg, 1924.

KRANEFELDT, WOLFGANG M. *Secret Ways of the Mind.* Translated [from *Die Psychoanalyse, psychoanalytische Psychologie*] by Ralph M. Eaton. New York, 1932; London, 1934.

KROLL, JOSEF. *Gott und Hölle. Der Mythos von Descensuskampfe.* (Studien der Bibliothek Warburg, 20.) Leipzig and Berlin, 1932.

KRUEGER, GUSTAV. *Das Dogma von der Dreieinigkeit und Gottmenschheit in seiner geschichtlichen Entwicklung dargestellt.* (Lebensfragen; Schriften und Reden, edited by Heinrich Weinel.) Tübingen, 1905.

KUEKELHAUS, HUGO. *Urzahl und Gebärde.* Berlin, 1934.

LACINIUS, JANUS. See BONUS, PETRUS.

LEGGE, FRANCIS (trans.). *Philosophumena; or, The Refutation of All Heresies.* (Formerly attributed to Origen but now to Hippolytus.) London and New York, 1921.

LEGGE, JAMES (trans.). *The Sacred Books of Confucianism: Part II. The Yi King.* (Sacred Books of the East, 16.) Oxford, 1882; 2nd edn., 1899.

LEISEGANG, HANS. *Denkformen.* Berlin, 1928.

———. *Die Gnosis.* Leipzig, 1924.

———. *Der Heilige Geist.* Leipzig, 1919.

———. *Pneuma Hagion.* (Veröffentlichungen der Forschungsinstituts für vergleichende Religionsgeschichte an die Universität Leipzig, 4.) Leipzig, 1922.

LÉVY-BRUHL, LUCIEN. *How Natives Think.* Translated by Lilian A. Clare [from *Les Fonctions mentales dans les sociétés inférieures*]. London, 1926.

——. *Primitive Mentality.* Translated by Lilian A. Clare. London and New York, 1923.

——. *La Mythologie primitive.* Paris, 1935.

"Liber de arte chymica." See (*A*) "Artis auriferae," **vii.**

"Liber Platonis quartorum." See (*A*) "Theatrum chemicum," **xiv.**

LIDDELL, HENRY GEORGE, and SCOTT, ROBERT. *A Greek-English Lexicon.* New (9th) edn., revised by Sir Henry Stuart Jones and Roderick McKenzie. Oxford, 1940. 2 vols.

LIPPMANN, EDUARD OSKAR VON. *Entstehung und Ausbreitung der Alchemie.* Berlin, 1919–31. 2 vols.

LIPSIUS, RICHARD ADELBERT, and BONNET, MAX. *Acta Apostolorum Apocrypha.* Leipzig, 1891–1903. 2 parts in 3 vols.

LO, L. C. (trans.). "Liu Hua Yang, Hui Ming King. Das Buch von Bewusstsein und Leben," *Chinesische Blätter für Wissenschaft und Kunst.* Edited by Richard Wilhelm (China-Institut, Frankfurt a. M.; pub. at Darmstadt), I : 3 (1926), 104–14.

LÜ PU-WEI (Lü Bu We). *Frühling und Herbst des Lü Bu We.* Edited by Richard Wilhelm. Jena, 1928.

LULL, RAYMOND. See (*A*) *Theatrum chemicum,* **ix.**

MACROBIUS. *Commentarium in Somnium Scipionis.* For translation, see:

——. *Commentary on the Dream of Scipio.* Translated by William Harris Stahl. (Records of Civilization, Sources and Studies, 48.) New York, 1952.

MADATHANUS. "Aureum saeculum redivivum." See (*A*) *Musaeum hermeticum,* **i.**

MAIER, MICHAEL. *Atalanta fugiens, hoc est, Emblemata nova de secretis naturae chymica.* Oppenheim, 1618.

——. *De circulo physico quadrato.* Oppenheim, 1616.

——. *Secretioris naturae secretorum scrutinium chymicum.* Frankfurt a. M., 1687.

——. *Symbola aureae mensae duodecim nationum.* Frankfurt a. M., 1617.

MAITLAND, EDWARD. *Anna Kingsford, Her Life, Letters, Diary, and Work.* London, 1896. 2 vols.

MEAD, G. R. S. *Fragments of a Faith Forgotten.* 3rd edn., London, 1931.

——. *Pistis Sophia.* 2nd edn., London, 1921.

MEIER, C. A. "Spontanmanifestationen des kollektiven Unbewussten," *Zentralblatt für Psychotherapie* (Leipzig), XI (1939), 284–303.

MEYER, WILHELM. "Die Geschichte des Kreuzholzes vor Christus," *Abhandlungen der philosophisch-philologischen Classe der königlich Bayerischen Akademie der Wissenschaft* (Munich), XVI, 2 (1882), 107–8.

MICRERIS. "Tractatus Micreris." See (*A*) *Theatrum chemicum,* **xiii.**

MIGNE, JACQUES PAUL (ed.). *Patrologiae cursus completus.*
[*P.L.*] Latin Series. Paris, 1844–64. 221 vols.
[*P.G.*] Greek Series. Paris, 1857–66. 166 vols.
(These works are referred to in the text and in this bibliography as "Migne, *P.L.*" and "Migne, *P.G.*" respectively. References are to columns, not to pages.)

Missale Romanum (*The Roman Missal*). For translation, see: *The Missal in Latin and English.* Edited by J. O'Connell and H. P. R. Finberg. London, 1949.

MORET, ALEXANDRE. *Du caractère religieux de la royauté pharaonique.* (Annales du Musée Guimet, Bibliothèque d'études, 15.) Paris, 1902.

MYLIUS, JOHANN DANIEL. *Philosophia reformata.* Frankfurt a. M., 1622.

The Mysteries. Translated by Ralph Manheim and R. F. C. Hull. (Papers from the Eranos Yearbooks, 2.) New York (Bollingen Series XXX) and London, 1955.

NELKEN, JAN. "Analytische Beobachtungen über Phantasien eines Schizophrenen," *Jahrbuch für psychoanalytische und psychopathologische Forschung* (Vienna and Leipzig), IV (1912), 504ff.

NEUMANN, ERICH. *The Origins and History of Consciousness.* Translated by R. F. C. Hull. New York (Bollingen Series XLII) and London, 1954.

NIELSEN, [CHRISTIAN] DETLEF. *Der Dreieinige Gott.* Copenhagen, 1922–42. 2 vols. (Vol. I, *Die dreigöttlichen Personen;* Vol. II, *Die drei Naturgottheiten.*)

NIETZSCHE, FRIEDRICH WILHELM. *Human, All-too-Human.* Translated by Helen Zimmern and Paul V. Cohn. (Complete Works, 6, 7.) London and New York, 1909, 1911. 2 vols.

———. *Thus Spake Zarathustra.* Translated by Thomas Common and revised by Oscar Levy and John L. Beevers. London, 1931.

———. *Werke.* Edited by Alfred Baeumler. Leipzig, [1930–32]. 8 vols. ("Dem unbekannten Gott" appears in Vol. 5, p. 457.)

NIKLAUS VON FLÜE. See KLAUS, BROTHER.

NINCK, MARTIN. *Wodan und germanischer Schicksalsglaube.* Jena, 1935.

NORDEN, EDUARD. *Die Geburt des Kindes.* (Studien der Bibliothek Warburg, 3.) Leipzig and Berlin, 1924.

NUKARIYA, KAITEN. *The Religion of the Samurai.* London, 1913.

ŌHAZAMA, SHŪEI [Ohasama, Schûej]. *Zen: Der lebendige Buddhismus in Japan.* Translated from Japanese into German by August Faust. Gotha and Stuttgart, 1925.

ONIANS, RICHARD BROXTON. *The Origins of European Thought.* Cambridge, 1951.

OPICINUS DE CANISTRIS. See Codices and Manuscripts, **viii.**

ORIGEN. *Contra Celsum.* See Migne, *P.G.,* vol. 11, cols. 657–1632. For translation, see:

———. *Origen, Contra Celsum.* Translated by Henry Chadwick. Cambridge, 1953.

———. *In Jeremiam Homiliae.* See Migne, *P.G.,* vol. 13, cols. 255–544.

———. *De Principiis.* See Migne, *P.G.,* vol. 11, cols. 115–414. For translation, see:

———. *On First Principles.* Translated by G. W. Butterworth. London, 1936.

ORTHELIUS. See (*A*) *Theatrum chemicum,* **xviii**; MANGETUS, *Bibliotheca chemica,* **x.**

OTTO, RUDOLF. *The Idea of the Holy.* Translated by John W. Harvey. 4th impr., Oxford, 1926.

PALANQUE, J. R., and others. *The Church in the Christian Roman Empire.* Vol. I: *The Church and the Arian Crisis.* Translated by Ernest C. Messenger. London, 1949.

PANTHEUS, JOANNES AUG. *Ars transmutationis metallicae.* Venice, 1519.

PAULI, W. "The Influence of Archetypal Ideas on the Scientific Theories of Kepler," translated from the German by Priscilla Silz. In: *The Interpretation of Nature and the Psyche.* New York (Bollingen Series LI) and London, 1955.

PEARCY, HENRI REUBELT. *A Vindication of Paul.* New York, 1936.

PERCIVAL, MILTON A. *William Blake's Circle of Destiny.* New York, 1938.

PERERIUS, BENEDICTUS, S. J. *De Magia: De observatione somniorum et de divinatione astrologica libri tres.* Cologne, 1598.

PETRUS BONUS. See BONUS.

PEUCER, KASPAR. *Commentarius de praecipuis generibus divinationum . . .* Wittenberg, 1560.

PICINELLI, FILIPPO. *Mondo simbolico.* Milan, 1669. Translated into Latin as: PHILIPPUS PICINELLUS. *Mundus symbolicus.* Cologne, 1680–81.

Pistis Sophia. See MEAD.

PITRA, JEAN-BAPTISTE. *Analecta sacra Spicilegio Solesmensi parata.* Paris, 1876–91. 8 vols.

PIUS XII, POPE. *Apostolic Constitution "Munificentissimus Deus."* Translated into English. Dublin (Irish Messenger Office), 1950.

PLATO. *Symposium.*

——. *Timaeus and Critias. The Thomas Taylor Translation.* (Bollingen Series III.) New York, 1944.

——. *Timaeus und Kritias.* Translated (into German) by Otto Apelt. (Philosophische Bibliothek, 179.) Leipzig, 1922.

——. See also CORNFORD.

PLATO, pseud. "Liber Platonis quartorum." See (*A*) *Theatrum chemicum,* **xiv.**

PLUTARCH. *De defectu oraculorum.* In: *Moralia.* With an English translation by Frank Cole Babbitt. (Loeb Classical Library.) Cambridge (Mass.) and London, 1936ff. 14 vols. (Vol. V, pp. 350ff.)

——. *Quaestiones convivales.* In: *Plutarchi Moralia.* Edited by C. Hubert and others. Vol. IV. Leipzig, 1925.

POPELIN, CLAUDIUS. *Le Songe de Poliphile.* Paris, 1883. 2 vols.

PORTMANN, ADOLF. "Die Bedeutung der Bilder in der lebendigen Energiewandlung," *Eranos-Jahrbuch* (Zurich), XXI (1953), 325–57.

POWELL, JOHN WESLEY. *Annual Reports of the Bureau of Ethnology to the Secretary of the Smithsonian Institution, Washington.* Vols. V (1883–84) and VIII (1886–87). Washington, 1887, 1891.

PREISENDANZ, KARL. *Papyri Graecae Magicae.* Leipzig and Berlin, 1928–31. 2 vols.

PREISIGKE, FRIEDRICH. *Vom göttlichen Fluidum nach ägyptischer Anschauung.* (Papyrusinstitut Heidelberg, Schrift I.) Berlin and Leipzig, 1920.

——. *Die Gotteskraft der frühchristlichen Zeit.* (Papyrusinstitut Heidelberg, Schrift VI.) Berlin and Leipzig, 1922.

PRZYWARA, ERICH. *Deus semper major.* Freiburg i. B., 1938. 3 vols.

PSELLUS, MICHAEL. *De daemonibus.* In: *Iamblichus de mysteriis Aegyptiorum, Chaldaeorum, Assyriorum, etc.* Edited by Marsilio Ficino. Venice, 1497.

RAHNER, HUGO. *Griechische Mythen in christlicher Deutung.* Zurich, 1945.

——. "Mysterium Lunae," *Zeitschrift für katholische Theologie* (Innsbruck and Leipzig), LXIV (1940), 80.

[RAMAKRISHNA PARAMAHAMSA.] *The Gospel of Ramakrishna.* Authorized edn., New York, 1907.

[——.] *Worte des Ramakrishna.* Edited by Emma von Pelet. Zurich, 1930.

REITZENSTEIN, RICHARD. *Poimandres.* Leipzig, 1904.

REUSNER, HIERONYMUS. *Pandora, das ist, die edelst Gab Gottes, oder der werde und heilsame Stein der Weysen.* Basel, 1588.

RHINE, J. B. *The Reach of the Mind.* London and New York, 1948.

Rig-Veda. See: NICOL MACNICOL (ed.). *Hindu Scriptures.* (Everyman's Library.) London and New York, 1938.

RIPLEY, GEORGE. *Opera omnia chemica.* Kassel, 1649.

Rituale Romanum (The Roman Ritual.) Editio typica. Vatican City, 1952.

ROMANUS, SAINT. See PITRA.

Rosarium philosophorum. Secunda pars alchimiae . . . cum figuris. Frankfurt a. M., 1550. See also (*A*) Manget, *Bibliotheca chemica,* vi; and *Artis auriferae,* **viii.**

ROSCHER, W. H. (ed.) . *Ausführliches Lexikon der griechischen und römischen Mythologie.* Leipzig, 1884–1937. 6 vols.

ROSENCREUTZ. See ANDREAE.

"Rosinus ad Sarratantam." See (*A*) *Artis Auriferae,* v.

ROSSI, GIOVANNI BATTISTA DE'. *Musaici cristiani delle Chiese di Roma anteriori al secolo XV.* Rome, 1899.

RULAND, MARTIN. *Lexicon alchemiae, sive Dictionarium alchemisticum.* Frankfurt a. M., 1612. For translation, see: *A Lexicon of Alchemy or Alchemical Dictionary* [London, 1892].

RÜCKER, ADOLF. See THEODORE, BISHOP OF MOPSUESTIA.

RUPERT, ABBOT OF DEUTZ (Rupertus Abbas Tuitiensis). *Commentarium in Joannem.* In Migne, *P.L.,* vol. 169, cols. 205–826.

RUPESCISSA, JOANNES DE. *La Vertu et la propriété de la quinte essence.* Lyons, 1581.

RUSKA, JULIUS. *Tabula Smaragdina: ein Beitrag zur Geschichte der hermetischen Literatur.* Heidelberg, 1926.

———. *Turba Philosophorum; ein Beitrag zur Geschichte der Alchemie.* (Quellen und Studien zur Geschichte der Naturwissenschaften und der Medizin, 1.) Berlin, 1931.

RUYSBROECK, JOHN OF. *The Adornment of the Spiritual Marriage, etc.* Translated by C. A. Wynschenck Dom. London, 1916.

SALOMON, RICHARD. *Opicinus de Canistris: Weltbild und Bekenntnisse eines avignonesischen Klerikers des 14. Jahrhunderts.* London, 1936.

SALZER, ANSELM. *Die Sinnbilder und Beiworte Mariens.* Linz, 1893.

Samyutta-Nikāya. *The Book of the Kindred Sayings* (*Samyutta-Nikāya*). Part II: The Nidāna Book (Nidāna-Vagga). Translated by Mrs. Catherine F. Rhys Davids and F. H. Woodward. (Pali Text Society, Translation Series, 10.) London, 1922.

SCHAER [SCHÄR], HANS. *Erlösungsvorstellungen und ihre psychologischen Aspekte.* (Studien aus dem C. G. Jung-Institut, II.) Zurich, 1950.

———. *Religion and the Cure of Souls in Jung's Psychology.* Translated by R. F. C. Hull. New York (Bollingen Series XXI) and London, 1951.

SCHÄRF, RIWKAH. "Die Gestalt des Satans im Alten Testament." In: C. G. JUNG. *Symbolik des Geistes.* Zurich, 1953.

SCHILLER, FRIEDRICH. *Wallensteins Tod.* 1799.

SCHOLEM, GERSHOM G. *Major Trends in Jewish Mysticism.* New York, 1941; 3rd edn., 1954.

SCHOLZ, HEINRICH. *Die Religionsphilosophie des Als-Ob.* Leipzig, 1921.

SCHOPENHAUER, ARTHUR. "On the Fourfold Root of the Principle of Sufficient Reason." In: *Two Essays by Arthur Schopenhauer.* Translated anon. (Bohn's Philosophical Library.) London, 1889. (Pp. 1–189.)

SCHULTZ, WOLFGANG. *Dokumente der Gnosis.* Jena, 1910.

SCOTT, WALTER (ed.). *Hermetica.* Oxford, 1924–36. 4 vols.

SENDIVOGIUS. See (*A*) *Musaeum Hermeticum,* **ii, iii**; *Theatrum chemicum,* **xviii**; MANGETUS, *Bibliotheca chemica,* **viii, ix.**

The Shatapatha-Brāhmana. Translated by Julius Eggeling. Vol. V. (Sacred Books of the East, 44.) Oxford, 1900.

SHAW, GEORGE BERNARD. *Saint Joan.* London, 1938.

SIGISMUND [DULLINGER] OF SEON. *Trithemius sui-ipsius Vindex.* Ingolstadt, 1616.

SILBERER, HERBERT. *Der Traum.* Stuttgart, 1919.

SINGER, CHARLES (ed.). *Studies in the History and Method of Science.* Oxford, 1917.

SMITHSONIAN INSTITUTION. See POWELL.

Solomon, Odes of. See BERNARD, JOHN HENRY.

SOSNOSKY, THEODOR VON. *Die rote Dreifaltigkeit: Jakobiner und Bolscheviken.* Einsiedeln, 1931.

SPAMER, ADOLF (ed.). *Texte aus der deutschen Mystik des 14. und 15. Jahrhunderts.* Jena, 1912.

SPIELREIN, SABINA. "Über den psychologischen Inhalt eines Falls von Schizophrenie," *Jahrbuch für psychoanalytische und psychopathologische Forschung* (Leipzig and Vienna), III (1912), 329–400.

Spirit and Nature. Translated by Ralph Manheim and R. F. C. Hull. (Papers from the Eranos Yearbooks, 1.) New York (Bollingen Series XXX), 1954; London, 1955.

"Splendor solis." See (*A*) *Aureum vellus,* **i.**

STEEB, JOANNES CHRISTOPHORUS. *Coelum sephiroticum hebraeorum.* Mainz, 1679.

STERN, LUDWIG. "Die koptische Apokalypse des Sophonias," in *Zeitschrift für Ägyptische Sprache und Alterthumskunde* (Leipzig), XXIV (1886), 115–36.

STOECKLI, ALBAN. *Die Visionen des seligen Bruder Klaus.* Einsiedeln, 1933.

STOLCIUS DE STOLCENBERG, DANIEL. *Viridarium chymicum figuris cupro incisis adornatum et poeticis picturis illustratum . . .* Frankfurt a. M., 1624.

STRACK, H. L., and BILLERBECK, PAUL. *Kommentar zum neuen Testament aus Talmud und Midrasch.* Munich, 1922–28. 4 vols.

SUZUKI, DAISETZ TEITARO. *Essays in Zen Buddhism.* Three series. London, 1949–53.

——. *An Introduction to Zen Buddhism.* London and New York, 1949.

——. *The Training of the Zen Buddhist Monk.* Kyoto, 1934.

TAYLOR, F. SHERWOOD. "A Survey of Greek Alchemy," *Journal of Hellenic Studies* (London), L (1930), 109–39.

TERTULLIAN. *Adversus Judaeos.* In Migne, *P.L.,* vol. 2, cols. 595–642. For translation, see: *The Writings of Tertullianus.* Translated by S. Thelwall, P. Holmes, and others. Vol. III. (Ante-Nicene Christian Library, 18.) Edinburgh, 1870.

——. *Apologeticus adversus Gentes pro Christianis.* In Migne, *P.L.,* vol. 1, cols. 257–536.

——. *De Carne Christi.* In Migne, *P.L.,* vol. 2, cols. 751–92.

——. *De testimonio animae.* In Migne, *P.L.,* vol. 1, cols. 607–18. For translation, see:

——. *Tertullian.* Translated by C. L. Dodgson. (Library of Fathers of the Holy Catholic Church.) Oxford, 1842.

[THEODORE, BISHOP OF MOPSUESTIA.] *Ritus Baptismi et Missae quem descripsit Theodorus ep. Mopsuestanus in sermonibus catecheticis.* Translated by Adolf Rücker. (Opuscula et textus, series liturgica, 2.) Münster, 1933.

Theologia Germanica. Translated by Susanna Winkworth; revised and edited by Willard R. Trask. New York, 1949; London, 1950.

Theologische Zeitschrift. Basel.

Thomas, Acts of. See *Acts of Thomas*; JAMES; MEAD.

THOMAS AQUINAS, SAINT. *Quaestiones de veritate.* In: *Sancti Thomae Aquinatis Quaestiones disputatae.* Edited by P. Mandonnet. Paris, 1925. 3 vols. (Vol. I.)

———. *Summa theologica.* Paris, 1868. 9 vols. For translation, see:

———. *The Summa Theologica of St. Thomas Aquinas.* Literally translated by the Fathers of the English Dominican Province. London, 1911–22. 18 vols.

THOMAS AQUINAS, pseud. "Aurora, sive Aurea hora." In: [H. CONDEESYANUS, pseud. i.e., J. Grasseus.] *Harmoniae inperscrutabilis chymico-philosophicae, sive Philosophorum antiquorum consentientium* . . . Decas I . . . collectae ab H.C.D. . . . Decas II . . . collecta studio et industria Joannis Rhenani, M.D. Frankfurt a. M., 1625. (Decas II, pp. 175–242.) See also: (*A*) *Artis auriferae,* **iv**; Codices and Manuscripts, **vi, xiii.**

THORNDIKE, LYNN. *A History of Magic and Experimental Science.* New York, 1923–41. 6 vols.

TONQUÉDEC, JOSEPH DE. *Les Maladies nerveuses ou mentales et les manifestations diaboliques.* Paris, 1938.

"Tractatulus Avicennae." See (*A*) *Artis auriferae,* **vi.**

Tractatus aureus. See HERMES TRISMEGISTUS.

"Tractatus Micreris." See (*A*) *Theatrum chemicum,* **xiii.**

TRISMOSIN, SOLOMON. "Splendor solis." See (*A*) *Aureum vellus,* **i.** For translation, see:

———. *Alchemical Treatises of Solomon Trismosin.* With explanatory notes by J. K. London, 1920.

"Turba philosophorum." See RUSKA; (*A*) *Artis auriferae,* **i**; MANGETUS, *Bibliotheca chemica,* **iii.**

"Viridarium chymicum." See STOLCIUS DE STOLCENBERG.

"Visio Arislei." See (*A*) *Artis auriferae,* **iii, viii.**

WAITE, ARTHUR EDWARD. *The Hermetic Museum Restored and Enlarged.* London, 1893. 2 vols.

———. *The Secret Tradition in Alchemy.* London, 1926.

———. (ed. and trans.). *The New Pearl of Great Price.* London, 1894.

WHITE, VICTOR. *God and the Unconscious.* London, 1952; Chicago, 1953.

WHITE, WILLIAM. *Emanuel Swedenborg: His Life and Writings.* London, 1867. 2 vols.

WICKHOFF, FRANZ. "Das Apsismosaik in der Basilica des H. Felix zu Nola," *Römische Quartalschrift* (Rome), III (1889), 158–76.

WIEDERKEHR, KARL. *Die leibliche Aufnahme der allerseligsten Jungfrau Maria in den Himmel.* Einsiedeln, 1927.

WILHELM, RICHARD (trans.). *The I Ching or Book of Changes.* Translated into English by Cary F. Baynes. New York (Bollingen Series XIX) and London, 1950. 2 vols.

———. *The Secret of the Golden Flower.* With a European commentary by C. G. Jung. London and New York, 1931.

———. See also LÜ PU-WEI.

WOLFF, TONI. "Einführung in die Grundlagen der Komplexen Psychologie." In: *Die Kulturelle Bedeutung der Komplexen Psychologie.* (Festschrift zum 60. Geburtstag von C. G. Jung.) Berlin, 1935. (Pp. 1–168.)

WOOLLEY, SIR LEONARD. *Abraham: Recent Discoveries and Hebrew Origins.* London, 1936.

ZELLER, EDUARD. *Die Philosophie der Griechen.* Tübingen and Leipzig, 1856–68. 3 vols. Partially translated as: *A History of Greek Philosophy.* Translated by S. F. Alleyne. London, 1881. 2 vols.

ZIMMER, HEINRICH. *The Art of Indian Asia.* Completed and edited by Joseph Campbell. (Bollingen Series XXXIX.) New York, 1955. 2 vols.

———. *Kunstform und Yoga im indischen Kultbild.* Berlin, 1926.

———. *Myths and Symbols in Indian Art and Civilization.* Edited by Joseph Campbell. (Bollingen Series VI.) New York, 1946.

ZÖCKLER, OTTO. *The Cross of Christ.* Translated by Maurice J. Evans. London, 1877.

ZOSIMOS. "Rosinus ad Sarratantam." See (*A*) *Artis auriferae,* **v.**

INDEX

INDEX

In entries relating to the books of the Bible, the numbers in parentheses indicate the chapter and verse(s) referred to.

B

D

G

I

J

K

N

O

S

U

W

The Collected Works of C. G. Jung

1. Psychiatric Studies
2. Experimental Researches
3. Psychogenesis in Mental Disease
4. Freud and Psychoanalysis
5. Symbols of Transformation
6. Psychological Types
7. Two Essays on Analytical Psychology
8. The Structure and Dynamics of the Psyche
9. PART I. Archetypes and the Collective Unconscious
9. PART II. Aion: A Historical Inquiry into the Symbolism of the Self
10. Civilization in Transition
11. Psychology and Religion: West and East
12. Psychology and Alchemy
13. Alchemical Studies
14. Mysterium Coniunctionis
15. The Spirit in Man, Art, and Literature
16. The Practice of Psychotherapy
17. The Development of Personality

Final Volumes: Miscellaneous Works, Bibliography, and General Index

THE COLLECTED WORKS OF

C. G. JUNG

THE PUBLICATION of the first complete collected edition, in English, of the works of C. G. Jung has been undertaken by Routledge and Kegan Paul, Ltd., in England and by the Bollingen Foundation, Inc., through Pantheon Books, Inc., in the United States. The edition contains revised versions of works previously published, such as *Psychology of the Unconscious,* which is now entitled *Symbols of Transformation;* works originally written in English, such as *Psychology and Religion;* works not previously translated, such as *Aion;* and, in general, new translations of the major body of Professor Jung's writings. The author has supervised the textual revision, which in some cases is extensive. Sir Herbert Read, Dr. Michael Fordham, and Dr. Gerhard Adler compose the Editorial Committee; the translator is R. F. C. Hull.

Every volume of the Collected Works contains material that either has not previously been published in English or is being newly published in revised form. In addition to *Aion,* the following volumes will, entirely or in large part, be new to English readers: *Psychiatric Studies; Archetypes and the Collective Unconscious; Alchemical Studies; Mysterium Coniunctionis; The Spirit in Man, Art, and Literature;* and *The Practice of Psychotherapy.*

The volumes are not being published in strictly consecutive order; but, generally speaking, works of which translations are lacking or unavailable are given precedence. The price of the volumes varies according to size; they are sold separately, and may also be obtained on standing order. Several of the volumes are extensively illustrated. Each volume contains an index and, in most cases, a bibliography; the final volumes will contain a complete bibliography of Professor Jung's writings and a general index of the entire edition. Subsequent works of the author's will be added in due course.

1. PSYCHIATRIC STUDIES *

On the Psychology and Pathology of So-Called Occult Phenomena

On Hysterical Misreading

Cryptomnesia

On Manic Mood Disorder

A Case of Hysterical Stupor in a Prisoner in Detention

On Simulated Insanity

A Medical Opinion on a Case of Simulated Insanity

A Third and Final Opinion on Two Contradictory Psychiatric Diagnoses

On the Psychological Diagnosis of Facts

2. EXPERIMENTAL RESEARCHES

STUDIES IN WORD ASSOCIATION

The Associations of Normal Subjects (by Jung and Riklin)

Experimental Observations on Memory

On the Determination of Facts by Psychological Means

Analysis of the Associations of an Epileptic

The Association Method

Reaction-Time in Association Experiments

On Disturbances in Reproduction in Association Experiments

The Significance of Association Experiments for Psychopathology

Psychoanalysis and Association Experiments

Association, Dream, and Hysterical Symptoms

PSYCHOPHYSICAL RESEARCHES

On Psychophysical Relations of the Association Experiment

Psychophysical Investigations with the Galvanometer and Pneumograph in Normal and Insane Individuals (by Peterson and Jung)

Further Investigations on the Galvanic Phenomenon and Respirations in Normal and Insane Individuals (by Ricksher and Jung)

* Pulished 1957.

* Published 1956.

The Battle for Deliverance from the Mother
The Dual Mother
The Sacrifice
Epilogue
Appendix: The Miller Fantasies

6. PSYCHOLOGICAL TYPES

PART I

Introduction
The Problem of Types in the History of Classical and Medieval Thought
Schiller's Ideas upon the Type Problem
The Apollonian and the Dionysian
The Type Problem in the Discernment of Human Character
The Problem of Types in Poetry
The Type Problem in Psychiatry
The Problem of Typical Attitudes in Aesthetics
The Problem of Types in Modern Philosophy
The Type Problem in Biography

PART II

General Description of the Types
Definitions
Conclusion
Four Papers on Psychological Typology

7. TWO ESSAYS ON ANALYTICAL PSYCHOLOGY *

The Psychology of the Unconscious
The Relations between the Ego and the Unconscious
Appendix: New Paths in Psychology; The Structure of the Unconscious

8. THE STRUCTURE AND DYNAMICS OF THE PSYCHE

On Psychic Energy
A Review of the Complex Theory
General Aspects of Dream Psychology
The Nature of Dreams
Instinct and Unconscious
The Psychological Foundation of Belief in Spirits
The Structure of the Psyche
Basic Postulates of Analytical Psychology

* Published 1953.

(continued)

8. (*continued*)

The Real and the Surreal
The Soul and Death
Analytical Psychology and Weltanschauung
The Stages of Life
Spirit and Life
On the Nature of the Psyche
The Transcendent Function
Synchronicity: An Acausal Connecting Principle
The Significance of Heredity and Constitution in Psychology
Psychological Factors Determining Human Behaviour

9. PART I. ARCHETYPES AND THE COLLECTIVE UNCONSCIOUS * *Illustrated*

The Concept of the Collective Unconscious
Archetypes of the Collective Unconscious
Concerning the Archetypes, with Special Reference to the Anima Concept
Psychological Aspects of the Mother Archetype
Concerning Rebirth
The Psychology of the Child Archetype
The Psychological Aspects of the Kore
The Phenomenology of the Spirit in Fairy Tales
On the Psychology of the Trickster Figure
The Conscious Mind, the Unconscious, and Individuation
A Study in the Process of Individuation
Concerning Mandala Symbolism

9. PART II. AION * *Illustrated*

A HISTORICAL INQUIRY INTO THE SYMBOLISM OF THE SELF

The Ego
The Shadow
The Syzygy: Anima and Animus
The Self
Christ, a Symbol of the Self
The Sign of the Fishes
The Prophecies of Nostradamus
The Historical Significance of the Fish
The Ambivalence of the Fish Symbol
The Fish in Alchemy
The Alchemical Interpretation of the Fish

* To be published 1958.

* Published 1958.

(*continued*)

11. *(continued)*

Psychoanalysis and the Cure of Souls
Answer to Job

EASTERN RELIGION

Psychological Commentary on "The Tibetan Book of the Great Liberation"
Psychological Commentary on "The Tibetan Book of the Dead"
Yoga and the West
Foreword to Suzuki's "Introduction to Zen Buddhism"
The Psychology of Eastern Meditation
The Holy Men of India: Introduction to Zimmer's "Der Weg zum Selbst"
Foreword to the "I Ching"

12. PSYCHOLOGY AND ALCHEMY * *Illustrated*

Introduction to the Religious and Psychological Problems of Alchemy
Individual Dream Symbolism in Relation to Alchemy
Religious Ideas in Alchemy
Epilogue

13. ALCHEMICAL STUDIES *Illustrated*

Commentary on "The Secret of the Golden Flower"
The Spirit Mercurius
Some Observations on the Visions of Zosimos
Paracelsus as a Spiritual Phenomenon
The "Arbor philosophica"

14. MYSTERIUM CONIUNCTIONIS

The Components of the *Coniunctio*
The Paradox
The Personification of Opposites:
Introduction; Sol; Sulphur; Luna; Sal; Rex; Regina; Adam and Eve
The Conjunction

15. THE SPIRIT IN MAN, ART, AND LITERATURE

Paracelsus
Paracelsus the Physician
Sigmund Freud: A Cultural Phenomenon
Sigmund Freud: An Obituary

* Published 1953.

Richard Wilhelm: An Obituary
Psychology and Literature
On the Relation of Analytical Psychology to the Poetic Art
Picasso
"Ulysses"

16. THE PRACTICE OF PSYCHOTHERAPY * *Illustrated*

GENERAL PROBLEMS OF PSYCHOTHERAPY

Principles of Practical Psychotherapy
What Is Psychotherapy?
Some Aspects of Modern Psychotherapy
Aims of Modern Psychotherapy
Problems of Modern Psychotherapy
Psychotherapy and a Philosophy of Life
Medicine and Psychotherapy
Psychotherapy Today
Fundamental Questions of Psychotherapy

SPECIFIC PROBLEMS OF PSYCHOTHERAPY

The Therapeutic Value of Abreaction
The Practical Use of Dream-Analysis
Psychology of the Transference

17. THE DEVELOPMENT OF PERSONALITY *
Psychic Conflicts in a Child
Introduction to Wickes' "Analyse der Kinderseele"
Child Development and Education
Analytical Psychology and Education: Three Lectures
The Gifted Child
The Significance of the Unconscious in Individual Education
The Development of Personality
Marriage as a Psychological Relationship

Final Volumes. MISCELLANEOUS WORKS, BIBLIOGRAPHY, AND GENERAL INDEX

SELECTED LETTERS AND SEMINARS
REVIEWS, SHORT ARTICLES, ETC., OF THE PSYCHOANALYTICAL PERIOD
LATER INTRODUCTIONS, ETC.
BIBLIOGRAPHY OF C. G. JUNG'S WRITINGS
GENERAL INDEX OF THE COLLECTED WORKS

* Published 1954.